Praise for the First Edition

"Overall, *Java Development with Ant* is an excellent resource...rich in valuable information that is well organized and clearly presented."

—Slashdot.org

"If you are using Ant, get this book."

—Rick Hightower, co-author of
Java Tools for eXtreme Programming

"This is the indispensable Ant reference."

—Nicholas Lesiecki, co-author of
Java Tools for eXtreme Programming

"*Java Development with Ant* is essential for anyone serious about actually *shipping* Java applications. I wish I could say I wrote it."

—Stuart Halloway
Chief Technical Officer, DevelopMentor
Author, *Component Development
for the Java Platform*

"Erik and Steve give you the answers to questions you didn't even know you have. Not only is the subject of Ant covered almost in its entirety, but along the way you pick up all these juicy little tidbits that only one who's used Ant in production environments would know."

—Ted Neward
.NET & Java Author, Instructor

"This should be required reading for all Java developers."

—Denver Java Users Group

Ant in Action

Second Edition of
Java Development with Ant

STEVE LOUGHRAN
ERIK HATCHER

MANNING

Greenwich
(74° w. long.)

For online information and ordering of this and other Manning books, please go to
www.manning.com. The publisher offers discounts on this book when ordered in
quantity. For more information, please contact:

Special Sales Department
Manning Publications Co.
Sound View Court 3B   Fax: (609) 877-8256
Greenwich, CT 06830   Email: orders@manning.com

Manning Publications Co.   Copyeditor: Laura Merrill
Sound View Court 3B   Typesetter: Denis Dalinnik
Greenwich, CT 06830   Cover designer: Leslie Haimes

ISBN 1-932394-80-X

Printed in the United States of America
1 2 3 4 5 6 7 8 9 10 – MAL – 11 10 09 08 07

*To my wife, Bina, and our little deployment project, Alexander.
You've both been very tolerant of the time I've spent
on the computer, either working on the book
or on Ant itself.*

brief contents

contents

preface to the second edition

Gosh, is it time for a new edition already? That's one of the odd aspects of writing about open source projects: the rapid release cycles and open development process mean that things date fast—and visibly. In a closed source project, changes are invisible until the next release ships; in open source, there's a gradual divergence between the code at the head of the repository and that covered in a book.

Java Development with Ant shipped in 2002, at the same time as Ant 1.5. Both the build tool and the book were very successful. Ant became the main way people built and tested Java projects, and our book showed how to use Ant in big projects and how to solve specific problems.

Ant 1.6 came along, and people started asking how some of the scalability improvements changed the build, and we would say "it makes it easier" without having any specifics to point to. At the same time, other interesting technologies came along to help, such as Ivy for dependency management, and other tools for deployment and testing. Java development processes had improved—and it was time to document the changes.

So I did. Erik, having just finished *Lucene in Action*, took a break from the Ant book series, leaving me the sole author of the second edition. I was blessed with a good start: all the text from the first edition. This text was a starting place for what turned out to be a major rewrite. Along with the changes to Ant, I had to deal with the changes in Enterprise Java, in XML schema languages, as well as in deployment and testing tools and methodologies. This made for some hard choices: whether to stay with JUnit and Java EE or whether to switch to Spring, OSGi, and TestNG as the way to package, deliver, and test applications. I chose to stay with the conventional ecosystem, because people working in Java EE need as much help as they can get, and because the tooling around JUnit 3 is excellent. If and when we do a third edition, things may well change yet again.

This book is now completely updated to show how to build, test, and deploy modern Java applications using Ant 1.7. I'm excited by some of the advanced chapters, especially chapters 10 and 11, which show Ant and Ivy working together to build big projects, managing library dependencies in the process. Chapter 16, deployment, is a favorite of mine, because deployment is where I'm doing my research. If you can automate deployment to a three-tier machine, you can automate that deployment to a pay-as-you-go infrastructure, such as Amazon's EC2 server farm. If your application is designed right, you could even roll out the application to a grid of 500 servers hosting the application on their spare CPU cycles!

That's why building and testing Java applications is so exciting. It may seem like housekeeping, something that an IDE can handle for you, but the projects that are the most interesting and fun, are the ones where you attempt to do things that nobody has done before. If you are going to be innovative, if you want to be leading edge, you will need tools that deliver both power and flexibility. Ant does both and is perfect for developing big Java applications.

But enough evangelization. I've enjoyed writing this book, and hope you will enjoy reading it!

STEVE LOUGHRAN

foreword to the first edition

Ant started its life on a plane ride, as a quick little hack. Its inventor was Apache member James Duncan Davidson. It joined Apache as a minor adjunct—almost an afterthought, really—to the codebase contributed by Sun that later became the foundation of the Tomcat 3.0 series. The reason it was invented was simple: it was needed to build Tomcat.

Despite these rather inauspicious beginnings, Ant found a good home in Apache, and in a few short years it has become the *de facto* standard not only for open source Java projects, but also as part of a large number of commercial products. It even has a thriving clone targeting .NET.

In my mind four factors are key to Ant's success: its extensible architecture, performance, community, and backward compatibility.

The first two—extensibility and performance—derive directly from James's original efforts. The dynamic XML binding approach described in this book was controversial at the time, but as Stefano Mazzocchi later said, it has proven to be a "viral design pattern": Ant's XML binding made it very simple to define new tasks and, therefore, many tasks were written. I played a minor role in this as I (along with Costin Manolache) introduced the notion of nested elements discussed in section 17.6. As each task ran in the same JVM and allowed batch requests, tasks that often took several minutes using Make could complete in seconds using Ant.

Ant's biggest strength is its active development community, originally fostered by Stefano and myself. Stefano acted as a Johnny Appleseed, creating build.xml files for numerous Apache projects. Many projects, both Apache and non-Apache, base their Ant build definitions on this early work. My own focus was on applying fixes from any source I could find, and recruiting new developers. Nearly three dozen developers have become Ant "committers," with just over a dozen being active at any point in time. Two are the authors of this book.

Much of the early work was experimental, and the rate of change initially affected the user community. Efforts like Gump sprang up to track the changes and have resulted in a project that now has quite stable interfaces.

The combination of these four factors has made Ant the success that it is today. Most people have learned Ant by reading build definitions that had evolved over time and were largely developed when Ant's functionality and set of tasks were not as rich as they are today. You have the opportunity to learn Ant from two of the people who know it best and who teach it the way it should be taught—by starting with a simple build definition and then showing you how to add in just those functions that are required by your project.

You should find much to like in Ant. And if you find things that you feel need improving, then I encourage you to join Erik, Steve, and the rest of us and get involved!

SAM RUBY
Director, Apache Software Foundation

preface to the first edition

In early 2000, Steve took a sabbatical from HP Laboratories, taking a break from research into such areas as adaptive, context-aware laptops to build web services, a concept that was very much in its infancy at the time.

He soon discovered that he had entered a world of chaos. Business plans, organizations, underlying technologies—all could be changed at a moment's notice. One technology that remained consistent from that year was Ant. In the Spring of 2000, it was being whispered that a "makefile killer" was being quietly built under the auspices of the Apache project: a new way to build Java code. Ant was already in use outside the Apache Tomcat group, its users finding that what was being whispered was true: it was a new way to develop with Java. Steve started exploring how to use it in web service projects, starting small and slowly expanding as his experience grew and as the tool itself added more functionality. Nothing he wrote that year ever got past the prototype stage; probably the sole successful deliverable of that period was the "Ant in Anger" paper included with Ant distributions.

In 2001, Steve and his colleagues did finally go into production. Their project— to aggressive deadlines—was to build an image-processing web service using both Java and VB/ASP. From the outset, all the lessons of the previous year were applied, not just in architecture and implementation of the service, but in how to use Ant to manage the build process. As the project continued, the problems expanded to cover deployment to remote servers, load testing, and many other challenges related to realizing the web service concept. It turned out that with planning and effort, Ant could rise to the challenges.

Meanwhile, Erik was working at eBlox, a Tucson, Arizona, consulting company specializing in promotional item industry e-business. By early 2001, Erik had come to Ant to get control over a build process that involved a set of Perl scripts crafted by the sysadmin wizard. Erik was looking for a way that did not require sysadmin effort to modify the build process; for example, when adding a new JAR dependency. Ant solved this problem very well, and in the area of building customized releases for each of eBlox's clients from a common codebase. One of the first documents Erik encountered on Ant was the infamous "Ant in Anger" paper written by Steve; this document was used as the guideline for crafting a new build process using Ant at eBlox.

At the same time, eBlox began exploring Extreme Programming and the JUnit unit-testing framework. While working on JUnit and Ant integration, Erik dug under the covers of Ant to see what made it tick. To get JUnit reports emailed automatically from an Ant build, Erik pulled together pieces of a MIME mail task submitted to the ant-dev team. After many dumb-question emails to the Ant developers asking such things as "How do I build Ant myself?" and with the help of Steve and other Ant developers, his first contributions to Ant were accepted and shipped with the Ant 1.4 release.

In the middle of 2001, Erik proposed the addition of an Ant Forum and FAQ to jGuru, an elegant and top-quality Java-related search engine. From this point, Erik's Ant knowledge accelerated rapidly, primarily as a consequence of having to field tough Ant questions. Soon after that, Erik watched his peers at eBlox develop the well-received Java Tools for Extreme Programming book. Erik began tossing around the idea of penning his own book on Ant, when Dan Barthel, formerly of Manning, contacted him. Erik announced his book idea to the Ant community email lists and received very positive feedback, including from Steve who had been contacted about writing a book for Manning. They discussed it, and decided that neither of them could reasonably do it alone and would instead tackle it together. Not to make matters any easier on himself, Erik accepted a new job, and relocated his family across the country while putting together the book proposal. The new job gave Erik more opportunities to explore how to use Ant in advanced J2EE projects, learning lessons in how to use Ant with Struts and EJB that readers of this book can pick up without enduring the same experience. In December of 2001, after having already written a third of this book, Erik was honored to be voted in as an Ant committer, a position of great responsibility, as changes made to Ant affect the majority of Java developers around the world.

Steve, meanwhile, already an Ant committer, was getting more widely known as a web service developer, publishing papers and giving talks on the subject, while exploring how to embed web services into devices and use them in a LAN-wide, campus-wide, or Internet-wide environment. His beliefs that deployment and integration are some of the key issues with the web service development process, and that Ant can help address them, are prevalent in his professional work and in the chapters of this book that touch on such areas. Steve is now also a committer on Axis, the Apache project's leading-edge SOAP implementation, so we can expect to see better integration between Axis and Ant in the future.

Together, in their "copious free time," Erik and Steve coauthored this book on how to use Ant in Java software projects. They combined their past experience with research into side areas, worked with Ant 1.5 as it took shape—and indeed helped shape this version of Ant while considering it for this book. They hope that you will find Ant 1.5 to be useful—and that Java Development with Ant will provide the solution to your build, test, and deployment problems, whatever they may be.

acknowledgments

Writing a book about software is similar to a software project. There's much more emphasis on documentation, but it's still essential to have an application that works.

Writing a second edition of a book is a form of software maintenance. You have existing code and documentation—information that needs to be updated to match a changed world. And how the world has changed! Since the last edition, what people write has evolved: weblogs, REST services, XMPP-based communications, and other technologies are now on the feature lists of many projects, while deadlines remain as optimistic as ever. The Java building, testing, and deployment ecosystem has evolved to match.

I've had to go back over every page in the first edition and rework it to deal with these changes, which took quite a lot of effort. The result, however, is a book that should remain current for the next three-to-five years.

Like software, books are team projects. We must thank the Manning publishing team: Laura Merrill; Cynthia Kane; Mary Piergies; Karen Tegtmeyer; Katie Tennant; Denis Dalinnik; and, of course, Marjan Bace, the publisher. There are also the reviewers and the members of the Manning Early Access Program, who found and filed bug reports against early drafts of the book. The reviewers were Bas Vodde, Jon Skeet, Doug Warren, TVS Murthy, Kevin Jackson, Joe Rainsberger, Ryan Cox, Dave Dribin, Srinivas Nallapati, Craeg Strong, Stefan Bodewig, Jeff Cunningham, Dana Taylor, and Michael Beauchamp. The technical reviewer was Kevin Jackson.

The Ant team deserves to be thanked for the ongoing evolution of Ant, especially when adding features and bug fixes in line with the book's needs. I'd like to particularly thank Stefan Bodewig, Matt Benson, Peter Reilly, Conor MacNeill, Martijn Kruithof, Antoine Levy-Lambert, Dominique Devienne, Jesse Glick, Stephane Balliez, and Kevin Jackson. Discussions on Ant's developer and user mailing lists also provided lots of insight—all participants on both mailing lists deserve gratitude.

Alongside Ant come other tools and products, those covered in the book and those used to create it. There's a lot of really good software out there, from operating systems to IDEs and networking tools: Linux and the CVS and Subversion tools deserve special mention.

I'd also like to thank my HP colleagues working on SmartFrog for their tolerance of my distracted state and for their patience when I experimented with their build process. The best way to test some aspects of big-project Ant is on a big project, and yours was the one I had at hand. This book should provide the documentation of what the build is currently doing. Julio Guijarro, Patrick Goldsack, Paul Murray, Antonio Lain, Kumar Ganesan, Ritu Sabharwal, and Peter Toft—thank you all for being so much fun to work with.

Finally, I'd like to thank my friends and family for their support. Writing a book in your spare time is pretty time-consuming. Now that it is finished, I get to rest and spend time with my wife, my son, our friends, and my mountain bike, while the readers get to enjoy their own development projects, with their own deadlines. Have fun out there!

about this book

This book is about Ant, the award-winning Java build tool. Ant has become the centerpiece of so many projects' build processes because it's easy to use, is platform-independent, and addresses the needs of today's projects to automate testing and deployment. From its beginnings as a helper application to compile Tomcat, Apache's Java web server, it has grown to be a stand-alone tool adopted across the Java community, and in doing so has changed people's expectations of their development tools.

If you have never before used Ant, this book will introduce you to it, taking you systematically through the core stages of most Java projects: compilation, testing, execution, packaging, and delivery. If you're an experienced Ant user, we'll show you how to "push the envelope" in using Ant. We place an emphasis on how to use Ant as part of a large project, drawing out best practices from our own experiences.

Whatever your experience with Ant, we believe that you will learn a lot from this book and that your software projects will benefit from using Ant as the way to build, test, and release your application.

WHO SHOULD READ THIS BOOK

This book is for Java developers working on software projects ranging from the simple personal project to the enterprise-wide team effort. We assume no prior experience of Ant, although even experienced Ant users should find much to interest them in the later chapters. We do expect our readers to have basic knowledge of Java, although the novice Java developer will benefit from learning Ant in conjunction with Java. Some of the more advanced Ant projects, such as building Enterprise Java applications and web services, are going to be of interest primarily to the people working in those areas. We'll introduce these technology areas, but we'll defer to other books to cover them fully.

HOW THIS BOOK IS ORGANIZED

We divided this book into three parts. Part 1 introduces the fundamentals of Ant and shows how to use it to build, test, package, and deliver a Java library. Part 2 takes the lessons of Part 1 further, exploring how to use Ant to solve specific problems, including coordinating a multi-project build, and deploying and testing web and Enterprise applications. Part 3 is a short but detailed guide on how to extend Ant in scripting languages and Java code, enabling power users to adapt Ant to their specific needs, or even embed it in their own programs.

Part 1

In chapter 1, we first provide a gentle introduction to what Ant is, what it is not, and what makes Ant the best build tool for building Java projects.

Chapter 2 digs into Ant's syntax and mechanics, starting with a simple project to compile a single Java file and evolving it into an Ant build process, which compiles, packages, and executes a Java application.

To go further with Ant beyond the basic project shown in chapter 2, Ant's abstraction mechanisms need defining. Chapter 3 introduces Ant's properties and datatypes, which let build-file writers share data across parts of the build. This is a key chapter for understanding what makes Ant shine.

Ant and test-centric development go hand in hand, so chapter 4 introduces our showcase application alongside JUnit, the tool that tests the application itself. From this chapter onwards, expect to see testing a recurrent theme of the book.

After packaging the Java code in chapter 5, we look in chapter 6 at launching Java and native programs. Chapter 7 takes what we've packaged and distributes it by email and FTP and SCP uploads.

It's often difficult to envision the full picture when looking at fragments of code in a book. In chapter 8, we show a single build file that merges all the stages of the previous chapters. Chapter 8 also discusses the issues involved in migrating to Ant and adopting a sensible directory structure, along with other general topics related to managing a project with Ant.

Part 2

The second part of the book extends the core build process in different ways, solving problems that different projects may encounter. Chapter 9 starts by showing how to extend Ant with optional and third-party tasks to perform new activities, such as checking out files from revision control, auditing code, and adding iteration and error-handling to a build file.

Chapter 10 looks at big-project Ant—how to build a big project from multiple subsidiary projects. This chapter is complemented by Chapter 11, which uses the Ivy libraries to address the problem of library management. Having a tool to manage your library dependencies and to glue together the output of different projects keeps Java projects under control, especially large ones.

Web development is where many Java developers spend their time these days. Chapter 12 shows how to package, deploy, and then test a web application. You can test a web application only after deploying it, so the development process gets a bit convoluted.

Chapter 13 discusses a topic that touches almost all Java developers: XML. Whether you're using XML simply for deployment descriptors or for transforming documentation files into presentation format during a build process, this chapter covers it.

Chapter 14 is for developers working with Enterprise Java; it looks at how to make an application persistent, how to deploy it on the JBoss application server, and how to test it with Apache Cactus.

The final two chapters of Part 2 look at how to improve your development processes. Chapter 15 introduces continuous integration, the concept of having a server automatically building and testing an application whenever code is checked in. Chapter 16 automates deployment. This is a topic that many developers neglect for one reason or another, but it typically ends up coming back to haunt us. Automating this—which is possible—finishes the transformation of how a Java project is built, tested, and deployed.

Part 3

The final part of our book is about extending Ant beyond its built-in capabilities. Ant is designed to be extensible in a number of ways. Chapter 17 provides all the information needed to write sophisticated custom Ant tasks, with many examples.

Beyond custom tasks, Ant is extensible by scripting languages, and it supports many other extension points, including Resources, Conditions, FilterReaders, and Selectors. Monitoring or logging the build process is easy to customize, too, and all of these techniques are covered in detail in chapter 18.

At the back

Last but not least are three appendices. Appendix A is for new Ant users; it explains how to install Ant and covers common installation problems and solutions. Because Ant uses XML files to describe build processes, appendix B is an introduction to XML for those unfamiliar with it. All modern Java integrated development environments (IDEs) now tie in to Ant. Using an Ant-enabled IDE allows you to have the best of both worlds. Appendix C details the integration available in several of the popular IDEs.

What we do not have in this edition is a quick reference to the Ant tasks. When you install Ant, you get an up-to-date copy of the documentation, which includes a reference of all Ant's tasks and types. Bookmark this documentation in your browser, as it is invaluable.

ONLINE RESOURCES

There's a web site that accompanies this book: http://antbook.org/. It can also be reached from the publisher's web site, www.manning.com/loughran. You'll find links to the source and the author forum plus some extra content that isn't in the book, including a couple of chapters from the previous edition and a bibliography with links. Expect more coverage of Ant-related topics as time progresses.

This antbook.org web site links to all the source code and Ant build files in the book, which are released under the Apache license. They are hosted on the Source-Forge open source repository at http://sourceforge.net/projects/antbook.

The other key web site for Ant users is Ant's own home page at http://ant.apache.org/. Ant and its online documentation can be found here, while the Ant user and developer mailing lists will let you meet other users and ask for help.

CODE CONVENTIONS

`Courier` typeface is used to denote Java code and Ant build files. **`Bold Courier`** typeface is used in some code listings to highlight important or changed sections.

Code annotations accompany many segments of code. Certain annotations are marked with numbered bullets. These annotations have further explanations that follow the code.

AUTHOR ONLINE

Purchase of *Ant in Action* includes free access to a private web forum run by Manning Publications where you can make comments about the book, ask technical questions, and receive help from the authors and from other users. To access the forum and subscribe to it, point your web browser to www.manning.com/loughran. This page provides information on how to get on the forum once you are registered, what kind of help is available, and the rules of conduct on the forum.

Manning's commitment to our readers is to provide a venue where a meaningful dialog between individual readers and between readers and the authors can take place. It is not a commitment to any specific amount of participation on the part of the authors, whose contribution to the AO remains voluntary (and unpaid). We suggest you try asking the authors some challenging questions, lest their interest stray!

The Author Online forum and the archives of previous discussions will be accessible from the publisher's web site as long as the book is in print.

about the authors

STEVE LOUGHRAN works at HP Laboratories in Bristol, England, developing technologies to make deployment and testing of large-scale servers and other distributed applications easier. His involvement in Ant started in 2000, when he was working on early web services in Corvallis, Oregon; he is a long-standing committer on Ant projects and a member of the Apache Software Foundation. He holds a degree in Computer Science from Edinburgh University, and lives in Bristol with his wife Bina and son Alexander. In the absence of any local skiing, he makes the most of the off-road and on-road cycling in the area.

ERIK HATCHER, an Apache Software Foundation Member, has been busy since the first edition of the Ant book, co-authoring *Lucene in Action,* becoming a dad for the third time, and entering the wonderful world of humanities computing. He currently works for the Applied Research in Patacriticism group at the University of Virginia, and consults on Lucene and Solr through eHatcher Solutions, Inc. Thanks to the success of the first edition, Erik has been honored to speak at conferences and to groups around the world, including JavaOne, ApacheCon, OSCON, and the No Fluff, Just Stuff symposium circuit. Erik lives in Charlottesville, Virginia, with his beautiful wife, Carole, and his three wonderful sons, Blake, Ethan, and Jakob. Erik congratulates Steve, his ghost writer, for single-handedly tackling this second edition.

about the cover illustration

The figure on the cover of *Ant in Action* is a "Paysan de Bourg de Batz," an inhabitant from the city of Batz in Brittany, France, located on the Atlantic coast. The illustration is taken from the 1805 edition of Sylvain Maréchal's four-volume compendium of regional dress customs. This book was first published in Paris in 1788, one year before the French Revolution.

The colorful diversity of the illustrations in the collection speaks vividly of the uniqueness and individuality of the world's towns and regions just 200 years ago. This was a time when the dress codes of two regions separated by a few dozen miles identified people uniquely as belonging to one or the other. The collection brings to life a sense of isolation and distance of that period—and of every other historic period except our own hyperkinetic present.

Dress codes have changed since then and the diversity by region, so rich at the time, has faded away. It is now often hard to tell the inhabitant of one continent from another. Perhaps, trying to view it optimistically, we have traded a cultural and visual diversity for a more varied personal life. Or a more varied and interesting intellectual and technical life.

We at Manning celebrate the inventiveness, the initiative, and the fun of the computer business with book covers based on the rich diversity of regional life of two centuries ago, brought back to life by the pictures from this collection.

Introduction to the Second Edition

WELCOME TO ANT IN ACTION

We took a rest after the first edition of this book, *Java Development with Ant*. Erik went on to work on *Lucene in Action*, (Manning Publications Co., 2005) exploring the index/search tool in wonderful detail. Steve returned to HP Laboratories, in the UK, getting into the problem of grid-scale deployment.

In the meantime, Ant 1.6 shipped, not breaking anything in the first edition, but looking slightly clunky. There were easier ways to do some of the things we described, especially in the area of big projects. We finally sat down and began an update while Ant 1.7 was under development.

Starting the update brought it home to us how much had changed while we weren't paying attention. Nearly every popular task has had some tweak to it, from a bit of minor tuning to something more fundamental. Along with Ant's evolution, many of the technologies that we covered evolved while we weren't looking—even the Java language itself has changed.

We had to carefully choose which technologies to cover with this book. We've put the effort into coverage of state-of-the-art build techniques, including library management, continuous integration, and automated deployment.

We also changed the name to *Ant in Action*. Without the wonderful response to the first edition, we would never have written it. And we can say that without the wonderful tools at our disposal—Ant, JUnit, IntelliJ IDEA, jEdit, and Eclipse—we wouldn't have been able to write it so well. We owe something to everyone who has worked on those projects. If you're one of those people, remind us of this fact if you ever happen to meet us, and we shall honor our debt in some way.

The Application: A Diary

We're going to write a diary application. It will store appointments and allow all events on a given day/range to be retrieved. It will not be very useful, but we can use it to explore many features of a real application and the build process to go with it: persistence, server-side operation, RSS feeds, and whatever else we see fit. We're writing this Extreme Programming-style, adding features on demand and writing the tests as we do so. We're also going to code in an order that matches the book's chapters. That's the nice thing about XP: you can put off features until you need them, or, more importantly, until you know exactly what you need.

All the examples in the book are hosted on SourceForge in the project antbook and are available for download from http://antbook.org/. Everything is Apache licensed; do with it what you want.

What's changed since the first edition?   The first edition of this book, *Java Development with Ant*, was written against the version of Ant then in development, Ant 1.5. This version, *Ant in Action*, was written against Ant 1.7. If you have an older version, upgrade now, as the build files in this book are valid only in Ant 1.7 or later.

To show experienced Ant users when features of Ant 1.6 and 1.7 are being introduced, we mark the appropriate paragraph. Here's an example:

The spawn attribute of the <java> task lets you start a process that will outlive the Ant run, letting you use Ant as a launcher of applications.

If you've been using Ant already, all your existing build files should still work. Ant is developed by a rigorous process and a wide beta test program. That's one of the virtues of a software build tool as an open source project: it's well engineered by its end users, and it's tested in the field long before a product ships. Testing is something that Ant holds dear.

PART 1

Learning Ant

Welcome to *Ant in Action*, an in-depth guide to the ubiquitous Java build tool. In this book, we're going to explore the tool thoroughly, using it to build everything from a simple little Java library to a complete server-side application.

Chapters 1 through 8 lay the foundation for using Ant. In this section, you'll learn the fundamentals of Java build processes—including compilation, packaging, testing, and distribution—and how Ant facilitates each step. Ant's reusable datatypes and properties play an important role in writing maintainable and extensible build files. After reading this section, you'll be ready to use Ant in your own projects.

C H A P T E R   1

Introducing Ant

Welcome to the future of your build process.

This is a book about Ant. It's more than just a reference book for Ant syntax, it's a collection of best practices demonstrating how to use Ant to its greatest potential in real-world situations. If used well, you can develop and deliver your software projects better than you have done before.

Let's start with a simple question: what is Ant?

1.1   WHAT IS ANT?

Ant is a *build tool*, a small program designed to help software teams develop big programs by automating all the drudge-work tasks of compiling code, running tests, and packaging the results for redistribution. Ant is written in Java and is designed to be cross-platform, easy to use, extensible, and scalable. It can be used in a small personal project, or it can be used in a large, multiteam software project. It aims to automate your entire build process.

The origin of Ant is a fascinating story; it's an example of where a spin-off from a project can be more successful than the main project. The main project in Ant's case is Tomcat, the Apache Software Foundation's Java Servlet engine, the reference implementation of the Java Server Pages (JSP) specification. Ant was written by James Duncan Davidson, then a Sun employee, to make it easier for people to compile

Tomcat on different platforms. The tool he wrote did that, and, with help from other developers, became the way that Apache Java projects were built. Soon it spread to other open source projects, and trickled out into helping Java developers in general.

That happened in early 2000. In that year and for the following couple of years, using Ant was still somewhat unusual. Nowadays, it's pretty much expected that any Java project you'll encounter will have an Ant build file at its base, along with the project's code and—hopefully—its tests. All Java IDEs come with Ant support, and it has been so successful that there are versions for the .NET framework (NAnt) and for PHP (Phing). Perhaps the greatest measure of Ant's success is the following: a core feature of Microsoft's .NET 2.0 development toolchain is its implementation of a verson: MSBuild. That an XML-based build tool, built in their spare time by a few developers, is deemed worthy of having a "strategic" competitor in the .NET framework is truly a measure of Ant's success.

In the Java world, it's the primary build tool for large and multiperson projects—things bigger than a single person can do under an IDE. Why? Well, we'll get to that in section 1.2—the main thing is that it's written in Java and focuses on building and testing Java projects.

Ant has an XML syntax, which is good for developers already familiar with XML. For developers unfamiliar with XML, well, it's one place to learn the language. These days, all Java developers need to be familiar with XML.

In a software project experiencing constant change, an automated build can provide a foundation of stability. Even as requirements change and developers struggle to catch up, having a build process that needs little maintenance and remembers to test everything can take a lot of housekeeping off developers' shoulders. Ant can be the means of controlling the building and deployment of Java software projects that would otherwise overwhelm a team.

1.1.1 The core concepts of Ant

We have just told you why Ant is great, but now we are going to show you what makes it great: its ingredients, the core concepts. The first is the design goal: Ant was designed to be an extensible tool to automate the build process of a Java development project.

A *software build process* is a means of going from your source—code and documents—to the product you actually deliver. If you have a software project, you have a build process, whether or not you know it. It may just be "hit the compile button on the IDE," or it may be "drag and drop some files by hand." Neither of these are very good because they aren't automated and they're often limited in scope.

With Ant, you can delegate the work to the machine and add new stages to your build process. Testing, for example. Or the creation of XML configuration files from your Java source. Maybe even the automatic generation of the documentation.

Once you have an automated build, you can let anyone build the system. Then you can find a spare computer and give it the job of rebuilding the project *continuously*. This is why automation is so powerful: it starts to give you control of your project.

Ant is Java-based and tries to hide all the platform details it can. It's also highly extensible in Java itself. This makes it easy to extend Ant through Java code, using all the functionality of the Java platform and third-party libraries. It also makes the build very fast, as you can run Java programs from inside the same Java virtual machine as Ant itself.

Putting Ant extensions aside until much later, here are the core concepts of Ant as seen by a user of the tool.

Build Files

Ant uses XML files called *build files* to describe how to build a project. In the build file developers list the high-level various goals of the build—the *targets*—and actions to take to achieve each goal—the *tasks*.

A build file contains one project

Each build file describes how to build one project. Very large projects may be composed of multiple smaller projects, each with its own build file. A higher-level build file can coordinate the builds of the subprojects.

Each project contains multiple targets

Within the build file's single project, you declare different targets. These targets may represent actual outputs of the build, such as a redistributable file, or activities, such as compiling the source or running the tests.

Targets can depend on other targets

When declaring a target, you can declare which targets have to be built first. This can ensure that the source gets compiled before the tests are run and built, and that the application is not uploaded until the tests have passed. When Ant builds a project, it executes targets in the order implied by their dependencies.

Targets contain tasks

Inside targets, you declare what work is needed to complete that stage of the build process. You do this by listing the tasks that constitute each stage. When Ant executes a target, it executes the tasks inside, one after the other.

Tasks do the work

Ant tasks are XML elements, elements that the Ant runtime turns into actions. Behind each task is a Java class that performs the work described by the task's attributes and nested data. These tasks are expected to be smart—to handle much of their own argument validation, dependency checking, and error reporting.

New tasks extend Ant

The fact that it's easy to extend Ant with new classes is one of its core strengths. Often, someone will have encountered the same build step that you have and will have written the task to perform it, so you can just use their work. If not, you can extend it in Java, producing another reusable Ant task or datatype.

To summarize, Ant reads in a build file containing a project. In the project are targets that describe different things the project can do. Inside the targets are the tasks, tasks that do the individual steps of the build. Ant executes targets in the order implied by their declared dependencies, and the tasks inside them, thereby building the application. That's the theory. What does it look like in practice?

1.1.2 Ant in action: an example project

Figure 1.1 shows the Ant build file as a graph of targets, each target containing tasks. When the project is built, Ant determines which targets need to be executed, and in what order. Then it runs the tasks inside each target. If a task somehow fails, Ant halts the build. This lets simple rules such as "deploy after compiling" be described, as well as more complex ones such as "deploy only after the unit tests have succeeded."

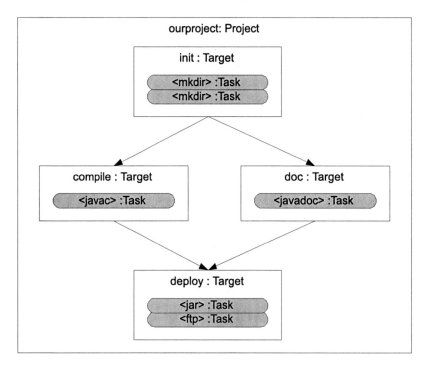

Figure 1.1 Conceptual view of a build file. The project encompasses a collection of targets. Inside each target are task declarations, which are statements of the actions Ant must take to build that target. Targets can state their dependencies on other targets, producing a graph of dependencies. When executing a target, all its dependents must execute first.

Listing 1.1 shows the build file for this typical build process.

Listing 1.1   A typical scenario: compile, document, package, and deploy

```xml
<?xml version="1.0" ?>
<project name="ourproject" default="deploy">

  <target name="init">
    <mkdir dir="build/classes" />         Create two output
    <mkdir dir="dist" />                  directories for
  </target>                               generated files

  <target name="compile" depends="init">
    <javac srcdir="src"
      destdir="build/classes"/>          Compile the Java source
  </target>

  <target name="doc" depends="init" >
    <javadoc destdir="build/classes"     Create the
             sourcepath="src"            javadocs of all
             packagenames="org.*" />     org.* source files
  </target>

  <target name="package" depends="compile,doc" >
    <jar destfile="dist/project.jar"     Create a JAR file
         basedir="build/classes"/>       of everything in
  </target>                              build/classes

  <target name="deploy" depends="package" >
    <ftp server="${server.name}"
         userid="${ftp.username}"
         password="${ftp.password}">     Upload all files in
      <fileset dir="dist"/>              the dist directory
    </ftp>                               to the ftp server
  </target>
</project>
```

While listing 1.1 is likely to have some confusing pieces to it, it should be mostly comprehensible to a Java developer new to Ant. For example, packaging (`target name="package"`) depends on the successful javac compilation and javadoc documentation (`depends="compile,doc"`). Perhaps the most confusing piece is the `${...}` notation used in the FTP task (`<ftp>`). That indicates use of Ant properties, which are values that can be expanded into strings. The output of our build is

```
> ant -propertyfile ftp.properties
Buildfile: build.xml

init:
    [mkdir] Created dir: /home/ant/ex/build/classes
    [mkdir] Created dir: /home/ant/ex/dist
```

```
compile:
    [javac] Compiling 1 source file to /home/ant/ex/build/classes

doc:
  [javadoc] Generating Javadoc
  [javadoc] Javadoc execution
  [javadoc] Loading source files for package
            org.example.antbook.lesson1...
  [javadoc] Constructing Javadoc information...
  [javadoc] Building tree for all the packages and classes...
  [javadoc] Building index for all the packages and classes...
  [javadoc] Building index for all classes...
package:
      [jar] Building jar: /home/ant/ex/dist/project.jar
deploy:
      [ftp] sending files
      [ftp] 1 files sent

BUILD SUCCESSFUL
Total time: 5 seconds.
```

Why did we invoke Ant with -propertyfile ftp.properties? We have a file
called ftp.properties containing the three properties server.name, ftp.
username, and ftp.password. The property handling mechanism allows parame-
terization and reusability of our build file. This particular example, while certainly
demonstrative, is minimal and gives only a hint of things to follow. In this build, we tell
Ant to place the generated documentation alongside the compiled classes, which isn't a
typical distribution layout but allows this example to be abbreviated. Using the
-propertyfile command-line option is also atypical and is used in situations
where forced override control is desired, such as forcing a build to upload to a different server. This example shows Ant's basics well: target dependencies, use of properties, compiling, documenting, packaging, and, finally, distribution.

For the curious, here are pointers to more information on the specifics of this
build file: chapter 2 covers build file syntax, target dependencies, and <javac> in
more detail; chapter 3 explains Ant properties, including -propertyfile; chapter 5
delves into <jar> and <javadoc>; and, finally, <ftp> is covered in chapter 7.

Because Ant tasks are Java classes, the overhead of invoking each task is quite
small. For each task, Ant creates a Java object, configures it, then calls its execute()
method. A simple task such as <mkdir> would call a Java library method to create a
directory. A more complex task such as <ftp> would invoke a third-party FTP
library to talk to the remote server, and, optionally, perform dependency checking
to upload only files that were newer than those at the destination. A very complex
task such as <javac> not only uses dependency checking to decide which files
to compile, it supports multiple compiler back ends, calling Sun's Java compiler in
the same Java Virtual Machine (JVM), or executing a different compiler as an external executable.

These are implementation details. Simply ask Ant to compile some files—how Ant decides which compiler to use and what its command line is are issues that you rarely need to worry about. It just works.

That's the beauty of Ant: it just works. Specify the build file correctly, and Ant will work out target dependencies and call the targets in the right order. The targets run through their tasks in order, and the tasks themselves deal with file dependencies and the actual execution of the appropriate Java package calls or external commands needed to perform the work. Because each task is usually declared at a high level, one or two lines of XML is often enough to describe what you want a task to do. Ten lines might be needed for something as complex as creating a database table. With only a few lines needed per task, you can keep each build target small, and keep the build file itself under control.

That is why Ant is popular, but that's not the only reason.

1.2   WHAT MAKES ANT SO SPECIAL?

Ant is the most popular build tool in Java projects. Why is that? What are its unique attributes that helped it grow from a utility in a single project to the primary build system of Java projects?

Ant is free and Open Source

Ant costs nothing to download. It comes with online documentation that covers each task in detail, and has a great online community on the Ant developer and user mail lists. If any part of Ant doesn't work for you, you can fix it. All the Ant developers got into the project by fixing bugs that mattered to them or adding features that they needed. The result is an active project where the end users are the developers.

Ant makes it easy to bring developers into a project

One of the benefits of using Ant comes when a new developer joins a team. With a nicely crafted build process, the new developer can be shown how to get code from the source code repository, including the build file and library dependencies. Even Ant itself could be stored in the repository for a truly repeatable build process.

It is well-known and widely supported

Ant is the primary build tool for Java projects. Lots of people know how to use it, and there is a broad ecosystem of tools around it. These tools include third-party Ant tasks, continuous-integration tools, and editors/IDEs with Ant support.

It integrates testing into the build processes

The biggest change in software development in the last few years has been the adoption of test-centric processes. The *agile* processes, including Extreme Programming and Test-Driven Development, make writing tests as important as writing the functional code. These *test-first* processes say that developers should write the tests before the code.

Ant doesn't dictate how you write your software—that's your choice. What it does do is let anyone who does write tests integrate those tests into the build process. An Ant build file can mandate that the unit tests must all pass before the web application is deployed, and that after deploying it, the functional tests must be run. If the tests fail, Ant can produce a nice HTML report that highlights the problems.

Adopting a test-centric development process is probably the most important and profound change a software project can make. Ant is an invaluable adjunct to that change.

It enables continuous integration

With tests and an automated build that runs those tests, it becomes possible to have a machine rebuild and retest the application on a regular basis. How regularly? Nightly? How about every time someone checks something into the code repository?

This is what continuous integration tools can do: they can monitor the repository and rerun the build when something changes. If the build and tests work, they update a status page on their web site. If something fails, developers get email notifying them of the problem. This catches errors within minutes of the code being checked in, stopping bugs from hiding unnoticed in the source.

It runs inside Integrated Development Environments

Integrated Development Environments (IDEs) are great for editing, compiling, and debugging code, and they're easy to use. It's hard to convince users of a good IDE that they should abandon it for a build process based on a text file and a command line prompt. Ant integrates with all mainstream IDEs, so users do not need to abandon their existing development tools to use Ant.

Ant doesn't replace an IDE; a good editor with debugging and even refactoring facilities is an invaluable tool to have and use. Ant just takes control of compilation, packaging, testing, and deployment stages of the build process in a way that's portable, scalable, and often reusable. As such, it complements IDEs. The latest generation of Java IDEs all support Ant. This means that developers can choose whatever IDE they like, and yet everyone can share the same automated build process.

1.3   WHEN TO USE ANT

When do you need Ant? When is an automated build tool important? The approximate answer is "whenever you have any project that needs to compile or test Java code." At the start of the project, if only one person is coding, then an IDE is a good starting point. As soon as more people work on the code, its deliverables get more complex, or the test suite starts to be written, then its time to turn to Ant. This is also a great time to set up the continuous integration server, or to add the project to a running one.

Another place to use Ant is in your Java programs, if you want to use its functionality in your own project. While Ant was never designed with this reuse in mind, it can be used this way. Chapter 18 looks at embedding Ant inside another program.

1.4 WHEN NOT TO USE ANT

Although Ant is a great build tool, there are some places where it isn't appropriate.

Ant is not the right tool to use outside of the build process. Its command line and error messages are targeted at developers who understand English and Java programming. You should not use Ant as the only way end-users can launch an application. Some people do this: they provide a build file to set up the classpath and run a Java program, or they use Ant to glue a series of programs together. This works until there's a problem and Ant halts with an error message that only makes sense to a developer.

Nor is Ant a general-purpose workflow engine; it lacks the persistence or failure handling that such a system needs. Its sole options for handling failure are "halt" or "ignore," and while it may be able to run for days at a time, this is something that's never tested. The fact that people do try to use Ant for workflow shows that there's demand for a portable, extensible, XML-based workflow engine. Ant is not that; Ant is a tool for making development easier, not solving every problem you can imagine.

Finally, setting up a build file takes effort. If you're just starting out writing some code, it's easier to stay in the IDEs, using the IDE to set up your classpath, to build, and to run tests. You can certainly start off a project that way, but as soon as you want HTML test reports, packaging, and distribution, you'll need Ant. It's good to start work on the build process early, rather than try to live in the IDE forever.

1.5 ALTERNATIVES TO ANT

Ant is not the only build tool available. How does it fare in comparison to its competition and predecessors? We'll compare Ant to its most widely used comptetitors—IDEs Make, and Maven.

1.5.1 IDEs

IDEs are the main way people code: Eclipse, NetBeans, and IntelliJ IDEA are all great for Java development. Their limitations become apparent as a project proceeds and grows.

- It's very hard to add complex operations, such as XSL stylesheet operations, Java source generation from IDL/WSDL processing, and other advanced tricks.
- It can be near-impossible to transfer one person's IDE settings to another user. Settings can end up tied to an individual's environment.
- IDE-based build processes rarely scale to integrate many different subprojects with complex dependencies.
- Producing replicable builds is an important part of most projects, and it's risky to use manual IDE builds to do so.

All modern IDEs have Ant support, and the IDE teams all help test Ant under their products. One IDE, NetBeans, uses Ant as its sole way of building projects, eliminating any difference between the IDE and Ant. The others integrate Ant within their own build process, so you can call Ant builds at the press of button.

1.5.2 Make

The Unix Make tool is the original build tool; it's the underpinnings of Unix and Linux. In Make, you list targets, their dependencies, and the actions to bring each target up-to-date.

The tool is built around the file system. Each target in a makefile is either the name of a file to bring up-to-date or what, in Make terminology, is called a *phony target*. A named target triggers some actions when invoked. Make targets can depend upon files or other targets. Phony targets have names like `clean` or `all` and can have no dependencies (that is, they always execute their commands) or can be dependent upon real targets.

One of the best parts of Make is that it supports pattern rules to determine how to build targets from the available inputs, so that it can infer that to create a `.class` file, you compile a `.java` file of the same name.

All the actions that Make invokes are actually external programs, so the rule to go from `.java` files to `.class` files would invoke the javac program to compile the source, which doesn't know or care that it has been invoked by Make.

Here's an example of a very simple GNU makefile to compile two Java classes and archive them into a JAR file:

```
all: project.jar

project.jar: Main.class XmlStuff.class
        jar -cvf $@ $<

%.class: %.java
        javac $<
```

The makefile has a phony target, `all`, which, by virtue of being first in the file, is the default target. It depends upon `project.jar`, which depends on two compiled Java files, packaging them with the JAR program. The final rule states how to build class (`.class`) files from Java (`.java`) files. In Make, you list the file dependencies, and the tool determines which rules to apply and in what sequence, while the developer is left tracking down bugs related to the need for invisible tab characters rather than spaces at the start of each action.

When someone says that they use Make, it usually means they use Make-on-Unix, or Make-on-Windows. It's very hard to build across both, and doing so usually requires a set of Unix-compatible applications, such as the Cygwin suite. Because Make handles the dependencies, it's limited to that which can be declared in the file: either timestamped local files or phony targets. Ant's tasks contain their own dependency logic. This adds work for task authors, but benefits task users. This is because specialized tasks to update JAR files or copy files to FTP servers can contain the code to decide if an entry in a JAR file or a file on a remote FTP server is older than a local file.

Ant versus Make

Ant and Make have the same role: they automate a build process by taking a specification file and using that and source files to create the desired artifacts. However, Ant and Make do have some fundamentally different views of how the build process should work.

With Ant, you list sequences of operations and the dependencies between them, and you let file dependencies sort themselves out through the tasks. The only targets that Ant supports are similar to Make's phony targets: targets that are not files and exist only in the build file. The dependencies of these targets are other targets. You omit file dependencies, along with any file conversion rules. Instead, the Ant build file states the stages used in the process. While you may name the input or output files, often you can use a wildcard or even a default wildcard to specify the source files. For example, here the <javac> task automatically includes all Java files in all subdirectories below the source directory:

```
<?xml version="1.0" ?>
<project name="makefile" default="all">
  <target name="all">
    <javac srcdir="."/>
    <jar destfile="project.jar" includes="*.class" />
  </target>
</project>
```

Both the <javac> and <jar> tasks will compare the sources and the destinations and decide which to compile or add to the archive. Ant will call each task in turn, and the tasks can choose whether or not to do work. The advantage of this approach is that the tasks can contain more domain-specific knowledge than the build tool, such as performing directory hierarchy-aware dependency checking, or even addressing dependency issues across a network. The other subtlety of using wildcards to describe source files, JAR files on the classpath, and the like is that you can add new files without having to edit the build file. This is nice when projects start to grow because it keeps build file maintenance to a minimum.

Ant works best with programs that are wrapped by Java code into a task. The task implements the dependency logic, configures the application, executes the program, and interprets the results. Ant does let you execute native and Java programs directly, but adding the dependency logic is harder than it is for Make. Also, with its Java focus, there's still a lot to be said for using Make for C and C++ development, at least on Linux systems, where the GNU implementation is very good, and where the development tools are installed on most end users' systems. For Java projects, Ant has the edge, as it is portable, Java-centric, and even redistributable if you need to use it inside your application.

1.5.3 Maven

Maven is a competing build tool from Apache, hosted at http://maven.apache.org. Maven uses templates—archetypes—to define how a specific project should be built. The standard archetype is for a Java library, but others exist and more can be written.

Like Ant, Maven uses an XML file to describe the project. Ant's file explicitly lists the stages needed for each step of the build process, but neglects other aspects of a project such as its dependencies, where the source code is kept under revision control, and other things. Maven's Project Object Model (POM) file declares all this information, information that Maven plugins use to manage all parts of the build process, from retrieving dependent libraries to running tests and generating reports.

Central to Maven is the idea that the tools should encode a set of best practices as to how projects should be laid out and how they should test and release code. Ant, in comparison, has no formal knowledge of best practices; Ant leaves that to the developers to decide on so they can implement their own policy.

Ant versus Maven

There is some rivalry between the two Apache projects, though it is mostly good-natured. The developer teams are friends, sharing infrastructure bits and, sometimes, even code.

Ant views itself as the more flexible of the two tools, while Maven considers itself the more advanced of the pair. There are some appealing aspects to Maven, which can generate a JAR and a web page with test results from only a minimal POM file. It pulls this off if the project is set up to follow the Maven rules, and every library, plugin, and archetype that it depends upon is in the central Maven artifact repository. Once a project starts to diverge from the templates the Maven team have provided, however, you end up looking behind the curtains and having to fix the underpinnings. That transition from "Maven user" to "plugin maintainer" can be pretty painful, by all accounts.

Still, Maven does have some long-term potential and it's worth keeping an eye on, but in our experience it has a hard time building Java projects with complex stages in the build process. To be fair, building very large, very complex Java projects is hard with any tool. Indeed, coping with scale is one of the ongoing areas of Ant evolution, which is why chapters 10 and 11 in this book are dedicated to that problem.

1.6 THE ONGOING EVOLUTION OF ANT

Ant is still evolving. As an Apache project, it's controlled by their bylaws, which cover decision-making and write-access to the source tree. Those with write-access to Ant's source code repository are called *committers*, because they're allowed to commit code changes directly. All Ant users are encouraged to make changes to the code, to extend Ant to meet their needs, and to return those changes to the Ant community.

As table 1.1 shows, the team releases a new version of Ant on a regular basis. When this happens, the code is frozen during a brief beta release program. When they come out, public releases are stable and usable for a long period.

Table 1.1 The release history of Ant. Major revisions come out every one to two years; minor revisions release every three to six months.

Date	Ant version	Notes
March 2000	Ant 1.0	Really Ant 0.9; with Tomcat 3.1
July 2000	Ant 1.1	First standalone Ant release
October 2000	Ant 1.2	
March 2001	Ant 1.3	
September 2001	Ant 1.4	Followed by Ant 1.4.1 in October
July 2002	Ant 1.5	Along with the first edition of *Java Development with Ant*
September 2003	Ant 1.6	With regular 1.6.x patches
June 2005	Ant 1.6.5	Last of the 1.6 branch
December 2006	Ant 1.7.0	The version this edition of the book was written against

New releases come out every 12–24 months; point releases, mostly bug fixes, come out about every quarter. The team strives to avoid breaking existing builds when adding new features and bug fixes. Nothing in this book is likely to break over time, although there may be easier ways of doing things and the tool will offer more features. Build files written for later versions of Ant do not always work in older releases—this book has targeted Ant 1.7.0, which was released in December 2006. Users of older versions should upgrade before continuing, while anyone without a copy of Ant should download and install the latest version. If needed, Appendix A contains instructions on how to do so.

1.7 SUMMARY

This chapter has introduced Ant, a Java tool that can build, test, and deploy Java projects ranging in size from the very small to the very, very large.

- Ant uses XML *build files* to describe what to build. Each file covers one Ant *project*; a project is divided into *targets*; targets contain *tasks*. These tasks are the Java classes that actually perform the construction work. Targets can depend on other targets. Ant orders the execution so targets execute in the correct order.

- Ant is a free, open source project with broad support in the Java community. Modern IDEs support it, as do many developer tools. It also integrates well with modern test-centric development processes, bringing testing into the build process.

- There are other tools that have the same function as Ant—to build software—but Ant is the most widely used, broadly supported tool in the Java world.
- Ant is written in Java, is cross platform, integrates with all the main Java IDEs, and has a command-line interface.

Using Ant itself does not guarantee a successful Java project; it just helps. It is a tool and, like any tool, provides greatest benefit when used properly. We're going to explore how to do that by looking at the tasks and types of Ant, using it to compile, test, package, execute, and then redistribute a Java project. Let's start with a simple Java project, and a simple build file.

CHAPTER 2

A first Ant build

Let's start this gentle introduction to Ant with a demonstration of what it can do. The first chapter described how Ant views a project: a project contains targets, each of which is a set of actions—tasks—that perform part of the build. Targets can depend on other targets, all of which are declared in an XML file, called a *build file*.

This chapter will show you how to use Ant to compile and run a Java program, introducing Ant along the way.

2.1 DEFINING OUR FIRST PROJECT

Compiling and running a Java program under Ant will introduce the basic concepts of Ant—its command line, the structure of a build file, and some of Ant's tasks.

Table 2.1 shows the steps we will walk though to build and run a program under Ant.

The program will not be very useful, but it will introduce the basic Ant concepts. In normal projects, the build file will be a lot smaller than the source, and not the other way around.

Table 2.1   The initial steps to building and running a program

Task	Covered in
Step zero: creating the project directory	Section 2.2
Step one: verifying the tools are in place	Section 2.3
Step two: writing your first Ant build file	Section 2.4
Step three: running your first build	Section 2.5
Step four: imposing structure	Section 2.6
Step five: running our program	Section 2.7

2.2 STEP ZERO: CREATING THE PROJECT DIRECTORY

Before doing anything else, create an empty directory. Everything will go under here: source files, created output files, and the build file itself. All new Java/Ant projects should start this way.

Our new directory, `firstbuild`, will be the base directory of our first project. We then create some real Java source to compile. In the new directory, we create a file called `Main.java`, containing the following minimal Java program:

```java
public class Main {

    public static void main(String args[]) {
        for(int i=0;i<args.length;i++) {
            System.out.println(args[i]);
        }
    }
}
```

The fact that this program does nothing but print the argument list is unimportant; it's still Java code that we need to build, package, and execute—work we will delegate to Ant.

2.3 STEP ONE: VERIFYING THE TOOLS ARE IN PLACE

Ant is a command-line tool that must be on the path to be used. Appendix A describes how to set up an Ant development system on both Unix and Windows. To compile Java programs, developers also need a properly installed Java Development Kit.

To test that Ant is installed, at a command prompt type

```
ant -version
```

A good response would be something listing a recent version of Ant, version 1.7 or later:

```
Apache Ant version 1.7 compiled on December 13 2006
```

A bad response would be any error message saying Ant is not a recognized command, such as this one on a Unix system:

```
bash: ant: command not found
```

On Windows, the error contains the same underlying message:

```
'ant' is not recognized as an internal or external command,
operable program or batch file.
```

Any such message indicates you have not installed or configured Ant yet, so turn to Appendix A: Installation, and follow the instructions there on setting up Ant.

2.4 STEP TWO: WRITING YOUR FIRST ANT BUILD FILE

Now the fun begins. We are going to get Ant to compile the program.

Ant is controlled by providing a text file that tells how to perform all the stages of building, testing, and deploying a project. These files are *build files*, and every project that uses Ant must have at least one. The most minimal build file useful in Java development is one that builds all Java source in and below the current directory:

```xml
<?xml version="1.0"?>
<project name="firstbuild" default="compile" >
  <target name="compile">
    <javac srcdir="." />
    <echo>compilation complete!</echo>
  </target>
</project>
```

This is a piece of XML text, which we save to a file called build.xml. It is not actually a very good build file. We would not recommend you use it in a real project, for reasons revealed later in this chapter, but it does compile the code.

It's almost impossible for a Java developer to be unaware of XML, but editing it may be a new experience. Don't worry. While XML may seem a bit hard to read at first, and it can be an unforgiving language, it isn't very complex. Readers new to XML files should look at our brief overview in Appendix B. Now let's examine the build file.

2.4.1 Examining the build file

Let's look at that first build file from the perspective of XML format rules. The <project> element is always the *root* element in Ant build files, in this case containing two attributes, name and default. The <target> element is a child of <project>. The <target> element contains two child elements: <javac> and <echo>.

This file could be represented as a tree, which is how XML parsers represent XML content when a program asks the parser for a Document Object Model (DOM) of the file. Figure 2.1 shows the tree representation.

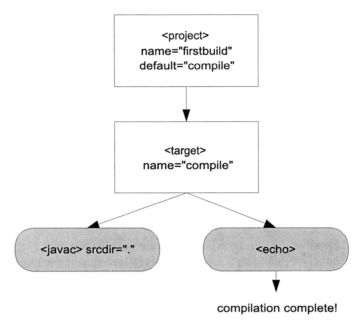

Figure 2.1 The XML Representation of a build file is a tree: the project at the root contains one target, which contains two tasks. This matches the Ant conceptual model: projects contain targets; targets contain tasks.

The graphical view of the XML tree makes it easier to look at a build file, and so the structure of the build file should become a bit clearer. At the top of the tree is a <project> element, which has two attributes, name and default. All Ant build files must contain a single <project> element as the root element. It tells Ant the name of the project and, optionally, the default target.

Underneath the <project> element is a <target> with the name compile. A target represents a single stage in the build process. It can be called from the command line or it can be used internally. A build file can have many targets, each of which must have a unique name.

The build file's compile target contains two XML elements, one called <javac> and one called <echo>. The names of these elements should hint as to their function: one calls the javac compiler to compile Java source; the other echoes a message to the screen. These are the *tasks* that do the work of this build. The compilation task has one attribute, srcdir, which is set to ".", and which tells the task to look for source files in and under the current directory. The second task, <echo>, has a text child node that will be printed when the build reaches it.

In this build file, we have configured the <javac> task with attributes of the task: we have told it to compile files in the current directory. Here, the <echo> task uses the text inside it. Attributes on an element describe options and settings that can only set once in the task. A task can support multiple nested elements, such as a list of files to delete. The attributes and elements of every built-in task are listed in Ant's online documentation. Bookmark your local copy of this documentation, as you will use it regularly when creating Ant build files. In the documentation, all *parameters* are XML attributes, and all *parameters specified as nested elements* are exactly that: nested XML elements that configure the task.

Now, let's get our hands dirty by running the build.

2.5   STEP THREE: RUNNING YOUR FIRST BUILD

We've just covered the basic theory of Ant: an XML build file can describe targets to build and the tasks used to build them. You've just created your first build file, so let's try it out. With the Java source and build file in the same directory, Ant should be ready to build the project. At a command prompt in the project directory, type

```
ant
```

If the build file has been typed correctly, then you should see the following response:

```
Buildfile: build.xml

compile:
    [javac] Compiling 1 source file
     [echo] compilation complete!

BUILD SUCCESSFUL

Total time: 2 seconds
```

There it is. Ant has compiled the single Java source file in the current directory and printed a success message afterwards. This is the core build step of all Ant projects that work with Java source. It may seem strange at first to have an XML file telling a tool how to compile a Java file, but soon it will become familiar. Note that we did not have to name the source files; Ant just worked it out somehow. We will spend time in chapter 3 covering how Ant decides which files to work on. For now, you just need to know that the <javac> task will compile all Java files in the current directory and any subdirectories. If that's all you need to do, then this build file is adequate for your project. You can just add more files and Ant will find them and compile them.

Of course, a modern project has to do much more than just compile files, which is where the rest of Ant's capabilities, and the rest of this book, come in to play. The first is Ant's ability to report problems.

2.5.1   If the build fails

When you're learning any new computer language, it's easy to overlook mistakes that cause the compiler or interpreter to generate error messages that don't make much sense. Imagine if somehow the XML was mistyped so that the <javac> task was misspelled, as in

```
<javaac srcdir="." />
```

With this task in the target, the output would look something like

```
Buildfile: build.xml

compile:

BUILD FAILED
compile:

BUILD FAILED
C:\AntBook\firstbuild\build.xml:4:
  Problem: failed to create task or type javaac
Cause: The name is undefined.
Action: Check the spelling.
Action: Check that any custom tasks/types have been declared
Action: Check that any <presetdef>/<macrodefs> declarations have taken
place
```

Whenever Ant fails to build, the BUILD FAILED message appears. This message will eventually become all too familiar. Usually it's associated with Java source errors or unit test failures, but build file syntax problems result in the same failure message.

If you do get an error message, don't worry. Nothing drastic will happen: files won't be deleted (not in this example, anyway!), and you can try to correct the error by looking at the line of XML named and at the lines on either side of the error. If your editor has good XML support, the editor itself will point out any XML language errors, leaving the command line to find only Ant-specific errors. Editors that are Ant-aware will also catch many Ant-specific syntax errors. An XML editor would also catch the omission of an ending tag from an XML element, such as forgetting to terminate the target element:

```
<?xml version="1.0"?>
<project name="firstbuild" default="compile" >
  <target name="compile">
    <javac srcdir="." />
    <echo>compilation complete!</echo>
</project>
```

The error here would come from the XML parser:

```
C:\AntBook\firstbuild\xml-error.xml:6:
  The element type "target" must be terminated by the matching
  end-tag "</target>".
```

Well-laid-out build files, formatted for readability, help to make such errors visible, while XML-aware editors keep you out of trouble in the first place.

One error we still encounter regularly comes from having an attribute that isn't valid for that task. Spelling the srcdir attribute as sourcedir is an example of this:

```
    <javac sourcedir="." />
```

If the build file contains that line, you would see this error message:

```
compile:

BUILD FAILED

C:\AntBook\firstbuild\build.xml:4:
 The <javac> task doesn't support the "sourcedir" attribute.
```

This message indicates that the task description contained an invalid attribute. Usually this means whoever created the build file typed something wrong, but it also could mean that the file's author wrote it for a later version of Ant, one with newer attributes or tasks than the version doing the build. That can be hard to fix without upgrading; sometimes a workaround isn't always possible. It's rare that an upgrade would be incompatible or detrimental to your existing build file; the Ant team strives for near-perfect backwards compatibility.

The error you're likely to see most often in Ant is the build halting after the compiler failed to compile your code. If, for example, someone forgot the semicolon after the `println` call, the compiler error message would appear, followed by the build failure:

```
Buildfile: build.xml
compile:
 [javac] Compiling 1 source file
 [javac] /home/ant/firstbuild/Main.java:5: ';' expected
 [javac] System.out.println("hello, world")
 [javac]                                    ^
 [javac] 1 error

BUILD FAILED
/home/ant/firstbuild/build.xml:4: Compile failed, messages
     should have been provided.

Total time: 4 seconds
```

The build failed on the same line as the error in the previous example, line 4, but this time it did the correct action. The compiler found something wrong and printed its messages, and Ant stopped the build. The error includes the name of the Java file and the location within it, along with the compiler error itself.

The key point to note is that failure of a task will usually result in the build itself failing. This is essential for a successful build process: there's no point packaging or delivering a project if it didn't compile. In Ant, the build fails if a task fails. Let's look at the successful build in more detail.

2.5.2 Looking at the build in more detail

If the build does actually succeed, then the only evidence of this is the message that compilation was successful. Let's run the task again, this time in verbose mode, to see what happens. Ant produces a verbose log when invoked with the -verbose parameter.

This is a very useful feature when figuring out what a build file does. For our simple build file, it doubles the amount of text printed:

```
> ant -verbose

Apache Ant version 1.7 compiled on December 19 2006
Buildfile: build.xml
Detected Java version: 1.5 in: /usr/java/jdk1.5.0/jre
Detected OS: Linux
parsing buildfile /home/ant/firstbuild/build.xml with URI = file:////home/
ant/firstbuild/build.xml
Project base dir set to: /home/ant/firstbuild/
Build sequence for target(s) 'compile' is [compile]
Complete build sequence is [compile, ]

compile:
    [javac] Main.class skipped - don't know how to handle it
    [javac] Main.java omitted as Main.class is up-to-date.
    [javac] build.xml skipped - don't know how to handle it
     [echo] compilation complete!

BUILD SUCCESSFUL
Total time: 0 seconds
```

For this build, the most interesting lines are those generated by the `<javac>` task. These lines show two things. First, the task did not compile `Main.java`, because it felt that the destination class was up-to-date. The task not only compiles all source files in a directory tree, but it also uses simple timestamp checking to decide which files are up-to-date. All this is provided in the single line of the build file, `<javac srcdir="." />`.

The second finding is that the task explicitly skipped the files `build.xml` and `Main.class`. All files without a `.java` extension are ignored.

What is the log in verbose mode if Ant compiled the source file? Delete `Main.class` then run Ant again to see. The core part of the output provides detail on the compilation process:

```
[javac] Main.java added as Main.class doesn't exist.
[javac] build.xml skipped - don't know how to handle it
[javac] Compiling 1 source file
[javac] Using modern compiler
[javac] Compilation arguments:
[javac] '-classpath'
[javac] '/home/ant/ant/lib/ant-launcher.jar:
  /home/ant/ant/lib/ant.jar:
  /home/ant/ant/lib/xml-apis.jar:
  /home/ant/ant/lib/xercesImpl.jar:
  /usr/java/jdk1.5.0/lib/tools.jar'
[javac] '-sourcepath'
[javac] '/home/ant/firstbuild'
[javac] '-g:none'
```

```
[javac]
[javac] The ' characters around the executable and arguments are
[javac] not part of the command.
[javac] File to be compiled:
[javac]     /home/ant/firstbuild/Main.java
 [echo] compilation complete!
```

BUILD SUCCESSFUL

This time the `<javac>` task does compile the source file, a fact it prints to the log. It still skips the `build.xml` file, printing this fact out before it actually compiles any Java source. This provides a bit more insight into the workings of the task: it builds a list of files to compile, which it passes to the compiler along with Ant's own classpath. The Java-based compiler that came with the Java Development Kit (JDK) is used by default, running inside Ant's own JVM. This keeps the build fast.

The log also shows that we're now running on a Unix system, while we started on a Windows PC. Ant doesn't care what platform you're using, as long as it's one of the many it supports. A well-written build file can compile, package, test, and deliver the same source files on whatever platform it's executed on, which helps unify a development team where multiple system types are used for development and deployment.

Don't worry yet about running the program we compiled. Before actually running it, we need to get the compilation process under control by imposing some structure on the build.

2.6   STEP FOUR: IMPOSING STRUCTURE

The build file is now compiling Java files, but the build process is messy. Source files, output files, and the build file: they're all in the same directory. If this project gets any bigger, things will get out of hand. Before that happens, we must impose some structure. The structure we're going to impose is quite common with Ant and is driven by the three changes we want to make to the project.

- We want to automate the cleanup in Ant. If done incorrectly, this could accidentally delete source files. To minimize that risk, you should always separate source and generated files into different directories.

- We want to place the Java source file into a Java package.

- We want to create a JAR file containing the compiled code. This should be placed somewhere that also can be cleaned up by Ant.

To add packaging and clean-build support to the build, we have to isolate the source, intermediate, and final files. Once source and generated files are separated, it's safe to clean the latter by deleting the output directory, making clean builds easy. These are more reliable than are incremental builds as there is no chance of content sneaking into the output. It's good to get into the habit of doing clean builds. The first step, then, is to sort out the source tree.

2.6.1 Laying out the source directories

We like to have a standard directory structure for laying out projects. Ant doesn't mandate this, but it helps if everyone uses a similar layout. Table 2.2 shows what we use, which is fairly similar to that of Ant's own source tree.

Table 2.2 An Ant project should split source files, compiled classes files, and distribution packages into separate directories. This makes them much easier to manage during the build process.

Directory name	Function
src	Source files
build	All files generated in a build that can be deleted and recreated
build/classes	Intermediate output (created; cleanable)
dist	Distributable files (created; cleanable)

The first directory, src, contains the Java source. The others contain files that are created during the build. To clean up these directories, the entire directory trees can be deleted. The build file also needs to create the directories if they aren't already present, so that tasks such as <javac> have a directory to place their output.

We want to move the Java source into the src directory and extend the build file to create and use the other directories. Before moving the Java file, it needs a package name, as with all Java classes in a big project. Here we have chosen org.antbook. welcome. We add this name at the top of the source file in a package declaration:

```
package org.antbook.welcome;
public class Main {

    public static void main(String args[]) {
        for(int i=0;i<args.length;i++) {
            System.out.println(args[i]);
        }
    }
}
```

Next, we save the file in a directory tree beneath the source directory that matches that package hierarchy: src/org/antbook/welcome. The dependency-checking code in <javac> relies on the source files being laid out this way. When the Java compiler compiles the files, it always places the output files in a directory tree that matches the package declaration. The next time the <javac> task runs, its dependency-checking code looks at the tree of generated class files and compares it to the source files. It doesn't look inside the source files to find their package declarations; it relies on the source tree being laid out to match the destination tree.

NOTE For Java source file dependency checking to work, you must lay out source in a directory tree that matches the package declarations in the source.

Only when the source is not in any package can you place it in the base of the source tree and expect <javac> to track dependencies properly, which is what we've been doing until now. If Ant keeps recompiling your Java files every time you do a build, it's probably because you haven't placed them correctly in the package hierarchy.

It may seem inconvenient having to rearrange your files to suit the build tool, but the benefits become clear over time. On a large project, such a layout is critical to separating and organizing classes. If you start with it from the outset, even on a small project, you can grow more gently from a small project to a larger one. Modern IDEs also prefer this layout structure, as does the underlying Java compiler.

Be aware that dependency checking of <javac> is simply limited to comparing the dates on the source and destination files. A regular clean build is a good practice—do so once a day or after refactoring classes and packages.

With the source tree set up, the output directories follow.

2.6.2   Laying out the build directories

Separate from the source directories are the build and distribution directories. We'll configure Ant to put all intermediate files—those files generated by any step in the build process that aren't directly deployed—in or under the build directory. We want to be able to clean up all the generated files simply by deleting the appropriate directory trees. Keeping the directories separate and out of the control of any Software Configuration Management (SCM) tool makes cleanup easy but means that we need to tell Ant to create these directories on demand.

Our project will put the compiled files into a subdirectory of build, a directory called "classes". Different intermediate output types can have their own directories alongside this one.

As we mentioned in section 2.5.2, the Java compiler lays out packaged files into a directory tree that matches the package declarations in the source files. The compiler will create the appropriate subdirectories on demand, so we don't need to create them by hand. We do need to create the top-level build directory and the classes subdirectory. We do this with the Ant task <mkdir>, which, like the shell command of the same name, creates a directory. In fact, it creates parent directories, too, if needed:

```
<mkdir dir="build/classes">
```

This call is all that's needed to create the two levels of intermediate output. To actually place the output of Ant tasks into the build directory, we need to use each task's attribute to identify a destination directory. For the <javac> task, as with many other Ant tasks, the relevant attribute is destdir.

2.6.3   Laying out the distribution directories

The dist directory contains redistributable artifacts of the project. A common stage in a build process is to package files, placing the packaged file into the dist directory. There may be different types of packaging—JAR, Zip, tar, and WAR, for example—and so a subdirectory is needed to keep all of these files in a place where they can be identified and deleted for a clean build. To create the distribution directory, we insert another call to <mkdir>:

```
<mkdir dir="dist">
```

To create the JAR file, we're going to use an Ant task called, appropriately, <jar>. We've dedicated chapter 5 to this and the other tasks used in the packaging process. For this introductory tour of Ant, we use the task in its simplest form, when it can be configured to make a named JAR file out of a directory tree:

```
<jar destfile="dist/project.jar" basedir="build/classes" />
```

Doing so shows the advantage of placing intermediate code into the build directory: you can build a JAR file from it without having to list what files are included. This is because all files in the directory tree should go in the JAR file, which, conveniently, is the default behavior of the <jar> task.

With the destination directories defined, we've now completed the directory structure of the project, which looks like the illustration in figure 2.2. When the build

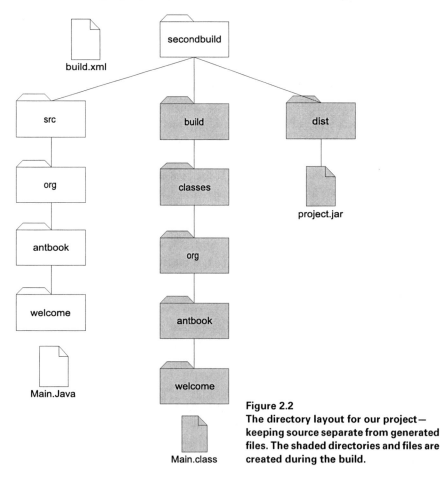

Figure 2.2
The directory layout for our project—keeping source separate from generated files. The shaded directories and files are created during the build.

is executed, a hierarchy of folders will be created in the class directory to match the source tree, but since these are automatically created we won't worry about them.

This is going to be the basic structure of all our projects: source under `src/`, generated files under `build/`, with the compiled classes going under `build/classes`. Future projects will have a lot more files created than just `.class` files, and it's important to leave space for them. With this structured layout, we can have a new build file that creates and uses the new directories.

2.6.4   Creating the build file

Now that we have the files in the right places and we know what we want to do, the build file needs to be rewritten. Rather than glue all the tasks together in one long list of actions, we've broken the separate stages—directory creation, compilation, packaging, and cleanup—into four separate targets inside the build file.

```xml
<?xml version="1.0" ?>
<project name="structured" default="archive" >

  <target name="init">
    <mkdir dir="build/classes" />        Creates the output
    <mkdir dir="dist" />                 directories
  </target>

  <target name="compile" depends="init" >
    <javac srcdir="src"
      destdir="build/classes"           Compiles into the output directories
      />
  </target>

  <target name="archive" depends="compile" >
    <jar destfile="dist/project.jar"
      basedir="build/classes" />         Creates the archive
  </target>

  <target name="clean" depends="init">
    <delete dir="build" />              Deletes the output
    <delete dir="dist"  />             directories
  </target>

</project>
```

This build file adds an `init` target to do initialization work, which means creating directories. We've also added two other new targets, `clean` and `archive`. The `archive` target uses the `<jar>` task to create the JAR file containing all files in and below the `build/classes` directory, which in this case means all `.class` files created by the `compile` target. The `clean` target cleans up the output directories by deleting them. It uses a new task, `<delete>`. We've also changed the default target to `archive`, so this will be the target that Ant executes when you run it.

As well as adding more targets, this build file adds another form of complexity. Some targets need to be executed in order. How do we manage this?

2.6.5 Target dependencies

In our current project, for the archive to be up-to-date, all the source files must be compiled, which means the `archive` target must come after the `compile` target. Likewise, `compile` needs the directories created in `init`, so Ant must execute `compile` after the `init` task. *Ant needs to know in what order it should execute targets.*

These are dependencies that we need to communicate to Ant. We do so by listing the direct dependencies in the `depends` attributes of the targets:

```
<target name="compile" depends="init" >
<target name="archive" depends="compile" >
<target name="clean" depends="init">
```

If a target directly depends on more than one target, then we list both dependencies, such as `depends="compile,test"`. In our project, the archive task depends upon both `init` and `compile`, but we don't bother to state the dependency upon `init` because the `compile` target already depends upon it. If Ant must execute `init` before `compile` and `archive` depends upon `compile`, then Ant must run `init` before `archive`. Put formally: *dependencies are transitive.*

What isn't important is the order of targets inside the build file. Ant reads the whole file before it builds the dependency tree and executes targets. There's no need to worry about forward references to targets.

If you look at the dependency tree of targets in the current example, it looks like figure 2.3. Before Ant executes any target, it executes all its predecessor targets. If these predecessors depend on targets themselves, Ant considers those and produces an order that satisfies all dependencies. If two targets in this execution order share a common dependency, then that predecessor will execute only once.

Experienced users of Unix's Make tool will recognize that Ant targets resemble that tool's "pseudotargets"—targets in a makefile that you refer to by name in the dependencies of other targets. Usually in Make, you name the source files that a target depends on, and the build tool

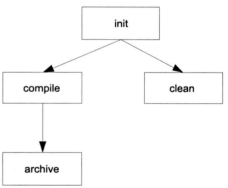

Figure 2.3 Once you add dependencies, the graph of targets gets more complex. Here `clean` depends upon `init`; `archive` depends on `compile`, and, indirectly, `init`. All of a target's dependencies will be executed ahead of the target itself.

itself works out what to do to create the target file from the source files. In Ant, you name stages of work as targets, and the tasks inside each target determine for themselves what their dependencies are. Ant builds what is known in computer science circles as a Directed Acyclic Graph (DAG). A DAG is a graph in which the link between nodes has a specific direction—here the *depends* relationship—and in which there are no circular dependencies.

Interlude: circular dependencies

What happens if a target directly or indirectly depends on itself? Does Ant loop? Let's see with a target that depends upon itself:

```xml
<?xml version="1.0" ?>
<project name="loop" default="loop" >

  <echo>loop test</echo>

  <target name="loop" depends="loop">
    <echo>looping</echo>
  </target>

</project>
```

Run this and you get informed of an error:

```
      [echo] loop test

BUILD FAILED
Circular dependency: loop <- loop

Total time: 0 seconds
Process ant exited with code 1
```

When Ant parses the build file, it builds up the graph of targets. If there is a cycle anywhere in the graph, Ant halts with the error we've just seen.

Any tasks placed in the build files outside of any target will be executed before the target graph is created and analyzed. In our experiment, we had an `<echo>` command outside a target. Ant executes all tasks outside of any target in the order they appear in the build file, before any target processing begins.

With a loop-free build file written, Ant is ready to run it.

2.6.6 Running the new build file

Now that there are multiple targets in the build file, we need a way of specifying which to run. You can simply list one or more targets on the command line, so all of the following are valid:

```
ant
ant init
ant clean
ant compile
ant archive
```

Calling Ant with no target is the same as calling the target named in the `default` attribute of the `<project>`. In the following example, it is the `archive` target:

```
> ant
Buildfile: build.xml

init:
    [mkdir] Created dir: /home/ant/secondbuild/build/classes
    [mkdir] Created dir: /home/ant/secondbuild/dist

compile:
    [javac] Compiling 1 source file to /home/ant/secondbuild/build/classes

archive:
      [jar] Building jar: /home/ant/secondbuild/dist/project.jar

BUILD SUCCESSFUL
Total time: 5 seconds
```

This example demonstrates that Ant has determined the execution order of the targets. As both the `compile` and `archive` targets depend upon the `init` target, Ant calls `init` before it executes either of those targets. It orders the targets so that first the directories get created, then the source is compiled, and finally the JAR archive is built.

The build worked—once. What happens when the build is run a second time?

2.6.7   Incremental builds

Let's look at the log of the build if it's rerun immediately after the previous run:

```
init:

compile:

archive:

BUILD SUCCESSFUL

Total time: 1 second
```

Ant goes through all the targets, but none of the tasks say that they are doing any work. Here's why: all of these tasks in the build file check their dependencies, and do nothing if they do not see a need. The `<mkdir>` task doesn't create directories that already exist, `<javac>` compiles source files when they're newer than the corresponding `.class` file, and the `<jar>` task compares the time of all files to be added to the archive with the time of the archive itself. No files have been compiled, and the JAR is untouched. This is called an *incremental build*.

If you add the `-verbose` flag to the command line, you'll get more detail on what did or, in this case, did not take place.

```
> ant -v
Apache Ant version 1.7 compiled on December 13 2006
Buildfile: build.xml
Detected Java version: 1.5 in: /usr/java/jdk1.5.0/jre
Detected OS: Linux
```

```
parsing buildfile /home/ant/secondbuild/build.xml with
 URI = file:///home/ant/secondbuild/build.xml
Project base dir set to: /home/ant/secondbuild
Build sequence for target(s) 'archive' is [init, compile, archive]
Complete build sequence is [init, compile, archive, clean]

init:

compile:
[javac] org/antbook/welcome/Main.java omitted as
  org/antbook/welcome/Main.class is up-to-date.

archive:
  [jar] org omitted as org/ is up-to-date.
  [jar] org/antbook omitted as org/antbook/ is up-to-date.
  [jar] org/antbook/welcome omitted as
    org/antbook/welcome/ is up-to-date.
  [jar] org/antbook/welcome/Main.class omitted as
    org/antbook/welcome/Main.class is up-to-date.

BUILD SUCCESSFUL
Total time: 1 second
Process ant exited with code 0
```

The verbose run provides a lot of information, much of which may seem distracting. When a build is working well, you don't need it, but it's invaluable while developing that file. Here the build lists the order of target evaluation, which we've boldfaced, and it shows that the <jar> task is also dependency-aware: the JAR file was not modified since every file inside it was up-to-date. That shows a powerful feature of Ant: many tasks are dependency-aware, with special logic to handle problems such as timestamps inside Zip/JAR files or to remote FTP sites.

TIP   If ever you are unsure why a build is not behaving as expected, add the -v or -verbose option to get lots more information.

Now that the build file has multiple targets, another question arises. Can we ask for more than one target on the command line?

2.6.8   Running multiple targets on the command line

Developers can run multiple targets in a single build, by listing the targets one after the other on the command line. But what happens when you type ant compile archive at the command line? Many people would expect Ant to pick an order that executes each target and its dependencies once only: [init, compile, archive]. Unix Make would certainly do that, but Ant does not. Instead, it executes each target and dependents in turn, so the actual sequence is init, compile, then init, compile, archive:

```
> ant compile archive
Buildfile: build.xml
```

```
init:
    [mkdir] Created dir: /home/ant/secondbuild/build/classes
    [mkdir] Created dir: /home/ant/secondbuild/dist

compile:
    [javac] Compiling 1 source file to
      /home/ant/secondbuild/build/classes

init:

compile:

archive:
      [jar] Building jar: /home/ant/secondbuild/dist/project.jar

BUILD SUCCESSFUL
Total time: 4 seconds
```

This behavior is a historical accident that nobody dares change. However, if you look closely, the second time Ant executes the compile target it does no work; the tasks get executed but their dependency checking prevents existing outputs from being rebuilt.

The final question is this: when a target lists multiple dependencies, does Ant execute them in the order listed? The answer is "yes, unless other dependencies prevent it." Imagine if we modified the archive target with the dependency attribute depends="compile,init". A simple left-to-right execution order would run the compile target before it was initialized. Ant would try to execute the targets in this order, but because the compile target depends upon init, Ant will call init first. This subtle detail can catch you off guard. If you try to control the execution order by listing targets in order, you may not get the results you expect since explicit dependencies always take priority.

Being able to run multiple targets on the command line lets developers type a sequence of operations such as ant clean execute to clean the output directory, rebuild everything, and run the program. Of course, before they can do that, Ant has to be able to run the program.

2.7   STEP FIVE: RUNNING OUR PROGRAM

We now have a structured build process that creates the JAR file from the Java source. At this point the next steps could be to run tests on the code, distribute it, or deploy it. We shall cover those later. For now, we just want to run the program.

2.7.1   Why execute from inside Ant?

We could just call our program from the command line, stating the classpath, the name of the entry point, and the arguments:

```
>java -cp build/classes org.antbook.welcome.Main a b .
a
b
.
```

Calling Java programs from the command line isn't hard, just fiddly. If we run our program from the build file, we get some immediate benefits:

- A target to run the program can depend upon the compilation target, so we know we're always running the latest version of the code.
- It's easy to pass complex arguments to the program.
- It's easy to set up the classpath.
- The program can run inside Ant's own JVM.
- You can halt a build if the return code of the program isn't zero.

Integrating compiling with running a program lets you use Ant to build an application on demand, passing parameters down, including information extracted from other programs run in earlier targets. Running programs under Ant is both convenient and powerful.

2.7.2 Adding an "execute" target

To run the program, we add a new target, execute, which depends upon compile. It contains one task, <java>, that runs our class Main.class using the interim build/classes directory tree as our classpath:

```
<target name="execute" depends="compile">
  <java
    classname="org.antbook.welcome.Main"
    classpath="build/classes">
    <arg value="a"/>
    <arg value="b"/>
    <arg file="."/>
  </java>
</target>
```

We have three <arg> tags inside the <java> task; each tag contains one of the arguments to the program: "a", "b", and ".", as with the command-line version. Note, however, that the final argument, <arg file="."/>, is different from the other two. The first two arguments use the value attribute of the <arg> tag, which passes the value straight down to the program. The final argument uses the file attribute, which tells Ant to resolve that attribute to an absolute file location before calling the program.

Interlude: what can the name of a target be?

All languages have rules about the naming of things. In Java, classes and methods cannot begin with a number. What are Ant's rules about target names?

Ant targets can be called almost anything you want—their names are just strings. However, for the sake of IDEs and Ant itself, here are some rules to follow:

- Don't call targets " " or " , " because you won't be able to use them.
- Don't use spaces in target names.
- Targets beginning with a minus sign cannot be called from the command line. This means a target name "-hidden" could be invoked only by other tasks, not directly by users. IDEs may still allow access to the task.

Ant's convention is to use a minus sign (-) as a separator between words in targets, leading to names such as "build-install-lite" or "functional-tests". We would advise against using dots in names, such as "build.install", for reasons we won't get into until the second section of the book entitled, "Applying Ant."

With the execute target written, we can compile and run our program under Ant. Let's try it out.

2.7.3   Running the new target

What does the output of the run look like? First, let's run it on Windows:

```
C:\AntBook\secondbuild>ant execute
Buildfile: build.xml

init:

compile:

execute:
    [java] a
    [java] b
    [java] C:\AntBook\secondbuild
```

The compile task didn't need to do any recompilation, and the execute task called our program. Ant has prefixed every line of output with the name of the task currently running, showing here that this is the output of an invoked Java application. The first two arguments went straight to our application, while the third argument was resolved to the current directory; Ant turned "." into an absolute file reference. Next, let's try the same program on Linux:

```
[secondbuild]> ant execute
Buildfile: build.xml

init:

compile:

execute:
    [java] a
    [java] b
    [java] /home/ant/secondbuild
```

Everything is identical, apart from the final argument, which has been resolved to a different location, the current directory in the Unix path syntax, rather than the DOS one. This shows another benefit of starting programs from Ant rather than from any batch file or shell script: a single build file can start the same program on multiple platforms, transforming filenames and file paths into the appropriate values for the target platform.

This is a very brief demonstration of how and why to call programs from inside Ant, enough to round off this little project. Chapter 6 will focus on the topic of calling Java and native programs from Ant during a build process.

We've nearly finished our quick introduction to Ant, but we have one more topic to cover: how to start Ant.

2.8   ANT COMMAND-LINE OPTIONS

We've already shown that Ant is a command-line program and that you can specify multiple targets as parameters. We've also introduced the -verbose option, which allows you to get more information on a build. We want to do some more to run our program. First, we want to remove the [java] prefixes, and then we want to run the build without any output unless something goes wrong. Ant's command-line options enable this.

Ant can take a number of options, which it lists if you ask for them with ant -help. The current set of options is listed in table 2.3. This list can expand with every version of Ant, though some of the options aren't available or relevant in IDE-hosted versions of the program. Note also that some of the launcher scripts, particularly the Unix shell script, provide extra features, features that the ant -help command will list.

Table 2.3   Ant command-line options

Option	Meaning
-autoproxy	Bind Ant's proxy configuration to that of the underlying OS.
-buildfile *file*	Use the named buildfile, use -f as a shortcut.
-debug, -d	Print debugging information.
-diagnostics	Print information that might be helpful to diagnose or report problems.
-Dproperty=value	Set a property to a value.
-emacs	Produce logging information without adornments.
-find *file*	Search for the named buildfile up the tree. The shortcut is -s.
-help, -h	List the options Ant supports and exit.
-inputhandler *classname*	The name of a class to respond to <input> requests.
-keep-going, -k	When one target on the command line fails, still run other targets.

continued on next page

Table 2.3 Ant command-line options *(continued)*

Option	Meaning
`-listener` *classname*	Add a project listener.
`-logfile` *file*	Save the log to the named file.
`-logger` *classname*	Name a different logger.
`-main` *classname*	Provide the name of an alternate main class for Ant.
`-nice  <number>`	Run Ant at a lower or higher priority.
`-noclasspath`	Discard the CLASSPATH environment variable when running Ant.
`-nouserlib`	Run Ant without using the jar files from .ant/lib under the User's home directory.
`-projecthelp`	Print information about the current project.
`-propertyfile` *file*	Load properties from file; -D definitions take priority.
`-quiet, -q`	Run a quiet build: only print errors.
`-verbose, -v`	Print verbose output for better debugging.
`-version`	Print the version information and exit.

Some options require more explanation of Ant before they make sense. In particular, the options related to properties aren't relevant until we explore Ant's properties in chapter 3. Let's look at the most important options first.

2.8.1 Specifying which build file to run

Probably the most important Ant option is `-buildfile`. This option lets you control which build file Ant uses, allowing you to divide the targets of a project into multiple files and select the appropriate build file depending on your actions. A shortcut to `-buildfile` is `-f`. To invoke our existing project, we just name it immediately after the `-f` or `-buildfile` argument:

```
ant -buildfile build.xml compile
```

This is exactly equivalent to calling `ant compile` with no file specified. If for some reason the current directory was somewhere in the source tree, which is sometimes the case when you are editing text from a console application such as `vi`, `emacs`, or even `edit`, then you can refer to a build file by passing in the appropriate relative filename for your platform, such as `../../../build.xml` or `..\..\..\build.xml`. It's easier to use the `-find` option, which must be followed by the name of a build file. This variant does something very special: it searches the directory tree to find the first build file in a parent directory of that name, and invokes it. With this option, when you are deep into the source tree editing files, you can easily invoke the project build with the simple command:

```
ant -find build.xml
```

Note that it can be a bit dangerous to have a build file at the root of the file system, as the -find command may find and run it. Most other command-line options are less risky, such as those that control the log level of the program.

2.8.2 Controlling the amount of information provided

We stated that we want to reduce the amount of information provided when we invoke Ant. Getting rid of the [java] prefix is easy: we run the build file with the -emacs option. This omits the task-name prefix from all lines printed. The option is called -emacs because the output is now in the emacs format for invoked tools, which enables that and other editors to locate the lines on which errors occurred.

For our exercise, we only want to change the presentation from the command line, which is simple enough:

```
> ant -emacs execute
Buildfile: build.xml

init:

compile:

execute:
    a
    b
    /home/ant/secondbuild

BUILD SUCCESSFUL
Total time: 2 seconds.
```

This leaves the next half of the problem—hiding all the output. Three of the Ant options control how much information is output when Ant runs. Two of these (-verbose and -debug) progressively increase the amount. The -verbose option is useful when you're curious about how Ant works or why a build isn't behaving. The -debug option includes all the normal and verbose output and much more low-level information, primarily only of interest to Ant developers. To see nothing but errors or a final build failed/success message, use -quiet:

```
> ant -quiet execute

BUILD SUCCESSFUL
Total time: 2 seconds
```

In quiet runs, not even <echo> statements appear. One of the attributes of <echo> is the level attribute, which takes five values: error, warning, info, verbose, and debug control the amount of information that appears. The default value info ensures that messages appear in normal builds and in -verbose and -debug runs. By inserting an <echo> statement into our execute target with the level set to warning, we ensure that the message appears even when the build is running as -quiet:

```
<echo level="warning" message="running" />
```

Such an <echo> at the warning level always appears:

```
>ant -q
    [echo] running
```

To eliminate the [echo] prefix, we add the -emacs option again, calling

```
>ant -q -emacs
```

to get the following output:

```
running

BUILD SUCCESSFUL
Total time: 2 seconds.
```

Asking for -quiet builds is good when things are working; asking for -verbose is good when they are not. Using <echo> to log things at level="verbose" can provide extra trace information when things start going wrong. The other way to handle failure is to use the -keep-going option.

2.8.3 Coping with failure

The -keep-going option tells Ant to try to recover from a failure. If you supply more than one target on the command line, Ant normally stops the moment any of these targets—or any they depend upon—fail. The -keep-going option instructs Ant to continue running any target on the command line that doesn't depend upon the target that fails. This lets you run a reporting target even if the main build didn't complete.

2.8.4 Getting information about a project

The final option of immediate relevance is -projecthelp. It lists the main targets in a project and is invaluable whenever you need to know what targets a build file provides. Ant lists only those targets containing the optional description attribute, as these are the targets intended for public consumption.

```
>ant -projecthelp
Buildfile: build.xml
Main targets:

Other targets:

 archive
 clean
 compile
 execute
 init
Default target: archive
```

This isn't very informative, which is our fault for not documenting the file. If we add a description attribute to each target, such as description="Compiles the source code" for the compile target, and a <description> tag right after the project declaration, then the target listing includes these descriptions, marks all the described targets as "main targets," and hides all other targets from view:

```
> ant -p
Buildfile: build.xml
Compiles and runs a simple program
Main targets:

 archive  Creates the JAR file
 clean    Removes the temporary directories used
 compile  Compiles the source code
 execute  Runs the program

Default target: archive
```

To see both main and sub targets in a project, you must call Ant with the options `-projecthelp` and `-verbose`. The more complex a project is, the more useful the `-projecthelp` feature becomes. We strongly recommend providing description strings for every target intended to act as an entry point to external callers, and a line or two at the top of each build file describing what it does.

Having looked at the options, especially the value of the `-projecthelp` command, let's return to the build file and add some descriptions.

2.9 EXAMINING THE FINAL BUILD FILE

Listing 2.1 shows the complete listing of the final build file. In addition to adding the description tags, we decided to make the default target run the program. We've marked the major changes in bold, to show where this build file differs from the build files and build file fragments shown earlier.

> **Listing 2.1 Our first complete build file, including packaging and executing a Java program**

```
<?xml version="1.0" ?>
<project name="secondbuild" default="execute" >
<description>Compiles and runs a simple program</description>

  <target name="init">
    <mkdir dir="build/classes" />
    <mkdir dir="dist" />
  </target>

  <target name="compile" depends="init"
     description="Compiles the source code">
    <javac srcdir="src"
      destdir="build/classes"
      />
  </target>

  <target name="archive" depends="compile"
     description="Creates the JAR file">
```

```
        <jar destfile="dist/project.jar"
          basedir="build/classes"
          />
      </target>

      <target name="clean" depends="init"
          description="Removes the temporary directories used">
        <delete dir="build" />
        <delete dir="dist" />
      </target>

      <target name="execute" depends="compile"
          description="Runs the program">
        <echo level="warning" message="running" />
        <java
          classname="org.antbook.welcome.Main"
          classpath="build/classes">
          <arg value="a"/>
          <arg value="b"/>
          <arg file="."/>
        </java>
      </target>

    </project>
```

That's forty-plus lines of Ant XML to compile ten lines of Java, but think of what those lines of XML do: they compile the program, package it, run it, and can even clean up afterwards. More importantly, if we added a second Java file to the program, how many lines of code need to change in the build file? Zero. As long as the build process doesn't change, you can now add Java classes and packages to the source tree to build a larger JAR file and perform more useful work on the execution parameters, yet you don't have to make any changes to the build file itself. That is one of the nice features of Ant: you don't need to modify your build files whenever a new source file is added to the build process. It all just works. It even works under an IDE.

2.10 RUNNING THE BUILD UNDER AN IDE

Most modern Java IDEs integrate with Ant. One, NetBeans, is built entirely around Ant. Others, including Eclipse and IntelliJ IDEA, let you add build files to a project and run them from within the GUI.

To show that you can run this Ant under an IDE, figure 2.4 shows a small picture of the "execute" target running under Eclipse.

Appendix C covers IDE integration. All the examples in this book were run from the command line for better readability. However, most of the build files were written in IDEs and often were tested there first. Don't think that adopting Ant means abandoning IDE tools; instead you get a build that works everywhere.

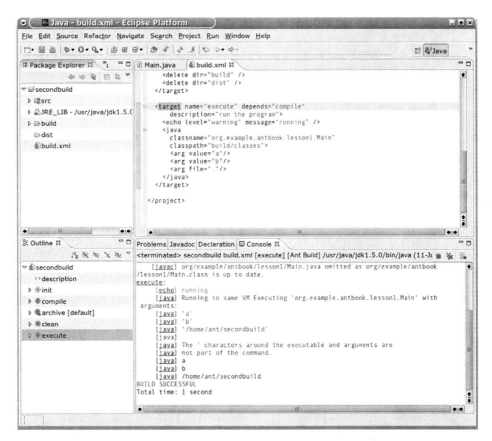

Figure 2.4 Our build file hosted under Eclipse. Consult Appendix C for the steps needed to do this.

2.11 SUMMARY

Ant is told what to build by an XML file, a *build file*. This file describes all the actions to build an application, such as creating directories, compiling the source, and determining what to do afterwards; the actions include making a JAR file and running the program.

The build file is in XML, with the root <project> element representing a Ant *project*. This project contains *targets*, each of which represents a stage of the project. A target can depend on other targets, which is stated by listing the dependencies in the depends attributes of the target. Ant uses this information to determine which targets to execute, and in what order.

The actual work of the build is performed by Ant *tasks*. These tasks implement their own dependency checking, so they only do work if it is needed.

Some of the basic Ant tasks are <echo> to print a message, <delete> to delete files and directories, <mkdir> to create directories, <javac> to compile Java source, and `<jar>` to create an archive file. The first three of these tasks look like XML versions of shell commands, but the latter two demonstrate the power of Ant. They contain dependency logic, so that `<javac>` will compile only those source files for which the destination binary is missing or out of date, and `<jar>` will create a JAR file only if its input files are newer than the output.

Running Ant is called *building*; a build either succeeds or fails. Builds fail when there's an error in the build file, or when a task fails by throwing an exception. In either case, Ant lists the line of the build file where the error occurred. Ant can build from the command line, or from within Java IDEs. The command line has many options to control the build and what output gets displayed. Rerunning a build with the `-verbose` option provides more detail as to what is happening. Alternatively, the `-quiet` option runs a build nearly silently. The most important argument to the command line is the name of the targets to run—Ant executes each of these targets and all its dependencies.

After this quick introduction, you're ready to start using Ant in simple projects. If you want to do this or if you have deadlines that insist on it, go right ahead. The next two chapters will show you how to configure and control Ant with its properties and datatypes, and how to run unit tests under it. If your project needs these features, then please put off coding a bit longer, and keep reading.

CHAPTER 3

Understanding Ant datatypes and properties

In the last chapter, we used Ant to build, archive, and run a Java program. Now we're going to look at how to control that process through Ant's datatypes and properties.

In programming language terms, Ant's tasks represent the functionality offered by the runtime libraries. The tasks are useful only with data, the information that they need to know what to do. Java is an object-oriented language where data and functions are mixed into classes. Ant, although written in Java, differentiates between the tasks that do the work and the data they work with—data represented as *datatypes*. Ant also has the approximate equivalent of variables in its *properties*.

To pass data to tasks, you need to be able to construct and refer to datatypes and properties in a build file. As with tasks, datatypes are just pieces of XML, pieces that list files or other resources that a task can use. This chapter introduces datatypes and properties. It does go into some depth, so don't be afraid to skip bits and return to them later. We'll start with the basic concepts.

3.1 PRELIMINARIES

Just as Java has classes and variables, Ant has datatypes and properties, which are at the core of its capabilities. All build files make use of them in one way or another, and all Ant users need to understand them. Let's start with an overview of them both.

3.1.1 What is an Ant datatype?

An Ant *datatype* is equivalent to a Java class—behind the scenes they're actually implemented as such. Datatypes store complex pieces of information used in the build—for example, a list of files to compile or a set of directories to delete. These are the kinds of things Ant has to manage, so build files need a way to describe them. Ant datatypes can do this. The datatypes act as parameters to tasks. You can declare them inside a task or define them outside, give them a name, and then pass that name to a task. This lets you share a datatype across more than one task.

A typical Ant build has to handle files and paths, especially the notorious classpath. Ant datatypes can handle files and paths natively. The *fileset* and *path* datatypes crop up throughout Ant build files.

The fileset datatype can enumerate which files to compile, package, copy, delete, or test. Defining a fileset of all Java files, for example, is straightforward:

```
<fileset id="source.fileset" dir="src" includes="**/*.java" />
```

By providing an id attribute, we're defining a *reference*. This reference name can be used later wherever a fileset is expected. For example, copying our source code to another directory using the same source.fileset is

```
<copy todir="backup">
  <fileset refid="source.fileset"/>
</copy>
```

This will work only if the fileset was defined previously in the build, such as in a predecessor target. Otherwise, Ant will fail with an error about an undefined reference.

That's a quick introduction to datatypes, which we'll be using throughout the book. Now, let's look at what a property is.

3.1.2 Property overview

An Ant *property* represents any string-specified item. Ant properties are essential not just to share information around the build, but to control build files from the outside. For example, changing a build to use a different version of a third-party library, perhaps for testing purposes, can be made as trivial as this:

```
ant -Dhost=localhost
```

We could set the property inside the file using

```
<property name="host" value="localhost" />
```

In either case, the Ant property host is now bound to the value localhost. To use this value in a build file, we can use it inside any string

```
<echo>host=${host}</echo>
```

If the property is defined, the ${host} is replaced with its value; if it isn't, it stays as is.

Unlike Java variables, Ant properties are *immutable:* you cannot change them. The first task, project, or person to set a property fixes it for that build. This rule is the opposite of most languages, but it's a rule that lets you control build files from the outside, from tools such as IDEs, or from automated build systems. It's also the key to letting different users customize a build file to work on their system, without editing the build file itself. Simply by defining the appropriate property on the command line, you can change the behavior of your own or someone else's build file. Inside the build file, properties let you define a piece of information once and share it across many tasks. This makes maintenance easier and reduces errors.

Now that we've defined datatypes and properties, let's use them to get Ant to compile a program.

3.2 INTRODUCING DATATYPES AND PROPERTIES WITH <JAVAC>

Compiling Java source is central to all Java projects and is supported with the <javac> task. This task provides a front end to many Java compilers, including the normal JDK compiler and alternatives such as Jikes and gjc. Most of the differences in invocation and command-line parameters are handled by the task, so users can use whichever compiler they prefer without the build file author having to know or care.

To compile Java source on the command line, you have to specify the source files and usually a destination directory. Other common options control whether debugging information is included, and what the classpath for the compiler is.

Here's how we would go about compiling some Java source on the command line:

```
javac -d build/classes
  -classpath build/classes
  -sourcepath src
  -g:lines,vars,source
  src/d1/core/*.java
```

We declare the destination directory and add it to our classpath, say that our source package hierarchy begins in the src directory, and that we want full debugging information. Finally, we declare that we want all Java files in a single directory compiled. Sun's javac program is helpful, in that it automatically compiles source files you didn't tell it to compile, if import statements imply that they're needed. Other compilers, such as that from the Kaffe JVM, aren't so greedy, and we would need to specify every .java file.

Now, let's build in Ant. We'll start by looking at the mapping between `javac` options and those of `<javac>`, as shown in table 3.1.

Table 3.1 Sun's javac compared to Ant's wrapper `<javac>` task. Note the similarities between the parameters. Also note Ant's way of using domain-specific terminology for concepts such as classpath.

Option	JDK's javac switch	Ant's `<javac>` syntax
Debugging info	`-g` (generate all debugging info)	`debug="true"`
	`-g:none` (generate no debugging info)	`debug="false"`
	`-g:{lines,vars,source}` (generate only some debugging info)	`debug="true"` `debuglevel="lines,` `vars,source"`
Generate no warnings	`-nowarn`	`nowarn="true"`
Output compiler messages	`-verbose`	`verbose="true"`
Provide detail on deprecated API use	`-deprecation`	`deprecation="true"`
Specify where to find referenced class files and libraries	`-classpath <path>`	`<classpath>` `<pathelement` `location="log.jar"` `/>` `</classpath>`
Specify where to find input source files	`-sourcepath <path>`	`<src path="src"/>`
Override location of bootstrap class files	`-bootclasspath <path>`	`<bootclasspath …/>`
Override location of installed extensions	`-extdirs <dirs>`	`<extdirs …/>`
Specify where to place generated class files	`-d <directory>`	`destdir="build"`
Specify character encoding used by source files	`-encoding <encoding>`	`encoding="…"`
Generate class files for specific VM version	`-target 1.1`	`target="1.1"`
Enable Java 1.4 assertions	`-source 1.4`	`source="1.4"`
Enable Java 5 language	`-source 1.5`	`source="1.5"`
Cross compile to J2ME	`-cldc1.0`	(no equivalent)

NOTE Ant itself is not a Java compiler; it simply contains a facade over compilers such as Sun's javac. You need a Java compiler such as the JDK javac program. See appendix A for installation and configuration information in order to use `<javac>`.

The <javac> syntax introduces several new attributes, as well as several child elements of <javac>. Most of these attributes are Boolean in nature—debug, optimize, nowarn, verbose, and deprecation. Ant allows flexibility in how Booleans can be specified with *on*, *true*, and *yes* all representing true and any other value mapping to false. The elements <classpath>, <src>, <bootclasspath>, and <extdirs> introduce one of Ant's greatest assets—its path- and file-handling capability. Each of these elements represents a *path*.

Using this information, we can write the following piece of a build file:

```
<property name="build.classes.dir"        ❶
    location="build/classes" />


<path id="compile.classpath">
  <pathelement location="lib/junit.jar"/>   ❷
</path>


<mkdir dir="${build.classes.dir}"/>    ←❸


<target name="compile" >
  <javac
        destdir="${build.classes.dir}"    ←❹
        debug="true"       ❺
        srcdir="src">     ←┘
    <classpath refid="compile.classpath"/>    ←❻
  </javac>
</target>
```

This <javac> example is more than a simple translation: we've started to adapt it to Ant's way of working. To explain this example, we'll have to introduce some new concepts.

First, we set an Ant property to the directory where we want to compile our source ❶. Next, we declare a path for JARs to use in the compile. It contains one item, junit.jar ❷. We use the <mkdir> task to create a directory ❸. The directory is specified by the property defined previously. The "${...}" notation denotes a use of an Ant property; the property is expanded in the string where the reference appears. The same property ${build.classes.dir} is used to tell the <javac> task where to place the output ❹.

The srcdir attribute ❺ implicitly defines a *fileset* containing all files in the specified directory tree. The <classpath> element ❻ declares the classpath for the compiler by referring to the path declared earlier with the id "compile.classpath".

This single fragment of a build file contains most of the core concepts of Ant. One of the central ones is the *path* datatype.

3.3 PATHS

A path, sometimes called a *path-like structure* in Ant's documentation, is an ordered list of elements, where each element can be a file or a directory. It describes paths such as the Java CLASSPATH, or the PATH environment variable of Unix and Windows. It may have a task-specific name, such as `<classpath>` above, or it may just have the simple name `<path>`.

An example of a path definition is:

```
<path>
  <pathelement location="lib/junit.jar"/>
</path>
```

This definition contains one element, whose `location` attribute can specify a single file or directory. You can also extend a path with another path, using `path` instead of `location`:

```
<path>
  <pathelement path="build/classes;lib/junit.jar"/>
</path>
```

This `path` attribute separates its parameters into individual elements, using either a semicolon (;) or colon (:) to split them. There's some special handling for a Windows-style `c:\winnt`; this will be treated as a single directory, and not *c* and *winnt*. Directories can be separated by either a forward-slash (/) or a back-slash (\), regardless of operating system; a build file shouldn't have to care what system it runs on.

If a path structure consists of only a single `path` or `location`, it can be specified using a shortcut form as in

```
<path location="lib/junit.jar" />
```

or with multiple files separated by either the : or ; path separator:

```
<path path="build/classes:lib/junit.jar" />
```

Paths can include a set of files:

```
<path>
  <fileset dir="lib">
    <include name="*.jar"/>
  </fileset>
</path>
```

This set of files creates a path containing all JAR files in the `lib` directory. This is a path built from a *fileset*, which we're about to introduce.

Ant makes no order guarantees within a `<fileset>`. Each element in a path is ordered from the top and down so that all files within a fileset would be grouped together in a path. However, the order within that fileset isn't guaranteed. The result in this example is that the path would contain all the JAR files, but the order cannot be predicted.

That's a path defined. Now, how do you use one?

3.3.1 How to use a path

There are two ways to use a path. A standalone path declaration can be given a name via its `id` attribute. This name has to be unique across all Ant datatypes given ID values; this is a separate namespace from property and target names.

```
<path location="lib/junit.jar" id="junit.path"/>
```

The name can be referenced whenever a path is needed:

```
<path refid="junit.path" />
```

The `refid` attribute references the defined path; if no such path has been defined at that point in the build, Ant will fail with an error.

The other way to use a path is inline, in any task that takes a nested element of the path type. These elements may not be called `path`. They may have other names, though the word *path* is usually in there. Our ongoing example, the `<javac>` task, has the elements `<classpath>`, `<sourcepath>`, `<bootclasspath>` and `<extdirs>`. The latter path element shows that not all path elements end in the word path—this is a special case for compatibility with the command-line version. It also shows that the online manual (or an Ant-aware text editor) is important to have when writing build files.

When using the task, we could declare two `<src>` tags to compile two separate directory trees of source code into a single output directory:

```
<javac destdir="build/classes">
  <src path="src"/>
  <src path="test"/>
</javac>
```

The task will then compile both source paths together. There are lots of permutations of all the ways in which these fileset and path capabilities can work together to accomplish precisely choosing the files desired. We'll expose you to some of these variations throughout this book.

The other ubiquitous Ant datatype is the *fileset*. While a path represents a list of files or directories, a fileset represents a general-purpose collection of files, such as all the Java files in a source tree. It's the main way to pass a collection of files to an Ant task.

3.4 FILESETS

Most build processes operate on sets of files, either to compile, copy, delete, or manipulate in any number of other ways. These processes are so central that Ant provides the fileset as a built-in datatype, one of the more generic sets of *resource types*.

A *fileset* is a set of files rooted from a single directory. By default, a fileset specified with only a root directory will include all the files in that entire directory tree, including files in all subdirectories recursively. For a concrete running example that will demonstrate fileset features as we discuss them, let's copy files from one directory to another:

```
<copy todir="newweb">
  <fileset dir="web"/>
</copy>
```

In its current form, all files from the web directory are copied to the newweb directory. This example will evolve into copying only specific files, altering them during the copy with token replacement, and flattening the directory hierarchy in the newweb directory.

Selecting all files in a directory is a bit of a blunt instrument. Many filesets restrict their selection to a subset of the files by using a patternset.

3.4.1 Patternsets

A fileset can contain multiple *patternsets*, which restrict the files in the fileset to those that match or don't match a specified pattern. We can use one to include all JSP files under a web directory:

```
<copy todir="newweb">
  <fileset dir="web" includes="**/*.jsp"/>
</copy>
```

This patternset is equivalent to

```
<copy todir="newweb">
  <fileset dir="web">
    <include name="**/*.jsp"/>
  </fileset>
</copy>
```

Had we specified just *.jsp, only the JSP files in the web directory would have been copied, but the files in any subdirectories wouldn't have been copied.

Patternsets may be nested within one another, such as

```
<patternset>
  <include name="**/*.gif"/>
  <include name="**/*.jpg"/>
  <patternset>
    <exclude name="**/*.txt"/>
    <exclude name="**/*.xml"/>
  </patternset>
</patternset>
```

A patternset is just a collection of file-matching patterns. The patternset itself doesn't refer to any actual files until it's nested in a fileset and, therefore, rooted at a specific directory. The patterns it supports are simple regular expressions on a directory path. The "*.jar" and "**/*.jsp" strings we've just been using are some of these expressions.

The rules for pattern matching in the strings are as follows:

- "*" matches zero or more characters.
- "?" matches a single character.

- "`**`", used as the name of a directory, represents matching of all directories from that point down, matching zero or more directories.
- A pattern ending with a trailing "`/`" or "`\`" implies a trailing "`**`". That is, a directory includes its subdirectories.
- The directory separators "`/`" and "`\`" are converted into the correct separator for the local platform.
- Everything else is treated as simple text.

As well as being embedded inside filesets, patternsets can be specified independently as standalone datatypes. Table 3.2 lists the attributes available on the `<patternset>` element.

Table 3.2 Patternset attributes. Including and excluding patterns allows filesets to be defined precisely to encompass only the files desired.

Attribute	Description
`includes`	Comma-separated list of patterns of files that must be included. All files are included when omitted.
`excludes`	Comma-separated list of patterns of files that must be excluded. No files (except default excludes) are excluded when omitted.
`includesfile`	The name of a file; each line of this file is taken to be an include pattern. You can specify more than one include file by using nested `includesfile` elements.
`excludesfile`	The name of a file; each line of this file is taken to be an exclude pattern. You can specify more than one exclude file by using nested `excludesfile` elements.

Exclusion patterns take precedence, so that if a file matches both an `include` and `exclude` pattern, the file is excluded.

The `<patternset>` datatype also has elements for every aspect of the pattern, which makes it easy to list multiple patterns inside a single `<patternset>`. The elements are `<include>`, `<exclude>`, `<includesfile>`, and `<excludesfile>`. Each of these elements has a name attribute. For `<include>` and `<exclude>`, the name attribute specifies the pattern to be included or excluded, respectively. For the `<includesfile>` and `<excludesfile>` elements, the name attribute represents a filename. Each of these elements has `if`/`unless` attributes, which are covered in the conditional patternset section later in this chapter.

Here is an example of a patternset:

```
<patternset>
  <include name="*.jsp"/>
</patternset>
```

This patternset includes all JSP pages in a single directory. Here's another patternset:

```
<patternset>
  <include name="**/*.jsp"/>
  <exclude name="**/test/broken?.jsp"/>
</patternset>
```

This one includes all JSP pages in a directory tree, except any in the directory `test` and the local name consisting of `broken?.jsp`, such as `broken1.jsp`, or `brokenC.jsp`. As you can see, explicit exclusion is a powerful tool.

One thing that's important to know is that some file types are excluded by default, the *default excludes* patterns. In many builds, special or temporary files end up in your source tree from IDEs and Software Configuration Management (SCM) systems such as CVS and Subversion. To avoid having to always explicitly exclude these, exclude patterns are enabled by default for some common patterns. The standard patterns are shown in table 3.3.

Table 3.3 Default exclude patterns, which are used in filesets to match files that aren't used, copied or deleted by default. If you want to add files that match these patterns to a fileset, then set defaultexcludes="no".

Pattern	Typical program that creates and uses these files
`**/*~`	jEdit and many other editors, used as previous version backup
`**/#*#`	Editors
`**/.#*`	Editors
`**/%*%`	Editors
`**/CVS/`	CVS (Concurrent Version System) metadata
`**/.cvsignore`	CVS, contains exclusion patterns for CVS to ignore during routine operations
`**/SCCS/`	SCCS metadata
`**/vssver.scc`	Microsoft Visual SourceSafe metadata file
`**/._*`	Mac OS/X resource fork files
`**/.svn/`	Subversion files (can be `**/_svn` on some systems)
`**/.DS_Store`	OS/X Folder Information

Many users have been bitten by the confusion caused when a fileset omits files because they match one of these default exclude patterns. The `<fileset>` element has a `defaultexcludes` attribute for turning off this behavior. Simply use `defaultexcludes="no"` to turn off the automatic exclusions. If needed, you can change the set of `defaultexcludes` files using the `<defaultexcludes>` task. You can add files:

```
<defaultexcludes add="**/*.iml"/>
```

You can remove a pattern:

```
<defaultexcludes remove="**/.svn"/>
```

You can reset the set of patterns:

```
<defaultexcludes default="true"/>
```

And you can even print the list of current patterns:

```
<defaultexcludes echo="true"/>
```

We recommend extending only the list, and only then if your SCM system or editor creates different file types to exclude. If you get the list wrong, you can end up excluding all files!

Filesets in use

Having covered filesets and patternsets, we can apply the information to the `<javac>` task. This task is one of the many *implicit fileset* tasks. Rather than requiring you to add a fileset of source files as a nested element, the task itself supports many of the attributes and elements of a fileset:

```
<javac srcdir="src" destdir="build/classes">
  <include name="org/antbook/**/*.java"/>
  <exclude name="org/antbook/broken/*.java"/>
</javac>
```

This task has `<javac>` acting as a fileset, including some files and excluding some others. Note: you can't reliably use `excludes` patterns to tell `<javac>` which files *not* to compile. If a Java file you include needs another file, Sun's `javac` compiler will search the source tree for it, even if it's been excluded from the fileset. This is a feature of the compiler, and not Ant. We can exclude only the classes in the `org.antbook.broken` package because they aren't imported into any class in the fileset.

Another thing to know is that filesets resolve their files when the declaration is first evaluated. This may not be when it's declared, but when it's first used. Once resolved, the set is never updated. This is important to know when referring to a previously defined fileset, as new files and directories matching the patterns may have appeared between the resolution and reference; these new files do not appear in the fileset.

Filesets and paths are some of the most common of Ant's datatypes and are often passed down to tasks within nested elements.

Datatype elements in tasks

Ant tasks accept datatypes as nested parameters, sometimes in the name of the type, such as `<fileset>`, which is how the task to create JAR archives, `<jar>`, accepts filesets. Other tasks name their parameters from the role of the data. The `<javac>` task supports the `<src>`, `<classpath>`, and `<extdirs>` elements, which are all nested paths, for source, classpath files, and external directories respectively.

`<javac>` is also a task with an *implicit fileset*: it has the attributes `includes`, `excludes`, `includesfile`, and `excludesfile` as well as nested `<include>`, `<exclude>`, `<includesfile>`, and `<excludesfile>` elements. Normally, a `<fileset>` has a mandatory root `dir` attribute, but in the case of `<javac>` this is specified with the `srcdir` attribute. Confusing? Yes. However, it was done this way in order to remove ambiguity for build file writers. Would a `dir` attribute on `<javac>` have represented a source directory or a destination directory?

Most tasks with implicit filesets can be recognized by their `dir`, `includes`, and `excludes` attributes. A lot of the core Ant tasks take arguments this way, though it's no longer encouraged in new tasks because nested datatypes are preferred.

Regardless of how they're passed down, datatypes are the main way of configuring Ant tasks, and the fileset and path are ubiquitous. The fileset is the most common datatype that build file authors will write. One of its strengths is that it can select which files to work on by much more than just the name of the file.

3.5 SELECTORS

Filenames are a common way of selecting files for operations, but not always enough. Sometimes you want to delete out-of-date files or upload only changed files to a remote site. What if you want to delete files, leaving directories in their place? You can do all these things by refining the fileset with *selectors*. Each selector is a test that's applied to each file in the fileset (or other selector container). It narrows down the selection of files in the fileset. The selectors are listed in table 3.4.

These selectors can be combined inside *selector containers* to provide grouping and logic. The containers are `<and>`, `<or>`, `<not>`, `<none>`, `<selector>`, and `<majority>`. Containers may be nested inside containers, enabling complex selection logic. Rather than detailing every available selector, container, and their options,

Table 3.4 Ant's built-in selectors. Any fileset can be restricted by these selectors to choose only those files that match the specific tests.

Selector	Description
`<filename>`	Works like a patternset `<include>` or `<exclude>` element to match files based on a pattern
`<depth>`	Selects files based on a directory depth range
`<size>`	Selects files that are less, equal to, or more than a specified size
`<date>`	Selects files (and optionally directories) that have been last modified before, after, or on a specified date
`<present>`	Selects files if they exist in another directory tree
`<depend>`	Selects files that are newer than corresponding ones in another directory tree
`<contains>`	Selects files that contain a string
`<containsregexp>`	Select files that contain a regular expression-described string
`<different>`	Selects files that are different from those in another directory
`<type>`	Selects by type of file or directory
`<modified>`	Calculates (and caches) checksums for files; selects those that have changed
`<signedselector>`	Selects signed JAR files, optionally naming the signatory
`<scriptselector>`	Inline script language containing a selection rule

CHAPTER 3   UNDERSTANDING ANT DATATYPES AND PROPERTIES

we refer you to Ant's documentation for this information. We will, however, provide a couple of examples showing how selectors work, and we'll use them in the book where needed.

To compare two directory trees and copy the files that exist in one tree but not in another, we use a combination of <not> and <present>:

```
<copy todir="newfiles" includeemptydirs="false">
  <fileset dir="web">
    <not>
      <present targetdir="currentfiles"/>
    </not>
  </fileset>
</copy>
```

This <copy> task will copy only the files from the web directory that don't exist in the currentfiles directory. Using the <contains> selector, we choose only those files containing a certain string:

```
<copy todir="currentfiles" includeemptydirs="false">
  <fileset dir="web">
    <contains text="System"/>
  </fileset>
</copy>
```

Only the files containing the text "System" in the web directory are copied to the currentfiles directory. By default <contains> is case-sensitive, but it can be changed using casesensitive="no".

All rules must be satisfied before a file is considered part of a fileset, so when using selectors in conjunction with patternsets, the file must match the include patterns, must not match any exclude patterns, and the selector rules must test positively. If you don't find the current selectors adequate, you can write a custom one in Java.

These are pretty much all of Ant's <fileset> types which, along with <path>, are the main way of referring to files. There are a few other file and directory datatypes that crop up in special cases, which we'll explore next.

3.6   ADDITIONAL ANT DATATYPES

We've covered the Ant datatypes that are frequently used by Ant tasks, but there are several other datatypes that are used by a smaller number of tasks. Here's a brief overview of the most important ones: filelist, dirset, and filterset.

Filelist

A sibling of the fileset is the *filelist*. These are ordered lists of files and directories that may or may not exist. They're useful when you need to order a set of files. The datatype is supported in the <concat>, <dependset>, and <pathconvert> tasks, among others, as well as a nested element within the <path> datatype.

```
<touch>
  <filelist dir="." files="1.txt,2.txt">
    <file name="white spaced file.txt" />
    <file name="*.txt" />
  </filelist>
</touch>
```

This task will create four files: `"1.txt"`, `"2.txt"`, `"white spaced file.txt"`, and `"*.txt"`. The latter file shows that filename expansion doesn't take place in filesets. The other big difference is that while a fileset finds all existing files that match a pattern, a filelist can contain filenames that don't yet exist.

Dirset

The fileset datatype incorporates both files and directories, but some tasks prefer to only operate on directories. The `<dirset>` datatype is used only in the `<javadoc>` and `<pathconvert>` tasks. The path datatype also supports a nested `<dirset>`, which allows for easier construction of classpath elements for multiple directories.

Filterset

During the build process, you sometimes need to dynamically fill in values of a file, often with timestamps and version information; sometimes with tuning code for a specific project. Ant has a type for this, *filterset,* with support in the `<copy>` and `<move>` tasks. Three situations typically take advantage of filtered copy:

- Putting the current date or version information into files bundled with a build, such as documentation
- Conditionally "commenting out" pieces of configuration files
- Simple generation of source or data files

A filter operation replaces tokenized text in source files during either a `<move>` or `<copy>` to a destination file. In a filtered `<copy>`, the source file isn't altered. A token is defined as text surrounded by beginning and ending token delimiters. These delimiters default to the at-sign character (@), but can be altered using the `begintoken` and `endtoken` attributes of `<filterset>`.

That concludes our overview of the main datatypes of Ant. Filesets and paths are the most common and are the ones that will soon become familiar. Although we'll return to datatypes later in the chapter, looking at datatype references and Ant's resources model, we now have enough to get started. Before doing that, it's time to look at properties, because together with filesets and paths, they form the core of Ant's configuration data.

3.7 PROPERTIES

One of the most important concepts in Ant is that of *properties*. Ant properties contain string values that can be used wherever a string is needed in a build file. They can be set in tasks or on the command line, and can both control the build process and configure it.

Ant provides various built-in properties, properties that the runtime sets for you. These are listed in table 3.5.

Table 3.5 Ant's built-in properties. Build files can rely on these being set, although sometimes IDE-hosted Ant runs can find that this isn't always the case.

Name	Definition
ant.file	The absolute path of the build file.
ant.home	The path to executing version of Ant's root directory. Some IDEs don't set this.
ant.java.version	The JVM version Ant detected; currently it can hold the values 1.1, 1.2, and so on.
ant.project.name	The name of the project that's currently executing; it's set in the name attribute of <project>.
ant.version	The version of Ant.
basedir	The absolute path of the project's base directory, the directory from which relative filenames are resolved.

Properties are expanded by surrounding them with ${}, such as in the string "ant.file = ${ant.file}". Properties written like this will be expanded in all string assignments to task attributes, and inside most task text elements. For example, to examine the built-in properties, we can use the <echo> task:

```
<target name="echo">
  <echo message="ant.file = ${ant.file}"/>
  <echo message="ant.home = ${ant.home}"/>
  <echo message="ant.java.version = ${ant.java.version}"/>
  <echo>basedir = ${basedir}</echo>
</target>
```

This task generates output similar to this:

```
echo:
     [echo] ant.file = /home/ant/datatypes/properties.xml
     [echo] ant.home = /home/ant/ant
     [echo] ant.java.version = 1.5
     [echo] basedir = /home/antbook/datatypes
```

This example was run with the -file command-line option to specify a different build file name, as shown in ant.file. The basedir property defaults to the path of the current build file—it can be changed by adding a basedir attribute on the <project> element.

All JVM system properties are provided as Ant properties, letting your build files determine user's home directory path and the current username. The JVM system properties will vary from platform to platform, but there are many that you can rely on, for example,

```
<echo message="user.name = ${user.name}"/>
<echo message="user.home = ${user.home}"/>
<echo message="java.home = ${java.home}"/>
```

Here are sample results from running this code on a Windows machine:

```
[echo] user.name = erik
[echo] user.home = C:\Documents and Settings\erik
[echo] java.home = c:\jdk\jre
```

If you're curious about the set of properties at any point in a build file, the `<echoproperties>` task can list the current set to the console or to a file. On its own, this task will list all properties in the order they're stored in the hashtable:

```
<target name="echoall">
  <echoproperties />
</target>
```

The XML output is sorted, which makes it easy to browse. You could also save the list to a file to compare against a previous version.

```
<target name="echoxml">
  <echoproperties format="xml"
    destfile="current-properties.xml" />
</target>
```

Listing properties or saving them to a file is useful while learning about properties and for diagnostics. We often have a diagnostics target that lists the current set of properties.

Being able to read properties is only half the problem. How do you set them?

3.7.1 Setting properties with the <property> task

The `<property>` task is the normal way to set properties. It provides many ways to assign properties, the most popular being

- Name/value assignment
- Name/location assignment
- Loading a set of properties from a properties file
- Reading environment variables

Setting and using a simple property

A common action in a build file is selecting one of two choices, such as whether to compile debug information into the .class files. Development releases need this, while production builds may opt to omit it. This choice can be managed through a property. We can define a property named `build.debug` and set its value to `true`.

```
<property name="build.debug" value="true"/>
```

This property can be passed to the `debug` attribute in a `<javac>` task:

```
<javac srcdir="src" debug="${build.debug}"/>
```

The `<property value>` assignment is the easiest way to set a property in the build file, and it's ideal for simple values. However, it isn't the best way to set filenames or paths, where the `location` attribute is preferable.

Setting a property to a filename

The `location` attribute of the `<property>` task converts a relative path into an absolute location and converts directory separators to that of the target platform. Build file authors can choose between forward slashes (/) or backslashes (\) based on personal preference:

```
<property name="release.dir" location="../release" />
```

When run from a Windows build in the directory `c:\erik\ch02`, the property will be set to `C:\erik\release`. On a Unix system, the path could be something like `/home/erik/release`.

This resolved path can be passed down to native programs or Java code, as it's now absolute and platform-specific. The directory against which relative paths are resolved is the base directory of the project, which is typically the directory where `build.xml` resides. The built-in property `basedir` is set to this directory.

In this book, file locations are always set using `<property location>`. You can often get away with using the `value` attribute instead; many build files do. We use `<property location>` to make the files more readable and to avoid problems when properties are passed across build files—something that's done in chapter 9 of this book. Consider it a best practice, rather than an absolute requirement.

In addition to setting properties in the build file, Ant can be configured by properties in external files.

Loading properties from a properties file

Loading properties from a Java properties file is a common way of customizing builds. We can create a file named `build.properties` in the root directory of our project, alongside the build file. This file has a comment and some properties:

```
#properties for the build
build.debug=false
```

Ant's `<property>` task will load the file in the `file` attribute:

```
<property file="build.properties"/>
```

Property values in the properties file are expanded during the load. Consider a properties file containing these lines:

```
build.dir=build
output.dir=${build.dir}/output
```

When loaded, `output.dir` will have the value `build/output`. Forward-referencing property values may be used in a single properties file as well; if the previous lines had been in opposite order, the same results would be obtained. Circular definitions will cause a build failure.

All properties loaded from a properties file are loaded as simple string values, as if they were set by the `<property value>` operation. To turn them into absolute values, the build file would have to reassign them.

```
<property name="output.dir.absolute" location="${output.dir}" />
```

This would resolve it to a path such as `/home/erik/ch02/build/output`.

There are two other issues with property file loading that developers need to know. One is that to use a backslash in the file, it must be repeated twice:

```
release.dir=..\\release
```

This is because the file is loaded using the `java.util.Properties` class, which requires this. Consult the class's JavaDocs for the complete file syntax.

The other quirk is that if you misspell the name of the file, with something such as `<property file="build.propertoes"/>`, Ant doesn't stop the build. Indeed, it doesn't even warn of a problem, except when you run Ant in verbose (`-v`) mode. This seems like a bug, but it's actually deliberate. It lets you offer the option to control the build, without making it mandatory. To understand how to do that, you need to understand Ant's unusual property assignment model.

Why overriding a property doesn't work

First, a little test—examine the following code lines and guess their output given the properties file just defined, the one that sets build.debug to `false`:

```
<target name="override">
  <property file="build.properties"/>
  <property name="build.debug" value="true"/>
  <echo message="build.debug is ${build.debug}"/>
</target>
```

We wouldn't have asked this question had it been completely straightforward. The result is:

```
[echo] build.debug is false
```

A property's value doesn't change once set: *properties are immutable*. Whoever sets a property first, sets it for the duration of the build. Understanding this rule and how to take advantage of it is essential for using Ant. It causes a lot of confusion and frustration with new users, with build files that appear not to be working, when really it's just the "first property assignment wins" rule at work.

Why does Ant have such a rule, one at odds with most other languages? It could just be a historical accident, but in fact it has proven to be very powerful when controlling a build. Why? Because you can manipulate the build file from the outside. To do a single build with debugging turned off, just set it on the command line

```
ant -Dbuild.debug=false
```

In that build, the property build.debug is frozen to false, regardless of what assignments are made.

> **NOTE** Once a property has been set, either in the build file or on the command line, it cannot be changed. Whoever sets a property first fixes its value. This is the direct opposite of variables in a program, where the last assignment becomes its value.

Ant's property override rule turns every property into a place in which someone can deliberately override the build file to meet their needs. Common customizations are

- Choosing which compiler to compile Java source
- Changing the output directories for files
- Choosing to compile against different JAR files in a build
- Giving the generated distributable files a specific version name

All these things can be enabled through a judicious use of Ant properties. We'll define many build file settings via properties in order to give users a way of controlling the build and to encourage Ant users to do the same.

We can also configure Ant through environment variables.

Loading environment variables

The <property> task can import environment variables into Ant properties. In order to avoid colliding with existing Ant properties, environment variables are loaded with a name prefix. The convention is to use the prefix env:

```
<property environment="env"/>
```

All environment variables are loaded into Ant's internal properties with the prefix env. (including the trailing period). This gives us properties like env.PATH, or, on Windows NT platforms, env.Path. Tasks in the build can use these settings and change them before executing native and Java programs.

Extracting environment variables is one of the early setup actions most build files do. Another is examining the local system to see what state it's in, which the <available> or <condition> tasks can do.

3.7.2   Checking for the availability of files: <available>

We've been busy setting Ant properties with the <property> task. Many tasks set properties in the course of their work; it's one of the main ways of passing data between tasks. Two useful tasks are <available> and <condition>, which set a property if a test is successful, and, on failure, leave it unset. The <available> task can check for the existence of a Java class or resource in a classpath or for the existence of a file or directory in the file system.

One use of <available> is to check for a particular class in a classpath. This could let Ant skip targets when a prerequisite is missing. The task can look for a class in Ant's own classpath or another supplied path:

```
<available property="junit.present"
        classname="junit.framework.TestCase" />
<echo message="junit.present = ${junit.present}"/>
```

If the junit.framework.TestCase class is found, junit.present is set to true. If it is absent, the property isn't touched and remains undefined.

NOTE   An undefined property will not be expanded, and the string ${property.name} will be used literally.

The <available> task can also look for files or directories:

```
<available property="lib.properties.present"
        file="${lib.dir}/lib.properties"
        type="file"/>
```

The file attribute specifies the file or directory to locate. The optional type attribute can require the file to be of a specific type—either a file or dir for file and directory, respectively.

The final availability check is for a Java resource, which is any file that can be found on the classpath. You can check for the availability of configuration files:

```
<available property="resource.exists"
  resource="log4j.properties" />
```

You can even look for a class without loading it, by giving the path to the implementation class:

```
<available property="junit.found"
  resource="junit/framework/TestCase.class" />
```

This is equivalent to the classname probe we've already seen, except the .class file itself must be requested, and package separators replaced with forward slashes.

The <available> task is essentially one of Ant's many *conditions*. It's an Ant task, but it also can be nested inside the <condition> task. Most other conditions only work inside an Ant task that supports them. There are lots of other conditions, which can be used to set properties or control other aspects of a build.

3.7.3 Testing conditions with <condition>

Most of Ant's tests are grouped under the <condition> task, which will set a named property if a nested condition holds true. A complex condition can be built up using the logical operators <and>, <or>, <xor>, and <not>. Here's a test that sets the property os to the value "windows" if the underlying OS is either of the two Windows platforms, or "other" if it is anything else:

```
<condition property="os"
    value="windows"
    else="other">
  <or>
    <os family="win9x" />
    <os family="winnt" />
  </or>
</condition>
```

The conditions that Ant's conditional tasks support are listed in table 3.6, along with the version of Ant they appeared in.

Table 3.6 Ant's conditions. The list of tests began in Ant 1.4 and has grown over time to let you test everything from Ant's version to the availability of remote computers.

Element	Definition	Version
<and>	Evaluates to true if all nested conditions are true; returns false immediately after reaching the first failed condition	1.4
<antversion>	Tests that the version of Ant matches expectations	1.7
<available>	Exactly the same semantics and syntax as the <available> task, except property and value are ignored; evaluates to true if the resource is available	1.4
<checksum>	Uses the same syntax as the <checksum> task, evaluating to true if the checksum of the file(s) match	1.4
<contains>	Tests whether one string contains another; optionally case-sensitive	1.6
<equals>	Evaluates to true if both properties have the same value	1.4
<filesmatch>	Byte-for-byte file comparison between two files	1.6
<hasfreespace>	Tests for a disk having the specified amount of free space (Java 1.6+)	1.7
<hasmethod>	Tests for a class implementing a named method or field	1.7
<http>	Checks for a URL being reachable without an error code	1.5
<isfailure>	Tests a property for matching the platform's specific values of the failure response codes of an executed program	1.7
<isfalse>	The negation of <istrue>	1.5
<isfileselected>	Tests that a named file is selected in a specific selector	1.6.3
<isreachable>	Checks that a remote machine is reachable (Java 1.5+)	1.7

continued on next page

Table 3.6   Ant's conditions. The list of tests began in Ant 1.4 and has grown over time to let you test everything from Ant's version to the availability of remote computers. *(continued)*

Element	Definition	Version
`<isreference>`	Tests for a datatype reference being valid	1.6
`<isset>`	Evaluates to true if the property exists	1.6
`<issigned>`	Evaluate to true if a named file is signed	1.7
`<istrue>`	Evaluates to true if the value is on, true, or yes	1.5
`<length>`	Checks that the length of a string or file matches expectations	1.6.3
`<matches>`	Tests whether a string matches a regular expression	1.7
`<not>`	Inverts the result of the nested condition	1.4
`<or>`	Evaluates to true if any nested condition is true; returns true after reaching the first successful condition	1.4
`<os>`	Evaluates to true if the OS family (mac, windows, dos, netware, os/2, or unix), name, architecture, and version match	1.4
`<parsersupports>`	Tests for the XML parser supporting a named feature	1.7
`<resourcecount>`	Verifies that the number of resources matches expectations	1.7
`<resourcesmatch>`	Byte-by-byte (or text mode) equality test of two resources	1.7
`<scriptcondition>`	Inline script to evaluate anything	1.7
`<socket>`	Checks for a socket listener on a specified port and host	1.5
`<typefound>`	Tests that a type or task is known	1.7
`<uptodate>`	Exactly the same semantics and syntax as the `<uptodate>` task, except property and value are ignored; evaluates to true if file(s) are up-to-date	1.4
`<xor>`	Exclusive or of the nested conditions	1.7

We'll use conditions throughout the book. Here's one example test:

```
<property name="server.port" value="8080" />
<fail message="no server at ${server.port}" >
  <condition>
    <not>
      <socket port="${server.port}"
        server="127.0.0.1"/>
    </not>
  </condition>
</fail>
```

We've put a condition inside the `<fail>` task, a task that halts the build with an error message if its nested `<condition>` is true. The test tells Ant to halt the build unless there's something listening for inbound TCP connections on port 8080 on the local machine. We use the property `server.port` to hold the port to test; anyone who runs the server on a different port can override this property and the test will adapt.

As we already stated, the `<available>` and `<condition>` tasks are two of the Ant tasks that set a property during their work. Many other tasks do this, of which a simple one is `<tstamp>`, which creates build timestamps for naming files or including in messages.

3.7.4 Creating a build timestamp with `<tstamp>`

The `<tstamp>` task sets a named property to the current time, information that can be used to create files with timestamps in their names. In its simplest form, `<tstamp>` takes no parameters:

```
<tstamp/>
```

It sets three properties automatically based on the current date/time. These properties are listed in table 3.7.

Table 3.7 Ant properties set by the `<tstamp>` task, unless you provide a specific pattern

Property	Value format (based on current date/time)
DSTAMP	"yyyymmdd"
TSTAMP	"hhmm"
TODAY	"month day year"

The `<tstamp/>` task also allows any number of nested `<format>` elements, which define properties given a format specification. For example, to create a property with only the day of the week, use `<format property="..." pattern="...">`:

```
<tstamp>
  <format property="dayofweek" pattern="EEEE"/>
</tstamp>
<echo message="It is ${dayofweek}"/>
```

This results in the following:

```
[echo] It is Monday
```

The `pattern` is specified using the format described in the JavaDocs for `java.text.SimpleDateFormat`. The `<format>` element also supports `locale` and `offset` attributes to change the time zone or the output format—refer to the task reference for these specifics.

We like to set timestamps in the ISO 8601 time representation, which are common in XML documents described in the XML Schema language. We can save it in a properties file inside the application, then embed it into generated files. The `<tstamp>` task creates an ISO 8601 timestamp when given the right pattern:

```
<tstamp>
  <format property="buildtime"
          pattern="yyyy-MM-dd'T'HH:mm:ss" />
</tstamp>
<echo message="buildtime = ${buildtime}"/>
```

This produces output similar to

```
[echo] buildtime = 2006-12-13T17:17:21
```

If we set the `file` attribute of `<echo>`, we can print this to a file, where it can be included in the application's distribution package.

The `<tstamp>` task is a useful example of how many Ant tasks set properties when they run. Many other tasks do this; they'll be introduced as we automate other aspects of the build process. Another way of setting properties is on the command line.

3.7.5 Setting properties from the command line

Ant users can set Ant properties on the command line before Ant does any work. For example, you may want to test against a different version of a library, or supply a password to an FTP upload. Ant has two command-line options to set properties: `-D` and `-propertyfile`.

Nothing can override a property set from the command line. Ant has two classes of properties, *user* properties and *standard* properties. User properties consist of system properties and command-line defined properties, as well as properties overridden using `<ant>`. Properties defined on the command line get set as user properties and are truly immutable, ignoring even the immutability exceptions noted earlier.

You can also name files of properties to load, using the `-propertyfile` option and following it with a filename:

```
ant -propertyfile build.properties -f properties.xml echoall
```

This will load the property file before the build file itself is executed. This trick has the following rules:

1 Properties defined with `-Dname=value` options take precedence.

2 If the property file is missing, a warning is printed but the build continues.

3 Properties in the loaded file aren't expanded.

Items (2) and (3) are different behaviors from that of `<property file>` file loading, which is more common. The fact that property expansion doesn't take place can cause surprises.

Ant properties, whether they're set on the command line or by a task, are the main way to control Ant. How do we do that?

3.8 CONTROLLING ANT WITH PROPERTIES

We've been showing lots of ways to set properties, sometimes to values and paths, but sometimes to the results of various tests in the `<condition>` task or with `<available>`. How can we use these properties to control Ant?

There are three main ways in which properties can help control builds.

- Conditional target execution
- Conditional build failure
- Conditional patternset inclusion/exclusion

In all the techniques, the value of a property is usually unimportant. Most of Ant's conditional execution assumes that a property being set equals *true* and unset equals *false*. As tasks like <condition> and <available> set properties when true, this matches up with their output.

Now, let's go through the three main ways Ant can be controlled by properties.

3.8.1 Conditional target execution

All Ant targets can be made conditional, so they execute only if a property is set or unset. This is done by setting their if and/or unless attributes to *the name of the property*—that is, a string such as property and not ${property}. It's easy to get this wrong, and Ant does nothing to warn you that your conditions are being ignored.

Here's how to use the if attribute to conditionally include source code in a JAR file:

```
<target name="init">
  <mkdir dir="build/classes"/>
  <mkdir dir="dist"/>
</target>

<target name="compile" depends="init">
  <javac srcdir="src" destdir="build/classes"/>
</target>

<target name="copysource" depends="init" if="copy.source">
  <copy todir="build/classes">
    <fileset dir="src"/>
  </copy>
</target>

<target name="jar" depends="compile,copysource">
  <jar basedir="build/classes" jarfile="dist/our.jar">
</target>
```

Each target's conditions are evaluated just prior to the target's execution. This allows dependent targets to control their successors through properties. In this little demonstration, the copysource target could be enabled by setting copy.source. The value is irrelevant—even "false" would enable it. This could be done from the command line:

```
ant -Dcopy.source=true jar
```

Alternatively, the copy.source property could be defined by using one of the many variants of <property>.

Users of conditional targets often get burned by three mistakes. One is by using an expression if="${property}" rather than just the property name:

`if="property"`. The next is that a condition is met if a property is defined; its value is irrelevant. Finally, some people expect that if a target's condition isn't met, then its dependencies should not execute. This isn't the case. All proceeding targets get processed before the test is looked at.

Conditional targets can execute or skip work on demand. Alternatively, a property value can be used to stop the build.

3.8.2 Conditional build failure

We've already used `<fail>` to halt the build depending upon a nested `<condition>`. Ant also has `if` and `unless` attributes to block the build when a property is defined or undefined. Here we fail if two needed libraries are absent:

```
<target name="init">
  <condition property="all.dependencies.present">
    <available classname="junit.framework.TestCase" />
  </condition>

  <fail message="Missing dependencies"
    unless="all.dependencies.present"/>
</target>
```

The `if`/`unless` attributes used to be the only way to make failure conditional other than placing it in a conditional target. You may encounter it in existing projects, although a nested `<condition>` is usually easier to use.

We can also use properties to control which files get pulled into filesets, which lets you choose which files to work on based on the state of the system.

3.8.3 Conditional patternset inclusion/exclusion

As mentioned in section 3.4.1, patternsets have an `if` and `unless` property on their `<include>` and `<exclude>` elements. This is a useful feature for including or excluding files from compilation depending on the existence of libraries.

```
<javac srcdir="src"
       destdir="${build.dir}/classes"
  <exclude name="org/example/antbook/junit/*.java"
           unless="junit.present" />
</javac>
```

This example takes advantage of `<javac>` acting as an implicit fileset, but the `if`/`unless` technique can configure the files that go into any fileset, and hence into any task that supports them.

Overall, conditional patternsets, targets, and tasks are among the main ways that properties can configure a build, skipping files or tasks when not needed. Another way that properties configure tasks is through inline string expansion, which can be used in attributes or elements. Together, they make properties the main way to share information across tasks. The other way to share data across tasks is by using shared datatypes, passing references to the types to multiple tasks.

3.9　REFERENCES

Every Ant datatype declaration can have a unique identifier, which can be used as a *reference*. A common use is with paths. We can give our compile classpath an `id` attribute of `"compile.classpath"` to give it a name that can be referenced:

```
<path id="compile.classpath">
  <fileset dir="lib">
    <include name="*.jar"/>
  </fileset>
</path>
```

This path defines the dependencies needed to compile the application. To feed it into the `<javac>` task, we pass in a reference to the path:

```
<javac destdir="${build.classes.dir}"
       srcdir="src">
  <classpath refid="compile.classpath"/>
</javac>
```

This lets us share the classpath across tasks. The path can also be referenced in other datatype declarations, such as when the test classpath is set up:

```
<path id="test.classpath">
  <path refid="compile.classpath"/>
  <pathelement location="${build.dir}/classes"/>
  <pathelement location="${build.dir}/test/classes"/>
</path>
```

All Ant datatypes support the `refid` and `id` attributes. Anywhere a datatype is declared, it can have an `id` associated with it, which can then be used later. Normally referenced datatypes are defined outside any task, in a target that gets executed before the tasks that refer to the data. That includes the `<property>` task, oddly enough.

3.9.1　Viewing datatypes

Ant properties aren't datatypes. While properties and datatypes are independent from one another for most practical purposes, there are a couple of interesting intersections between them. The ubiquitous `<property>` task can convert any reference to its string representation by calling the `toString()` operation on the datatype. As an example, let's turn a path into a string. First, the path:

```
<path id="the.path">
  <pathelement path="some.jar;another.jar"/>
</path>
```

A `<property>` and an `<echo>` can display the value:

```
<property name="path.string" refid="the.path"/>
<echo message="path = ${path.string}"/>
```

The `<path>` datatype resolves all relative items to their absolute paths and converts all file and path separators to the local platform, and so the result on our platform is

```
[echo] path = /home/ant/ch03/some.jar: /home/ant/ch03/another.jar
```

On Windows, the result would be different, something like

```
[echo] path = C:\ch03\some.jar;C:\ch03\another.jar
```

The path elements have been converted to the local form, resolved to absolute locations, and separated by the current `${path.separator}` value. Printing properties is invaluable for diagnosing path problems.

Converting datatype references to their string value is such a common activity that Ant has a shortcut to let you do it. To have the `toString()` method called on any datatype, just call `${toString:id}`, where `id` is the name of the reference:

```
<echo message="the.path is ${toString:the.path}"/>
```

This technique works for any Ant datatype that has a useful `toString()` value.

We can also use references across patternsets, and use the same string conversion trick. Let's see how.

Using references for nested patternsets

Patternsets provide a nice abstraction for file and directory name matching for use inside of filesets. Defining a patternset only once with an `id` allows it to be reused in any number of filesets. Nesting patternsets allows for patternset grouping. Here's an example:

```
<patternset id="image.files" includes="**/*.gif,**/*.jpg"/>

<patternset id="binary.files">
  <exclude name="**/*.txt"/>
  <exclude name="**/*.xml"/>
  <patternset refid="image.files"/>
</patternset>

<echo level="verbose">
  binary.files = ${toString:binary.files}
</echo>
```

The `binary.files` patternset excludes both .txt and .xml files, and the files included or excluded by the `image.files` patternset. In this case, `binary.files` will also include .jpg and .gif files. The string representation of a patternset is useful for debugging purposes, so defining a property using the patternset `refid` yields these results:

```
[echo] binary.files = patternSet{ includes:
    [**/*.gif, **/ *.jpg] excludes: [**/*.txt, **/*.xml] }
```

If you don't know why an Ant build doesn't do what you expect, print it in `<echo>`. If you echo at `level="verbose"`, then the message doesn't appear except on a

`-verbose` build. One of the things we like to print out at this level is our path of libraries, as the `<path>` datatype is the main way to set up the classpath for compiling and running code.

3.10   MANAGING LIBRARY DEPENDENCIES

Most Java projects depend on other Java libraries and JAR files. Some may only be needed at build time, others during testing or when executing the final program. The Ant build file needs to set up the classpath for the tasks that perform all these operations; otherwise the build will fail. How should this be done?

The simplest (and most common) way to manage libraries is to have a directory (by convention, the directory `lib`), into which you put all dependent libraries. To add a new JAR to the project, drop it into the directory.

To include these files on our compilation classpath, we declare a path that includes every JAR file in the directory:

```
<path id="compile.classpath">
  <fileset dir="lib">
    <include name="*.jar"/>
  </fileset>
</path>
```

This path can then be fed to the compiler by referring to it in the `<javac>` task:

```
<javac destdir="${build.classes.dir}"
       srcdir="src">
  <classpath refid="compile.classpath"/>
</javac>
```

With this technique, it's easy to add new JAR files, and you can see what libraries a project uses. If you check the JARs in the `lib` directory into the source code repository, all developers will get the files they need—and any updates.

Dropping JAR files into a single directory does have its limitations, and in big projects it's too simple a solution. When that time comes, we'll look at alternative solutions. One technique to help you prepare for that is this:

> *Give every library that you put in the lib/ directory a version number in the filename, if it doesn't have one already.*

As an example, if you add version 3.8.2 of `junit.jar` to the directory, rename it `junit-3.8.2.jar`. This lets you see at a glance which versions of the libraries you're using.

We're going to stick with this technique of JAR file management throughout the first section of the book. In the second section, *Applying Ant*, we'll return to the problem of library management.

Having introduced Ant's main datatypes and its property mechanism, we've introduced enough of Ant's type system to be able to build complex applications. There's one other thing that's useful to know a bit about, and that is Ant's model of *resources*. These are just a set of Ant datatypes with standard Java interfaces, interfaces that enable tasks to use them as sources of data. It's an attempt at fitting a unified data/file access model to Ant, including the existing datatypes.

3.11 RESOURCES: ANT'S SECRET DATA MODEL

Ant works with files—files in the file system, files in JAR, Zip, or tar archives, and files joined together to make a path. We've just seen many of the datatypes that work with files: `<fileset>`, `<filelist>`, and `<path>` in particular. It can be very confusing. Why doesn't Ant have a simple, consistent model of data sources?

The answer is simple: nobody was thinking that far ahead. Solving one problem at a time, Ant has slowly acquired all the different types without any unified model of them. For Ant 1.7, one of the developers[1] sat down and unified the Java classes behind the file datatypes, creating a conceptual model that links them all: *resources*. Everything you can use as a data source is a *resource*, and everything that groups resources together is a *resource collection*.

A resource collection is something that holds resources? What does that mean? Well, it means that there are some common things that can be grouped together and fed into tasks. A task that's "resource-enabled" can accept one or more resources—and work with the content the resource refers to—without worrying about what kind of resource it's dealing with.

This is all pretty abstract. If it had been in Ant from the outset, we'd have a simpler conceptual model to explain. Instead, we have one view of Ant's types, "there are things like `<filesets>` and `<filelists>`," and another view that says "everything is just a resource, only some are in the file system."

We're going to stick to the first view for now, the classic model of how Ant works. While the vision of resources is appealing—you can feed any data source or destination to a task—the reality is that most things work best with filesets and filelists, because the code behind most tasks expects to read and write files, using the files' timestamps to provide dependency information. We'll return to the resource concept in chapter 5, with a look at using the `<copy>` task to work with data from arbitrary sources.

3.12 BEST PRACTICES

We've probably scared readers off the Ant datatypes, but we've tried to give a brief yet complete introduction to them. Here are some things that we recommend in order to make effective use of them:

---

[1] Matt Benson—he managed to do a major rewrite of Ant's internals with almost nothing breaking!

- Ant properties are the key to making builds customizable and controllable. Use them copiously.
- Remember that properties are almost always immutable. Whoever sets them first wins.
- Use `<property location="..."/>` to define files and directories. Use the `value` variant for other string values, including filename fragments if needed.
- Reuse datatype definitions. You should have to declare a path or fileset only once.
- Using `<filterset>` to perform simple text substitutions during a build can accomplish powerful things like inserting dates or other dynamic build-time information. Be careful not to use it on binary files, however.
- Use conditions and conditional targets and tasks to adapt to the environment. Build files can be made more robust, or fail with better diagnostics messages.
- Carefully consider the directory structure of your project, including how properties will map to top-level or subordinate directories. By planning this well, a parent build can easily control where it receives the output of the child build.
- A simple, yet effective, way to manage JAR files in a single project is to place them all in a subdirectory, usually called `lib`, and include all these JAR files in the classpath used to build and run programs.

3.13 SUMMARY

This chapter has introduced the foundational Ant concepts of paths, filesets, patternsets, filtersets, properties, and references. Let's look at how they all get used together. Our compilation step utilizes all of these facilities, either directly or indirectly:

```
<target name="compile" depends="init">
  <javac destdir="${build.classes.dir}"
         debug="${build.debug}"
         includeAntRuntime="yes"
         srcdir="src">
    <classpath refid="compile.classpath"/>
  </javac>
</target>
```

We use a property, `build.debug`, to control whether compilation is performed with debug on or off. Typically, the `includeAntRuntime` value should be set to no, but our compilation is building a custom Ant task and requires `ant.jar`. The `<javac>` task acts as an implicit fileset, with `srcdir` mapping to `<fileset>`'s `dir` attribute. All files in the `src` tree are considered for compilation because no `excludes` or explicit `includes` were specified. A reference to a previously defined path, `compile.classpath`, is used to define our compilation classpath.

From this chapter, several important facts about Ant should stick with you throughout this book and on into your build file writing:

- Ant uses *datatypes* to provide rich, reusable parameters to tasks.
- `<javac>` is a task that utilizes most of Ant's datatypes.
- *Paths* represent an ordered list of files and directories. Many tasks can accept a classpath, which is an Ant path. Paths can be specified in a cross-platform manner—the MS-DOS conventions of semicolon (;) and backslash (\) or the Unix conventions of colon (:) and forward slash (/); Ant sorts it all out at runtime.
- *Filesets* represent a collection of files rooted from a specified directory. Tasks that operate on sets of files often use Ant's fileset datatype.
- *Patternsets* represent a collection of file-matching patterns. Patternsets can be defined and applied to any number of filesets.
- The actual element names used for datatypes within a task may vary, and a task may have several different elements all using the same datatype. Some tasks even implicitly represent a path or fileset. Ant's documentation clearly defines the types each attribute and element represents and is the best reference for such details.
- *Properties* are the heart of Ant's extensibility and flexibility. They provide a mechanism to store variables and load them from external resources including the environment. Unlike Java variables, they're immutable.

Several additional datatypes have been introduced, but we haven't provided a lot of detail yet. We'll cover them as it's time to use them; look to chapter 5 in particular. You already should have a general knowledge of Ant's abstractions, which will enable you to define your build process at a high level. Over the next few chapters, we'll show you how to do just that.

With Ant's datatypes introduced and the `<javac>` task thoroughly explored, we know how to build a simple program. It's time to start the main project of the book, which is what the next chapter will do—a diary application and web site. More importantly, the next chapter will cover writing and running the tests for the main application, as we're going to write our code test first!

C H A P T E R   4

Testing with JUnit

> *"Any program feature without an automated test simply doesn't exist."*
>
> —Kent Beck, *Extreme Programming Explained*

At this point we've learned how Ant can build and run an application. But does the application work? Does it do what we wanted? Sure, we can use Ant to run the program after the compile, and we can then check the output, but is that adequate?

You can write code, but unless you're going to write tests or formal proofs of correctness, you have no way of knowing if it works. You can pretend it does, but your end users will discover the truth. Unless you like fielding support calls, you need to be testing your code. Ant and JUnit make this possible. JUnit provides the test framework to write your tests in Java, and Ant runs the tests. The two go hand in hand. JUnit makes it easy to write tests. Ant makes it easy to run those tests, capture the results, and halt the build if a test fails. It will even create HTML reports.

This chapter is going to look at testing, introduce JUnit, and show you how and why testing can and should be central to every software project. It will introduce the program that will be developed through the book. Using this program—a diary—it will show how Ant can integrate this testing into the build process so that every time you type ant, the source is compiled and tested. This makes it easy to run the tests and makes it impossible to ship code that fails those tests.

4.1 WHAT IS TESTING, AND WHY DO IT?

Testing is running a program or library with valid and invalid inputs to see that it behaves as expected in all situations. Many people run their application with valid inputs, but that's just demonstrating that it can be made to work in controlled circumstances. Testing aims to break the application with bad data and to show that it's broken. *Automated testing* is the idea that tests should be executed automatically, and the results should be evaluated by machines. Modern software development processes all embrace testing as early as possible in the development lifecycle. Why?

To show that code works

With a test, you can pass in parameters that are designed to break the program, to stress it at the corners, and then you can see what happens. A well-written test often reveals bugs in your code that you can fix.

To replicate bugs

If you can write a unit test that replicates the bug, you are one step closer to fixing it. You have a way of verifying the problem, and you have some code you can step into to find out what's going wrong. The best part? The test remains, stopping the bug from creeping back.

To avoid proofs-of-correctness

In theory, formal methods can let you prove that a piece of code works. In practice, they can't. The complexity of a modern system implies that you need to have studied something like the pi-calculus to stand a chance. Even if you have the skills, are you really going to prove everything *still* works after every change?

We believe formal logic has a place in software. However, we also think that the people writing the `java.util.concurrent` libraries should do the proofs, not us.

To test on different platforms

If you've automated tests, you can run them on all target platforms. That includes Java versions, application/web server releases, and operating systems. People always criticize Java as "write once, test everywhere," but once testing becomes easy, testing everywhere becomes possible. At that point, you really do have code that runs everywhere.

To enable regression testing

A new Java release comes out every six to twelve months. Libraries in a big project may be updated every month or two. How do you know that your program still works whenever a piece is upgraded? Regression testing, that's how. Regression tests verify that an application still works the way it used to, that there have been no *regressions*. All bug-replication tests become regression tests the moment the bug is fixed.

To enable refactoring

Refactoring is now a well-known concept: the practice of rearranging your code to keep it clean and to help it adapt to change. As defined by Martin Fowler, refactoring is "the restructuring of software by applying a series of internal changes that do not affect its observable behavior" (Fowler 1999). That is, it changes the internals of a program without changing what it does.

If you're going to refactor your program, large portions of your source can change as they're moved around, restructured, or otherwise refactored—often at the click of a button in the IDE. After you make those changes, how can you be sure that everything is still working as before? The only way to know is through those tests that you wrote before you began refactoring, the tests that used to work.

Automated testing transforms how you develop programs. Instead of writing code and hoping that it works, or playing with a program by hand to reassure yourself that all is well, testing can show how much of a program really is working. Ant goes hand in hand with this concept, because it integrates testing with the build process. If it's easy to write tests and easy to run them, there's no longer any reason to avoid testing.

4.2 INTRODUCING OUR APPLICATION

This is the first place in our book where we delve into the application that we built to accompany this text. We're going to use this application through most of the remaining chapters.

Why is the "testing" chapter the right place to introduce our application? Because the tests were written alongside our application: the application didn't exist until this chapter.

4.2.1 The application: a diary

We're going to write a diary application that will store appointments somewhere and print them out. Later on, the diary will save data to a database and generate RSS feeds and HTML pages from that database. We'll add these features as we go along, extending the application, the tests, and the build file in the process.

Using an agile process doesn't mean we can skip the design phase. We just avoid overdesigning before implementing anything we don't immediately need. Accordingly, the first step for the application is to sketch out the architecture in a UML tool. Figure 4.1 shows the UML design of the library.

The core of our application will be the `Events` class, which will store `Event` instances. Every `Event` *must* have a non-null `id`, a `date`, and a `name`; extra `text` is optional. The operation `Event.equals()` compares only the ID values; the `hashCode()` value is also derived from that. The `Event.compareTo` operator is required to have the same semantics as the `equals` operator, so it too works only on the ID value. To sort events by time, we must have a special `Comparator` implementation, the `DateOrder` class. We mark our `Event` as `Serializable` to use

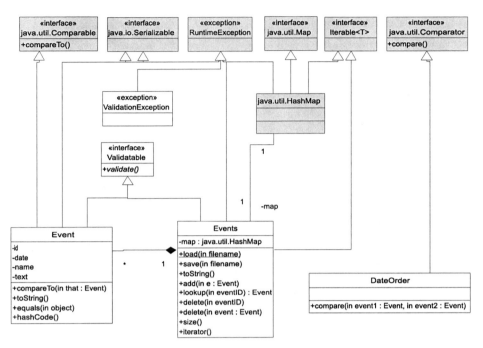

Figure 4.1   UML diagram of the core of our diary. Interfaces and classes in grey are those of the Java libraries. We're going to assume they work and not test them ourselves.

Java's serialization mechanism for simple persistence and data exchange. Oh, and the ID class itself is the `java.util.UUID` GUID class.

We aggregate events in our `Events` class, which provides the manipulation options that we currently want. It's also `Serializable`, as is the class to which it delegates most of the work, a `java.util.HashMap`. Provided all elements in the collection are serializable, all the serialization logic is handled for us. Two methods, `Events.load()` and `Events.save()` aid serialization by saving to/from a file. We don't override the `equals()`/`hashCode()` logic in our `Events` class; it's too much effort. In keeping with XP philosophy, we avoid writing features until they're needed; if they're not needed, we omit them. This is also why the class exports very few of the operations supported by its internal map; initially it exports only `size()` and `iterator()`.

The Java package for the application is `d1` for "diary-1"; the core library that will go into the package is `d1.core`.

There. That's a sketch of the initial design of our program. Is it time to start coding? Almost. We just have to think about how to test the program before we write a line of code, as that's the core philosophy of test-first development.

4.3 HOW TO TEST A PROGRAM

Test-first development means writing the tests before the code, wherever possible. Why? Because it makes developers think about testing from the outset, and so they write programs that can be tested. If you put off testing until afterwards, you'll neglect it. When someone does eventually sit down to write a test or two, they'll discover that the application and its classes may be written in such a way that its almost impossible to test.

The classic way to show that a program works is to write special `main` methods on different classes, methods that create an instance of the class and check that it works as expected. For example, we could define a `main` method to create and print some files:

```
public class Main {

    public static void main(String args[]) throws Exception {
        Events events = new Events();
        events.add(new Event(UUID.randomUUID(),
                        new Date(), "now", null));
        events.add(new Event(UUID.randomUUID(),
                new Date(System.currentTimeMillis() + 5 * 60000),
                "Future", "Five minutes ahead"));
        System.out.println(events);
    }
}
```

We can run this program from the command-line:

```
java -cp build\classes;build\test\classes d1.core.test.Main
```

It will print something we can look at to validate:

```
Wed Feb 16 16:15:37 GMT 2005:Future - Five minutes ahead
Wed Feb 16 16:10:37 GMT 2005:now -
```

This technique is simple and works with IDEs. But it doesn't scale. You don't just want to test an individual class once. You want to test all your classes, every time you make a change, and then have the output of the tests analyzed and presented in a summary form. Manually trying to validate output is a waste of time. You should also want to have your build stop when the tests fail, making it impossible to ship broken programs.

Ant can do this, with help. The assistant is JUnit, a test framework that should become more important to your project than Ant itself. The two tools have a long-standing relationship: JUnit made automated testing easy, while Ant made running those tests part of every build.

Before exploring JUnit, we need to define some terms.

- *Unit tests* test a piece of a program, such as a class, a module, or a single method. They can identify problems in a small part of the application, and often you can run them without deploying the application.

- *System tests* verify that a system as a whole works. A server-side application would be deployed first; the tests would be run against that deployed system, and may simulate client behavior. Another term for this is *functional testing*.

- *Acceptance tests* verify that the entire system/application meets the customers' acceptance criteria. Performance, memory consumption, and other criteria may be included above the simple "does it work" assessment. These are also sometimes called *functional tests*, just to cause extra confusion.

- *Regression testing* means testing a program to see that a change has not broken anything that used to work.

JUnit is a unit-test framework; you write tests in Java to verify that Java components work as expected. It can be used for regression testing, by rerunning a large test suite after every change. It can also be used for some system and acceptance testing, with the help of extra libraries and tools.

4.4   INTRODUCING JUNIT

JUnit is one of the most profound tools to arrive on the Java scene. It single-handedly took testing mainstream and is the framework that most Java projects use to implement their test suites. If you consider yourself a Java developer and you don't yet know JUnit, now is the time to learn. We'll introduce it briefly. (If you wish to explore JUnit in much more detail, we recommend *JUnit in Action* by Vincent Massol.) Ant integrates JUnit into a build, so that you don't neglect to run the tests and to give you nice HTML reports showing which tests failed.

JUnit is a member of the xUnit testing framework family and is now the *de facto* standard testing framework for Java development. JUnit, originally created by Kent Beck and Erich Gamma, is an API that makes it easy to write Java test cases, test cases whose execution can be fully automated.

JUnit is just a download away at http://www.junit.org. All JUnit versions can be downloaded from http://prdownloads.sourceforge.net/junit/. The archive contains junit.jar—which is the JAR file you need—the JavaDocs, and the source (in src.jar). Keep the source handy for debugging your tests. We're using JUnit 3.8.2, not the version 4.x branch.

Why use JUnit 3.8.2 and not JUnit 4.0?

This book uses JUnit 3.8.2 throughout. JUnit 4.0, released in February 2006, is the successor to this version, as are versions 4.1 and beyond. So why aren't we using the 4.x branch? Primarily, because the new version isn't very backwards-compatible with the existing JUnit ecosystem. JUnit 3.x has been stable for so long that many tools have built up around it—including Ant itself. Because Ant is designed to work on all versions of Java from 1.2 upwards, Ant and its own test suite haven't migrated to the JUnit 4.x branch.

Ant's `<junit>` task does work with JUnit 4, so you can run JUnit 4 tests under Ant. However the generated reports aren't perfect, as Ant is still running and reporting the tests as if they were JUnit 3.x tests. A new task for JUnit 4 is needed, one that will probably be hosted in the JUnit codebase itself.

JUnit's architecture

Figure 4.2 shows the UML model of the JUnit 3.8.2 library. The abstract `TestCase` class is of most interest to us.

The `TestCase` class represents a test to run. The `Assert` class provides a set of assertions that methods in a test case can make, assertions that verify that the program is doing what we expect. Test case classes are what developers write to test their applications.

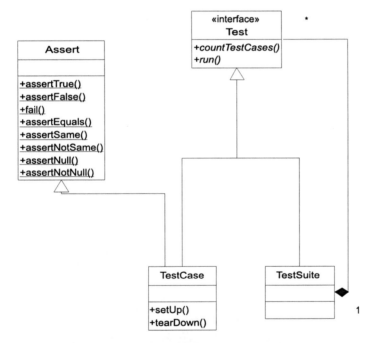

Figure 4.2 JUnit UML diagram depicting the composite pattern utilized by `TestCase` and `TestSuite`. A `TestSuite` contains a collection of tests, which could be either more TestSuites or TestCases, or even classes simply implementing the test interface. The Assert class provides a set of static assertions you can make about your program.

4.4.1 Writing a test case

The first thing we must do with JUnit is write a test case, a class that contains test methods. This is easy to do. For a simple test case, we follow three steps:

- Create a subclass of `junit.framework.TestCase`.
- Provide a constructor, accepting a single String name parameter, which calls `super(name)`.
- Write some public no-argument `void` methods prefixed by the word `test`.

Here is one such test case, the first one for our application:

```
package d1.core.test;

import junit.framework.TestCase;
import d1.core.Event;                          Extend the
                                               TestCase
public class SimpleTest extends TestCase {  ←⏋

    public SimpleTest(String s) {         String constructor
        super(s);                         that invokes the parent
    }                                     String constructor

    public void testCreation() {          This is the
        Event event=new Event();          test method
    }
}
```

This test actually performs useful work. We have a single test, `testCreation`, in which we try to create an event. Until that class is written, the test case won't compile. If the `Event` constructor throws a `RuntimeException`, the test won't work. Merely by trying to instantiate an object inside a test case, we're testing parts of the application.

With the test case written, it's time to run it.

4.4.2 Running a test case

Test cases are run by way of JUnit's `TestRunner` classes. JUnit ships with two built-in test runners—a text-based one, `junit.textui.TestRunner`, and a GUI one, `junit.swingui.TestRunner`. From the Windows command-line, we could run the text `TestRunner` like this:

```
java -cp build\classes;build\test\classes;
    %ANT_HOME%\lib\junit-3.8.2.jar junit.textui.TestRunner
    d1.core.test.SimpleTest

.
Time: 0.01

OK (1 test)
```

The '.' character indicates a test case is running; in this example only one exists, `testCreation`. The Swing `TestRunner` displays success as green and failure as red

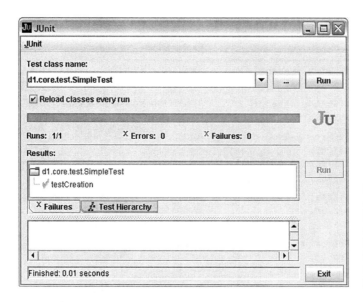

Figure 4.3
JUnit's Swing GUI has successfully run our test case. A green bar indicates that all is well. If there was a red bar, we would have a problem.

and has a feature to reload classes dynamically so that it can pick up the latest test case classes whenever you rebuild. For this same test case, its display appears in figure 4.3.

Ant uses its own `TestRunner`, which runs the tests during the build, so the GUI isn't needed. Java IDEs come with integrated JUnit test runners. These are good for debugging failing test cases. Ant can do something the GUIs can't do: bulk-test hundreds of tests and generate HTML reports from the results. That is our goal: to build and test our program in one go.

4.4.3 Asserting desired results

A test method within a JUnit test case *succeeds* if it completes without throwing an exception. A test *fails* if it throws a `junit.framework.AssertionFailed-Error` or derivative class. A test terminates with an *error* if the method throws any other kind of exception. Anything other than success means that something went wrong, but failures and errors are reported differently.

`AssertionFailedError` exceptions are thrown whenever a JUnit framework assertion or test fails. These aren't Java `assert` statements, but inherited methods that you place in tests. Most of the assertion methods compare an actual value with an expected one, or examine other simple states of `Object` references. There are variants of the `assert` methods for the primitive datatypes and the `Object` class itself.

Diagnosing why a test failed is easier if you provide meaningful messages with your tests. Which would you prefer to deal with, an assertion that "expected all records to be deleted," or "AssertionFailedError on line 423"? String messages become particularly useful when you have complex tests with many assertions, especially those created with `assertTrue()`, `assertFalse`, and `fail()`, for which there is no automatically generated text. Table 4.1 lists JUnit's built-in assertions.

Table 4.1 Assertions that you can make in a JUnit test case

Assertion	Explanation
`assertTrue([String message],` `    boolean condition)`	Asserts that a condition is true.
`assertFalse([String message],` `    boolean condition)`	Asserts that a condition is false.

`assertNull([String message],`
`    Object object)`
`assertNotNull([String message],`
`    Object object)`
	Asserts that an object reference is null. The complementary operation asserts that a reference is not null.

`assertEquals([String message],`
`    Type expected,`
`    Type actual)`
	Asserts that two primitive types are equal. There are overloaded versions of this method for all Java's primitive types except floating point numbers.

`assertEquals([String message],`
`    Object expected,`
`    Object actual)`
	States that the test `expected.equals(actual)` returns true, or both objects are null.

`assertEquals([String message],`
`    FloatType expected,`
`    FloatType actual,`
`    FloatType delta)`
	Equality assertion for floating point values. There are versions for `float` and `double`. The values are deemed equal if the difference is less than the delta supplied. If an infinite value is expected, the delta is ignored.

`assertSame([String message],`
`    Object expected,`
`    Object actual)`
	Asserts that the two objects are the same. This is a stricter condition than simple equality, as it compares the object identities using `expected == actual`.

`assertNotSame([String message],`
`    Object expected,`
`    Object actual`
	Asserts that the two objects have different identities, that is, `expected != actual`.

`fail()` `fail(String message)`	Unconditional failure, used to block off a branch of the test.

Every test case should use these assertions liberally, checking every aspect of the application.

Using the assertions

To use the assertions, we have to write a test method that creates an event with sample data, then validates the event:

```
public class LessSimpleTest extends TestCase {

    public LessSimpleTest(String s) {
        super(s);
    }

    public void testAssignment() {
        final Date date = new Date();
```

```
Event event = new Event(UUID.randomUUID(),
            date, "now", "Text");
assertEquals("self equality failed",
            event,
            event);
assertEquals("date not retained",
            date,
    event.getDate());
String eventinfo = event.toString();
assertTrue("Event.name in toString() "
        + eventinfo,
        eventinfo.contains("now"));
    }
}
```

**Test that Event.equals()
works for comparing
an object to itself**

**Test that the date we supplied
in the constructor was used**

**Evaluate event.toString()
and verify that the name
of the event is returned**

It's important to keep test methods as simple as you can, with many separate test methods. This makes analysis easier: there should be only one reason for any test to fail.

For thorough testing, you need lots and lots of tests. In a well-tested project, the amount of test code may well be bigger than the main source itself. It's certainly not trivial to write good, thorough tests. Everyone on the team needs to think it's important—all the developers, all the management. If anyone thinks that writing tests is a waste of time, you won't get the support or coverage you need. You'll need to convince them otherwise by showing how testing gets applications working faster than shipping broken code and waiting for support calls. The only way to do that is to write those tests, then run them.

The lifecycle of a TestCase

JUnit runs every test method in the same way. It enumerates all test methods in a test class (here, our LessSimpleTest class) and creates an instance of that class for each test method, passing the method name to the constructor. Then, for every test method, it runs the following routine:

```
public void runBare() throws Throwable {
    setUp();
    try {
        runTest();
    }
    finally {
        tearDown();
    }
}
```

That is, it calls the method public void setUp(), runs the test method through some introspection magic, and then calls public void tearDown(). The results are forwarded to any classes that are listening for results.

You can add any number of test methods to a TestCase, all beginning with the prefix test. Methods without this prefix are ignored. You can use this trick to turn off tests or to write helper methods to simplify testing. JUnit 4.0 and TestNG let you use Java 5 annotations to mark the tests to run, but JUnit 3.8.x simply tests every method beginning with the word test.

Test methods can throw any exception they want: there's no need to catch exceptions and turn them into assertions or failures. What you do have to make sure of is that the method signature matches what's expected: no parameters and a void return type. If you accidentally add a return type or an argument, the method is no longer a test.

> **TIP** If you have an IDE that has macros or templates, write a template for a testcase. For example, with IntelliJ IDEA you can map something like "test" to:
>
> ```
> public void test$NAME$() throws Throwable {
>     $END$
> }
> ```
>
> This creates a stub test method and prompts us to fill in the name. Declaring that it throws an Exception lets our test throw anything. Eclipse ships with a similar template predefined.

To create or configure objects before running each test method, you should override the empty TestCase.setUp method and configure member variables or other parts of the running program. You can use the TestCase.tearDown method to close any open connections or in some way clean up the machine, along with try {} finally {} clauses in the methods themselves. If, for example, we wanted to have a configured Event instance for each test, we could add the member variable and then create it in an overridden setUp() method. Because an instance of the class is created for every test method before any of the tests are run, you can't do setup work in the constructor, or cleanup in any finalizer.

To summarize: the setUp and tearDown methods are called before and after every test method and *should be the only place where you prepare for a test and clean up afterwards*.

Once the tests are written, it's time to run the tests. This is where Ant comes into play.

4.4.4 Adding JUnit to Ant

Ant has a task to run the JUnit tests called, not surprisingly, <junit>. This is an *optional task*. Ant has three categories of tasks.

- *Core tasks* are built into ant.jar and are always available.
- *Optional tasks* are tasks that are supplied by the Ant team, but are either viewed as less important or they depend on external libraries or programs. They come in the ant-optional.jar or a dependency-specific JAR, such as ant-junit-jar.
- *Third-party tasks* are Ant tasks written by others. These will be introduced in chapter 9.

The `<junit>` task is an optional task, which depends upon JUnit's JAR file to run the tests.

Older versions of Ant required `junit.jar` to be in Ant's classpath by placing it in a directory that Ant loaded at startup. Ant 1.7 has changed this, so that now a copy of JUnit in the classpath that you set up for compiling and running the test code is all that's needed. Unfortunately, a lot of existing build files assume that the `junit.jar` is always on Ant's classpath, so they don't bother to add it. Given how important JUnit is, you may as well copy it and place it where Ant can load it. This is a good time to introduce how Ant adds libraries to its classpath.

When you type `ant` at the command line, it runs Ant's launcher code in `ant-launcher.jar`. This sets up the classpath for the rest of the run by

- Adding every JAR listed in the `CLASSPATH` environment variable, unless the `-noclasspath` option is set
- Adding every JAR in the `ANT_HOME/lib` directory
- Adding every JAR in `${user.home}/.ant/lib`, where `${user.home}` is the OS-specific home directory of the user, unless the `-nouserlib` option is set
- Adding every JAR in every directory listed on the command line with the `-lib` option

The key thing to know is that all JAR files in `ANT_HOME/lib` and `${user.home}/.ant/lib` are added to Ant's classpath automatically. If `junit.jar`, or any other library is placed there, then it's available to Ant and its tasks. It can also be picked up by any build file that uses Ant's own classes when compiling or running programs.

All we need to do then is download `junit.jar`, stick it in the correct place and have Ant's `<junit>` task pick it up. This is something that can be done by hand, or it can be done by asking Ant to do the work itself.

Interlude: how to automatically fetch JAR files for use with Ant. If you're online and a proxy server is not blocking outbound HTTP connections, change to Ant's home directory, then type:

```
ant -f fetch.xml all
```

This code runs a special build file that fetches all the libraries that Ant needs and saves them in `ANT_HOME/lib`. If you need to save the JAR files in your personal `.ant/lib` directory, add the `-Ddest=user` clause. Welcome to the world of automated JAR-file downloading!

If you work in a security-sensitive organization, you shouldn't download and install files without first authenticating them. You might even want to consider downloading the source and building the files yourself.

To see what is on Ant's classpath, type:

```
ant -diagnostics
```

This tells Ant to look at its internal state and print out useful information. One section in the listing analyzes the availability of tasks and lists any tasks that are missing or unable to run. It also prints out system properties, including Ant's Java classpath. If there is no `junit.jar` listed there, the `<junit>` task will work only if it's explicitly added to the test classpath.

This concludes our little interlude. Optional tasks often need external JAR files, which are best installed by adding them to ANT_HOME/lib or ${user.home}/lib. Now, on with the coding.

4.4.5   Writing the code

We've already written our first tests. Now let's write the first bit of our Event class.

```java
public class Event implements Serializable {
    private UUID id;
    private Date date;
    private String name;
    private String text;

    public Event() {
    }

    public Event(UUID id, Date date, String name, String text) {
        this.id = id;
        this.date = date;
        this.name = name;
        this.text = text;
    }

    public Date getDate() {
        return date;
    }

    public void setDate(Date date) {
        this.date = date;
    }

    public String toString() {
        return "Event #" +
                id + " - "+
                (date != null ? date.toString() : "(no date)")
                " - "
                + (text != null ? text : "");
    }
}
```

Once we implement this much of our class, the tests compile. If we run the tests, Ant should be happy. In the eyes of the tests, we're finished. Let's get Ant building and running the tests to see if our implementation is adequate.

4.5   THE JUNIT TASK: <JUNIT>

The <junit> task is an "optional" task, one that is so important you must have it and junit.jar in your Ant distribution. The task runs one or more JUnit tests, then collects and displays the results. It can also halt the build when a test fails.

To execute the test case that we've just written via Ant, we can declare the task with the name of the test and its classpath, like this:

```
<property name="test.suite"
  value="d1.core.test.AllTests" />

<target name="test-basic" depends="test-compile">
  <junit >
    <classpath refid="test.classpath"/>
    <test name="${test.suite}"/>
  </junit>
</target>
```

When we run it, we see the following:

```
test-basic:
    [junit] Test d1.core.test.AllTests FAILED
BUILD SUCCESSFUL
```

This tells us two things. First, our code is broken and second, we need <junit> to tell us what failed and stop the build afterwards.

Before fixing these problems, we need to get our directory structure and Ant build file set up to accommodate testing.

Interlude: how to lay out source and test directories.   Once you start writing tests, you have two sets of source files for every project, the main source and the test source. It's essential to control how everything is laid out in the file system to avoid contaminating the release software with test code.

Test code must be kept separate from production code to keep the test code out of the production binary distributions and to let you compile the tests and source separately. Tests should also use a Java package hierarchy, as with normal source.

One strategy is to place tests in their own source tree but in the same package as the codes they test. This gives the tests package-level access privileges to the code being tested so the tests can test classes and methods that aren't public.

The other strategy is to place tests in their own source tree, *in different packages*. This forces the tests to use the public API of the classes. It also keeps the tests running when the main files are archived into signed JAR files.

In our projects, we have the following layout:

- The main source tree is under the directory src.
- These files are compiled into build/classes.
- Test files go into the directory tree test.

- Tests are put into test packages under the packages they test.
- Test files are compiled into `build/test/classes`.

It's essential to keep project source and test source separate and to be consistent across projects. Ant can use this proposed layout to build and package the source and test classes separately and to keep all generated files, including test results, away from the original content.

4.5.1 Fitting JUnit into the build process

With this new layout, we need to add a few additional targets to initialize the testing directory structure, compile the test code, and then execute the tests and generate the reports. Figure 4.4 illustrates the target dependency graph of the build file.

We use Ant properties and datatypes to make writing our test targets cleaner, to avoid hard-coded paths, and to allow flexible control of the testing process.

First, we assign properties to the various directories used by our test targets:

```
<property name="test.dir" location="${build.dir}/test" />
<property name="test.classes.dir" location="${test.dir}/classes" />
<property name="test.data.dir" location="${test.dir}/data" />
<property name="test.reports.dir" location="${test.dir}/reports" />
```

Declaring the directories this way gives individual developers flexibility. For example, by overriding `test.reports.dir` we could place reports in a directory served by a web server.

We need a different classpath for our tests than for the main source. We need JUnit's JAR file for compilation and execution, and the `test/classes` directory for execution. How do we do this? We rely on `junit.jar` being on Ant's classpath. As long as we include Ant's classpath in our tasks, we get JUnit for free. This is cheating and only works provided all projects can use the same version of JUnit.

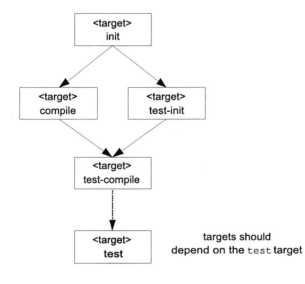

Figure 4.4
Adding test targets to the build process. Tests can be compiled only after the main source is compiled; the test run depends on the tests being compiled.

targets should
depend on the `test` target

Let's start with the classpath for compiling our library. It includes all JARs in the `lib` subdirectory.

```
<path id="compile.classpath">
  <fileset dir="lib">
    <include name="*.jar"/>
  </fileset>
</path>
```

To compile the tests, we need to add in the compiled classes:

```
<path id="test.compile.classpath">
  <path refid="compile.classpath"/>
  <pathelement location="${build.classes.dir}"/>
</path>
```

To run the tests, we also need the compiled tests on the classpath:

```
<path id="test.classpath">
  <path refid="test.compile.classpath"/>
  <pathelement location="${test.classes.dir}"/>
</path>
```

This technique of chaining classpaths is very effective. If we add a dependency to the core project, the classpaths to compile and run the tests pick it up immediately.

Before compiling tests, we need to create the relevant directories:

```
<target name="test-init">
  <mkdir dir="${test.classes.dir}"/>
  <delete dir="${test.data.dir}"/>
  <delete dir="${test.reports.dir}"/>
  <mkdir dir="${test.data.dir}"/>
  <mkdir dir="${test.reports.dir}"/>
</target>
```

This target creates all the output directories. Most unusually, it deletes two of them before recreating them. This is a brute-force purge of the directories' contents to make sure the results of previous test runs aren't mixed in with the latest run.

Our `test-compile` target uses `test.classpath` as well as `test.dir`:

```
<target name="test-compile" depends="compile,test-init">
  <javac destdir="${test.classes.dir}"
         debug="true"
         includeAntRuntime="true"
         srcdir="test">
    <classpath refid="test.compile.classpath"/>
  </javac>
</target>
```

The `includeAntRuntime="true"` flag is a sign that we're pulling in Ant's own classpath in order to get one file, `junit.jar`. The alternative is to add `junit.jar` to the projects `lib` directory.

Having set up the directories and the various classpaths, we're ready to set up `<junit>` to stop the build after tests fail and to present the results.

4.5.2   Halting the build when tests fail

If we care about testing, the build must stop when the tests fail. We don't want to package or release a program that doesn't work.

By default, `<junit>` doesn't halt the build when tests fail. There's a reason for this: you may want to format the results before halting. For now, we can set the `haltonfailure` attribute to `true` to stop the build immediately.

Let's add both `haltonfailure="true"` and `printsummary="true"` to our `<junit>` declaration

```
<junit printsummary="true" haltonfailure="true">
  <classpath refid="test.classpath"/>
  <test name="${test.suite}"/>
</junit>
```

We now get the following output:

```
test-summary:
    [junit] Running d1.core.test.AllTests
    [junit] Tests run: 2, Failures: 1, Errors: 0,
            Time elapsed: 0.02 sec

BUILD FAILED
```

The build halted because the test case failed, exactly as it should. The summary output provides slightly more details: how many tests were run, and how many didn't pass. We need more information than this, which `<junit>` will gladly provide.

4.5.3   Viewing test results

To analyze why tests fail, we need to see the results in detail, including the names of the failing tests, stack traces of exceptions and anything printed to the output and error streams.

The JUnit task outputs test results through *formatters*. One or more `<formatter>` elements can be nested either directly under `<junit>` or under its `<test>` and `<batchtest>` elements. Ant includes the three formatters shown in table 4.2.

Table 4.2   Ant <junit> result formatters can output the test results in different ways.

<formatter>	Description
brief	Summarizes test failures in plain text
plain	Provides text details of test failures and statistics of each test run
xml	Creates XML results for post-processing

By default, `<formatter>` output is directed to files, but it can be directed to Ant's console instead. To get detailed console output, we change the task slightly:

```
<junit printsummary="false" haltonfailure="true">
  <classpath refid="test.classpath"/>
  <formatter type="brief" usefile="false"/>
  <test name="${test.suite}"/>
</junit>
```

Formatters normally write their output to files in the directory specified by the `<test>` or `<batchtest>` elements, but `usefile="false"` tells them to write to the Ant console. We turn off the `printsummary` option because it duplicates and interferes with the console output. The result is the following:

```
[junit] Testsuite: d1.core.test.AllTests
[junit] Tests run: 2, Failures: 1, Errors: 0,
        Time elapsed: 0.02 sec

[junit] Testcase:
     testAssignment(d1.core.test.LessSimpleTest):        FAILED
[junit] Event.name in toString()
        Event #44134602-3860-4326-8745-c7829f299a33 -
        Sat Mar 03 22:43:59 GMT 2007  - Text
[junit] junit.framework.AssertionFailedError:           ❶
        Event.name in toString()
        Event #44134602-3860-4326-8745-c7829f299a33 -
        Sat Mar 03 22:43:59 GMT 2007 - Text
[junit]       at d1.core.test.LessSimpleTest
              .testAssignment(LessSimpleTest.java:23)
[junit]       at sun.reflect.NativeMethodAccessorImpl
              .invoke0(Native Method)
[junit]   ...
```

Now we can see the problem. The `testAssignment()` test threw an `Assertion-FailedError` containing the message "`Event.name in toString()`" ❶, causing the test to fail. Looking at the source of this test, we can find the line that caused the problem:

```
    public void testAssignment() {
        Date date = new Date();
        Event event = new Event(UUID.randomUUID(),
            date, "now", "Text");
        String eventinfo = event.toString();
        assertTrue("Event.name in toString() " + eventinfo,
            eventinfo.contains("now"));
    }
```

It is the test of `toString()` that is failing, because we forgot to include the event name in the string. We can fix that now, and we'll know when it's fixed, as the tests will pass and the `<junit>` task will not fail. Detailed test results are the best way of determining where problems lie. The other thing that can aid diagnosing the problem is the application's output, which we can also pick up from a test run.

Viewing System.out and System.err output

Lots of Java code prints information to the console, either directly to `System.out` and `System.err` or via logging libraries. All this output is invaluable when trouble-shooting failures. With no formatters specified and `printsummary` either on or off, the `<junit>` task swallows all console output. If `printsummary` is set to `"withOutAndErr"`, `<junit>` will forward everything through Ant's console. If we inserted a print `System.out.println(eventinfo)` into our failing test method, we would see it in the test summary:

```
[junit] Running d1.core.test.AllTests
[junit] Tests run: 2, Failures: 1, Errors: 0, Time elapsed: 0.1 sec
[junit] Output:
[junit] Event #972349e6-00e8-449f-b3bc-d1aac4595109 -
       Sat Mar 03 22:45:00 GMT 2007 - Text
```

The brief formatter also captures the log:

```
[junit] Tests run: 2, Failures: 1, Errors: 0, Time elapsed: 0.1 sec

[junit] ------------- Standard Output ---------------
[junit] Event #972349e6-00e8-449f-b3bc-d1aac4595109 -
       Sat Mar 03 22:45:00 GMT 2007
[junit] ------------- ---------------- ---------------
[junit] Testcase:
    testAssignment(d1.core.test.LessSimpleTest):      FAILED
```

Printed output is great for diagnostics after a test has failed. Don't be afraid to log messages inside a test. All Ant's formatters will capture the log for output.

The next thing we need to do is run all the tests in the project in a single `<junit>` task.

4.5.4 Running multiple tests with <batchtest>

So far, we've only run one test case using the `<test>` tag. You can specify any number of `<test>` elements inside a `<junit>` declaration, but that's inefficient. Developers should not have to edit the build file when adding new test cases. Likewise, you can write `TestSuite` classes, but again, who wants to edit Java source unless they need to? Why not delegate all the work to the machine?

Enter `<batchtest>`. You can nest filesets within `<batchtest>` to include all your test cases.

> **TIP** Standardize the naming scheme of your test case classes for easy fileset inclusion. The normal naming-convention scheme calls for test cases to end with the word "Test". Here, `SimpleTest` and `LessSimpleTest` are our test cases, and `CoreTestCase` is the abstract base class. We use `TestCase` as the suffix for our abstract test cases and declare the classes as `abstract` so that IDEs do not try to run them either.

The `<junit>` task has now morphed into

```
<junit printsummary="false" haltonfailure="true">
  <classpath refid="test.classpath"/>
  <formatter type="brief" usefile="false"/>
  <batchtest todir="${test.data.dir}">
    <fileset dir="${test.classes.dir}"
      includes="**/test/*Test.class"/>
  </batchtest>
</junit>
```

The `includes` pattern, `"**/test/*Test.class"`, ensures that only our concrete test cases in the test directory are considered, and not our abstract `Core-TestCase` class, as its name doesn't match the pattern. The `<junit>` task fails if it's told to run a class that's abstract or that isn't a test case.

Setting up a batch test pattern makes adding new test cases to a project trivial. The `<javac>` task compiles all source and test source files in the appropriate directory trees, and now `<junit>` will run any test class whose name matches the pattern. Developers can now add new test cases without editing the build file. The easier it is to add and run test cases, the more likely they are to be written.

Making it easy to add new test cases has one little side effect. Before long, there will be many test cases, which results in an increase in the time to run the tests and an explosion in the size of the test output. Developers cannot be expected to sit staring at the console watching results scroll by, so we need a better way of presenting the results—such as HTML pages.

4.6 GENERATING HTML TEST REPORTS

Being able to read the text output is useful, as you encounter these results quite often, including in emails from other people. But it doesn't scale to hundreds of tests. For that we need something better.

Enter the XML formatter for JUnit. This formatter creates an XML file for every test class. We can add it alongside the brief formatter:

```
<junit printsummary="false" haltonfailure="false">
  <classpath refid="test.classpath"/>
  <formatter type="brief" usefile="false"/>
  <formatter type="xml"/>
  <batchtest todir="${test.data.dir}">
    <fileset dir="${test.classes.dir}"
      includes="**/test/*Test.class"/>
  </batchtest>
</junit>
```

The effect of adding the XML formatter is the creation of an XML file for each `<test>` element. For us, the filename is `${test.data.dir}/TEST-d1.core.test.AllTests.xml`.

XML files are not what we want; we want human-readable HTML reports. This is a bit of post-processing that `<junitreport>` does for us. It applies some XSL transformations to the XML files generated by the XML `<formatter>`, creating HTML files summarizing the test run. You can browse tests, see which ones failed, and view their output. You can also serve the HTML files up on a web site.

Adding the reporting to our routine is simply a matter of setting `halton-failure="false"` in `<junit>` so the build continues after the failure, then declaring the `<junitreport>` task after the `<junit>` run:

```
<junitreport todir="${test.data.dir}">
  <fileset dir="${test.data.dir}">
    <include name="TEST-*.xml"/>
  </fileset>
  <report format="frames" todir="${test.reports.dir}"/>
</junitreport>
```

The `<fileset>` is necessary and should normally include all files called `TEST-*.xml`. The `<report>` element instructs the transformation to use either `frames` or `noframes` Javadoc-like formatting, with the results written to the `todir` directory. Figure 4.5 shows the framed report of our test run.

Navigating to a specific test case displays results such as those shown in figure 4.6. You get a summary of all tests and can zoom in on a test case of interest. Note the timestamp field; it can warn you of old results. The hostname is there in case you're collating results from different machines.

There are three limitations with `<junit>` and `<junitreport>`. Firstly, `<junit>` doesn't have any dependency logic; it always runs all tests. Secondly,

Name	Tests	Errors	Failures	Time(s)	Time Stamp	Host
EventsTest	6	0	0	0.040	2005-04-07T16:35:18	Zermatt
EventTest	12	0	0	0.210	2005-04-07T16:35:18	Zermatt
JavaAssertTest	1	0	0	0.020	2005-04-07T16:35:18	Zermatt
LessSimpleTest	1	0	1	0.030	2005-04-07T16:35:18	Zermatt
MainTest	3	0	0	0.090	2005-04-07T16:35:18	Zermatt
PropertyTest	9	0	0	0.020	2005-04-07T16:35:18	Zermatt
SimpleTest	1	0	0	0.030	2005-04-07T16:35:18	Zermatt

Figure 4.5 The test results presented by `<junitreport>`. The main page summarizes the test statistics and hyperlinks to test case details.

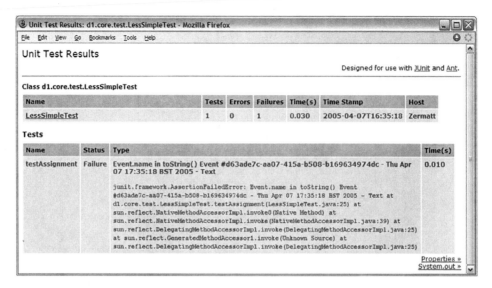

Figure 4.6 Test case results showing the assertion that failed, and the stack trace. The output log is under the System.out link. Keep an eye on the Time Stamp to make sure you're not viewing old test results.

<junitreport> simply aggregates XML files without any knowledge of whether the files it's using have any relation to the tests that were just run. Cleaning up the old test results before running new tests gives you better reports.

The final problem is more subtle. We've had to turn off haltonfailure in order to run <junitreport>. How can we generate reports *and* stop the build if the tests failed?

4.6.1   Halting the builds after generating reports

To halt the build after creating the HTML pages, we make the <junit> task set an Ant property when a test fails, using the failureProperty and errorProperty attributes. A test failure means an assertion was thrown, while an error means that some other exception was raised in the test case. Some teams like to differentiate between the two, but we don't. We just want to halt the built if a test failed for any reason, which we can ask for by naming the same property on both attributes. We also need to set haltOnFailure="false", or, given that false is the default value, omit the attribute entirely.

Using the properties set by <junit>, we can generate the reports before we fail the build. Listing 4.1 shows the complete target needed to run the tests, create the reports, and halt the build on failure.

Listing 4.1 Integrated testing, reporting, and failure

```
<target name="test-reporting" depends="test-compile">
  <junit printsummary="false"
        errorProperty="test.failed"           Name the properties
        failureProperty="test.failed">         to set on failure
    <classpath>
      <path refid="test.classpath"/>
    </classpath>
    <formatter type="brief" usefile="false"/>
    <formatter type="xml"/>
    <batchtest todir="${test.data.dir}" >
      <fileset dir="${test.classes.dir}"
        includes="**/test/*Test.class"/>
    </batchtest>
  </junit>

  <junitreport todir="${test.data.dir}">
    <fileset dir="${test.data.dir}">
      <include name="TEST-*.xml"/>
    </fileset>
    <report format="frames"
      todir="${test.reports.dir}"/>
  </junitreport>

  <fail if="test.failed">                       Conditional <fail>
  Tests failed. Check ${test.reports.dir}       task triggered when
  </fail>                                        the property is set
</target>
```

Running this target will run the tests, create the report, and halt the build if any test raised an error or failed. It even prints the name of the directory into which the reports went, for pasting into a web browser.

The HTML reports are the nicest way to view test results. Be aware that the XSL transformation can take some time when there are a lot of tests to process. The plain text output is much faster. Sometimes we split the testing and report creation in two in order to let us run the tests without creating the HTML reports.

With HTML output, the core of Ant's JUnit coverage is complete. Projects can use what we've covered—batch execution of test cases and HTML output—for most of their needs. There are a few more advanced topics that may be of interest. Once you have testing up and running in a project, come back to this section and think about using them to improve the test process.

4.7   ADVANCED <JUNIT> TECHNIQUES

Before closing off our JUnit introduction, there are a few more tricks to know about running JUnit under Ant. These are all optional extras, described in no particular order, but useful to have on hand when needed.

Running a single test case

Once your project has a sufficiently large number of test cases, you may need to isolate a single test case to run when ironing out a particular issue. This feat can be accomplished using the if/unless clauses on <test> and <batchtest>. Our <junit> task evolves again:

```
<junit printsummary="false"
       errorProperty="test.failed"
       failureProperty="test.failed"
       fork="${junit.fork}"
       forkmode="${junit.forkmode}">
  <classpath>
    <path refid="test.classpath"/>
    <!-- include our current JVM's options -->
    <pathelement path="${java.class.path}"/>
  </classpath>
  <formatter type="brief" usefile="false"/>
  <formatter type="xml"/>
  <test name="${testcase}" todir="${test.data.dir}" if="testcase"/>
  <batchtest todir="${test.data.dir}" unless="testcase">
    <fileset dir="${test.classes.dir}"
      includes="**/test/*Test.class"/>
  </batchtest>
</junit>
```

By default, the testcase property is undefined, the <test> element will be skipped, and the <batchtest> tests will execute. To run a single test case, we just define the name of the test on the command line by setting the testcase property:

```
ant test -Dtestcase=d1.core.test.SimpleTest
```

This is a good technique for a big project—even Ant's own build file does it!

Running JUnit in its own JVM

The <junit> task, by default, runs within Ant's JVM. It's a lot more robust to run tests in a new JVM, which we can do with the attribute fork="true". This term, *forking*, comes from Unix, where a process can *fork* into two identical processes. Java doesn't implement Unix's fork() operation, but Ant comes close and uses the term in some of its tasks.

The fork attribute can be used in the <junit> tag to control all test cases, or it can be used in the <test> and <batchtest> tags, controlling the fork option of a specific set of tests. Forking unit tests let developers do the following:

- Use a different JVM than the one used to run Ant (jvm attribute)
- Set timeout limitations to prevent tests from running too long (timeout attribute)
- Test in low memory configurations (maxmemory attribute)

- Test different instantiations of a singleton or other situations where an object may remain in memory and adversely affect clean testing
- Set up a path for loading native libraries and test Java Native Interface (JNI) code

We like to fork our code because it makes things more robust; the test run cannot break Ant, and Ant's state doesn't affect the test code. Running tests in a new process does cause some problems, because the classes needed by the formatters and the test cases themselves must be in the classpath. One way to do this is to adjust the classpath for running tests:

```
<classpath>
  <path refid="test.classpath"/>
  <pathelement path="${java.class.path}"/>
</classpath>
```

The JVM-provided property `java.class.path` is handy to make sure the spawned process includes the same classpath used by the original Ant JVM. If you want to be more selective about classpaths, include `ant-junit.jar` and `junit.jar`. You also need the Apache Xerces XML parser or an equivalent. Since this is now built into the Java runtime, there's no need to explicitly ask for it.

What happens when `<junit>` forks? Unless you say otherwise, every test case class is run in its own JVM. This can be slow, especially when there's a lot of static startup code in the application being tested. You can control this behavior with the `forkMode` attribute, which takes any of the values listed in table 4.3.

Table 4.3 Options for the `forkMode` attribute of `<junit>`, controlling how often a new JVM is created during the run. The `once` and `perBatch` modes are fastest.

perTest	Fork a new JVM for every test (default)
perBatch	Fork a new JVM for every batch of tests
once	Fork a new JVM once

The `once` option starts a new JVM for every set of tests which have matching JVM configuration options, so it may need to start a few if the `<junit>` declaration is complex. It does run tests faster and should be played with. Just don't rely on a single JVM lasting for all tests.

Passing information to test cases

One common problem in a test run is passing configuration information down to the test.

How can test cases be configured? It may be OK to hard code values into the test source, but not things that vary on a per-system basis, such as the path to a file on the local drive or the port that a server is listening on. To configure tests dynamically, we pass the information down as Java system properties, using the `<sysproperty>` element. This is the equivalent of a -D argument to a Java command-line program.

```
<junit printsummary="false"
       errorProperty="test.failed"
       failureProperty="test.failed">
  <classpath refid="test.classpath"/>
  <sysproperty key="test.url" value="http://localhost:8080/"/>
  <sysproperty key="debug" value="true"/>
  <sysproperty key="data.dir" file="./data"/>
  <formatter type="xml"/>
  <formatter type="brief" usefile="false"/>
  <test name="${testcase}" if="testcase"/>
  <batchtest todir="${test.data.dir}" unless="testcase">
    <fileset dir="${test.dir}" includes="**/test/*Test.class"/>
  </batchtest>
</junit>
```

To read these values, our tests call `System.getProperty` or `Boolean.get-Boolean()`:

```
String url = System.getProperty("test.url");
String dataDir = System.getProperty("data.dir");
boolean debug = Boolean.getBoolean("debug");
```

It is often useful to have a helper method that asserts that the property actually exists:

```
public String getProperty(String property) {
    String value=System.getProperty(property);
    assertNotNull("Property "+property+" is undefined",value);
    return value;
}
```

If you use this method, any absent property is detected immediately and raised as a test failure. Filename properties can be handled with an extension of this technique that looks for a property naming a file that must exist:

```
public File getFileProperty(String property) {
    String value = getProperty(property);
    File file=new File(value);
    assertTrue("File "+file+" does not exist",file.exists());
    return file;
}
```

Checks like these are valuable when you run JUnit from IDEs, as they'll have their own way of configuring properties, and a bit of rigor here stops problems from sneaking in.

We can also use Java language assertions in JUnit tests. There's no benefit in using Java `assert` statements inside JUnit tests, but libraries may contain them.

Enabling Java Assertions

You can enable Java assertions in a forking `<junit>` task; the request is ignored when `fork="false"`. Assertions are enabled and configured with an `<assertions>` element in the `<junit>` declaration:

```
<assertions enableSystemAssertions="true">
  <enable/>
  <enable package="d1.core"/>
  <disable class="d1.core.Events"/>
</assertions>
```

Here we're turning on all assertions in the runtime, including all those in everything else (`<enable/>`) and all in package `d1.core` except for those in the class `d1.core.events`. If your libraries have assertions, turn them on during testing!

Our final bit of advanced `<junit>` concerns reporting.

Customizing the *<junitreport>* reports

Sometimes the HTML reports are too verbose or they lack the custom layout a team needs so it can publish it straight onto their web site. You can customize the pages generated by `<junitreport>` by using different XSL files. The XSL files used by the task are embedded in Ant's ant-junit.jar and ship in the etc/ directory of the installation for customization. To customize, either copy the existing junit-frames.xsl and junit-noframes.xsl files to another directory or create new ones. You *must* use these exact filenames. To use your custom XSL files, simply point the styledir attribute of the `<report>` element at them. Here we have a property junit.style.dir that is set to the directory where the XSL files exist:

```
<junitreport todir="${test.data.dir}">
  <fileset dir="${test.data.dir}">
    <include name="TEST-*.xml"/>
  </fileset>
  <report format="frames"
      styledir="${junit.style.dir}"
      todir="${test.reports.dir}"/>
</junitreport>
```

If you reach the limit of what XML+XSLT can do in terms of report generation, there's one more option: writing your own result formatter.

Creating your own test result formatter

The `<formatter>` element has an optional classname attribute, which you can specify instead of type. You must specify a fully qualified name of a class that implements the JUnitResultFormatter interface and get that class into the classpath of the JVM that runs the unit tests. Examine the code of the existing formatters to learn how to develop your own, if you ever have the urge.

4.8   BEST PRACTICES

We love JUnit. It's easy to learn, and once you start using it you cannot help wondering why you never used it before.

Ant makes unit testing simple by running JUnit, capturing the results, and halting the build if a test fails. It will even create fancy HTML reports. By integrating testing with your build process, you can be sure that the tests are run every build, making testing as central and foundational as compiling the Java source. This is what we think developers should do:

- Think about testing from the beginning. You can design programs to make them easier to test; you can also design programs to make testing nearly impossible.
- Separate test code from production code. Give them each their own unique directory tree with an appropriate package-naming structure.
- Test *everything* that could possibly break.
- Write a well-written test. If all your tests pass the first time, you're probably not testing vigorously enough.
- Add a new test case for every bug you find.
- When a test case fails, track down the problem by writing more tests before going to the debugger. The more tests you have, the better.
- Use informative names for tests. It's better to know that `testFileLoad` failed, rather than `test17` failed.
- Pick a unique naming convention for test cases; we use "*Test.java." We can use this pattern with `<batchtest>` to run only the files that match the naming convention.

From an Ant perspective, the most important thing to do is write build files that run tests every build. Don't make running the tests something only one person in the team does, and then only once a week.

If you need to retrofit tests to an existing application, don't panic. Add tests as you continue to evolve the application. Before adding new code, write tests to validate the current behavior and verify that the new code doesn't break this behavior. When a bug is found, write a test case to identify it clearly, then fix the bug and watch the test pass. Keep at it and you'll slowly build up test coverage of the application.

Now, there's one more little topic to cover before we finish this chapter: JUnit versions.

4.8.1 The future of JUnit

This book uses JUnit 3.8.2 throughout. The JUnit 3 branch of JUnit is the version of the framework most broadly used and is widely supported in Ant, IDEs, and other tools. There is a newer version, JUnit 4; at the time of writing, JUnit 4.2 was the latest release. It lets developers use Java 5 annotations as a way of marking up test classes and methods. Why hasn't this book adopted the latest version of JUnit?

The main reason for sticking with the JUnit 3.8 branch is because it's been so successful that it has become integrated with much of the Java development infrastructure. IDEs recognize test classes and can run them; Ant's tasks are built for JUnit 3 and added only incomplete JUnit 4 support in Ant 1.7. Most critically, there are extension tools such as Apache Cactus, which work only with JUnit 3.8.x. Apache Cactus is an extension for JUnit that can run tests inside an application server; it's invaluable for some server-side testing, and something which we'll look at in chapter 14. There are other extensions which have yet to migrate, such as HttpUnit, XmlUnit, and DbUnit. If you need these extensions, you need to stick with the JUnit 3.8.x branch.

When will these extensions move to JUnit 4? We don't know. It will require them to move to Java 1.5 and be incompatible with the Java 1.4 world, so isn't a decision to be made lightly—especially when there is an alternative.

TestNG, from http://testng.org/, is another Java test framework. Like JUnit 4, it supports Java 5 annotations for marking up tests. It also runs under Java 1.4, using Javadoc annotations for test markup. Furthermore, like JUnit 4, it can run JUnit 3 tests case classes.

TestNG has its own task, which is built into the test framework. The XML reports that the task generates feed into Ant's existing <junitreport> task, so TestNG integrates with Ant as well as JUnit does. We're not going to cover TestNG in this book. However, it has some interesting features, and anyone thinking of moving to JUnit 4 should also look closely at TestNG before making a decision.

4.9   SUMMARY

In this chapter, we started writing a diary application by writing the JUnit tests for these classes at the same time as the application itself and integrating the tests into the build process so that Ant compiles both source trees and runs the tests, generating HTML report pages.

We'll extend this application through the book, packaging and running it, redistributing it, then using it in a web application with the Enterprise Java APIs adding persistence. Throughout all these changes, we'll know the moment any change breaks the basic functionality of the system, because the test cases written in this chapter will highlight problems the moment any change breaks the core. This is why testing is better than debugging manual "experiments" with an application: tests pay for themselves many times over.

Test-centric development transforms how you write code, usually for the better. Here are some key points to keep in mind:

- JUnit is Java's main testing framework; it integrates tightly with Ant.
- The more tests you have, the better.
- Tests are most useful if you run them after every change, which is where Ant joins in.
- <junit> runs JUnit test cases, captures results, and can set a property if tests fail.
- The <sysproperty> element can pass information from Ant to the test cases.
- <junitreport> generates HTML test reports and allows for customization of the reports generated via XSLT.

One of the surprising and disappointing things we discover as we encounter new projects is how many projects have yet to adopt a test-centric development process. JUnit makes it so easy! The benefits of tests are so tangible! Yet again and again, we join some project, ask for the tests and hear, "Oh, we haven't written them yet." Writing tests takes time, but so does debugging. Moving to a test-centric process is a key way to improve product quality. For that reason, if there's one message we want readers to remember from this entire book, it is not "We should build with Ant"; it is "We should build *and test* with Ant."

CHAPTER 5

Packaging projects

We can now compile and test our diary classes, using Ant, `<javac>`, and `<junit>`. This code can be turned into a JAR library. It can be used inside our application, or it can be redistributed for other people to use.

This brings us and our build file to the next problem: packaging a program for reuse and redistribution. We want to take the compiled classes and create a JAR file that can itself be bundled into some source and binary redistribution packages—such as Zip and tar files—for different platforms. We will then be able to execute the JAR file and upload the Zip and tar files to servers. We are effectively releasing our diary as a library, on the basis that having passed its tests, it's ready for use.

What else does a project need to do before releasing a Java program?

- Create the documentation.
- Write any platform-specific bootstrap scripts, batch files, or programs.
- Write any installer configuration files, such as Java Web Start files.
- Build the application and package it into a JAR file.
- Pass the test suite.
- Bundle the JAR, the documentation, and any other files into redistributable packages (usually Zip and tar files).

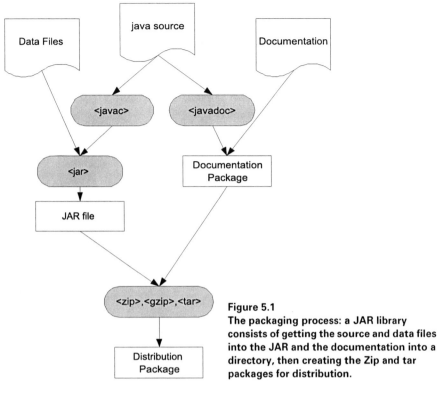

Figure 5.1
The packaging process: a JAR library
consists of getting the source and data files
into the JAR and the documentation into a
directory, then creating the Zip and tar
packages for distribution.

Ant can handle the activities in figure 5.1. It can take the source files and create .class files and JavaDoc documentation, then package everything up as redistributables. Along the way it can copy, move, and delete files and directories.

The build file can already compile the source and run the tests; in this chapter we'll look at the rest of the packaging problem. We'll start with file system operations to get everything into the right place.

5.1 WORKING WITH FILES

The basis of the packaging and deployment process is copying and moving files around. Ant has a set of tasks to do this, most of which operate on filesets. We can use them to prepare directories and files for the packaging steps in the build.

Creating Directories

Before we can distribute, we need a destination for our distributable files. Let's create a subdirectory dist with another doc for documentation under it. As usual, we declare these locations through properties to provide override points.

```
<property name="dist.dir" location="dist" />
<property name="dist.doc.dir" location="${dist.dir}/doc" />
```

```
<mkdir dir="${dist.dir}"/>
<mkdir dir="${dist.doc.dir}"/>
```

This XML will create all the distribution directories. The `<mkdir>` task creates all parent directories in its `dir` attribute, so when the task is executed with `dir="dist/doc"`, the whole directory tree would be created on demand.

This same recursive creation applies to deletion, where the entire distribution directory can be deleted all at once.

5.1.1 Deleting files

We've been deleting files since chapter 2, using the `<delete>` task. This task can delete an individual file with a single `file` attribute:

```
<delete file="${dist.doc.dir}/readme.txt" />
```

It can just as easily delete an entire directory with

```
<delete dir="${dist.dir}" />
```

This task is dangerous, as it can silently delete everything in the specified directory and those below it. If someone accidentally sets the `dist.dir` property to the current directory, then the entire project will be destroyed. Be careful of what you delete.

For more selective operations, `<delete>` takes a fileset as a nested element, so you can specify a pattern, such as all backup files in the source directories:

```
<delete>
  <fileset dir="${src.dir}"
           includes="*~"
           defaultexcludes="false" />
</delete>
```

This fileset has the attribute `defaultexcludes="false"`. Usually, filesets ignore the editor- and SCM-generated backup files that often get created, but when trying to delete such files you need to turn off this filtering. Setting the `defaultexcludes` attribute to false has this effect.

Three attributes on `<delete>` handle failures: `quiet`, `failonerror`, and `deleteonexit`. The task cannot delete files if another program has a lock on the file, so deletion failures are not unheard of, especially on Windows. When the `failonerror` flag is true, as it is by default, Ant halts the build with an error. If the flag is false, then Ant reports the error before it continues to delete the remaining files. You can see that something went wrong, but the build continues:

```
<delete defaultexcludes="false"
  failonerror="false" >
  <fileset dir="${dist.dir}" includes="**/"/>
</delete>
```

The `quiet` option is nearly the exact opposite of `failonerror`. When `quiet="true"`, errors aren't reported and the build continues. Setting this flag implies you don't care whether the deletion worked or not. It's the equivalent of rm -q in Unix. The final flag, `deleteonexit`, tells Ant to tell the JVM to try to delete the file again when the JVM is shut down. You can't rely on this cleanup being called, but you could maybe do some tricks here, such as marking a file that you know is in use for delayed deletion. Things may not work as expected on different platforms or when Ant is run from an IDE.

There's also a `verbose` flag to tell the task to list all the files as it goes. This can be useful for seeing what's happening:

```
<delete failonerror="false"
  verbose="true">
  <fileset dir="${dist.dir}" includes="**/"/>
</delete>
```

Deleting files is usually a housekeeping operation. Its role in packaging is to clean up destination directories where files can go before adding the directory contents to JAR, Zip, or tar archives. Create a clean directory with a `<delete>` command and a `<mkdir>` command, then copy all the files to be packaged into this directory tree.

5.1.2 Copying files

The task to copy files is, not surprisingly, `<copy>`. At its simplest, you can copy files from one place to another. You can specify the destination directory; the task creates it and any parent directories if needed:

```
<copy file="readme.html" todir="${dist.doc.dir}"/>
```

You can also give it the complete destination filename, which renames the file during the copy:

```
<copy file="readme.html" tofile="${dist.doc.dir}/README.HTML"/>
```

To do a bulk copy, declare a fileset inside the copy task; all files will end up in the destination directory named with the `todir` attribute:

```
<copy todir="${dist.doc.dir}">
  <fileset dir="doc" >
    <include name="**/*.*"/>
  </fileset>
</copy>
```

By default, `<copy>` is timestamp-aware; it copies only the files that are newer than those of the destination. At build time this is what you want, but if you're using the task to install something over a newer version, set `overwrite="true"`. This will always overwrite the destination file.

Copied files' timestamps are set to the current time. To keep the date of the original file, set `preservelastmodified="true"`. Doing so can stop other tasks from thinking that files have changed. Normally, it isn't needed.

If you want to change the names of files when copying or moving them, or change the directory layout as you do so, you can specify a `<mapper>` as a nested element of the task. We'll cover mappers in section 5.2.

One limitation of Ant is that `<copy>` doesn't preserve Unix file permissions, because Java doesn't let it. The `<chmod>` task can be used to set permissions after a copy—a task that is a no-op on Windows—so it can be inserted where it's needed. Similarly, Ant cannot read permissions when creating a tar archive file, a problem we'll solve in a different way.

Related to the `<copy>` task is the `<move>` task, which enables you to move or rename files.

5.1.3 Moving and renaming files

Ant's `<move>` task can move files around. It first tries to rename the file or directory; if this fails, then it copies the file and deletes the originals. An unwanted side effect is that if `<move>` has to copy, Unix file permissions will get lost.

The syntax of this task is nearly identical to `<copy>`, as it's a direct subclass of the `<copy>` task, so any of the examples listed in section 5.1.1 can be patched to move files instead:

```
<move file="readme.txt" todir="${dist.doc.dir}"/>
```

As with `<copy>`, this task uses timestamps to avoid overwriting newer files unless `overwrite="true"`.

The `<move>` task is surprisingly rare in build files, as copying and deleting files are much more common activities. Its main role is renaming generated or copied files, but since `<copy>` can rename files during the copy process and even choose a different destination directory, there's little need for the task.

5.2   INTRODUCING MAPPERS

We've shown how filesets can select files to copy or move, but what if you want to rename them as they're moved? What if you want to flatten a directory so that all JAR files are copied into one single directory? These are common operations in preparing files for packaging. To do these operations you need *mappers*.

Ant's mappers generate a new set of filenames from source files. Any time you need to move sets of files into a new directory hierarchy, or change parts of the filename itself, such as an extension, look for an appropriate mapper. Table 5.1 shows the built-in mapper types. They are used by `<uptodate>`, `<move>`, `<copy>`, `<apply>`, and several other tasks.

Table 5.1   Mapper types. Mappers implement file-renaming algorithms, telling tasks like `<copy>` how files should be renamed during the operation.

Type	Description
identity	The target is identical to the source filename.
flatten	Source and target filenames are identical, with the target filename having all leading directory paths stripped.

continued on next page

Table 5.1 Mapper types. Mappers implement file-renaming algorithms, telling tasks like <copy> how files should be renamed during the operation. *(continued)*

Type	Description
merge	All source files are mapped to a single target file specified in the to attribute.
glob	A single asterisk (*) used in the from pattern is substituted into the to pattern. Only files matching the from pattern are considered.
package	A subclass of the glob mapper, package functions similarly except that it replaces path separators with the dot character (.) so that a file with the hierarchical package directory structure can be mapped to a flattened directory structure while retaining the package structure in the filename.
regexp	Both the from and to patterns define regular expressions. Only files matching the from expression are considered.
unpackage	Replaces dots in a Java package with directory separators.
composite	Applies all nested mappers in parallel.
chained	Applies all nested mappers in sequence.
filter	Applies a list of 'pipe' commands to each filename.
scriptmapper	Creates an output filename by running code in a scripting language.

Mappers are powerful, and it's worthwhile looking at them in detail. If a project has any need to rename files and directories or move files into a different directory tree, a mapper will probably be able to do it. Let's explore them in some more detail.

Identity mapper

The first mapper is the *identity* mapper, which is the default mapper of <copy> and <move>. It's used when a task needs a mapper, but you don't need to do any filename transformations:

```
<identitymapper/>
```

Because it's the default mapper of <copy>, the following declarations are equivalent:

```
<copy todir="new_web">
  <fileset dir="web" includes="**/*.jsp"/>
  <identitymapper/>
</copy>

<copy todir="new_web">
  <fileset dir="web" includes="**/*.jsp"/>
</copy>
```

It's fairly rare to see the identity mapper because you get it for free.

The next mapper, the *flatten* mapper, is used when collecting files together in a single directory, such as when collecting JAR files to go into the WEB-INF/lib directory of a web application.

Flatten mapper

The flatten mapper strips all directory information from the source filename to map to the target filename. This is one of the most useful mapping operations, because it collects files from different places and places them into a single directory. If we wanted to copy and flatten all JAR files from a library directory hierarchy into a single directory ready for packaging, we would do this:

```
<copy todir="dist/lib">
  <fileset dir="lib" includes="**/*.jar"/>
  <flattenmapper />
</copy>
```

If multiple files have the same name in the source fileset, only one of them will be mapped to the destination directory—and you cannot predict which one.

Although it copies everything to a single directory, the flatten mapper doesn't rename files. To do that, use either the glob or regexp mapper.

Glob mapper

The very useful *glob* mapper can do simple file renaming, such as changing a file extension. It has two attributes, to and from, each of which takes a string with a single asterisk (*) somewhere inside. The text matched by the pattern in the from attribute is substituted into the to pattern:

```
<globmapper from="*.jsp" to="*.jsp.bak"/>
```

The glob mapper is useful for making backup copies of files by copying them to new names, as shown in the following example. Files not matching the from pattern are ignored.

```
<copy todir="new_web">
  <fileset dir="web" includes="**/*.jsp"/>
  <globmapper from="*.jsp" to="*.jsp.bak" />
</copy>
```

This task declaration will copy all JSP pages from the web directory to the new_web directory with each source .jsp file given the .jsp.bak extension.

If you have more complex file-renaming problems, it's time to reach for the big brother of the glob mapper, the regexp mapper, which can handle arbitrary regular expressions.

Regexp mapper

The *regexp* mapper takes a regular expression in its from attribute. Source files matching this pattern get mapped to the target file. The target filename is built using the to pattern, with pattern substitutions from the from pattern, including \0 for the fully matched source filename and \1 through \9 for patterns matched with enclosing parentheses in the from pattern.

Here's a simple example of a way to map all `.java` files to `.java.bak` files. It has the same effect as the glob mapper example, shown above:

```
<regexpmapper from="^(.*)\.java$" to="\1.java.bak"/>
```

The `<copy>` example for the glob mapper can be rewritten this way:

```
<copy todir="new_web">
  <fileset dir="web" includes="**/*.jsp"/>
  <regexpmapper from="^(.*)\.jsp$" to="\1.jsp.bak" />
</copy>
```

Quite sophisticated mappings can be done with this mapper, such as removing a middle piece of a directory hierarchy and other wacky tricks. To find the pattern syntax, look up `java.util.regex.Pattern` in the JDK documentation.

One conversion is so common it has its own mapper: the package mapper.

Package mapper

The *package* mapper transforms the * pattern in its `from` attribute into a dotted package string in the `to` pattern. It replaces each directory separator with a dot (.). The result is a flattening of the directory hierarchy where Java files need to be matched against data files that have the fully qualified class name embedded in the filename. This mapper was written for use with the data files generated by the `<junit>` task's XML formatter.

The data files resulting from running a test case with `<junit>` are written to a single directory with the filename TEST-*fully qualified classname*.xml. The package mapper lets you map from Java classnames to these files:

```
<packagemapper from="*.java" to="${results.dir}/TEST-*.xml" />
```

Another use would be to create a flat directory tree of all the source code:

```
<copy todir="out">
  <fileset dir="src" includes="**/*.java"/>
  <packagemapper from="*.java" to="*.java" />
</copy>
```

Running this target would copy a file such as `src/org/d1/core/Constants.java` to `out/core.d1.Constants.java`.

This mapper has an opposite, the *unpackagemapper*, which goes from dotted filenames to directory separators.

All the mappers covered so far focus on renaming individual files in a copy. Mappers can do more than this, as they can provide any mapping from source filenames to destination names. One mapper, the merge mapper, maps every source file to the same destination mapper.

Merge mapper

The *merge* mapper maps all source files to the same destination file, which limits its value in a <copy> operation. However, it comes in handy in the <uptodate> task. This is a task that compares a fileset of source files to a mapped set of destination files and sets a property if the destination files are as new as the source files. This property indicates that the destination files are up-to-date.

With the merge mapper, <uptodate> lets us test if an archive file contains all the latest source files:

```
<uptodate property="zip.notRequired">
  <srcfiles dir="src" includes="**/*.java"/>
  <mergemapper to="${dist.dir}/src.zip"/>
</uptodate>
```

The property will not be set if the Zip file is out of date, a fact that can be used to trigger the execution of a conditional target that will create the Zip file only on demand.

Mappers can also go the other way, generating multiple names from a single source, which lets you map a source file to multiple destinations.

Composite mapper

The *composite* mapper takes multiple mappers inside it and returns the result of mapping the source file to every mapper. The more source files you have, the more mapped filenames you end up with: it's the "or" operation of mapping. Here we copy our source files to their original name and into the same directory with a .java.txt suffix:

```
<copy todir="dist/source">
  <fileset dir="src" includes="**/*.java" />
  <compositemapper>
    <identitymapper />
    <globmapper from="*.java" to="*.java.txt"/>
  </compositemapper>
</copy>
```

There's one other mapper that takes nested mappers, the chained mapper.

Chained Mapper

The *chained* mapper lets you chain together a list of other mappers to create the final set of filenames. We could use this mapper to copy the source files into a flat directory using <flattenmapper>, then change the extension to .txt using the <globmapper>:

```
<copy todir="dist/source">
  <fileset dir="src" includes="**/*.java" />
    <chainedmapper>
      <flattenmapper/>
      <globmapper from="*.java" to="*.txt" />
    </chainedmapper>
</copy>
```

This is good for composing complex filename transformations.

There are a few more mappers listed in the documentation but rarely used. Chapter 18 covers one of these, the script mapper. The script mapper lets you describe the mapping logic in any scripting language that Java supports. If you have a complex renaming problem that the regexp mapper can't handle, script mapper offers you a way to solve it without writing a new mapper in Java.

The whole mapper concept may seem a bit complex, but it gives <move> and <copy> operations complete control over the name, the location, and even the number of copied files. We can even have the tasks change the contents of the files by *filtering* them.

5.3   MODIFYING FILES AS YOU GO

It's good to customize the text files that go with a library, inserting the current date and version into them. These are the files that people read, and people like to know they have the current release. We can customize text files in Ant by patching the files on the fly.

Both the <move> and <copy> tasks can be set up to act as token filters for files. These are something we introduced in section 3.6. When filtering, the tasks replace tokens in the file with absolute values. You do this by nesting a <filterset> element inside the <copy> task.

In our diary project, we have a text file called doc/readme.html with some release notes. When creating the distribution packages, we want to insert a timestamp into this file. The <copy> task can do that. Here's the file:

```
<html>
  <head><title>d1 Diary Release Notes</title></head>
  <body>
    This product was built on: @DATE@ - @TIME@
  </body>
</html>
```

The @DATE@ and @TIME@ in the file are "tokens," which can be replaced during the copy:

```
<tstamp/>
<copy todir="${dist.doc.dir}" overwrite="true">
  <fileset dir="doc" includes="**/*.html"/>
  <filterset>
    <filter token="DATE" value="${DSTAMP}"/>
    <filter token="TIME" value="${TSTAMP}"/>
  </filterset>
</copy>
```

The <tstamp> task sets the DSTAMP and TSTAMP properties to the current date and time. The <copy> task contains a <filterset> element, which lists each token to replace and the value to use; we get the value from the properties.

The other trick in the task declaration is that it disables dependency checking by setting `overwrite="true"`. This is because we want the filtered copy to always overwrite the destination file, even if it exists.

Applying this filtered copy on the HTML template produces the following:

```
<html>
  <head><title>d1 Diary Release Notes</title></head>
  <body>
    This product was built on: 20061219 - 2248
  </body>
</html>
```

Adding information to a generated file is good for support because you can tell when something was built. If a project keeps version information in a properties file, the build version can also be included in the filter. Keeping this data out of text files lets you update the version in a single place and have it propagate to the documentation automatically.

Replacing text in a file can be tricky, which is why Ant's filters search for the filter tokens within a pair of delimiters. The default delimiter is the "at" sign (@), so the filterset will only replace occurrences of @TIMESTAMP@ in the file. If you want, you can supply a new prefix and suffix in the filterset declaration. For example, to replace the string `[[TIMESTAMP]]` with a real timestamp, the declaration would be

```
<tstamp>
  <format property="timestamp.isoformat"
    pattern="yyyy-mm-dd'T'HH:mm:ss" locale="en"/>
</tstamp>

<filterset begintoken="[[" endtoken ="]]">
  <filter token="TIMESTAMP" value="${timestamp.isoformat}"/>
</filterset>
```

One thing you must never do is try to filter a binary file; it may get corrupted. This essentially means *do not copy binary files with a filter set.*

In the Ant manual, there's a `<filter>` task that lets you specify a default filter for *every* move and copy that follows. Since this filter applies even to binary files, *DO NOT USE IT!* Once a global `<filter>` is set, you cannot copy a binary file without bad things happening.

That completes our overview of the basic file operations, `<copy>`, `<move>`, and `<delete>`, and the mappers and filters that can be used with them. It's time to use the tasks to prepare our code for packaging.

5.4   PREPARING TO PACKAGE

When preparing to distribute code, always do a clean build first. We want no relics of previous builds. Our `clean` target should clean up all the output directories:

```
<target name="clean"
  description="Deletes files generated by the build.">
```

```
    <delete dir="${build.dir}"
      defaultexcludes="false" />
    <delete dir="${dist.dir}"
      defaultexcludes="false" />
  </target>
```

This target purges our directories of all files. We've opted not to set `failonerror=`
`"false"` on the deletions, because we've chosen to find out if the delete fails.

When run, the `clean` target guarantees that there's nothing in the directories that
Ant will build into. The `<javac>` task will build everything again, so the `.class` files
in `build/classes` will be current. We need to accompany those files with any
resources in the source tree; we do so with a `<copy>` action.

5.4.1 Adding data files to the classpath

Alongside the generated `.class` files, developers often need to include data files in
the Java package hierarchy and, in so doing, copy them into the JAR. These files, which
are called *resources* when they are on the classpath, can then be retrieved with a call to
`this.getClass().getResource()` or `getResourceAsStream()`. The nor-
mal way to work with these files is to keep them all in the source directory and copy
them into the compiled classes directory after compiling the Java code. First, we
define a property containing the pattern to include:

```
    <property name="source.files.tocopy"
      value="**/*.properties,**/*.dtd,**/*.xml,**/*.xsd,**/*.jpg" />
```

We declare this as a property for ease of reuse. For the source, we add:

```
<copy todir="${build.classes.dir}">
  <fileset dir="src"
    includes="${source.files.tocopy}"/>
</copy>
```

This target copies the data files into the `build/classes` directory, and so onto the
classpath or into the JAR we're about to make. Make sure the pattern includes all the files
you want to distribute and none that you do not. If we include resources with our test
classes, we need to do the same action, albeit with a different source and destination:

```
<copy todir="${test.classes.dir}">
  <fileset dir="test"
    includes="${source.files.tocopy}"/>
</copy>
```

We normally do this copy immediately after compiling the source, right after the
`<javac>` task. There's never any situation in which we would not want to copy
the resources over, so having a unified target is good.

After compiling the code we need to generate the JavaDoc HTML files that both
the source and binary distribution packages can redistribute.

5.4.2 Generating documentation

To create the JavaDoc files, we turn to the `<javadoc>` task, which offers complete access to the `javadoc` program. Its basic use is quite straightforward. As usual, we have to declare and create a destination directory in our `init` target:

```
<mkdir dir="${javadoc.dir}"/>
<mkdir dir="${javadoc.dir}"/>
```

Then we declare a new target to create the documentation.

```
<target name="javadocs" depends="compile"
    description="make the java docs" >
  <javadoc
      access="private"
      sourcepath="src"            ❶
      destdir="${javadoc.dir}"    ❷
      packagenames="d1.*"
      use="true"
      version="true"
      windowtitle="${ant.project.name}"
      failonerror="true">
    <classpath refid="compile.classpath"/>   ❸
  </javadoc>
</target>
```

We aren't going to cover how to use the `<javadoc>` task because it would take far too long. It has 50-odd parameters and over a dozen nested elements that show how complex creating the documentation can be. The underlying `javadoc` program has about 25 arguments; the complexity in the task is mainly to provide detailed control as to what that program does.

Fortunately, most of this stuff is irrelevant. The task needs only three things—the source directories ❶, the destination directory ❷, and a list of files to document. It also likes the classpath used by `<javac>` to compile the application ❸.

The `<source>` nested element is where you can list the Java files to document, but specifying packages is usually much easier, especially when you can give a wildcard to import an entire tree. You can specify a package in three ways, as listed in table 5.2. For any complex project, the standard tactic is to list the packages to

Table 5.2 Ways to specify packages to include. The final option, packagelist, is not usually used; it exists to make it easier to migrate from Ant.

Attribute/element	Specification	Example
packagenames	List of packages; wildcards OK.	packagenames="org.*,com.*"
<package>	One package; wildcards OK.	<package name="d1.core.*"/>
packagelist	File listing the packages to import. This is handed directly to the javadoc program using the @ command.	packagelist="packages.txt" packages.txt= d1. d1.core

compile with nested <package> elements, using wildcards to keep the number of declarations to a minimum.

For <javadoc> to work, it needs access to all the libraries used in the application. If the task cannot resolve references to classes, it prints out warnings and the documentation ends up incomplete. To minimize this, we pass the task the compile classpath via the classpathref attribute. By placing the <javadoc> task in a target called javadocs, with a dependency declaration of depends="compile", the task is only called when the classpath is set up and the source compiled.

One big choice to make is what level of methods and fields to document—internal versus external. We've set access="private" to expose everything; the other options being package, protected, and public.

Figure 5.2 shows the result: HTML pages that cover our library.

This documentation can be included in the redistributables, or served up on the team's web site. Many projects do both.

Existing documents can be packaged as is, or get copied through a filterset to expand common tokens such as a release version. There's one other change for some files: fixing the line endings.

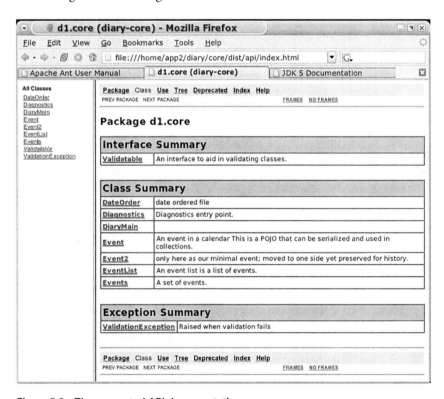

Figure 5.2   The generated API documentation

5.4.3 Patching line endings for target platforms

Shell scripts and plain text documentation have one extra need: their lines must end with the appropriate line endings for the target platform. Files intended for use on Windows should have \r\n line endings; Unix files need \n terminators.

The task for adjusting line endings is <fixcrlf>; this task can be set to convert to the Unix (\n), MSDOS (\r\n), or Mac OS (\r) line endings, depending on the setting of the eol option. If that option is not set, the task defaults to setting the line ending of the local system.

For our project, we currently have only a Python script, but we may want to add some more. We're ready for Unix and Windows scripts, with different patterns for each:

```
<property name="unix.scripts"
  value="**/*.sh,**/*.pl,**/*.py" />
<property name="dos.scripts"
  value="**/*.bat,**/*.cmd" />
```

These patterns are used in our "scripts" target, which does three things. It copies the files into the distribution directory, patches the name of the JAR file we are creating, and then fixes the line endings before finally making the Unix files executable:

```
<target name="scripts" depends="init">
  <copy todir="${dist.dir}" overwrite="true">
    <fileset dir="bin" includes="${unix.scripts},${dos.scripts}"/>
    <filterset begintoken="[[" endtoken ="]]">
      <filter token="TARGET.NAME" value="${target.name}"/>
    </filterset>
  </copy>
  <fixcrlf srcdir="${dist.dir}" eol="unix"
    includes="${unix.scripts}" />
  <fixcrlf srcdir="${dist.dir}" eol="dos"
    includes="${dos.scripts}" />
  <chmod dir="${dist.dir}"  perm="a+x"
    includes="${unix.scripts}" />
</target>
```

The <fixcrlf> task overwrites the destination files if the existing line endings don't match those in the eol attribute. If the file is already patched, <fixcrlf> does nothing. Unless you specify a directory in the destdir attribute, this will mean it overwrites the original files.

Now, what if we want to create text files and scripts for both Windows and Unix?

Creating multiple versions for multiple targets

If you create distributions with scripts and text files that are targeted at multiple operating systems, you may need to create multiple copies of the relevant files, each with the correct line endings in the target.

Listing 5.1 shows a target that takes a readme template and creates the Unix file README and a Windows version, README.TXT, each with the appropriate line endings. This target also uses another service provided by the task, the conversion of tabs to spaces. Tab conversion lets you avoid layout surprises when the recipient views a file in an editor with different tab spacing parameters than normal.

Listing 5.1 Example target to generate Unix and Windows Readme files from the same original

```
<target name="fix-docs" depends="dist-docs,javadocs">
  <property name="readme.windows.file"
    location="${dist.doc.dir}/readme.txt" />
  <property name="readme.unix.file"
    location="${dist.doc.dir}/README" />
  <copy file="${readme.windows.file}"
    tofile="${readme.unix.file}"/>
  <fixcrlf eol="crlf" file="${readme.windows.file}"
    tab="remove" tablength="4" />
  <fixcrlf eol="lf" file="${readme.unix.file}"
    tab="remove" tablength="2" />
</target>
```

Tab conversion inside Java source files receives special treatment by `<fixcrlf>`. If you need to do it, look at the `javafiles` attribute in the documentation. We prefer to leave redistributed source untouched, as it makes it much easier to incorporate submitted patches.

Creating Javadoc files and patching text files are pretty much the limit of Ant's built-in document processing facilities. In chapter 13, we'll use its XML tasks to create HTML and Java source files from XML source documents, which is another way to create documentation. For anything more advanced, consider Apache Forrest.

Creating Dynamic Content with Apache Forrest

There's another Apache project, Apache Forrest, that provides a tool to create documentation as PDF files and web pages from content written in various XML formats, such as the DocBook and OpenOffice.org formats. It uses Apache Cocoon for the XML processing, Apache Batik for rendering SVG drawings into images, and Apache FOP for creating the PDF files. The tool uses Ant to start everything off, and it includes its own version of Ant for that purpose.

Forrest is good for any project that has complex documentation requirements, because you can handwrite documents in the OpenOffice.org word processor and design graphics using an SVG editing tool, such as Inkscape. This content can be integrated with machine-generated content, all of which can be converted to HTML and PDF and published at build time or served dynamically.

Because Forrest is based on Ant, it can be integrated with an Ant-based build process. We're not going to use Forrest, but we will point people to the web site, http://forrest.apache.org/. If you have a project with lots of documentation, investigate it.

Assuming all the documentation is ready, it's now time to create the archives JAR, tar, and Zip.

5.5 CREATING JAR FILES

The JAR file is the central redistributable of Java. It has derivatives, the most common of which are the WAR and EAR files for web applications and Enterprise applications, respectively. Underneath, they're all Zip archives (figure 5.3). Zip files/archives are the ubiquitous archive files of DOS and, more recently, Windows. They can store lots of files inside by using a choice of compression algorithms, including "uncompressed."

The JAR, WAR, and EAR archives are all variations of the basic Zip file, with a text manifest to describe the file and potentially add signing information. The WAR and EAR files add standardized subdirectories to the JAR file to store libraries, classes, and XML configuration files. This can make the WAR and EAR files self-contained redistributables.

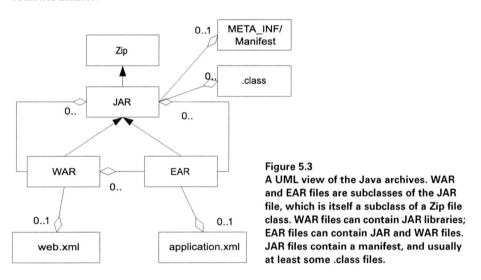

Figure 5.3
A UML view of the Java archives. WAR and EAR files are subclasses of the JAR file, which is itself a subclass of a Zip file class. WAR files can contain JAR libraries; EAR files can contain JAR and WAR files. JAR files contain a manifest, and usually at least some .class files.

Building and manipulating JAR files is a common activity; anyone who uses Ant to build a project will soon become familiar with the `<zip>` and `<jar>` tasks. The full set of packaging tasks have the implementation class hierarchy of figure 5.4.

A JAR file stores classes in a simple tree resembling a package hierarchy, with any metadata added to the `META-INF` directory. This directory contains a manifest file `MANIFEST.MF`, which describes the JAR file to the classloader.

We've been generating JAR files since chapter 2, using the `<jar>` task. At its simplest, it archives an entire tree of files, usually the output of the build.

```
<target name="jar" depends="compile">
  <jar destfile="${dist.dir}/d1-core.jar"
       duplicate="preserve"
       compress="false">
```

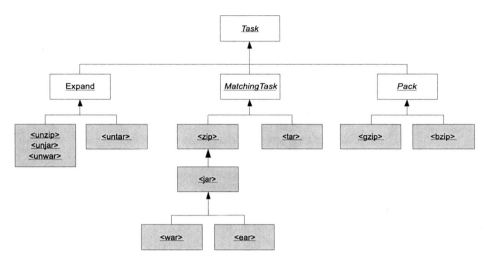

Figure 5.4 The implementation hierarchy of Ant's packaging classes and tasks. The <zip>, <jar>, <war> and <ear> task hierarchy resembles that of their respective file types.

```
        <fileset dir="${build.classes.dir}"/>
    </jar>
</target>
```

The task creates a manifest file unless you explicitly provide one. The `compress` attribute controls whether the archive is compressed. By default `compress= "true"`, but an uncompressed archive may be faster to load. Compressed files do download faster, however.

The current preferred practice for libraries is to create an archive filename from a project name along with a version number in the format `dl-core-0.1.jar`. This lets users see at a glance what version a library is. We can support this practice with some property definitions ahead of the `jar` target:

```
<property name="project.name" value="${ant.project.name}" />
<property name="project.version" value="0.1alpha" />
<property name="target.name"
  value="${project.name}-${project.version}.jar" />
<property name="target.jar"
  location="${dist.dir}/${target.name}" />
```

Ant automatically defines the property `ant.project.name` from the `<project>` declaration in the build file; we reassign this property to a new property to give developers the opportunity to pick a different name. The project version is also something we want to allow for easy overrides. To create the JAR file, we use the `target.jar` property to pass its name to the `destfile` attribute:

```
<target name="jar" depends="compile">
  <jar destfile="${target.jar}"
       duplicate="preserve"
       compress="true">
```

```
        <fileset dir="${build.classes.dir}"/>
    </jar>
</target>
```

This target will now create the JAR file dist/diary-core-0.1alpha.jar. The
<jar> task is dependency-aware; if any source file is newer than the JAR file, the JAR
is rebuilt. Deleting source files doesn't constitute a change that merits a rebuild; a
clean build is needed to purge those from the JAR file.

There is an update attribute that looks at dependencies between source files and
files stored inside the archive. It can be used for incremental JAR file updates, in
which only changed files are updated. Normally, we don't bother with things like
this; we just rebuild the entire JAR when a source file changes. JAR creation time only
becomes an issue with big projects, such as in EAR files or WAR files.

One thing that is important is that all the <jar> targets in this book have
duplicate="preserve" set. The duplicate attribute tells Ant what to do when
multiple filesets want to copy a file to the same path in the archive. It takes three values

- add: silently add the duplicate file. This is the default.
- preserve: ignore the duplicate file; preserve what is in the archive.
- fail: halt the build with an error message.

The default option, add, is dangerous because it silently corrupts JAR files. Ant itself
will ignore the duplicate entry, and so will the JDK jar program. Other tools, such as
the javac compiler, aren't so forgiving, and will throw an IndexOutOfBounds-
Exception or some other obscure stack trace if they encounter duplicate entries. If
you don't want to have users of your application or library making support calls, or
want to waste mornings trying to track down these problems in other people's libraries, change the default value! The most rigorous option is fail, which warns of a
duplication; preserve is good for producing good files without making a fuss.

Once created, we need to check that the JAR file contains everything it needs.

5.5.1   Testing the JAR file

Just as there's a <jar> task, there's an <unjar> task to expand a JAR, a task which is
really an alias of <unzip>. The task expands the Zip/JAR file into a directory tree,
where you can verify that files and directories are in place either manually or by using
the <available> and <filesmatch> conditions. Graphical tools may be easier
to use, but they have a habit of changing the case of directories for usability, which can
cause confusion. WinZip is notorious for doing this, making any all-upper-case directory lower-case and leading to regular bug reports in Ant, bug reports that are always
filed as "INVALID".[1]

---

[1] There is an online bug reporting system for Ant, but all the developers are working in their spare time,
     for free. INVALID and WORKSFORME are two ways defects can be closed. If your bug report gets
     closed this way, don't take it personally.

Expanding a file is easy:

```
<target name="unjar" depends="dist" >
  <unjar
     src="${target.jar}"
     dest="${build.dir}/unjar"/>
</target>
```

The `<unjar>` task takes a source file, specified by `src`, and a destination directory, `dest`, and unzips the file into the directory, preserving the hierarchy. It's dependency-aware; newer files are not overwritten, and the timestamp of the files in the archive is propagated to the unzipped files.

You can selectively unzip parts of the archive, which may save time when the file is large. To use the task to validate the build process after the archive has been unzipped, you should check for the existence of needed files or, perhaps, even their values:

```
<target name="test-jar" depends="jar" >
  <property name="unjar.dir"
    location="${build.dir}/unjar"/>
  <unjar
    src="${target.jar}"
    dest="${unjar.dir}">
    <patternset>
      <include name="d1/**/*"/>
    </patternset>
  </unjar>
  <condition property="jar.uptodate">
    <filesmatch
    file1="${build.classes.dir}/d1/core/Event.class"
    file2="${unjar.dir}/d1/core/Event.class"
    />
  </condition>
  <fail unless="jar.uptodate" message="file mismatch in JAR"/>
</target>
```

Here we expand classes in the archive and then verify that a file in the expanded directory tree matches that in the tree of compiled classes. Binary file comparison is a highly rigorous form of validation, but it can be slow for large files.

To be honest, we rarely bother with these verification stages. Instead, we include the JAR file on the classpath when we run our unit tests. This is the best verification of them all. If we left something out of the JAR, the unit tests will let us know. We'll modify our test run to do this in section 5.6, once the JAR file has the manifest and a signature.

5.5.2 Creating JAR manifests

The `<jar>` task creates a JAR manifest if needed. It will contain the manifest version and the version of Ant used to build the file:

```
Manifest-Version: 1.0
Ant-Version: Apache Ant 1.7
Created-By: 1.5.0_09 (Sun Microsystems Inc.)
```

Sometimes this isn't enough, such as when you want to specify the default entry point of the JAR or add version information to the manifest, as is covered in the JDK document *Java Product Versioning Specification*. You also need to provide a manifest if you want to add extension libraries, following the even more complex Java extension specification *Extension Mechanism Architecture*.

Adding a manifest to the JAR file is trivial; point the `manifest` attribute of the task at a predefined manifest file:

```
<target name="dist-with-manifest"
  depends="compile"
    description="make the distribution" >
  <jar destfile="${jarfile.path}"
      duplicate="preserve"
      index="true"
      manifest="src/META-INF/MANIFEST.MF">
    <fileset dir="${build.classes.dir}"/>
  </jar>
</target>
```

This target needs a manifest file here in `src/META-INF/MANIFEST.MF`

```
Manifest-Version: 1.0
Created-By: Antbook Development Team      ❶
Sealed: true                           ↵
Main-Class: d1.core.Diagnostics   ←❷
```

The `Sealed: true` entry in the manifest marks non-empty packages as *sealed* ❶. The classloader won't allow any other JAR files to contain classes in the `d1.core` package, not even our own test classes. They are allowed in their own package under `d1.core`, which is why the test classes are defined in the `d1.core.test` package. We've set our default entry point to a diagnostics class ❷.

When Ant runs the `<jar>` task, it will parse and potentially correct the manifest before inserting it into the JAR file. If the manifest is invalid, you'll find out now, rather than when you ship.

This process has one weakness: someone has to create the manifest first. Why not create it during the build process, enabling us to use Ant properties inside the manifest? This is where the `<manifest>` task comes in.

```
<target name="jar-dynamic-manifest"
    depends="compile" >
  <property name="manifest.mf"
    location="${build.dir}/manifest.mf" />
  <manifest file="${manifest.mf}" >
    <attribute name="Built-By" value="${user.name}"/>
    <attribute name="Sealed" value="true"/>
    <attribute name="Built-On" value="${timestamp.isoformat}"/>
    <attribute name="Main-Class" value="${main.class}"/>
  </manifest>
  <jar destfile="${target.jar}"
```

```
      duplicate="preserve"
      manifest="${manifest.mf}">
      <fileset dir="${build.classes.dir}"/>
    </jar>
</target>
```

The outcome of this task will be something like the following manifest, although the exact details depend on who created the file, when they created it, and the version of Ant and Java used:

```
Manifest-Version: 1.0
Ant-Version: Apache Ant 1.7
Created-By: 1.5.0_09 (Sun Microsystems Inc.)
Built-By: stevel
Sealed: true
Built-On: 2006-12-20T00:15:28
Main-Class: dl.core.Diagnostics
```

For complex manifests, the task can create manifest sections, using the `<section name="...">` nested element, which can contain attributes and values of a separate section in the manifest. The task can also be used as an element inside the `<jar>` task, avoiding the need to save the manifest to a temporary file. We prefer the stand-alone action, as it's easier to examine the generated content.

Another recurrent bug report raised against Ant is that "`<jar>` wraps long manifest entries," usually related to the classpath attribute. The task follows the specification to the letter, especially the rule "No line may be longer than 72 bytes." If you encounter a problem with something failing to parse a manifest, and the cause is wrapped lines, then it is usually the third-party application that's at fault.

NOTE   Ant's `<jar>` task creates manifest files that follow the specification exactly, and fixes up any supplied manifest where appropriate. This is exactly what you want, except in the special case where the system reading the manifest doesn't comply with the specification. Some mobile phones with J2ME runtimes suffer from this problem. If you want a handwritten manifest in the JAR, without any changes, use the `<zip>` task instead of `<jar>`.

The `MANIFEST.MF` file is the main piece of metadata JAR files use. Sometimes you may need to add extra content to the `META-INF` directory, alongside the manifest, which the `<jar>` task can cope with.

5.5.3   Adding extra metadata to the JAR

There's a nested fileset element, `<metainf>`, which lets you specify the metadata files to add to the JAR.

```
<jar destfile="${target.jar}"
  duplicate="preserve"
  manifest="src/META-INF/MANIFEST.MF">
  <fileset dir="${build.classes.dir}"/>
  <metainf dir="src/META-INF/"/>
</jar>
```

We still declared the manifest file, even though the `<metainf>` element appeared to import the manifest. There's special handling in the `<jar>` task of manifest files that it encounters in any fileset: it silently skips them. There's an attribute, `fileset-manifest`, that lets you control this behavior: `skip`, `merge`, and `merge-withoutmain` are the three options. If you need to merge manifests, look at this attribute. Otherwise, we recommend explicit naming of the manifest, rather than relying on merging possibly taking place.

5.5.4 JAR file best practices

There are four things to consider for better `<jar>` tasks:

- Copy all the files you want to include in the JAR into one place before building. This makes it easier to see what will be included.

- Create your own manifest, either in a file or in Ant, and explicitly ask for it with the `manifest` attribute. If you leave it to the `<jar>` task, you get a minimal manifest.

- Always set `duplicate="preserve"`. It keeps duplicate entries out of a file and avoids possible problems later on.

- Finally, and arguably most importantly, give your libraries a version number at the end.

When we get into repository-based downloading, in chapter 11, you'll see how version-labeled JAR files can be used. It pays off in your own project the moment you start trying to track down bugs related to versions of libraries. If every JAR file has a version, including your own, it's much easier to replicate a problem.

Now that we've built the JAR, we can sign it.

5.5.5 Signing JAR files

Signing is useful when you redistribute stuff through Java Web Start or by other means. It doesn't take much effort to add signing support, but it's important to start doing it early on. Signed JAR files are loaded slightly differently, with the classloader preventing other JAR files from declaring classes in the same packages. It's important, therefore, to start signing early on—even if the key is made up just for the purpose. It avoids our creating fundamental design errors that only show up later on in the project.

To sign JAR files, we need a public/private key pair in a password-protected keystore, and Ant will need that password. One thing you don't want to do is put that in the build file itself—anyone with access to the source repository will see it. This isn't what you want in your build file:

```
<property name="keystore.password" value="secret" />
```

Instead, you need the `<input>` task to prompt the user.

```
<target name="get-password" >
  <input addproperty="keystore.password" >password for
```

```
keystore:</input>
  <echo level="verbose">password = ${keystore.password}</echo>
</target>
```

This task pauses the build with a prompt; the user then has to enter a string. In a -verbose run, we echo this back:

```
get-password:
    [input] password for keystore:    │ This is echoed
more-secret                           ←┘ user input
    [echo] password = more-secret
```

The task has two problems. First, it doesn't work properly in older IDEs or in automated builds, but we can work around that. More seriously, the string you type in gets echoed to the console. Anyone looking over your shoulder can see the password. We cannot avoid this, not until Ant adds a Java 6-specific input handler

For unattended builds, you need to know that <input> doesn't halt with a prompt if the property is already set. If we define the property in a properties file that's not in your SCM system and that's protected from all other users, we can read it in before the <input> task, and so skip the prompt. Here we use ${user.home}/.secret, a location which is restricted to the user on a Windows NTFS file system. For Unix, we want to make it readable only by us. For that, we declare a <chmod> operation to lock it down. This task runs the chmod program to set file or directory permissions, but only on platforms that support it. On Windows, it's a harmless no-op. We look for a keystore.properties file in this directory and save the keystore there to keep it private:

```
<target name="init-security">
  <property name="keystore.dir" location="${user.home}/.secret" />
  <mkdir dir="${keystore.dir}" />
  <chmod file="${keystore.dir}" perm="700"/>
  <property name="keystore"
     location="${keystore.dir}/local.keystore" />
  <property file="${keystore.dir}/keystore.properties" />
  <property name="keystore.alias" value="code.signer"/>
</target>
```

After changing the get-password target to depend upon this new init-security target, the file keystore.properties will be read before the <input> operation. If we put the relevant declaration in there (keystore.password=hidden.secret), this is what we see at input time:

```
get-password:
    [input] skipping input as property keystore.password
            has already been set.
    [echo] password = hidden-secret
```

The <chmod> task is encountered very rarely in Ant projects. Because Java 5 and earlier has no API to read or write Unix file permissions, all of Ant's file operations drop their values. This includes <copy> as well as the <tar> and <zip> tasks we'll cover in section 5.8. For this reason, <zip> and <tar> offer ways to declare the permission on files in the archives. If you want to set permissions on a local file, <chmod> must be the last Ant task to manipulate the file.

With the password in a property, we're nearly ready to sign the JAR. We just need a certificate and the <signjar> task. First, the certificate.

Generating a signing key

To authenticate JARs in a Java runtime, you have to buy a certificate from one of the approved vendors. For testing purposes or for private use, you can generate a self-signed certificate using Sun's keytool tool, which Ant wraps up into the <genkey> task. This task adds a key into a keystore, creating the store if needed:

```
<target name="create-signing-key" depends="get-password">
  <genkey
    alias="${keystore.alias}"
    keystore="${keystore}"
    storepass="${keystore.password}"
    validity="366" >
    <dname>
      <param name="CN" value="autosigner"/>
      <param name="OU" value="Steve and Erik"/>
      <param name="O"  value="Apache Software Foundation"/>
      <param name="C"  value="EU"/>
    </dname>
  </genkey>
</target>
```

This task creates a new alias in the keystore, with a certificate that's valid for 366 days. Although these keys are cryptographically sound, tools such as the Java Web Start don't trust them. If you're verifying JAR files in your own application, you're free to use self-generated keys, and within an organization or community you may be able to convince end users to add your certificate (or private certification authority) to the trusted list.

What we can do with an untrusted key is sign the JAR and verify that our application works with signed JAR files and the classloader complications that follow.

Signing the file

The <signjar> task signs JAR files. It checksums all the entries in the file, signs these checksums, and adds them to the manifest. It also adds signature information to the META-INF directory in the JAR file. The task needs the location and the password of the keystore file, and the alias and any optional extra password for the signature itself. It will then modify the JAR file in place by invoking the jarsigner tool in the JDK:

```
<target name="sign-jar" depends="jar,get-password">
  <signjar jar="${target.jar}"
```

```
        alias="${keystore.alias}"
        keystore="${keystore}"
        storepass="${keystore.password}" />
</target>
```

Our manifest now contains digest signatures of the classes inside the JAR, and there are new files in the META-INF directory, including the public certificate of the generated pair. The `<signjar>` task can bulk sign a set of JAR files, using a nested fileset element. It also performs basic dependency checking, by not attempting to sign any files that are already signed by the user. It doesn't check to see if the file has changed since the last signing. This means that you should not mix JAR signing with incremental JAR creation: the `update` flag in the `<jar>` task must remain at `false`.

Java behaves differently with signed JARs, and some applications can break. To be sure that this has not happened, we must take the signed JAR file of the diary classes and run our existing tests against it.

5.6 TESTING WITH JAR FILES

Running JUnit against a signed JAR file, rather than the raw classes, lets us test more things. It lets us test that the classes were added to the JAR file, that we've remembered to add any resources the application needs, and that the signing process has not broken anything. It also lets us state that the tests were run against the redistributables, which is something to be proud of.

It is very easy to test against the JAR file. Recall that in chapter 4, we set up our classpath for compiling and running tests like this:

```
<path id="test.compile.classpath">
  <path refid="compile.classpath"/>
  <pathelement location="${build.classes.dir}"/>
</path>
```

We need to change one line to run against the generated JAR file:

```
<path id="test.compile.classpath">
  <path refid="compile.classpath"/>
  <pathelement location="${target.jar}"/>
</path>
```

We also have to declare that the test targets depend upon the JAR file being created:

```
<target name="test-init" depends="sign-jar">
```

As all the test targets, including `test-compile`, depend upon this `test-init` target, we are now set up to compile and run the tests against the JAR file.

To verify everything works, run `ant clean test`. As clean builds are usually fast, don't be afraid to run them regularly.

Since the tests still appear to be working, we can say that we've finished our process of generating the JAR file. Next comes redistributing the JAR file inside Zip and tar packages.

5.7 CREATING ZIP FILES

Ant creates Zip files as easily as it creates JAR files, using `<jar>`'s parent task, `<zip>`. All attributes and elements of `<zip>` can be used in `<jar>`, but the JAR-specific extras for the manifest and other metadata aren't supported. What the `<zip>` and `<jar>` tasks support is the `<zipfileset>` element. The `<zipfileset>` extends the normal fileset with some extra parameters, as listed in table 5.3. It lets you add the contents of one Zip file to another, expanding it in the directory tree where you choose, and it lets you place files imported from the file system into chosen places in the Zip file. This eliminates the need to create a complete directory tree on the local disk before creating the archive.

Table 5.3 Extra attributes in <zipfileset> compared to a <fileset>

Attribute	Meaning
prefix	A directory prefix to use in the Zip file
fullpath	The full path to place the single file in archive
src	The name of a Zip file to include in the archive
encoding	The encoding to use for filenames in the Zip file; default is the local encoding
filemode	Unix file system permission; default is 644
dirmode	Unix directory permission; default is 755

The last two attributes let you declare the Unix file permissions. The values are interpreted by the Info-ZIP implementations of the zip and unzip programs that are common on Unix and Linux systems. In theory, you could set the permissions for executables and files, and when unzipped on the command line, they would be set.

We tend to use the tar file format when setting permissions, but that could just be a historical quirk of ours. If you create a Zip file with permissions, you may not need to make a tar file at all.

Planning the redistribution

To create the Zip file in our build, the first step is to define the names of the new output files. We use the plural, as we plan to create two files for distribution: a binary redistributable and a source edition. We do so by adding properties to the start of the project, declaring a full path to each Zip file.

First, we realize that the combination of project-name and version is going to be used so often it needs factoring into its own property

```
<property name="project.name-ver"
  value="${project.name}-${project.version}"
```

Then we create properties naming both the Zip files we're about to create

```
<property name="target.zip"
  location="${dist.dir}/${project.name-ver}.zip" />
<property name="src.zip"
  location="${dist.dir}/${project.name-ver}-src.zip" />
```

These files will be fed into the tasks to create the Zip files and follow-on tasks that will expand the same files for testing. There are two Zip files to create—binary and source—with two targets.

5.7.1   Creating a binary Zip distribution

Our binary distribution contains the project's JAR file, all the documentation, and any scripts in the `bin` directory. Listing 5.2 contains the target to do this.

Listing 5.2   Creating a binary Zip distribution

```
<target name="create-bin-zipfile" depends="sign-jar,fix-docs"
  description="create the distributable for Windows">
  <zip destFile="${target.zip}"
    duplicate="preserve">
    <zipfileset file="${target.jar}"
      prefix="${project.name-ver}" />
    <zipfileset dir="${dist.doc.dir}"
      includes="**/*"
      prefix="${project.name-ver}/docs" />
    <zipfileset dir="${javadoc.dir}"
      includes="**/*"
      prefix="${project.name-ver}/docs/api" />
  </zip>
</target>
```

This target depends on the signed JAR created in the `"sign-jar"` target of section 5.5.5 and the `"fix-docs"` target of section 5.4.3. We want the signed JAR and the documents that were patched with DOS file endings.

We've given every `zipfileset` the prefix of the project name and version. This is the Unix tradition: the redistributable should expand into a directory containing the name and title of the project. This is very useful for having versions of programs side by side, which is why it's a common technique.

To verify that this task works, we create a target to unzip the file:

```
<property name="unzip.dir" location="${build.dir}/unzip" />
<property name="unzip.bin.dir" location="${unzip.dir}/bin" />

<target name="unzip-bin-zipfile" depends="create-bin-zipfile">
  <unzip src="${target.zip}" dest="${unzip.bin.dir}" />
</target>
```

The result should be that the contents of the file are unzipped into the directory `build/unzip/bin/diary-core-0.1alpha`. We could go on to test using the same techniques for verifying that JAR worked: either with `<available>` tests or, better, by using the unzipped files in the next stage of the project.

Our Zip file is ready for redistribution. If we depended on other libraries we'd have to include them as another `<zipfileset>` in the `<zip>` target and then worry about the license implications. If you use a GPL- or LPGL-licensed library, this is where you discover whether its license applies to your own code.

Hand in hand with the binary distribution goes the source distribution.

5.7.2   Creating a source distribution

In the open-source world, there's often little difference between source and binary distributions. In closed-source software there is a difference, but the source is still regularly distributed, just not as broadly.

A source-only distribution contains the source tree and the build file(s); the recipient has to compile everything. Open-source projects may want to consider a single distribution containing the source and the binaries, delivering a quick start from the JAR files, yet offering the opportunity of editing the source to all users.

We're going to include the JAR file; then the components for our source build file become clear. They are: the source, test, and documentation directory trees; the build file; and the binary Zip file itself:

```
<target name="create-src-zipfile" depends="sign-jar">
  <zip destfile="${src.zip}"
    duplicate="preserve">
    <zipfileset file="${target.jar}"
      prefix="${project.name-ver}" />
    <zipfileset dir="."
      includes="src/**,test/**,doc/**,*.xml"
      prefix="${project.name-ver}" />
  </zip>
</target>
```

The result is a file that runs out of the box but which contains the entire source and, of course, the build file. We can verify this by unzipping the file:

```
<target name="unzip-src-zipfile" depends="create-src-zipfile">
  <unzip src="${src.zip}" dest="${build.dir}/src" />
</target>
```

There's one little extra trick we can do to validate a source distribution: we can run Ant in it and verify that it works. This is wonderfully recursive; however, it uses the `<ant>` task, which will not be formally introduced until chapter 10. At the risk of a forward reference, here's the target to run the unzipped copy of our own build file:

```
<target name="validate-src-zipfile" depends="unzip-src-zipfile">
  <ant dir="${build.dir}/src/${project.name-ver}"
    antfile="core-chapter5.xml"
    inheritall="false" >
    <propertyset>
```

```
        <propertyref prefix="keystore"/>
      </propertyset>
    </ant>
</target>
```

There's some magic there to deal with passing down the password and other signing information, which is where the <ant> task gets complicated and why we won't return to it for five more chapters.

5.7.3 Zip file best practices

Here are some tips to make creating Zip files easier:

- Copy all files you want to include in the JAR into one place before building. This makes it easier to test that the needed files have been copied.
- Don't distribute JAR files with a .zip extension—it causes confusion.
- Use the <zipfileset> element for more control over the entries in the Zip file.
- Create a subdirectory for everything, with the name and version of the project. This is what files will be unzipped into.
- Set the attribute duplicate="fail" or duplicate="preserve" to handle duplicate entries more robustly.
- Include the Unix documents and scripts alongside the Windows ones. Set the permissions for these scripts in a <zipfileset>, even if you cannot rely on them being set by the unzip programs.

Zip is a good format for distributing Java packages. Everything that runs Java can expand the files by using the jar tool if need be, and they're supported on Windows, Unix, and other platforms. Even so, there's some value in producing Unix-specific source and binary distribution packages, which Ant can do as easily as it can create a Zip file.

5.8   PACKAGING FOR UNIX

The preferred archive format for Unix systems is the tar file, while many Linux distributions can install RPM or .deb packages. Projects may want to produce these files alongside .zip distributions. Doing so makes the files more acceptable to Unix users. It also can give you some statistics that measure Unix and Linux package downloads alongside Windows ones if you're distributing via a web site that collects download statistics.

The main format to consider is the tar file.

5.8.1   Tar files

Tar files are the classic distribution format of Unix. The archive includes not only the folder hierarchy, but also the file permissions, including the files that are executable. A version of the tar program can be found on every Unix platform, and it's even

cross-compiled for Windows. Ant can create tar files, including permissions, using its
`<tar>` task. This task takes an implicit fileset with attributes such as `includes` and
`excludes` to control which files to include. We prefer a more verbose and explicit
policy of listing filesets as nested elements. This is more than simply a style policy for
better maintenance; it's a way of having more control over the build. At the same
time, we want to minimize maintenance. Although we could create the tar file by
copying fileset declarations from the `<zip>` task of listing 5.2, we do not want to do
that. That would force us to keep both the tar and Zip processes synchronized, or else
we may accidentally leave something out of a distribution. Also, we can't reference
`<zipfileset>` declarations inside the `<tar>` task. So how can we reuse all the Zip
file work to create a tar file?

Well, after creating the Zip distribution, we unzipped it, to verify it was all there.
What if we were to create a tar file from that directory tree, adding file permissions
as we go? That might seem like cheating, but from the extreme programming perspective, it's exactly the kind of lazy coding developers should be doing. Listing 5.3 shows
the target that we use to create the archive of the binary distribution, giving shell
scripts execute permissions as we do so.

Listing 5.3 Creating a tar file from our expanded Zip file

```
<property name="target.tar"
  location="${dist.dir}/${project.name-ver}.tar" />

<target name="create-bin-tar"
  depends="unzip-bin-zipfile">
  <tar destfile="${target.tar}"
    longfile="gnu">
    <tarfileset dir="${unzip.bin.dir}"
      excludes="${executables}" />
    <tarfileset dir="${unzip.bin.dir}"
      includes="${executables}"
      filemode="755"/>
  </tar>
</target>
```

The `<tar>` task extends the usual `<fileset>` element with the `<tarfileset>`:
a fileset with `filemode` and `dirmode` attributes for Unix permissions. The file permission is in the base-8 format used in Unix API calls. The default permission is 644
(read/write to the owner, read to everyone else), and the default identity is simply the
empty string. A mask of 755 adds an executable flag to this permission list, whereas
777 grants read, write, and execution access to all. The `<tarfileset>` element also
supports the `prefix` element found in `<zipfileset>`, which lets you place files
into the archive in a directory with a different name from their current directory. If
you want to set user and group names and identities, `<tarfileset>` has four
attributes of relevance, as shown in table 5.4.

ANT 1.7

Table 5.4 Attributes in a <tarfileset> to set the user and group owners of files

Attribute	Meaning	example
username	user name as a string	`"mysql"`
group	group name as a string	`"users"`
uid	decimal user ID	`"60"`
gid	decimal group ID	`"100"`

We normally ignore these options, worrying only about file permissions. First, we include everything but the executable files with default permissions, then we include the executable files with the relevant mask. We must not include the executables in the first fileset, because if we did, the files would be included twice with unpredictable results.

Problems with tar files

The original tar file format and program doesn't handle very long path names. There's a 100-character limit, which is easily exceeded in any Java source tree. The GNU `tar` program supports longer filenames, unlike the original Unix implementation. You can tell the `<tar>` task what to do when it encounters this situation with its `longfile` attribute, which takes any of the values listed in table 5.5.

Table 5.5 Values for the longfile attribute. Although optional, setting this attribute shows that you have chosen an explicit policy. Of the options, fail, gnu, and warn make the most sense.

Longfile value	Meaning
fail	Fail the build
gnu	Save long pathnames in the gnu format
omit	Skip files with long pathnames
truncate	Truncate long pathnames to 100 characters
warn	Save long pathnames in the gnu format, and print a warning message [default]

If you choose to use the GNU format, add a warning note on the download page about using GNU `tar` to expand the library. Also, tell whomever deals with support calls about the issue, because not enough people read the documentation. The usual sign is a bug report about missing source files, primarily on Solaris, AIX, or HP/UX. The problem never surfaces on Linux, as GNU `tar` is the only `tar` tool there.

Tar files are also a weak format for sharing, because they're uncompressed, and so can be overweight compared to Zip files. This issue is addressed by compressing them.

Compressing the archive

Redistributable tar files are normally compressed by using either the gzip or bzip2 algorithms as `.tar.gz` and `.tar.bz2` files, respectively. This process is so ubiquitous that the GNU `tar` tool has the options `--gzip` and `--ungzip` to do the `.gz` compression and decompression, along with the tar creation or extraction operations.

Ant can compress the `.tar` file by using the `<gzip>` and `<bzip2>` tasks:

```
<property name="target.tar.gz"
  location="${target.tar}.gz"/>
<property name="target.tar.bz2"
  location="${target.tar}.bz2"/>

<target name="compress-tar" depends="create-bin-tar">
  <gzip src="${target.tar}"
    destfile="${target.tar.gz}"/>
  <bzip2 src="${target.tar}"
    destfile="${target.tar.bz2}"/>
</target>
```

Apart from the different compression algorithms, the `<gzip>` and `<bzip2>` tasks behave identically. They take a single source file in the `src` attribute and an output file in either the `destfile` or `zipfile` attribute. When executed, these tasks create a suitably compressed file whenever the destination file is absent or older than the source.

We do, of course, have to check that the compressed tar file is usable. Ant has a task called `<untar>` to reverse the tar operation, and others called `<gunzip>` and `<bunzip2>` to uncompress the files first. You can use these tasks to verify that the redistributable files are in good condition. For example, here's the `.tar.gz` file expanded into a directory tree:

```
<property name="untar.dir" location="${build.dir}/untar" />

<target name="untar-bin.tar.gz" depends="compress-tar">
  <mkdir dir="${untar.dir}" />
  <gunzip src="${target.tar.gz}"
    dest="${untar.dir}" />
  <untar src="${untar.dir}/${project.name-ver}.tar"
    dest="${untar.dir}" />
</target>
```

Because Ant doesn't set permissions on untarred files, these tasks aren't quite as useful as Unix and GNU `gunzip` and `tar` commands.

Projects have to be ruthless and ask if creating tar files is worth the effort, or if using a Zip file is adequate. Every project will have to answer this for itself. Simple projects should find that Zip files are an adequate cross-platform redistributable, especially if you're targeting other Java users. Creating tar files is an act of political correctness: Unix users may expect it, and the JPackage group (see below) likes to use it as a starting place for its RPM files.

Projects should always create Zip files. Not only are they the only files that work on Windows, every JDK comes with the `jar` tool. Therefore, wherever there's a JDK, there's a way to expand the file. Tar files, on the other hand, are an optional extra.

The other important file format is the Linux RPM package.

5.8.2 Generating RPM Packages

Closing the subject of packaging for Linux, we note that there's a task, `<rpm>`, that runs the RedHat Package manager, generating an RPM file. These are files that can be installed by using the application management tools of RedHat, SuSE, and other RPM-based Linux distributions.

The authors never use `<rpm>`, because we don't create RPM packages. It's a personal choice. The RPM format is great for managing native programs on Linux. But only system administrators can install RPM files, and they affect the whole system. In Java, it's a lot easier to have personal installations with personal copies of all needed JAR files, even private JREs for separate projects. You don't often need system-wide installation on a self-managed box.

The JPackage project team (http://jpackage.org/) has a different opinion on the matter. They're trying to integrate Java projects with Linux distributions. If you want to start creating RPM files, look at what they do and join their mailing list. You should also be aware that recent Linux distributions often include the JPackage artifacts, which can be a help or a hindrance depending on how you adapt to them. Consult the JPackage team for its advice on how to redistribute JPackage-friendly code, especially if you want to integrate with Linux distributions or management tools.

Together, the JAR, Zip, and tar files form the core of Ant's packages. JAR is universal, as most projects create JAR files of one form or other. The other archives are more for redistribution.

There's one more thing we can do with all these archives, and that is read the data back. Tasks like `<unzip>`, and `<untar>` can expand the entire archives, but that's sometimes a bit of overkill. What if we just need to get one file from inside a JAR and feed it into another task? Do we really have to create a temporary directory, expand the JAR, pass the file reference, and remember to clean up afterwards? Isn't there an easier way?

There is an easier way: *Ant resources*.

5.9   WORKING WITH RESOURCES

Back in section 3.11 we mentioned that Ant 1.7 retrofitted Ant with a coherent model behind `<filesets>`, `<filelists>`, and other *resources*, but we didn't provide any more details. Now it's time to explore the topic, since our project has things like JAR, Zip, and tar files. Why? Because these files can contain Ant resources.

5.9.1   A formal definition of a resource

We're going to peek under the covers of Ant for a moment and describe what a resource is in terms of Java classes and interfaces.

1 The `org.apache.tools.ant.types.resources` package contains the base classes and interfaces that define resources.

2 A *resource* is anything that can act as a source and possibly a destination for reading and writing data. Some resources are *touchable*, meaning they implement the Touchable interface with its method touch() to set the time of the resource.

3 Files, URLs, and files inside Zip and tar archives are some of Ant's built-in resource types.

4 A *resource collection* is anything that acts as a container for resources. Formally, it is any datatype that implements the ResourceCollection interface, with its methods size(), iterator(), and isFileSystemOnly(). Filesets are one such resource collection.

5 The Resource class itself claims to be a ResourceCollection with one resource—itself.

6 A *resource-enabled task* is a task that's been written or updated to support resources and/or resource collections. Many such tasks accept resource collections that refer to only those resources that are in the local file system—that is, whose isFileSystemOnly() test returns true.

From the build file perspective, this means there's a new way of defining a data source or destination—resources and resource collections. These collections can be used in resource-enabled tasks that no longer have to care where or how the data gets into the task. You can feed the contents of a property to a task as easily as pointing it at a file.

From a packaging perspective, there are built-in resources to access the individual entries in a JAR, Zip, or tar archive. These resources enable build files to access files inside the archives without expanding them.

5.9.2 What resources are there?

Table 5.6 lists the built-in resources. These resources can be passed directly to any resource-enabled task, or grouped into a resource collection. Every resource is something that can act as a source of data. Some can act as output streams; those that are touchable can be used in the <touch> task to set their timestamps.

Table 5.6 Ant's built-in resources

Resource name	Description	Access
<resource>	The base of all resources	only if implemented in derivatives
<bzip2resource>	Dynamically compresses/uncompresses a nested resource	read/write
<file>	A normal file or a directory	read/write
<gzipresource>	Dynamically compresses/uncompresses a nested resource	read/write

continued on next page

Table 5.6 Ant's built-in resources *(continued)*

Resource name	Description	Access
`<javaresource>`	Anything that can be loaded off a classpath, such as class or property files	read-only
`<property>`	A resource view of an Ant property	writeable once
`<stringentry>`	A string whose contents act as the input stream	read-only
`<tarentry>`	Anything inside a tar file	read-only
`<url>`	A URL to remote data	read/write
`<zipentry>`	Anything inside a Zip file	read-only

The `<file>` resource is nothing special, but the `<javaresource>`, `<zipentry>`, and `<tarentry>` resources are new: they let you refer to something inside an archive or classpath, and they feed it directly to a task. The `<property>` and `<stringentry>` resources make it possible to generate source data in Ant without having to `<echo>` into a file. The `<url>` resource lets you use any URL that the Java runtime supports as a source of data.

To actually use any of these resources, you need to declare them inside a resource collection, which is an Ant datatype that supports nested resources.

5.9.3 Resource collections

Resources can be collected into resource collections, and this is where it gets interesting. Some of the resource collections are things that we've already encountered: `<fileset>`, `<filelist>`, `<path>`, `<zipfileset>`, and `<tarfileset>`. These resource collections are essentially different ways to describe a set of resources to a task. The best bit comes when you look at the ability to restrict, combine, and sort resources.

Table 5.7 Resource collections: ways to group resources

Resource collection name	Description
`<resources>`	A collection of resources of arbitrary type.
`<filelist>`	An ordered list of file resources.
`<files>`	A collection of files—essentially a `<fileset>` without the `basedir` attribute.
`<fileset>`	The ubiquitous `<fileset>` datatype. All filesets have a base directory and contain a list of file resources.
`<path>`	The `<path>` type: a list of file resources.
`<tarfileset>`	Things in a tar file: `<file>` or `<tarentry>` resources.
`<zipfileset>`	Things in a Zip or JAR file: `<file>` or `<zipentry>` resources.
`<difference>`	Examines multiple resource collections and returns only those that appear in one collection.

continued on next page

Table 5.7 Resource collections: ways to group resources *(continued)*

Resource collection name	Description
`<intersect>`	Returns the intersection of two or more resource collections.
`<restrict>`	Restricts another collection by selection criteria. Restrictions include resource name, existence, size, modified date, and others.
`<sort>`	Sorts a set of resources. Sort comparisons can be on attributes of the resource or its actual content.
`<tokens>`	String tokens extracted from nested resources.
`<union>`	Merges resource collections into a larger one.

The `<union>`, `<difference>`, and `<intersect>` collections provide the classic set operations to resource collections nested or referred to inside them.

To summarize where we are so far: resources represent sources (and sometimes destinations) of data; they can be aggregated in resource collections. The built-in resources can refer to files, strings, properties, or files stored inside packaged tar or Zip files. We can use the resource collections to access these resources.

Making use of resources

To use resource collections, you declare them inside a resource-enabled task. In an ideal world, you wouldn't need to differentiate between filesets, paths, filelists, and other collection types—you'd just pass them to a task. Nor would you worry about whether source files for `<javac>` compile or an `<xslt>` transformation came from local files, entries inside a Zip archive, or from remote `http://` URLs. This ideal world doesn't exist.

A unified model of resources is new to Ant, and it's only gradually being added to Ant's tasks. Many tasks can work only with files or resource collections that contain file system resources; the `<move>` and `<delete>` tasks are examples. This file-centric view of the world is not just restricted to Ant: tools like Sun's Java compiler work only with files in the file system, not remote URLs or source in a Zip file. The only way to move such programs to support arbitrary resources would be to provide a complete new virtual file system underneath.

This sounds a bit demoralizing, but don't worry. The `<copy>` task is fully resource-enabled; it will copy content from any resource to a file or directory. You can use `<copy>` to get anything onto the local file system for other tasks to work with. This is the primary way that non-file resources are used in Ant today. When we write new tasks in chapter 17, they'll be resource-enabled from the outset.

We've used `<unzip>`, `<gunzip>`, and `<untar>` to remove files from Zip and tar files. Can we treat everything as a resource and use `<copy>` instead? Yes. Here's a target that uses one `<copy>` to extract the `.tar` file from inside the `.gz` file, then extracts all the entries inside the tar file:

```
<target name="untar-with-copy" depends="compress-tar">
  <mkdir dir="${untar.dir}"/>
```

```
<copy todir="${untar.dir}" >
  <gzipresource>
    <file file="${target.tar.gz}"/>
  </gzipresource>
  <mapper type="glob" from="*.gz" to="*"/>
</copy>

<copy todir="${untar.dir}" preservelastmodified="true" >
  <tarfileset src="${untar.dir}/${project.name-ver}.tar"
      includes="**/*"/>
  </copy>
</target>
```

We have to remember to provide a `<mapper>` to the gunzip `<copy>` so that it knows to remove the `.gz` ending for the file. In the second `<copy>`, we need to set the `preserveLastModified` flag to keep the normal policy of `<untar>` and `<unzip>`: that of giving extracted files the timestamps they have in the archive.

We're going to use resources in the future when they solve specific problems. The whole resource concept will take time to propagate through tasks, especially third-party ones. Tasks that accept resource collections rather than just, say, filesets, are much more flexible as they can accept data from so many more sources. Build file authors will be able to do tricks, such as pull source files straight from a JAR or Zip file and feed them straight into another task. Resources can be used in another interesting way: developers can provide new resources or resource collections to represent new sources of data.

For now, the primary use of the concept is in `<copy>`. It can extract resources from any collection and save them to a file. Most other tasks, especially those that wrap existing code, can only handle in-file-system resources.

The immediate benefit from the resource and resource collection concepts is, therefore, that the `<filelist>`, `<fileset>`, and `<path>` lists of files are essentially interchangeable in a resource-enabled task.

5.10   SUMMARY

Packaging your Java classes into JAR files is the first step to using or distributing your code. Ant's `<jar>` task is the foundation for creating a JAR, and `<signjar>` is the means of signing it, if that's desired.

Once the JAR is made, you can use it in other programs or execute it. We'll cover those uses next. What we've covered in this chapter is the full spread of distribution packaging, from Zip to tar. Zip is the most uniformly supported and the one to start with; tar is also popular in Unix.

Building a redistributable package can go wrong—usually due to errors in the build file. There are three ways of addressing this problem: manual tests, automated tests, or shipping the product and waiting for complaints. We like the automated test system, and we've shown some ways to verify that the process works. Even if you don't bother with testing the tar and Zip files, using the JAR files in your test target is essential for ensuring that your JAR files have been correctly assembled.

Finally, we've introduced the resource and resource collection model of Ant. These form the conceptual model behind the fileset and other collections of data sources and destinations in Ant. Resource-enabled tasks, such as <copy>, are able to use arbitrary resources as data sources, which lets build files work directly with files straight out of JAR, Zip, or tar archives. Although new to Ant, resources will become more broadly supported over time and will lead to a better conceptual model of data sources and destinations.

With our diary JAR file created and the source and binary distributions put together, our build is in a position to do two things. The JAR can be executed, and the distribution packages redistributed. This is what the next two chapters will cover.

C H A P T E R   6

Executing programs

So far, our code compiles and the tests pass. Ant is packaging it into JAR files and then into Zip and tar packages for distribution.

This means it's time to explore the capabilities of Ant to execute programs, both Java and native. Ant is one of the best tools for starting programs in Java; it wraps all the platform-specific details into a few tasks. It's so useful that it's often used behind the scenes in many applications.

Ant's execution services come in three tasks, `<java>`, `<exec>`, and `<apply>`, that together meet most projects' needs for running Java and native code. Let's start with an overview of the problem, get into `<java>`, and then look at native code.

6.1   RUNNING PROGRAMS UNDER ANT— AN INTRODUCTION

Ant does a lot of work in its own libraries, in the Java code behind tasks. You don't need to explicitly run external programs on every line of a build file just to get the application compiled, packaged, and tested the way you'd have to do with the Make tool. Yet eventually, projects need to use external programs.

The most common program to run from inside Ant is the one you're actually building, such as our diary application. You may also need a native compiler, a Perl script, or just some local utility program. There are also other Java programs to which Ant can delegate work, such as tools like javac in the JDK.

When you need to run programs from inside Ant, there are two solutions. One option is to wrap it in a custom Ant task. We'll cover this subject in chapter 18. It's no harder than writing any other Java class, but it does involve programming, testing, and documentation. It's the most powerful and flexible means of integrating with Ant, and the effort is sometimes worthwhile. It's a great way of making software easy for other developers to use.

The other option—the easy option—is using Ant's <java> or <exec> task to run the program straight from a build file. Ant can run Java and native programs with ease. Java programs can even run inside Ant's own JVM for higher perfor-mance. Figure 6.1 illustrates the basic conceptual model of this execution. Many Ant tasks work by calling native programs or Java programs. As a case in point, the <javac> task can run Sun's javac compiler in Ant's JVM, or IBM's Jikes com-piler as a native application.

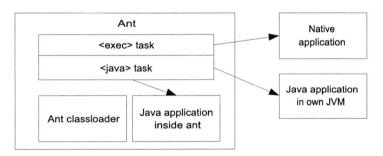

Figure 6.1 Ant can spawn native applications, while Java programs can run inside or outside Ant's JVM.

When running a program, Ant normally halts the build until it finishes. Console out-put from the program goes to the Ant logger, which forwards it to the screen, while input data goes the other way. Users can specify input sources and output destina-tions, whether they're files, Ant properties, or *filter chains*, which are Ant components to process incoming data.

Before we can run our diary, we need an entry point—a method that the Java runtime can invoke to start the program running. Listing 6.1 shows this entry point in its class DiaryMain.

Listing 6.1   An entry point to add events to our diary

```
public static void main(String args[])
        throws Exception {
    DiaryMain diaryMain = new DiaryMain("calendar.dl");
    diaryMain.load(false);
    if (args.length > 0) {
```

```
        String time = args[0];
        String name = null;
        name = args.length > 1 ? args[1] : "event";
        String text = null;
        text = args.length > 2 ? args[2] : null;
        diaryMain.add(time, name, text);
    }
    diaryMain.save();
    System.out.println(diaryMain.toString());
}
```

This method will create or update the calendar file `calendar.dl` with the appointment passed in as arguments. If no arguments are passed down, it lists the current diary; otherwise it tries to create one from the time, name, and text arguments passed in.

This entry point turns the JAR file into a program, one that can be run from the command line. It also can be run from Ant, which lets us integrate it with the build and which allows us to have Ant provide arguments from Ant properties and datatypes.

6.1.1   Introducing the \<java\> task

The central task for running Java applications is called, not surprisingly, `<java>`. It has many options and is well worth studying. We used it in our introductory build file in chapter 2. In this chapter, we're going to run our diary entry point with it, an entry point that gets compiled into the JAR file created in chapter 5:

```
<target name="java-example-1" depends="sign-jar">
  <echo>running the diary program</echo>
  <java classname="dl.core.DiaryMain" />
</target>
```

The task takes the name of the entry point class via its `classname` attribute. What happens when we run this target? First Ant runs the targets that build the JAR file. Then Ant reaches the `java-example-1` target itself:

```
java-example-1:
    [echo] running the diary program
    [java] Could not find dl.core.DiaryMain.
           Make sure you have it in your classpath
```

Oops! We left out the classpath and get to see Ant's error message when this happens. Welcome to classpath-related pain. If you're new to Java, this will be a new pain, but to experienced Java developers, it should be a very familiar sensation. To run our program, we have to set up the classpath for `<java>`.

6.1.2   Setting the classpath

Why did the `<java>` task fail? Why couldn't it find our entry point? For almost any use of the `<java>` task, you'll need a custom classpath. The basic `<java>` task runs only with Ant's classpath, which is as follows:

- Ant's startup JAR file, `ant-launcher.jar`.
- Everything in the `ANT_HOME/lib` directory (or more accurately, the directory containing the version of `ant-launcher.jar` that's running).
- All JAR files in `${user.home}/.ant/lib`. On Unix, that's "`~/.ant/lib`", while on Windows it's something like "`c:\Documents and Settings\USER\.ant\lib`"; the exact location varies with the user name and locale.
- All directories or JAR files named with `-lib` options on the command line.
- Everything in the `CLASSPATH` environment variable, unless `-noclasspath` is set on the command line.
- Any libraries an IDE hosting Ant saw fit to include on the classpath.
- If Ant can find it, `JAVA_HOME/lib/tools.jar`.

Adding classpaths is easy: you just fill out the `<java>` task's `<classpath>` element, or set its `classpath` attribute to a path as a string. If you're going to use the same classpath in more than one place, declare the path and then refer to it using the `classpathref` attribute. This is simple and convenient to do.

One common practice is to extend the compile-time classpath with a second classpath that includes the newly built classes, either in archive form or as a directory tree of .class files. We do this by declaring two classpaths, one for compilation and the other for execution:

```
<path id="compile.classpath">
  <fileset dir="lib" includes="*.jar" />
</path>

<path id="run.classpath">
  <path refid="compile.classpath"/>
  <pathelement location="${target.jar}"/>
</path>
```

The compile classpath will include any libraries we depend upon to build; then the run classpath extends this with the JAR just built. This approach simplifies maintenance; any library used at compile time automatically propagates to the runtime classpath.

With the new classpath defined, we can modify the `<java>` task and run our program:

```
<target name="java-example-2" depends="sign-jar">
  <echo>running with classpath ${toString:run.classpath}</echo>
  <java classname="d1.core.DiaryMain"
```

```
        classpathref="run.classpath" />/>
    </target>
```

The successful output of this task delivers the results we want:

```
java-example-2:
    [echo] running with classpath
            /home/ant/diary/core/dist/diary-0.1alpha.jar
    [java] File :calendar.dl

BUILD SUCCESSFUL
Total time: 1 second
```

Our program worked: it listed the empty diary. We also printed out the classpath by using the `${toString:run.classpath}` operation. When Ant expands this, it resolves the reference to `run.classpath`, calls the datatype's `toString()` method, and passes on the result. For Ant paths, that value is the path in a platform-specific path form. The result is we can see what the classpath will be.

NOTE When running `<java>` with a custom classpath, nearly everything on Ant's classpath other than the `java` and `javax` packages are excluded. Compare this to `<javac>`, which includes Ant's classpath unless it's told not to with `includeAntRuntime="false"`.

Setting up the classpath and the program entry point are the two activities that must be done for every `<java>` run. To pass data to a running program, the task needs to be set up with the arguments for the `main()` method and any JVM system properties that the program needs.

6.1.3 Arguments

The argument list is the main way of passing data to a running application. You can name arguments by a single value, a line of text, a filename, or a path. These arguments are passed down in one or more `<arg>` elements, an element that supports the four attributes listed in table 6.1. Ant resolves the arguments and passes them on in the order they're declared.

Table 6.1 The attributes of the `<arg>` element of `<java>`

`<arg>` attribute	Meaning
value	String value
file	File or directory to resolve to an absolute location before invocation
path	A string containing files or directories separated by colons or semicolons
pathref	A reference to a predefined path
line	Complete line to pass to the program

Let's feed some of them to our program.

```
<java classname="d1.core.DiaryMain"
  classpathref="run.classpath" >
  <arg value="2006-07-31-08:30" />
  <arg file="." />
  <arg path="${user.home};/" />
</java>
```

This uses three of the options.

```
<arg value="2006-07-31-08:30" />
```

String arguments are the simplest. Any string can be passed to the invoked program. The only tricky spot is handling those symbols that XML does not like. Angle brackets need to be escaped, substituting < for < and > for >.

The second argument used the `file` attribute to pass down a filename—the current directory:

```
<arg file="." />
```

As with `<property location>` assignments, this attribute can take an absolute or relative path. Ant will resolve it to an absolute location before passing it to the program.

The `path` attribute passes an entire path down. It generates a single argument from the comma- or colon-separated file path elements passed in

```
<arg path="${user.home};/" />
```

As with other paths in Ant, relative locations are resolved, and both Unix or MS-DOS directory and path separators can be used. The invoked program receives a path as a single argument containing resolved filenames with the directory and path separators appropriate to the platform. If we had wanted to pass a predefined path down, we could have used the `pathref` attribute instead:

```
<arg pathref="run.classpath" />
```

Ant will retrieve the path and add it as another argument.

Returning to our Ant target, and running it on Windows, this is what we see:

```
[java] Event #3ca33f56-21a1-41f8-bf1a-7e3c2c3dc207
       - Mon Jul 31 09:30:00 BST 2006
       - C:\app2\diary\core
       - C:\Documents and Settings\ant;C:\
```

What do we see on a Unix box?

```
[java] Event #0d1aec19-0c51-46b4-a3d3-c48e49a2319f
       - Mon Jul 31 09:30:00 BST 2006
       - /home/ant/diary/core
       - /home/ant/:/
```

All the files and paths are resolved relative to the project directory and converted to the platform-specific representation before any invoked program sees them. We also have encountered one little quirk of Ant path mapping: what does "/" resolve to? In

Unix, this is the root directory; every file in a mounted drive is underneath this directory. But in Windows, it resolves to the root directory of the current disk. There's no single root directory for Windows systems. This can cause a problem if you want to create a single fileset spanning content in two Windows disks, such as C: and D: because it cannot be done.

There is one other way to pass arguments down, using the `line` attribute. This takes a single line, which is split into separate arguments wherever there's a space between values:

```
<java classname="${main}" classpathref="run.classpath" >
  <arg line ="2006-07-31-08:30 . ${user.home};/" />
</java>
```

Is this equivalent? Not where the home directory has a space in it:

```
[java] Event #2c557ace-8aa1-4501-a99c-2e7449761442
       - Mon Jul 31 09:30:00 BST 2006
       - .
       - C:\Documents
```

The line was split by spaces *after* property expansion and the trailing `"and Settings\ant"` portion of the path was turned into argument number four on the command line, where it got lost. What's insidious here is that the target worked properly on Unix; we've written a brittle build file, which works only on systems where the current directory and `user.home` directory are without spaces. Note also that our local directory has not been expanded, and if we had escaped that last argument with single quotes (`"2006-07-31-08:30 . '${user.home};/'"`), the result would still not be a valid path for the local platform.

> **ISSUE** `<arg value>` *is not* `<arg line>`—People are often disappointed that `<java>` or `<exec>` doesn't correctly pass the contents of an argument like `<arg value="some commands here">` down to the program. They were expecting Ant to pass a series of all arguments down to the program, but Ant passed them down as a single argument. Learn the differences between the different argument options, and use the right one for each problem.

Avoid using the `<arg line="">` option. The only reason for using it is to support an unlimited number of arguments—perhaps from a property file or prompted input. Anyone who does this had better hope that spaces aren't expected in individual arguments.

The other way to pass data down is through JVM system properties.

6.1.4 Defining system properties

Java system properties are set on the Java command line as `-Dproperty=value` arguments. The `<java>` task lets you use these properties via the `<sysproperty>`

element. This is useful in configuring the JVM itself, such as controlling how long network addresses are cached:

```
<sysproperty key="networkaddress.cache.ttl" value="300"/>
```

There are two alternate options instead of the `value` parameter: `file` and `path`. Just as with `<arg>` elements, the `file` attribute lets you name a file. Ant will pass down an absolute filename in the platform-specific format. The `path` attribute is similar, except that you can list multiple files, and it will convert the path separator to whatever is appropriate for the operating system:

```
<sysproperty key="configuration.file" file="./config.properties"/>
<sysproperty key="searchpath"
    path="build/classes:lib/javaee.jar" />
```

We used these elements in chapter 4, passing information down to test cases running under `<junit>`. It shouldn't be a surprise to readers to discover that `<junit>` makes use of the `<java>` task internally.

We can also pass Ant properties down in bulk.

Propertysets

A *propertyset* is an Ant datatype that represents a set of properties. You can use it inside the `<java>` task to pass down a set of Ant properties

```
<syspropertyset >
  <propertyref builtin="commandline" />
  <propertyref prefix="proxy.*" />
</syspropertyset>
```

This declaration passes down to the program all Ant properties beginning with `"proxy"` and all properties on Ant's own command line. The `<propertyset>` datatype has a few more features that make it useful. Being a datatype, you can declare it in one location with an `id` attribute and reuse it via `idref` attributes. You can also use a mapper to rename the properties in the set.

Some Java properties, such as `java.endorsed.dirs`, are interpreted by the JVM itself, not the application. For these to be picked up reliably, we need to run our code in a new Java process, a new JVM instance. In Ant, this is called a *forked* JVM.

6.1.5 Running the program in a new JVM

The `<java>` task runs inside Ant's JVM unless the `fork` attribute is set to true. Non-forked code can be faster and shares more of the JVM's state. Forking offers the following advantages:

- You get perfect isolation from Ant's own classloader and code.
- Forked Java programs can run in a new working directory, with different JVM options and environment.
- Forked Java programs can run in a different version of Java than Ant itself.

- You cannot run a JAR ("-jar something.jar") in the Ant's JVM.
- Memory-hungry programs can run in their own JVM and not use Ant's memory.
- Forked programs can be killed if they don't finish in a specified time period.

Let's run the diary in a new JVM:

```
<target name="java-example-fork" depends="build">
  <property name="classpath-as-property" refid="run.classpath" />
  <java classname="d1.core.DiaryMain"
    classpathref="run.classpath"
    fork="true">
    <arg value="2005-06-31-08:30" />
    <arg file="." />
    <arg path="${user.home};/" />
  </java>
</target>
```

In informal experiments on a single machine, the time to build and run the program usually appears to be two seconds, rather than the one second that the original version took. That could be a doubling of execution time, but it's only an extra second, as measured with Ant's single-second clock. Does a second or so of delay matter that much?

We prefer to always fork our Java programs, preferring isolation over possible performance gains. This reduces the time spent debugging obscure problems related to classloaders and JVM isolation. It also lets us tune JVM options.

6.1.6 JVM tuning

Once we fork <java>, we can change the JVM under which it runs and the options in the JVM. This gives us absolute control over what's going on.

You can actually choose a Java runtime that's different from the one hosting Ant by setting the jvm attribute to the command that starts the JVM. This lets you run a program under a different JVM.

In addition to choosing the JVM, you can configure it. The most commonly used option is the amount of memory to use, which is so common that it has its own attribute, the maxmemory attribute. The memory option, as per the java command, takes a string that lists the number of bytes, kilobytes (k), or megabytes (m) to use. Usually, the megabyte option is the one to supply, with maxmemory="64m" setting a limit of 64MB on the process.

Other JVM options are specific to individual JVM implementations. A call to java -X will list the ones on your local machine. Because these options can vary from system to system, they should be set via properties so that different developers can override them as needed. Here, for example, we set the default arguments for memory and the server JVM with incremental garbage collection, using properties to provide an override point for different users:

```
<target name="java-example-jvmargs" depends="build">
  <property name="jvm" value="java" />
  <property name="jvm.gc.args" value="-Xincgc"/>
```

```
<property name="jvm.memory" value="64m"/>
<property name="jvm.type" value="-server"/>
<java
  classname="d1.core.DiaryMain"
  classpathref="run.classpath"
  fork="true"
  jvm="${jvm}"
  dir="${build.dir}"
  maxmemory="${jvm.memory}">
  <jvmarg value="${jvm.type}" />
  <jvmarg line="${jvm.gc.args}"/>
  <arg value="2005-06-31-08:30" />
  <arg file="."/>
</java>
</target>
```

You supply generic JVM arguments using `<jvmarg>` elements nested inside the `<java>` task. The exact syntax of these arguments is the same as for the `<arg>` elements. We use the `line` attribute, despite the negative things we said about it earlier, as it permits a single property to contain a list of arguments. Developers can override the `jvm.gc.args` property in their `build.properties` file to something like

```
-XX:+UseConcMarkSweepGC -XX:NewSize=48m -XX:SurvivorRatio=16
```

This would transform their garbage collection policy, without affecting anyone else.

We've also changed the starting directory of the program with the `dir` attribute. This lets you use relative file references in your code and have them resolved correctly when running. If you run this example, you may be surprised to see from the output that the file argument `<arg file="."/>` still resolves to the directory `diary/core`, not the build directory in which the JVM is running. Only the new JVM picks up the directory change, not Ant itself.

None of these JVM options have any effect when `fork="false"`; only a warning message is printed. If they don't seem to work, look closely at the task declaration and see if forking needs to be turned on. Ant's `-verbose` flag will provide even more details.

Regardless of whether the program runs in Ant's own JVM or a new process, we can still capture the return code of the program, which can be used to pass information back to the caller or signal an error.

6.1.7   Handling errors

What's going to happen if we pass a bad parameter to our program? Will the build break? First, we try to create an event on a day that doesn't exist:

```
<java classname="d1.core.DiaryMain"
  classpathref="run.classpath" >
  <arg value="2007-02-31-08:30" />
  <arg file="Event on February 31" />
</java>
```

Running this, we get a stack trace, but the build still thinks it succeeded.

```
[java] Exception in thread "main"
       java.lang.IllegalArgumentException:
       "2007-02-31-08:30" is not a valid representation of
       an XML Gregorian Calendar value.
[java]   at com.sun.org.apache.xerces.internal.jaxp.datatype.
         XMLGregorianCalendarImpl.<init>
[java]   at com.sun.org.apache.xerces.internal.jaxp.datatype.
         DatatypeFactoryImpl.newXMLGregorianCalendar
[java]   at d1.core.Event.parseIsoDate(Event.java:187)
[java]   at d1.core.Event.setDate(Event.java:175)
[java]   at d1.core.DiaryMain.add(DiaryMain.java:61)
[java]   at d1.core.DiaryMain.main(DiaryMain.java:97)
[java] Java Result: 1

BUILD SUCCESSFUL
```

The program failed, but Ant was successful. What happened?

Many Ant tasks have an attribute, `failonerror`, which controls whether the failure of the task breaks the build. Most such tasks have a default of `failonerror="true"`, meaning any failure of the task breaks the build, resulting in the familiar BUILD FAILED message.

The `<java>` task is one such task, halting the build if `failonerror="true"` and the return value of the Java program is non-zero. That happens if `System.exit()` is called with a non-zero argument or if the JVM failed, as it does when the entry point throws an exception, or if the command line arguments to the JVM are invalid. To get this behavior, developers must explicitly set the attribute, as shown here:

```
<target name="java-example-failonerror" depends="build">
  <java classname="d1.core.DiaryMain"
    classpathref="run.classpath"
    fork="true"
    failonerror="true">
    <arg value="2007-02-31-08:30" />
    <arg file="Event on February 31" />
  </java>
</target>
```

Calling this target, we get an error message and a halted build:

```
[java] Exception in thread "main"
       java.lang.IllegalArgumentException:
       "2007-02-31-08:30" is not a valid representation of
       an XML Gregorian Calendar value.
[java]   at com.sun.org.apache.xerces.internal.jaxp.datatype.
         XMLGregorianCalendarImpl.<init>
[java]   at com.sun.org.apache.xerces.internal.jaxp.datatype.
         DatatypeFactoryImpl.newXMLGregorianCalendar
[java]   at d1.core.Event.parseIsoDate(Event.java:187)
```

```
[java]    at d1.core.Event.setDate(Event.java:175)
[java]    at d1.core.DiaryMain.add(DiaryMain.java:61)
[java]    at d1.core.DiaryMain.main(DiaryMain.java:97)
[java] Java Result: 1
```

BUILD FAILED
/home/ant/diary/core/core-chapter6.xml:128: Java returned: 1

This is normally what you want, so set `failonerror="true"` on all uses of `<java>`. Alternatively, we could capture the return value and act on it in follow-up tasks.

Capturing the return code

Sometimes, you want to know if the program returned a status code or what the value was without halting the build. Knowing this lets you do conditional actions on the return code or run programs that pass information back to Ant. To get the return code, set the `resultproperty` attribute to the name of a property and leave `failonerror="false"`:

```
<target name="java-resultproperty" depends="build">
  <java classname="d1.core.DiaryMain"
    classpathref="run.classpath"
    fork="true"
    resultproperty="result" >
    <arg value="2007-02-31-08:30" />
    <arg file="Event on February 31" />
  </java>
  <echo>result=${result}</echo>
</target>
```

This will print out the result. We could use a `<condition>` to test the return value and act on it, or pass the property to another task.

6.1.8   Executing JAR files

So far, we've been executing Java programs by declaring the entry point in the `classname` attribute of the `<java>` task. There's another way: running a JAR file with an entry point declared in its manifest. This is equivalent to running `java -jar` on the command line. Ant can run JAR files similarly, but only in a forked JVM. To tell it to run a JAR file, set the `jar` attribute to the location of the file:

```
<target name="java-jar" depends="build">
  <java
    jar="${target.jar}"
    fork="true"
    failonerror="true">
    <arg value="2007-06-21-05:00" />
    <arg file="Summer Solstice" />
  </java>
</target>
```

For this to work, the manifest must be set up correctly. We declared a `Main` class when we created our JAR files in section 5.5, but now we've changed the manifest to point to `dl.core.DiaryMain`. When we run this new target, we get the same output as before.

If our JAR file depended upon other libraries, we must declare these dependencies in the manifest by providing a list of relative URLs in the `Class-Path` attribute of the `Main` section in the JAR manifest. There's no other way to set the classpath for JAR files, as `java` itself ignores any command-line classpath when running JAR files via `-jar`. Running Java programs this way is simple but inflexible. We normally use the `classname` attribute and set up the classpath in Ant.

That's the core of `<java>` execution covered. Now it's time to introduce `<exec>`, which can run native executables. Both tasks have a lot in common, so many of the concepts will be familiar. We'll return to `<java>` when we look at features common to both tasks.

6.2 RUNNING NATIVE PROGRAMS

A *native program* is any program compiled for the local system, or, in Unix, any shell script marked as executable. Many Ant tasks call them behind the scenes, including `<java>` itself when it starts a new JVM for a forked `<java>` call. There are many other programs that can be useful, from a command to mount a shared drive, to a native installer program. Ant can call these programs with the parameters you desire.

To run an external program in Ant, use the `<exec>` task. It lets you declare the following options:

- The name of the program and arguments to pass in
- The directory in which it runs
- Whether the application failure halts the build
- The maximum duration of a program
- A file or a property to store the output
- Other Ant components to act as input sources or destinations
- Environment variables
- A string that should be in the name of the OS

The syntax of `<exec>` is similar to `<java>`, except that you name an executable rather than a Java class or JAR. One use of the task is to create a symbolic link to a file for which there is no intrinsic Java command:

```
<exec executable="ln">
  <arg value="-s"/>
  <arg location="execution.xml"/>
  <arg location="symlink.xml"/>
</exec>
```

You don't need to supply the full path to the executable if it's on the current path. You can use all the options for the `<arg>` nested element as with the `<java>` task, as covered in section 6.1.3.

We can even use the task to start Java programs.

6.2.1 Running our diary as a native program

If a Java program has a shell script to launch the program, `<exec>` can start it. We can use it to start our diary application via a Python script. This script will launch the diary JAR via a `java -jar` command, passing down all arguments.

To run this script from Ant (Unix only), we invoke it after it's been prepared by the `"scripts"` target, which uses `<chmod>` to make the file executable:

```
<target name="exec-python" depends="scripts,sign-jar">
  <exec executable="${dist.dir}/diary.py"
    dir="${build.dir}"
    failonerror="true">
    <arg value="2007-12-21-12:00" />
    <arg value="Midwinter" />
  </exec>
</target>
```

We need to give the full path to the script or program to run. If we didn't, `<exec>` would fail with some OS-specific error code if the executable couldn't be found. The `executable` attribute doesn't convert its value to a file or location but executes it as is. This is inconvenient at times, but it does let us run anything on the path.

As with `<java>`, the `<exec>` task has `failonerror="false"` by default. Again, we normally set `failonerror="true"`.

There's a second problem with execution. What happens if a program cannot be run, because it's not there? This is a separate failure mode from the return code of a program that actually starts, which is what `failonerror` cares about. There's a different attribute, `failIfExecuteFails`, which controls whether the actual execution failures are ignored. It's true by default, which is where most people should leave it.

One common use of `<exec>` is issuing shell commands, which is unexpectedly tricky.

6.2.2 Executing shell commands

We've reached the point where we can use `<exec>` to start a program. Can we also use it to run shell commands? Yes, with caveats. Many shell commands aren't native programs; rather, they're instructions to the shell itself. They can contain shell-specific wildcards or a sequence of one or more shell or native commands glued together using shell parameters, such as the pipe (|), the angle bracket (>), double angle brackets (>>), and the ampersand (&).

For example, one might naively try to list the running Java processes and save them to a file by building a shell command, and use this shell command in `<exec>` as a single command, via the (deprecated) `command` attribute:

```
<exec command="jps &gt; processes.txt"
  failonerror="false"/>
```

This won't work. In addition to getting a warning for using the `command` attribute, the whole line needs to be interpreted by a shell. You'll probably see a usage error from the first program on the line—in this case the `jps` command:

```
exec-ps:
    [exec] The command attribute is deprecated.
    [exec] Please use the executable attribute and nested arg
           elements.
    [exec] Malformed Host Identifier: >processes.txt
    [exec] usage: jps [-help]
    [exec]         jps [-q] [-mlvV] [<hostid>]
    [exec] Definitions:
    [exec]      <hostid>:        <hostname>[:<port>]
```

The trick is to make the shell the command and to pass in a string containing the command you want the shell to execute. The Unix `sh` program lets you do this with its `-c` command, but it wants the commands to follow in a quoted string. XML doesn't permit double quotes inside a double quote–delimited literal, so you must use single quotes, or delimit the whole string in the XML file with single quotes:

```
<exec executable="sh"
  failonerror="true"/>
  <arg line="-c 'jps &gt; processes.txt'" />
</exec>
```

A command that uses both single and double quotes needs to use the `&quot;` notation instead of the double quote. Our simple example doesn't have this problem.

The Windows NT command shell CMD is similar to the Unix one:

```
<exec executable="cmd"
  failonerror="true"/>
  <arg line="/c jps &gt; processes.txt" />
</exec>
```

A lot of people encounter problems trying to run shell commands on Ant; it keeps the user mailing list busy on a regular basis. All you have to do is remember that shell commands aren't native programs. It's the shell itself that Ant must start with the `<exec>` task.

Running shell scripts shows another problem: the program we want to run varies with the underlying platform. Can you run such programs and keep your build file portable? The answer is "Maybe, if you try hard enough."

6.2.3 Running under different Operating Systems

The `<exec>` task can keep build files portable by letting you list which operating systems a program runs on. If Ant isn't running on a supported OS, the program isn't started. There are two attributes for this situation. The first attribute, `os`, takes a list of operating systems. Before the task is executed, Ant examines the value of the os.name system property and executes the program only if that property is found in the os string. A valid os attribute would have to be something such as "Linux AIX Unix", based on your expectations of which OS versions would be used. This method is very brittle and usually breaks when a new OS ships.

The newer osfamily attribute lets you declare which particular family of operating systems to use, according to the families listed in table 6.2. This method is much more robust, as an osfamily="winnt" test will work for all current and future NT-based Windows operating systems.

Table 6.2 Operating system families recognized by Ant. The <os> condition accepts these in its family attribute, as does the osfamily attribute of <exec> and its descendants.

Attribute value	Platform
windows	Windows 9x or NT-based systems
win9x	Windows 95-98, Windows ME, and WinCE
winnt	Windows NT-based systems (Including Win2K, XP, Vista, and successors)
mac	Apple Macintosh (all versions)
unix	All Unix systems, including Linux and Macintosh
os/2	OS/2
netware	Novell Netware
openvms	HP (originally DEC) OpenVMS
os/400	IBM OS/400 minicomputer OS
z/os	IBM z/OS and OS/390
tandem	HP (formerly Tandem) nonstop OS

We can use this attribute to restrict a program to a specific OS family. Doing so allows us to have different versions for different platforms side by side. Here, for example, is a target that runs the Windows or Unix time commands:

```
<target name="time">
  <exec executable="cmd"
    failonerror="true"
    osfamily="winnt">
    <arg value="/c"/>
    <arg value="time"/>
    <arg value="/t" />
  </exec>
  <exec executable="date"
    failonerror="true"
    osfamily="unix">
    <arg value="+%H:%M" />
  </exec>
</target>
```

CHAPTER 6 EXECUTING PROGRAMS

The Windows command is actually implemented by the shell, so we have to execute the `cmd` program with the appropriate arguments. The Unix program is a self-contained executable. By having the two tasks in the same target, each guarded by its own `osfamily` attribute, the relevant target will be run. The result will be the time according to the OS, something like

```
date:
    [exec] 15:27
```

If you have a lot of `<exec>` code in your build and you want to make it multiplatform, use this `osfamily` attribute to make it somewhat portable. Ant tasks such as `<chmod>` use it internally to avoid breaking under Windows.

Incidentally, the same operation system test can be used in an Ant condition.

The `<os>` condition

The Ant condition `<os>` can examine the operating system. This can be used to skip targets, depending on the underlying operating system. Here's a simple target that you can use to see what Ant thinks a system is:

```
<target name="os" >
  <condition property="is.unix">
    <os family="unix" />
  </condition>
  <condition property="is.nt">
    <os family="winnt" />
  </condition>
  <condition property="is.mac">
    <os family="mac" />
  </condition>
  <echo>
os.name=${os.name}
os.arch=${os.arch}
os.version=${os.version}

is.unix=${is.unix}
is.winnt=${is.winnt}
is.mac=${is.mac}
  </echo>
</target>
```

This target will produce different output on the various platforms, such as here, the Mac OS/X listing:

```
    [echo]
    [echo]    os.name=Mac OS X
    [echo]    os.arch=ppc
    [echo]    os.version=10.3.8
    [echo]
    [echo]    is.unix=true
    [echo]    is.winnt=${is.winnt}
    [echo]    is.mac=true
    [echo]
```

The combination of a new Java version and a new OS can sometimes break all this logic. There's no specific test for a platform being Windows- or Unix-based in Java, so Ant makes guesses based on OS names and path and directory separators. When a new version of Java gives an OS a new name, Ant can guess wrong. That's always a good time to upgrade Ant.

We can also use conditions to set up `<exec>` itself, either by checking for the OS or by looking for the program.

6.2.4   Probing for a program

Sometimes, you want to run a program, but you are prepared to continue the build if it isn't there. If you know where the program must be, then an `<available>` test can look for it. But what if the only requirement is that it must be on the path? The `<available>` task or condition can search a whole file path for a named file, so probing for a program's existence is a simple matter of searching for its name in the environment variable PATH. Of course, in a cross-platform manner, nothing is ever simple; Windows and Unix name executables and even the PATH variable differently. Taking this into account, looking for a program becomes a multiple-condition test. The test needs to look for the executable with and without the `.exe` extension, across two different environment variables converted to Ant properties:

```
<target name="probe_for_python" >
  <property environment="env" />
  <condition property="python.found" >
    <or>
      <available file="python"     filepath="${env.PATH}" />
      <available file="python.exe" filepath="${env.Path}" />
    </or>
  </condition>
  <echo>python.found = ${python.found}</echo>
</target>
```

If we run this, it tells us if the `python` program is ready to run:

```
probe_for_python:
    [echo] python.found = true
```

You can then write dependent targets that skip some work if the program is absent:

```
<target name="python" depends="probe_for_python" if="python.found">
  <exec executable="python" ... />
</target>
```

We do this in our build files to probe for programs, if they really are optional. If we have to have them present, we just let `<exec>` fail with an error message, as it saves work.

We've covered the basics of `<exec>`. We've also looked at how to use `<exec>` to run a program, to run a shell script, and to skip the execution if the operating system is unsupported or the program is missing. Along with the `<java>` task, readers now have enough information to use the tasks to run their own and other people's programs, both Java and native.

The tasks can do a lot more, though. You can tell Ant to kill the programs if they take too long, change the environment in which they execute, or pipe data between the program and Ant. These are advanced features offered by both tasks.

6.3 ADVANCED <JAVA> AND <EXEC>

Running programs is one of the most complex things that Ant can do. Programs don't run in isolation: they operate in an environment that can change their behavior. They have a stream giving them text, and two output streams—one for normal text, one for errors. Developers may need to link those inputs and outputs to files or other things that can produce or consume the data. Sometimes, programs hang, so the build needs to kill the programs if they take too long. Sometimes, the program may be expected to outlast the build itself. These are needs developers have, so they are problems that Ant has to address.

The <java> and <exec> tasks round off their ability to run programs with the attributes and elements needed for total control of how they run programs. Let's run through them, starting with environment variables.

6.3.1 Setting environment variables

All programs run in an environment, one in which the PATH variable controls the search path for executables, and JAVA_HOME defines the location of the JDK. Ant normally passes its own environment down to new processes that it starts. We can change that, passing a new environment down to child processes, which is useful when running some programs. What we cannot do is change Ant's own environment—this is fixed when Ant is run.

You can set environment variables inside <java>, <junit> and <exec> by using the element <env>. The syntax of this element is identical to that of the <sysproperty> element:

```
<java classname="d1.core.DiaryMain"
  classpathref="run.classpath"
  fork="true">
  <env key="JAVA_HOME" value="${user.home}/JDK" />
  <env key="PATH" path="${dist.dir};${env.PATH}"/>
  <env key="Path" path="${dist.dir};${env.Path}"/>
  <arg value="2006-06-31-08:30" />
  <arg file="." />
  <arg path="${user.home};/" />
</java>
```

In <java> and <junit>, the PATH environment variable controls where native libraries are loaded by the JNI facility. Setting the path on a forked program—and it must be forked—lets us load new JNI libraries in the program that's run by <java>.

The feature is invaluable in <exec>, as many native programs read the environment variables. You also can choose whether the program inherits Ant's current environment through the newenvironment attribute. Usually, you pass down all current environment settings, such as PATH and TEMP, but sometimes you may want absolute control over the parameters:

```
<exec executable="preprocess"
  newenvironment="true" >
  <env key="PATH" path="${dist.dir};${env.PATH}"/>
  <env key="Path" path="${dist.dir};${env.Path}"/>
  <env key="USER" value="self"/>
</exec>
```

Setting environment variables lets us control how some programs run. We also like to control how programs stop, killing them if they take too long.

6.3.2   Handling timeouts

How do you deal with programs that hang? You can stop a running build by hand, but unattended builds need to take care of themselves. To address this issue, the <exec> and <java> tasks support timeout attributes, which accept a number in milliseconds. The <java> task also needs fork="true" for timeout protection; <exec> always forks, so this is a non-issue.

When a program is executed with the timeout attribute set, Ant starts a watchdog thread that sleeps for the duration of the timeout. When it wakes up, this thread will kill the program if it has not yet finished. When this happens, the return code of the <exec> or <java> call is set to the value "1". If failonerror is set to true, this will break the build. Here's a somewhat contrived example, using the Unix sleep command to sleep for fifteen seconds, with a timeout of two seconds[1]:

```
<target name="sleep-fifteen-seconds" >
  <echo message="sleeping for 15 seconds" />
  <exec executable="sleep"
    failonerror="true"
    timeout="2000">
    <arg value="15" />
  </exec>
</target>
```

Running this target produces an error when the timeout engages:

```
sleep-fifteen-seconds:
    [echo] sleeping for 15 seconds

BUILD FAILED
core-chapter6.xml:195: Timeout: killed the sub-process
```

---

[1] If you really need to insert a pause into a build, the <sleep> task works across all platforms.

```
Total time: 3 seconds
Process ant exited with code 1
```

It's useful to have timeouts for all programs that run in automated builds, especially those programs you write yourself—since they may be less stable. We often do timeouts for `<junit>` runs too, for a similar reason. Nobody likes to find the background build has hung for the entire weekend because a test went into an infinite loop.

Long-lived programs don't have to block Ant if we run them in the background.

6.3.3 Running a program in the background

During testing or if you want to use Ant as a launcher of Java programs, you may want Ant to run the program in the background, perhaps even for it to outlive the Ant run itself. In Ant terminology, this is called *spawning*. Spawning can be accomplished by setting the spawn attribute to true. After starting the program, Ant detaches the program from its own process completely so that when Ant exits, the spawned program will keep going.

Spawning has a price, which is complete isolation from all further interaction between Ant and the spawned program. Here are the consequences:

- There's no way to kill a spawned process from Ant.
- There's no notification when the process terminates.
- Result codes aren't accessible.
- You cannot capture any output from the program.
- You cannot set the timeout attribute.

Both `<exec>` and `<java>` support the spawn attribute, though with `<java>` you must also set `fork="true"`:

```
<java
  jar="${target.jar}"
  fork="true"
  spawn="true">
  <arg value="2038-01-19-03:14" />
  <arg value="32-bit signed time_t wraps around" />
</java>
```

Here we're lucky: our program terminates of its own accord. If it did not, we would have to find the process using the appropriate OS tools and kill it. GUI applications are much easier to deal with, as you can just close their windows. As an example, the jconsole program that comes with Java is something that developers may want to run against the JVM of a process under development:

```
<target name="jconsole" >
  <exec executable="jconsole"
    spawn="true" />
</target>
```

The way that Ant completely forgets about the program is a bit brutal, as it's hard to stop the program afterwards. We do sometimes use spawned programs in functional testing. You start the program/application server, then run the unit tests, then run a special program to shut down the application. If you're not careful, your builds can leak spawned applications, so use the spawn option with care.

The other advanced features of the tasks are all related to integrating the program with Ant. Ant can pass data to the program and capture the results, letting us pull those results into files and Ant properties.

6.3.4 Input and output

Running <java> and <exec> programs can interact with the user, getting input from the console and feeding their output through Ant's logging system. What if we want Ant itself to capture the output, perhaps to feed it into another task? That and generating input for the program are both possible under Ant. You can feed the program input data from a file or property, and then save the output to different files or properties. The attributes to configure all this are listed in table 6.3.

Table 6.3 Attributes of <java> and <exec> for sharing data with Ant

input	A file to use as a source of input
inputstring	A string to use as a source of input
output	File to save the output
outputproperty	Name of a property in which to store output
error	File to save error (stderr/System.err) output
errorproperty	Name of a property in which to store error output
append	Set to true, will append the output to the files, rather than overwrite existing files
logerror	Force error output to the log while capturing output

To provide input to a program, we can identify a file with the input attribute, or a string with inputstring. Setting inputstring="" is a way to tell Ant not to pass any data down.

The core attributes for capturing output are output and outputProperty. If they alone are set, then all output from an application, both the "normal" and "error" streams (System.out and System.err), are redirected. If you still want to see error output on the log, set the logerror attribute to true and Ant will still log it.

We can also remove the error log from the normal output by setting either the error filename attribute or the errorproperty property name. The named destination will get the error stream, and the output destination will get the System.out messages.

Let's add some of these attributes to the <exec> of the Python script that runs our diary program:

```
<exec executable="${dist.dir}/diary.py"
  dir="${build.dir}"
  inputstring=""
  outputproperty="output"
  logerror="true"
  failonerror="false"
  resultproperty="result">
  <arg value="2007-12-21-12:00" />
  <arg value="Midwinter" />
</exec>
<echo>
output=${output}
result=${result}
</echo>
```

This target provides the empty string as input, and then logs output to a property that's echoed afterwards. Setting `logerror="true"` ensures that any error text still goes to Ant's output stream. We've set `failonerror="false"` and declared a property for the result with `resultproperty`. This property will pick up the exit value of the application, which we could feed into another task.

These properties are fairly simple to learn and use. If you want to chain programs and tasks together, save the output to a file or property then pass it into another. Normally, the files and properties are sufficient for managing program I/O. Sometimes, they're not. In those situations, reach for an I/O Redirector.

6.3.5   Piped I/O with an I/O redirector

The I/O Redirector is the power tool of I/O for those special emergencies. We're not going to cover it in detail; instead we'll refer the reader to Ant's own documentation.

An I/O redirector is a `<redirector>` element that can be nested inside the `<java>` and `<exec>` tasks to set up their entire I/O system. It supports all the I/O-related attributes of the tasks listed in table 6.3 and adds an extra input-related attribute, `loginputstring`, which stops the input string from being logged by Ant on its way to the program, for extra security. There are also three extra attributes, `inputencoding`, `outputencoding` and `errorencoding` which manage the encoding of the source and destination files.

The real power of the task comes in its nested mapper and filter elements. The `<inputmapper>`, `<outputmapper>` and `<errormapper>` elements let you control the names of the source and destination files. Alongside these are three optional *FilterChain* elements, elements that let you attach Ant filters to the input and output streams.

This is effectively the same as Unix pipe operations; anyone who is used to typing in commands like "`tail -500 log | less`" will know the power of piping. Ant's FilterChain mechanism has the same underlying ability; yet, as a relatively recent addition, it isn't broadly used. Accordingly, it doesn't have a broad set of filters to apply. This isn't too problematic, as one of the filters executes scripts. This lets us post-process the output from a program.

Here, for example, we can use JavaScript to convert the program's output to uppercase:

```
<java
    jar="${target.jar}"
    fork="true"
    failonerror="true">
    <arg value="2006-06-21-05:00" />
    <arg value="Summer Solstice" />
    <redirector>
      <outputfilterchain>
        <tokenfilter>
          <scriptfilter language="javascript">
              self.setToken(self.getToken().toUpperCase());
          </scriptfilter>
        </tokenfilter>
      </outputfilterchain>
    </redirector>
</java>
```

The result is returned in uppercase:

```
[java] FILE :CALENDAR.D1
[java] EVENT #E18CA8B7-A68C-45A6-889B-3A881F9EF38F
       - WED JUN 21 06:00:00 BST 2006 - SUMMER SOLSTICE -
```

This is very powerful. Run Ant with any needed script libraries, and suddenly you can add inline pre- or post-processing to Java or native code. Developers could have some fun there.

You don't need to write JavaScript to post-process the output if Ant has built-in support for the transformation. There are nearly twenty operations that you can use in a FilterChain—that is, twenty FilterReaders—that can take the output of a program and transform it. These operations can be used for changing the output of an execution or the contents of a file into the form that a follow-on task can use.

6.3.6   FilterChains and FilterReaders

Many common operations perform against files, such as stripping out all comments, searching for lines with a specific value, or expanding Ant properties. These are operations that Ant can perform against files while they're being moved or loaded, and against the input and output streams of the executed program. We used one in the previous section to run some JavaScript code against the output of our application, but there are other actions that are available in a FilterChain.

A FilterChain is an Ant datatype that contains a list of *FilterReaders*. Each Filter-Reader is something that can add, remove, or modify text as it's fed through the chain. The result is that the chain can transform all text that's passed through it.

Table 6.4 shows the built-in FilterReaders. They can be used in any task that takes nested FilterChain elements, currently `<concat>`, `<copy>`, `<move>`, `<loadfile>`, `<loadproperties>`, `<exec>`, and `<java>`.

Table 6.4   Ant's built-in FilterReaders

FilterReader	Description
`<classconstants>`	Generates `"name=value"` lines for basic and String datatype constants found in a class file.
`<concatfilter>`	Saves a stream to the beginning or end of a named file.
`<deletecharacters>`	Deletes named characters from the stream.
`<escapeunicode>`	Converts non-ASCII character to a \u1234-style declaration.
`<expandproperties>`	Replaces Ant property values.
`<filterreader>`	Provides a custom FilterReader by declaring its classname.
`<fixcrlf>`	Converts the carriage return, line feed and tab content of the data, just as the `<fixcrlf>` task can do for individual files.
`<headfilter>`	Extracts the first specified number of lines.
`<linecontains>`	Passes through only those lines containing the specified string.
`<linecontainsregexp>`	Passes through only those lines matching specified regular expression(s).
`<prefixlines>`	Prepends a prefix to all lines.
`<replacetokens>`	Replaces tokens on the stream.
`<scriptfilter>`	Passes the text though inline script in a supported language.
`<stripjavacomments>`	Removes Java-style comments.
`<striplinebreaks>`	Removes line breaks, that is \r and \n, but different characters can be stripped if desired.
`<striplinecomments>`	Removes lines beginning with a specified set of characters.
`<tabstospaces>`	Replaces tabs with a specified number of spaces.
`<tailfilter>`	Extracts the last specified number of lines.
`<tokenfilter>`	Splits the input stream into tokens (by default, separate lines), and passes the tokens to nested string filters.

One use is stripping all comments from Java source files, which can be done by using the `<stripjavacomments>` FilterReader within a `<copy>`:

```
<copy dir="src" todir="build/src" includes="**/*.java" >
  <filterchain>
    <stripjavacomments />
  </filterchain>
</copy>
```

After this operation, the copied Java source files will not contain any comments.

The `<redirector>` element of `<java>` and `<exec>` supports three FilterChains:

- `<inputfilterchain>` A FilterChain to create data for input to the program
- `<outputfilterchain>` A FilterChain to handle the standard output stream
- `<errorfilterchain>` A FilterChain to handle the error output stream

These FilterChains can be used to set up data for a program or to clean up the output. Compared to Unix pipes, Ant's filtering is limited. In particular, there's currently no way to directly link two or more `<exec>` or `<java>` processes.

That's the end of our coverage of the `<java>` and `<exec>` tasks. We've looked at running them, passing arguments, handling failure, and now handling I/O. There's one more execution task of interest, and that's `<apply>`, which is a version of `<exec>` that operates on many files at once.

6.4 BULK OPERATIONS WITH `<APPLY>`

What do we do if we want to execute the same program against a number of files in a bulk operation? In a command shell, we'd use a wildcard, such as *.xml. In Ant, we'd want to use its built-in methods to represent groups of files or other resources, such as filesets and other resource collections.

For this special problem of passing a list of files to an external executable, there's an extension of `<exec>` called `<apply>`. This task takes a resource collection and either invokes the application once for every entry in the collection, or passes the entire collection to the application as its arguments.

All the attributes of `<exec>` can be used with `<apply>`, with the additional feature of bulk execution. We could use this task to create a .tar file by using the Unix tar program instead of the `<tar>` task, and so—on Unix only—pick up file permissions from the file system:

```
<target name="native-tar" depends="build" >
  <property name="native.tar" location="${dist.dir}/native.tar"/>
  <apply executable="tar"
    relative="true"
    parallel="true"
    dir="${build.classes.dir}"
     >
    <arg value="-cf" />
    <arg value="${native.tar}"/>
    <srcfile/>
    <fileset dir="${build.classes.dir}"
      includes="**/*.class"/>
  </apply>
</target>
```

This `<apply>` task looks almost like a normal `<exec>` operation. Apart from the nested fileset listing the parameters, there's a `<srcfile/>` element in the argument list to show the task where to put the expanded files in the list of arguments. The `parallel` attribute declares that we want all files supplied at once, instead of executing the tar program once for every file. Similarly, we set the directory of the task as the base directory of the source code and then the relative attribute to true so that only the relative path to the files is passed down, not the absolute path. This would package up the files with the wrong paths. How did we know which attributes to apply? Trial and error, in this case.

To see the task at work, we run Ant with the -verbose option:

```
native-tar:
    [apply] Current OS is Linux
    [apply] Executing 'tar' with arguments:
    [apply] '-cf'
    [apply] '/tmp/diary/core/dist/native.tar'
    [apply] 'd1/core/DateOrder.class'
    [apply] 'd1/core/Diagnostics.class'
    [apply] 'd1/core/DiaryMain.class'
    [apply] 'd1/core/Event.class'
    [apply] 'd1/core/Event2.class'
    [apply] 'd1/core/EventList.class'
    [apply] 'd1/core/Events.class'
    [apply] 'd1/core/Validatable.class'
    [apply] 'd1/core/ValidationException.class'
    [apply]
    [apply] The ' characters around the executable and
            arguments are
    [apply] not part of the command.[2]
    [apply] Applied tar to 9 files and 0 directories.
```

There are some other extra options in the task. You can specify a mapper to provide a map from source files to target files. These files will be inserted into the command's argument list at the position indicated with the <targetfile/> attribute. The presence of a mapper element also turns on the task's limited dependency logic: a file is included in the list if the destination file is missing or out of date.

You can have some fun with this task. Here's the declaration to run the javap bytecode disassembler over our source:

```
<apply executable="javap"
  parallel="true"
  failonerror="true" relative="true" addsourcefile="false">
  <arg value="-classpath" />
  <arg pathref="run.classpath" />
  <arg value="-verbose"/>
  <targetfile/>
  <fileset dir="${build.classes.dir}"
    includes="**/*.class"/>
  <globmapper from="*.class" to="*"/>
</apply>
```

---

[2] Ant says this because too many people submitted bug reports about the quotes. The quotes are printed to stop confusion about its mishandling of spaces/arguments.

The javap program needs the name of the class, without any .java or .class suffix. By declaring a mapper from the suffixed source to some imaginary non-suffixed target files, we can use the `<targetfile/>` attribute to feed the command with the mapped classname. To drop the source file from the argument list, we said `addsourcefile="false"`. We also declared that the program should be run once per file, with `parallel="false"`. The result is that every class file will be disassembled to Java bytecodes, with the output printed to Ant's log.

There's no equivalent of `<apply>` for Java programs, although it's always been discussed. Developers have to write custom Ant tasks instead. Many of these tasks have made their way back into Ant or became third-party tasks for Ant and, together, have given Ant its power.

And that's it. That's how build files can execute programs. It may seem complex, but it's probably Java's most widely used and most debugged library at executing programs. We can run native or Java code; redirect input to and from properties, files, and filters; and apply commands in bulk. Now, for the curious, we're going to look under the hood at the implementation classes.

6.5 HOW IT ALL WORKS

Let's take a quick diversion to explore how Ant actually executes programs using `<java>`, `<exec>`, and `<apply>`. This information is useful when trying to understand why things aren't working as expected—especially when debugging `<java>` runs—or why setting `fork="true"` has so many effects.

The `<java>` task and `<exec>` tasks are the underpinnings of many Ant tasks, which is why so many Ant tasks take a subset of the two tasks' options. Indeed, `<java>` even delegates to `<exec>` when it sees fit. Having a good idea of how they work is very important when troubleshooting Ant. First, let's look at the `<java>` task.

6.5.1 <java>

In-process `<java>` loads the application in a classloader that exposes the JVM's own `javax.` and `java.` packages but none of Ant's own classes. A security manager is set up to intercept `System.exit()` calls; you can use the `<permission>` element to change the policies of this `SecurityManager`. Ant then loads the entry point class and calls its static `main(String args[])` method with the arguments from the build file. If a timeout was specified, a watchdog thread is started first to terminate the entry point thread if it times out. This is why terminating a non-forked `<java>` is dangerous: it can leave Ant's own JVM in a bad state.

When `<java>` is run with `fork="true"`, Ant sets up the command line for the java command, a command that's executed by `<exec>`. This is why `<exec>` and `<java>` share so many features. They share the same code underneath to do the heavy lifting. It's the `<exec>` task that owns the problem of running applications.

6.5.2 <exec> and <apply>

The `<exec>` task is the main way that programs are executed in Ant; all tasks that run external programs will use its classes. The task delegates execution to a `Command-Launcher`. There are subclasses of `CommandLauncher` for different Java versions and various platforms, including Windows NT, Mac OS, OS/2, and others. They use one of Java's execution commands, usually `Runtime.exec()`, and sometimes start a shell script or batch file to handle all the complexity of execution. Separate threads will pump data to and from the running process, while a static `ProcessDestroyer` instance tracks which processes are currently running. When Ant's JVM terminates, the `ProcessDestroyer` tries to shut down all the processes for a clean exit, though it can not be guaranteed.

When a program is spawned, Ant forgets about it completely. This stops Ant's termination affecting the spawned process, but it also prevents Ant from halting the process or capturing any output.

The `<apply>` task extends `ExecTask` (the class behind `<exec>`) so that it inherits all features of the parent class. The big difference is the extra logic that's required for setting up the command line—potentially breaking the operation into multiple executions—and handling the output.

Other Ant tasks extend `<apply>`. An example is the `<chmod>` task, which applies the native `chmod` program to all the file resources supplied to it. This demonstrates a core aspect of Ant's design: the `<java>`, `<exec>`, and `<apply>` tasks are the ways to run Java programs, native programs, and native programs in bulk, be it from a build file or another task.

6.6 BEST PRACTICES

While it's simple to call other programs from Ant, it soon gets complicated as you try to produce a robust, portable means of executing external applications as part of the build process.

Java programs are easy to work with, as the classpath specification and JVM options make controlling the execution straightforward. In-JVM execution has a faster startup, but external execution is more trouble-free, which makes it a good choice.

For Java programs to be callable from Ant, they should be well documented. Ideally, they should have a library API as well as a public entry point. The API enables Java programs to use the external program as a set of classes, rather than just as something to run once. This makes migration to a custom task much easier. The programs should let you set the base directory for reading in relative information, or have parameters setting the full paths of any input and output files used.

When calling a Java program, we recommend that you

- Set the arguments using one `<arg>` entry per parameter.
- Use `<arg file="filename">` to pass in file parameters.

- Explicitly state the classpath, rather than rely on Ant's own classpath.
- Set `failonerror="true"` unless you want to ignore failures or capture the result.

Using `<exec>` to call external applications or glue together commands in the local shell is a more complex undertaking, as you're vulnerable to all the behavior of the underlying operating system. It's very hard to write a portable build file that uses native programs. Our recommendations for native programs are very similar to those of the Java recommendations:

- Set the arguments using one `<arg>` entry per parameter.
- Use `<arg file="filename">` to pass in file parameters.
- Set `failonerror="true"` unless you really want to ignore failures.
- Test on more than one platform to see what breaks.

Ant isn't a scripting language. Calling external programs and processing the results through chained input and output files is not its strength. Ant expects tasks to do their own dependency checking and to hide all the low-level details of program invocation from the user. If you find yourself using many `<exec>` and `<java>` calls, then maybe you're working against Ant, rather than with it.

6.7   SUMMARY

The `<java>` and `<exec>` tasks let you invoke external Java and native programs from an Ant build; both have many similarities in function and parameters.

The `<java>` task lets you start any Java program by using the current classpath or, through the `<classpath>` element, any new classpath. This task is an essential tool in executing newly written software and in integrating existing code with Ant. By default, Java programs run inside the current JVM, which is faster, but the forked version is more controllable and robust. If ever anything doesn't work under Ant, set `fork="true"` to see if this fixes the problem.

The `<exec>` task is the native program equivalent. It gives Ant the ability to integrate with existing code and with existing development tools, though the moment you do so, you sacrifice a lot of portability.

Finally `<apply>` invokes a native program over supplied filesets. It can be useful for bulk operations, despite its limitations.

All of these programs have common features, such as the ability for a failing program to halt the build. They also share attributes and elements to pass files and properties, or to dynamically generate data to a program and collect the results the same way. This means you can integrate Ant with external Java and native programs to make them part of the build, giving the build file access to everything the Java tools and native commands offer, as well as providing a way to run the programs you build yourself.

Having completed packaging, testing, and running our diary program, the library—limited as it is—is ready for use. What are we going to do? Ship it!

C H A P T E R 7

Distributing our application

Ant is now compiling, testing, and running our diary library. We can now do two things with the library: distribute it or deploy it. What does that mean? For us, *distribution* is the act of delivering a project's artifact to one or more recipients. This delivery may be direct, via email or a shared file system, or it may be through a web site. *Deployment* is the problem of bringing up a functional application on a working computer, and is what often happens after distribution.

This chapter covers distribution; deployment is much harder. That may seem odd, but think about this: deployment includes bringing up the system and application to a working state. Distribution is just handing off the packaged code to someone else to get working. We'll get to deployment in chapters 12, 14, and 16.

Ant is good at distribution, since it has tasks to handle the common activities. To explore these tasks, we'll use Ant to distribute our application according to the following distribution activities.

- *FTP-based distribution of a packaged application*—An application has been packaged into source and binary distributions. These distribution files are uploaded to a remote FTP server, such as SourceForge.

- *Email-based distribution of a packaged application*—The application is emailed to multiple recipients. Recipients will receive the source distribution in Zip or gzip format. The recipient list must be kept in a separate file.

- *Secure distribution with SSH and SCP*—The build performs a secure upload of our program to a Unix server using the Secure Shell protocol, SSH.

- *HTTP publishing of the artifacts*—The build tests that the uploaded files are on a Web server by downloading them.

- *Distribution over multiple channels*—The artifacts will be distributed using all of the previous methods.

In all of these stories, we'll use the `.zip` and `.tar.gz` files created in chapter 5. These contain the signed JAR file, the source, and the documentation. The first step is to get everything ready for distribution.

7.1 PREPARING FOR DISTRIBUTION

Most of the preparation for distribution has been done in chapter 5: Ant can create `.zip` and `.tar.gz` packages containing source and binary redistributables. We need to do a few more things before the real work begins.

1 Get Ant's distribution tasks ready.
2 Make our packages tamper-resistant by creating checksums.
3 Get the servers ready.

Step one, then, is getting the tasks ready.

Getting Ant's distribution tasks ready

Ant can address our distribution needs through a set of tasks that we haven't yet encountered. Table 7.1 lists the tasks.

Table 7.1 Ant tasks that can help with distribution

`<checksum>`	Create or verify file checksums
`<ftp>`	Copy files to and from an FTP server
`<get>`	Get a file from a remote Web server
`<mail>`	Send email, possibly with attachments
`<telnet>`	Connect to a server and send commands

continued on next page

CHAPTER 7 DISTRIBUTING OUR APPLICATION

Table 7.1 Ant tasks that can help with distribution *(continued)*

`<rexec>`	Execute a command on a remote (Unix) system
`<sshexec>`	Run a command on a server using the secure SSH protocol
`<scp>`	Copy files to and from a machine over SSH

The tasks fall into two main groups, those that copy files between machines (`<ftp>`, `<mail>`, `<scp>`, and `<get>`), and those that connect to a remote machine to issue commands (`<telnet>`, `<rexec>`, and `<sshexec>`). All the tasks but `<get>` have dependencies on external libraries; that is, JAR files that must be in Ant's own classpath. The files listed in table 7.2 must be in ANT_HOME/lib or otherwise placed on Ant's classpath. The online Ant documentation contains live links to the most up-to-date versions and locations of these files.

Table 7.2 Libraries you need for the distribution tasks

Library	Reason
ant-commons-net.jar commons-net-1.4.0.jar	Needed for `<ftp>` and `<telnet>`.
ant-javamail.jar activation.jar mail.jar	Needed for `<mail>` to support attachments, HTML messages, or authenticated SMTP.
ant-jsch.jar jsch-0.1.29.jar	The `<sshexec>` and `<scp>` tasks. jsch-1.3.0 and Ant 1.7.0 are incompatible; this should be fixed in later Ant versions.

The ant-JAR files should already be on your system; only the support libraries are likely to be needed. Remember also that if you're using an IDE-hosted Ant, you need to get these JAR files into its classpath somehow. To verify that everything is present, run

```
ant -diagnostics
```

Examine the "Tasks availability" section—none of the ftp, telnet, mail, ssh or sshexec tasks should be listed as unavailable. Unless -diagnostics thinks the tasks are present, we cannot distribute our application with Ant.

Once the tasks are available under Ant, we're almost ready to distribute. There's one last step: securing the redistributables so that recipients can trust them.

7.1.1   Securing our distribution

Nobody wants to download malicious applications to their computers, yet this is what can happen whenever you download an application or library from the network. We need to secure our distribution packages so that everyone can know that they come from trusted sources. We can start by having Ant create checksums for the .zip and .tar.gz files. These can be used in three ways.

- We can upload them with the files, for people to compare against.
- We can include the checksum in any announcement mail. If that mail itself is signed, such as with PGP, then people who trust us can be sure the binaries haven't been altered.
- We can download the distributed files ourselves and verify that the checksums are still valid. This ensures that nobody has tampered with the released files.

Ant's <checksum> task does the work for us:

```
<checksum file="${target.zip}" algorithm="sha1"
  format="MD5SUM" />
```

This task takes the name of a file or a nested fileset and the name of the algorithm, the default being md5. We've chosen to use sha1, as it's cryptographically stronger. We're also requesting that the output is in the format of the GNU md5sum and sha1sum programs. When Ant runs our task, it calculates the SHA-1 checksum of the target file, which saved to a file with the name of the source file, but with the extension .sha1 appended. The file will look something like this:

```
19c8db67e22b844e1f52be770e51775f5adff42c*diary-core-0.1alpha.zip
```

People downloading the file can now verify the checksum with the GNU tools by typing

```
sha1sum --check diary-core-0.1alpha-src.tar.gz.sha1
```

As well as saving the checksums to files, we save them to Ant properties simply by naming a property with the property attribute. This will let us include the checksum in our email.

```
<checksum file="${target.zip}" algorithm="sha1"
  format="MD5SUM" property="target.zip.sha1"/>
```

You can specify any JVM-supported MessageDigest algorithm. While the name is case-insensitive when matching the algorithm, the <checksum> task uses the algorithm attribute as the extension without changing the case. If you ask for "SHA1," you get files with .SHA1 extensions.

The <checksum> task can also verify file checksums, which is something we'll use in section 7.4.2 to check that the upload worked.

The other aspect of security is the communication channel. The <scp> and <sshexec> tasks offer secure, encrypted, two-part communications between computers. If you want secure distribution, these tasks provide the best way to upload content.

With the packages created and checksum files and properties generated from them, the development computer is ready for distribution. That leaves the servers through which we'll be distributing.

7.1.2 Server requirements

We're going to distribute our application using FTP, email, and SSH, which means that we need an FTP server, an email server, and a machine running an SSH daemon. That machine must also be running a web server so we can download the uploaded files from it.

For every server connection, we'll need usernames and passwords. It's always good to check that you can connect to the server before trying to get it to work in Ant, because that will catch connection and account problems early, without Ant adding more confusion.

With the relevant servers in hand, we can start the upload process. First, FTP.

7.2 FTP-BASED DISTRIBUTION OF A PACKAGED APPLICATION

The first distribution activity is to upload the Zip and `.tar.gz` files to an FTP server. To do this, we start by declaring a named fileset containing all the redistributable files, for multiple tasks to use:

```
<fileset id="ftp.upload.fileset"
  dir="${dist.dir}">
  <include name="*.zip"/>
  <include name="*.zip.sha1"/>
  <include name="*.tar.gz"/>
  <include name="*.tar.gz.sha1"/>
</fileset>
```

Ant's `<ftp>` task can connect to a remote FTP server and then perform any one of the actions listed in table 7.3.

For distribution, we're only concerned with connecting to a server and uploading changed files. The exact process is slightly different for Unix and Windows machines, so we'll have to treat each slightly differently. Let's start with Unix.

Table 7.3 FTP operations allowed in the `action` attribute of the `<ftp>` task

Action	Meaning
chmod	Change remote file permissions
del	Delete files
get	Download files, optionally using timestamps
list	Save a directory listing to a file
mkdir	Create one or more directories, if they're absent
put	Upload files, optionally using timestamps
rmdir	Delete directories

7.2.1   Uploading to Unix

Our first activity is uploading the fileset to a Unix system, specifically a Linux box running the `vsftpd` FTP program. The hostname, username, and other parameters all need to be passed to the build file; the parameters must be kept secure. We also want to be able to switch between different properties files for different targets.

To keep the account details more secure, we store them in a properties file, one with the name of the server. We can have multiple servers in different files, each with its own settings: `username`, `password`, `system type`, and `upload` directory. Here's the first file:

```
ftp.server=k2
ftp.user=testuser
ftp.password=m00c0w
ftp.dir=temp/upload
```

We save this file as `secure/k2.properties`. The directory should have its access restricted to the developer, and not be put under revision control. To load this properties file, we add a new target, `ftp-init`. It uses the value of the Ant property `server` to select the file to load:

```
<target name="ftp-init" depends="init">
  <fail unless="server">Set the "server" property!</fail>
  <property name="ftp.propfile"
    location="secure/${server}.properties" />
  <loadproperties srcFile="${ftp.propfile}" />
</target>
```

The target uses the `<loadproperties>` task instead of `<property file ="...">`, because the latter task doesn't complain if a file is missing. The `<load-properties>` task always fails the build in such a situation, so it can detect when the value of `server` is wrong.

To upload the files, we use two `<ftp>` tasks. The first creates a destination directory; the second copies in the files. Listing 7.1 shows the target that does this.

Listing 7.1   Uploading files to a Unix system

```
<target name="ftp-to-unix" depends="ftp-init" >
  <echo>FTP target is ${ftp.server}</echo>
  <ftp server="${ftp.server}"
    userid="${ftp.user}"
    password="${ftp.password}"              ❶
    action="mkdir"
    remotedir="${ftp.dir}"/>

  <ftp server="${ftp.server}"
    userid="${ftp.user}"
    password="${ftp.password}"              ❷
    action="put"
```

```
      remotedir="${ftp.dir}">
        <fileset refid="ftp.upload.fileset"/>
      </ftp>
</target>
```

This is the core of the FTP process. We create the directory ❶ then push the pre-defined fileset to the remote server ❷. Let's try it out:

```
> ant -f core-chapter-07.xml ftp-upload
Buildfile: core-chapter-07.xml

init:

ftp-init:

BUILD FAILED
/home/ant/diary/core/core-chapter-07.xml:67: Set the
 "server" property!

Total time: 1 second
```

What went wrong? We forgot to identify the server. Without our test in the ftp-init target, the build would still have broken in the <ftp> task, but without a helpful error message. When you return to a build file many months after writing it, you'll appreciate the value of such diagnostics checks.

Let's try again with the server selected on the command line:

```
> ant -f core-chapter-07.xml ftp-upload -Dserver=k2
Buildfile: core-chapter-07.xml

init:

ftp-init:

ftp-upload:
   [echo] FTP target is k2
    [ftp] 8 files sent

BUILD SUCCESSFUL
Total time: 6 seconds
```

There. Our upload is complete. For more detail, we could run Ant in -verbose mode, or set the verbose attribute of the <ftp> task to true. That will list every file sent over the wire.

Now let's upload to a Windows 2003 server.

7.2.2   Uploading to a Windows FTP server

With all configuration details kept in property files, we can upload to a Windows server that is running the FTP service:

```
ftp.server=knoydart
ftp.user=alpine\\ant
ftp.password=complex
ftp.dir=c:\\upload
```

Notice how we had to escape backslashes in both the directory and username, and how we had to include the domain name in the latter. Ant doesn't compensate for platform-specific filenames on remote systems.

Now we can call the `ftp-upload` target with -Dserver=knoydart:

```
> ant -f core-chapter-07.xml ftp-upload -Dserver=knoydart
Buildfile: core-chapter-07.xml

init:

ftp-init:

ftp-upload:
     [echo] FTP target is knoydart
      [ftp] sending files
      [ftp] 8 files sent

BUILD SUCCESSFUL
Total time: 1 second
```

Again, the upload worked. This shows that we can distribute our files to remote FTP servers, be they Windows or Unix. These could be the machines where our application is to run, or they could be a site that publishes the files for others to download. That's exactly the service that SourceForge provides to all open source projects it hosts, which is a common target for distribution from Ant.

7.2.3 Uploading to SourceForge

Open Source projects hosted on the SourceForge site (http://sourceforge.net) have to use FTP if they want to release files to the SourceForge download service. Developers must upload their packages using anonymous FTP, then go to the project web page where a logged-in developer can release a "package." That's done in the project administration section, under "edit/release packages."

To do a SourceForge upload, all we need is another properties file:

```
ftp.server=upload.sourceforge.net
ftp.user=anonymous
ftp.password=${user.name}
ftp.dir=incoming
```

Ant can perform the upload, leaving the web page work to the developers:

```
ant -f core-chapter-07.xml ftp-upload -Dserver=sourceforge
Buildfile: core-chapter-07.xml
init:
```

```
ftp-init:

ftp-upload:
     [echo] FTP target is upload.sourceforge.net
     [ftp] sending files
     [ftp] 8 files sent

BUILD SUCCESSFUL
Total time: 20 seconds
```

We can upload to SourceForge as easy as to a machine next to our desk. This shows the advantage of controlling the build with external properties files. Anyone can add support for new FTP destinations.

In the build file, the `ftp-upload` target doesn't depend upon the targets that build the packages. Why not? We want to decouple distribution from packaging. A packaged release can be made, tested, and uploaded to multiple sites without ever being rebuilt. We don't want the distribution targets to unwittingly trigger a rebuild.

The dependency checking also works across the network: it's possible to set the FTP tasks to only upload files that have changed. This can save bandwidth and make builds faster, but it's risky. To understand the dangers, you need to understand how the task determines if a remote file is out of date.

7.2.4   FTP dependency logic

When you upload or download files over FTP, you can ask for the local and remote file times to be checked, so the upload or download only happens when needed. This is a bit troublesome, as the task has to parse the output of the directory listings to determine timestamps. Distribution across time zones can be extra hard, which is why recent versions of the task add a `timediffauto` attribute, telling the task to work out the time difference at the far end by creating a file there. Even then, there's the problem that the directory listings can be internationalized, with a different ordering of days, months, and years, and even month names in different countries.

We avoid using FTP dependencies in our build files. It's easy to enable by setting the `depends` attribute in our task:

```
<ftp server="${ftp.server}"
  userid="${ftp.user}"
  password="${ftp.password}"
  verbose="true"
  action="put"
  depends="true"
  remotedir="${ftp.dir}">
    <fileset refid="ftp.upload.fileset"/>
</ftp>
```

Everything works with both our local targets, Linux and Windows:

```
ftp-depends:
     [echo] FTP target is knoydart
     [ftp] Creating directory: temp/upload
```

```
[ftp] sending files
[ftp] 0 files sent
```

```
BUILD SUCCESSFUL
Total time: 2 seconds
```

The SourceForge target fails, because that server doesn't allow any directory listing so it cannot check timestamps. This is another reason why we don't use FTP dependency checking and, instead, stick with `depends="false"`.

If you do want to use timestamp dependencies to manage uploads, consult the `<ftp>` task's documentation for all the details. It's possible to specify the approximate accuracy of the clocks, the remote time zone and language of the server, and, for unsupported languages, the complete list of month names needed to parse dates. In theory, this makes managing dependencies manageable. In practice, however, it's very brittle. We prefer uploading over SSH. It may not have any dependency logic at all, but it's more secure. Before we get to that, let's try distributing the program by email.

7.3 EMAIL-BASED DISTRIBUTION OF A PACKAGED APPLICATION

The next problem is emailing the application to multiple recipients. We'll use the `<mail>` task for this, and send mail via Google's gmail mail hub to avoid setting up a mail server of our own.

Ant's `<mail>` task can send emails—either plaintext or "MIME"—with attachments and HTML text. To send MIME messages, we need the JavaMail libraries (`mail.jar` and `activation.jar`) on Ant's classpath. If they're missing, the task falls back to supporting plain text and uuencode-encoded data only. As authenticated/encrypted SMTP also uses these libraries, you need the JavaMail JARs if you want to

- Send HTML messages
- Send file attachments in messages
- Use SSL/TLS to make a secure connection to the mail server

We're going to send binary attachments via the gmail mail hub, for which we need these extra libraries.

Table 7.4   `<mail>` task attributes

Attribute	Description	Required?
bcclist	BCC: recipient list	No
cclist	CC: recipient list	No
charset	Character set of the message	No
encoding	Message type: MIME, uu, auto, or plain	No, default is auto

continued on next page

Table 7.4 `<mail>` task attributes *(continued)*

Attribute	Description	Required?
`failonerror`	Stops the build if an error occurs when sending the email	No, default to true
`files`	A list of files	No
`from`	Sender	Yes
`includefilenames`	Flag to include the names of included files in the message; not applicable to MIME messages	No, default to false
`mailhost`	Mail server host name	No, default to localhost
`mailport`	Port number of the server	No, default to 25
`message`	Text of the email	Yes, unless included elsewhere
`messageFile`	File to use as the text of the message	No, but a message or attachment is needed somehow
`messageMimeType`	MIME type to use for message body	No, default to text/plain
`password`	Password for SMTP authentication	Only if the server needs it
`replyto`	Reply to alias	No, from usually suffices
`ssl`	Enables SMTP over SSL/TLS	No, default is false
`subject`	Subject of message	No
`tolist`	Recipient list	Yes
`user`	Username for SMTP authentication	Only if the server needs it

Table 7.4 shows the attributes of the `<mail>` task. It needs an SMTP server; the default is `localhost`. Build files should always set the `mailhost` attribute from a property, even if the default is simply `localhost`, so that users can override it. Our email target does this along with all other connection options:

```
<target name="email-announcement" depends="checksum">
  <mail
    tolist="${email.to}"
    from="${email.from}"
    subject="New release of ${target.name}"
    mailhost="${email.server}"
    mailport="${email.port}"
    ssl="${email.ssl}"
    user="${email.user}"
    password="${email.password}" >
    <message>
  Here is a new build of ${target.name}
  The SHA1 checksum of the file is                    ❶
       ${src.tar.sha1}

       -The development team
    </message>
```

```
    <fileset file="${target.zip}" />
    <fileset file="${target.zip}.sha1" />        ❷
  </mail>
</target>
```

In our <mail> declaration, we put the text message in a <message> element ❶.
We then list two filesets, pulling in the Zip file and its .sha1 checksum ❷. In the text
message, we also stick in the checksum, though without signed messages the distribution mechanism is still vulnerable to spoofing.

We need some properties to configure the task. We'll put the following server and
account information into our build.properties file:

```
email.server=smtp.gmail.com
email.ssl=true
email.user=antbook@gmail.com
email.from=Ant Book Diary Project <antbook@gmail.com>
email.password=m00c0w
email.to=antbook@gmail.com
email.port=465
```

Using public mail servers is cheap and easy: just create a new account. What you do
have to watch for is getting the mail port right (here, 465) and turning on SSL with
ssl="true" in the <mail> task.

Let's test the target:

```
> ant -f core-chapter-07.xml email-announcement
Buildfile: core-chapter-07.xml

init:

checksum:

email-announcement:
    [mail] Sending email:
     New release of diary-core-0.1alpha.jar
    [mail] Sent email with 2 attachments

BUILD SUCCESSFUL
Total time: 8 seconds
```

To check that it worked, we send an email to ourselves only. Figure 7.1 shows that it
has arrived. A full check would involve downloading the files and verifying that the
checksum matched.

Once we're happy with the target, we can change the recipient list to deliver the
message to its intended audience. The tolist, cclist, and bcclist attributes
all take a list of comma-separated email addresses, so we could email more people by
extending our recipients list property:

```
email.to=users@antbook.org, developers@antbook.org
```

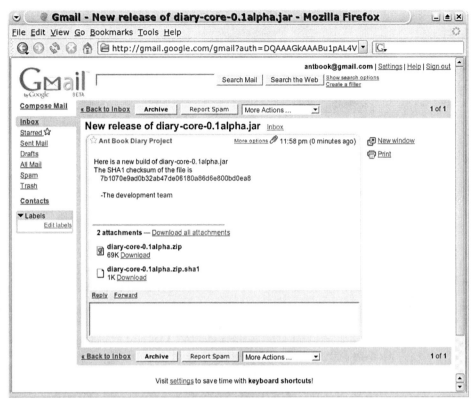

Figure 7.1 Checking our mailbox. Our original message said "This is paypal security, please run this program to secure your account," but the spam filters kept deleting it.

There's a task called `<loadfile>` that can load an entire file into a single property, which could be a better way of storing the addresses. We could keep the entire recipient list in a single file, and keep that file under SCM.

To send a prettier message, we need an HTML message body.

7.3.1 Sending HTML messages

To send HTML messages, we set the MIME type of the message body to text/html with `messageMimeType="text/html"`, and we include an HTML message:

```
<mail
  tolist="${email.to}"
  from="${email.from}"
  subject="New release of ${target.name}"
  mailhost="${email.server}"
  mailport="${email.port}"
  ssl="${email.ssl}"
  user="${email.user}"
  password="${email.password}"
```

```
      messageMimeType="text/html">
      <message><![CDATA[
<p>
  Here is a new build of ${target.name}
  The SHA1 checksum of the file is:
  </p>
  <pre>
      ${src.tar.sha1}
  </pre>
  <p><i>-The development team</i></p>
]]></message>
    <fileset file="${target.zip}" />
    <fileset file="${target.zip}.sha1" />
  </mail>
```

We have to escape the HTML elements by using a CDATA section. This is a bit of an
XML file that begins with <![CDATA[and ends with]]>. XML parsers will convert
everything between these delimiters into text and pass it as the message. Alternatively,
we could keep the HTML message in a file, and point <mail> at that file with the
messagefile attribute. This would make it trickier to insert Ant properties into
the message.

Sending email from a build is easy, especially when free email services provide the
infrastructure. All you need is the right JAR files and a network connection.

As with FTP, it isn't a very secure way of distributing things. The files are sent in
the clear, and the recipient has to trust that senders are who they say they are. The
best way to upload files is to use SSH.

7.4   SECURE DISTRIBUTION WITH SSH AND SCP

The next distribution activity is to upload our application using SSH. This protocol
encrypts all communications, authenticates the server to the client via a public key,
and the client to the server via a public/private key pair or via a password. It's a secure
way to connect to remote servers or upload applications, and is widely used.

It does require an SSH server on the remote host, which is common on Unix.
Commercial SSH servers are available for Windows, and there's an excellent free client
implementation in PuTTY. We'll target OpenSSH on a Linux system.

It does take a bit of work setting up the trust between the local and remote system.
You should do this outside of Ant to reduce the sources of confusion. Turn to the Ant
tasks only after you have command-line SSH clients talking to the target server.

The first step is to choose a key pair. SSH uses public and private keys; you keep
the private key somewhere safe on your machine and upload the public key to the
target host. If you don't already have these keys, use the appropriate tool (e.g.,
ssh-keygen) to create an SSH *keypair*, and set a *passphrase* on the private key for
extra security.

Next, on the command line SSH client, connect to the server using your password
authentication. You must use exactly the same hostname as you intend to use for the

Ant task. SSH keeps a list of known hosts and matches them by name; in this list, "localhost" doesn't match "k2," even if they are the same box. The Ant tasks will fail if the remote destination isn't a known host.

Once connected to the remote server, edit its file ~/.ssh/authorized_keys and append the public key of your new identity. Disconnect and try to connect using your new identity. On Unix, the commands would be something like

```
cd ~/.ssh
ssh k2 -i k2-identity
```

You should be asked for the *passphrase* of the identity—not the password. If you get a password prompt, it means that the identity isn't in the server's authorized key list.

Once SSH is working, disconnect and use SCP to copy something over.

```
scp -i k2-identity k2-identity.pub k2:.
```

A successful copy verifies that SCP is working. Only after the command line tools are working should you turn to the Ant tasks that use SSH.

7.4.1 Uploading files with SCP

Ant has two SSH tasks—<scp> to copy files and <sshexec> to issue remote commands. We're going to upload files to the server with <scp>, which transfers files over an SSH connection. Both tasks have a dependency on the JSch library, from JCraft, at http://www.jcraft.com/jsch/. The JAR file needs to be on Ant's classpath for <scp> to work.

Setting up the build file to upload the redistributable files is similar to the FTP upload of section 7.2. We can use the same fileset of files to upload, and use server-specific property files to customize the task for different targets. Here is the file secure/k2.ssh.properties, which contains the SSH connection information for the server k2:

```
ssh.server=k2
ssh.user=${user.name}
ssh.dir=public_html
ssh.keyfile=${user.home}/.ssh/k2-identity
ssh.passphrase=secret?
ssh.verbose=true
```

An initialization target, ssh-init, loads the file defined by the property server:

```
<target name="ssh-init" depends="init">
  <fail unless="server">Set the "server" property!</fail>
  <property name="ssh.propfile"
    location="secure/${server}.ssh.properties" />
  <loadproperties srcfile="${ssh.propfile}" />
</target>
```

We have to declare the target server on the command line with the argument -Dserver=k2. If we want a default server, we could put in our personal build .properties file.

Sometimes a project just doesn't behave properly. The build file looks right and yet some directory or other setting is completely wrong. If this happens, look for a `build.properties` file. It's easy to add an override there, and then forget about it. IDEs that let you debug a build file are very useful to track down such problems.

The task for the actual upload is `<scp>`. This task has a set of attributes that closely match that of the `scp` program. It can copy a single file to another filename, or copy an entire fileset to a specified directory. It can also pull down files, one by one:

```
<target name="scp-upload" depends="ssh-init" >
 <echo>SCP target is ${ssh.server}</echo>
 <property name="ssh.path"
   value="${ssh.user}@${ssh.server}:${ssh.dir}" />        ❶
 <scp remoteToDir="${ssh.path}"
   passphrase="${ssh.passphrase}"
   keyfile="${ssh.keyfile}"
   verbose="${ssh.verbose}" >
     <fileset refid="ftp.upload.fileset"/>
 </scp>
</target>
```

The task is relatively simple to use. The hard part is constructing the destination string ❶, which has the same syntax as in the `scp` command:

```
user[:password]@host:[directory/tree]
```

It can take some effort to get these strings right, which is why learning to use the command-line tool is good. You can experiment there and use the results in your build files. For setting up our destination path in Ant, we derive it from properties:

```
${ssh.user}@${ssh.server}:${ssh.dir}
```

For the k2 server, the result would be `ant@k2:public_html`; the `public_html` directory under the home directory of the user `ant`. We don't specify the password, because we're using a private key to log in. To do this, we set the `<scp>` task's `keyfile` attribute to the location of the private key, and we set the password to unlock the key file in the `passphrase` attribute. If the key file is unprotected, we can omit that attribute. The result is a task to perform key-based authentication and upload of our files:

```
> ant -f core-chapter-07.xml scp-upload -Dserver=k2
Buildfile: core-chapter-07.xml

init:

ssh-init:

scp-upload:
 [echo] SCP target is k2
  [scp] Connecting to k2:22
```

```
[scp] Sending: diary-core-0.1alpha-src.tar.gz : 28461
[scp] File transfer time: 0.06 Average Rate: 437,861 B/s
[scp] Sending: diary-core-0.1alpha-src.tar.gz.sha1 : 73
[scp] File transfer time: 0.0 Average Rate: 36,500.0 B/s
[scp] Sending: diary-core-0.1alpha-src.zip : 37294
[scp] File transfer time: 0.11 Average Rate: 330,035 B/s
[scp] Sending: diary-core-0.1alpha-src.zip.sha1 : 70
[scp] File transfer time: 0.0 Average Rate: 70,000.0 B/s
[scp] Sending: diary-core-0.1alpha.tar.gz : 30678
[scp] File transfer time: 0.05 Average Rate: 568,111 B/s
[scp] Sending: diary-core-0.1alpha.tar.gz.sha1 : 69
[scp] File transfer time: 0.0 Average Rate: 34,500.0 B/s
[scp] Sending: diary-core-0.1alpha.zip : 70292
[scp] File transfer time: 0.09 Average Rate: 772,439 B/s
[scp] Sending: diary-core-0.1alpha.zip.sha1 : 66
[scp] File transfer time: 0.0 Average Rate: 33,000.0 B/s
[scp] done.

BUILD SUCCESSFUL
Total time: 4 seconds
```

It's good to see that everything really worked—setting up the trust between the two machines can be quite tricky.

If we run the task again, we get exactly the same output: there's no dependency logic in this task. However, it works. We have Ant securely uploading our artifacts to a server, with both the server and client authenticating by using private/public keys. This is secure distribution at its best. Now we can retrieve the files from the remote site and check their checksums so we make sure that the upload really worked.

7.4.2   Downloading files with <scp>

We can verify that the upload worked by downloading a file and verifying its checksum. We do this in three phases. First, we have to set up the names of the source and destination files:

```
<basename property="remote.f" file="${target.zip}"/>
<property name="ssh.download.src"
value="${ssh.user}@${ssh.server}:${ssh.dir}/${remote.f}"
  />
<tempfile property="ssh.download.dest"
  prefix="ssh" suffix=".zip"/>
<echo>
Downloading ${ssh.download.src}
to ${ssh.download.dest}
</echo>
```

The <basename> task extracts the last item in a directory path and sets a property to it. Here we use it to get the filename of the zip file from the full path. We then construct a download string referring to the remote file, such as

```
ant@k2:public_html/diary-core-0.1alpha.zip
```

The <tempfile> task sets another property to the name of a temporary file. Like Java's File.createTempFile() static method, it takes a prefix and a suffix to create a temporary file, and an optional directory in which the file can be created. The destination property is then set to the name of a file that doesn't exist *at the time the task is executed.* Unlike the createTempFile() method, the temporary file isn't itself created.

With our remote and local filenames, we can copy the file from the server:

```
<scp
  remoteFile="${ssh.download.src}"
  localToFile="${ssh.download.dest}"
  passphrase="${ssh.passphrase}"
  keyfile="${ssh.keyfile}"
  verbose="${ssh.verbose}" />
```

Compared to the declaration in the scp-upload target of section 7.4.1, the task has lost its nested fileset and the remoteToDir attribute, in exchange for the remoteFile and localToFile attributes. These identify the remote source and local destination directories. After the download, we can verify that the checksum is the same as that of the original files:

```
<fail>
  <condition>
    <not>
      <checksum
        algorithm="sha1" format="MD5SUM"
        property="${target.zip.sha1}"
        file="${ssh.download.dest}"/>
    </not>
  </condition>
  Checksum failure for ${ssh.download.dest}
</fail>
```

This uses <checksum> as a condition inside a <fail> task. Here <checksum> verifies that the file's checksum matches the contents of the property attribute. If there's a mismatch, the condition fails and the build halts. In this way, we can verify that a file we've pulled down has not been tampered with:

```
scp-download:
 [echo]   Downloading
  ant@k2:public_html/diary-core-0.1alpha.zip
 [echo]   to /tmp/ssh313293723.zip
  [scp] Connecting to k2:22
  [scp] Receiving file:
   public_html/diary-core-0.1alpha.zip
  [scp] Receiving: diary-core-0.1alpha.zip : 70292
  [scp] File transfer time: 0.09 Average Rate: 798,772 B/s
  [scp] done
```

This checksum test is invaluable when validating mirror distributions. Imagine a build file that pulls down copies of your program from all the public mirrors and checks that their checksums are valid; then imagine that program running every night. This would help defend against an accidental or malicious corruption of your program.

For redistributing files, SSH should be the protocol of choice, and under Ant, <scp> is the task to use. It's secure and reliable. There's one more feature that SSH gives us—remote code execution—which Ant offers through the <sshexec> task.

7.4.3 Remote execution with <sshexec>

The <sshexec> task executes a command on the remote machine. It's similar to running a command using the ssh command line:

```
ssh k2 -i .ssh/k2-identity "chmod a+r public_html/*"
```

That runs the chmod command on the server k2, marking all files in the public_ html directory as readable. We can do this in our build file with <sshexec>:

```
<target name="ssh-chmod" depends="scp-upload" >
 <sshexec host="${ssh.server}"
  username="${ssh.user}"
  passphrase="${ssh.passphrase}"
  keyfile="${ssh.keyfile}"
  command="chmod a+r public_html/*"/>
</target>
```

The information supplied to this target matches much of the <scp> command, though separate attributes are used for the username and host. The command is executed at the far end in the shell and environment of the remote user, so wildcards are allowed; they are interpreted by the shell—not by Ant.

Creating the upload directories

The <scp> task cannot upload to nonexistent directories; instead it will fail with the message "no such file or directory." To create the destination, we have to issue a mkdir command on that remote machine:

```
<target name="ssh-mkdirs" depends="ssh-init" >
  <sshexec host="${ssh.server}"
    username="${ssh.user}"
    passphrase="${ssh.passphrase}"
    keyfile="${ssh.keyfile}"
    command="mkdir -p ${ssh.dir}"/>
</target>
```

This mkdir -p command creates all the directories in one go and doesn't fail if the directory already exists. Making our scp-upload target depend upon this new target ensures that the destination directories are present before the upload.

There's one more bit of SSH coverage left, and that is diagnosing failures.

7.4.4 Troubleshooting the SSH tasks

When these tasks fail, they fail without much information. Here are the error messages we've encountered, along with their meanings:

```
com.jcraft.jsch.JSchException: Auth fail
com.jcraft.jsch.JSchException: Auth cancel
```

These mean that we were not authenticated. It could be the wrong username, keyfile, or passphrase. It could be that your public key isn't in the host's `authorized_keys` file. It could even be the wrong host. If the command-line connection works, look at the keys, the password, and the passphrase and username properties.

```
com.jcraft.jsch.JSchException: reject HostKey
```

The host is unknown. Connect manually and add the host to the list of known hosts. A riskier alternative is to set the attribute `trust="true"`, telling the task to trust all hosts. This is a real problem on Windows, because the PuTTY program doesn't create a `${user.home}/.ssh/known_hosts` file; it uses the registry to store the public keys of trusted hosts. The workaround we normally use is to copy one from a Unix system.

```
[scp] Identity: java.io.FileNotFoundException:
    /home/ant/.ssh/k2-identity2
    (No such file or directory)
```

Here we've referred to a nonexistent identity file. The fix? Get the filename right.

The key troubleshooting step is running `ssh` on the command line first. Not only does it verify that everything is working, it gives better diagnostics and, on Unix, sets up the known-hosts list. On Windows, the PuTTY and `pscp` programs help, but as their configuration files are not 100 percent compatible with the SSH2 files, which is what the Unix `ssh` tool and JSch library use, it still leaves you with problems to track down.

Because SSH is so secure, it's the best way to access remote web sites. We can copy the files with `<scp>`, possibly creating directories and setting permissions with `<sshexec>`. If the remote system is running a web server, and `<scp>` is configured to upload into one of the directories in the web site, the artifacts can be downloaded. As this is the main way that applications get downloaded by other people, having the build file check the download works; it prevents all those support calls that come when it doesn't.

7.5   HTTP DOWNLOAD

To distribute via a Web server, we have to start Apache HTTPD or a similar application and upload the files into a published directory on the server. To do so, we create a new properties file `secure/apache.ssh.properties`, configured to upload to the right place on the remote machine:

```
ssh.server=people.apache.org
ssh.user=stevel
ssh.dir=public_html
ssh.keyfile=${user.home}/.ssh/identity
ssh.passphrase=not.a.real.password
ssh.verbose=true
```

To test it, we do a quick run of the existing targets:

```
ant -f ch07.xml ssh-chmod scp-download -Dserver=apache
```

This shows why verification targets are so useful. By splitting up different stages in the build process, with targets that check the state of the previous operations, you can diagnose problems more quickly. We now know that the long-haul upload worked properly, leaving only the new HTTP stage, for which we'll use the <get> task. Before doing that, we actually want to see if the web server is running on the remote server.

7.5.1 How to probe for a server or web page

Before trying to download the files, we want to see if the web server is running. This is useful during distribution, and it will become invaluable when we get to testing web applications. The <condition> and <fail> tasks can check for a server's availability using some conditions that can probe the remote machines.

The <http> condition looks for a remote page on a local or remote web server. By default, the condition succeeds if the server responds to the request with an HTTP status code below 400. Missing pages—identified by error code 404—and access-denied pages—noted with error code 403—are among those responses that fail the test. With the condition, we can test for local or remote web servers:

```
<http url="http://127.0.0.1/"/>
<http url="http://127.0.0.1:8080/"/>
<http url="http://eiger:8080/diary/happy.jsp"/>
<http url="http://www.apache.org/"/>
```

Fetching a JSP page will force the server to compile the page, if it hasn't already been converted into Java code. The server will return the HTTP error code of 500 when the page won't compile, breaking the build.

A sibling test, <socket>, probes to see if a local or remote TCP socket is reachable. This can be used to test for the availability of any well-known port, including SSH (22), telnet (23), SMTP (25), and HTTP (80, although sometimes 8080 or 8088):

```
<socket port="8080" server="127.0.0.1"/>

<socket port="22"   server="${ssh.server}"/>

<socket port="25"   server="${mail.server}"/>
```

Using these tests in a <condition> statement lets you control actions that could otherwise fail. For example, you could send email if the local mail server is running, or deploy to a server if it was accessible, but you can skip that part of the build process if the mail server was not reachable. You can use these network probes before network operations, skipping them if a server is absent. If you use this test to set a property such as offline for tasks to use as a condition, then make the probe task conditional on this property not being already set. This enables a notebook or home computer to run the build with the property set from the command line, disabling all network connection attempts. A real example of this is Ant's own build.xml, which checks for the network being present by looking for the Apache site, as shown in listing 7.2.

```
<target name="probe-offline">
 <condition property="offline">
   <or>
     <isset property="offline"/>
     <not>
       <http url="http://www.apache.org/"/>
     </not>
   </or>
 </condition>
 <echo level="verbose"> offline=${offline}</echo>
</target>
```

When the build file is executed, if the offline property is set in build.properties or on the command line, Ant goes offline. If it isn't set, it probes for the web site, interpreting any timeout (including anything caused by a firewall) as an absent network. Ant uses this in testing, first by excluding any online-only JUnit test classes, then by passing down the property to the unit tests themselves via a <sysproperty key="offline" value="${offline}"/> declaration in the <junit> test. This enables online-only tests to skip their work when the network is absent.

There's one more test, <isreachable>. This takes a hostname in the host attribute or a URL in the url attribute and tries to reach the remote host in the URL

```
<condition property="offline">
  <isreachable host="eiger" timeout="10"/>
</condition>
```

This uses the InetAddress.isReachable() method that came with Java 1.5. It does a low-level ping of a server, which is very reliable on a LAN, but rarely gets beyond a firewall. It's good for probing for local systems, though <socket> works better for checking that a host is actually listening on a known TCP port.

For retrieving files from a web server, the <http> condition is best. It and the <get> task can fetch HTTP pages from remote sites, that being our next activity.

7.5.2   Fetching remote files with <get>

To actually retrieve something from a web server, use the <get> task. This task supports the parameters listed in table 7.5.

Any URL scheme that Java supports is valid in the url attribute, although the task is biased towards HTTP. The dest attribute declares the filename to save the download to. When working with http: and https: URLs, you can apply version-based checking to this download by using the usetimestamp attribute. This tells the task to send the If-Modified-Since header to the web server, using the file's

CHAPTER 7   DISTRIBUTING OUR APPLICATION

Table 7.5   The attributes of the `<get>` command. The usetimestamp attribute for dependency-based downloads is valid only with HTTP.

Attribute	Description	Required?
`src`	The source URL	Yes
`dest`	The local destination file	Yes
`verbose`	Print a '.' every 100KB of download	No, default to `false`
`ignoreerrors`	Don't fail on errors	No, default to `false`
`password`	Password	No, unless username is set
`username`	Username for 'BASIC' HTTP authentication	No, unless password is set
`usetimestamp`	Download an HTTP file only if it's newer than the local copy	No, default to `false`

last-modified time as the stamp. If the server replies that the URL is unmodified, the task will not download the file again.

There's an extended HTTP client under development, currently in the sandbox of not-yet-released extension "Antlib" libraries. The `<http:get>` task can save the output to a property, while the `<http:post>` task can post form or XML data to a site. Go to Ant's web site or SVN repository for details on this if you have complex HTTP requirements.

Sticking with the built-in task, we want to `<get>` the file that we uploaded in section 7.4 with the `<scp>` task.

7.5.3   Performing the download

To download our redistributable file, we need to build a URL to the remote copy. We add a new property to each of the properties files used for SSH uploads. This property, `http.base.url`, contains the base URL for retrievals. Here's the version for the apache site:

```
http.base.url=http://people.apache.org/~${ssh.user}
```

> **NOTE**   Take full advantage of the fact that Ant properties can be used inside property files that Ant reads in. *Don't Repeat Yourself*, as the Pragmatic Programmers say.

To ensure that this property is set, our download target must depend on the ssh-init target to load the server-specific property file, and the checksum target that creates the validation checksums. It uses a `<get>` to get the file, and `<checksum>` in a `<fail>` test to validate it:

```
<target name="http-download" depends="ssh-init,checksum" >
  <basename property="http.filename"
   file="${target.zip}"/>
  <tempfile property="http.download.dest"
    prefix="http" suffix=".zip"
    destDir="${java.io.tmpdir}"/>
```

```
<property name="http.url"
  value="${http.base.url}/${http.filename}" />
<get src="${http.url}" dest="${http.download.dest}"
  verbose="true" />
<fail>
  Downloaded file ${http.download.dest}
  From URL ${http.url}
  does not match its expected checksum
  <condition>
    <not>
      <checksum
        algorithm="sha1" format="MD5SUM"
        property="${target.zip.sha1}"
        file="${http.download.dest}" />
    </not>
  </condition>
</fail>
</target>
```

Because we set the verbose flag on the <get> task, the output includes a progress marker and source and destination information:

```
>ant -f core-chapter-07.xml http-download -Dserver=apache
Buildfile: core-chapter-07.xml

init:

ssh-init:

checksum:

http-download:
  [get] Getting:
  http://people.apache.org/~stevel/diary-core-0.1alpha.zip
  [get] To: /tmp/http1798828968.zip
  [get] .............................................

BUILD SUCCESSFUL
Total time: 2 seconds
```

This output shows that the public web server is serving up the Zip file we uploaded earlier. The SCP upload worked, and the web server is working. This is a fully functional remote distribution, with automated testing alongside the upload operation. If the upload and download targets succeed, we'll know that everything works, without having to do any manual checks.

That completes our four redistribution activities: FTP, SSH/SCP, email, and HTTP. All that's left is to set up the build file so we can run all operations in one single build. If we can do that, we have a completely hands-free distribution process.

7.6 DISTRIBUTION OVER MULTIPLE CHANNELS

We have created a set of targets to distribute the files using FTP, email, and SCP. Now we want to invoke them all, for a one-stop redistribute-everywhere target. This seems straightforward, except for one little problem. How do we run the same targets more than once with different values of the `server` property?

We know we can do this from the command line, with a series of repeated `ant` runs:

```
ant ftp-upload -Dserver=aviemore
ant ftp-upload -Dserver=sourceforge
ant email-announcement
ant scp -Dserver=k2
ant scp -Dserver=apache
```

How do we do this *inside* Ant itself? With the task `<antcall>`, a task that runs any target and its dependencies, potentially with different properties.

7.6.1 Calling targets with `<antcall>`

Normally, Ant decides which order to run targets, based on their declared dependencies. It builds a big graph of all the targets, then it executes them in an order that guarantees that no target will be executed before its dependencies.

This works well, most of the time. Sometimes, however, a different problem comes up. To upload our files to multiple hosts, we need to run the same target, multiple times, with different properties. This is what the `<antcall>` task enables. It takes the name of a target and runs that target and all its dependencies. You can specify new properties and whether to pass down existing property definitions and datatype references.

The `<antcall>` task can call any target in the build file, with any property settings you choose. This makes it equivalent to a subroutine call, except that instead of passing parameters as arguments, you have to define "well known properties." Furthermore, any properties that the called target sets will not be remembered when the call completes.

A good way to view the behavior of `<antcall>` is as if you're actually starting a new version of Ant, setting the target and some properties on the command line. When you use this as a model of the task's behavior, it makes more sense that when you call a target, *its dependent targets are called also*.

To illustrate the behavior, let's use a project containing a target—"do-echo"— that prints out some properties potentially defined by the project's predecessors.

```xml
<project name="antcall" default="do-echo">
  <target name="init">
    <property name="arg3" value="original arg3" />
  </target>

  <target name="do-echo" depends="init">
    <echo>${arg1} - ${arg2} - ${arg3}</echo>
```

```
  </target>
</project>
```

When you call the do-echo target directly, the output should be predictable:

```
init:
do-echo:
    [echo] ${arg1} - ${arg2} - original arg3
```

Now add a new target, which invokes the target via `<antcall>`:

```
<target name="call-echo" depends="init">
  <property name="arg1" value="original arg1" />
  <property name="arg2" value="original arg2" />
  <echo>calling...</echo>
  <antcall target="do-echo">
   <param name="arg1" value="overridden"/>
  </antcall>
  <echo>...returned</echo>
</target>
```

This target defines some properties and then calls the do-echo target with one of the parameters overridden. The `<param>` element inside the `<antcall>` target is a direct equivalent of the `<property>` task: all named parameters become properties in the called target's context, and all methods of assigning properties in that method (value, file, available, resource, location, and refid) can be used. In this declaration, we've used the simple, value-based assignment.

The output of running Ant against that target is

```
init:
call-echo:
    [echo] calling...
init:
do-echo:
    [echo] overridden - original arg2 - original arg3
    [echo] ...returned
```

The first point to notice is that the init target has been called twice, once because call-echo depended upon it, and a second time inside the new `<antcall>` context because do-echo depended upon it.

The second point of interest is that the previously undefined properties, arg1 and arg2, have been set. The arg1 parameter was set by the `<param>` element inside the `<antcall>` declaration; the arg2 parameter *was inherited from the current context*. The final observation is that the final trace message in the call-echo target appears only after the echo call has finished. Ant has executed the entire dependency graph of the do-echo target as a subsidiary build within the new context. This notion of Ant contexts is very similar to that of an *environment* in LISP or Scheme. In those languages, an environment represents the complete set of definitions in which a function is evaluated. Ant's contexts are not so well isolated: Ant runs in a shared JVM; type definitions are global, and only properties and datatype references

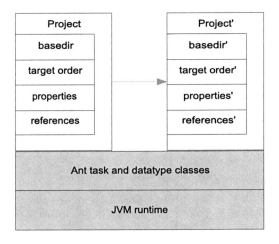

Figure 7.2
**A model of how <antcall>
creates a new project, with
its own internal state**

can be changed within a context. Figure 7.2 illustrates what's taking place. Some parts
of the project are new, but the JVM is still shared.

It's important to remember that all properties set in an <antcall> are local to
that call. Changes to the properties or references of the child project don't propagate
back up the calling build. Information from the parent project can be passed down,
if done carefully.

Managing inheritance in <antcall>

The <antcall> task has one mandatory attribute, target, which names the target to call, and two optional attributes, inheritall and inheritrefs. The
inheritall flag can prevent the task from passing all existing properties down to
the invoke target, that being the default behavior. If the attribute is false, only
new properties defined in the task declaration are passed down. To demonstrate this
behavior, we add another calling target:

```
<target name="call-echo2" depends="init">
  <property name="arg1" value="original arg1" />
  <property name="arg2" value="original arg2" />
  <echo>calling...</echo>
  <antcall target="do-echo"
    inheritall="false">
   <param name="arg1" value="newarg1"/>
  </antcall>
  <echo>...returned</echo>
</target>
```

When you execute this target, the log showed that do-echo didn't know the definition of arg2, as it was not passed down:

```
[echo] newarg1 - ${arg2} - original arg3
```

Note that arg3 is still defined, because the second invocation of the init target will
have set it; all dependent tasks are executed in an <antcall>.

Regardless of the inheritance flag setting, Ant always passes down any properties set on the command line. This means that anything manually set on the command line stays set, regardless of how you invoke a target. Take, for example, the command line

```
ant call-echo2 -Darg2=predefined -Darg1=defined
```

This results in an output message of

```
[echo] defined  - predefined - original arg3
```

Any properties defined on the command line *always* override anything set in the build file, no matter how hard the build file tries to avoid it. This is actually very useful when you do want to control a complex build process from the command line, as you don't need to care about how the build file is implemented internally.

You can also pass references down to the invoked target. If you set `inheritrefs="true"`, all existing references are accessible in the new context. You can create new references from existing ones by including a `<reference>` element in the `<antcall>` declaration, stating the name of a new reference to be created using the value of an existing path or other reference:

```
<reference refid="compile.classpath"
  torefid="exec.classpath" />
```

Creating new references is useful if the invoked target needs to use some path or patternset as one of its customizable parameters.

For the distribution problem, `<antcall>` will let us run the distribution targets against different servers by calling the targets multiple times, with the `server` property set to a different server on each call. We just need a single target to issue the calls.

7.6.2   Distributing with <antcall>

Listing 7.3 shows a target that runs each of the `"scp"` and `"ftp-upload"` targets twice, each time with a new destination set in the `server` property.

Listing 7.3   Using <antcall> to manage a series of distribution actions

```
<target name="distribute" depends="email-announcement">
  <antcall target="ftp">
    <param name="server" value="knoydart"/>
  </antcall>
  <antcall target="ftp-upload">
    <param name="server" value="sourceforge"/>
  </antcall>
  <antcall target="scp">
    <param name="server" value="k2"/>
  </antcall>
  <antcall target="scp">
    <param name="server" value="apache"/>
  </antcall>
</target>
```

If we had made all the distribution targets dependent on the complete compile, test, and package run, this would trigger four separate rebuilds of the entire application, which would make for a slow build indeed. Having the minimal dependencies on each <antcall> target keeps the build fast and guarantees that the same artifacts are distributed to every server. Once you start using <antcall>, the normal dependency rules of Ant are thrown out the window.

We're not going to show the entire trace of the build, because it's both verbose and repetitive. Here's a bit of the build—the two FTP "antcalls":

```
init:

ftp-init:

ftp-upload:
     [echo] FTP target is knoydart
     [ftp] sending files
     [ftp] 8 files sent

init:

ftp-init:

ftp-upload:
     [echo] FTP target is upload.sourceforge.net
     [ftp] sending files
     [ftp] 8 files sent

BUILD SUCCESSFUL
Total time: 1 minute 40 seconds
```

As you can see, the ftp-upload target and its two predecessors, init and ftp-init, have run twice within a single build. All told, it took less than two minutes to publish the packages to two local and two remote sites, and to email out the news. This is what distribution should be: fully automated and available at the push of a button.

The build also shows how to use <antcall>, namely when you want to invoke the same target(s) more than once, perhaps with different properties. Any project that uses <antcall> as the main way of chaining targets together isn't using Ant or <antcall> correctly.

Now, there's one more aspect of <antcall> to look at: determining when its use is inappropriate.

Best practices: effective <antcall>

In most projects, <antcall> is a rare occurrence. If you see it a lot, something has gone wrong. The common mistake is to use it to order all stages of a build:

```
<target name="main">
  <antcall target="compile" />
  <antcall target="jar" />
```

```
      <antcall target="test" />
      <antcall target="zip" />
      <antcall target="ship" />
</target>
```

As Ant creates a new project on every `<antcall>`, the build will be slow and memory hungry, with common targets being called repeatedly.

Except for targets that you want to call more than once, especially with different parameters, let Ant handle the order of targets by listing them in the `dependencies` attributes of other tasks.

7.7 SUMMARY

Distribution is a common activity in a build process, which means that it should be automated. We've distributed our diary Zip and tar files in three ways—by FTP using `<ftp>`, by email using `<mail>`, and by SSH with `<scp>` and `<sshexec>`. We've also used `<get>` to retrieve a published archive, then `<antcall>` to chain everything together into a big distribution activity.

A key theme in this process is security. Nobody should be running programs from sites or people that they don't trust. MD5 and SHA1 checksums can help, as they provide a basis for verifying that files haven't been tampered with en route.

The chapter also introduced the `<antcall>` task. This task lets you re-enter your build file, calling a named target with any properties you choose. The `<antcall>` task is powerful and useful for some operations. However, it does make a build slower and more complex. Use `<antcall>` sparingly, remember that a target's dependencies are also invoked, and don't expect properties to be passed back to the caller.

With distribution out of the way, we've covered the entire process of using Ant to build, test, package, run, and distribute a Java program. What we haven't done is shown a single build file that does all of these activities. It's time for a quick review of all that we need Ant to do, with a single build file to do everything. This review also will let us discuss how to write usable build files and how to migrate to Ant.

CHAPTER 8

Putting it all together

We've introduced the basic concepts, tasks, and types of Ant. We've shown how it reads build files containing targets and tasks, showing Ant what needs to be done to build a project. We've looked at Ant's tasks, targets, properties, and datatypes, and we've shown you how to automate the build and compile, test, package, and distribute a Java project. You should now be able to create build files to accomplish the most common build-related tasks, such as `<javac>`, `<copy>`, `<zip>` and `<jar>`.

What we haven't shown you is a single build file that incorporates all these things. This chapter provides a higher-level view of our sample application's build process, reviews the techniques that we've already presented, and introduces some new concepts. The first concept is the most important: the art of writing good build files.

8.1   HOW TO WRITE GOOD BUILD FILES

An Ant build file is meant to automate the process by which you build, test, distribute, and deploy your software. It should not become a maintenance project all of its own. If you spend more time maintaining the build file than writing code, tests, or documentation, something has gone wrong. There are several key ideas that we want to convey with our build file examples.

Begin with the end in mind

Your build file exists to build something. Start with that goal and work backwards as you write your targets. The goal of our build file is to build a distributable JAR library that we can use in other build files and publish via SSH and email. That gives us a `dist` target to create the distributables and a `publish` target to publish the file. The `dist` target will need code that we `compile`, `test`, and `package`, giving us more targets and the dependencies between them. And, of course, we need a `clean` target to clean up. You can work backwards from the final goals into the stages of the build, each stage becoming a target. Into the targets you can place the tasks needed to reach the current goal.

Integrate tests with the build

We cannot overemphasize the importance of automated testing. By putting testing into your build processes early, developers can write and execute tests without having to worry about the mechanics of how to run them. The easier you make testing, the more tests get written, and the more tests get run. This will directly improve the quality of the code and, hopefully, result in something you can ship sooner rather than later.

Keep it portable

Ant runs on many platforms, hiding many details such as what the operating system uses as a file separator or how different platforms report errors differently. As a result, build files are inherently portable. Be wary of using <exec> and <apply>, as they can reduce portability.

Enable customization

Ant properties allow for user, project, and per-build customizations. Individual developers can override options in the build file by editing their `build.properties` files or by setting options with -D arguments on the command line. You can also adapt to different machines by reading environment variables and Java system properties.

These are all practices that our example build files follow.

8.2   BUILDING THE DIARY LIBRARY

We're writing the core classes of a diary application, classes to represent a calendar with events. This library can be used in other applications once it's packaged, tested, and distributed. This chapter's build file does all of that, integrating everything covered in the previous chapters. It will compile and sign the JAR, run the tests, package everything into Zip files, then upload these to a remote site. For a single library, it's complete.

8.2.1   Starting the project

Projects begin with a name, a description, and, optionally, a default target. Always give build files a unique name to avoid confusion when you work across projects. Some text in the <description> element is useful, as it's printed when Ant is passed the -p or the -projecthelp parameter.

```xml
<project name="core-diary" default="default">

<description>
  This build file compiles, tests, packages and
  distributes the core library of the diary application.
</description>
```

You can have any name for the default target; we often use `default` because it avoids having to remember what the default target is when you ask for it on the command line:

```
ant clean default
```

This command asks for the `clean` target, then the `default` one. Ant will first run `clean` and its dependencies, then `default` with its dependencies. Any shared target will be executed twice.

After the description come the public entry point targets and the initialization targets.

8.2.2 The public entry points

The *entry point* targets are those targets we expect people to call on the command line or our IDE. All of our entry points have `description` attributes. This ensures that they're always listed in the project help listings, and Ant-aware IDEs often highlight them. Listing 8.1 shows the main entry points for the project: `default`, `dist`, `publish`, `test`, and `clean`.

Listing 8.1 The entry-point targets for the build file

```xml
<target name="default" depends="dist"
  description="package everything and checksum it" />

<target name="dist" depends="package-everything,checksum"
  description="create the distributables" />

<target name="publish"
  depends="email-announcement-html"
  description="publish the files">
  <antcall target="scp">
    <param name="server" value="k2"/>
  </antcall>
  <antcall target="scp">
    <param name="server" value="apache"/>
  </antcall>
  <antcall target="ftp-upload">
    <param name="server" value="knoydart"/>
  </antcall>
  <antcall target="ftp-upload">
    <param name="server"
        value="sourceforge"/>
  </antcall>
</target>
```

This target uses `<antcall>` to upload the files to remote SSH and FTP Servers

```
<target name="test" depends="unit-tests"
    description="compile and run the tests"/>

<target name="clean"
  description="Delete all generated files">
  <delete dir="${build.dir}"/>
  <delete dir="${dist.dir}"/>
  <delete dir="${test.data.dir}"/>
  <delete dir="${test.reports.dir}"/>
</target>
```

Delete all directories into which things are built

The final target, `clean`, uses properties that haven't been declared yet, and doesn't depend upon any other target. All the properties it uses are to be declared outside of any target, later on in the build file. Ant executes all out-of-target tasks before running any target, regardless of the relative location of targets and out-of-target tasks in the file. This means that we can reorder targets for a most readable file, placing entry points ahead of the rest of the build file.

8.2.3 Setting up the build

The next portion of the build file is dedicated to setting up the build by defining the main properties, paths and other datatypes of the project. More datatypes may be defined inside targets; there's no general rule for when to declare properties and types. Having everything at the start makes it easier to locate declarations, but in-target declarations define properties closer to where they're used, and allow you to incorporate the output of previous tasks and targets.

We like control of our build files, even if the original author felt they knew the right answers to everything. How do we manage this? By having the build file load an optional properties file, `build.properties`. This is the key to enabling customization. We can tune the build file to our needs by setting properties in this file before the rest of the build file gets a look in:

```
<property file="build.properties" />
```

Developers may not have a `build.properties` file, so the build file must be able to work without it being present. There must be `<property>` tasks for every property the build file needs, with `build.properties` entirely optional.

Next we define the common properties of the project, the directories into which things go, and any other options we want to define in one place. Here's listing 8.2, containing the relevant tasks.

Listing 8.2   Setting Ant properties to the locations and values of the build file

```
<property name="build.dir" location="build" />
<property name="build.classes.dir"
  location="${build.dir}/classes" />
<property name="test.dir" location="${build.dir}/test" />
<property name="test.classes.dir"
  location="${test.dir}/classes" />
```

```
<property name="test.data.dir" location="${test.dir}/data" />
<property name="test.reports.dir"
  location="${test.dir}/reports" />

<!-- set up distribution targets -->
<property name="dist.dir" location="dist" />
<property name="dist.doc.dir" location="${dist.dir}/doc" />

<property name="javadoc.dir" location="${dist.dir}/api" />

<property name="project.name" value="diary-core" />
<property name="project.version" value="0.1alpha" />     ⟵❶
<property name="project.name-ver"
  value="${project.name}-${project.version}" />
<property name="target.name"
  value="${project.name-ver}.jar" />
<property name="target.jar"
  location="${dist.dir}/${target.name}" />

<property name="target.zip"
  location="${dist.dir}/${project.name-ver}.zip" />
<property name="src.zip"
  location="${dist.dir}/${project.name-ver}-src.zip" />
<property name="unjar.dir"
  location="${build.dir}/unjar"/>

<property name="build.debug" value="true"/>

<!-- what is our fork policy for junit -->
<property name="junit.fork" value="true"/>
<property name="junit.forkmode" value="once"/>
<property name="test.suite"
  value="d1.core.test.AllTests" />

<!-- pattern of source files to copy -->
<property name="source.files.tocopy"
value="**/*.properties,**/*.dtd,**/*.xml,**/*.xsd,**/*.jpg" />
  <property name="bin.dir" location="bin" />
<property name="unix.scripts"
  value="**/*.sh,**/*.pl,**/*.py" />
<property name="dos.scripts"
  value="**/*.bat,**/*.cmd" />

<property name="unzip.dir" location="${build.dir}/unzip" />
<property name="unzip.bin.dir" location="${unzip.dir}/bin" />
<property name="unzip.src.dir" location="${unzip.dir}/src" />
<property name="untar.dir" location="${build.dir}/untar" />
<property name="unjar.dir" location="${build.dir}/unjar"/>
<property name="main.class"value="d1.core.Diagnostics"/>
```

This listing shows the central definition of most properties used in the build. They are properties that developers may want to override in their build.properties file.

For example, the version of the program is defined in this list ❶. We could change it from 0.1alpha to 1.0 by editing `build.properties` to override it:

```
project.version=1.0
```

The one thing we cannot reliably do in a properties file is set relative file locations. Whenever Ant encounters a `<property>` task that uses the location attribute, such as `location=".."`, it resolves the location to an absolute path. If the build file ran in `/home/ant/diary/core`, then the value of the property would be `"/home/ant/diary/"`.

What would happen if we set the `build.properties` file to a different relative path?

```
parent=../..,
```

After Ant loads the file, the value of `parent` would be `"../.."`. It would still be a relative path. For a reliable build, you have to declare the full path:

```
parent=/home/ant/diary/newdir
```

This declaration ensures that the path is absolute, however it's used.

After the property definitions come the datatypes, the paths, and filesets.

Declaring the datatypes

In listing 8.3, we set the compile and test classpaths by chaining each path together for reduced maintenance. Any JAR added to `compile.classpath` is picked up by the rest.

Listing 8.3 **Declaring the datatypes for the project: the paths and filesets that will be referred to by `refid` references in tasks.**

```
<path id="compile.classpath">
  <fileset dir="lib">
    <include name="*.jar"/>
  </fileset>
</path>

<path id="test.compile.classpath">
  <path refid="compile.classpath"/>
  <pathelement location="${target.jar}"/>
</path>

<path id="test.classpath">
  <path refid="test.compile.classpath"/>
  <pathelement location="${test.classes.dir}"/>
</path>

<path id="test.forking.classpath">
  <path refid="test.classpath"/>
  <pathelement path="${java.class.path}"/>
</path>
```

```
<patternset id="failing.tests">
  <exclude unless="run.failing.tests"
    name="d1/core/test/JavaAssertTest.*"/>
</patternset>

<fileset id="ftp.upload.fileset" dir="${dist.dir}">
  <include name="*.zip"/>
  <include name="*.zip.sha1"/>
  <include name="*.tar.gz"/>
  <include name="*.tar.gz.sha1"/>
</fileset>
```

We have to make sure that all paths, patternsets, filesets, and other datatypes have different id attributes. It's OK to clash with property names, but not with the ID of another datatype.

We also define a timestamp here for inserting into generated text files.

```
<tstamp>
  <format property="timestamp.isoformat"
    pattern="yyyy-mm-dd'T'HH:mm:ss" locale="en"/>
</tstamp>
```

This definition will set the timestamp.isoformat property to a time such as 2006-12-22T17:52:93, which can then be used in messages and generated text documents.

None of these out-of-target tasks have any side effects. Any activity that does, such as creating a directory or compiling source, has been moved into a target. Why? Because whenever Ant runs any build file, even just to get the -p target listing, it executes all tasks outside of a target. It's a bit unexpected if something as minor as running ant -p triggers some action such as creating all the output directories.

We tuck all such actions safely away in our init target:

```
<target name="init">
  <mkdir dir="${build.dir.dir}"/>
  <mkdir dir="${build.classes.dir}"/>
  <mkdir dir="${dist.dir}"/>
  <mkdir dir="${dist.doc.dir}"/>
  <mkdir dir="${javadoc.dir}"/>
</target>
```

This target creates the main directories of the build. It doesn't bother to create all the directories, such as those for test results and reports. We've chosen to leave those to the targets that run the tests. That's just a personal preference. It does create the build/compile directory for compiled classes, because compiling the Java source is the next action in the build.

8.2.4 Compiling and testing

Compiling and testing are the core features of most Ant builds, just as they are the core of most Java projects. Listing 8.4 combines the work of chapters 2, 4, and 5 to compile the code, create a JAR, and test against that JAR.

The classpath used at compile time is that of the `compile.classpath` path datatype declared previously in listing 8.3; it must include all libraries that we need.

Listing 8.4   Compiling the source and creating a JAR file

```
<target name="compile" depends="init">
  <condition property="build.debuglevel"
     value="lines,source"
     else="lines,vars,source" >
    <isset property="release.build" />
  </condition>
  <echo level="verbose">debug level=${build.debuglevel}</echo>
  <javac destdir="${build.classes.dir}"
    debug="true"
    debuglevel="${build.debuglevel}"
    includeAntRuntime="false"
    srcdir="src">
    <classpath refid="compile.classpath"/>
  </javac>
  <copy todir="${build.classes.dir}">
      <fileset dir="src"
        includes="${source.files.tocopy}"/>
    </copy>
  </target>

<target name="jar"
    description="create the JAR file"
    depends="compile" >
  <property name="manifest.mf"
    location="${build.dir}/manifest.mf" />
  <manifest file="${manifest.mf}" >
    <attribute name="Built-By" value="${user.name}"/>
    <attribute name="Sealed" value="true"/>
    <attribute name="Built-On" value="${timestamp.isoformat}"/>
    <attribute name="Main-Class" value="${main.class}"/>
  </manifest>
  <jar destfile="${target.jar}"
    manifest="${manifest.mf}">
    <fileset dir="${build.classes.dir}"/>
  </jar>
</target>

<target name="unjar" depends="init" >
  <unjar
```

```
      src="${target.jar}"
      dest="${unjar.dir}">
  </unjar>
</target>
```

The `compile` target also copies over all resources from the source directory into
`build/classes`; the `jar` target creates the JAR from this directory. The JAR is
ready to be tested, which is the role of the targets of listing 8.5.

Listing 8.5   Running the unit tests and creating the reports

```
<target name="test-init" depends="jar">
  <mkdir dir="${test.classes.dir}"/>
  <delete dir="${test.data.dir}"/>
  <delete dir="${test.reports.dir}"/>
  <mkdir dir="${test.data.dir}"/>
  <mkdir dir="${test.reports.dir}"/>
</target>
```
**Create the test classes and
data directories, deleting
the data directories first to
clean out old results**

```
<target name="test-compile" depends="compile,test-init">
  <javac destdir="${test.classes.dir}"
    debug="true"
    includeAntRuntime="yes"
    srcdir="test">
    <classpath refid="test.compile.classpath"/>
  </javac>
  <copy todir="${test.classes.dir}">
    <fileset dir="test" includes="${source.files.tocopy}"/>
  </copy>
</target>
```

```
<target name="unit-tests" depends="test-compile">
  <junit printsummary="false"
    errorProperty="test.failed"
    failureProperty="test.failed"
    fork="${junit.fork}"
    forkmode="${junit.forkmode}">
```
**Run junit
logging failures
to a property**
```
    <classpath refid="test.forking.classpath" />
    <assertions enableSystemAssertions="true">
     <enable package="d1.core"/>
     <enable />
     <disable class="d1.core.Events"/>
    </assertions>
```
**Assertions are turned on
except for one class**
```
    <sysproperty key="debug" value="true"/>
    <sysproperty key="data.dir" file="./data"/>
```
**Pass down
properties**
```
    <formatter type="brief" usefile="false"/>
    <formatter type="xml"/>
    <test name="${testcase}" todir="${test.data.dir}"
      if="testcase"/>
```
Run one test

```
    <batchtest todir="${test.data.dir}"
        unless="testcase">
      <fileset dir="${test.classes.dir}" >
        <include name="**/test/*Test.class"/>
        <patternset refid="failing.tests" />
      </fileset>
    </batchtest>
  </junit>

  <junitreport todir="${test.data.dir}">
    <fileset dir="${test.data.dir}">
      <include name="TEST-*.xml"/>
    </fileset>
    <report format="frames"
      todir="${test.reports.dir}"/>
  </junitreport>
  <fail if="test.failed">
  Tests failed. Check ${test.reports.dir}
  </fail>
</target>
```

Run all test cases
called *Test except
those known to fail

Create the HTML
test report

Fail if any of the
tests failed

In a test-centric process, these test targets are key. Only when all tests are working can we move on to the next stage: creating a distribution.

8.2.5   Packaging and creating a distribution

The distribution targets create the documentation and the redistributable files. We've chosen to only distribute Zip files to keep the build file leaner.

Listing 8.6 shows the first bit of work: getting the JavaDocs and other documentation into shape, converting the line endings on text files scripts into the right format for the target systems, and copying the patched files into a directory where they can be added to the Zip files.

Listing 8.6   Preparing the documentation and scripts

```
<target name="javadocs" depends="compile"
  description="make the java docs" >
  <javadoc
    access="private"
    destdir="${javadoc.dir}"
    packagenames="d1.*"
    sourcepath="src"
    windowtitle="${ant.project.name}"
    failonerror="true">
    <classpath refid="compile.classpath"/>
  </javadoc>
</target>

<target name="dist-docs" depends="init"
  description="patch documents while copying" >
```

Create the
javadocs

```xml
  <tstamp/>
  <copy todir="${dist.doc.dir}" overwrite="true">
    <fileset dir="doc" includes="**/*.html"/>
    <filterset>
      <filter token="DATE" value="${DSTAMP}"/>
      <filter token="TIME" value="${TSTAMP}"/>
    </filterset>
  </copy>
  <copy todir="${dist.doc.dir}" overwrite="true">
    <fileset dir="doc" includes="**/*.txt"/>
    <filterset begintoken="[[" endtoken ="]]">
      <filter token="TIMESTAMP"
          value="${timestamp.isoformat}"/>
    </filterset>
  </copy>
</target>

<target name="scripts" depends="init">
  <copy todir="${dist.dir}" overwrite="true">
    <fileset dir="bin"
      includes="${unix.scripts},${dos.scripts}"/>
    <filterset begintoken="[[" endtoken ="]]">
      <filter token="TARGET.NAME"
        value="${target.name}"/>
    </filterset>
  </copy>
  <fixcrlf srcdir="${dist.dir}" eol="unix"
    includes="${unix.scripts}" />
  <fixcrlf srcdir="${dist.dir}" eol="dos"
    includes="${dos.scripts}" />
  <chmod dir="${dist.dir}"  perm="a+x"
    includes="${unix.scripts}" />
</target>

<target name="fix-docs" depends="dist-docs,javadocs">
  <property name="readme.windows.file"
    location="${dist.doc.dir}/readme.txt" />
  <property name="readme.unix.file"
    location="${dist.doc.dir}/README" />
  <copy file="${readme.windows.file}"
    tofile="${readme.unix.file}"/>
  <fixcrlf eol="crlf" file="${readme.windows.file}"
    tab="remove" tablength="4" />
  <fixcrlf eol="lf" file="${readme.unix.file}"
    tab="remove" tablength="2" />
</target>

<target name="docs" depends="fix-docs"/>
```

Copy HTML files with filtering

Copy and filter text files

Replace JAR file name in scripts and batch files

Fix script's line endings and permissions

After running these targets, the files are all ready for packaging, with both Windows and Unix versions of all the text files. We could avoid most of the fixup if all of our documentation was in HTML files, which are cross-platform.

Alongside the text files and JavaDocs, the distribution takes the source and the JAR file, a file that we want to sign.

Signing the JAR files

Signing the JAR file authenticates it and enables uses such as Java Web Start deployment. The build file uses the <input> task to prompt for a password, rather than hard code the password into the build file. This is where developer customization in the build.properties file really kicks in. If the keystore.password property is set to the password there, the <input> prompt is skipped and the signing is fully automated. Listing 8.7 shows the targets.

Listing 8.7   Signing the JAR files

```
<target name="init-security">
  <property name="keystore.dir"
   location="${user.home}/.secret" />
  <mkdir dir="${keystore.dir}" />
  <chmod file="${keystore.dir}" perm="700"/>
  <property name="keystore"
    location="${keystore.dir}/local.keystore" />
  <property file="${keystore.dir}/keystore.properties" />
  <property name="keystore.alias" value="code.signer"/>
</target>

<target name="get-password" depends="init-security" >
  <input addproperty="keystore.password" >password:</input>
</target>

<target name="create-signing-key" depends="get-password">
  <genkey
    alias="${keystore.alias}"
    keystore="${keystore}"
    storepass="${keystore.password}"
    validity="366" >
    <dname>
      <param name="CN" value="autosigner"/>
      <param name="OU" value="Steve and Erik"/>
      <param name="O"  value="Apache Software Foundation"/>
      <param name="C"  value="EU"/>
    </dname>
  </genkey>
</target>

<target name="delete-keystore" depends="init-security" >
  <delete file="${keystore}" />
</target>
```

```
<target name="sign-jar" depends="jar,get-password">
  <fail>
    no keystore ${keystore}, run create-signing-key " >
    <condition>
      <not><available file="${keystore}" /></not>
    </condition>
  </fail>
  <signjar jar="${target.jar}"
    alias="${keystore.alias}"
    keystore="${keystore}"
    storepass="${keystore.password}" />
</target>
```

Many projects skip the signing stage. However, it's hard to retro-fit security into a Java project later on, because signed JARs are loaded differently. If there's any possibility of needing signed JARs, it's better to start signing sooner rather than later.

With the JAR signed, the Zip files can be created.

Creating the Zip files

The final packaging activity uses the `<zip>` task to create the binary and source Zip files. This is the work of the targets in listing 8.8.

Listing 8.8   Creating the Zip files

```
<target name="package-everything"
  description="package everything"
  depends="create-src-zipfile,create-bin-zipfile" />

<target name="create-bin-zipfile"
  depends="sign-jar,docs,scripts"
  description="create the distributable Zip files">
  <zip destFile="${target.zip}" >
    <zipfileset file="${target.jar}"
      prefix="${project.name-ver}" />
    <zipfileset dir="${dist.doc.dir}"
      includes="**/*"
      prefix="${project.name-ver}/docs" />
    <zipfileset dir="${javadoc.dir}"
      includes="**/*"
      prefix="${project.name-ver}/docs/api" />
  </zip>
</target>

<target name="unzip-bin-zipfile" depends="create-bin-zipfile">
  <unzip src="${target.zip}" dest="${unzip.bin.dir}" />
</target>

<target name="create-src-zipfile" depends="sign-jar">
  <zip destfile="${src.zip}">
```

```
    <zipfileset file="${target.jar}"
      prefix="${project.name-ver}" />
    <zipfileset dir="."
      includes="src/**,test/**,doc/**,*.xml"
      prefix="${project.name-ver}" />
  </zip>
</target>

<target name="unzip-src-zipfile" depends="create-src-zipfile">
  <unzip src="${src.zip}" dest="${unzip.src.dir}" />
</target>
```

We have two targets, unzip-src-zipfile and unzip-bin-zipfile, that will expand the Zip files and let you see what you created. Once you start building Zip, JAR, or tar files using filesets from many places, it's easy to pull too many or too few files into the artifacts. Having a look at what's produced is always wise, especially before you cut a release. Nobody wants to upload or email Zip files that accidentally have 16MB of unneeded JAR files.

8.2.6 Distribution

The diary project distributes its Zip files by emailing them out to known recipients and publishing them to a server using <scp>, the secure copy task. These targets don't depend on the packaging targets—they rely on the artifacts already existing. By removing the dependencies, we can use <antcall> to invoke the targets with different properties, which lets us distribute the same Zip files to multiple destinations.

What we do need is a target that creates the checksums for the most recent Zip files.

```
<target name="checksum" depends="init">
  <checksum file="${target.zip}"
    algorithm="sha1" format="MD5SUM"  />
  <checksum file="${src.zip}"
    algorithm="sha1" format="MD5SUM" />
  <checksum file="${target.zip}"
    algorithm="sha1" format="MD5SUM"
    property="target.zip.sha1"/>
  <checksum file="${src.zip}" algorithm="sha1" format="MD5SUM"
    property="src.zip.sha1"/>
</target>
```

Because the <checksum> task fails if the file attribute names a nonexistent file, this target implicitly checks that the Zip files are present. This check stops us from uploading files that haven't yet been created.

The email announcement

Listing 8.9 contains the target to email an announcement from section 7.3; it sends out an HTML message and the Zip file.

Listing 8.9   The target to email the Zip file with a covering note

```
<target name="email-announcement-html" depends="checksum">
  <mail
    tolist="${email.to}"
    from="${email.from}"
    subject="New release of ${target.name}"
    mailhost="${email.server}"
    mailport="${email.port}"
    ssl="${email.ssl}"
    user="${email.user}"
    password="${email.password}"
    messageMimeType="text/html">
    <message><![CDATA[
<p>
  Here is a new build of ${target.name}
  The SHA1 checksum of the file is:
  </p>
  <pre>
      ${target.zip.sha1}
  </pre>
  <p><i>-The development team</i></p>
]]></message>
    <fileset file="${target.zip}" />
    <fileset file="${target.zip}.sha1" />
  </mail>
</target>
```

Some organizations, including Apache, sign their redistributable packages and emails with GNU Privacy Guard, to authenticate the checksums and provide an audit trail. This behavior could be addressed with an <exec> call.

After the email comes the work to upload the files to a remote site.

File upload

The targets in listing 8.10 to upload files using <scp> are from section 7.4. After the upload, we copy it back to see that the checksums match.

Listing 8.10   Targets to upload the files to a remote server

```
<target name="ssh-init" depends="init">
  <fail unless="server">Set the "server" property!</fail>
  <property name="ssh.propfile"
    location="secure/${server}.ssh.properties" />
  <loadproperties srcFile="${ssh.propfile}" />
  <property name="tmp.dir" location="${build.dir}/tmp" />
  <mkdir dir="${tmp.dir}" />
</target>

<target name="ssh-mkdirs" depends="ssh-init" >
  <sshexec host="${ssh.server}"
```

```
            username="${ssh.user}"
            passphrase="${ssh.passphrase}"
            keyfile="${ssh.keyfile}"
            command="mkdir -p ${ssh.dir}"/>
  </target>

  <!-- insert trust="true" to turn on trust -->
  <target name="scp-upload" depends="ssh-init,ssh-mkdirs" >
    <echo>SCP target is ${ssh.server}</echo>
    <property name="ssh.path"
      value="${ssh.user}@${ssh.server}:${ssh.dir}" />
    <scp remoteToDir="${ssh.path}"
      passphrase="${ssh.passphrase}"
      keyfile="${ssh.keyfile}"
      verbose="${ssh.verbose}" >
        <fileset refid="ftp.upload.fileset"/>
    </scp>
  </target>

  <target name="ssh-chmod" depends="scp-upload" >
    <sshexec host="${ssh.server}"
      username="${ssh.user}"
      passphrase="${ssh.passphrase}"
      keyfile="${ssh.keyfile}"
      command="chmod a+r public_html/*"/>
  </target>

  <target name="scp-download" depends="ssh-init,checksum" >
    <basename property="remote.f" file="${target.zip}"/>
    <property name="ssh.download.src"
     value="${ssh.user}@${ssh.server}:${ssh.dir}/${remote.f}" />
    <tempfile property="ssh.download.dest" prefix="ssh"
      suffix=".zip" destDir="${java.io.tmpdir}"/>
    <echo>
    Downloading ${ssh.download.src}
    to ${ssh.download.dest}
    </echo>
    <fail>
      <condition>
        <not>
          <checksum
            algorithm="sha1" format="MD5SUM"
            property="${target.zip.sha1}"
            file="${ssh.download.dest}"/>
        </not>
      </condition>
      Checksum failure for ${ssh.download.dest}
    </fail>
  </target>

  <target name="scp" depends="ssh-chmod,scp-download"
    description="upload the file then download it using SCP"/>
```

We've left out the follow-on targets from section 7.5, which assumed that the scp-upload target published the files on a web page and used `<get>` to retrieve them. Projects that do publish this way should add the `http-download` target from that section to round off the upload. For this build file, the scp targets are the last targets in the project.

Closing the file

At the end of the file, the root element of the XML document must be closed, to make the document "well-formed XML."

```
</project>
```

We cannot add any tasks, targets, or even comments after this closing tag.

That's it! We've just walked through a complete build file, one that encodes the entire build, test, and distribution process of a library. It shows how we've used the tool in one of our projects. Now, how are you going to use it in your project?

8.3   ADOPTING ANT

When you use Ant, you get the opportunity to write a build file that describes how your project is built, tested, distributed, and deployed. It may be a brand new application, or it may be a project that already builds under an IDE or by some other means. You need to bring up the XML editor, and, starting with an empty `<project>` element, write the targets and tasks to automate your build process.

When you start with a new build file, you have complete control as to what it will do. Where should you begin? Look at what the project has to deliver, and think about how Ant can help you do that.

Determine your deliverables

A software project *delivers* things. Usually the application or library is the main deliverable, perhaps packaged in a Zip or tar file. If you're planning to host your application on a server, your deliverable needs to be a WAR or EAR file, which you then have to deploy. Many projects have non-code deliverables, such as test results and handwritten and JavaDoc-created documents,

The type of application you're writing determines what the deliverables are and how you deploy or deliver these outputs. Table 8.1 shows the outputs and distribution routes for common project types.

These are the things Ant has to handle. It has to create the deliverables and the *artifacts*, and then distribute or deploy them.

As an example, let's imagine a calendar application that uses the diary library. It will have a Swing GUI with supporting code and some HTML documentation. We'll package it as a JAR, then a Zip file, and distribute it by an SSH upload. Each of these activities becomes a stage in the build.

Table 8.1 Common application types, their deliverables, and deployment routes. Ant can handle all of this, with help from other tools.

Application Type	Deliverables	Distribution
Client application	JAR, Zip, tar; PDF, and HTML documentation	Upload to web site; email; Java Web Start
Applet	JAR, documentation	Upload to web server
Web application	WAR, code+JSP, SQL data	Copy to web server; set up database
Enterprise application	EAR file with JAR and WAR files, SQL data	Copy to application server; set up database

Determine the build stages

Once you have deliverables, you can list the stages needed to make them and the dependencies between them. These become your targets. Start with the common states a project can be in, such as `compiled`, `tested`, and `deployed`, and think of the steps needed to achieve these goals. Each major step in the build should have its own target for individual testing and use.

For our example client application, the entry-point targets would be `all`, `test`, `dist`, `upload`, and `clean`. We would have internal targets: `compile`, `archive`, `doc`, and `init`, with more to come when needed. The `compile` and `test` targets are central to our development process, as we want to run the tests whenever we build the application.

Plan the tests

It's never too early to start thinking about testing. In Java, JUnit and sometimes TestNG are the foundations for testing, adding extension libraries to test specific technologies. For our hypothetical client application, we have to test a Swing GUI. A good model-view split lets us test the model with normal unit tests, leaving only the view as a problem. An early action in the project will be to browse to explore the current options for testing Swing applications. With luck, we should be able to perform the core GUI tests from a `<junit>` call.

The test will form its own source tree, alongside the application source. This forces us to think about what makes a good directory structure for the program sources and for the generated files.

Lay out the source

We need to think about the source layout right from the outset. In particular, we should think about the Java package structure. For our application, we could put everything under `org.antbook.calendar`, but split the Swing GUI from the model, with packages such as `model` and `view` underneath. Doing so prevents contamination of the model by the view.

Ant likes Java source to be stored in a directory tree matching the package hierarchy—here org/antbook/calendar—with /model and /view underneath. Dependency checking relies on this layout.

If you want to access package-scoped classes and methods, you need to place tests into the same package as the classes they test. As we've explained before, we like to put our tests into sub-packages because it forces us to use the public APIs and it lets us test even when our JARs are signed. We'll place all tests in child packages called test.

The test classes should all follow a standard naming pattern, so that a wildcard such as **/test/*Test.class can include them in <junit>. In our client application, we would have the layout illustrated in figure 8.1.

The build directory will be the destination for all intermediate files. Having a single place for them makes cleaning up easy; a <delete dir="${build.dir}" />

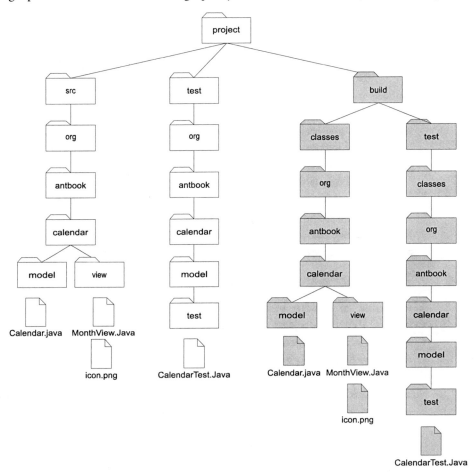

Figure 8.1 How to lay out classes in a large project. The files and directories in white are the source; those in grey are created in the build. Source and test source code trees are split up and compiled into different directories. Unit Test cases are in /test packages.

will do the trick. Again, there are separate trees for the source and test files, so we don't get test classes in the redistributable JAR. We also need to save space for the XML test logs and the resulting HTML test reports, all of which can find a place under `build/test`.

With the directory layout and basic design of the build in place, we can now create the build file for the project.

Creating the core build file

We can start a project by taking a team's standard build file and customizing it. If no such file exists, we start by coding the basic set of targets needed to get everyone building and testing code. Other targets can follow as the need arises.

We don't need to wait for the code before we start on the build file. With no source for compiling or testing, Ant will still create the output directories and build an empty JAR file.

At this point, we have the foundation for our project: now it's time to start coding.

Evolving the build file

Nobody in the team should be afraid of editing the build file. As they do so, they should try to keep the build file concise yet readable by using only a few pages to tell Ant how to build the project. A build file for a project gets big and complex only if the build process itself is complicated. When that happens, there are ways to manage the complexity, ways we shall explore in later chapters.

One problem with editing a build file is knowing which tasks to use. Start by looking in the Ant documentation: there are so many tasks, you may find what you want. There are also many tasks written by other people, tasks you can add to a build. We'll start exploring these tasks in chapter 9 once we've finished looking at how best to adopt Ant. The next problem is how to move an existing project to the tool.

8.4 BUILDING AN EXISTING PROJECT UNDER ANT

Migrating an existing project to Ant is possibly harder than starting with a new project. Existing projects already have deliverables such as JAR and Zip files, test reports, and deployment processes that Ant needs to automate. You aren't in a position to make radical changes to the application design or directory layout; you rarely have much time for the migration; and if you break something, the team will give you a hard time. This makes people reluctant to change an existing process, even if it's hard work to use and extend. In fact, the uglier and more complex the build process is, the more scared people are of fixing it. This fear is unfounded: the uglier and more complex the build process is, the more it needs Ant.

We've found that it usually doesn't take that long to move an existing project to Ant—that is, for a build file to compile, run, and archive an application. Extending that build file with automated tests and deployment does take effort, but that will be ongoing effort.

If there were one suggestion we would make about migration, it would be "do it after a deadline." There's almost always some slack time after a milestone to write a build file, or perhaps you can suggest an interim postmortem to see if any aspects of the project could be improved. Most likely, any project would benefit from more tests, automated testing, and automated deployment, so suggest Ant as the means of controlling these tasks.

Migrating to Ant is mostly a matter of following a fairly simple and straightforward process. The ten steps of migration are listed in table 8.2.

Table 8.2   Steps to migrate an existing project to Ant

Migration step	Purpose
1. Check in	Check everything in and tag it with a BEFORE_ANT label.
2. Clean up	Clean out the old .class files to prevent confusion; copy the old JAR files somewhere for safety. There should be no generated files in the project at this point.
3. Determine the deliverables	From examining your existing build tool, make a list of your project outputs and the stages in creating them; build a list of Ant targets and dependencies from this.
4. Define directories	Define your directory structure and the property names used to refer to these different directories.
5. Design the build file	Make an initial design of your build file or reuse an existing one.
6. Arrange the source	If you need to place the source into new directories, do so now.
7. Implement the build file	Create the build file that you've defined or customize one you're reusing.
8. Run a verbose build	Run the build and verify that it's working with the -verbose flag.
9. Add some tests	Start writing tests if there were none already.
10. Evolve the build file	Add more targets as you need them.

The key thing is to automate the basic bits of the build—creating the existing artifacts—without adding new things like testing until the basics are working and everyone is happy. Try to move to Ant simply by adding a new build.xml file at the base of the project. Moving directories around is far more disruptive. If the project already has JUnit tests, bring them up under <junit> and start creating reports with <junitreport>. After that, it's time to go live and start evolving the build file.

During the life of the project, you should rarely need to edit the build file to include new source files, documents, or tests; they should all be accommodated automatically. If you do need to keep editing the build file for such changes, then something is wrong with your task declarations—usually fileset and path declarations. The only reasons for build file maintenance should be new deliverables, new processing steps, and refactorings to clean up the process, such as moving all hard-coded paths and filenames into properties for easier overriding. This latter instance is when a working build is most likely to break; as with source, tests help verify that the changes worked. Testing after every little change is the key to a successful build file refactoring.

8.5 SUMMARY

This chapter walked through a complete build file, one that contains

- An initial setup of the build, with properties and datatypes to configure Ant.
- A compile stage, which compiles files, copies resources, and JARs the file up. The build file also signs the JAR.
- Test targets, which run JUnit and create HTML reports.
- Targets to package the JAR and documentation into source and binary Zip files.
- Distribution targets that email and upload the Zip file.

The information covered in this chapter shows what Ant can do: it can cover the gamut of build activities, from compilation to redistribution.

Readers should have the knowledge and tools necessary to build sophisticated, production-quality build files. While there certainly are more tools and techniques available, they all rely upon the fundamentals we've already covered. In the next section of this book, we'll apply Ant and the techniques we've covered to a number of common development situations, such as code generation, Web applications, XML manipulation, Enterprise Java, and much more.

PART **2**

Applying Ant

In the first part of this book, we introduced Ant, using it to compile, package and redistribute a library. In chapters 9 to 16, we will use that library as the basis for a web application, and later an Enterprise Java application, showing how Ant can rise to the challenges such applications entail. To build and test such applications, we need to automate many more activities, from managing builds that span more than one build file, to setting up the database and application server before we can deploy our application and run our tests.

Welcome to big-project, big-system, Ant!

CHAPTER 9

Beyond Ant's core tasks

At this point in the book, we have a build file that can build, test, package, run, and distribute a Java library. In the next few chapters, we'll use it in a bigger application, building, deploying, and testing web and Enterprise Java applications.

Before then we're going to look at more of Ant's tasks, exploring the different kinds of tasks that Ant supports: built-in, optional, and third-party. The tasks we're going to cover can all improve our application's build in little ways: automating other steps in the process such as patching property and text files, or auditing the source. Together they can automate even more steps of the process of getting software out the door. They also will give the reader a clearer understanding of the nature of the tasks that constitute Ant's functionality.

Concepts covered in this chapter, especially the different types of tasks and how to load tasks that do not come with Ant, are going to be used throughout the rest of the book. Therefore, even if you aren't interested in the specific tasks we cover here, please skim the chapter and become familiar with the terminology.

9.1 THE MANY DIFFERENT CATEGORIES OF ANT TASKS

What is Ant? It's an XML language to describe a build, an engine that interprets the language, and the tasks that the runtime executes to perform useful work. It is the tasks that build the project. Accordingly, Ant is only as useful as its tasks.

You can accomplish a great deal with an out-of-the-box Ant installation. However, eventually you'll need more than it offers through its built-in tasks. Ant's *optional tasks* provide a set of extra features, many of which need extra libraries installed in Ant's library directory.

There also are a growing number of Ant tasks—*third-party tasks*—which are written by other people. These are often part of Java projects and make their applications more usable under Ant. The broad variety of third-party tasks gives Ant its real power.

Altogether, there are four types of Ant tasks and datatypes:

- *Core*—Tasks that work out of the box and are immediately available for use. We've used many core tasks, such as `<javac>`, `<jar>`, and `<copy>`.

- *Optional*—Tasks that ship with Ant but typically require libraries or external programs that do not ship with Ant. We've already been using some of these tasks—`<junit>`, `<junitreport>`, `<ssh>`, and `<ftp>` are all optional.

- *Third-party*—Tasks that were developed by others and which can be dropped into an Ant installation.

- *Custom*—Tasks developed for your own projects. We'll cover these in chapter 17.

This chapter introduces optional and third-party tasks. We also cover a few technical hitches that can occur when using optional and third-party tasks. First, we'll dig into the optional tasks.

Optional Tasks

In early versions of Ant, "optional" tasks were distributed as an add-on library (`optional.jar`) that users had to download separately. Currently, Ant ships with a complete set of core and optional tasks. Even so, there are still distinctions between the two task types. Ant's optional tasks come in different JAR files and the online documentation splits the tasks into two lists, core and optional. With current distributions, this distinction may seem odd or unnecessary, but there are some remaining differences. Table 9.1 shows most of Ant's optional tasks.

Most optional tasks need an extra library or program to work, and they come in JAR files that group them by their dependencies. For example, the `<scp>` task of chapter 7 lives in `ant-jsch.jar` and depends upon the `jsch.jar` SSH library.

Optional tasks that don't depend on third-party JAR files are all packaged into `ant-optional.jar`. Normally this is invisible to users, unless they spend time browsing around Ant's directories.

Table 9.1 Ant's optional tasks. Most of these tasks require installation of additional components.

Task Category	Examples	Covered
Source Code Management[†]	ClearCase, Continuus, Perforce, PVCS, StarTeam, and Visual SourceSafe tasks. `<cvs>` is a core task	Chapter 9
Packaging	`<cab>`, `<rpm>`, `<ejbjar>`	
Compilers and Grammars	`<antlr>`, `<depend>`, `<javacc>`, `<javah>`, `<jspc>`, `<icontract>`, `<netrexxc>`, `<jdepend>`	
Utilities	`<propertyfile>`, `<image>`, `<sound>`, `<splash>`	
Text manipulation	`<native2ascii>`, `<replaceregexp>`, `<translate>`	
Testing	`<junit>`, `<junitreport>`	Chapter 4
XML Processing	`<xmlvalidate>`, `<schemavalidate>`	Chapter 13
Networking	`<telnet>`, `<ftp>`, `<sshexec>`, `<scp>`, `<setproxy>`, `<rexec>`	Chapter 7
Scripting	`<script>`, `<scriptdef>`	Chapter 18

Those tasks that depend on extra libraries usually need them in Ant's own classpath. That means they must be in one of the directories from which Ant loads JAR files, a directory named on the command line with the -lib option, or listed in the CLASSPATH environment variable. Ant's documentation lists dependencies, which can change from release to release. As Ant is built with the latest released versions of the external libraries, it's good to upgrade these libraries when upgrading Ant.

The final difference between core and optional tasks is that many optional tasks do not get used or tested as much as the core set. New tasks are added into the optional group either when they have an external dependency or when they're viewed as less important than the core set. In both cases, the number of users may be less than for other tasks, which means the support for and documentation of those tasks *may* be behind that of the main Ant tasks. *May* does not mean that this is always the case. The JUnit tasks `<junit>` and `<junitreport>` are both examples of broadly used and well-supported Ant tasks. You just need to be aware that if you use an optional task, you might have to do more of the maintenance yourself.

Third-party tasks

The Ant team maintains the Ant runtime and the many core and optional tasks, but it lacks the time and skills to maintain all the other tasks that projects may need. Third-party tasks are a common addition to many Ant-based projects. Many Java libraries and applications include Ant tasks. This gives Ant users tasks that are tightly bound to the product and are maintained by the same development team, which results in high-quality tasks.

As a consequence, many of the most interesting things you can now do with Ant require third-party tasks. We'll explore some of these tasks throughout this section of the book.

Some people fear third-party tasks, preferring to use only the tasks that ship with Ant itself. They do this because they believe that third-party tasks are lower in quality than those that Ant bundles, and that Ant builds should use only those tasks that Ant bundles. This isn't the case. Many open source and commercial products provide Ant tasks to work with their products, and these are often well-written tasks that integrate seamlessly with the products themselves. The quality, integration, and documentation for these tasks can be equal to or better than those that ship with Ant. Don't be afraid of using them.

Third-party tasks, like optional tasks, are distributed in JAR files. Traditionally, you've had to modify Ant build files to tell Ant about any new types in the JAR by using the <tasksdef> and <typedef> tasks.

Since Ant 1.6, a new task-loading mechanism, *Antlib*, makes this process much simpler. An Antlib is a JAR file whose type and task declarations are picked up by Ant when you declare the appropriate package URL in an XML namespace declaration. The mechanism also lets library developers declare more than just the tasks; they can declare datatypes and define tasks in scripting language or XML, rather than just Java. The Ant project itself is starting to distribute extension libraries as Antlibs, blurring the distinction between optional and third-party tasks.

After looking at some of Ant's optional tasks, we'll explore some third-party tasks. First, we'll look at the problem of getting an optional task installed.

9.2 *INSTALLING OPTIONAL TASKS*

To use most optional tasks, you must download and install extra libraries or programs. The JAR containing the task itself isn't always enough: any extra libraries that an optional task depends on must be on the classpath of Ant or you'll see an error message.

If the optional task is present but a library that it depends on is missing, Ant will inform you of this fact. Here, for example, is the error message if the <scp> task cannot load a version of the jsch.jar library:

```
build.xml:288: Problem: failed to create task or type scp
Cause: Could not load a dependent class com/jcraft/jsch/UserInfo
    It is not enough to have Ant's optional JARs
    you need the JAR files that the optional tasks depend upon.
    Ant's optional task dependencies are listed in the manual.
Action: Determine what extra JAR files are needed, and place
 them in one of:
   -C:\Java\Apache\Ant\lib
   -C:\Documents and Settings\ant\.ant\lib
   -a directory added on the command line with the -lib argument

Do not panic, this is a common problem.
The commonest cause is a missing JAR.

This is not a bug; it is a configuration problem
```

Ant doesn't directly identify or download the missing library—you need to consult Ant's documentation to see what's needed and where it can be retrieved.

If the `ant-jsch.jar` file itself was missing, the class implementing the `<scp>` task wouldn't be found, so the message and suggested action would be slightly different:

```
build.xml:288: Problem: failed to create task or type scp
Cause: the class org.apache.tools.ant.taskdefs.optional.ssh.Scp
    was not found.
    This looks like one of Ant's optional components.
Action: Check that the appropriate optional JAR exists in
    -C:\Java\Apache\Ant\lib
    -C:\Documents and Settings\ant\.ant\lib
    -a directory added on the command line with the -lib argument

Do not panic, this is a common problem.
The commonest cause is a missing JAR.

This is not a bug; it is a configuration problem
```

Ant assumes that any task implemented in its own packages is one of its own tasks, so Ant prints this special message. It has not recognized that the task will need `jsch.jar`; it will only discover that fact once `ant-jsch.jar` is present.

Once you have the main set of optional JAR files for your projects, these error messages should be rare. The only time they'll surface is if you're running Ant under an IDE and the relevant JAR files aren't on the classpath. In this situation, you'll need to add them to the classpath through the appropriate IDE settings dialogs.

You can explicitly probe for a task by using the `<typefound>` condition. This condition verifies that there's a task matching that of the name attribute and that Ant can instantiate it, and it lets the build file fail with a helpful error message:

```
<target name="check-scp" >
  <fail>
    SCP support not found; the scp task needs
      1. ant-jsch.jar
      2. jsch.jar from
      http://www.jcraft.com/jsch/
    <condition>
      <not><typefound name="scp" /></not>
    </condition>
  </fail>
</target>
```

This example checks for the presence of the `<scp>` task and shows where the task and JAR come from. If you run the target with verbose output (`ant -v check-scp`) you'll see the detailed diagnostics that Ant normally prints when a task cannot be created.

If you encounter problems, the cause is likely to be one of a common set.

9.2.1 Troubleshooting

Here are the special problems you may encounter with optional tasks.

Missing mandatory helper library

This is the most common problem. When working with optional tasks, check the online documentation for information on which libraries are needed.

Missing optional helper library

Some tasks will load but not work if a library is absent. For example, the `<mail>` task needs `mail.jar` and `activation.jar` to send MIME messages, and it can send only plain text with attachments as UUENCODE-encoded files. Tasks usually degrade gracefully or fail with task-specific error messages in these situations.

Out-of-date helper library

Ant is built and tested against the latest release and development versions of all other open source Java libraries. The latest versions of those libraries will have more fixed, new features and sometimes a changed API. Check for library updates whenever you upgrade Ant.

Missing task implementation

Ant packages optional tasks by the names of their dependencies into files such as `ant-junit.jar`. If one of these libraries is missing, none of the Ant tasks in it will be found. Even if the JAR is there, it may not contain all the implementation classes. This happens when someone makes their own build of Ant. Official Ant releases should not suffer from this.

Library version conflicts

If there are different versions of library classes on the classpath, Ant may end up running with an older version of the library. This may happen if a JAR file—such as `jython.jar`—ships with some library classes (in this case the Jakarta-ORO regular expression classes). The Ant documentation warns whenever a JAR file has this problem. The only fix is to strip the particular library files, usually in a Zip file editor.

Failed build when running Ant under an IDE

We recommend setting up your IDEs to use the version of Ant that you use on the command line, with all the files in `ANT_HOME/lib` on the classpath. Not all IDEs load JAR files under `${user.home}/.ant/lib`. You may need to manually add these files to the IDE.

Missing executables

Tasks that depend on an executable being on the path will fail with a platform-specific error if the program is absent or if the user's path isn't set up correctly. On Windows, a message with "Error code 2" is the usual cue for this problem.

The power tool for tracking down many of these problems is `ant -diagnostics`. If users of your build file are encountering problems, ask them to save the output of a diagnostics run to a file so that you can examine their configuration at your leisure.

There is also a `<diagnostics>` task, which runs the diagnostics code inside Ant itself:

```
<target name="diagnostics" description="diagnostics">
  <diagnostics/>
</target>
```

This task is invaluable for troubleshooting Ant under an IDE, as it shows how the IDE has configured the tool.

Now that we've covered how to troubleshoot optional tasks, let's use some.

9.3 *OPTIONAL TASKS IN ACTION*

We've already used a few optional tasks in the book, first `<junit>` and `<junitreport>` in chapter 4; then `<ftp>`, `<scp>`, and `<sshexec>` in chapter 7. Here we'll explore a few more that often come in handy in a project:

- `<propertyfile>`
- `<depend>`
- `<replaceregexp>`

Most of these tasks illustrate the optional nature of the tasks and require additional components to be installed in order to function properly. For each task, we discuss the specific requirements it has and how to configure your system to run it.

9.3.1 Manipulating property files

One of the easiest and most common methods of configuring Ant and Java are Java property files. The `<propertyfile>` task lets you create and manipulate property files, even incrementing numbers and dates. Java programs can then read these files via the `java.util.Properties` class.

We can use `<propertyfile>` to save the build date and time, machine name, user, and operating system into a properties file. Listing 9.1 shows how to do this.

Listing 9.1   Using `<propertyfile>` to capture build-time information

```
<property environment="env"/>
<property name="env.COMPUTERNAME" value="${env.HOSTNAME}"/>

<propertyfile comment="Build Information"
              file="${build.classes.dir}/build.properties">
  <entry key="build.date"
     type="date"
     pattern="EEEE MMM dd, yyyy"
     value="now"/>
  <entry key="build.time"
```

```
        type="date"
        pattern="kk:mm:ss"
        value="now"/>
    <entry key="build.host" value="${env.COMPUTERNAME}"/>
    <entry key="build.user.name" value="${user.name}"/>
    <entry key="build.os.name" value="${os.name}"/>
</propertyfile>
```

The `<propertyfile>` task takes the name of a file to create an optional comment string to appear at the top of the task. It then takes a list of `<entry>` elements, all of which must have a `key` and `value`. Every entry may also have a `type`, which can be `"string"`, `"int"`, or `"date"`. The default type, `string`, just saves the value straight to the properties file—escaping it according to the rules of the `java.util`
`.Properties` class. With this file created under `${build.classes.dir}`, it will be pulled into the JAR we create, and so provide an audit trail as to who built the application, and when.

The `date` type is interesting, because it dynamically evaluates and formats the date; with `value="now"` it sets it to the current date or time. When we get a support call related to this JAR, we can find out who built it, and when. We could even have some Java code in the application to load the properties from the classpath, and print the information in a diagnostics screen.

While updating the file, the task doesn't set any Ant properties. To use the properties in Ant, we have to load the file using `<property file="..."/>`, perhaps setting the `prefix` attribute to keep the entries from clashing with already-existing properties.

It's nice to have a properties file in a JAR with audit information—but how about setting some advanced properties, such as an auto-incrementing build number? Whenever the application is rebuilt, the number would increment. We might also want to include an expiration date that our software could use to restrict the life of a demo version, or act as a trigger to probe for an updated release.

The `<propertyfile>` task can do both of these things, as it has the ability to increment numbers and dates. Ant also includes a `<buildnumber>` task to increment build numbers more concisely. In listing 9.2, we use both tasks to create/update a properties file at build-time, which not only stores the build number, but also sets an expiration date in the file.

> **Listing 9.2   Using `<propertyfile>` to increment a build number and set a future date in the same file**

```
<property name="metadata.dir" location="metadata"/>

<property name="buildprops.file"
          location="${metadata.dir}/build.properties"/>
<property name="buildnum.file"
          location="${metadata.dir}/build.number"/>
```

```
<buildnumber file="${buildnum.file}"/>          Increments a build counter

<echo message="Build Number: ${build.number}"/>

<delete file="${buildprops.file}"/>
<propertyfile comment="Build Information"
              file="${buildprops.file}">          Opens the property file

  <entry key="build.number"
    value="${build.number}"/>          Writes the build number

  <entry key="expiration.date"
      type="date"
      operation="+"                    Creates an expiry date
      value="1"                        by adding one month
      default="now"                    to today's date
      unit="month" />
</propertyfile>
```

The `<entry>` element of the `<propertyfile>` task supports an `operation` attribute, which must be either `"+"`, `"-"`, or the default of `"="`. Date types also support a `unit` attribute to define the value of the addition. By setting the `expiration.date` entry to be the operation of "now+1 month", we've set it to a date in the future.

Existing properties are untouched unless modified explicitly with an `<entry>` item. All comments are lost, however; they are stripped out when the original is read in, and so they cannot be recreated.

The next optional task we're going to look at is `<depend>`, which adds extra dependency logic onto `<javac>`.

9.3.2 Improving `<javac>` with dependency checking

The `<javac>` task passes `.java` files to the compiler if the corresponding `.class` file is older or absent. It doesn't rebuild classes—such as a parent class or an imported class—when the files that they depend upon change. The `<depend>` task fixes this. Rather, it looks at the generated `.class` files, extracts the references to other classes from them, and then deletes the class files if they're out of date compared to their references. This process clears out files for `<javac>` to rebuild. One disadvantage of this is that because compile-time constants, such as primitive datatype values and string literals, are inlined at compile time, neither `<javac>` nor `<depend>` can tell when a definition such as `Constants.DEBUG` has changed from `true` to `false`.

In situations where there's a large number of Java source files and when clean builds take a long time, the `<depend>` task is a great benefit to ensure incremental builds compile the correct files. Adding the dependency check to the build process is fairly simple; we just paste it into the compile target above the `<javac>` call, as shown here:

```
<depend srcdir="src"
  destdir="${build.classes.dir}"
  cache="${build.dir}/dependencies"
  closure="true">
  <classpath refid="compile.classpath"/>
</depend>
<javac destdir="${build.classes.dir}"
  debug="true"
  debuglevel="${build.debuglevel}"
  includeAntRuntime="false"
  srcdir="src">
  <classpath refid="compile.classpath"/>
</javac>
```

The <depend> task requires two attributes, srcdir, which points to the Java source, and destdir, which points to the classes. The cache attribute names a directory that is used to cache dependency information between runs; this directory is created on demand.

The <depend> task analyzes the .class files to determine which classes they depend on, and as this information doesn't change when the source is unchanged, it can be safely cached from run to run to speed up the process. Because it does speed up the process, however, we highly recommend that you always specify a cache directory.

The final attribute we're using is closure, which tells the task whether to delete .class files if an indirect dependency has changed. The merits of this attribute are unclear: it may be safer to set closure=true, but faster to leave it unset.

There's also a nested attribute to specify a classpath. This isn't mandatory; <depend> isn't compiling the source and it doesn't need to know where all the packages the source depends upon are stored. Instead, the task uses any supplied classpath as a list of classes that may also have changed. It looks inside JAR files to see the timestamps of classes, deleting local .class files if imports from the JAR have changed. For faster dependency checking, list those JAR files that change regularly.

You can also include or exclude source files from the dependency checking by using nested <includes> and <excludes> elements, though we never bother with this.

Running the target adds one more line to the compilation target's output, here stating that seven files were deleted:

```
compile:
  [depend] Deleted 7 out of date files in 0 seconds
  [javac] Compiling 7 source files to
          /home/ant/diary/core/build/classes
```

This task makes incremental builds more effective. Keep in mind, however, that it cannot detect dependencies on imported constants—primitive types declared as static and final. Therefore, a regular clean build is always a good idea.

These two tasks give a bit of the flavor of Ant's optional tasks. It's very much a mixed bag of tasks that are viewed as "sometimes useful" alongside other tasks that are almost essential—<junit> being one of these—but which have external dependencies.

One set of useful optional tasks is the Software Configuration Management task family, which can be used to work with version control repositories to let a build run, check out, check in, or tag files.

9.4 SOFTWARE CONFIGURATION MANAGEMENT UNDER ANT

Ant works with most software configuration management (SCM) systems. There are a multitude of tasks that enable developers to make calls to the repositories from inside Ant. These tasks can check in and check out code, and sometimes even add labels. The exact set of services available depends on the particular SCM tool in use: each tool has a unique set of corresponding Ant tasks, most of which are implemented as optional tasks.

Ant directly supports CVS, Perforce, ClearCase, SourceSafe, SourceOffsite, StarTeam, Serena PVCS, and Continuus. Each has its own tasks and its own set of operations. Table 9.2 lists the corresponding Ant tasks showing which SCM systems support tasks for the comment actions of *update*, *check out*, *check in*, and *label*.

We're not going to cover all the tasks, because there are many of them and some of the products are pretty obscure. We'll just look at CVS and mention its forthcoming successor, Subversion.

All the SCM tasks need external programs or libraries to run. Most rely on native executables on the path, such as cvs, p4, svn, or cleartool.

Table 9.2 Ant-supported SCM systems and their common operations

SCM System	Update	Check out	Check in	Label
ClearCase	<ccupdate>	<cccheckout>	<cccheckin>	
Continuus		<ccmcheckout>	<ccmcheckin>	
CVS	<cvs command= "update">	<cvs command= "checkout">	<cvs command= "commit">	<cvs command= "label">
Perforce	<p4sync>	<p4edit>	<p4submit>	<p4label>
PVCS	<pvcs>			
SourceOffSite	<sosget>	<soscheckout>	<soscheckin>	<soslabel>
SourceSafe	<vssget>	<vsscheckout>	<vsscheckin>	<vsslabel>
StarTeam		<stcheckout>	<stcheckin>	<stlabel>
Subversion	<svn subcommand= "update" />	<svn subcommand= "checkout"/>	<svn subcommand= "commit"/>	<svn subcommand= "copy"/>

During the development of this book, we used CVS servers as the repositories for source and the book's chapters themselves. We added a task to check out the code from the repository into a temporary directory, which makes it easy for developers to create a read-only copy of the source. This method also enables you to check that the contents of the repository build properly. Chapter 15 will automate this checkout and build as part of the continuous integration process, but a manual checkout is still useful to isolate SCM problems from those of the continuous integration server.

Here is the Ant script to check out the application using the <cvs> task:

```
<property name="root.dir" location="${env.TEMP}"/>
<property name="cvs.user" value="anonymous"/>
<property name="cvs.host" value="antbook.sourceforge.net"/>
<property name="cvs.root"
  value=":pserver:${cvs.user}@${cvs.host}:/cvsroot/antbook"/>
<property name="cvs.passfile" value="../.cvspass"/>
<property name="cvs.dir" location="${root.dir}"/>
<property name="cvs.package" value="examples/diary"/>


<cvs cvsRoot="${cvs.root}"
     command="checkout"
     dest="${root.dir}"
     package="${cvs.package}"
     passfile="${cvs.passfile}"
     failonerror="true" />
```

We've told <cvs> to check the files out into a temporary directory, and set failonerror="true" to ensure that a <cvs> failure is fatal. When run, the <cvs> task will check out our project using the normal Windows/Unix CVS program, or fail with an error.

The <cvs> command also lets us label the repository and check in files. Adventurous Ant users could have builds that automatically label the repository after a build, or check files in after updating them.

There are also two CVS reporting tasks, <cvschangelog> and <cvstagdiff>. The <cvschangelog> task generates an XML file containing all the changes that have occurred within a specified date range on CVS modules. The <cvstagdiff> task generates an XML file containing the differences between two CVS tags. Ant ships with two XSL files, changelog.xsl and tagdiff.xsl, both in ANT_HOME/etc, which turn these XML files into attractive hypertext markup language (HTML) reports. You'll need to refer to Ant's documentation for more details on these tasks, but we leave you with the following example of how to generate a report from a CVS change log:

```
<cvschangelog destfile="build/changelog.xml"/>
<xslt in="build/changelog.xml"
      out="build/changelog.html"
      style="${ant.home}/etc/changelog.xsl">
```

```
  <param name="title" expression="AntBook ChangeLog"/>
  <param name="module" expression="AntBook"/>
</xslt>
```

Chapter 13 covers the `<xslt>` task in more detail.

If CVS isn't on the path, the `<cvs>` tasks—as with the other SCM tasks—fail with an OS-specific error code. In Windows, "Create Process" and "code=2" usually appear somewhere in the message.

The standard way of debugging any of these SCM tasks is to

1 Type `cvs`, `svn`, or the equivalent on the command line to verify the program is found.

2 Run the Ant target in `-verbose` mode to see the full command.

3 Run this full command on the command line to see why it doesn't work.

If the executable is present, the usual cause of failure is either misconfiguration of the Ant task, or, for those tools that need some kind of password, incomplete authentication of the user. Don't try to use any of the SCM tasks until you have it working on the command line.

You can also give up on the tasks and just call the programs using `<exec>`:

```
<exec executable="cvs" failonerror="true">
  <arg line="-r -z7 update -dP" />
</exec>
```

We generally delegate SCM work (especially updates and labeling) to the continuous integration server. Even so, it's nice to have a task to use in some parts of the process, such as when labeling the repository before we make a release.

Although the book's source was developed using CVS, at some point it will be migrated to Subversion. Subversion, also known as *svn*, is the ultimate successor to CVS for open source and in-house projects. Ant does not and will not ship with Subversion support out of the box. Instead, a separate *Antlib* provides tasks that act as a thin wrapper around the `svn` command-line tool. This library can be found on the Ant web site. It's effectively a *third-party task*, which we'll explore next.

9.5   USING THIRD-PARTY TASKS

Ant's core and optional tasks ship with Ant. However, you can also use third-party tasks, which are any tasks that don't come with Ant itself. We mentioned them earlier in the chapter, and now it's time to look at some in more detail.

There is an incredibly broad set of third-party Ant tasks. In fact, there are more third-party tasks than there are core and optional tasks. They cover almost everything you need to do in a project, from auditing your source code style to deploying web applications. In this chapter we'll look at logic and iteration tasks, then at code auditing. In later chapters we'll explore many other third-party task suites.

Three steps are all it takes to make third-party tasks usable in a build file:

1 Finding the tasks

2 Adding the libraries to Ant's classpath

3 Telling Ant about the tasks

The final two stages can be merged into one if you keep the JAR files in a well-known place, such as a directory in your SCM repository, and declare this classpath when you tell Ant about the tasks.

The first step is finding the tasks you want. If you download a development tool or other product you want to use, look for the Ant tasks in the download or see if they're mentioned on the web site. The online documentation of Ant lists some tasks, but, as with any web site, the information listed at http://ant.apache.org/external.html soon goes out of date. If you can't find what you're looking for online, you can turn to search engines and the Ant user mailing list.

The Ant tasks should come in a JAR file, perhaps with some other library dependencies, and they need to be on the classpath. The standard ways to make this happen are

- Drop the JAR files into `ANT_HOME/lib`. Do this only if the library is to be used by all users of a machine on all projects. Otherwise, it may lead to library version conflicts.

- Drop the JAR files into `${user.home}/.ant/lib`. This is per-user, but it still applies across all projects and is still dangerous.

- Keep the files in a private directory and add the directory's contents to the path via Ant's `-lib` option. You can include this directory in the `ANT_ARGS` environment variable for automatic inclusion.

These three options automatically add the task libraries to the classpath, so all you need to do in your build file is declare the mapping from task name to implementation class. However, there's one more trick you can use, though it requires a little extra coding in the build file: you can explicitly load the tasks using a classpath you set up in the build file. This is the best tactic for a team project, because the JAR files can live in the SCM repository, and the build file declares them. There's no need for any work by the individual developers.

Adding the files to Ant's classpath doesn't make the tasks automatically available inside the build file. Every build file that uses a third-party task must tell Ant to load the tasks, providing the names and/or XML namespaces to use. This is called *defining a task*, which can be done in several ways.

9.5.1 Defining tasks with <taskdef>

Ant is preconfigured with the knowledge of which Java class implements each of the core and optional tasks. To use a new third-party task in a build file, you need to tell Ant about it. This is what the core tasks `<taskdef>` and `<typedef>` do. To define a single task, you must specify the task's name and the class behind it. The task name can be arbitrary, but it must be unique within the build file.

To demonstrate how to declare a third-party task, we'll use the Ant-contrib tasks—tasks that provide a lot of extra functionality to Ant. We'll be exploring them in detail, but first let's cover the ways of loading them. Given the name of the implementing class, we can tell Ant to bind <if> to this class using <taskdef>:

```
<taskdef name="if"
    classname="net.sf.antcontrib.logic.IfTask"
    classpath="${ant-contrib.jar}"/>
```

Our build file now has the capability to use the <if> task in the same manner any other task is used. To use the other tasks in the library, we could add other <taskdef> declarations, but this is needless work. It's better if the task library lists all its tasks in a properties file, which can be loaded in bulk.

9.5.2 Declaring tasks defined in property files

The Ant-contrib tasks are all listed in a properties file stored as a resource in the JAR: net/sf/antcontrib/antcontrib.properties. It lists the tasks in the JAR and the names by which they should be used, including the <if> task we declared earlier. Here's a fragment of the file:

```
# Logic tasks
if=net.sf.antcontrib.logic.IfTask
foreach=net.sf.antcontrib.logic.ForEach
throw=net.sf.antcontrib.logic.Throw
trycatch=net.sf.antcontrib.logic.TryCatchTask
switch=net.sf.antcontrib.logic.Switch
```

The <taskdef> command can do the bulk of this entire file, defining all the tasks in one go:

```
<taskdef resource="net/sf/antcontrib/antcontrib.properties"/>
  <classpath refid="tasks.classpath"/>
</taskdef>
```

Some projects also define datatypes in a separate file, which are declared with a <typedef> statement:

```
<typedef resource="org/example/types.properties">
  <classpath refid="tasks.classpath"/>
</typedef>
```

This statement will declare the Ant datatypes, but do this in a new classloader, not the one used for the tasks, even though the same classpath was used in both declarations. Having the classes loaded in separate classloaders can stop the tasks from using the types properly. To load them in the same classloader, set the loaderref attribute of both <typedef> and <taskdef> declarations to the same string. It doesn't matter what the string is, only that it's a unique name for the shared classloader.

Bulk loading of tasks through a properties file is efficient, and most third-party libraries come with a properties file for this purpose. One risk with this mechanism is that as the properties files name the tasks, there is no way to prevent clashes between the names of tasks defined in different libraries. This may seem unlikely, but as Ant continually adds new tasks and types, over time it's almost inevitable—unless we do something to avoid the problem. We need a way of telling Ant about third-party tasks yet keeping them separate from Ant's own tasks. This is where XML namespaces can help.

9.5.3 Defining tasks into a unique namespace

What happens if you try to define a task or type if something of the same name has already been defined?

- If the new definition is identical to the original, then the redefinition is silently ignored.
- If the new definition is identical except for a different classpath, a warning message "Trying to override old definition" appears, and the new definition is accepted.
- In any other circumstance, the definition is silently accepted.

The result is that you can redefine new tasks with the same name as old ones. This guarantees that a new version of Ant will not break your old build files, even if a third-party task used a name that is now claimed by Ant itself. There's a price of course: the price of confusion. You won't be able to use the new tasks, and tools and users of the build file may not realize that a third-party task is being used.

One solution is to give tasks very unique names, often a prefix such as ac—for the Ant-contrib tasks—a prefix that has to be used inside the properties file that defines the tasks. The alternative is to use XML namespaces. Since Ant 1.6, it's been possible to declare tasks into their own namespace. Once that's done, its "local" name can be the same as any task in any other namespace, yet there will be no name collision.

To recap the basic rules of XML namespaces that are covered in Appendix B: XML elements and attributes can be declared in a *namespace*, by first defining a prefix mapping to a URI, then qualifying the element or attribute declaration with the prefix.

For example, when Ant-contrib's <switch> task is declared in the default Ant namespace, its appears in the file as just the task's name:

```
<switch> … </switch>
```

If the task were declared in a namespace, the task would need to be accessed via a prefixed name:

```
<target name="identify-SCM-tool" depends="define-ac"     Declare the
  xmlns:ac="http://antcontrib.sf.net">                   namespace
  <ac:switch value="${scm}">     <-- Qualify the task wherever it is used
    <case value="cvs">     <-  Nested elements do
      <echo>using CVS</echo>      not need qualification
    </case>
```

```
      <ac:case value="svn">     <─── Unless you want to
        <echo>using Subversion</echo>
      </ac:case>
      <default>
        <echo>No SCM system defined</echo>
      </default>
    </ac:switch>     ┌─ Remember: the closing tag
  </target>          │  needs the prefix too!
```

Elements and attributes inside the task do not need to be prefixed, unless you want to include a type or task from a different namespace, or to make things clearer to readers. Furthermore, the name of the prefix doesn't matter, only the URI to which it's bound. You can reuse the same namespace prefix in different parts of the build file, and in different build files.

To declare a task or type in a namespace, set the `uri` attribute of the `<taskdef>` or `<typedef>` to the namespace you want the task to be defined in. For the task above, we would need to declare it in the `http://antcontrib.sf.net` namespace:

```
<target name="define-ac">
  <taskdef resource="net/sf/antcontrib/antcontrib.properties"
    uri="http://antcontrib.sf.net" />
</target>
```

One complication with XML namespaces is that the namespace needs to be declared, either in the element using the namespace, or in an XML element that contains it. In the example above we've declared it in the target, but usually we declare them in the `<project>` declaration. This lets you use the task anywhere in the project without having to re-declare the namespace.

In this book, we declare most third-party tasks into new namespaces. It may seem complicated at first, but there are long-term benefits with guaranteed unique names. The real benefit comes with Antlib libraries, which we are about to explore.

9.5.4   Defining tasks from an Antlib

Prior to Ant 1.6, the main way for declaring third-party tasks was via property files. This has now been supplemented with *Antlibs*, which are JARs containing Ant tasks and types—tasks and types that are listed in an XML file. Antlib task declarations are much better because

- A single Antlib XML file can contain `<taskdef>`, and `<typedef>` declarations of tasks, types, and conditions, and `<macrodef>` and `<presetdef>` declarations that build up tasks from other Ant tasks. We'll cover the latter two tasks in the next chapter.
- Everything in the library is loaded in the same classloader.
- Ant can automatically load Antlib declarations from special `antlib:` URIs.

Automatic library loading can dramatically simplify how you use third-party tasks. Instead of having to use `<taskdef>` or `<typedef>` in a build file, all you need to do is declare the namespace:

```
xmlns:ac="antlib:net.sf.antcontrib"
```

From then on, you can declare tasks or types in that namespace. When Ant first encounters an Antlib namespace declaration, it tries to load the library but silently ignores all failures (it's exactly equivalent to setting `onerror="ignore"` inside `<typedef>`). The moment Ant actually tries to instantiate a task or type in the namespace, it will try again, this time failing with an error message if something went wrong. This will be the usual "failed to create task or type" error message, with an extra Antlib-specific paragraph:

```
This appears to be an antlib declaration.
Action: Check that the implementing library exists in ANT_HOME/lib or in
        C:\Documents and Settings\ant\.ant\lib
```

Antlib libraries can still be manually installed using the `<typedef>` task. This allows skilled developers to do advanced things such as set up an explicit path if the library isn't already in Ant's classpath, or to use the library in the same build file in which the tasks are compiled and packaged.

Let's explore this in a real set of tasks, the Ant-contrib suite, which provides useful functionality to build files.

9.6   THE ANT-CONTRIB TASKS

One of the most popular suites of third-party tasks is the Ant-contrib Antlib, from http://ant-contrib.sourceforge.net.

These are invaluable in a big project because they add extra logic and decision-making operations to Ant, including iteration and exception handling. Ant-contrib is a long-standing project, with stable tasks that are widely used. It contains some tasks that aren't in the Ant core. The reason is that they're viewed as "too procedural," which is in opposition to the declarative goal of Ant. Another reason is that they violate Ant's "rules," such as the one about properties being immutable. They also cover things that Ant doesn't, such as C++ compilation and mathematical operations. As a result, any complex project is likely to find something of use in these third-party tasks.

The core of the Ant-contrib suite is its logic tasks. These provide extra structure to Ant, with `<for>`, `<if><then><else>`, and `<try>`/`<catch>` tasks. Table 9.3 lists the tasks that extend Ant's logic and execution abilities.

Alongside logic come the property operations of table 9.4, tasks that offer simple mathematics and dynamic property evaluation.

The `<var>` task does something that's completely against all of Ant's immutability rules. Chapter 10 looks at when it's appropriate to use `<var>` and how.

Table 9.3   The Logic/Execution tasks offered by Ant-contrib

Task	Function
`<antcallback>`	`<antcall>` with declared properties extracted from the called build and passed into the calling project. This lets you get return values from `<antcall>`
`<antfetch>`	`<ant>` with return values.
`<assert>`	An assertion facility for Ant. Very similar to `<fail>` with nested conditions, but you can enable or disable all assertions in a build file by setting the property `ant.enable.asserts` to true or false.
`<foreach>`	Ant-contrib's original iterator task: calls a target, `<antcall>` style, once for each element in a list, fileset, or iterator supplied.
`<for>`	Iterative execution of a nested sequence of tasks. This is the successor to `<foreach>` and is much more efficient.
`<forget>`	Start a sequence of tasks in a separate thread.
`<if>`	Conditional if/then/else/elseif execution of tasks.
`<limit>`	Run (nested) tasks with a specified time limit.
`<outofdate>`	Compare target files with source files, and execute nested tasks if the target files are considered out of date.
`<runtarget>`	Run a new target (and any dependencies) within the current environment.
`<switch>`	Switch on the value of a string, executing different tasks for each declared case.
`<throw>`	`<fail>` with the added ability to throw an exception caught in a `<catch>` statement.
`<timestampselector>`	Not a task: a new selector that selects the oldest or youngest file(s), from a larger set.
`<trycatch>`	Exception handling with try/catch/finally.

Table 9.4   Property tasks of Ant-contrib

Task	Function
`<math>`	Simple equation evaluation.
`<osfamily>`	Set a property to the OS family; the `<os family>` condition renders this obsolete.
`<propertycopy>`	Copy properties. Property expansion can be used in naming the source or destination, which lets you do simple array-like retrieval.
`<propertyselector>`	A selector of property names that match a specified regular expression.
`<pathtofileset>`	Create a fileset from a path.
`<propertyregex>`	Evaluate a regexp expression.
`<sortlist>`	Sort a list of items into their natural order as defined by the current locale of Ant. Sort orders are not consistent across languages.
`<urlencode>`	Convert a string into an x-www-form-urlencoded escaped representation.
`<var>`	Make a variable or unset Ant properties.

There are some extra conditions in the library, all listed in table 9.5. They can be used in `<condition>`, `<fail>`, `<waitfor>`, and Ant-contrib's own `<if>` tasks—anywhere a normal Ant condition can be used.

Table 9.5   Extra Ant-contrib conditions to use in build files

Task	Function
`<isgreaterthan>`	Numeric or string (platform's locale) comparison.
`<islessthan>`	Numeric or string (platform's locale) comparison.
`<ispropertyfalse>`	Test for a property being false. Ant's own `<isfalse>` condition can determine this.
`<ispropertytrue>`	Test for a property being false. Ant's own `<istrue>` condition can determine this.

Finally, there are a few other tasks, which are not so easy to classify. We're not going to cover any of them, but they're available if ever you have a need for them. There's also a listener that records how long tasks take to execute. Table 9.6 lists all the tasks.

All these tasks are a download away, at http://ant-contrib.sourceforge.net/. At the time of writing, the version of their library was 1.0b2. Some of the tasks also require extra libraries and dependencies that are listed in the documentation, which you should pick up alongside the `ant-contrib.jar` file.

Table 9.6   Ant-contrib's other tasks

Task	Function
`<anteclipse>`	Extract classpaths from an eclipse project file.
`<antserver>`/`<remoteant>`	Listen for Ant build requests from outside hosts and execute them. There's no security around these tasks, so they should be treated with caution.
`<cc>`	Published separately: a powerful, portable C/C++ compilation module. Also supports IDL compiles. We covered `<cc>` in the first edition of this book, but have now removed the chapter from this edition. Download it from the book's website.
`<inifile>`	Edit windows .ini files.
`<post>`	HTTP post.
`<shellscript>`	Declare a shell-script/batch file inline; this will be saved to a file and executed. Not portable, but possibly useful in some low-level situations.
`<stopwatch>`	Start and stop timing of task execution.
`<verifydesign>`	Examines .class files to verify that parts of a project are decoupled and that there are no imports of some packages by classes in others. This can enforce a strict separation of model and view, or persistence layer and model.

The easiest way to use the tasks is to copy `ant-contrib.jar` into Ant's lib directory. We may also need to tell the IDE about it too, adding it to its Ant classpath. We can then use the libraries in any project, by declaring an XML namespace with the URI `antlib:net.sf.antcontrib`. This is because it's an *Antlib* library:

```
<project name="core-chapter-09"
  basedir="." default="default"
  xmlns:ac="antlib:net.sf.antcontrib" >
```

To explicitly import the tasks from a different location, we would need to set a path to the location of the JAR, then use a `<typedef>` declaration:

```
<target name="load-antcontrib" >
  <typedef
    resource="net/sf/antcontrib/antlib.xml"
    uri="antlib:net.sf.antcontrib"
    onerror="failall">
    <classpath path="${ant-contrib.jar}" />
  </typedef>
</target>
```

The `onerror` attribute of `<typedef>`/`<taskdef>` has four values: `"ignore"`, `"report"`, `"fail"`, and `"failall"`. The first one does nothing if the tasks cannot be defined for any reason. The `report` option prints errors but continues the build, while the final two will halt the build if trouble is detected. The default is `"fail"`. It will raise an exception if the task or type does not load but do nothing if the resource itself isn't found. The strictest option, `failall`, raises an immediate error if the identified resource/URI isn't resolvable, and is the best choice for immediately finding a problem. The other options are relevant only for backwards compatibility or for skipping a premature `<typedef>` in projects in which custom tasks are actually compiled.

Once the tasks are loaded, they can be used alongside core and optional tasks.

9.6.1 The Ant-contrib tasks in action

We'll now have a quick look at some of the most useful Ant-contrib tasks. This only scratches the surface of the suite, so don't be afraid to look around the documentation whenever you get a chance. If there's something you want to do in Ant that it doesn't appear to do out of the box, the Ant-contrib library should be the next place to look.

For now, we'll look at how to copy properties, some of the extra logic operations, and exception handling to give readers an idea of what the Antlib can do.

Copying properties

One thing Ant lacks is pointers (or array indexing), there's no way to refer to a property by way of another property. That's the kind of weakness that the Ant-contrib team view as a challenge. Their `<propertycopy>` task lets you use property names to indirectly reference a property, which is a crude way of having pointers or arrays:

```
<target name="property-copy">
  <property name="X" value="Y"/>
  <property name="Y" value="Z"/>
  <ac:propertycopy name="A" from="${X}"/>
  <echo message="A = ${A}"/>
</target>
```

The value of ${X} is "Y". The `from` attribute of `<propertycopy>` refers to an Ant property name, "Y" in this example. The value of the property Y is "Z", so the output is "A = Z". People use this to do array-like tricks, using `<propertycopy>` to read and write properties like "hostname[${index}]".

Using if/then/else logic

Another recurrent problem in Ant is performing if/then/else tests and switching logic. This is something the language was never designed for. The logic tasks from Ant-contrib make it possible, so we could fetch a web page only if the server is present and serving up pages without an error code:

```
<target name="if-get" >
  <property name="localhost" value="http://localhost:8080/" />
  <ac:if>
    <http url="${localhost}" />
    <ac:then>
      <tempfile property="temp.file" suffix=".html"/>
      <get src="${localhost}" dest="${temp.file}" />
    </ac:then>
    <ac:else>
      <echo >skipping fetch of ${localhost}</echo>
    </ac:else>
  </ac:if>
</target>
```

The `<ac:if>` element takes a single condition, which can be anything that the `<condition>` task accepts, including the `<and>` or `<or>` constructs. If the condition evaluates to true, all tasks within the `<ac:then>` section are executed; otherwise the ones within the `<ac:else>` section execute.

You can accomplish the same thing with conditional targets with their `if` and `unless` attributes set to the name of a condition evaluated in a predecessor. The Ant-contrib approach eliminates the temporary property and the need for multiple targets at the expense of hiding the conditional nature of the execution from Ant-aware tools.

Multiple value switching

Along the same vein as the `<if>` task, the `<switch>` task controls the execution flow based on a string value:

```
<target name="identify-SCM">                    Switch on the
  <ac:switch value="${scm}">          ◁┘        value attribute
```

CHAPTER 9 BEYOND ANT'S CORE TASKS

```
      <ac:case value="cvs">
        <echo>using CVS</echo>                    Value="cvs"
      </ac:case>
      <ac:case value="svn">
        <echo>using Subversion</echo>             Value="svn"
      </ac:case>
      <ac:default>
        <echo>No SCM system defined</echo>        Any other
      </ac:default>                               value
    </ac:switch>
</target>
```

The `<case>` task container specifies the value that must equal the `<switch>` value for the containing tasks to be executed. The tasks under `<default>` run if the value doesn't match any of the `<case>` values. Unlike Java, there's no fall-through from one case to another, so there's no need for a `<break/>` element.

Catching task exceptions

A failing Ant task normally immediately stops the build with a BUILD FAILED banner. If you want the build to continue when a task fails, turn to Ant-contrib's `<trycatch>` task. Mirroring Java's exception handling facilities, `<trycatch>` has nested `<catch>` and `<finally>` containers to allow tasks to execute in those two conditions. Returning to the example of a web page download, we could use it to clean up if a `<get>` request fails:

```
<target name="trycatch" >
  <property name="localhost" value="http://localhost:8080/" />
  <tempfile property="temp.file" suffix=".html"/>
  <ac:trycatch
    property="exception.message"
    reference="exception.ref" >

    <ac:try>
      <get src="${localhost}" dest="${temp.file}" />
      <!-- more processing here -->
    </ac:try>

    <ac:catch>
      <echo>Caught: ${exception.message}</echo>
      <ac:throw refid="exception.ref" />
    </ac:catch>

    <ac:finally>
      <echo>cleanup</echo>
      <delete file="${temp.file}" />
    </ac:finally>
  </ac:trycatch>
</target>
```

Executing this target produces this output when there's no server:

```
trycatch:
   [get] Getting: http://localhost:8080/
   [get] To: C:\diary\core\null1319877082.html
   [get] Error getting http://localhost:8080/ to
         C:\diary\core\null1319877082.html
  [echo] Caught: java.net.ConnectException: Connection refused: connect
  [echo] cleanup

BUILD FAILED
C:\diary\core\core-chapter-09.xml:118:
   java.net.ConnectException: Connection refused: connect
```

The <get> failed, invoking the <catch> clause. After printing out the error, we threw the exception again using the <throw> task, which also comes from Ant-contrib. This is an extension of <fail> that takes a reference to an existing exception to throw. At that point, the <finally> clause was executed, invoking the <echo> and <delete> tasks.

If there was a functional HTTP server, the <finally> clause would still run after all tasks in the <try> section:

```
trycatch:
   [get] Getting: http://localhost:8080/
   [get] To: C:\diary\core\null2021604881.html

  [echo] cleanup
[delete] Deleting: C:\diary\core\null2021604881.html

BUILD SUCCESSFUL
```

The <trycatch> task is invaluable where you need to clean up when something goes wrong, such as stopping a program or removing temporary files after tests fail.

Iterative execution

Sometimes, you may find yourself wishing there was a way to perform a set of Ant tasks for every file in a fileset, or iterating over a list of values. With the Ant-contrib <for> and <foreach> tasks, such iteration is easy. Both of these tasks will take anything iterable: a list, a list of paths, or any Java datatype that has a method Iterator iterator(). The <for> task is the oldest one; it will invoke a named target once for every item by invoking <ant> and creating a full clone of the project's current state. This is needlessly inefficient, hence its replacement, the <foreach> task. This takes a sequence of tasks inline, running them once for every item.

Here's an iteration over the list [1, 5 ,10], sleeping for the specific number of milliseconds:

```
<target name="for">
  <ac:for list="1,5,10" param="delay"
            delimiter=",">
   <sequential>
    <sleep milliseconds="@{delay}" />
```

```
    <tstamp>
      <format pattern="HH:mm:ss.SSSS"
        property="tstamp.@{delay}" />
    </tstamp>
    <echo>@{delay}: ${tstamp.@{delay}}</echo>
    </sequential>
  </ac:for>
</target>
```

The name of the iteration's value is specified in the `parameter` attribute. This names a special "@" parameter for the nested sequence. This parameter isn't an immutable property; it's a value that changes every iteration. When used in the `<sleep>` statement, setting the delay to @{delay}, it's expanded to the current value.

Properties set in the sequence are still immutable; any property set in the first iteration will not change the next time through the loop. We'll look at this problem with Ant's macro facility in chapter 10.

```
for:
    [echo]  1
    [echo]  5
    [echo]  10
```

The task also takes a path, running the sequence for every file in the path. This is useful for some bulk operations. Here's a target that will print out every source file:

```
<target name="for-files">
  <ac:for param="name">
   <path>
    <fileset dir="src" includes="**/*.java" />
   </path>
   <sequential>
    <echo>@{name}</echo>
   </sequential>
  </ac:for>
</target>
```

Developers could use this task to distribute files to a list of FTP sites or to pass a set of files to a `<java>` program, one after the other. If the option `parallel="true"` is set, the iterations are run in parallel. Most Ant tasks are never designed to be thread-safe, so be very careful with this.

Handling out-of-date artifacts

The final Ant-contrib task that we'll cover is the `<outofdate>` task. This task runs a nested sequence of tasks if any target files are out of date compared to a set of source files.

Ant's `<uptodate>` task compares a set of source files against a single destination file, setting a property if the destination file is up-to-date compared to all the source files. A successor target can be made conditional on this scenario. Ant-contrib's

`<outofdate>` task extends that with multiple destination files, an optional mapper to specify a mapping from source to destination files, and the ability to declare the actions inline.

One use for it is to add dependency logic to tasks that lack it, such as javadoc:

```
<target name="javadocs-outofdate" depends="compile"
  description="make the java docs" >
  <ac:outofdate>
    <sourcefiles>
      <fileset dir="src" includes="**/*.java" />
    </sourcefiles>
    <mapper type="glob"
      dir="src" from="*.java" to="${javadoc.dir}/*.html"/>
    <sequential>
      <javadoc
          access="private"
          destdir="${javadoc.dir}"
          packagenames="d1.*"
          sourcepath="src"
          use="true"
          version="true"
          windowtitle="${ant.project.name}"
          failonerror="true">
        <classpath refid="compile.classpath"/>
      </javadoc>
    </sequential>
  </ac:outofdate>
</target>
```

Wrapping the `<javadoc>` task with an `<outofdate>` task, we declare that the source files are all our Java files. Instead of declaring any destination files, we list a mapper from our Java files to the generated HTML pages. The result? javadoc runs only when one of the HTML pages is older than the Java file it documents or when it's actually absent. This is a simple use of the task; it offers many more options. Note that `<outofdate>` is not only a task—it's a condition. You can use the test part of the task inside anything conditional, including `<fail>`, `<condition>`, and `<waitfor>`.

Overall, Ant-contrib represents a way to boost Ant with a broadly usable set of tasks. This quick overview of the library has only explored some of the main tasks it offers. If you're writing build files for complex projects, there is likely to be something of immediate relevance in there. Download it and see!

Alongside such general-purpose libraries come many that are designed for one specific purpose. We'll encounter some of those in future chapters. We'll close this chapter with one such library, Checkstyle, to audit Java source code, as it's a useful addition to any project.

9.7   CODE AUDITING WITH CHECKSTYLE

Imagine, whenever you wrote some Java source, the "code police" would review your code and see if it broke any rules set by the team. They could enforce code style policies and highlight possible design errors. This could either be very irritating or very useful, especially on a large project. With consistent code it's easier for people to work on different parts of the application, and no bits of the application would degrade to low-quality code while the rest of the team was distracted.

Few projects have any full time code police. It's exactly the kind of repetitive work best delegated to software—in this case a tool called Checkstyle, from http://checkstyle .sourceforge.net. It works as a command-line tool, an Ant task, and an IDE-plugin. It has the capability to check the following, and more:

- Unused and duplicate import statements
- Imports of forbidden libraries (such as sun.*)
- Proper and preferred javadoc tag usage
- The presence of license headers in all modules
- The preferred placement of curly brackets
- The existence of tabs
- Line lengths
- Naming conventions for classes, methods, and variables
- The ordering of modifiers such as public final static
- Code policies, such as final parameters, whether inline ?: conditions that are allowed or "magic numbers" in the source
- Bad class designs, including mutable exceptions and public fields

Checkstyle is configured by an XML file that declares which of its built-in or plug-in modules should be run over your code and what options each module has. It ships with a default policy that implements Sun's coding conventions (http://java.sun.com/docs/codeconv/) and the style rules of Effective Java (2001). Listing 9.3 shows the targets to audit our application.

> Listing 9.3   Checkstyle.xml: checking our coding style standards

```
<target name="checkstyle-init">
  <typedef resource="checkstyletask.properties"        Declaring the
          uri="antlib:com.puppycrawl.checkstyle"       checkstyle task
          onerror="failall"/>
  <property name="xml.dir" location="../xml"/>              The directory
  <property name="checkstyle.policy"                       containing our
          location="${xml.dir}/checkstyle-policy.xml"/>     policy file and
  <property name="checkstyle.xsl"                          style sheets
          location="${xml.dir}/checkstyle-frames.xsl"/>
  <property name="build.checkstyle.dir"
```

```
        location="${build.dir}/checkstyle" />
    <mkdir dir="${build.checkstyle.dir}" />
    <property name="checkstyle.report.xml"
        location="${build.checkstyle.dir}/checkstyle.xml" />
    <property name="checkstyle.report.html"
        location="${build.checkstyle.dir}/checkstyle.html" />
</target>

<target name="checkstyle-run" depends="checkstyle-init"
        xmlns:cs="antlib:com.puppycrawl.checkstyle">        ◁─┐ Use the checkstyle
    <cs:checkstyle                                               │    namespace
        failOnViolation="false"
        failureProperty="checkstyle.failed"                      Run checkstyle
        config="${checkstyle.policy}"                            over our source,
        classpathref="test.compile.classpath">                  printing out to
        <formatter type="plain"/>                                the console and
        <formatter type="xml"                                    to an XML file
            toFile="${checkstyle.report.xml}"/>
            <fileset dir="src" includes="**/*.java"/>
        </cs:checkstyle>
    </target>

<target name="checkstyle-report"  depends="checkstyle-run"
    if="checkstyle.failed">                      ◁─┐ Generate reports and
    <xslt style="${checkstyle.xsl}"                   halt the build if the
        in="${checkstyle.report.xml}"                 checkstyle.failed
        out="${checkstyle.report.html}" />            property is set
    <fail>
 Checkstyle reported style failures. See
 ${checkstyle.report.html}
    </fail>
</target>

<target name="checkstyle" depends="checkstyle-report" />
```

The <checkstyle> task takes multiple source filesets; we omitted the test fileset for
simplicity and because we may want some different rules there. Passing down the
classpath of the compiled code is optional, but it helps with some design checks,
particularly one that examines thrown exceptions to see if they're derived from
RuntimeException and hence don't need to be declared. Like <junitreport>,
the task has formatters write its output to the console or log file, as well as to XML format for integrated reporting. We can then use XSLT to generate HTML pages. The
XSL file to do this is one of those that comes with Checkstyle.

   We've taken both the XSL sheets and the sample Checkstyle policy file and put
them in a directory under SCM. We then commented out most of the checks, especially the whitespace ones. When you start adding this to an existing project, you get
a lot of whitespace errors, most of which are irrelevant. Listing 9.4 shows our minimal
coding policy.

Listing 9.4   Our checkstyle-policy.xml policy file

```xml
<!DOCTYPE module PUBLIC
    "-//Puppy Crawl//DTD Check Configuration 1.2//EN"
    "http://www.puppycrawl.com/dtds/configuration_1_2.dtd">

<module name="Checker">
  <module name="TreeWalker">
    <module name="ConstantName"/>
    <module name="LocalVariableName"/>
    <module name="MemberName"/>
    <module name="MethodName"/>
    <module name="PackageName">
      <property name="format"
          value="[a-z]+(\.[a-z_0-9]*)*$"/>
    </module>
    <module name="ParameterName"/>
    <module name="StaticVariableName"/>
    <module name="TypeName"/>
    <module name="EmptyStatement"/>
    <module name="IllegalInstantiation"/>
    <module name="InnerAssignment"/>
    <module name="MagicNumber"/>
    <module name="MissingSwitchDefault"/>
    <module name="IllegalImport"/>
    <module name="RedundantImport"/>
    <module name="UnusedImports"/>
    <module name="LineLength"/>
    <module name="ModifierOrder"/>
    <module name="RedundantModifier"/>
    <module name="InterfaceIsType"/>
    <module name="VisibilityModifier"/>
    <module name="UpperEll"/>
  </module>
</module>
```

It's up to every project to choose the rules and the options they want. Individuals cannot override these, which is exactly what you want. Project-wide code rules, by their very nature, should not be something that developers can customize. If you want to see a stricter policy, Ant's own checkstyle-config can be found in its source tree, under `src/etc/checkstyle.config`. In an open source project, having machine-enforced rules is one way of making it easier for outsiders to read the source. It can also ensure that any patches submitted to the project follow the rules.

Installing and running Checkstyle

You can obtain the latest Checkstyle release version from http://checkstyle.sourceforge .net; we used version 4.0beta5. The tool comes with a lot of extra JAR files; we were reluctant to put them all into our main `antlib` directory. Instead we just add Checkstyle's directory to the classpath when we run the targets.

```
ant -lib ~/bin/checkstyle-4.0-beta5 checkstyle
```

When we run this, we get a trace of errors, some generated reports and finally a halted build. Figure 9.1 shows a report on one file.

Checkstyle is useful in any team project. Adopting it can be painful, as it can throw many errors at the beginning. Start by commenting out most of the rules and focusing on the serious problems. Ant itself uses a far stricter policy set than that of listing 9.4, but it doesn't require the task to succeed before releasing a distribution. A very strict project may want to do just that.

One thing to remember about Checkstyle is that it's a style checker. It doesn't check that the code works, only that the source looks right. Other tools, such as EMMA, can do that (http://emma.sourceforge.net). However, Checkstyle does look at the code and, as figure 9.1 demonstrates, it can find many defects. Indeed, the biggest problem in retrofitting it to an existing project is just how many problems it finds.

It takes only a few more lines in a build file to add code-auditing from Checkstyle to a project, and it can find bugs that haven't been caught in testing. It's a fantastic example of a new feature a team can add to a build once Ant is in charge of the compile and test process. It also shows how third-party tasks can radically improve what the build file does for the developer team.

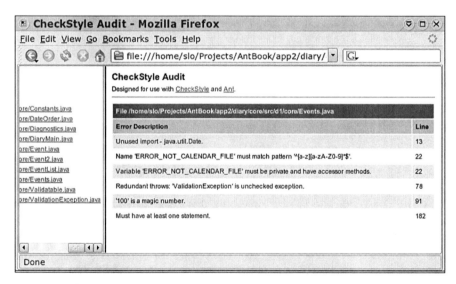

Figure 9.1 Stop! It's the code police! The tool also has caught the fact that we've forgotten to make a constant final. The case rule of constants (all capitals) did not match that of a variable.

CHAPTER 9   BEYOND ANT'S CORE TASKS

9.8   SUMMARY

Ant provides core tasks compiled into `ant.jar` and also ships with optional tasks that typically require additional components in order to function properly. Many third-party tasks also exist, adding extra functionality to your build process.

To use third-party tasks, you need to add the libraries to the classpath, either by adding them to a suitable directory, using the `-lib` argument or by adding them explicitly in a `<taskdef>` or `<typedef>` statement. These two tasks are how you can tell Ant about new task libraries. With the Antlib feature, you can even have task libraries loaded just by stating the right URL in an XML namespace declaration.

In this chapter, we looked at the various SCM tasks as a sample of Ant's optional tasks, then we looked at two useful third-party libraries: Ant-contrib, and Checkstyle. Ant-contrib provides many extra features to Ant—features big and complex projects can use—while Checkstyle automates the "code police." Both are great.

Ant's web site documentation and Ant's web site itself list many third-party tasks. If Ant doesn't provide what you need, check with the Ant web site or with the vendor of the product you're automating around. If all else fails, check with the Ant user email list.

Best practices with third-party and optional tasks

We routinely use Ant's optional tasks, as well as third-party and custom tasks. Some of the optional tasks, such as `<junit>` and `<junitreport>`, are almost mandatory.

Don't be put off by tasks that require you to download additional dependencies. Typically, dropping JAR files into `ANT_HOME/lib` is all that it takes to get up and running with the optional tasks that require an external library, such as `<ftp>`. Third-party tasks can also be added to this directory, or added to the classpath with a `-lib` argument. Explicitly declaring the classpath in a `<taskdef>` declaration adds some work, but doing so can help the build file being used by other developers.

In this book, we declare all third-party tasks into their own namespaces. This will cleanly separate Ant tasks from third-party tasks. It also enables the Antlib library loading mechanism, whereby the tasks and types of a library are automatically loaded just by identifying the package in an `antlib:` URL. More and more third-party tasks provide `antlib.xml` descriptors to enable this feature.

If you can, keep task libraries and their dependencies under source code control. Building your system should be as easy as checking out the repository and typing `ant` or maybe `ant -lib` with an SCM-managed directory.

CHAPTER 10

Working with big projects

Scalability is one of the classic challenges of software engineering. Every time you think you've solved it, the problem scales up: people expect even more the next time.

When this book introduced Ant, it started off with a small project—a diary library. As the chapters added more features, the project itself grew. It's now becoming a big project, as we're planning to use it in a web application. We now have the problem of scale to deal with, which is where this chapter comes to our aid. It looks at how to use Ant with big projects. That means projects that use multiple Ant build files to build different parts of a big system. Somehow, we want Ant to integrate those separate builds into one big application.

Ant was written to deal with the problem of building a large Java project across multiple platforms. Now that that's possible, the next problem arises. How do you build *very* large projects? How do you manage library dependencies? How do you manage the many build files you end up with? These are the problems that big projects encounter. Ant itself is continually evolving to address these problems, as developers use it for larger and larger projects. Don't wait until your project gets big before adopting features in Ant that are needed in big projects; small projects can benefit too. Indeed, the earlier you start to use some of the techniques, the better.

Building a large project is hard

A build system is a means to an end. The end is your project's deliverables, and as a project gets bigger, the structure of the application itself has to change. You may break the code into different modules, each comprising its own JAR/WAR/EAR file. You may split the project into subprojects, each with its own source tree. You may even have different release schedules for the subprojects. But no matter what, you will still need to test it all. Ant should not dictate how you organize your project; instead it has to adapt to you.

Here are the key problems in large-scale Ant projects:

- Delegating work to build files in subprojects
- Building subprojects in the correct order
- Ensuring build files are easy to maintain
- Managing libraries

We're going to look at all of these. (Library management is such a complex topic that it merits its own chapter, chapter 11.) In this chapter we'll cover the other problems, starting with that of delegating work across build files.

10.1 MASTER BUILDS: MANAGING LARGE PROJECTS

Large projects create their own problems. There's more to do, there are more people on the team, and the integration issues are worse. A small project could have one artifact, such as a JAR file, and its documentation. A large project could have client-side and server-side components, native library add-ins, and a database somewhere. These all need to be built, tested, and deployed together. If the build process is inadequate, the effort of managing the build can spiral out of control.

Can Ant manage the build for a big project? Yes. It may be great for small to medium projects, but it also scales up to work with large ones. Like any software scaling exercise, scaling up doesn't come automatically: you need to plan. You also need the other foundational tools of a large project—source control management, defect tracking, and some planning—that we'll assume you have in place.

Our diary project is slowly becoming a large project. It has a core library, and we're now about to write a web-based front end and, perhaps, data persistence. We still want to be able to run a single build file to bring it all up-to-date.

The standard solution to size in any system is to break it into smaller, more manageable modules. In Ant, that means dividing the application into child projects, each with its own set of deliverables. For our example application, penciling in some future subprojects gives us a number of child projects, as shown in table 10.1.

These projects need to build in the right order, with the generated artifacts passed down to those projects that depend upon them. We'll do this with a master build file that can call the subprojects in the order that the file's authors specify, with significant control over these invoked builds. The key to this is the <ant> task.

Table 10.1 Subprojects within our example project

Child project	Function	Deliverables
core	Diary core	diary-core.jar
webapp	Web application	diary-webapp.war
persist	Data persistence	diary-persist.jar
ear	Everything as an Enterprise Archive	diary-ear.ear

10.1.1 Introducing the <ant> task

We covered the `<antcall>` task in chapter 7. It can invoke a target and all its dependencies with a new set of properties. The `<ant>` task extends `<antcall>` by allowing you to specify the build file to use. This enables you to divide your build file into subprojects, one for each of the child projects of the actual software project, and call them from other build files.

The basic use of the `<ant>` task is simple: you use it to call any target in any other build file, passing in properties and references, if you desire. When you call a target with it, you implicitly invoke any other target in the build file that the invoked target depends on. That means if we use `<ant>` to call the `dist` target of another build file, that build file will run every target required to create the distribution.

To use `<ant>`, we have to know the name of a target to call, which means every project must have a standard set of targets. These entry points are listed in table 10.2.

Table 10.2 Our unified set of entry points. These are implemented across all child projects.

Target Name	Function
default	The default entry point
all	Builds and tests everything; creates a distribution
clean	Deletes all generated files and directories
dist	Produces the distributables
docs	Generates all documentation
test	Runs the unit tests
noop	Does nothing but print the name of the project

The `default` target is going to be the default for each project, and will usually depend on `dist` to create a distribution. The `noop` target is a special target added to test the whole build process. In code, the stub targets look like those in listing 10.1

Listing 10.1 An initial set of entry-point targets

```
<target name="default" depends="dist"
  description="default: Make everything" />

<target name="all" depends="dist"
  description="build everything"/>
```

```
<target name="test" depends="dist"
  description="run tests" />

<target name="docs" depends="javadocs"
  description="generate documentation" />

<target name="default" depends="all"
    description="default: build 'all'"/>

<target name="clean"
  description="clean up"/>

<target name="noop">
  <echo>in ${basedir}</echo>
</target>
```

We now add similar targets for the other projects, resulting in a set of entry points whose meaning is consistent across the projects.

With all the projects laid out under a root directory, diary, we can create a basic master build file that calls the targets. Listing 10.2 shows a master build file that builds the five subprojects.

Listing 10.2   Using <ant> to build subprojects

```
<?xml version="1.0"?>
<project name="master" default="delegate">

  <target name="delegate"  description="Build everything">
    <property name="target" value="all" />
    <ant dir="core"   target="${target}"  inheritAll="false"/>
    <ant dir="persist" target="${target}" inheritAll="false"/>
    <ant dir="webapp" target="${target}"  inheritAll="false"/>
    <ant dir="ear" target="${target}"  inheritAll="false"/>
  </target>

</project>
```

This build file contains one target that invokes the subprojects. We ordered the <ant> calls to ensure that all predecessor projects are built before those that depend on them. Although the default target here is all, we use a property so that it can be overridden on the command line. To run, say, the noop target, we would run Ant, explicitly selecting the noop target in our subsidiary build files by way of the target property:

```
C:\diary\> ant -Dtarget=noop
```

This produces a trace of all the targets that are run:

```
delegate:

noop:
     [echo] in c:\diary\core

noop:
     [echo] in c:\diary\persist

noop:
     [echo] in c:\diary\webapp

noop:
     [echo] in c:\diary\ear
```

Ant doesn't show which subprojects are being built, unless you ask for it with a -verbose option. This can be very confusing at times. A good trick is for every build file to print out its filename/directory with an <echo> statement outside any target.

This shows how Ant, a master build file, can delegate down to a set of child build files. It's the secret for breaking things up into modules, yet coordinating work between them. To manage that work, we need to keep the master build file under control.

10.1.2   Designing a scalable, flexible master build file

We have a master build file that can delegate to child projects, but the ordering of those projects is done by hand. Why not use Ant's target structure to model dependencies between subprojects? If there's a target defined in the master build file for each subproject, invoking it with <ant>, then we can use their depends attributes to state how they depend on each other. Ant will then control the order in which targets are run and, hence, subprojects are built.

The first step is to determine the direct dependencies between projects, as shown in figure 10.1.

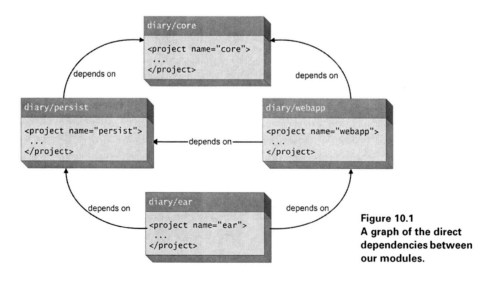

**Figure 10.1
A graph of the direct dependencies between our modules.**

Listing 10.3 shows our reworked master build file, now with each `<ant>` call split into its own target, mirroring the dependency graph.

Listing 10.3   Dependency logic inside a master build file

```xml
<target name="init">
  <fail unless="target">no target to delegate</fail>
</target>

<target name="do-core" depends="init">
  <ant dir="core" target="${target}"
    inheritAll="false"/>
</target>

<target name="do-persist" depends="do-core">
  <ant dir="persist" target="${target}"
    inheritAll="false"/>
</target>

<target name="do-webapp" depends="do-persist,do-core">
  <ant dir="webapp" target="${target}"
    inheritAll="false"/>
</target>

<target name="do-ear" depends="do-persist,do-webapp">
  <ant dir="ear" target="${target}"
    inheritAll="false"/>
</target>

<target name="delegate" depends="do-ear" />
```

Just as before, a call to `ant delegate -Dtarget=clean` will run the target `"clean"` on all delegate systems, only now Ant handles the correct order of child project invocation.

We can then write entry points to the build file, each using `<antcall>` to invoke the `delegate` target, setting the `target` parameter for us:

```xml
<target name="noop"
    description="do nothing">
  <antcall target="delegate">
    <param name="target" value="noop"/>
  </antcall>
</target>

<target name="clean"
    description="clean up">
  <antcall target="delegate">
    <param name="target" value="clean"/>
  </antcall>
</target>
```

```
<target name="all"
    description="clean up">
  <antcall target="delegate">
    <param name="target" value="clean"/>
  </antcall>
</target>

<target name="default"
    description="default actions">
  <antcall target="delegate">
    <param name="target" value="default"/>
  </antcall>
</target>
```

At this point, we can use the master build file to coordinate the overall build. Calling a target such as all will delegate down to the child projects, calling the same target in each of them, in the order that the projects depend on each other. This means that Ant can handle the problems of ordering the child projects—which becomes more important the more projects you have. The master build file can do one other thing: it can control those child builds by passing data down to them.

10.2   CONTROLLING CHILD PROJECT BUILDS

We've just shown how to subdivide a project into a number of standalone child projects—each with its own build file—with one master build file to integrate them all and execute them in the right order.

If there's a problem in this design, it's that we don't want to have to declare the same properties and tasks in all the different child projects. There are ways to do this, which we shall now explore.

10.2.1   Setting properties in child projects

Master build files can control their child projects through properties. Because of Ant's property immutability rule, a child project cannot override any property set by a master build file. This lets you write master build files that control complex details of the child project, even child projects that were never written to be called from a master build file. As an example, figure 10.2 shows a build file that sets the dist.dir property for two child projects. The outcome of this operation will be that the two child projects will place all their final distribution files into a single directory, rather than into their own directories.

In all our uses of the <ant> task so far, we've carefully declared inheritall= "false" without explaining why. We actually introduced this attribute in chapter 7, when looking at property inheritance in <antcall> target. The <antcall> task actually uses <ant> to do its work, so the property inheritance model for both is identical.

Although the two tasks share the same implementation code, when creating a master build file you use them slightly differently. The <antcall> task can call targets

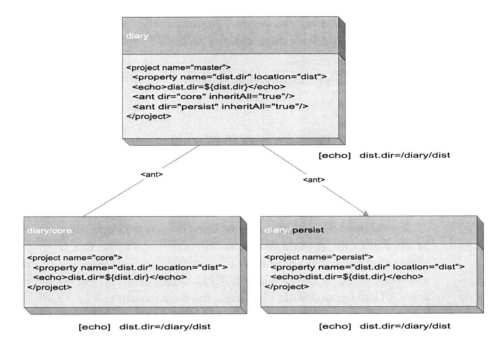

```
diary
<project name="master">
  <property name="dist.dir" location="dist">
  <echo>dist.dir=${dist.dir}</echo>
  <ant dir="core" inheritAll="true"/>
  <ant dir="persist" inheritAll="true"/>
</project>
```

[echo] dist.dir=/diary/dist

<ant>   <ant>

```
diary/core
<project name="core">
  <property name="dist.dir" location="dist">
  <echo>dist.dir=${dist.dir}</echo>
</project>
```

```
diary/persist
<project name="persist">
  <property name="dist.dir" location="dist">
  <echo>dist.dir=${dist.dir}</echo>
</project>
```

[echo] dist.dir=/diary/dist   [echo] dist.dir=/diary/dist

Figure 10.2 A master build can set the properties for the child projects, even if those projects try to override them. If the master build had accidentally used value instead of location, the directory location would have still been resolved in the client build files relative to their own directory, which would be a bug.

inside the current build file with new parameters. The <ant> task can invoke a completely separate build file.

Any of the properties and references that the <ant> task sets for the invoked project are immutable. You can control the settings of a child project by predefining any property or path before its own initialization code tries to define it. If the <ant> call defines a dest.dir property and all child projects use that property to name the directory for their redistributables, then that location becomes the destination directory for all distribution files—even if the child build files try to redefine it.

To use this feature, you need to know the rules by which properties are passed down:

- Properties set on the command line are always passed down and can never be overridden.

- If inheritAll is true, all properties set in the master build file are passed to the child projects.

- Any properties defined inside <ant> override those set in the master build, but not the command line.

- If inheritAll is false, only those properties defined inside the <ant> declaration and the command line are passed down.

The command-line rule means that you can configure the master build from the command line and have those changes propagate down to all the child builds, as shown here:

```
ant -Ddist.dir=/projects/CDimage/dist
```

Of course, this works only if projects are designed to be overridden.

Designing a project for easy overriding

Controlling where the projects place their distribution packages is one common control option for a master build; others are which tests to run and which servers to deploy against. For a child project to be controllable, it needs to make extensive use of properties.

A good build file should already be using properties to define any string, attribute, or file that's used in multiple places. For easy integration into a larger project, any option that could sensibly be overridden should first be defined with a property and then referred to, giving the master build an option to change the value. To make this work, all child project build files should use the same names for the same controllable options. It's no use if `core/build.xml` used `dest.dir` for the destination directory, and `webapp/build.xml` used `destination.dir`.

To make overriding work better, use `<property location>` to define file locations, rather than `<property value>`. In a single build file, using the `value` attribute to define a file location works, because when these properties are resolved to file locations, it will be in the same build file. When you're passing properties around to other build files, using the `location` attribute ensures that relative paths are resolved in the build file declaring the property, not in the build file using the property.

Sometimes, overridden projects get corrupted by some of the properties of the parent project. This happens if the parent accidentally sets a property that's used in the internal workings of the project. Imagine if the child used a property `tests .failed` to log whether the unit tests failed. If the parent project set the same property, the child project would think that the tests had failed.

The way to avoid this is to have standard names for properties that parent build files are expected to configure in children, and for the parent build files to not pass down any other properties.

If you call a project with `<ant>` without setting `inheritall="false"`, all properties defined by the parent file will propagate to the child project. This is dangerous as it increases the risk of an accidental property overwrite. This is why setting `inheritall="false"` is so important: the best way to pass information down is inside the `<ant>` call.

10.2.2 Passing down properties and references in `<ant>`

The `<ant>` task lets you declare properties to pass down with the `<property>`, `<propertyset>`, and `<reference>` nested elements. To anyone using `<antcall>`, this should seem familiar, although in that task the equivalent of the `<property>` element is called `<param>`.

The `<property>` element of `<ant>` resembles a normal `<property>` task: it can set properties to a value, a location, a file, or a resource. You can even use `<property env="env">` to load the environment variables. Loading properties from a file is powerful, because a single file can then control which properties are set. For example, we could modify our targets to load a common file, the values of which would be set in all the child projects:

```
<target name="do-core" depends="init">
  <ant dir="core" target="${target}"
    inheritAll="false"/>
    <property file="master.properties"/>
  </ant>
</target>
```

All properties declared in the file `master.properties` will be set in the child project. For example, it could be

```
build.compiler=modern
dist.dir=/projects/CDimage/dist
```

This would force all projects to stick their distributables into the same target directory. We cannot place relative file references in the file, as all properties are treated as simple values. You must use absolute paths in a property file. Relative paths can be used in an inline declaration:

```
  <ant dir="core" target="${target}"
      inheritAll="false">
  <property name="dest.dir" location="dest" />
  <property file="master.properties"/>
  </ant>
```

To pass a datatype reference down, declare the type in the build file and then insert a `<reference>` tag:

```
  <ant dir="core" target="${target}"
      inheritAll="false">
  <property name="dest.dir" location="dest" />
  <property file="master.properties"/>
  <reference refid="main.classpath"/>
  </ant>
```

This will pass the classpath `main.classpath` down to the child project. You can rename a reference with the `torefid` attribute:

```
  <ant dir="core" target="${target}"
      inheritAll="false">
  <property name="dest.dir" location="dest" />
  <property file="master.properties"/>
  <reference refid="main.classpath" torefid="compile.classpath"/>
  </ant>
```

The <propertyset> element can be used to pass down a whole set of properties defined in the current build. It lets you specify a prefix or regular expression for properties, which is useful for bulk propagation of values. Some example <propertyset> declarations are

```
<propertyset>
  <propertyref prefix="test."/>          ⟵┐  Everything beginning
</propertyset>                                with "test."

<propertyset>
  <propertyref regex="*.host"/>          │   Everything ending
</propertyset>                                in ".host"

<propertyset>                             ┌   A single property,
  <propertyref name="test.host"/>        ⟵┘   "test.host"
</propertyset>
```

The last of these examples passes down a single property, but only if it's defined. If it's undefined, the property is unset. Ant's own documentation covers a few more features and examples; consult them if you have any complicated property propagation needs.

The other way to configure child projects is to have each one pull in a configuration file from the parent directory. This ensures that every child project shares common settings, even when not invoked from a parent build file. It becomes a single place to set project-wide settings. Here's how we load the file:

```
<project name="base" default="all">

  <echo>Building ${ant.file}</echo>

  <property file="build.properties"/>            ⟵❶
  <property name="root.dir" location=".."/>      ⟵❷
  <property name="settings.file"                      ❸
    location="${root.dir}/master.properties"/>
  <property file="${settings.file}"/>            ⟵❹
```

This is quite a complex process. First, we load our local properties ❶. Next we set a property root.dir to the parent directory ❷, *unless it was set to something else in our build.properties file*. If you move a project, you can point to the original root.dir location in your local build.properties file.

We then declare a property to be the build.properties file in that root directory (another override point) ❸, and finally we actually load it ❹. This file can contain all the shared settings across projects, and, provided every child project uses the root.dir property to identify the root directory, that property's file can use the value ${root.dir} to declare paths:

```
build.compiler=modern
dist.dir=${root.dir}/dist
```

This is a highly effective way of eliminating repetition across projects.

Overall, <ant> forms the basis for sharing work across build files. That doesn't just include those of a single project. There's nothing to stop a project taking an existing project from a third party, such as an open source project, and rebuilding it with customized settings. There are some other tasks, built-in and third-party, that extend <ant> with more complex delegations. Ant developers should know of them in case they have a need to use them.

10.3 ADVANCED DELEGATION

Three other tasks that can assist with delegation are <subant>, which is built into Ant, and the <antcallback> and <antfetch> tasks from the Ant-contrib project. Let's take a quick look at them.

<subant>

The <subant> task exists to make delegation to an entire set of build files easier. It looks very similar to <ant>, with various enhancements and with some corrections of default values that are, with hindsight, wrong:

- You can nominate multiple <fileset> or <filelist> listings of directories/build files to run.
- You can run the same "generic" build file in all the specified directories.
- If you set failonerror="false", failures in child projects will be ignored.
- Setting target="" will invoke the default target of the project; <ant> would try to run a target called "" instead.
- By default, nothing is inherited by child projects. That is, inheritall="false".

This task offers opportunities. Want to build the default target of all projects under the extensions directory, ignoring failures? It takes only three lines:

```
<subant target="" failonerror="false">
  <fileset dir="extensions" includes="*/build.xml" />
</subant>
```

Applying it to our build file, we can use <subant> to delegate all our work.

```
<filelist id="children">
  <file name="core"/>
  <file name="persist"/>
  <file name="webapp"/>
  <file name="ear"/>
</filelist>

<target name="delegate"  description="Delegate the build">
  <fail unless="target">no target to delegate</fail>
  <subant target="${target}" verbose="true">
```

```
      <filelist refid="children" />
    </subant>
  </target>
```

In chapter 11 we'll introduce an advanced way of ordering child builds, using the Ivy library management Antlib to create a list of projects sorted correctly for their internal dependencies. The `<subant>` task can take this list and invoke the children in the right order. Accordingly, we'll return to this task in the next chapter.

10.3.1 Getting data back

The Ant-contrib team has added its own tasks to the mix: `<antcallback>` and `<antfetch>` are tasks that extend `<antcall>` and `<ant>`, respectively, by adding a new attribute called `return`. `return` takes a list of properties to copy back from the invoked target into the calling project—effectively a function call.

Here's an example of using `return` to get some checksum values back from our core project:

```
<project name="fetch"
  xmlns:ac="antlib:net.sf.antcontrib">

  <ac:antfetch
    dir="core"
    target="checksum"
    return="target.zip.sha1, target.tar.sha1"/>

  <echo>target.zip.sha1=${target.zip.sha1}</echo>

</project>
```

As with the other Ant-contrib tasks, they need the Ant-contrib library introduced in chapter 9. The two tasks are used much less frequently than the other delegation tasks, but enable something that isn't built into Ant—the ability to use build files as function calls.

In the projects we work on, we find `<ant>` and `<subant>` do most of the work, the latter in conjunction with the Ivy tasks forthcoming in chapter 11. In either case, we try not to delegate too deeply: the master build file manages dependencies between the build files, and the individual build files assume that they are being called in the right order. Any team that tries too hard to chain work together across too many build files is going to end up confused about what's going on, and end up with a build that doesn't behave.

What we do strive for across all our build files is code reuse by sharing and extending template build files. Rather than copy and paste a working build file across ten projects, we try to have one build file that acts a bit like "base class" for the child projects. How can we do that? With the `<import>` task.

10.4 *INHERITING BUILD FILES THROUGH <IMPORT>*

Once you have more than one build file, you have a problem keeping them synchronized. If you deal with this problem by copying and pasting values, your project is doomed to become a build file maintenance nightmare, just as when you use copy-and-paste coding throughout your Java source.

The solution, in build files as well as Java, is this: *"Don't Repeat Yourself!"*

This is a phrase from *The Pragmatic Programmer*, and it's an important rule to remember. If you find yourself doing something by hand—repeatedly—you should try to find a better solution. Manual repetition creates errors and increases maintenance costs.

Even with a fully automated build, it's hard to stop repetition from creeping into large projects. Once a project has more than one build file, you tend to want the same targets in each. Unless you can share these targets, you'll end up with duplicate targets in different files.

You need to avoid the following things:

- Repeated options, such as the names of files or directories
- Repeated fragments of XML in different build files
- Repeated declarations of tasks, with the same or slightly different parameters
- Repeated fragments of XML in a build file

Repeated options is the easiest of these to deal with: use properties to avoid declaring the same constant text more than once, which is what we've been doing in the book up till now. More advanced features of Ant are needed to address the others. The first of these will deal with the problem of repeated fragments of XML in different build files.

The first step to doing this is to know that in pure XML, the only way to share data between files is to use XML entities. Ant supports this, although its use is now discouraged.

10.4.1 XML entity inclusion

XML parsers let you declare references to fragments of XML text, text that will be inserted into the document when the declared entity is used.

First we must declare the entity at the beginning of the file, after the `<?xml?>` header and before the XML data itself:

```
<?xml version="1.0"?>
<!DOCTYPE project [
    <!ENTITY properties SYSTEM "../properties.xml">
]>
<project name=" application " default="default" basedir=".">
```

This doesn't insert the file yet; it merely makes it known to the XML parser using the name `properties`. We'll use this entity name when inserting the text. The path to the file must be an absolute or relative URL and cannot contain Ant properties.

To insert the XML text inside the build file, we must declare the entity name between an ampersand (&) and a semicolon (;)—just as if we were inserting characters into the XML file, such as the `&gt;` and `&lt;` angle brackets:

```
<project name="application" default="default" basedir=".">
```

```
    &properties;
```

When parsing the file, the XML parser will replace all entity references with the text behind them. Ant sees everything from the included file as if it were pasted directly into the main XML file.

This technique is very limited, primarily because the XML parser does all the work. Only incomplete fragments of an XML document can be included. You can't use Ant properties in setting the path to the file you want to include, and there's no way of overriding included targets with new targets.

This mechanism is now obsolete, at least within Ant, which has its own solution—the `<import>` task.

10.4.2 Importing build files with <import>

The `<import>` task is the Ant-specific successor to XML entities. To import a build file into the current build file, you just use an `<import>` task outside any target:

```
<import file="${base-dir}/common.xml"/>
```

When Ant processes a build file, it runs through all declarations outside the targets before executing any requested target. Whenever Ant encounters an `<import>` declaration, it imports the referenced file by

1 Resolving the file reference, expanding any properties in the process

2 Retrieving and parsing the file

3 Inserting its (transformed) contents into the current file

4 Handling collisions between target names by renaming the targets of the imported file

On the surface, the task looks very similar to that of XML entities. How do they differ? Table 10.3 shows the differences.

At first glance, `<import>` doesn't appear significantly better than XML entities, but it is, because Ant is in control of the process. It happens as the containing build file is interpreted, so property expansion can be used to locate the file. Ant interprets the targets declared in the file specially, and provides what is effectively a simple inheritance model of build files. One of the big differences is that Ant lets you override the targets defined in a file that's pulled in via `<import>`.

Table 10.3   Comparing XML entity inclusion with Ant's <import>

XML Entities	<import>
Valid in any XML file	Ant only
Declare at top of document	Declare anywhere outside a target
Takes absolute or relative URL references	Takes absolute or relative filenames
Cannot use ${property} references in the URL	Can use ${property} references in the filename
Must resolve to a file	optional="true" imports will skip missing files
Must resolve to a fragment of an XML document	Must resolve to a complete Ant build file
It's an error to declare targets with the same name	Has a model for overriding target declarations
Are interpreted in the directory of the file into which they're imported	Has access to the original name and directory of the imported file through properties
Hard to track down problems	Slightly easier to debug

10.4.3   How Ant overrides targets

When we import a build file, it can add targets to our own build file. Ant allows us to override those imported targets with new ones. That gives build files a feature very similar to subclassing in Java itself. A base build file can define the default behavior for a project by using standard targets, and build files that import the project can override this behavior by redefining the targets.

Let's explore this behavior with a `base.xml` file containing the targets `init`, `all`, and `dist`:

```
<project name="basefile" basedir=".">

  <target name="init" >
    <mkdir dir="build" />
  </target>

  <target name="dist" depends="init"/>

  <target name="all" depends="dist" />

</project>
```

Now import `base.xml` into a new build file, which will import this project and define a new `dist` target:

```
<project name="app" basedir=".">
<import file="base.xml"/>

  <target name="dist">
    <echo>creating a distribution</echo>
```

```
    </target>

</project>
```

What's going to happen? If we run ant -f app.xml all, what is printed?

```
Buildfile: app.xml

dist:
    [echo] creating a distribution

all:

BUILD SUCCESSFUL
Total time: 0 seconds
```

The imported all target has run, as has its direct dependency, dist. But instead of the implementation from the same build file running, the one from the outer build file has been executed. And, because the new dist target did not depend upon the init target, that target wasn't called at all.

This demonstrates the following:

1 The targets in the imported file are available on the command line.

2 Targets in the imported file can depend upon targets in the main file, and vice versa.

3 If a target is already defined in the build file, then it overrides any in the imported file.

4 When such an override takes place, any dependencies of the overridden target are lost.

These are the main aspects of the behavior of <import>. These inheritances and overwritten rules let you selectively override targets of a base build file, creating extended build files.

10.4.4   Calling overridden targets

What if you don't want Ant to override a target? You cannot prevent that, but you can explicitly invoke the original target by prefixing the project name to the target. This is important: not the name of the file, exactly, but the name of the project as defined in the name attribute of the root <project> element of the build file:

```
<target name="dist" depends="basefile.dist">
  <echo>creating a distribution</echo>
</target>
```

With our overriding dist target declared as depending on the basefile.dist target of the imported file, our Ant build now invokes the imported target and all its dependencies:

```
init:
    [mkdir] Created dir: C:\big_projects\build
```

```
basefile.dist:

dist:
    [echo] creating a distribution

all:
```

You can't import two build files with the same project name; the build will fail if you try this. You can always be sure that a fully qualified target is the one you want, not one from another build file.

From Ant 1.7, every imported target can *always* be referred to by its fully qualified name. In Ant 1.6, only targets that were overridden got this treatment. The advantage of the new rule is that it allows build files to explicitly call specific targets, whether they are overridden or not. You can use this behavior to stop targets from being accidentally overridden:

```
<target name="all" depends="basefile.init,basefile.dist" />
```

If you don't want target dependencies in an imported project to be overridden, always use the full target name.

There's one other aspect to the <import> process that can be useful: the properties it defines in the process.

10.4.5   The special properties of <import>

Any imported build file can find out its original filename. When a file is imported, a new property is created that records the name of the file. First, you need to know that ant.file is a property that's always set to the full path of the build file that's executed. This is one of those things that Ant has always done. With <import>, Ant sets the property ant.file.*projectname* to the path of the imported file:

```
<project name="root" default="status">        ⟵┐ The name of
                                                  │ the project
<target name="status">
  <echo>ant.file=${ant.file}</echo>      ⟵— The original property
  <echo>ant.file.root=${ant.file.root}</echo>         ⟵┐ The root
  <echo>ant.file.imported=${ant.file.imported}</echo> │ project's file
</target>

</project>
```

The output of this build file is the path of the build file twice:

```
Buildfile: root.xml

status:
    [echo] ant.file=/tmp/root.xml
    [echo] ant.file.root=/tmp/root.xml
    [echo] ant.file.imported=${ant.file.imported}
```

Now let's create an import file in a subdirectory:

```
<project name="imported" >

<echo>*Imported file
*ant.file.imported=${ant.file.imported}
</echo>
</project>
```

We can use it in our main project:

```
project name="root" default="status">

<target name="status">
  <echo>ant.file=${ant.file}</echo>
  <echo>ant.file.root=${ant.file.root}</echo>
  <echo>ant.file.imported=${ant.file.imported}</echo>
</target>

<import file="subdir/imported.xml" />

</project>
```

What are we going to see now?

```
Buildfile: root.xml
     [echo] *Imported file
     [echo] *ant.file.imported=/tmp/subdir/imported.xml

status:
     [echo] ant.file=/tmp/root.xml
     [echo] ant.file.root=/tmp/root.xml
     [echo] ant.file.imported=/tmp/subdir/imported.xml
```

This output shows that the imported file's top-level declarations run before any targets. It also shows that Ant has created a new property, ant.file.imported, set to the path of the imported project. This property is visible across the merged build files from the <import> declaration onwards. We can use this in the <dirname> task to determine the base directory of an imported project. Here's how we do this in imported.xml:

```
<dirname property="imported.dir" file="${ant.file.imported}"/>
<echo>imported.dir=${imported.dir}</echo>
```

The extra line of output is

```
[echo] imported.dir=/tmp/subdir
```

Once you have the base directory, you can find files and directories relative to that location, instead of just relative to the outer build file.

There's one little caveat here: for all this to work, you cannot <import> projects with the same name into another project. Ant will halt the build if you try to do so. You must set the name of every <project> to something different.

That ends our introduction to `<import>`, a task that constitutes possibly the most radical change to Ant in recent years. Given it is so radical, we need to think about the best way to use it in real projects.

10.5   APPLYING `<IMPORT>`

The `<import>` task can pull in other build files, inserting its tasks and targets into the outer project in a way that allows Ant to override targets. How can we use `<import>` to make maintaining a big project easier?

There are three different ways of using `<import>` that regularly crop up in build files:

- Extending existing build files
- Creating a base build file for many projects
- Mixin build files

Let's run through each of these methods in turn.

10.5.1   Extending an existing build file

One use of the `<import>` task is to completely import an existing build file, just to stick a few more tasks on the end. Doing so guarantees that you don't break the existing build file and lets you add new targets to a build file that may not even be yours; it may be from another project that you just need to build.

The sample build files for chapter 5 onwards have used `<import>` this way. Anyone who looked at the sample files and saw the "ignore this for now" comments has now reached the point where we explain this situation.

As an example, here's the start of the chapter 7 build file, `core-chapter-07.xml`:

```
<project name="core-chapter07" default="default">

<description>
  This is the core build file for chapter 7.
  </description>

<!-- we don't cover imports until chapter 10
    If you are curious, what we are doing here
    is importing every single declaration of the
    imported build file, both toplevel and targets.
-->

<import file="core-chapter-06.xml" />

<target name="ftp-init" depends="init">
  <fail unless="server">Set the "server" property!</fail>
  <property name="ftp.propfile" location="secure/${server}.properties" />
  <loadproperties srcFile="${ftp.propfile}" />
</target>
```

We've included all the targets of the chapter 6 build file, which includes all the packaging, testing, and execution targets. By adding the distribution targets of chapter 7 to a separate file, we can be sure that no changes we make to the chapter 7 targets will have any effect on the build of chapter 6. Yet we can still make targets in our new build file depend on those in the original, such as where our `ftp-init` target depends on the base `init` target.

Isolating some parts of the build process, here, distribution, can help with some aspects of build-file maintenance. We can be sure that the side effects of changes to the distribution build file will be limited to that file and any that import it or call it with `<ant>`. What we cannot do is isolate the file from changes in the files it imports—any error in the chapter 6 build or changes to its `init` target could break our distribution build.

The second use of the `<import>` task is to create a reusable template file that can be extended by all the child build files in a large project.

10.5.2 Creating a base build file for many projects

Remember the master build file from section 10.1, which used `<ant>` to invoke build files for the project `core`, `persist`, `webapp`, and `ear`? Did we have to write stub build files for each project? Yes, but not very big stubs. What we did do was write the base build file, `diary/xml/base.xml`, a build file containing nothing other than the main entry points we want to implement across all projects.

```xml
<?xml version="1.0"?>
<project name="base" default="all">

  <echo>Building ${ant.file}</echo>

  <property file="build.properties"/>
  <property name="root.dir" location=".."/>
  <property name="settings.file"
    location="${root.dir}/master.properties"/>
  <property file="${settings.file}"/>

  <target name="default" depends="all"
    description="default: build 'all'"/>

  <target name="dist"  description="Build the distribution"/>

  <target name="all"  description="Build everything"
    depends="dist"/>

  <target name="diagnostics"
    description="diagnostics">
    <diagnostics/>
  </target>

  <target name="clean"
    description="clean up"/>
```

```
<target name="noop">
  <property name="dist.dir" location="dist"/>
  <echo>in ${basedir}</echo>
  <echo>dist.dir=${dist.dir}</echo>
</target>

</project>
```

All our child projects will import this target, allowing it to override any of the stub declarations with its actual implementations. Here, for example, is the file `persist/build.xml`, which currently does nothing other than import the targets.

```
<?xml version="1.0"?>
<project name="persist" default="default">

  <property file="build.properties" />
  <property name="root.dir" location=".." />
  <property name="xmlfiles.dir" location="${root.dir}/xml" />
  <!-- import our base file -->
  <import file="${xmlfiles.dir}/base.xml" />

  <!-- insert any new targets here -->
</project>
```

The initial property settings will read the per-project `build.properties` file before anything else, then set up the location of the base build file to import. This allows developers to move the entire child project somewhere else on their hard disk, yet still refer back to the original file. If the path had been hard-coded into the `<import>`, as the declaration `file="../../xml/base.xml"`, it would be impossible to move the project.

This behavior shows an unwelcome consequence of `<import>`. Once a project starts depending on XML files in parent or sibling directories, it's no longer self-contained. This prevents projects from releasing self-contained source distributions of child projects. The whole project tree needs to be included for a build to work. You can use the `optional` attribute of `<import>` to say that the build should continue if the imported file is missing, but that doesn't help, because everything contained in the file is now missing from the build. Source distributions need to include the whole source tree, including the common build files.

The other problem is that even with standardized target names, it becomes hard to manage the dependencies of targets across the base and extended build files.

Creating milestone targets for easier overrides

Once you embrace `<import>`, build files become deceptively complex. Just as a deep hierarchy of Java classes can be hard to visualize, so can a deep tree of `<import>` declarations and overridden targets. One technique that appears to make this more manageable is to have targets that represent states you want the project to be in.

Ant targets are usually named for actions or deliverables, such as `"jar"`, `"compile"`, and `"copy-files"`. They say what the target does. Once you start overriding things, however, it's not so clear what the targets do. Our solution to this situation is to declare what we call *milestone targets*. These targets represent the state of a build, such as *ready-to-compile* and *packaged*. Most importantly, these targets contain no tasks. Instead they just declare what targets need to run to reach the milestone. On a simple project, *ready-to-compile* is just a matter of setting up the classpath for the libraries. This would be described as

```
<target name="ready-to-compile" depends="classpaths-setup" />
```

On a more complex project, that state may be reached only if we generate Java source from XML files:

```
<target name="ready-to-compile"
  depends="classpaths-setup,generate-source" />
```

If the base build file declares the core milestones and basic sequence of actions, build files that `<import>` this file can define new steps that have to be taken to reach the goal, and can still inherit all the dependencies of the original milestone:

```
<target name="ready-to-compile"
  depends="base.ready-to-compile,javacc" />
```

This is why it's so important for these milestone targets to have no tasks inside them. When we override a milestone yet declare a dependency on the base milestone, we tell Ant that the overridden target depends on `base.ready-to-compile` and all its dependencies. It's the dependencies we want, but the only way to pull them in is to depend on the `base.ready-to-compile` target. If it did any work, such as a `<javac>` compile, it would run before the new `javacc` target and perhaps not work.

To use milestone targets, you have to define a set of states that are common across all projects. There is no standard set of milestones. Common ones we use include the following: `"ready-to-compile"`, `"compile-complete"`, `"classpaths-setup"`, `"dist"`, `"all"`, `"installed"`, `"tested"`, and `"deployed"`. The idea is that at the command line, you tell Ant what state you want the build to be in, such as

```
> ant deployed
```

The tool will do all the work needed to get the application into that state, be it the common steps of the base build file or custom steps of derivative build files.

There's one final way to use `<import>` that takes this notion of milestone targets and uses it to mix multiple template build files into a single project.

10.5.3 Mixin build files

The first two ways of using `<import>` are both quite similar: you take a build file and extend it, just as if you were extending a Java class. There's another way, one that bears more of a resemblance to C++ programming—*mixin build files*.

The *mixin* is a concept from C++, where you would extend a class just to get some extra methods in your own class. Because C++ lets you inherit from multiple classes, you could mix in many different parent classes, to make your class as an aggregation of all its parents.

Similarly, the <import> task lets you define *mixin build files*. These are build files that perform a specific function, such as creating an archive or deploying a web application to a local application server. They don't have to be self-contained; they can import other build files, which can mix in others. Each build file will be imported only once, even if there are multiple <import> statements doing it.

This is cutting-edge Ant build file development. We aren't going to show in detail how to do it or explain best practices, because nobody knows how to do this properly. We're all just learning. Where it does appear to work best is when the mixin file defines template tasks, using the <presetdef> and <macrodef> tasks we're about to introduce. This effectively makes new tasks available to the outer build files, which can glue them together in whatever order you choose.

10.5.4   Best practices with <import>

The consequences of adding <import> to Ant are profound. You can use the command to implement simple inheritance, so you now have a better way of managing projects with multiple subprojects. Ideally, each subproject should be nothing but a simple delegation to the base component. Some things to keep in mind when using <import> follow:

- Be very cautious about importing multiple files. The risk of clashes and unexpected overrides increases as you do so.

- Give every project a unique name attribute in the <project> declaration. It's easy to miss this when using an existing file as a template, and it can be very confusing.

- Provide clear, structured override points if you want to offer default targets that may need to be overridden.

- Be very, very, careful when maintaining a common build file that's imported into multiple projects. If you accidentally name a target the same as one in any of the projects that import it, your build will not work, and you'll have a hard time figuring out why.

Just as object-oriented design has flaws, inheritance and overriding of targets brings new dangers. Yet <import> also delivers the ability to scale projects better than Ant has been able to do so before. It's one of the key ways of keeping build files easy to maintain, which was listed as one of the problems of large-scale Ant projects. It can provide reusable targets, targets you can override when needed. The next way to keep maintenance down is to define template tasks, templates that can standardize the options of commonly used tasks—macros.

10.6 ANT'S MACRO FACILITIES

In this chapter, we've looked at `<ant>` and `<subant>`, which delegate work to self-contained builds. Next came the `<import>` task, to share and reuse targets across build files.

That still leaves a big problem. There's too much repetition in every task declaration. All too often, projects want standard values across all uses of a task, such as the `source="1.5"` for the `<java>` task. Even if everyone remembers to set this attribute correctly across all uses of `<java>` across multiple build files, what happens when the team moves to Java 7? Do we really have to edit every use of the task?

That's the final challenge of scale this chapter addresses, through Ant's macro facilities. Anyone who wrote C or C++ code will remember the `#define` preprocessor instruction. This was a tool of power—and, in the wrong hands, terror. The macro expansion took place before the language itself was parsed, so you could almost generate a new language if you got carried away.

Ant has a macro system, but it's more restrained. It lets you do two things, both of which take place *after* parsing. First, you can define new tasks with different defaults from existing tasks, using `<presetdef>`. Secondly, you can define a *macro task*, which is a sequence of other tasks. This macro can declare attributes—mandatory and optional—and elements, all of which will be accessible in the macro. In this way, you can build a new composite task from those that exist already. Both techniques have their place.

10.6.1 Redefining tasks with <presetdef>

We'll start with the `<presetdef>` task, which is the simpler of the two tasks. It lets you declare a new task based on an existing task. This new task can be used anywhere you would use a normal task and when it's executed, the task it wraps is invoked. If we were fixing the `<exec>` task, we could define a new task, `<robustExec>`, which would set `failonerror="true"`. Whenever we wanted to execute a program, we would declare it with `<robustExec>` and the `failonerror` attribute would be set for us. All other attributes and nested elements would still be the same as for the original task. We could even set `failonerror="false"`, in overriding the values set in the template defined with `<presetdef>`.

We like the `<presetdef>` task because it lets you lay down rules for what the default arguments to tasks should be, across all projects. It also allows us to change those defaults in one place—the build file that defines the `<presetdef>` tasks—and have those changes propagate. We use it a lot. It crops up in Ant's own build and test files a lot, too.

How do you actually use it? Well, let's fix the `<exec>` task. This task is useful, but it defaults to ignoring any failure code returned by the program. To fix that, we define a new task, with a different failure policy:

```
<presetdef name="robustExec">
   <exec failonerror="true"/>
</presetdef>
```

This gives a new task, `<robustExec>`. We can use it wherever we would normally use `<exec>`, and know that the failure-handling policy will be consistently set to what we want:

```
<robustExec executable="firefox" />
```

It can even be used inside another `<presetdef>` declaration: here defining a version that runs code only on Windows and which also checks the return codes:

```
<presetdef name="execOnWindows">
   <robustExec os="windows" />
</presetdef>
```

We can then use this wherever we see fit.

```
<execOnWindows executable="iexplore" />
```

This looks a bit like subclassing in object-oriented languages, but it isn't. We're just predefining values, values callers can still override and extend. Anyone can overwrite predefined attributes.

Defining new default values is invaluable when you want to lay down the rules for performing common operations, such as compiling code. A `<presetdef>` declaration of a new task can declare all the project policies. Here, for example, we declare a new set of defaults for the `<javac>` task, with various options (language, debug, deprecation, etc.) all set to what we want:

```
<presetdef name="javac" uri="http://antbook.org/d1/ext" >
  <javac debug="${javac.debug.mode}"
    nowarn="true"
    deprecation="${javac.deprecation.mode}"
    source="${javac.java.version}"
    target="${javac.java.version}"
    includeAntRuntime="false"
    >
  </javac>
</presetdef>
```

By setting the `uri` attribute, we've placed the new task into a namespace. This allows our task to coexist with the original name. When we use it, we have to use the task in our new namespace:

```
<target name="compile" depends="init"
  xmlns:ext="http://antbook.org/d1/ext" >
  <ext:javac
    classpathref="compile.classpath"
    srcdir="${src.dir}"
    destdir="${build.classes.dir}"
    >
```

```
    <src dir="${src.dir}">
  </ext:javac>
</target>
```

The `<presetdef>` task is invaluable in a large project, because it can keep options consistent across all projects. It also makes it easy to add a new default value to all build files, wherever a target is used. We regularly create new definitions for common tasks of `<javac>`, `<exec>`, `<java>`, and `<jar>` for this reason. That doesn't mean that it should be used everywhere; there are hazards to be aware of.

10.6.2   The hazards of \<presetdef\>

You may be so excited by the possibility of redefining the default options for every possible task that you'll want to bring up the build files in your editor and rapidly redefine everything. Don't! Wait until you've read more!

When a new task is declared with `<presetdef>`, the default attributes of a task can be redefined. Any user of the task is free to override these values when they use the task:

```
<execOnWindows executable="iexplore" failonerror="false"/>
```

The options that you set aren't absolute rules; they are merely hints. This is inadequate if you want to enforce rules across your projects.

Any nested element in the `<presetdef>` declaration is included in the task along with any new definitions. Unlike attributes, which can be overridden, nested elements get concatenated. If, for example, our task declared that the source directory was `${src.dir}`, there would be no way to override that declaration.

Another serious hazard is task name clashes. Imagine you decide to wrap up the `<jar>` task with a preset task, with the meaningful name `<archive>`. Now imagine a new version of Ant ships, with a task called `<archive>`. When `<archive>` is used, which one is going to be run? The answer: whichever got declared last. This can be somewhat unexpected. Now, you may think that unless Ant comes out with a new task this isn't a risk, but what if you import a build file that declares its own `<presetdef>` task called `<archive>`? Which is going to be used now? It may depend on the order the targets were executed. This is very important: you need to know the rules for inheritance of `<presetdef>` (and, soon, `<macrodef>`) declarations, which are as follows:

- Whoever declares a task most recently wins. This is the opposite of the property assignment model.
- A task stays defined through Ant processes that are started by `<ant>`, `<antcall>`, or `<subant>`.
- Ant warns if you redefine things, whether the definition is the same or different.

We prefer to define new tasks in private namespaces, to make it clear that they are not Ant's own tasks, and to isolate ourselves from Ant's own set of tasks.

Here are some effective ways to work with the `<presetdef>` task:

- Don't run out and declare <presetdef> wrappers for every task. The result is a build file that only you will understand.
- Do use <presetdef> when you want to lay down new rules for common tasks.
- Give tasks and macros meaningful names.
- Don't redefine an existing task in the default namespace. Bad things can happen.
- Declare the tasks in a new namespace, to isolate them from the built-in tasks.

As we said, <presetdef> is a wonderful thing. It just needs a bit of care to be used effectively. The other macro tool, <macrodef>, is equally powerful and needs to be treated with similar caution.

10.7 WRITING MACROS WITH <MACRODEF>

The <presetdef> declaration defines default values for an existing task. It doesn't let you create a completely new task from a sequence of existing tasks, nor does it hide any of the details of the underlying task. All you can do is predefine some settings.

If you want to do more, you need a different task: <macrodef>. This task lets you define a macro task, with optional and mandatory attributes and nested elements. Inside it, you can list a sequence of tasks. When the new task is used in a build file, Ant passes the task's parameters to the inner sequence of tasks, and your work is performed.

Here's an example:

```
<macrodef name="copy-useful-files" uri="http://antbook.org/d1/ext">
    <attribute name="src"/>
    <attribute name="dest"/>
    <attribute name="failonerror" default="false"/>
    <attribute name="pattern"
    default="**/*.ini,**/*.xml,**/*.dtd,**/*.xsd,**/*.properties" />
  <sequential>
    <echo level="verbose">copying @{pattern}
      from @{src} to @{dest}</echo>
    <copy todir="@{dest}" failonerror="@{failonerror}">
      <fileset dir="@{src}" includes="@{pattern}"/>
    </copy>
  </sequential>
</macrodef>
```

What does this do?

The <macrodef> begins the declaration; we then list four attributes. Two of the attributes, failonerror and pattern, have default values, which implicitly indicates that these attributes are optional and provides their value in such cases. Then follows a sequence of tasks, wrapped in the <sequential> container. One of the tasks is a simple <echo> to list the parameters when you run Ant in verbose mode; the other is a `<copy>` operation. As with `<presetdef>`, we've placed the declaration into a new namespace by setting the optional `uri` attribute.

This task copies all the files matching the macro's pattern from the source tree to the compiled classes' directory tree. If we don't specify a pattern, we get the default set:

```
<ext:copy-useful-files src="${src.dir}" dest="${build.classes.dir}"/>
```

We can change this to a different pattern:

```
<ext:copy-useful-files src="${src.dir}" dest="${build.classes.dir}"
    pattern="**/*.xslt,**/*.sxw"/>
```

This will completely replace the default value, which isn't available.

10.7.1 Passing data to a macro

Macros support attributes, elements, and nested text elements. Inside the macro, we can access attribute parameters by using the `@{attribute}` operation, which works almost like classic `${property}` property expansion, except that the case of the attribute is ignored. Ant expands macro parameters before properties, which lets you use a macro parameter to define the name of a property: `${@{property}}`. This is different from normal, where `${${nested-property}}` expansion is supported only in the Ant-contrib task `<propertycopy>`.

Nested text inside can be placed into a parameter named with the `<text>` element. This text can be made optional or not, and leading and trailing whitespace can be stripped with the `trim` attribute:

```
<macrodef name="verbose" uri="http://antbook.org/d1/ext">
  <text name="text.value" trim="false" optional="false" />
  <sequential>
    <echo level="verbose">@{text.value}</echo>
  </sequential>
</macrodef>
```

This macro prints out messages in verbose mode:

```
<ext:verbose>Reformatting hard drive</ext:verbose>
```

We could use this new task to add log messages to our build files, messages that will appear only in a `-verbose` run. Nested text can be very useful in a macro.

Alongside text and attributes, the `<macrodef>` task supports nested elements. First, we must declare an `<element>` parameter in the task, which says that an element called `<files>` is required:

```
<element name="files" optional="false"/>
```

We can then insert all XML under this element anywhere inside our sequence of targets, just by declaring the name of the element as an element inside the sequence:

```
<files/>
```

All the XML elements underneath the `<files/>` declaration get passed in, as if the declaration were inline[1]. Here's a simple demonstration that echoes out the XML passed in:

```
<macrodef name="exml" uri="http://antbook.org/d1/ext">
  <element name="files" optional="false"/>
  <sequential>
    <echoxml><x><files/></x></echoxml>
  </sequential>
</macrodef>
```

We can use this with any XML inside our `<files/>` element.

```
<ext:exml>
  <files>
    <fileset dir="." includes="*.xml" />
  </files>
</ext:exml>
```

The result of this run is what Ant's `<echoxml>` task does: it prints out the nested XML to the screen or a file:

```
exml:
<?xml version="1.0" encoding="UTF-8"?>
<x>
  <fileset dir="." includes="*.xml" />
</x>
```

You can declare one element parameter as implicit, meaning that it takes all the XML nested inside the macro that doesn't match any other element:

```
<macrodef name="do2" uri="http://antbook.org/d1/ext">
  <element name="commands" implicit="true"/>
  <sequential>
    <commands/>
    <commands/>
  </sequential>
</macrodef>
```

This states that the parameter `<commands/>` should be bound to all the nested XML. This macro executes the tasks supplied as parameters twice in a row, so we can use it like this:

```
<ext:do2>
  <echo>message</echo>
</ext:do2>
```

This shows that you can use the macro elements anywhere inside the macro, not just inside an Ant task or datatype:

---

[1] In Ant 1.6 and Ant1.7, top-level text gets lost—which is probably a bug—but elements are passed down along with their attributes and text.

```
do2:
    [echo] message
    [echo] message
```

Think of all the fun you can have with that. With this and the Ant-contrib tasks of chapter 10, Ant is almost a real programming language. It doesn't have local variables, but it does have something close to it.

10.7.2 Local variables

Anyone who writes a complex macro will end up using properties to pass information between the tasks in the macro. This works, once. The second time the macro runs, the old properties will still be set, because Ant's properties are immutable.

What can you do? Break the immutability rule. The `<var>` task from Ant-contrib creates a property that can be a real variable, meaning it can be changed. We can then unset a global property before calling any task that wants to use it. Take a macro to set a property to the full path of a file that has been "reparented" to a different directory. We need to use properties inside the macro here:

```
<macrodef name="reparent" uri="http://antbook.org/d1/ext">
  <attribute name="file" />
  <attribute name="destdir" />
  <attribute name="property" />
  <sequential>
    <ac:var name="var.reparent.dest" unset="true" />
    <property name="var.reparent.dest" location="@{destdir}" />
    <ac:var name="var.reparent.filename" unset="true" />
    <basename property="var.reparent.filename" file="@{file}"/>
    <property name="@{property}"
      location="${reparent.dest}/${var.reparent.filename}" />
  </sequential>
</macrodef>
```

We can use this task to determine the name that some files will have, after a copy operation. To make sure that our properties are acting as variables, we run the macro twice:

```
<target name="reparent" >
  <ext:reparent file="build.xml" property="copy1"
    destdir="${java.io.tmpdir}" />
  <ext:reparent
    file="ch10-macros.xml" property="copy2"
    destdir="${java.io.tmpdir}" />
  <echo>
   copy1=${copy1}
   copy2=${copy2}
  </echo>
</target>
```

When we run this macro, we get the appropriate results for each build file, showing that the macro is working:

```
reparent:
    [echo]
    [echo]      copy1=/tmp/build.xml
    [echo]      copy2=/tmp/ch10-macros.xml
    [echo]
```

Remember that the macro is still using global properties for its work, and that the `<var>` task will reset any properties' values. Always use obscure property names for properties used inside macros. One convention suggested by a reviewer[2] was to use `tmp.` or `var.` as the prefix, which is what we've done.

10.7.3   Effective macro use

Macros give you power. With power comes responsibility: use it carefully. Here are some tips on writing safe macros:

- Write macros to manage common sequences of operations.
- Don't write macros when you don't have any repetition in your build file.
- Declare macros in private namespaces.
- Use the Ant-contrib tasks for conditional logic, property resets with `<var>`, and other complex operations inside macros.

One obvious problem arises in a big project: where to declare the macros? This is where the mixin build files, mentioned in section 10.5.3, come into play. We have a build file, `xml/macros-mixin.xml`, that contains nothing but `<macrodef>` and `<presetdef >` declarations.

It begins by declaring the project and the namespaces of the macros and the Ant-contrib:

```
<project name="macros"
  xmlns:ext="http://antbook.org/d1/ext"
  xmlns:ac="antlib:net.sf.antcontrib">

<property name="macros-mixin.uri" value="http://antbook.org/d1/ext" />
```

The file contains all of our `<macrodef>` and `<presetdef>` declarations, declaring them in the XML namespace `http://antbook.org/d1/ext`. Any build file can import this file to get all the tasks:

```
<import file="../xml/macros-mixin.xml"/>
```

This gives all build files in the project access to the predefined tasks, providing us with a single point of control over how the core tasks of Ant are used in all build files across the projects. Together, `<presetdef>`, `<macrodef>`, and `<import>` give you control of big project builds.

---

[2] Jon Skeet, committer emeritus on the Ant project.

10.8 SUMMARY

Scaling up a software project is always troublesome. Ant can scale to meet the needs of big projects, if used carefully. We have enumerated four problems with big projects:

- Delegating work to build files in subprojects
- Building subprojects in the correct order
- Ensuring build files are easy to maintain
- Managing libraries

The <ant> and <subant> tasks can delegate work to other build files, with the ability to control the invoked file by predefining properties and passing down datatype declarations.

Once you have multiple child projects, you have another problem—avoiding duplication of work. The <import> task comes to your aid here. It lets you import a shared build file into multiple build files, providing a base set of targets that can be (optionally) overridden. We have looked at three ways to use <import>:

- To extend an existing build file with new follow-on functionality—such as deployment or distribution targets. This isolates the deployment and distribution from the other work.

- To override a base build file with specific actions at various stages in the application's build. This is similar to inheritance and overriding in object-oriented languages and can bring in similar complexity. The use of a common state model, with milestone targets, can alleviate some of the problems.

- As a way of writing mixin build files that define targets or tasks that can be used from any build file, without any dependencies on the state of the application at the time that they're invoked.

Finally, we've introduced two tasks, <presetdef> and <macrodef>, that let you define new tasks from existing ones. The <presetdef> task can be used to set task policies across projects, while the <macrodef> task lets you build up complex sequences of operations from other tasks. Together they strive to keep the build files you write simple and consistent.

That leaves the final problem: managing libraries. That little problem is going to take up the whole of the next chapter.

CHAPTER 11

Managing dependencies

One topic that this book has been avoiding is this: how to manage library dependencies in Ant. We've avoided it because it's hard to get right. We've covered the basic mechanics of setting up a classpath, but not where those JAR files should come from and how to look after them. It's time to face the challenge of managing JAR dependencies properly.

The first step is to define the problems we have. What do we need to know?

1 How to set up the build with the JAR files that are needed to compile, test, and run the application

2 How to pass a JAR file created in one project into other projects built on the same machine, or even to other developers in a team

3 How to build child projects that depend on each other in the right order

4 How to switch library versions on demand

A single product addresses these issues, but it isn't built into Ant. It's an extension Antlib called Ivy. Before we introduce it, we have to look at the underlying problem: managing JAR files.

How to add libraries to an Ant classpath

The simplest way to manage libraries is to have a directory containing all the JAR files. To add new JARs, just drop them in. The classpath includes every JAR file in the directory:

```
<path id="compile.classpath">
 <fileset dir="lib" includes="**/*.jar" />
</path>
```

This is the main way of managing libraries in Ant. If the directory is kept under revision control, then all developers who check out the project get the JARs. They can roll back the library versions alongside the code, so old versions of an application stay synchronized with the libraries. This technique works for small to medium projects. However, it doesn't work for projects with multiple child projects, or when the classpaths for different parts of the build (compile, test, deploy, embedded-use, or standalone) are all radically different. In other words, it doesn't scale.

Now imagine if a server kept all the released versions of popular JAR files. You could have a task that took the name and version of a file and retrieved it. It could cache these files on the local disk, so laptops could still build when they were off the network. Finally, if this repository was writeable, team members could use it to share artifacts across projects.

Such a repository exists, as do the Ant tasks to work with them. The repository came from the Apache Maven project, whose developers wrote a build system for fixing what they saw as defects in Ant. One idea—the Maven repository—called for a centralized repository of open-source artifacts. Every artifact in the repository is accompanied by metadata in an XML file—the POM file. This file describes the artifact and even declares which versions of other libraries the JAR depends on. The result is that the build tool pulls down both the direct and the indirect dependencies of an application.

That's what Apache Maven does, and it's one of the selling points of Maven against Ant. Yet we aren't going to advocate a switch to Maven. There's certainly some appeal in its conformance-over-configuration vision: "Follow the rules of the Maven team exactly, and you don't need to write build files." But we have too many problems following their rules. They not only dictate how to lay out your source, but they have a strict notion of your development lifecycle. If your workflow is more complex, with activities such as creating Java source from XML files, making signed JARs of the test files, or even creating two JAR files from a single project, you end up fighting Maven's rules all the way.

We shouldn't have to switch to a different way of building, testing, and deploying applications just to get the classpaths in Ant set up. This is where Ivy comes into the picture. It manages dependencies and nothing else—and it does this job very well!

11.1 INTRODUCING IVY

Ivy is a tool to manage libraries in Ant and to coordinate Ant builds across related projects. It was created by Xavier Hanin, of the French company Jayasoft, in September 2004. In October 2006, it moved into the Apache Incubator as a way of joining the Apache organization. Once it has finished its incubation period, it should become a fully-fledged Apache project, possibly under the http://ant.apache.org site.

11.1.1 The core concepts of Ivy

The main concept behind Ivy is that Ivy files describe the dependencies of a Java library or application, something they term a *module*. Every module or child project in a big application has its own `ivy.xml` file. This file lists what configurations the module has, such as *compile*, *test*, *standalone*, or *embedded*. Each configuration lists the artifacts it depends on and the artifacts it generates. The dependencies can be used to set up the classpath for part of the project or to compile files for redistribution. The generated artifacts can be published to a repository, including the local file system. Other projects can declare a dependency on the published artifacts, listing the name of the project, the module, and the version required. They can also declare the configurations of a module on which they want to depend. A module not only exports its own artifacts, but it can also export those artifacts on which it depends. "Downstream" modules can get all of these dependencies too, if they want.

This is easier to demonstrate than explain. Let's get Ivy to manage our project.

Our first ivy.xml file

The first action is to create the `ivy.xml` file for `diary/core`, our core diary library. Listing 11.1 shows this file, which goes into the `diary/core` directory alongside the `build.xml` file. It states that the library has two dependencies and five configurations.

Listing 11.1 The `ivy.xml` file for the `diary-core` module

```
<ivy-module version="1.4">
  <info organisation="org.antbook" module="diary-core" />
  <configurations defaultconfmapping="default">
    <conf name="compile" visibility="private"/>
    <conf name="test" extends="compile" visibility="private"/>      <-❶
    <conf name="master" />
    <conf name="runtime" extends="compile"/>
    <conf name="default" extends="master,runtime"/>      <-❷
  </configurations>
  <publications>
    <artifact conf="master"/>      <-❸
  </publications>
  <dependencies>
    <dependency org="log4j" name="log4j" rev="1.2.13"
        conf="compile->default;runtime->default"/>
```

```
    <dependency org="junit" name="junit" rev="3.8.2"
        conf="test->default"/>
  </dependencies>
</ivy-module>
```

This `ivy.xml` file states that the project depends on revision 1.2.13 of `log4j` from the `log4j` team and version 3.8.2 of `junit`. We don't want to compile the main source against `junit-3.8.2.jar`, because only the test code should be using it. By adding a `conf` attribute to the `<dependency>` element, we can control which configurations add the JARs and their dependencies to the classpath. For Log4J, we say:

```
conf="compile->default;runtime->default"
```

This means that our `compile` configuration wants the `default` configuration of Log4J, as does the `runtime` configuration. Similarly, the `conf="test->default"` attribute for the JUnit library restricts JUnit to the `test` configuration. That configuration also needs Log4J on the classpath, but we haven't asked for it. Why not? Because `test` extends the `compile` configuration ❶. This tells Ivy that the `test` configuration wants to inherit every dependency of `compile`. Similarly, the `default` configuration extends both `master` and `runtime` ❷. The configuration will contain all artifacts in both inherited configurations.

The `master` configuration has no dependencies. This configuration contains nothing but the module's own artifact ❸, which tells Ivy that we publish the `diary-core` JAR file in this configuration. We don't need to bother stating the name of the artifact, as it defaults to that of the module, `diary-core`, from the organization called `org.antbook`. (Note that Ivy usually spells "organisation" with an "s" [European style] in its XML files.)

That's a lot of information in a few short lines. It's enough for Ivy to pull down the JARs needed for compiling and testing the library, to know what artifacts to publish. When someone else declares a dependency on the `diary-core` JAR from the `antbook.org` organization, they can get the JAR file itself, they can get everything it needs at runtime, or they can get both. We aren't just configuring Ivy for our own use, we're providing information—metadata—about our JAR for downstream developers.

How Ivy resolves dependencies

The metadata in the `ivy.xml` file can be used by Ivy to determine what libraries each configuration of a module needs. It can then look across repositories to find and fetch those files. Before it downloads the artifacts—usually JAR files—it looks for metadata on the repository about the file. It can read `ivy.xml` files and most Maven POM files. Both file types describe the configurations and dependencies of the artifacts that are being retrieved. Ivy looks at the metadata, determines what new dependencies there are, and follows them, building up a complete graph of the dependencies.

The tool then validates the graph, looking for errors such as cycles or unresolvable dependencies. It detects when more than one version of the same artifact is on the graph, which constitutes a *conflict*, and hands off the problem to a *conflict manager*, which is an Ivy component that decides what to do. Conflict managers decide which version of a file to use, such as the latest or the one asked for explicitly.

After all dependencies are resolved and all conflicts are addressed, Ivy can perform a number of activities. The key ones are generating an HTML report showing the dependencies of every configuration and downloading the needed artifacts.

The HTML report is good for developers, and it will be the first thing we'll work on. The second action, copying down the JAR files, is exactly what we need in order to set up the classpath. Ivy can copy over all the dependencies of a project, and then Ant can add them to its classpath through simple `<fileset>` declarations. Ivy does the dependency management, while Ant does the build.

Let's get Ant to set up the classpath for our `diary-core` module. Step one: install Ivy.

11.2 INSTALLING IVY

In early 2007, Ivy was moving into Apache, and its source was moving into the Apache Subversion server. This means that the location of the Ivy downloads is changing, and the final URL is still unknown. Start off at http://www.jayasoft.org/ivy, from where a link to the latest version will always be found. This chapter was written against Ivy 1.4.1, which was the last pre-Apache release.

The file `ivy-1.4.1-bin.zip` contained the JAR `ivy-1.4.1.jar`, which should be added to ANT_HOME/lib or ${user.home}/.ant/lib so that Ant will pick it up.

The JAR file contains the Ivy code and an `antlib.xml` file which declares the tasks. To use Ivy in an Ant build file, all we need to do is declare the XML namespace, currently:

```
xmlns:ivy="antlib:fr.jayasoft.ivy.ant"
```

Once this is at the top of the file, we can use any of the Ivy tasks in table 11.1.

Table 11.1 Ant tasks provided by Ivy 1.4.1. Expect more tasks in later releases

Task	Function
`<ivy:artifactproperty>`	Sets a set of properties to the full path of every loaded artifact, deriving the property names from a supplied pattern.
`<ivy:artifactreport>`	Creates an XML report of all the dependencies and configurations of a module.
`<ivy:buildlist>`	Creates an ordered list of targets to use (for <subant>). The root attribute declares the target for which everything needs to be built.

continued on next page

Table 11.1   Ant tasks provided by Ivy 1.4.1. Expect more tasks in later releases *(continued)*

Task	Function
`<ivy:buildnumber>`	Calculates a build number from the repository, one more than the latest version.
`<ivy:cachefileset>`	Creates a fileset containing the cached dependencies of a configuration.
`<ivy:cachepath>`	Creates a path containing the cached dependencies of a configuration.
`<ivy:configure>`	Configures Ivy for the rest of the build.
`<ivy:deliver>`	Generates a resolved Ivy file, expanding all properties and hard coding all dependencies.
`<ivy:findrevision>`	Sets a property to the revision number of a resolved artifact.
`<ivy:info>`	Sets some Ant properties from an `ivy.xml` file, including the organization, module name, and revision.
`<ivy:install>`	Copies a module from one repository to another.
`<ivy:listmodules>`	Creates a list of modules matching the criteria, and sets an ant property for each one.
`<ivy:publish>`	Publishes the current module's artifacts.
`<ivy:report>`	Creates an HTML report of all the dependencies and configurations of a module.
`<ivy:repreport>`	Generates a report across a big project.
`<ivy:resolve>`	Resolves artifacts to the local cache, print output.
`<ivy:retrieve>`	Copies resolved artifacts to a local location.

We'll focus on the core tasks to manage our dependencies and leave the rest for the online documentation. The first task, the one that must be called in every build, is called `<ivy:configure>`.

11.2.1   Configuring Ivy

Before it can download artifacts, Ivy needs to know where to find them and where to store them locally. This information comes from a configuration file, `ivyconf .xml`. Every module/child project has its own `ivy.xml` file, but `ivyconf.xml` should be shared between all projects of a big application. Listing 11.2 shows the diary's configuration.

Listing 11.2   The diary's Ivy configuration file, `diary/ivyconf.xml`

```
<ivyconf>
  <property name="ibiblio-maven2-root"
      value="http://www.ibiblio.org/maven2/" override="false"/>
  <property name="maven2.pattern"
   value="[organisation]/[module]/[revision]/[module]-[revision]"
    />
  <property name="maven2.pattern.ext"
```

```
        value="${maven2.pattern}.[ext]" />
<include url="${ivy.default.conf.dir}/ivyconf-local.xml"/>    <-❶
<conf defaultResolver="default"/>
<resolvers>
  <filesystem name="team">    <-❷
    ivys="true" artifacts="true" m2compatible="true" >
    <artifact pattern=
       "${ivy.conf.dir}/repository/${maven2.pattern.ext}"/>
    <ivy pattern=
      "${ivy.conf.dir}/repository/${maven2.pattern}.xml"/>
  </filesystem>
  <ibiblio name="maven2"    <-❸
      root="${ibiblio-maven2-root}"
      pattern="${maven2.pattern.ext}"
      m2compatible="true"
      />
  <chain name="default" dual="true">    <-❹
    <resolver ref="local"/>
    <resolver ref="team"/>
    <resolver ref="maven2"/>
  </chain>
  <chain name="internal">    <-❺
    <resolver ref="local"/>
    <resolver ref="team"/>
  </chain>
</resolvers>
<modules>
  <module organisation="org.antbook" name=".*"
      resolver="internal"/>
</modules>
</ivyconf>
```

The full details of this file are beyond the scope of this book. What's important is
that it defines the different resolvers for retrieving and publishing artifacts. They are
as follows:

❶ A <filesystem> resolver team, which contains shared artifacts belonging to the
team. This repository is under SCM; all developers get a copy.

❷ An <ibiblio> resolver called maven2 to download files from the Maven2 repository. The root of the repository is set to http://ibiblio.org/maven2.

❸ The local cache, whose definition is in the file ivyconf-local.xml. This
resolver is created by Ivy itself and defines the standard layout and location for downloaded artifacts.

❹ The default resolver is a chain resolver, a sequence of the local, team, and maven2
resolvers. Files are located by looking in the cache, the team repository, and, finally, in
the Maven2 repository.

❺ Another chain, internal, defines how to search the local repositories.

The `<modules>` listing adds one extra feature: it declares that artifacts belonging to the `org.antbook` organization should be searched for on the internal resolver, which searches only the local repository. This avoids searching the network for the files that we create ourselves.

Getting an `ivyconf.xml` file right is quite tricky. Start with a working example and tweak it carefully. There's an Apache Ivy-user mailing list where you can find help.

The `ivyconf.xml` file configures Ivy, but it needs to be passed to Ant. This is the role of the `<configure>` task. It sets up Ivy for the rest of the build to use the listed resolvers/repositories. It has to be called once per build, before any other Ivy task:

```
<target name="ivy-init">
  <property name="ivy.lib.dir" location="build/ivy/lib"/>
  <ivy:configure file="${root.dir}/ivyconf.xml"/>
</target>
```

This `ivy-init` target defines a directory for retrieved artifacts, and then calls `<ivy:configure>` against the shared `ivyconf.xml` file. Every build file that uses Ivy must have a target like this, and all targets that use other Ivy tasks must depend on it, so it gets called at startup:

```
ivy-init:
[ivy:configure] Loading jar:file:/C:/Java/Apache/Ant/lib/
                ivy-1.4.1.jar!/fr/jayasoft/ivy/ivy.properties
[ivy:configure] :: Ivy 1.4.1 - 20061109165313 ::
                http://ivy.jayasoft.org/ ::
[ivy:configure] :: configuring :: file = C:\diary\ivyconf.xml

BUILD SUCCESSFUL
```

If there's an error in the configuration, the task will print a message and the build will fail. If everything is successful, all the other tasks are available, of which the most fundamental is `<ivy:resolve>`. This resolves all of the dependencies of a single module.

11.3 RESOLVING, REPORTING, AND RETRIEVING

When the dependencies of a module are *resolved*, that means that Ivy has determined the complete set of dependencies for all configurations of the module. It has managed to locate all the artifacts, locally or remotely, and any associated metadata. Resolution, then, is the single most important action Ivy can do for a project, and something on which most of the Ivy tasks depend. For the diary application, that means that the dependencies get analyzed and the relevant versions of the JUnit and Log4J libraries retrieved—along with any of their dependencies.

To resolve the `ivy.xml` file, we use the `<resolve>` task, which only works if Ivy has been already configured with the `<configure>` task:

```
<target name="ivy-resolve" depends="ivy-init">
  <ivy:resolve/>
</target>
```

This operation will trigger a search for the file ivy.xml in the local directory, a parse of it, and a recursive resolve and parse of all dependencies.

```
ivy-resolve:
[ivy:resolve] :: resolving dependencies ::
  [ org.antbook | diary-core |working@Zermatt ]
[ivy:resolve]    confs: [compile, test, master, runtime, default]
[ivy:resolve]    found [ log4j | log4j | 1.2.13 ] in maven2
[ivy:resolve]    found [ junit | junit | 3.8.2 ] in maven2
[ivy:resolve] :: resolution report ::
-------------------------------------------------------------------
|              |         modules          ||    artifacts       |
|    conf      | number| search|dwnlded|evicted|| number|dwnlded|
-------------------------------------------------------------------
|   compile    |   1   |   0   |   0   |   0   ||   1   |   0   |
|    test      |   2   |   0   |   0   |   0   ||   2   |   0   |
|   master     |   0   |   0   |   0   |   0   ||   0   |   0   |
|   runtime    |   1   |   0   |   0   |   0   ||   1   |   0   |
|   default    |   1   |   0   |   0   |   0   ||   1   |   0   |
-------------------------------------------------------------------

BUILD SUCCESSFUL
```

The output is a brief summary of actions: what configurations there are, how many artifacts are depended upon, and how many files were downloaded. In this run everything was in the cache; if an artifact was not there, here's where it would be downloaded.

Once an ivy.xml file has been resolved, tasks that act on the resolved files and metadata can be used. One of these tasks is invaluable when setting up a build: <report>, which creates a report on all the dependencies.

11.3.1 Creating a dependency report

When setting up a project's dependency and configuration information in the ivy.xml file, you need to know what's happening. You need to know which files are in which configuration and whether there were any conflicts. Rather than analyze the build file logs or look at retrieved artifacts, the tool to use is Ivy's <report> task. This task creates an HTML report of the resolved system. There's also the <artifactreport> task, which outputs pure XML for further processing. For most developers, the HTML report is the most useful.

```
<target name="ivy-report" depends="ivy-resolve">
  <ivy:report todir="${build.dir}/ivy/report"/>
</target>
```

This target generates an HTML page for every configuration in the chosen output directory. Figure 11.1 shows the output for the default configuration, whose sole dependency is Log4J.

Only after the report matches your expectations should you move on to retrieving artifacts.

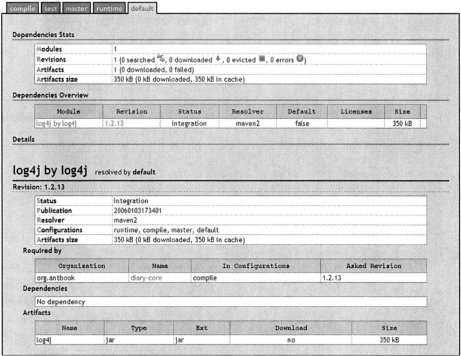

diary-core **by org.antbook**

resolved on 2006-11-13 00:07:36

Figure 11.1   Ivy reports the dependencies for one of the configurations

11.3.2   Retrieving artifacts

After resolution, a module's dependencies are all in the local Ivy cache, which is in
`${user.home}/.ivy/cache` by default. That's good, but it isn't directly where the
project can fetch them. Three tasks make these files accessible. The `<cachefileset>`
and `<cachepath>` tasks set up an Ant fileset or path to the list of dependencies for
a configuration:

```
<ivy:cachepath pathid="compile.classpath" conf="compile" />
```

The generated Ant datatype can be passed straight to tasks that take paths or filesets,
including `<java>` and `<taskdef>`.

For this chapter, we will use the `<ivy:retrieve>` task. It copies all of the
libraries of the selected configurations into a directory tree:

```
<target name="ivy-retrieve" depends="ivy-resolve">
  <ivy:retrieve
    pattern="${ivy.lib.dir}/[conf]/[artifact]-[revision].[ext]"
```

```
            sync="true"/>
  </target>
```

This copies the files from the cache into separate subdirectories, one for each configuration:

```
ivy-retrieve:
[ivy:retrieve] :: retrieving :: [ org.antbook | diary-core ] [sync]
[ivy:retrieve]  confs: [compile, test, master, runtime, default]
[ivy:retrieve]  5 artifacts copied, 0 already retrieved
```

If different configurations use the same artifacts, they get their own private copy from the local cache. When the task is run again, it won't copy the files if they already exist:

```
ivy-retrieve:
[ivy:retrieve] :: retrieving :: [ org.antbook | diary-core ] [sync]
[ivy:retrieve]  confs: [compile, test, master, runtime, default]
[ivy:retrieve]  0 artifacts copied, 5 already retrieved
```

We also can look into a directory to see what's there, such as the test configuration:

```
>ls build/ivy/lib/test
junit-3.8.2.jar  log4j-1.2.13.jar
```

Clearly, the dependencies are all set up. Incidentally, the `sync="true"` attribute of the `<retrieve>` task hands over complete control of the directory to Ivy. Ivy will delete from the destination directories any files that aren't currently part of the configuration's dependencies. This action lets us avoid having to clean up the directories when changing the dependencies of configurations; Ivy does it for us.

Once the artifacts are retrieved into directories, Ant can use the files.

11.3.3 Setting up the classpaths with Ivy

To compile using the retrieved libraries, we can use Ant's `<path>` datatype declaration to set up classpaths from the configuration directories:

```
<target name="classpaths" depends="ivy-retrieve">
  <path id="compile.classpath">
    <fileset dir="${ivy.lib.dir}/compile" includes="*.jar"/>
  </path>

  <path id="test.compile.classpath">
    <fileset dir="${ivy.lib.dir}/test" includes="*.jar"/>
    <pathelement location="${target.jar}"/>
  </path>

  <path id="test.classpath">
    <path refid="test.compile.classpath"/>
    <pathelement location="${test.classes.dir}"/>
  </path>
</target>
```

To test that everything is set up, we run ant clean test to run all unit tests against a fresh rebuild of the classes. As they pass, we know that the build is working, which means that the classpaths are set up right for the compile and test targets.

That's it! We've used Ivy to set up the classpaths for the different activities in our application: compiling and testing. One has Log4J; the other has Log4J and JUnit. Ivy resolves the dependencies for each configuration, including inheriting the dependencies of other configurations, downloads the files from repositories, adds the dependencies of those files to the configurations, and then creates status reports or copies the artifacts over for Ant to use. That's a pretty impressive set of operations.

We could stop there; it's powerful enough. But Ivy does more, much more. We can use it to glue together projects, feeding the artifacts of one project into another.

11.4   WORKING ACROSS PROJECTS WITH IVY

Ivy can pull down artifacts from the local cache, a team repository, or a remote server; it can be used to pass metadata and artifacts from one Ant project to another, each of which is, in Ivy terminology, a separate module with its own ivy.xml file. Each project's build needs to publish the JAR files and other artifacts it creates into a shared repository. The ivy.xml files of the other projects declare a dependency on the created artifacts, and Ivy will locate the files during resolution.

11.4.1   Sharing artifacts between projects

The <publish> task will copy the artifacts of a project to the repository identified by a named resolver, here the "local" resolver:

```
<target name="ivy-publish" depends="sign-jar,ivy-init">
  <ivy:publish resolver="local" pubrevision="${project.version}"
    overwrite="true"
    artifactspattern="${dist.dir}/[artifact]-[revision].[ext]"/>
</target>
```

This resolver is bound to a repository in ${user.home}/.ivy/local. All builds by the same user have access to the repository, unless their ivyconf.xml files say otherwise. Because it's shared by all of the user's projects, all the user's builds can retrieve the artifacts published to it.

The task requires a version number for the files, which is set with the pubrevision attribute. In our builds, we've been numbering all artifacts, but Ivy doesn't require this. You can create artifacts with simple names and have their revision number tacked on when the file is published. This is useful when retrofitting Ivy to an existing project. Ivy's <ivy:buildnumber> task can even determine a build number from a repository, by determining the version number of the latest artifact in the repository and setting an Ant property to that value plus one.

With our build files already using version numbers, we avoid that step. We do have to tell Ivy how to locate the files, which is where the artifactspattern attribute comes in. It contains a directory path and a pattern for finding artifacts. The pattern [artifact]-[revision].[ext] says that artifacts are created with the pattern of name-revision and the expected extension. Unnumbered artifacts would need the simpler pattern [artifact].[ext]. What we don't do is list the actual files that are created. This seems surprising, but it's because the ivy.xml file declared the artifact already in its <publications> element:

```
<publications>
  <artifact conf="master"/>
</publications>
```

This element declares that an artifact is published in the "master" configuration only. The artifact's name defaults to that of the module, and it also has the default extension/type of JAR. Projects can create artifacts with different names or extensions. In chapter 14, for example, we'll create the EAR file diary.ear:

```
<artifact name="diary" conf="master" type="ear" />
```

Again, this is invaluable when adding Ivy to existing code. There's no need to change the name of existing artifacts; you only need to add extra metadata and extend the build process with the <ivy:publish> task, a task which must be run as part of the local installation activities:

```
ivy-publish:
[ivy:publish] :: delivering :: [ org.antbook | diary-core |
  working@Zermatt ] :: 0.1alpha-SNAPSHOT :: integration
[ivy:publish]    delivering ivy file to C:\diary\core\dist
  /ivy-0.1alpha-SNAPSHOT.xml      <-❶
[ivy:publish] :: publishing :: [ org.antbook | diary-core ]
[ivy:publish]    published diary-core to
  C:\Documents and Settings\ant\.ivy/local/org.antbook
  /diary-core/0.1alpha-SNAPSHOT/jars/diary-core.jar      <-❷
[ivy:publish]    published ivy to C:\Documents and Settings\ant\
  .ivy/local/org.antbook/diary-core/0.1alpha-SNAPSHOT/ivys/ivy.xml      <-❸
```

This trace of the publish process shows the actions Ivy took:

❶ Ivy placed a copy of the ivy.xml file into the same directory in which the artifacts were created. All Ivy variables in this file are expanded, so all version numbers and other late-binding values are expanded.

❷ Ivy copied the JAR file to the specified repository.

❸ Ivy copied the XML file to the specified repository.

Sometimes Ivy doesn't seem to update the metadata before publishing the file. Deleting the entire dist directory fixed this. A clean build is always safest.

The <ivy:publish> operation placed the file in a user-specific repository. There's nothing to stop the task from publishing the file to a team repository, such as one on a shared file store. This would work well if it takes a long time to build some of the project's artifacts, and there's no need for every developer to rebuild every part of the application. The team repository would share the files for everyone to use. This brings up the next part of the problem: using the published files.

11.4.2 Using published artifacts in other projects

Published artifacts can be pulled into other projects simply by listing them in the <dependencies> section of the other project's ivy.xml files. The web application coming in chapter 12 uses the diary-core library, so the application's ivy.xml file declares a dependency upon the diary-core artifact:

```
<dependency org="org.antbook"
  name="diary-core"
  rev="latest.integration"      <-❶
  changing="true"                    <-❷
  conf="compile->master;runtime->master;war->master"/>    <-❸
```

This declaration has three unusual features. Instead of a hard-coded revision number, or even a property-driven value, the requested version is latest.integration ❶. This is a way of asking for the latest version published on the repository. Ivy will look at the repositories and find the latest version. As the ivyconf.xml file declares that org.antbook artifacts come from the local and team repositories only, Ivy doesn't poll any remote server. As well as asking for the latest version, we declare that the artifact and its metadata are changing ❷. Normally Ivy doesn't update metadata files once they're in the cache; instead it saves the complete dependency graph of every configuration to its own XML file nearby. For static dependencies, caching all the dependency information makes resolution much faster. For changing files and metadata, that cached data can stop changes being picked up. We need the most current copy from the repository, along with its metadata. Unless we used <ivy:buildnumber> or the current timestamp to create a new build number on every build—which is an option—we need to tell Ivy to poll for metadata and artifact changes on every build. This is what changing ="true" does.

Declaring the configuration to depend on

The final detail is that in every configuration, we ask for the "master" configuration of the diary-core module only ❸. That gives us nothing but diary-core.jar— not its dependencies. When Ivy publishes artifacts to the repository, it adds the module's dependency data. If we had compiled with the default configuration via a compile->default dependency, we would have had Log4J on the classpath.

> **NOTE** When you depend upon other modules, you get all the dependencies of the selected configuration, not just the published artifacts of the modules.

This is an important feature of dependency management tools. Their goal is to simplify your life by giving you all the files you need. There's a price: sometimes you get more than you want. As we don't need Log4J to compile the web application and we don't want it at runtime, we must ask for a configuration that contains the diary-core artifact but not its dependencies.

The choice of public configurations is based on those of Maven2, because whenever Ivy pulls in metadata from the Maven repositories, it parses the metadata and maps it to Ivy configurations. Maven only supports the configurations of table 11.2.

Table 11.2   Maven2's dependency configurations, as interpreted by Ivy

Configuration name	Meaning
default	The artifact and its runtime dependencies
master	The artifact itself
runtime	All the runtime dependencies of the artifact
compile	Dependencies used to compile the artifact
provided	Compile time dependencies to be pre-installed on the classpath
system	Runtime dependencies to be pre-installed on the classpath

Ivy doesn't mandate any specific configurations. We normally start off with the Maven team's configurations to be consistent with artifacts coming from the Maven repository. The master configuration has the artifacts with no dependencies, runtime has the dependencies with no artifact, and default has both. We use these standard configurations to make it possible to publish artifacts to the central repository, something that's beyond the scope of this book. We can still add private configurations for internal use (such as setting up a <taskdef> classpath) or to create new public configurations with different dependencies, such as embedded, redist, or webapp.

Having declared the dependencies on the master configuration only, we can run the new build.

Resolving the new project

The complete ivy.xml file for the diary web application is much more complex than the diary-core module. Running its ivy-resolve target creates a long list of dependencies:

```
ivy-resolve:
[ivy:resolve] :: resolving dependencies ::
              [ org.antbook | diary | working ]
[ivy:resolve]  confs: [default, compile, test, master, runtime,
               war, jing]
[ivy:resolve]   found [ org.antbook | diary-core |
                0.1alpha-SNAPSHOT ] in  local
[ivy:resolve]   [0.1alpha-SNAPSHOT]
                [ org.antbook | diary-core | latest.integration ]
[ivy:resolve]   found [ rome | rome | 0.8 ] in maven2
[ivy:resolve]   found [ jdom | jdom | 1.0 ] in maven2
[ivy:resolve]   found [ javax.servlet | servlet-api | 2.4 ]
                in maven2
[ivy:resolve]   found [ httpunit | httpunit | 1.6 ] in maven2
```

```
[ivy:resolve]      found [ xerces | xmlParserAPIs | 2.2.1 ] in maven2
[ivy:resolve]      found [ xerces | xercesImpl | 2.6.2 ] in maven2
[ivy:resolve]      found [ nekohtml | nekohtml | 0.9.1 ] in maven2
[ivy:resolve]      found [ xerces | xerces | 2.4.0 ] in maven2
[ivy:resolve]      found [ junit | junit | 3.8.2 ] in maven2
[ivy:resolve]      found [ rhino | js | 1.5R4.1 ] in maven2
[ivy:resolve]      found [ jtidy | jtidy | 4aug2000r7-dev ] in maven2
[ivy:resolve]      found [ thaiopensource | jing | 20030619 ]
                   in maven2
[ivy:resolve] downloading C:\Documents and Settings\ant\.ivy\local\
  org.antbook\diary-core\0.1alpha-SNAPSHOT\jars\diary-core.jar
[ivy:resolve] ... (12kB)
[ivy:resolve] .. (0kB)
[ivy:resolve] [SUCCESSFUL ] [ org.antbook | diary-core |
                   0.1alpha-SNAPSHOT ] /diary-core.jar[jar] (100ms)
[ivy:resolve] :: resolution report ::
[ivy:resolve] :: evicted modules:
[ivy:resolve] [ junit | junit | 3.8.1 ]
                   by [[ junit | junit | 3.8.2 ]] in [test]
[ivy:resolve] [ javax.servlet | servlet-api | 2.3 ]
                   by [[ javax.servlet | servlet-api | 2.4 ]] in [test]
```

This build log shows that the diary-core module was downloaded from the local repository. This is the artifact published earlier with the <ivy:publish> task; it can now go on the classpath of the web application.

The other interesting log item is that there were two "evicted modules." The artifact junit-3.8.1 was replaced by junit-3.8.2, and version 2.4 of the servlet API was used instead of version 2.3. The older dependencies came from HttpUnit, which is something we'll be using for testing the web application. It was built against older versions of the two libraries, versions picked up by the Ivy resolver. As newer versions were in the web application's ivy.xml, the older versions were evicted and the newer versions retained on the dependency graph. Eviction information is included in the HTML pages generated by <ivy:report>, so team members can see what versions are being used. Figure 11.2 shows the report. It highlights that the diary-core artifact was found on the local repository, and checked for changes ("searched"), while two artifacts were evicted.

Now that we are feeding the output of one project into the next, we can chain builds together just by running them in the right order. We can use the <subant> task to do this:

```
<presetdef name="delegate">
  <subant verbose="true">
    <filelist >
      <file name="core"/>
      <file name="webapp"/>
    </filelist>
  </subant>
</presetdef>
```

Dependencies Stats

Modules	11
Revisions	13 (1 searched 🔍, 0 downloaded ⬇, 2 evicted ▇, 0 errors ⊗)
Artifacts	11 (0 downloaded, 0 failed)
Artifacts size	3546 kB (0 kB downloaded, 3546 kB in cache)

Conflicts

Module	Selected	Evicted
servlet-api by javax.servlet	2.4	2.3
junit by junit	3.8.2	3.8.1

Dependencies Overview

Module	Revision	Status	Resolver	Default	Licenses	Size	
httpunit by httpunit	1.6	integration	maven2	false		401 kB	
--- jtidy by jtidy	4aug2000r7-dev	integration	maven2	false		135 kB	
--- js by rhino	1.5R4.1	integration	maven2	false		583 kB	
--- nekohtml by nekohtml	0.9.1	integration	maven2	false		66 kB	
------ xerces by xerces	2.4.0	integration	maven2	false		875 kB	
--- xercesImpl by xerces	2.6.2	integration	maven2	false		987 kB	
--- xmlParserAPIs by xerces	2.2.1	integration	maven2	false		81 kB	
--- servlet-api by javax.servlet	2.4	integration	maven2	false		95 kB	
--- servlet-api by javax.servlet	2.3					0 kB	▇
--- junit by junit	3.8.2	integration	maven2	false		118 kB	
--- junit by junit	3.8.1					0 kB	▇
servlet-api by javax.servlet	2.4	integration	maven2	false		95 kB	
rome by rome	0.8	integration	maven2	false		193 kB	
diary-core by org.antbook	0.1alpha-SNAPSHOT	integration	local	false		12 kB	🔍
junit by junit	3.8.2	integration	maven2	false		118 kB	

Figure 11.2   In this configuration, two obsolete modules are evicted.

This `<delegate> presetdef` can delegate targets down to the child components, building and perhaps publishing the core component before the web application.

Ordering the builds by hand works if the dependencies are simple and known by the author of the master build file, but doing so doesn't scale. Once you have more than a few projects, projects with different team members maintaining the `build .xml` and `ivy.xml` files, soon you have dependencies where you don't expect. If the list of build files to delegate to isn't kept synchronized, projects start building with outdated artifacts and developers start wondering why changes don't propagate, or worse: you ship old code.

11.4.3   Using Ivy to choreograph builds

If ordering builds by hand is unreliable, the solution is to have the machine work out the correct sequence. Every module's `ivy.xml` file lists that module's dependencies. If something were to look through all these files, it could see what modules were being built and which ones depended on others. It could then sort the list of modules in the order needed to ensure that all a module's predecessors were built before the module itself was built.

The `<buildlist>` task does this, creating a filelist of all the `build.xml` files ordered so that projects are built in the right sequence:

```
<ivy:buildlist reference="child.projects"
  skipbuildwithoutivy="true">
  <fileset dir="." includes="*/build.xml"/>
</ivy:buildlist>
```

We can use this task to create a `<presetdef>` task to delegate work to the build files:

```
<presetdef name="delegate" description="Delegate the build">
  <subant verbose="true">
    <buildpath refid="child.projects"/>
    <property file="master.properties"/>
  </subant>
</presetdef>
```

The path can also be printed out, to show the execution order:

```
<target name="show-order">
  <property name="child.projects.property"
   refid="child.projects" />
  <echo>The order to build the projects is
    ${child.projects.property}
  </echo>
</target>
```

Running this target shows the build order of the projects:

```
> ant -f ch11-ivy-masterbuild.xml show-order
Buildfile: ch11-ivy-masterbuild.xml
[ivy:buildlist] :: Ivy 1.4.1 - 20061109165313 ::
    http://ivy.jayasoft.org/ ::
[ivy:buildlist] :: configuring :: file = C:\diary\ivyconf.xml

show-order:
    [echo] The order to build the projects is
    [echo]    C:\diary\core\build.xml;
             C:\diary\persist\build.xml;
             C:\diary\persist-webapp\build.xml;
             C:\diary\webapp\build.xml
```

This run shows that Ivy can not only manage the problem of dependencies between projects, it also can use that same information to order builds.

There are a couple of aspects of the task to be aware of: looping and indirection.

Loops in project dependencies

If there's a loop—that is, if two or more modules create a cycle in the dependency— the order of those looped projects is undefined. Modules before the loop will be built in the right order, and modules after the loop will be ordered, but there's no way to predict the order Ivy will choose for those in the loop. This means that it's acceptable to have loops in a project, but Ivy will not order the dependencies correctly.

Loops are not unusual in Java library projects, especially if one configuration of a project depends upon the output of another, which itself depends on the first program. Often you can unroll the loop by creating a new module that depends on everything.

Indirect dependencies

Ivy doesn't order builds correctly if two projects have an indirect dependency via a module that isn't in the `<ivy:buildlist>` fileset. For example, the `persist-webapp` project coming in chapter 14 depends on `diary-core-persist`, which itself depends upon `diary-core`. If the `diary-core-persist` project was excluded from the `<ivy:buildlist>` fileset, the task wouldn't care that `persist-webapp` depended indirectly on `diary-core`, and not build the components in the right order.

To create a correct ordering of the build files, the fileset inside the task must contain all related projects. This doesn't mean that you have to build them all, because the `root` attribute can restrict the list to only those build files that matter for a chosen model:

```
<ivy:buildlist reference="root.projects"
    skipbuildwithoutivy="true"
    root="webapp" >
  <fileset dir="." includes="*/build.xml"/>
</ivy:buildlist>
```

This task passes in all build files with matching `ivy.xml` files, but only selects those projects that the `webapp` module depends on. The task can be used to build subsets of a system, using Ivy to manage the selection and ordering of the subset.

The `<ivy:buildlist>` task is the core Ivy task for complex projects. There's a reporting task `<ivy:repreport>`, which can create a report about all artifacts in a repository. If a project publishes all generated artifacts to a private repository, this reporting task will list everything that gets produced and show the dependencies between artifacts. This is a useful piece of documentation.

There are some other details about Ivy worth knowing about, which we'll take a quick look at.

11.5 OTHER ASPECTS OF IVY

There's a lot more about Ivy that's covered in its documentation, and there's no substitute for experience. Here are some techniques that are worth pulling out because they're so important.

11.5.1 Managing file versions through Ivy variables

Ivy files support *Ivy variables*. They are like Ant properties, but they're truly variable: they can be changed. They are expanded in strings just like Ant properties, so `${ivy.default.ivy.user.dir}` is bound to what in Ant would be `${user.home}/.ivy`. We set some properties in our `ivyconf.xml`, such as this pattern:

```
<property name="maven2.pattern.ext"
    value="${maven2.pattern}.[ext]" />
```

Ivy variables make configuration easier, especially as `ivyconf.xml` files can import other `ivyconf.xml` files, which may define properties as well as other parts of the system configuration. Where Ivy variables are invaluable is in setting properties inside an Ivy file from Ant, because all Ant properties are turned into Ivy variables. Whenever an Ivy task is invoked, it has access to all of Ant's properties. This behavior lets us control library versions through Ant properties. The build file can load a properties file of all library versions, and Ivy files resolved later will pick up these values. At the beginning of the build, we load in three files—one an optional file for user-specific customizations, one a child project-specific set of libraries, and the final one a declaration of versions for all projects/modules in the diary application:

```
<property file="build.properties"/>
<property file="libraries.properties"/>
<property file="../libraries.properties"/>
```

The shared `libraries.properties` file defines the default artifact versions:

```
junit.version=3.8.2
log4j.version=1.2.13
mysql.version=3.1.13
```

These properties can be used just as Ant properties in an `ivy.xml` file:

```
<dependency org="log4j" name="log4j" rev="${log4j.version}"
    conf="compile->default"/>
<dependency org="junit" name="junit" rev="${junit.version}"
    conf="test->default"/>
```

During resolution, Ivy expands the properties, so the resolved Ivy files and generated reports show exactly which version was used. It's essential to manage dependency versions this way, to provide a single place to upgrade all versions of a library, across all child projects. Doing so also lets developers experiment with new versions, such as a later release of JUnit:

```
ant clean release -Djunit.version=4.1
```

As it's now trivial to change from one version of an artifact to another, the hard problem is finding out what the name of an artifact is, and what versions of it are available. There are web sites and search tools to help with this.

11.5.2   Finding artifacts on the central repository

The best way to locate artifacts on the central Maven repository is to use one of the search engines, such as mvnrepository, http://mvnrepository.com/, and Maven Repo Search at http://maven.ozacc.com/. These repository search engines will take a name of an artifact and show the full organization and artifact name, as well as a list of public versions. You also can point a web browser at http://ibiblio.org/maven2 and browse around.

CHAPTER 11   MANAGING DEPENDENCIES

Usually the releases available on the repository lag public releases by a few days to a few months, depending on the project. When new artifacts do come out, the metadata with them can be a bit unstable; it can take time before the dependency information is correct. If one machine is building projects with different artifacts from the others, delete the machine's Ivy cache and rebuild everything; this will pull down the latest versions.

11.5.3 Excluding unwanted dependencies

The dependency report of figure 11.2 shows a problem. Two XML parsers are coming in: `xerces/XercesImpl-2.6.2.jar` and `xerces/xerces-2.4.0.jar`. Neither version is needed, as Java 1.5 ships with Xerces built in. Rather than switch to HttpUnit's `master` configuration and explicitly ask for all its other dependencies, we can drop the XML parsers by excluding artifacts coming from `xerces`.

```
<dependency org="httpunit"
  name="httpunit"
  rev="${httpunit.version}"
  conf="test->default">
  <exclude org="xerces"/>
</dependency>
```

An `<ivy:report>` run after this change shows that the files have been dropped. Artifacts to exclude can be specified by organization, module name, artifact name, or artifact extension, all of which can be given a regular expression containing wildcards for easier matching. A `conf` attribute can restrict exclusions to specific configurations.

The `<exclude>` element is invaluable. The more dependencies a project has, the more likely it is that unwanted files will end up on its classpath. Being able to selectively exclude artifacts addresses the problem without requiring a private repository with private metadata files, which is the other solution.

11.5.4 Private repositories

The central Maven2 repository on ibiblio.org has some problems. There is inadequate security for any security-conscious organization. There's the cost and bandwidth of connecting to the servers and the risk that they can be unavailable.

A private repository addresses these problems. It can contain all approved artifacts, with dependency metadata managed by the team, instead of the team having to rely on stability and availability of an external repository for successful builds. The private repository promises better security, as only audited artifacts could be placed on the repository, and it provides a place where private artifacts can be stored, including Sun artifacts that cannot be served on the public servers.

Most big Ivy projects end up creating a team repository because of the control it offers. One task, `<ivy:install>`, simplifies the process of setting up the repository, because it can copy artifacts and metadata from one repository (usually the remote one) to another repository. It can populate the repository with the base files and metadata, metadata that can then be hand-tuned to meet a team's needs.

11.5.5 Moving to Ivy

Existing Ant projects can add Ivy support. How hard is it to do so? It takes a few days of careful work. Here's a workflow for the migration that can be used as a starting point:

1 Start after a release or in a period of calm and relative code stability. Nobody should be editing the build files or changing dependencies.

2 Create a single `ivyconf.xml` file by copying a working example.

3 Define a common set of configurations for all projects, such as those of table 11.2.

A common set of configurations can be shared across `ivy.xml` files with the `<include>` element:

```
<configurations>
  <include file="../ivy/configurations.xml" />
  <configuration name="package" extends="runtime" />
<configurations>
```

Including configurations from a shared file keeps maintenance effort down and makes it easy to add new configurations to all applications. Unfortunately, Ivy 1.4.1 has a bug here: it tries to resolve relative paths in the project running the task, including `<ivy:buildlist>` in a parent directory. It should be fixed in a later release.

To summarize: migration to Ivy is manageable, but you should practice on something small first.

11.6   SUMMARY

At the beginning of this chapter, we listed four problems we wanted to address.

1 How to set up the build with the JAR files that it needs.

2 How to pass a JAR file created in one project into other projects.

3 How to build multiple projects in the right order.

4 How to be able to switch library versions on demand.

Together, Ant and Ivy can do all of these things.

1 If projects list their dependencies in an `ivy.xml` file, Ivy can retrieve them. Different configurations can be set up for the different paths and filesets a project needs.

2 JAR files and other artifacts can be published by using `<ivy:publish>`.

3 The `<buildlist>` task determines the correct order in which to build subsidiary projects.

4 If library versions are defined in a central properties file, a developer can switch library versions just by setting the appropriate version property to a different value.

We'll be using Ivy throughout the remainder of the book, though we won't go into quite so much detail about `ivy.xml` configurations. They are all available online, and we'll mention some aspects of Ivy configuration when it encounters a new feature or problem.

Now that we can set up libraries and dependencies between modules, it's time to use the techniques by writing a web application. This web application will use Ivy to pull in external dependencies and to add the `diary-core` JAR to the web application itself.

C H A P T E R 1 2

Developing for the Web

We now have a library to create entries in a diary, a build process that can handle multiple projects, and a way of sharing artifacts between them. What next? How about building a web site that uses the diary library and can publish events as an Atom feed?

It's time to build a Java Web Application, the public face of most server-side Java. This chapter looks at what you have to do to build and test one. Web applications are more complex to package than the simple JAR files we've done so far, and before they can be tested, they must be deployed. This makes the build process much harder than what we've done so far. Ant will have a more complex packaging problem to deal with, and it will have to deploy our code onto a web site before testing it. Solving problems like these are where Ant shows what it can really do!

What is a web application?

A Java web application is a web site packaged into a JAR file. The JAR file contains libraries, code, and resources—the pages, images, and other content that together form the web site. The resources provide the static parts of the web site, while the Java classes, libraries, and JSP/JSPX content form the dynamic part of the application.

Web applications are not standalone; a servlet container hosts them. This container, be it an embeddable servlet engine such as Jetty or a full-blown J2EE application server like JBoss, needs to know how to execute the web application. This requires a standard packaging mechanism: the WAR file, which is just a JAR file with a standardized layout. Everything in it, other than content under the WEB-INF and META-INF directories, is served up by the web server. The WEB-INF directory should contain a web.xml file describing the application to the server, while Java code goes under WEB-INF/classes and libraries into WEB-INF/lib. Table 12.1 lists some of the content commonly added to WAR files.

Table 12.1   Common content in web applications

Content type	Description
web.xml	An XML file that configures the application. Mandatory before version 2.5 of the servlet/web application API. Found in WEB-INF/web.xml.
Static content	Images, HTML pages, and similar files; content that never changes while the server is running. Saved in the WAR file outside the WEB-INF and META-INF directories.
JSP pages	HTML or XML pages that are dynamically generated whenever they receive an HTTP request. Saved alongside static content.
Java classes	Compiled Java classes. Placed in WEB-INF/classes.
Servlets	Java classes that serve up parts of the site, such as a directory tree or all files with a specific extension.
JAR files	Java libraries containing project or third-party code, including JSP tag libraries. Placed in WEB-INF/lib.

Building and deploying WAR files is the core of a Web application's build process. Packaging the file is primarily a matter of getting all the stuff into the appropriate place, and getting the web.xml file right. Deploying and testing rounds off the process. The first step is getting all the files together.

12.1   DEVELOPING A WEB APPLICATION

Figure 12.1 shows how to construct a web application, by hand or by Ant. Ant needs to compile the Java code with <javac>, then package the generated .class files into a WAR file. This WAR file must include any web content, any needed JAR libraries, and usually a web.xml manifest file.

After the WAR file is built, it can be deployed to a server. Then, and only then, can the application be tested. This is done with *functional testing*, by making requests of the site. You can do that by hand, and that is certainly the best way to see that things look right. You can also delegate much of the testing to the computer, to save time and also to compile all the JSP pages. This is a complex process—which is precisely why we need Ant to automate it.

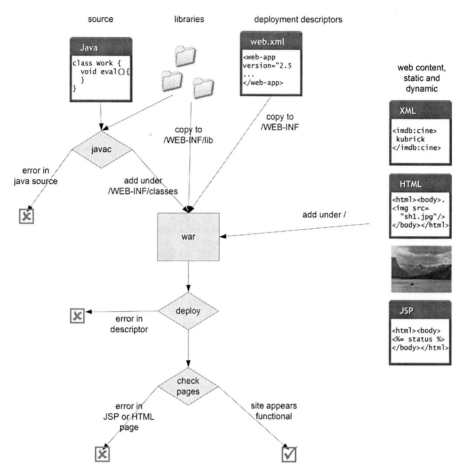

Figure 12.1   The basic workflow for constructing a web application

Designing the web application

The first step is to design the application. It will do one thing: publish the diary's events as an Atom feed so that subscribers can track up-and-coming events.

Our diary-core library provides the calendar, while the Atom support will come from Sun's Rome project, hosted at https://rome.dev.java.net/. This library can generate various XML feed streams that we can publish with a servlet we write ourselves. The library depends on JDOM, which is one of the many Java XML APIs.

Before we begin coding, we start with the housekeeping: setting up the source and destination directories.

- The web application goes into its own directory, `diary/webapp/`, alongside the `core/` and `xml/` directories. The master build file from chapter 10 will build the compound application.

- We need a subdirectory for static web content, /web. It will go under webapp/web.
- Java source files will go in the webapp/src directory.

We do, of course, need a new build file.

Creating the build file

The build file for this project takes full advantage of the Ant concepts of the previous two chapters. It uses `<import>` to pull in build files that declare common targets, common `<macrodef>` and `<presetdef>` templates for various tasks, and library tasks to manage its dependencies. Before it imports these files, it declares that the extension of the target JAR to be `war` and not `jar`, so that definitions of other properties, especially `target.jar`, pick up the intended type of the application:

```
<property file="build.properties"/>
<property name="project.name" value="diary"/>
<property name="target.extension"
          value="war"/>
<property name="root.dir" location=".."/>

<property name="xmlfiles.dir" location="${root.dir}/xml"/>
<import file="${xmlfiles.dir}/ivy-mixin.xml"/>
<!-- import the ivy dependency targets -->
<!--macros-->
<import file="${xmlfiles.dir}/macros-mixin.xml"/>

<!-- pull this in last so that any overrides get defined first-->
<import file="${xmlfiles.dir}/state.xml"/>
<import file="${xmlfiles.dir}/base.xml"/>
```

Next comes the declaration of the web-specific directories and files:

```
<property name="web.dir" location="web"/>
```

With these files imported, our common entry points and milestone targets, such as `compiled`, `dist`, and `test`, are defined. We just need to add any new code, set up the compile classpath, and build our application as normal. It's the packaging and testing that changes.

12.1.1 Writing a feed servlet

We want our web application to serve up the diary's events as an Atom XML feed. We can do this with the Rome syndication library, which can publish data in all the popular syndication/blog formats. Listing 12.1 shows a servlet we've written, which provides an Atom feed, the content generated by an `EventSyndicator` class. This is a class that creates an Atom entry for every event in the calendar. When deployed in the web application, the servlet will let anyone listen for forthcoming events.

Listing 12.1 A servlet to publish events as an Atom feed

```
package dl.webapp.servlets;

import com.sun.syndication.feed.synd.SyndFeed;
import com.sun.syndication.io.*;
import dl.webapp.*;

import javax.servlet.ServletException;
import javax.servlet.http.*;
import java.io.IOException;

public class EventFeedServlet extends HttpServlet {
  private EventSyndicator syndicator;

  public void init() throws ServletException {
    GroupEvents group = GroupEvents.getGroupEvents();
    syndicator = new EventSyndicator("Events",
                      group.getEvents());
  }

  protected void doGet(HttpServletRequest request,
                  HttpServletResponse response)
      throws ServletException, IOException {
    try {
      SyndFeed feed = syndicator.getFeed();
      feed.setFeedType("atom_1.0");
      response.setContentType("application/xml");
      SyndFeedOutput output = new SyndFeedOutput();
      output.output(feed, response.getWriter());
    }
    catch (FeedException e) {
      throw new ServletException("When creating feed", e);
    }
  }
}
```

The EventSyndicator takes events from the diary-core collection and can syndicate them

This is the handler for HTTP GET requests

Write out the event list as an Atom feed

Once the classpath is setup, a `<javac>` task in the `compile` target can compile the servlet, placing it in `${build.classes.dir}` as normal. To set that classpath up, we must look at the libraries a web application needs.

12.1.2 Libraries in web applications

Web applications can include libraries inside the WAR file, in the `WEB-INF/lib` directory. For a self-contained application, this directory should include every JAR the application needs beyond those provided by the container. Web servers usually offer the servlet API, the JSP engine, and perhaps the whole of the Java EE API, so those must stay out of the WAR. However, they're needed at compile time if the application imports their classes. The solution here is to create a new Ivy configuration, `war`, containing only those libraries we want in the WAR file.

CHAPTER 12 DEVELOPING FOR THE WEB

Our diary application needs the servlet API and the Rome and JDOM libraries when compiling the source. We have to set up the `<dependencies>` list in the `ivy.xml` file for the servlet API in the `compile` configuration, and Rome and the locally created diary-core library in the `compile`, `runtime`, and `war` configurations:

```
<dependency org="org.antbook"
  name="diary-core"
  rev="latest.integration"
  changing="true"
  conf="compile->master;runtime->master;war->master"/>
<dependency org="javax.servlet"
  name="servlet-api"
  rev="${servlet-api.version}"
  conf="compile->master"/>
<dependency org="rome"
    name="rome"
    rev="${rome.version}"
    conf="compile->master;runtime->default;war->default"/>
```

As JDOM is a declared dependency of Rome, there's no need to ask for it. Running the `ivy-resolve` target of chapter 11 will copy the dependencies of each configuration into separate directories, one of which is used to set up the compile classpath. The new `war` configuration is a private configuration that lists all libraries Ant will add to the WAR file.

Redistributing the libraries

The WAR file must include all the libraries that aren't provided by the application server. An `<ivy:retrieve>` operation can place them into a directory that's ready for adding to the WAR file. This time we don't want the version numbers on the files, so use a different pattern when retrieving them, asking only for the artifact and extension:

```
<target name="war-libraries" depends="ivy-resolve">
  <property name="war.lib.dir" location="${build.dir}/warlib"/>
  <ivy:retrieve conf="war"
      pattern="${war.lib.dir}/[artifact].[ext]" sync="true"/>
</target>
```

This target copies three files into the `build/warlib` directory: `rome.jar`, `diary-core.jar`, and `jdom.jar`. These will be used when the WAR is built. Before then: the web pages.

12.1.3 Writing web pages

Web applications usually contain web pages and graphics. Simple, static HTML pages are just text files. They go under the root directory of the WAR file, and, in this project, in the `web/` subdirectory of the SCM source tree. More interesting are JSP pages. These are HTML or XML pages mixed with JSP directives and Java code. When served up via a "JSP engine," they are executed, returning transformed content. There are two types of JSP content, the original *JSP Page* with a .jsp extension that normally returns HTML content, and *JSP Documents*. The latter is an XML version of JSP pages and has the extension .jspx. Most aspects of the original JSP syntax have equivalents in the JSPX files. We use the term "JSP File" to refer to both JSP pages and JSP documents.

All JSP files are processed by the "JSP engine," usually the Jasper runtime from Apache Tomcat. The engine includes a servlet that's bound to the *.jsp and *.jspx paths. The first time the servlet fields a request for a JSP file, it creates a Java file from the JSP source, compiles it into a .class file, and finally runs it. After that first time, processing a JSP file is as fast as other Java code, but that first fetch can be slow. It will also be the place where errors show up.

NOTE   The way to compile and test JSP content is to fetch them. Although Ant has a <jspc> task to compile web pages, and applications servers often have similar tasks, the only mechanism that has proven reliable is just to pull down the pages from the deployed application.

The ideal way to code in a JSP file is via new HTML/XML elements, *JSP tag libraries*. The worst way to do it, from a maintenance perspective, is to embed the Java source straight into the JSP file. But that's so very easy, which is why the happy.jsp page in listing 12.2 does it.

Listing 12.2   A JSP page, happy.jsp

```
<%@ page import="dl.webapp.FindClass" %>
<html>
 <head><title>Diary Happy Page</title></head>
<body>
  <table>
    <tr><td>
      <%= FindClass.locate("dl.core.Event")%>
    </td></tr>
    <tr><td>
      <%= FindClass.locate("com.sun.syndication.io.FeedException")%>
    </td></tr>
    <tr><td>
      <%= FindClass.locate("org.jdom.JDOMException")%>
    </td></tr>
  </table>
  <p>
    The diary application is succesfully deployed
  </p>
</body>
</html>
```

When this page is fetched, it calls a static method we've written called `dl.webapp`
`.FindClass.locate()`, passing in the name of a required class. If the named
class cannot be loaded, the method throws a `RuntimeException`, which is caught
and turned into an HTML error page by the servlet engine.

By locating classes from different libraries, this page verifies that the JARs the
application needs are present. If a needed class is missing, the server will return an
error instead of the page. We will use this page, the "happy page," when we deploy
the application. If the happy page can be fetched, then the application is not only
deployed, it considers itself to be healthy.

This JSP page goes into the web directory, along with any static content such as
graphics files. When building the WAR file, everything under that directory must be
copied into the WAR file, starting at the root. Before creating that WAR file, there's
one more thing to do: create the `web.xml` file.

12.1.4   Creating a web.xml file

The final part of the WAR File is an XML file to describe the web application, `WEB-`
`INF/web.xml`. Although it used to be mandatory, since the servlet 2.5 API, it's been
optional. Even so, most web applications will need one. There are two ways to create it:

- Write the `web.xml` file by hand.
- Add JavaDoc annotations to the source and use a tool called XDoclet to create a
  `web.xml` file from introspecting the `.class` files and parsing the source.

The XDoclet tool can create XML files from JavaDoc-annotated source. Prior to Java
1.5, it was the only way to generate the XML files that Web and Enterprise Java applications needed. With annotations added to the Java language, there's now a new way
to mark up code. Different annotations are being standardized to assist in integrating
a web or Java EE application with its hosting application server.

As of late 2006, annotations for web services and persistence were part of Java EE 5,
but there were none to eliminate `web.xml` files. Something may arrive in Java EE 6.
Until then, XDoclet is something to consider if you have many servlets or if you're
writing JSP tag libraries. Consult the book *XDoclet in Action* (Manning Publications)
and the XDoclet web sites (http://xdoclet.codehaus.org/ and http://xdoclet.sourceforge
.net/) for details.

For a simple `web.xml` file with a few servlets and mime types, XDoclet is overkill.
Instead, we have the hand-written file of listing 12.3.

Listing 12.3   The `web.xml` file, in `web/WEB-INF/web.xml`

```
<?xml version="1.0" encoding="UTF-8"?>
<web-app version="2.4" >
<servlet>
 <servlet-name>EventFeed</servlet-name>
 <servlet-class>dl.webapp.servlets.EventFeedServlet</servlet-class>
</servlet>
```

```
<servlet-mapping>
 <servlet-name>EventFeed</servlet-name>
 <url-pattern>/feed/</url-pattern>
</servlet-mapping>
</web-app>
```

■

This web.xml file declares the servlet of listing 12.1, on page 324, under the path feed/. With the file written, the application is ready to be turned into a WAR file.

12.2 BUILDING THE WAR FILE

A WAR file is just a JAR file, so you can build it with the <jar> task. An extension of this task, <war>, makes the process slightly easier. It has special handling for the content that goes under WEB-INF, including classes, libraries, and the web.xml file. Table 12.2 lists the elements of the <war> task that come into play when creating a WAR file. The new elements, <classes>, <libraries>, and <webinf>, are just filesets with specific target directories, so they can be replaced by <zipfileset> elements with the appropriate prefix.

There's an attribute, webxml, that takes the name of a file to turn into the WEB-INF/web.xml configuration file. The attribute and corresponding file are mandatory, unless the needxmlfile attribute is set to false.

Table 12.2 The primary elements of the <war> task

Element	Destination	Description
<fileset>	/	Web pages or other files
<zipfileset>	/ or anywhere else	Web pages or other files
<classes>	WEB-INF/classes	Compiled classes
<libraries>	WEB-INF/lib	Libraries
<webinf>	WEB-INF/	Configuration files

To create a WAR file, then, we can call the <war> task, filling in the different parts of the archive with the various data sources:

```
<target name="war" depends="ready-to-package"
    description="create a WAR file">
  <war destfile="${target.jar}"
      duplicate="fail"
      webxml="${web.dir}/WEB-INF/web.xml">     ⟵ web.xml

    <fileset dir="${web.dir}" />     ⟵ Web files

    <classes dir="${build.classes.dir}"/>     ⟵ Classes

    <lib dir="${war.lib.dir}">
      <include name="*.jar" />          │ Libraries
```

```
      </lib>
    </war>
  </target>
```

The task contains three filesets: the web pages, the classes, and the libraries. These have all been set up by earlier targets. As with `<zip>` and `<jar>`, the `duplicate` attribute declares that it's an error to have a duplicate entry in the WAR file.

Creating the WAR

To create the WAR file, we run the `dist` target:

```
compile:
[ext:javac] Compiling 4 source files to C:\diary\webapp\build\classes

war-libraries:
    [mkdir] Created dir: C:\diary\webapp\build\lib
     [copy] Copying 5 files to C:\diary\webapp\build\lib

ready-to-package:

war:
      [war] Building war:
            C:\diary\webapp\dist\diary-0.1alpha-SNAPSHOT.war

dist:
```

At this point, the WAR is built. We have a WAR file containing static content and JSP pages. Behind that we have a servlet, other classes, and bundled JARs. The one thing we don't yet have is a working application. How do we know that? Because we haven't tested it yet! We can test a web application only after it's deployed.

12.3 DEPLOYMENT

We have been writing code without doing any tests. This is a problem that comes with web applications. Before you can test the application, you need to deploy it.

The good news is the WAR file is ready to be deployed. For this chapter we'll deploy on Tomcat, http://tomcat.apache.org/. It's the application that Ant was written for, and it lets you deploy just by copying the WAR file into the right place.

The first deployment action is installing Tomcat itself. Download a current version of the "core" package in a form suitable for your platform; it comes as `.zip`, `.tar.gz`, and as a windows `.exe` installer. On Windows, the `.exe` installation installs Tomcat as a service, and it doesn't provide batch files to start or stop the program (you get a native Windows `.exe`). For development you need a version you put in a place of your choice, with the `.bat` files that the IDE needs for debugging. Use the `.zip` file instead.

You can start Tomcat by running `startup.sh` or `startup.bat`, as appropriate.

12.3.1   Deployment by copy

You can deploy onto Tomcat by copying the entire WAR file to the web application directory of the server. If Tomcat isn't running, the WAR will be loaded when Tomcat starts up. If it's running, the changes will be picked up within a few seconds.

Listing 12.4 shows a build file that deploys this way. It extends the main build file for this chapter by importing it ❶, then declaring a new `deploy` target that adds a dependency on the `deploy-by-copy` target. The target, in turn, copies the WAR file into the application server's directory, possibly renaming it in the process ❷.

> **Listing 12.4   The simplest way to deploy to Tomcat is by copying the WAR file to the web application directory of the sever**

```
<project name="deploy-by-copy" default="deploy">

  <import file="webapp-chapter-12.xml"/>       ◁─❶

  <target name="deploy" depends="deploy-by-copy"/>   ◁─❷

  <target name="deploy-properties" depends="init">
    <property name="deploy.files.dir" location="deploy"/>
    <property name="appserver" value="tomcat"/>
    <property file="${deploy.files.dir}/${appserver}.properties"/>
    <property name="deploy.name"
      value="${project.name}"/>
    <property name="deploy.destfile"
      location="${deploy.dir}/${deploy.name}.war"/>
    <property name="url.server" value="localhost" />
    <property name="application.url"
      value="http://${url.server}:${deploy.port}/${deploy.name}/"/>
  </target>

  <target name="deploy-by-copy"
      depends="ready-to-deploy,deploy-properties">
    <echo>
      Deploying ${target.jar} to ${deploy.destfile}
      URL: ${application.url}
    </echo>
    <copy file="${target.jar}"
        tofile="${deploy.destfile}"
        overwrite="true"/>
  </target>
<project>
```

Because the deployment options may vary with every user and application server, all the configuration options are stored in a directory `deploy/`, with different property files for different computers. The Windows test system uses Tomcat, with a file called `tomcat.properties`:

```
deploy.port=8080
deploy.dir=C:\\Apps\\tomcat\\webapps
```

The Linux server uses JBoss, which itself hosts Tomcat. It has a different deployment path, with the `jboss.properties` file providing the relevant settings:

```
deploy.port=8080
deploy.dir=/home/ant/jboss/server/default/deploy
```

We also need to override the `appserver` property in this system, which is something an entry in `webapp/build.properties` can do.

Undeployment

The opposite of deployment is, of course, undeployment. This will take the application offline. If we delete a WAR file from the Tomcat or JBoss deployment directories, the application server undeploys it by shutting down the web application. Deleting the WAR file is an easy target to write:

```
<target name="undeploy" depends="deploy-properties"
    description="undeploy">
  <delete file="${deploy.destfile}"/>
</target>
```

You don't actually need to undeploy an existing application before deploying an update; deploying the new WAR should suffice.

12.4 POST-DEPLOYMENT ACTIVITIES

We can now deploy the application. What can we do with it? It takes a lot of work to get a web application off the ground, so go look at its start page to see that, yes, it really is there. Now let's return to Ant and the tools it offers. There are two actions Ant can take after deployment:

- Probe for the availability/health of a web application
- Run tests against the application

Because it can take some seconds for the WAR file to deploy, Ant should delay running tests until the application is up. This is done by running both actions one after the other.

12.4.1 Probing for server availability

Chapter 7 introduced Ant's two conditions that probe for network servers, `<http>` and `<socket>`. These conditions can be used to block the tests until the application is running.

Spinning with the <waitfor> task

Any condition that Ant supports in the <condition> task can also be used in <waitfor>. This task evaluates a test repeatedly until it succeeds or the time limit is reached, sleeping between each test.

You can specify the maximum wait and sleep times in units ranging from milliseconds to weeks. It will support a nested condition, which it will test repeatedly. Here is a test that probes the local machine for a program listening on port 8080:

```
<target name="wait-for-server">
  <waitfor maxwait="30" maxwaitunit="second"
    timeoutproperty="server.missing">
    <socket port="8080" server="127.0.0.1"/>
  </waitfor>
  <fail if="server.missing">No server found</fail>
</target>
```

Table 12.3 lists the task's attributes. If the condition is met, the build continues executing. If not, the property named in timeoutproperty is set to true; Ant can <fail> on this.

Table 12.3 Attributes for the <waitfor> task. The maximum wait time often needs tuning for the particular use.

Attribute	Description
timeoutproperty	A property to set if the task times out.
maxwait	How long to keep waiting. Defaults to 180000 maxwaitunits; usually 180 seconds.
checkevery	How often to check. By default, 500 checkeveryunits; effectively twice a second.
maxwaitunit	The time unit used by the maxwait attribute, a millisecond by default. One of millisecond, second, minute, hour, day, or week.
checkeveryunit	The time unit used by the checkevery attribute, a millisecond by default. This takes the same options as the maxwaitunit.

We're going to use the <waitfor> task to spin for 15 seconds, waiting for the deployed application to be available, polling its URL. If the task times out, the build halts:

```
<target name="wait" depends="deploy">
  <property name="deploy.waittime" value="15" />
  <waitfor maxwait="${deploy.waittime}"
      maxwaitunit="second"
      timeoutproperty="server.missing">
    <http url="${application.url}" />
  </waitfor>
  <fail if="server.missing">Not found: ${application.url}</fail>
</target>
```

There's a race condition here: when doing a hot update, `<waitfor>` may succeed against the old application, not the new one. We need to wait a few seconds, before starting the `<waitfor>` loop.

12.4.2 Pausing the build with <sleep>

A `<sleep>` task can insert pauses into a build. The task will halt the thread executing the task/build file for the time set by the four attributes hours, minutes, seconds, and milliseconds:

```
<sleep hours="5" minutes="2" seconds="15" milliseconds="47" />
```

Our patched target has a short delay from `<sleep>` followed by a `<waitfor>` call to block until the application is ready.

```
<target name="wait" depends="deploy">
  <property name="deploy.sleep" value="5"/>
  <property name="deploy.waittime" value="10" />
  <sleep seconds="5"/>
  <waitfor maxwait="${deploy.waittime}"
      maxwaitunit="second"
      timeoutproperty="server.missing">
    <http url="${application.url}" />
  </waitfor>
  <fail if="server.missing">Not found: ${application.url}</fail>
</target>
```

The alternative tactic is to always call the undeploy target before deploy and have another target that waits for the application to be completely undeployed:

```
<target name="wait-undeploy" depends="undeploy">
  <property name="undeploy.waittime" value="30"/>
  <waitfor maxwait="${undeploy.waittime}"
      maxwaitunit="second">
    <not>
      <http url="${application.url}"/>
    </not>
  </waitfor>
</target>
```

Here the `<waitfor>` task has to use the inverse of the normal test, wrapping the `<http>` test in a `<not>` call. If our deploy target depends on this new target, it will wait until the application server has stopped the running application before we upgrade it. Either way, if the deploy target succeeds, the application server has deployed, so it's ready for testing.

12.5 TESTING WEB APPLICATIONS WITH HTTPUNIT

A web site is like any other piece of code: you don't know it works unless you test it. For web applications, we have to do system tests, tests that show how the entire system works. Unit tests are good for qualifying the parts used to build the system and to track down problems. They can find problems earlier, identify the area of trouble, and show that they are fixed. System tests can fetch web pages, simulate a remote user, and show that the application works on our chosen server.

JUnit can test the web application with the aid of an extension called HttpUnit, from http://www.httpunit.org/. HttpUnit allows test cases to interact with a web server as if it were a web browser. It can start a session with a server, fetch pages, fill in forms, and navigate around the site. Along the way, it can validate web pages, looking at elements in the page such as the title, forms, and text. You can write code to follow links, letting you validate further pages off your starting page. If you really know what you're doing, it will give you the actual XML Document Object Model (DOM) of the HTTP response.

Ant integrates testing with HttpUnit into the build process, by building and deploying the web application, running the JUnit/HttpUnit tests, and presenting the results. The effect is to make system testing of the web application no harder than unit testing the diary-core library.

12.5.1 Writing HttpUnit tests

To use HttpUnit, the first step is to download the latest version from http://httpunit.org and unzip it somewhere. It contains the documentation and the two files you need to run the tests `httpunit.jar` and `jtidy.jar`. the latter of which is a library to tidy up HTML pages.

The HttpUnit tests themselves are normal JUnit test cases. They use the HttpUnit classes to talk to a web server, fetching and testing HTML pages on the remote site—then validating the results against expectations.

As we're likely to write more than one test case, we start with an abstract base test class, which we name `WebTestBase`. It will contain the set-up logic to bind to a URL supplied to JUnit:

```
public abstract class WebTestBase extends TestCase {
    protected String url;
    protected WebConversation session;

    public WebTestBase(String name) {
        super(name);
    }
}
```

The class extends the JUnit `TestCase` class; the HttpUnit classes don't replace any existing aspects of the JUnit framework. Indeed, the classes work perfectly well outside the JUnit framework. Our `WebTestBase` class adds two fields to work with HttpUnit:

- `url`, which we will use to point to the base of our application
- `session`, which represents the ongoing conversation with the server—including any cookies set on the client

Next comes the setup method, which binds the `url` field to the `server.url` system property, configures HttpUnit, and starts a new session.

```
public void setUp() throws Exception {
    super.setUp();
    url=System.getProperty("server.url");
    assertNotNull("server.url not set", getUrl());
    HTMLParserFactory.setPreserveTagCase(false);
    HttpUnitOptions.setExceptionsThrownOnErrorStatus(true);
    HttpUnitOptions.setMatchesIgnoreCase(true);
    session=new WebConversation();
}
```

Finally, we add some utility methods to use throughout our tests:

```
protected GetMethodWebRequest requestPage(String page) {      Creates a
    return new GetMethodWebRequest(url +page);               request
}                                                            for a page
```

```
protected WebResponse getPage(String page)
        throws IOException, SAXException {                   Fetches a page
    WebRequest request = requestPage(page);                 under the web
    return session.getResponse(request);                    application
}
```

```
protected WebResponse getHomePage()
        throws IOException, SAXException {                   Fetches the
    return getPage("");                                     home page of
}                                                           the webapp
```

The key method is `getPage()`, which fetches a page under the web application. It will throw an exception if the request fails, so `getPage("happy.jsp")` is enough to fetch a page and implicitly assert that it returned successfully.

Next comes the first test class, `HappyPageTest`:

```
public class HappyPageTest extends WebTestBase {
    public HappyPageTest(String name) {
        super(name);
    }
}
```

Into this, we then add our test cases. The first test retrieves the `happy.jsp` page:

```
public void testHappy() throws Throwable {
    getPage("happy.jsp");
}
```

That's all JUnit needs to do its work. If the JSP page doesn't compile or if the page is unhappy, the server returns an HTTP 500 error code, which HttpUnit converts to an exception.

The second test fetches the root page of the application. This is what our `index.html` page looks like:

```
<html>
<head>
    <title>Diary Web Application</title>
    <link rel="alternate" type="application/atom+xml"
          title="Diary Atom Feed" href="feed/" />
</head>

<body>
<h1>Diary Web Application</h1>
<h3>XML Feeds</h3>
  <p><a href="feed/" id="atom">Feed</a></p>
<h3>Health</h3>
<ul>
    <li><a href="happy.jsp" id="happy">happy test</a></li>
    <li><a href="unhappy.jsp" id="unhappy">unhappy test</a></li>
</ul>
</body>
</html>
```

The test method fetches this page and then follows the links. By giving each link an id attribute, the test can ask for the links by ID:

```
public void testIndex() throws Throwable{
    WebResponse home = getHomePage();
    assertEquals("Diary Web Application",home.getTitle());    ←❶
    WebLink link=home.getLinkWithID("happy");    ←❷
    assertNotNull("Happy link missing",link);    ←❸
    WebRequest nextRequest=link.getRequest();
    WebResponse status=getSession().getResponse(nextRequest);    ⎫❹
}
```

The test checks the title of the page ❶ and then asks for the link with a given ID ❷. If the link is missing this will return null, which an assertion picks up ❸. Following the link ❹ causes HttpUnit to fetch the referenced page, or fail if it cannot be retrieved.

By following links this way, JUnit can validate links on a page. We could have looked up links by the text inside them, using a call such as home.getLinkWith ("happy test"). Doing so would enable us to avoid needing to add ID tags to links, but could break the test whenever the web page text changes.

Another test verifies that the unhappy.jsp page is working correctly, that it returns an error code when fetched:

```
public void testUnhappy() throws Throwable {
    try {
        getPage("unhappy.jsp");
        fail("should have raised an exception");
    } catch (HttpInternalErrorException e) {
        //success
    }
}
```

This test fetches the page and fails the test unless the attempt fails with a response code of 500. HttpUnit throws an `HttpUnitException` for HTTP errors, with specific subclasses for internal errors `HttpInternalErrorException` and `HttpNotFoundException`, on 500 and 404 error codes respectively.

Together these tests can verify that our web application deployed and that our index page is as we intended it to be. Because `happy.jsp` checks the health of the application, the tests effectively verify that the application considers itself healthy. These are the initial tests an application needs. Let's compile and run them.

12.5.2 Compiling the HttpUnit tests

Ivy needs two dependencies for the `test` configuration to add `junit-3.8.2` and `httpunit-1.6` to the classpath, and exclude an XML parser that we do not need:

```
<dependency org="httpunit" name="httpunit"
  rev="${httpunit.version}"
  conf="test->default">
  <exclude org="xerces"/>
</dependency>
<dependency org="junit" name="junit"
    rev="${junit.version}"
    conf="test->default"/>
```

This configuration doesn't depend on the web application because there's no code shared between them. The targets in listing 12.5 use the classpath Ivy creates from this configuration to compile and package the tests.

Listing 12.5 Targets to compile the tests into a JAR file

```
<target name="test-classpath" depends="ivy-retrieve">
  <path id="test.compile.classpath">
    <fileset dir="lib/test" includes="*.jar" />
  </path>
</target>

<target name="test-compile" depends="test-classpath">
  <ext:javac destdir="${test.classes.dir}"
      classpathref="test.compile.classpath"
      srcdir="test" includes="**/*.java/>"          ❶
  <ext:copy-useful-files src="test"
    dest="${test.classes.dir}"/>
</target>

<target name="test-jar" depends="test-compile">
  <jar destfile="${test.jar}">
    <fileset dir="${test.classes.dir}" includes="**/* "/>   ❷
  </jar>
</target>
```

```
<target name="test-classpaths" depends="test-jar">
  <path id="test.classpath">
    <path refid="test.compile.classpath"/>
    <pathelement location="${test.jar}"/>
  </path>

  <path id="test.forking.classpath">
    <path refid="test.classpath"/>
    <pathelement path="${java.class.path}"/>
  </path>
</target>
```
❸

The `compile` target ❶ should be familiar; after compiling the tests, Ant creates a test JAR file ❷ which is then added to the classpath for running the tests ❸. We can now run those tests and create the reports.

12.5.3 Running the HttpUnit tests

Running the tests is almost like running normal JUnit tests, with two differences. The application must be deployed before the tests, so the test target depends on the `deployed` target ❶. The other critical detail is that the URL to the server must be passed down to the unit tests, through a `<sysproperty>` element ❷:

```
<target name="test" depends="deployed,test-classpaths">     ◄─❶
  <junit printsummary="false"
      errorProperty="test.failed"
      failureProperty="test.failed"
      fork="true" >
    <classpath refid="test.forking.classpath"/>
    <sysproperty key="server.url" value="${application.url}"/>  ◄─❷
    <formatter type="brief" usefile="false"/>
    <batchtest todir="${test.data.dir}">
      <fileset dir="test">
        <include name="**/test/*Test.java"/>
      </fileset>
    </batchtest>
  </junit>
  <fail if="test.failed">
    Tests failed. Check ${test.reports.dir}
  </fail>
</target>
```

Apart from these details, the fact that the target is now testing the deployed code on a web server is almost invisible to the build process. Let's run the tests and see:

```
test:
  [junit] Testsuite: d1.webapp.test.EventFeedTest
  [junit] Tests run: 1, Failures: 0, Errors: 0, Time elapsed: 1.022 sec

  [junit] Testsuite: d1.webapp.test.HappyPageTest
  [junit] Tests run: 3, Failures: 0, Errors: 0, Time elapsed: 0.701 sec
```

```
[junit] Testsuite: dl.webapp.test.IndexTest
[junit] Tests run: 1, Failures: 0, Errors: 0, Time elapsed: 0.621 sec
```

BUILD SUCCESSFUL

All the tests are working. HttpUnit can now check our servlet and our JSP pages every time we rebuild, and so make sure that the application keeps working. We can also write more tests.

That's it! We have a complete build process for our web application, including deployment and testing. The application may not be ready to go live, but with a deploy and test process in place, we can start working on it.

12.6   SUMMARY

This chapter has covered web applications, and how to build, deploy and test them.

- The `<war>` task creates WAR files. The task is really just `<jar>` with some extra knowledge about how to lay out a WAR file.

- Web and application servers that support deploy-by-copy deployment, specifically Tomcat and JBoss, make deployment trivial. To deploy the WAR file, copy it to the right directory. To undeploy, delete the file.

- Ant's `<get>` task can fetch web pages and halt the build if an error is returned by the server.

- The `<waitfor>` task can pause the build until a condition is met. It can be used with the `<http>` or `<socket>` condition to pause the build until an application is ready for testing.

- The `<sleep>` task can also insert delays, which is sometimes useful.

- HttpUnit is the foundation for functional testing of web sites. You can use it to get pages, post forms, and to analyze the results.

There's an incredible amount of foundation work to get any web application off the ground. There's the coding and the whole WAR-file layout and creation process and the need to fetch JSP pages to force-compile them. The way to stay on top of this is to automate as much as you can, having Ant build, package, deploy, and test the application, which is what we've covered in this chapter.

What next? Well, we could go straight into making the application persistent, creating an Enterprise application. But before then, let's explore Ant's XML support. By doing so we can use Ant to validate the XML output of our web application and make more uses of XML in our build process.

C H A P T E R   1 3

Working with XML

In this chapter we're going to take a partial break from the web site and do some low-level XML work. Many Java projects need some XML processing at build time. It may be the need to create configuration files on the fly, or it could be the desire to generate Java source files from XML. This is essentially what all web service stacks do when they create Java classes from the XML files that describe the remote SOAP service.

We're going to explore XML processing in Ant. We'll see how to use Ant to validate the Atom feed of events coming off our diary web application, and to generate Java source files from XML templates. We'll also look at the basic ways that Ant can work with XML.

Ant can perform four main actions with XML data:

- Write some XML into a file
- Validate an XML document
- Read Ant properties from an XML file
- Transform XML content into other XML documents, HTML files, or plain text

This will give a taste of Ant's abilities and show its limits too. It will demonstrate where a bit of XML can benefit a Java application at build time, and how Ant can help.

13.1 Background: *XML-processing libraries*

Before beginning on XML processing, here's a quick recap of the current state of XML parsing in Java. This can explain why XML parsing and processing don't always work.

Java supports multiple XML parsers, Apache Xerces being the one that Java 5 and Ant ship with, but various vendors provide others. These parsers implement the SAX event-based parser in the `org.w3c.sax` packages and one or more versions of the World Wide Web Consortium (W3C) XML Document Object Model (DOM), a standard defined in the `org.w3c.dom` packages. More recently, the pull-model parsers implementing the StAX API, are emerging, with one built into Java 6.

Java 5 and 6 include a version of Xerces, while Ant distributions come with more recent versions; the `-diagnostics` command lists the name and location of the parser in use:

```
-------------------------------------------
 XML Parser information
-------------------------------------------
XML Parser : org.apache.xerces.jaxp.SAXParserImpl
XML Parser Location: /home/ant/ant/lib/xercesImpl.jar
```

Java IDEs may run Ant under a different XML parser, which can cause problems; a target with an inline `<diagnostics/>` task can be used to list the in-IDE state and so identify the parser.

Alongside the XML parser API is the API for transforming XML, TRaX. Apache Xalan is the standard XSLT engine used by Ant tasks; other implementations of TRaX may work, but they aren't so widely used. Java currently ships with a version of Xalan called XSLTC; this compiles XSL into Java. It's more memory-hungry than classic Xalan, which we believe works best with Ant. If a build runs out of memory when doing XSL work, increase Ant's memory in the `ANT_OPTS` environment variable or add Xalan to Ant's classpath.

With that little detail out of the way, let's start the XML work by creating an XML file.

13.2 Writing XML

The easiest way to create XML files in Ant is by using the `<echoxml>` task. You just declare the name of the file and embed the XML content inside the task:

```
<target name="echoxml">
  <property name="echoxml.xml"
    location="${build.dir}/echoxml.xml" />
  <echoxml file="${echoxml.xml}" >
    <xmlfile>
      <nested attribute="value">nested &gt;</nested>
    </xmlfile>
  </echoxml>
</target>
```

ANT 1.7

This would create the following file:

```
<?xml version="1.0" encoding="UTF-8"?>
<xmlfile>
  <nested attribute="value">nested &gt;</nested>
</xmlfile>
```

It's easy to use and, because the XML is inline in the XML build file, guarantees that the generated file is well-formed. The document is encoded in UTF-8, and any characters that need to escape are correctly escaped.

Unfortunately, the task is very limited; it was built from existing Ant code, and it has some problems.

- Support for XML namespaces is unreliable.
- XML Processor Instructions are stripped out when Ant's own build file is parsed.
- You cannot insert other declarations, such as the DOCTYPE declaration used to bind a file to a DTD.
- The order in which text elements and other nested child elements are included can vary.
- The only encoding is UTF-8.

Here's an example of the limitations in action. Can Ant generate the file we want?

```
<echoxml file="${build.dir}/xmlns.xml">
  <x:xmlfile xmlns:x="http://antbook.org/2006/01/01">
    text data
    <x:nested attribute="value">nested &gt; </x:nested>
    more text
    <?processing instruction?>
  </x:xmlfile>
</echoxml>
```

No, it can not:

```
<?xml version="1.0" encoding="UTF-8"?>
<x:xmlfile>
  <x:nested attribute="value">nested &gt;</x:nested>
text data


        more text</x:xmlfile>
```

This is a mess and, without the namespace information, an incorrect mess. For such complex XML, we're better off using the <echo> task. That task will print anything to a file, including XML data.

```
<echo file="${cdata.xml}"
    encoding="${enc}"
><![CDATA[<?xml version="1.0" encoding="${enc}"?>
<x:xmlfile xmlns:x="http://antbook.org/2006/01/01">
    text data
```

```
    <x:nested attribute="value">nested &gt;</x:nested>
    more text
    <?processing instruction?>
</x:xmlfile>]]>
  </echo>
```

The default encoding of <echo> is that of the local platform; you can ask for any encoding that the JVM supports; the JavaDocs for the class java.nio.charset.Charset list those supported in all systems: US-ASCII, UTF-8, UTF-16, and ISO-8859-1 are all guaranteed to be valid encodings.

Inside the <echo> task, the string <![CDATA[tells Ant's XML parser to accept all XML content as is, up until the closing]]> characters. This is an XML CDATA section, in which you can place anything (other than]]>). No XML elements will be processed by the parser, but Ant properties will still be expanded inline:

```
<?xml version="1.0" encoding="UTF-8"?>
<x:xmlfile xmlns:x="http://antbook.org/2006/01/01">
    text data
    <x:nested attribute="value">nested &gt;</x:nested>
    more text
    <?processing instruction?>
</x:xmlfile>
```

This XML has the correct namespace and layout. But even <echo> has some disadvantages:

- XML-based editors aren't active inside the CDATA section.

- You must not insert any spaces into the document ahead of the <?xml?> declaration. The <![CDATA[declaration must immediately follow the end of the <echo> tag, and the <?xml?> declaration must follow after that. There can be no newlines.

- There is no automatic escaping of data (like ampersands).

- It's easy to <echo> incorrect XML.

The biggest problem is that it's easy to create invalid documents, but that's something the Ant build file can check for us. Let's get to work.

13.3 VALIDATING XML

Ant build files are XML: *well-formed XML*. That means that the XML and elements in the document are correct according to the XML specification. There's an even stricter state of an XML document, *valid XML*, in which the XML has been validated according to some specification. XML parsers can do this validation, checking that an XML document is valid against a schema. Programmers can use this information to validate XML documents they work with, and Ant can use it to check XML documents it is handed.

Validating XML at build time is very useful. It can let you check that XML configuration files are valid before deployment or that test data stored in XML files is correct. It can also be used to check the output of an executed or deployed application. In our project, we will do this, validating an XML representation of forthcoming events in the calendar.

Table 13.1 lists the main ways of describing the validity of an XML document. The odd one out of the set is Schematron. It's a set of rules that can be used to test a document for being valid; rules can be used instead of a schema language or alongside one.

Table 13.1 Ways of describing XML documents

Specification language	File extension	Description	Ant tasks
Datatype Definition	DTD	The original non-XML language for describing XML languages. Not namespace- aware.	`<xmlvalidate>`
XML Schema	XSD	The W3C-approved successor to DTD. Powerful, but very complex.	`<schemavalidate>`
RelaxNG	RNG	An OASIS/ISO standard; a lightweight alternative to XSD.	`<jing>` (third-party task)
Schematron		A set of patterns that describe valid documents.	None

Ant can validate XML files against DTD and XSD descriptions by using the `<xmlvalidate>` and `<schemavalidate>` tasks. RelaxNG support comes from a third-party task, `<jing>`. Because of the way Schematron works, it doesn't have a direct validation task.

To check that the XML files are well formed, use the built-in task `<xmlvalidate>`. By asking for lenient processing, we ask the task to not validate the XML against any schema or DTD:

```
<target name="lenient" depends="echoxml,cdata,xmlns">
  <xmlvalidate lenient="true">
    <fileset dir="${build.dir}" includes="*.xml"/>
  </xmlvalidate>
</target>
```

The output is confirmation that every file we have so far created is well-formed XML:

```
lenient:
[xmlvalidate] 3 file(s) have been successfully validated.
```

This test is important when using `<echo>` to create the files, as it's easy to get something wrong.

If you do have a schema, a specification of what XML documents you allow, then Ant can go one step farther and validate the document. Ant supports two specification mechanisms out of the box, DTDs and XML Schema, with separate tasks to check each one.

13.3.1 Validating documents using DTD files

The classic language to describe a valid XML document is a Data Type Definition (DTD) file. Here's one that says that the valid elements in a document are `<xmlfile>` and `<nested>`:

```
<?xml version="1.0" encoding="UTF-8"?>
<!ELEMENT nested (#PCDATA) >
<!ATTLIST nested
  attribute CDATA #REQUIRED
>
<!ELEMENT xmlfile (nested) >
```

The `<xmlfile>` element supports `<nested>` elements inside; those elements can contain text and must have an attribute called `attribute`. We can use it to validate XML documents created with `<echo>`. We first need to declare the document type at the beginning of the file.

```
<target name="cdata-dtd" >
  <property name="cdata-dtd.xml"                        Declare the
   location="${build.dir}/cdata-dtd.xml"/>              filename

  <property name="enc" value="UTF-16"/>     <--  UTF-16 encoding

  <property name="dtd-name"                             The public
    value="-//antbook.org//DTD simple 1.0//EN" />       DTD identifier
  <echo file="${cdata-dtd.xml}"
    encoding="${enc}"
><![CDATA[<?xml version="1.0" encoding="${enc}"?>
<!DOCTYPE xmlfile PUBLIC "${dtd-name}" "simple.dtd">    <--❶
    <xmlfile>
      <nested attribute="value">nested &gt;</nested>
    </xmlfile>
]]>
  </echo>
</target>
```

Files that have a DTD must declare this in their `<!DOCTYPE>` declaration ❶, which states the name of the root element and whether it's a PUBLIC or a SYSTEM DTD. Public DTDs need a public ID to uniquely identify the document. For system DTDs all that's needed is a relative or absolute URL. In our example, we declare a public ID and a system reference, but the latter is invalid: there's no file of that name in our local directory.

When we run this `cdata-dtd` target, we get an XML file with a reference to our simple DTD:

```
<!DOCTYPE xmlfile PUBLIC "-//antbook.org//DTD simple 1.0//EN" "simple.dtd">
    <xmlfile>
      <nested attribute="value">nested &gt;</nested>
    </xmlfile>
```

To validate this, we again use the `<xmlvalidate>` task, which supports DTD validation with two nested elements.

- The `<dtd>` element lets you declare a public ID and a URL or file to the DTD.
- The `<xmlcatalog>` element needs the Apache XML project's `xml-resolver` JAR on the classpath. It will then resolve DTD IDs and other references/URIs in the file against a nested list of declarations and against any loaded XML catalog files. This makes it easier to manage large sets of DTDs.

We're going to stick to the simple `<dtd>` element. First, what happens when this element is missing? Here `<xmlvalidate>` tries to validate the document by resolving the system reference and retrieving the file:

```
<target name="validate-echo-no-dtd" depends="cdata-dtd" >
  <xmlvalidate file="${cdata-dtd.xml}"/>
</target>
```

This fails, because the DTD isn't there. The task doesn't give any reason for the failure, though in -verbose mode, the long stack trace of the underlying cause explains the problem:

```
[xmlvalidate] Validating cdata-dtd.xml...
BUILD FAILED
/home/ant/xml/build.xml:96: Could not validate document /home/ant/xml/
build/cdata-dtd.xml
  at org.apache.tools.ant.taskdefs.optional.XMLValidateTask.
    doValidate(XMLValidateTask.java:540)
  ...
Caused by: java.io.FileNotFoundException: /home/ant/xml/build/simple.dtd
(No such file or directory)
  at java.io.FileInputStream.open(Native Method)
  ...
```

This shows two things. First, `<xmlvalidate>` really is trying to validate the document against the DTD, and, second, if the DTD isn't found, validation fails. We need to tell the parser where to find the DTD:

```
<target name="validate-echo-dtd" depends="cdata-dtd" >
  <xmlvalidate file="${cdata-dtd.xml}">
    <dtd publicId="${dtd-name}"
        location="schemas/simple.dtd"/>
  </xmlvalidate>
</target>
```

By declaring a mapping from the `publicId` of the schema to the `location` where a local copy of the schema lives, the task can now verify that the document is valid.

Historically, DTD validation was all you needed to check all deployment descriptors and other documents before actually deploying programs to application servers. More recently, XML Schema has become the language for describing things such as the format of web.xml files since the Servlet 2.4 specification, leading to the next challenge: XML Schema validation.

13.3.2 Validating documents with XML Schema

The W3C XML Schema (usually abbreviated to XSD) is the Perl of XML description languages. You can describe nearly anything in it, but it's nearly impossible to read. You also get some interesting error messages. For example, an *invalid facet* error means that you have defined a pattern for a valid element or attribute (such as the regular expression of a telephone number), and the number in the document doesn't match the pattern. The other interesting error is a complaint about *ambiguous particles*. This means that there are two ways to parse a document, and the parser doesn't know what to do.

XML Schema is very hard to work with. Unfortunately, it's out there, it goes hand in hand with Web Services, and Java developers eventually encounter it. Accordingly, Ant needs to handle it. XSD is very namespace-centric, which means we need to decide whether a schema is going to be in a namespace from the outset, and then we need to work with it differently depending on the decision. It's initially easiest to avoid XML namespaces.

No-namespace validation with XML schema

To create an XML schema for our sample XML files, we used the ubiquitous *XML Spy* tool to reverse-engineer a schema.

> **Listing 13.1** An XML schema for a file with no namespace. This can validate any XML document that doesn't declare itself to be in any namespace.

```
<?xml version="1.0" encoding="UTF-8"?>
<xs:schema xmlns:xs="http://www.w3.org/2001/XMLSchema"
    elementFormDefault="qualified">
  <xs:element name="xmlfile">
    <xs:complexType mixed="true">
      <xs:choice minOccurs="0" maxOccurs="unbounded">
        <xs:element name="nested">
          <xs:complexType>
            <xs:simpleContent>
              <xs:extension base="xs:string">
                <xs:attribute name="attribute"
                  type="xs:string" use="optional"/>
              </xs:extension>
            </xs:simpleContent>
          </xs:complexType>
        </xs:element>
      </xs:choice>
    </xs:complexType>
  </xs:element>
</xs:schema>
```

We can use this schema, saved to the file `schemas/simple.xsd`, to validate the document created in the `echoxml` target of section 13.2. This requires the `<schemavalidate>` task, which extends `<xmlvalidate>` with some extra XSD options. The first of these is the ability to declare the schema used to validate all XML that is not in a namespace:

```
<target name="validate-echo-xsd" depends="echoxml" >
  <schemavalidate file="${echoxml.xml}"
    noNamespaceFile="schemas/simple.xsd"/>
</target>
```

When we run this target, if it succeeds nothing is printed at all. In `-verbose` mode, Ant prints out some more low-level details:

```
validate-echo-xsd:
[schemavalidate] Using SAX2 reader
                 org.apache.xerces.parsers.SAXParser
[schemavalidate] Validating echoxml.xml...
[schemavalidate] 1 file(s) have been successfully validated.
```

This declares that the file is valid. Now, what about XML content in namespaces?

Validating documents with namespaces

To validate XML in a namespace we need to create a new XML schema by copying the one from listing 13.1 into a new file, `namespace.xsd`, and binding it to a namespace. Listing 13.2 shows the file, with the extra line marked in bold.

Listing 13.2   A modified XSD file to declare the schema for a single namespace

```
<?xml version="1.0" encoding="UTF-8"?>
<xs:schema xmlns:xs="http://www.w3.org/2001/XMLSchema"
    targetNamespace="http://antbook.org/2006/01/01"
    elementFormDefault="qualified">
  <xs:element name="xmlfile">
    <xs:complexType mixed="true">
      <xs:choice minOccurs="0" maxOccurs="unbounded">
        <xs:element name="nested">
          <xs:complexType>
            <xs:simpleContent>
              <xs:extension base="xs:string">
                <xs:attribute name="attribute"
                  type="xs:string"
                  use="optional"/>
              </xs:extension>
            </xs:simpleContent>
          </xs:complexType>
        </xs:element>
      </xs:choice>
    </xs:complexType>
  </xs:element>
</xs:schema>
```

We can use this file to validate the document created by the `cdata` target, which declares its elements to be in the same namespace as the schema:

```
<target name="validate-cdata-xsd" depends="cdata" >
  <schemavalidate file="${cdata.xml}">
    <schema namespace="http://antbook.org/2006/01/01"
      file="schemas/namespace.xsd" />
  </schemavalidate>
</target>
```
❶

Instead of declaring the schema to use in the `noNamespaceFile` attribute, we've declared the namespace and file as a nested `<schema>` element ❶. This shows where XML Schema can work with namespaces: we can mix elements and attributes from multiple namespaces in the same document, validating it by declaring the namespace and schema file for every namespace. A good way to do this is to use `<presetdef>` to define the template for validation, which lists all schemas to use, and use this definition wherever files need to be validated. Listing 13.3 shows an example of this complex build process that validates a SOAP API defined in WSDL and XSD files.

Listing 13.3 A `<presetdef>` to validate documents against the SOAP1.2 specifications

```
<presetdef name="validate-soap">
  <schemavalidate>
    <schema namespace="http://www.w3.org/2003/05/soap-envelope"
      file="${soap12.xsd}"/>
    <schema namespace="http://schemas.xmlsoap.org/wsdl/"
      file="${soap.dir}/wsdl.xsd"/>
    <schema namespace="http://schemas.xmlsoap.org/wsdl/soap/"
      file="${soap.dir}/wsdlsoap.xsd"/>
  </schemavalidate>
</presetdef>
```

Issues with XSD not withstanding, it's a powerful language, being namespace-aware and capable of validating documents without any `<!DOCTYPE>` declaration. Validating deployment descriptors and other XML manifests can be a chore that Ant can automate with it. That leaves one remaining problem: those documents described by the RelaxNG schema language, which is exactly the problem we need to address for the diary web application.

13.3.3   Validating RelaxNG documents

The diary web application generates a RelaxNG document in need of validation. The Atom event feed servlet, the one that provides events to listening applications, generates an Atom 1.0 XML feed. And which schema language does that use? RelaxNG. If we could retrieve that feed and validate it against the specification, then we would know if the third-party syndication library we're using, Rome, is generating valid Atom data.

Ant has no built-in support for RelaxNG validation; it's handled by the Jing library from http://www.thaiopensource.com/relaxng/jing.html. This library contains a task called `<jing>` to validate XML files against RelaxNG schemas.

Declaring the Jing task

Because the needed JAR, `jing.jar`, is in the ibiblio artifact repository, Ivy can retrieve the file. We have to add a new configuration to the `ivy.xml` file:

```
<conf name="jing" description="libraries for the jing task"
  visibility="private"/>
```

This configuration has one dependency:

```
<dependency org="thaiopensource"
    name="jing"
    rev="${jing.version}"
    conf="jing->default"/>
```

The `libraries.properties` file needs to be updated too, with a reference to the latest Jing release:

```
jing.version=20030619
```

The retrieved artifacts are fed in to a `<taskdef>` declaration, setting up the `<jing>` task:

```
<target name="declare-jing" depends="ivy-retrieve" >
  <taskdef name="jing"
    classname="com.thaiopensource.relaxng.util.JingTask"
    uri="http://thaiopensource.com/">
    <classpath>
      <fileset dir="${ivy.lib.dir}/jing" includes="*.jar" />
    </classpath>
  </taskdef>
</target>
```

Running the `declare-jing` target will declare in the namespace `http://thaiopensource.com/` a new task, `<jing>`. This can verify the XML data generated by the web application once that data has been captured to a local file.

Fetching the XML feed

Fetching the XML feed is no harder than fetching any other web page with the `<get>` task. The only change is that the saved page is handed on to the validation target:

```
<target name="get-feed" depends="deployed" >
  <property name="feed.xml" location="${build.dir}/feed.xml" />
  <get src="${application.url}feed/" dest="${feed.xml}"/>
</target>
```

This target is in the sample build file `diary/webapp/webapp-chapter-13.xml`, which extends the deploy-by-copy targets of chapter 12 by importing that build file:

```
<import file="webapp-deploy-by-copy.xml"/>
```

As a result, because the `get-feed` target depends on the application being in the `deployed` state, Ant automatically rebuilds and redeploys the application before fetching the XML feed:

```
get-feed:
  [get] Getting: http://localhost:8080/diary/feed/
  [get] To: /home/ant/diary/webapp/build/feed.xml
```

That leaves two more actions: getting a local copy of the relevant schema file and validating `feed.xml` against it.

The IETF Atom specification contains the RelaxNG specification as an appendix. RelaxNG has two syntaxes, a pure-XML one and a compact syntax that's easier for people to read. The relevant bit of the document was copied by hand and pasted into a file in the test source tree, as `test/d1/webapp/test/atom.rng`. Why put it there? Because it turns out to be very handy to have all schemas and DTDs in the classpath when running unit tests since it lets developers validate XML data within the Java tests. Putting the schemas in the directory makes this possible, though we'll have to make sure `**/*.rng` is copied into the test JAR.

With the feed downloaded and the `.rng` specification in a local file, we can now check our diary's XML feed against the Atom standard:

```
<target name="validate-feed" depends="declare-jing,get-feed"
    xmlns:jing="http://thaiopensource.com/">
  <property name="atom.rng"
    location="test/d1/webapp/test/atom.rng" />
  <jing:jing rngfile="${atom.rng}"
      compactsyntax="true">
    <fileset file="${feed.xml}"/>
  </jing:jing>
</target>
```

This target uses the `<jing>` task, pointing it at the `atom.rng` file and stating that this is in the compact syntax and not XML. The nested fileset is then set to the single file we wish to validate. What happens when we run it? The build succeeds:

```
get:
    [get] Getting: http://localhost:8080/diary//happy.jsp
    [get] To: /home/ant/diary/webapp/build/happy.html

deployed:

get-feed:
    [get] Getting: http://localhost:8080/diary/feed/
    [get] To: /home/ant/diary/webapp/build/feed.xml

validate-feed:

BUILD SUCCESSFUL
Total time: 13 seconds
```

The target has succeeded, so we can be confident that the feed is a valid Atom 1.0 data source. This is why XML validation is useful. Any hand-written or machine-generated XML can be validated against its schema definitions. In Ant, the `<xmlvalidate>`, `<schemavalidate>`, and `<jing>` tasks will validate XML documents against DTDs, XSD, and RelaxNG schemas respectively.

13.4 READING XML DATA

Ant has the limited ability to read XML files into properties, which can be used to extract information from XML documents. If you have XML data files that contain values needed in your build process, the `<xmlproperty>` task may be able to help. It can create properties from the elements and attributes in the XML document, setting the property values to the values of the XML nodes. It has some limitations though: it doesn't perform local DTD resolution, and it merges elements if there are duplicate names. Here's an example data file, `schema/properties.xml`:

```
<?xml version="1.0" encoding="UTF-8" ?>
<data>
  <element attribute1="attribute1">element1</element>
  <element attribute2="attribute2">element2</element>
</data>
```

Ant can load this and print out the contents:

```
<target name="load-properties">
  <xmlproperty file="schemas/properties.xml"
    keepRoot="false"
    collapseAttributes="true"
    />
  <echo>
  element = ${element}
  element.attribute1 = ${element.attribute1}
  element.attribute2 = ${element.attribute2}
  </echo>
</target>
```

Running this target shows what Ant can extract from the XML document:

```
load-properties:
     [echo]
     [echo]    element = element1,element2
     [echo]    element.attribute1 = attribute1
     [echo]    element.attribute2 = attribute2
     [echo]
```

The two duplicate `<element>` declarations have been merged with a comma between them. In older versions of Ant, only the first declaration would have been retained. Both `attribute1` and `attribute2` are accessible, showing that this task can be handy when you have some simple XML data that you need to turn into Ant properties.

The task isn't namespace-aware; you can refer to elements loaded in a namespace-enabled XML document, but you need to know the prefix and use that prefix when evaluating a property. You can see this in a target that loads the namespace-enabled file `build/cdata.xml`. After loading, we use the `<echoproperties>` task to print out all properties with the prefix `x:`, that is, everything with that namespace alias:

```
<target name="load-cdata" depends="cdata">
  <xmlproperty file="${cdata.xml}"/>
  <echoproperties prefix="x:" />
</target>
```

The result is a listing of the properties. The `<echoproperties>` task escapes everything, just as a Java properties file requires, so every colon has a backslash that's just an artifact of the echoing:

```
x\:xmlfile=text data,more text
x\:xmlfile(xmlns\:x)=http\://antbook.org/2006/01/01
x\:xmlfile.x\:nested=nested >
x\:xmlfile.x\:nested(attribute)=value
```

In a build file, we omit the colons, fetching an attribute with the property `${x:xmlfile.x:nested(attribute)}`. This isn't a perfect way of referring to attributes, but unless someone wants to add XPath support to Ant, it's all there is.

We've now covered writing, reading, and validating XML from Ant. There's one more way that Ant can work with XML, and it is possibly the most powerful. It can transform the XML into other forms through XML Stylesheets (XSL). These XML files contain rules for turning one XML file into another document. Ant can apply these to XML files as part of the build.

13.5   TRANSFORMING XML WITH XSLT

XML is a great way to keep data separate from formatting. It's the ideal format for documentation because it lets you transform it into display or print formats, such as HTML and PDF. This can be done at runtime, perhaps with a framework such as Cocoon. It can also be done at build time, to convert XML into readable text or HTML. Indeed, that's exactly how `<junitreport>` works, turning test logs into HTML pages.

Ant's built-in `<xslt>` task performs XSL transformations. Transforming an entire fileset of XML files with a single XSL stylesheet is easy. Figure 13.1 shows the basic workflow: incoming XML files are transformed by an XSL stylesheet into new XML, HTML, or text files. Those text files can be documentation, or they can be something more sophisticated, such as Java source files.

The problem we're going to explore is exactly that: taking an XML source file, `constants.xml`, and creating Java source files and HTML documentation from it. What are the steps for doing this?

1 Define the structure and, perhaps, the DTD/Schema of the XML file.

2 Create the `constants.xml` file.

3 Create XSL style sheets to generate Java and HTML files.

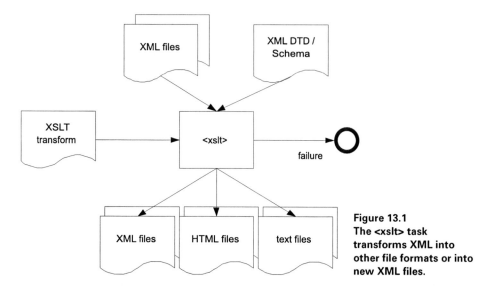

**Figure 13.1
The <xslt> task
transforms XML into
other file formats or into
new XML files.**

4 Define in the build file the locations of the XML and XSL files and the destination directories.

5 Write the `<xslt>` tasks to create the output files.

6 Compile the generated Java source.

Generating source from XML documents is a powerful technique. Here we'll define the XML namespaces of the Atom drafts, the standards, and some string values for XML elements in their feeds. For every URI in the `constants.xml` file, we'll define a `static final URI`, turning any exception from the constructor into a runtime exception.

13.5.1 Defining the structure of the constants file

Our XML file will have constants, either URIs or strings. Each will have a name, a value, and perhaps a description, the latter being multi-line.

From this, an approximate DTD falls out, as shown in listing 13.4.

Listing 13.4 The DTD for our constants, in `xml/format.dtd`

```
<!ELEMENT constants (string | uri )*>
<!ELEMENT string (description)*>
<!ATTLIST string
  name CDATA #REQUIRED
  value CDATA #REQUIRED >
<!ELEMENT uri (description)*>
<!ATTLIST uri
  name CDATA #REQUIRED
  value CDATA #REQUIRED >
<!ELEMENT description (#PCDATA) >
<!ELEMENT name (#PCDATA) >
```

CHAPTER 13 WORKING WITH XML

Having a DTD allows XML-aware editors to validate the file during editing, and it lets `<xmlvalidate>` check the `constants.xml` syntax before handing it off to the style sheets.

13.5.2 Creating the constants file

The `constants.xml` file goes into `webapp/xml`, the same directory as the file `format.dtd`. This allows us to use a local system reference for the DTD. Listing 13.5 shows the file.

Listing 13.5   The initial constants file. It defines three URIs and the names of three elements in some proposed XML.

```
<?xml version="1.0" encoding="UTF-8"?>
<!DOCTYPE constants SYSTEM "format.dtd">
<constants>
  <uri name="NS_ATOM_10"
   value="http://www.w3.org/2005/Atom">
    <description>Atom 1.0 Namespace</description>
  </uri>
  <uri name="NS_ATOM_03"
    value="http://purl.org/atom/ns#">
    <description>Atom 0.3 Namespace</description>
  </uri>
  <string name="ELEMENT_FEED" value="feed">
    <description>Atom XML element</description>
  </string>
  <string name="ELEMENT_TITLE" value="title">
    <description>Atom XML element</description>
  </string>
  <string name="ELEMENT_ENTRY" value="entry">
    <description>Atom XML element</description>
  </string>
</constants>
```

We'll be able to use these constants in the web application or its test code. To do that, we need the constants in our Java source. We could do that by hand, but that would just create maintenance problems. Every time we added a new constant, we would have to remember to edit the Java source and the HTML documentation, and then rebuild everything. What we want is something better: to create the Java source from the XML. This is what XSL can do for us.

13.5.3 Creating XSL style sheets

We need XSL style sheets for both Java and HTML files. Listing 13.6 shows the XSL file to create the Java source.

```xml
<?xml version="1.0" encoding="UTF-8"?>
<xsl:stylesheet
  xmlns:xsl="http://www.w3.org/1999/XSL/Transform"
  version="1.0">
  <xsl:output method="text" encoding="us-ascii"/>    ◄─❶


  <xsl:template match="/constants">    ◄─❷


package d1.webapp.generated;    ◄─❸
import javax.xml.namespace.QName;
import java.net.URI;                              ❹
import java.net.URISyntaxException;


public class Constants {
  private Constants() { }

  private static URI makeURI(String value) {
    try {
        return new URI(value);
    } catch (URISyntaxException e) {              ❺
        throw new RuntimeException(
          "Cannot instantiate URI to "+value,e);
    }
  }

  <xsl:apply-templates select="uri"/>       ❻
  <xsl:apply-templates select="string"/>

}                 ❼
</xsl:template>

<xsl:template match="uri">
  <xsl:apply-templates select="description"/>
  public static final URI
    URI_<xsl:value-of select="@name"/>              ❽
      = makeURI("<xsl:value-of select="@value"/>");
</xsl:template>

<xsl:template match="string">
  <xsl:apply-templates select="description"/>
  public static final String
  <xsl:value-of select="@name"/> =               ❾
   "<xsl:value-of select="@value"/>";
</xsl:template>

<xsl:template match="description">
  /**                                          ❿
    * <xsl:value-of select="."/>
```

```
    */
</xsl:template>        ↑ ⑩

</xsl:stylesheet>                                    ■
```

XSL stylesheets contain templates that match subsets of the document, subsets described by XPath patterns. The XSL engine matches and applies the templates, outputting XML, text, or HTML. For Java source, we need ASCII text ❶.

In the stylesheet, the /constants XPath matches the root element of the document, <constants>, so that template is applied first ❷. Inside that template goes the header of the Java document, the package declaration ❸, any imports ❹, and then the class declaration, a private constructor, and a static helper method ❺. Finally, just before the closing bracket of the class and the end of the template ❼, we apply all templates that match uri or string against the children of /constants ❻. That will apply the relevant templates for the child elements.

The URI ❽ and string ❾ templates are invoked for every <uri> and <string> declared in the constants file. Each of them creates a public static final constant, using a shared template ⑩. The <xsl:value-of> declarations in all these templates extract the text values of the XPath supplied in the select attribute. For the description element, the pattern <xsl:value-of select="."/> means "insert all my nested text here." The URI and string templates want to extract the values of attributes, so they use the XPath expression to do just that. For example, the URI template goes:

```
URI_<xsl:value-of select="@name"/>
```

For the <uri> element with the name attribute NS_ATOM_03, this will insert the text URI_NS_ATOM_03 into the Java source, which is the name of the constant that we want.

Creating an XSL file that generates syntactically correct Java is no easy task. Trying to produce code that lays out well is even harder. It may be possible, but it would probably make the XSL file itself very hard to read. The style sheet in listing 13.7 to generate HTML is much simpler.

> **Listing 13.7 The toHtml.xsl style sheet. It's a lot easier to generate HTML than Java.**

```
<?xml version="1.0" encoding="UTF-8"?>
<xsl:stylesheet xmlns:xsl="http://www.w3.org/1999/XSL/Transform"
  version="1.0">
 <xsl:output method="html" encoding="us-ascii"/>    ←❶

 <xsl:template match="/constants">
  <html>
  <head><title>Constants</title></head>
  <body>
```

```
         <h1>Constants</h1>
         <h2>URIs</h2>
         <table>
             <xsl:apply-templates select="uri"/>
         </table>
         <h2>Strings</h2>
         <table>
             <xsl:apply-templates select="string"/>
         </table>
   </body>
   </html>
 </xsl:template>

 <xsl:template match="uri|string">      ◄─❷
  <tr>
     <td><code>
       <xsl:value-of select="@name"/>
     </code></td>
     <td><code>
       <xsl:value-of select="@value"/>
     </code></td>
     <td>
     <xsl:value-of select="description"/>
     </td>
  </tr>
 </xsl:template>

</xsl:stylesheet>
```

There are two big changes to this file. First, the output format is explicitly "html" ❶. HTML is not XML, and you need to ask for it unless you want XHTML content. Second, there's only one template for both `<uri>` and `<string>` elements, even though each appears in its own table. By using the XPath `"uri|string"`, this template will be used for either element ❷.

With both XSL files written, Ant can generate the Java and HTML files from the constants file.

13.5.4   Initializing the build file

To create the XML, we need a new target to define all the various source and destination files, and we need to create the destination directories. Here's the XML:

```
<target name="init-constants" depends="init">
  <property name="xml.dir"
            location="xml"/>
  <property name="constants.xml"
            location="${xml.dir}/constants.xml"/>
  <property name="toJava.xsl"
            location="${xml.dir}/toJava.xsl"/>
  <property name="toHtml.xsl"
            location="${xml.dir}/toHtml.xsl"/>
```

```
<property name="build.src.dir"
  value="${build.dir}/src"/>
<property name="constants.java.dir"
  value="${build.src.dir}/d1/webapp/generated"/>
<property name="Constants.java"
        location="${constants.java.dir}/Constants.java"/>

<property name="constants.doc.dir"
  value="${build.dir}/doc"/>
<property name="constants.html"
        location="${constants.doc.dir}/constants.html"/>

<mkdir dir="${constants.java.dir}"/>
<mkdir dir="${constants.doc.dir}"/>
</target>
```

First, Ant defines properties for all the source files for ease of reference. Then, Ant creates the destination directories under `${build.dir}`. It's critical that the generated Java source goes into a directory with the same structure as the package name declared in the XSL file, here `d1/webapp/generated`. We never generate Java source into a package with hand-written code, and never, never, place the generated source into a directory under SCM. These generated files are created during the build process and do not need to be managed.

Finally, the target creates the destination directories. This means that Ant is ready to create the files.

Generating the source with <xslt>

After the complexity of the XSL files, the targets to run them come as a relief. For both the source and the documentation, we declare an `<xslt>` task, listing the input XML file, the output file, and the XSL stylesheet:

```
<target name="constants" depends="init-constants"
  description="create java constants from XML">
  <xmlvalidate file="${constants.xml}"/>
  <xslt in="${constants.xml}"
        out="${Constants.java}"
        style="${toJava.xsl}">
  </xslt>
  <xslt in="${constants.xml}"
        out="${constants.html}"
        style="${toHtml.xsl}">
  </xslt>
</target>
```

The `<xslt>` task is dependency-aware, which means that it will run if the destination file is absent or if it is older than either the source file or the stylesheet.

With the task written, we can run it.

```
constants:
[xmlvalidate] 1 file(s) have been successfully validated.
     [xslt] Processing /home/ant/diary/webapp/xml/constants.xml to
        /home/ant/diary/webapp/build/src/d1/webapp/generated/Constants.java
     [xslt] Loading stylesheet /home/ant/diary/webapp/xml/toJava.xsl
     [xslt] Processing /home/ant/diary/webapp/xml/constants.xml to
        /home/ant/diary/webapp/build/doc/constants.html
     [xslt] Loading stylesheet /home/ant/diary/webapp/xml/toHtml.xsl
BUILD SUCCESSFUL
```

This looks like it worked, but we should check to make sure. A web browser can check the HTML page, as shown in figure 13.2.

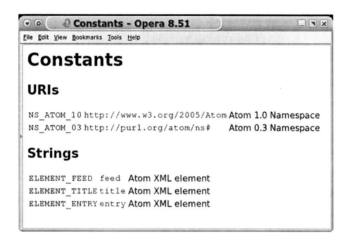

Figure 13.2
The generated HTML page. We can use this in developer documentation, or add it to the web site content.

The Java source is harder to verify. We can look at it; it appears valid, but it contains various constants laid out in a bit of a mess:

```java
/**
  * Atom 0.3 Namespace
  */

public static final URI
  URI_NS_ATOM_03
    = makeURI("http://purl.org/atom/ns#");

/**
  * Atom XML element
  */

public static final String
ELEMENT_FEED =
  "feed";
```

The best way to check is, of course, to compile the source.

Compiling the generated source

Adding generated code to the compile stage complicates the process. We need to make sure that the source is generated before `<javac>` gets called. We also need to run `<javac>` over both source trees, the main tree and the generated source, *at the same time*. We cannot do one before or after the other if we want to have them interdependent. Also, because we're extending-by-importing the webapp-chapter-12.xml build file, we need to override its existing `compile` target.

To ensure that the constants are processed before compilation, we redefine our `ready-to-compile` target, adding the `constants` target as a dependency:

```
<target name="ready-to-compile"
  depends="webapp-chapter-12.ready-to-compile,constants" />
```

Next comes a complete rewrite of the compile target, in order to change the `srcdir` property.

```
<target name="compile" depends="ready-to-compile">
  <ext:javac destdir="${build.classes.dir}"
          classpathref="compile.classpath"
          srcdir="src:${build.src.dir}"
          includes="**/*.java">
  </ext:javac>
  <ext:copy-useful-files src="src" dest="${build.classes.dir}"/>
</target>
```

Now, instead of a single directory, `src`, the `srcdir` attribute is set to a path: `src:${build.src.dir}`. This is a little secret of that attribute: it doesn't take a directory; it takes a path. It's important that both source directories are at the base of the package trees: if we had listed the actual directory into which the file `Constants.java` went, the code may have compiled, but the dependency logic would be broken.

Running the new target is a bit of an anti-climax, as all that happens is that Ant compiles one more file:

```
compile:
[ext:javac] Compiling 1 source file to
  /home/ant/diary/webapp/build/classes
```

This is exactly what we want. A Java file, whether handwritten or generated from an XML source via an XSL transformation, is just a Java file. We can now use these constants in our application.

Generating Java source from XML documents may seem like a lot of work. Once the process is set up, however, it becomes trivial to extend it to generate more complex types. Using XSL transformations to generate Java source is only one example of what XML+XSL can do in an Ant project. It just happens to be the one that's useful for many Java projects. The task can just as easily be used to generate HTML pages from XML documents or even CSV-formatted text files from the XML results of a JUnit run. Whenever your build needs to take XML files and create some kind of text, HTML, or XML file from it, turn to the `<xslt>` task!

13.6 SUMMARY

Although not an XML workflow engine, Ant can produce, consume, and transform XML during a build. This lets it handle the XML-related steps of the build process, from reading and writing XML files, to generating new content from XML source data.

You can create XML using <echoxml> and <echo>, which allow you to create custom XML files. The <xmlproperty> task lets you read XML back in to Ant properties, extracting information from the values of elements and attributes.

XML files can be checked for being well-formed and valid. There's built-in support for DTD-described files with <xmlvalidate> and XML Schema in <schemavalidate>. The third-party task, <jing>, can validate against RelaxNG schemas. These can all verify that XML files match the specification, or, alternatively, that the specification is adequate. If you're creating XML files in Ant, validating them lets you know immediately when the files are invalid, helping you to get the build working.

The <xslt> task will transform XML during the build. This lets you store content in XML form and then dynamically generate text, HTML, or XML files. We've shown how to use it to create both HTML content and Java classes from the same XML source. Dynamically generating Java source enables many new things.

Finally, remember this: Ant isn't a tool for general purpose XML processing. Products like Apache Cocoon (http://cocoon.apache.org/), and NetKernel (http://1060research.com/) are designed to work with XML from the ground up. Ant's XML processing is limited to a bit of XML work during the build process. If you find yourself reaching the limits of what Ant can do with XML, then take the time to look at tools that focus on XML processing, and see if you can delegate those parts of the build to them.

Now, where does the web application stand? This chapter added validation of the Atom feed, and we've got some constants we need being generated from XML. With the Atom feed working, that means that the web application can serve up data to any RSS client that supports the Atom protocol, including current versions of Mozilla FireFox and Internet Explorer. It's almost a diary. Unfortunately, without persistence, it cannot remember things reliably. If we want it to save and retrieve events to and from a database, we need to work on the back end of the application. We need to make it an Enterprise Java application.

Enterprise Java

It's time to move our application up a notch. We're going to make it an Enterprise application. One way to do this is to use Java Enterprise Edition (Java EE), the product formerly known as Java 2 Enterprise Edition (J2EE). According to Sun's web site (http:// java.sun.com/javaee/), "Java EE provides web services, component model, management, and communications APIs that make it the industry standard for implementing Enterprise-class service-oriented architecture (SOA) and Web 2.0 applications."

What that means is that the Java EE API provides all the APIs needed to make Java classes persistent to a database, and for the outside world to talk to the application over HTTP, CORBA, or the Web Service protocols. It doesn't provide implementations; Java EE applications work properly only inside an application server. This makes development and testing harder than it is for anything else we've covered so far.

There's been a bit of a backlash against Java EE, leading to the lightweight open-source alternatives of Hibernate and the Spring Application Framework. Ant works with those too. If you're using these frameworks, you can fast-forward to the deployment and testing sections (sections 14.6 and 14.7). All server-side frameworks have the same problem: you need to deploy and test them on an application server.

14.1 EVOLVING THE DIARY APPLICATION

We're going to make the diary Enterprise-ready by binding it to a database. This requires that we rework the web application to make the diary and its events persistent.

What's the plan?

1 Get the Java EE Software Development Kit (SDK) and related tools.

2 Make the Event class persistent.

3 Write a calendar API to provide access to the persistent data.

4 Integrate with the web application.

5 Package and deploy the application on an appropriate server.

6 Test the new application.

Ant, as we'll see in the later parts of the project, can help. But before we get to building, packaging, and testing the code, we need to install the SDK and write the application. Let's start with installing the SDK.

Installing the Java EE SDK

Enterprise Java comes with a whole new set of Java classes, mostly in the `javax` packages. The API is implemented in the file `javaee.jar`, which comes with the Java EE SDK. The first step is to download the Java EE SDK from http://java.sun.com/javaee.

The JAR file provides most of the APIs for Enterprise Java and some Java annotation declarations to accompany them. What it doesn't contain is any of the implementation classes. The Enterprise Java applications work only inside an *Application Server*, which is a program hosting the deployed Enterprise applications, creating Enterprise Java Bean (EJB) instances on demand, and implementing the various server-side APIs.

Selecting an application server

To use all of the Java EE services, we need an application server. We've chosen the popular JBoss application server. It runs on most platforms, is thoroughly documented, and is the most popular open source application server. A good alternative would have been Sun's Glassfish application server. It has a very nice web-based control panel as well as good support for current Java EE technologies.

Here are the core steps to follow to install JBoss:

1 Download and run the "installer JAR" from the JBoss site (http://labs.jboss .com/portal/jbossas/download); at the time of writing the installer was called `jems-installer-1.2.0.GA.jar`.

2 Select the "ejb3" option, to enable EJB3 support.

3 Use the recommended profile name, "default."

4 In the page "Isolation and Call by Value Semantics," you *must* check the "Enable deployment isolation/call by value" option. Things will not work properly unless that option is selected.

After installing, change to the created `jboss/bin` directory:

1 Start the server with `run.bat` or `./run.sh`.
2 Point a web browser at http://localhost:8080/ and verify that JBoss is up. If you see something other than a JBoss application server, then another web server is running locally. Turn it off and restart JBoss.
3 Try connecting from another system. If the page isn't visible, open up the firewall.

If the JBoss web page is visible, the server is installed and ready for deployment. For more information, you may want to check out the book *JBoss at Work* (Marrs and Davis, 2005). It covers configuring and managing JBoss 4 well.

Databases

We also need a database, which complicates deployment and testing. For deployment, you need to set up the database with the right tables and accounts. For testing, we need to add data setup and then clean up on teardown.

The chosen database is the "Hypersonic" HSQLDB. This is a pure-Java database that can run standalone or as a lightweight in-process datastore. It also has a non-persistent mode in which the data is discarded after the program ends. That makes it ideal for testing. The product's home page is http://hsqldb.org/; the version used was 1.8.0.7. The single JAR is all you need; it implements the Java Database Connectivity (JDBC) API for database access.

With all our tools set up, we're ready to turn the diary into an Enterprise application.

14.2   MAKING AN ENTERPRISE APPLICATION

To make our database persistent, we'll have to turn some classes into Enterprise Java Beans (EJB). There are three types of Enterprise beans, as listed in table 14.1

Table 14.1   The different types of Enterprise JavaBeans

Name	Function
Entity Bean	A class that can be saved to and loaded from a database; fields in the class map to columns in tables.
Session Bean	A class that provides access to the data through a local or remote interface. It can contain "business logic," meaning server-side code that works across beans or other parts of the system.
Message-Driven Bean	A class that is invoked when incoming messages are received.

In previous versions of J2EE, Enterprise beans were complex classes backed up by complex XML files. Java EE and EJB3.0 has moved to annotated classes. We can turn our `Event` class into an entity bean and design a session bean for access to this data. We need an interface, `CalendarSession`, and an implementation class, `Calendar-SessionBean`, which will work with the database through an `EntityManager`, a Java EE class that can bind entity beans to a database.

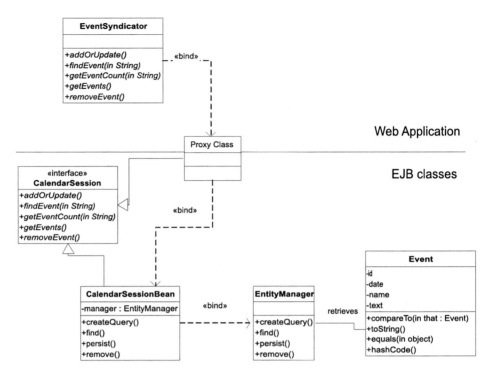

Figure 14.1 The new architecture of the diary application. The proxy class is created for us, and bridges from the web application to the session bean.

Figure 14.1 shows the design. The entity manager handles persistence; the application server hosts everything and connects the web application with the session bean. All we need to do is declare the data mappings for the `Event` class and write the `CalendarSessionBean`.

14.3 CREATING THE BEANS

To make the diary's `Event` class persistent, we mark it up with annotations from the Java Persistence API (JPA). Sun's 229-page *Java Persistence API Specification* covers these annotations in detail. The bare minima of markup needed to make a class persistent are the annotations to bind the class to a table and a mapping for every persistent field.

The first thing we have to do is declare that the `Event` is an entity bean by annotating the class with a `@javax.peristence.Entity` flag. A `@Table` declaration names the database table to use; the table we use here is called EVENTS:

```
package d1.persist;
import d1.core.*;
import java.io.Serializable;
import java.util.*;
import javax.persistence.*;
```

```
@Entity
@Table(name = "EVENTS")
public class Event implements Serializable,
                    Validatable, Comparable<Event>
```

We then define a mapping of the persistent fields to database columns, producing table 14.2.

Table 14.2 Class fields and types and their database equivalent

Field	Java type	Column name	Database type
Id	UUID	EVENT_ID	String: 48 chars
Name	String	EVENT_NAME	String: 255 chars
Text	String	EVENT_TEXT	String: 8192 chars
Date	Date	EVENT_DATE	timestamp

Every persistent attribute in the class gets a @Column annotation on its getter method, the method in the class offering access to the data. The annotation should state the database column to use for the attribute and, sometimes, details about the mapping:

```
@Column(name = "EVENT_NAME")
public String getName() {
    return name;
}

@Column(name = "EVENT_TEXT",length = 8192)
public String getText() {
    return text;
}

@Column(name = "EVENT_DATE")
@Temporal(value = TemporalType.TIMESTAMP)
public Date getDate() {
    return date;
}
```

The trickiest field is the ID field, which is stored in the database as a string instead of as a serialized java.util.UUID class. This is done by providing a getter and setter for a string attribute called key, marking that as the primary key with the @Id attribute. The method just converts the existing id field to a string.

```
@Id
@Column(name = "EVENT_ID", length = 48, unique = true)
public String getKey() {
    return id.toString();
}
```

A matching setter method rounds it off:

```
public void setKey(String id) {
    this.id = UUID.fromString(id);
}
```

We also need to declare the original ID attribute as transient—something not to be persisted:

```
@Transient
public UUID getId() {
    return id;
}
```

The result is to turn the key field into the primary key, which can be used in query strings.

Once annotated, the class is ready to be persisted. This brings Ant into the picture to build and package the class.

14.3.1 Compiling Java EE-annotated classes

Ant's normal <javac> task can compile classes marked up with Java EE annotations, provided the Java EE JAR is on the task's compile classpath. If the Java EE 1.5 library was on the ibliblio repository, adding the JAR should just be a line in the ivy.xml file:

```
<dependency org="sun" name="javaee" rev="${javaee.version}" />
```

Except it isn't in the repository—causing <ivy:resolve> to fail. The task prints out a list of missing artifacts and fails the build:

```
[ivy:resolve]  ::::::::::::::::::::::::::::::::::::::::::::::::::::::
[ivy:resolve]  ::           UNRESOLVED DEPENDENCIES          ::
[ivy:resolve]  ::::::::::::::::::::::::::::::::::::::::::::::::::::::
[ivy:resolve]  :: [ org.antbook | diary-core-persist |
                   latest.integration ]: not found
[ivy:resolve]  :: [ sun | javaee | 1.5 ]: not found
[ivy:resolve]  ::::::::::::::::::::::::::::::::::::::::::::::::::::::
```

There are two options here. One is to bypass Ivy and add it to the classpath by hand. The other is to install the file into a team repository. Chapter 11 raised the notion of a team repository as a way of providing secure artifacts or to offer better metadata. It also can serve up files that are not in any public repository.

The diary application has a repository set up under the CVS tree; everyone who checks out a file gets a copy. The log of the build shows where Ivy looked for the file, a search that included the team repository:

```
[ivy:resolve] C:\diary\repository\sun\javaee\1.5\javaee-1.5.jar
```

We need to create the directory sun/javaee/1.5 and copy in the javaee.jar from the SDK, renaming it javaee-1.5.jar. There's no need to add any ivy.xml file, unless we want to add dependencies and multiple configurations. The artifact on its own is sufficient. It's assumed to have no dependencies and one configuration, "default." This is how the diary-core-persist component declares a dependency on its own ivy.xml file:

```
<dependency org="org.antbook" name="diary-core"
  rev="latest.integration"
  conf="compile->default;runtime->default"/>
<dependency org="sun" name="javaee" rev="${javaee.version}"
  conf="compile->default"/>
```

With the classpath set up, a version of `<javac>` that is set to the project's default options with `<presetdef>` does the work:

```
<ext:javac destdir="${build.classes.dir}"
      srcdir="${src.dir}">
  <classpath refid="compile.classpath"/>
</ext:javac>
```

We can use the annotated `Event` class as a normal Java object, creating, modifying and serializing/deserializing it on demand. We also can use it as a persistent object, bound to a database through an `EntityManager`. This is a class that binds events to a database, with methods to find, delete, and update beans. The web application can work with one through a session bean.

14.3.2 Adding a session bean

Session beans are another part of the Enterprise Java Bean architecture. They are where local or remote callers can interact with the system. For the diary, a session bean can provide the public API, offering operations to add, remove, and find events. This API will be defined by an interface. Client applications will use the interface, with the Java EE container bridging between the interface and the implementation through a proxy class it creates—a proxy class that also implements the interface. Session beans also can be exported as web services, allowing remote callers access to the same services.

Listing 14.1 The interface for the calendar session bean

```
package d1.persist.session;

import d1.persist.Event;
import java.util.*;

public interface CalendarSession {
    void addOrUpdate(Event event);
    Event findEvent(String key);
    Event findEvent(UUID id);
    int getEventCount(String where);
    int getEventCount();
    List<Event> getEvents(String where);
    List<Event> getEvents();
    boolean removeEvent(String key);
}
```

Listing 14.1 shows the `CalendarSession` API. This is implemented in the session bean, which begins as follows:

```
package d1.persist.session;

import d1.persist.Event;
import javax.ejb.*;
import javax.persistence.*;
import java.util.List;

@Stateless
@Local(CalendarSession.class)

public class CalendarSessionBean implements CalendarSession

    @PersistenceContext
    public EntityManager manager;

    public CalendarSessionBean() {
    }
```

This class is declared with two annotations, `@Stateless` and `@Local` ❶. These annotations declare the class to be a stateless session bean with one local interface. That means that it doesn't preserve any state between method calls, which makes for easy reuse. The `@Local` attribute names the interface that we use for local invocation, that being all that we support.

The class itself extends the `CalendarSession` interface ❷, which we defined in listing 14.1. Users of the session bean work through this interface, an interface which the session bean will implement.

The most interesting declaration is where we declare an `EntityManager` ❸. We declare the manager in a field, *but we never set it to a value.* The application server will configure it for us, a technique known as *dependency injection.* Before every transaction begins, the container sets the bean's `manager` field to the current entity manager. The class uses this injected entity manager to work with the database:

```
public void addOrUpdate(Event event) {
    manager.persist(event);
}

public Event findEvent(String key) {
    Event loaded = manager.find(Event.class, key);
    return loaded;
}
```

As a result, `CalendarSessionBean` lets callers work with the persistent data, without forcing them to know how the data is stored.

Like the entity bean, this class compiles without any special steps, provided the Java EE JAR is on the classpath. What we cannot do with this class is run it outside an application server, which will do the dependency injection. This forces us to put off testing until the classes are packaged and integrated with the web application.

This also provides incentive to get on with the packaging. There's just an XML file left.

Writing a persistence.xml file

By marking up our classes with annotations, we can almost completely avoid writing new XML configuration files for our beans. We do still need one, `META-INF/persistence.xml`, to define the *persistence unit* of the library. The persistence unit describes how to bind the entity beans to a database, including server-specific customizations:

```
<persistence>
 <persistence-unit name="diary">
  <jta-data-source>java:/DefaultDS</jta-data-source>       Data binding
  <class>d1.persist.Event</class>                          class to persist

  <properties>
  <property name="jboss.entity.manager.factory.jndi.name"
    value="java:/DiaryEntityManagerFactory"/>             Jboss
  <property name="jboss.entity.manager.jndi.name"          options
    value="java:/DiaryEntityManager"/>

  <property name="hibernate.dialect"
    value="org.hibernate.dialect.HSQLDialect"/>            Hibernate
  <property name="hibernate.hbm2ddl.auto"                  options
    value="create-drop"/>
  </properties>
 </persistence-unit>
</persistence>
```

This file lets developers change the data binding without recompiling the application, although you still have to repackage it. A single `persistence.xml` file also can contain multiple `<persistence-unit>` elements, each one targeting a different runtime or application server, or exporting different classes into different persistence units.

Packaging the beans

With the code compiled and the XML file written, we can package everything with `<jar>`. Ant has a special task for creating the old EJB 2.x JAR file, `<ejb-jar>`, which is now obsolete—ignore it. All we need is the `<jar>` task, which creates a new JAR, `diary-core-persist.jar`. This is what the web application now needs to import and work with.

14.4   EXTENDING THE WEB APPLICATION

With the entity and session beans coded, the web application can become persistent. Here's what has to be done:

1 Add the persistent event and Java EE JARs to the compilation classpath.

2 Bind to a `CalendarSession` implementation at startup.

3 Use the `CalendarSession` to talk to the database in order to save, retrieve, and update events.

4 Build the new WAR file, with its enhanced `web.xml` file and appropriate class libraries.

5 Package the WAR file inside an Enterprise archive.

We're going to omit most of the coding changes made to the app, as they don't change the build process. However, the web application does need to change its dependencies, swapping the servlet API dependency for that of `javaee-1.5.jar` and the beans in the `diary-core-persist` library. Table 14.3 lists the dependencies that Ivy resolves to compile the web application.

Table 14.3 The dependencies in the compile configuration

Project	Artifact	Version	Comments
org.antbook	diary-core	latest.integration	built locally
org.antbook	diary-core-persist	latest.integration	built locally
rome	rome	0.8	
javaee	javaee	1.5	in the private repository

Updating the web application code itself is harder, especially in the area of event management. The `CalendarSession` interface provides access to the persistent data store; the web application needs access to an implementation. In a fully compliant Java EE 5 container, this can be done with dependency injection, just as the session bean is bound to the entity manager:

```
@EJB(name = "CalendarSessionBean")
CalendarSession session;
```

Unfortunately, here's when some server-specific details surface. JBoss 4 is not a complete Java EE 5 Container. To get the session bean, we need to look up the class by using the Java Naming and Directory Interface (JNDI) API:

```
public static CalendarSession getSession() {
    try {
        Context ctx = new javax.naming.InitialContext();
        CalendarSession calendar = (CalendarSession) ctx.lookup(
                "diary/CalendarSessionBean/local");
        return calendar;
    } catch (NamingException e) {
        throw new RuntimeException(e);
    }
}
```

We access this via a `JBoss4Calendar` class that acts as a session factory. By changing to a different calendar factory, we could bind to the session bean by using dependency injection on an application server that supported it, or we could use a different JNDI path. This JNDI-based binding mechanism appears so brittle that it caused lots of problems during development. Consult the latest JBoss documentation before copying this code, and use session injection as soon as it's working.

Assuming the lookup does work, we can now call `getSession()` when we need it, such as when creating an atom feed of all events:

```
private EventSyndicator createFeed(HttpServletRequest request) {
    String base = extractApplicationURL(request);
    CalendarSession session = JBoss4Calendar.getSession();    ◄—❶
    EventSyndicator feed;
    return new EventSyndicator("Events",base,
            session.getEvents());    ◄—┐
}                                        ❷
```

This code gets a calendar session ❶, to enumerate all events ❷. Similar changes to the code have to take place wherever the event list is used, and then the application is ready for compiling and packaging. With the path set up, compiling is trivial. Packaging is harder.

Packaging the new web application

The web application of chapter 12 included every JAR that it needed in the WAR file's `WEB-INF/lib` directory. The new web application has no `<lib>` element in the `<war>` task, as no JAR files are needed:

```
<target name="ready-to-package" depends="compile,xdoclet"/>

<target name="war" depends="ready-to-package"
    description="create a WAR file">
  <war destfile="${diary.war}"
       duplicate="fail"
       webxml="${web.xml}" >
    <classes dir="${build.classes.dir}"/>
    <webinf dir="${build.webinf.dir}"
        excludes="web.xml" />
    <fileset dir="${web.dir}" />
  </war>
</target>
```

This web application will work only when packaged inside an Enterprise application archive (EAR) containing its dependencies. Building that EAR file is the next activity.

14.5 BUILDING THE ENTERPRISE APPLICATION

EAR files can contain nearly everything an application needs to deploy server-side. They are JAR files with an `.ear` suffix, files that can contain the following artifacts:

- Web applications, each in a WAR file.

- Java libraries packaged as JAR files.

- JAR files containing Enterprise beans and related classes. These must include `META-INF/persistence.xml` files to define their entity beans.

- Resource adaptors for binding to non-Java systems, as `.rar` files.

- The optional file `META-INF/application.xml`, which lists the modules in the archive: bean JARs, WAR files, and JAR files for client applications.

The EAR file contains the entire application, becoming a single thing to distribute, deploy, and undeploy. JAR files in the EAR file are available to all other classes in the EAR, including the web applications. Not only do you avoid duplicating libraries, by using a common classloader the application code can pass objects between different parts of the program without serializing them.

Our diary application needs an EAR file containing the WAR file, the `diary-core-persist.jar` file with the session and entity beans, and any other runtime dependencies not satisfied by the application server. This seems fairly straightforward:

1 Collect all the JAR and WAR files needed for the application.

2 Create an `application.xml` descriptor.

3 Use Ant's `<ear>` task to create an EAR file.

However, differences between application servers complicate things. We need to know how to add JARs in the EAR onto the classpath of the beans and the web application. Here are what appear to be the rules for declaring artifacts in the `application.xml` file, and how the classloaders work:

- WAR files are declared as `<web>` modules, with their filename a context root in the web site. Everything in their `WEB-INF/lib` directory is added to its own classpath.

- EJB archives are defined as `<ejb-module>` modules.

- Client JARs are defined as `<java>` modules.

- If an `<ejb-module>` file declares a classpath in its JAR manifest, the JARs in the classpath are loaded relative to the EJB module. That can give different beans different classpaths, but requires the JARs to be patched with deployment-specific classpaths in their `META-INF/manifest.mf` files.

- BEA WebLogic adds all JAR files in `APP-INF/lib` to the classpath of all JARs.

- JBoss, in the "unified classloader" mode, builds up a classpath from all JARs listed as modules from within the `WEB-INF/lib` directories of all WAR files and from other deployed applications; there isn't a hierarchy.

- JBoss in the proper classloader mode adds all client `<java>` modules to the classpath.

- Java EE 5 adds a new element, `<library-directory>`, to `application.xml`, which can identify a subdirectory in the EAR containing JAR files to add on the classpath.
- The default library directory of a Java EE 5 EAR file is `/lib`.
- Application servers export their own classes; these may have priority over EAR libraries.
- If you need to include "endorsed" JAR files, you need to know about `Extension-List` entries in manifests, or use an endorsed directory on the server for the files.

There are a lot of rules about setting up dependencies. Chapter 8 of the Java EE Specification covers these in detail, though it ignores server-specific details, one of which is critical:

Every application server has a different set of bundled libraries on its classpath. Duplicating these JARs in the EAR or WAR file can cause problems. Furthermore, some artifacts, such as JDBC drivers, cannot be deployed in the EAR.

This means that if you want to deploy a JDBC database driver, it must be on the classpath in a place where the JDBC API can find it. It also means that if your application server includes something like Log4J and makes the class available, you must not include your own copy of Log4J in the EAR file. Otherwise, things will not work right.

This whole problem of classpath setup is why the notion of application server portability is a dangerous myth. It's a myth because you'll need to build different EAR files for different machines. It's dangerous because some people believe it, and it gets them into trouble. This leads us to our definition of an EAR file:

An EAR file is a JAR file that contains an enterprise application. The EAR file contains the WAR files, JAR files, and XML configuration data for a specific installation of a system.

That means we shouldn't think of an EAR file as a broadly reusable library, like a normal JAR file. It's a way of packaging the files for a target deployment.

Collecting the artifacts

The first step to building an EAR file is identifying which libraries we want and collecting them in one place. We want our own `diary-core-persist` and `diary-core` libraries, without Log4J or the Java EE artifacts. We want Rome with the JDOM XML library it needs. All of these tasks are handled by a new configuration in the `ivy.xml` file:

```
<conf name="ear" description="ear file libraries" />
```

The artifacts that we want to put in the EAR file get declared as being part of this configuration, resulting in the following `ivy.xml` dependencies:

```
<dependency org="org.antbook" name="diary-core"
    rev="latest.integration" changing="true"
    conf="compile->master;ear->master"/>
<dependency org="org.antbook" name="diary-core-persist"
    rev="latest.integration" changing="true"
    conf="compile->master;ear->master"/>
<dependency org="rome" name="rome" rev="${rome.version}"
    conf="compile->default;ear->default"/>
<dependency org="sun" name="javaee" rev="${javaee.version}"
  conf="compile->default"/>
```

This code declares that the EAR has all the same dependencies as compiling the web application, except for the unneeded Java EE JAR. We explicitly ask for the "master" configuration of the `diary-core` and `diary-core-persist` artifacts so that Log4J doesn't sneak in.

All of these artifacts need to go into the EAR file without any version numbers on the JAR files. Ivy's `<retrieve>` task can do this, with the `pattern` attribute set up to define the naming schemes of JARs as `[artifact].[ext]`:

```
<target name="ear-libraries" depends="ivy-resolve">
  <property name="ear.lib.dir"
    location="${build.dir}/ear/lib"/>
  <ivy:retrieve conf="ear"
      pattern="${ear.lib.dir}/[artifact].[ext]" sync="true"/>
</target>
```

This task will copy all JAR files into the directory `build/ear/lib`, except for the WAR file itself. To make the classes visible, these files need to be listed in the `application.xml` file.

Creating the application.xml descriptor

The `application.xml` file is the place to list web applications and EJB packages. In Java EE 5 runtimes, we also can point to a directory containing extra libraries, so we could trivially refer to all of the JARs by adding them to the `/lib` directory of the EAR. As JBoss 4.0.5 doesn't support that, we have to enumerate every artifact we want loaded. Listing 14.2 shows the `application.xml` file for the application.

Listing 14.2 An `application.xml` file targeting JBoss

```
<application xmlns="http://java.sun.com/xml/ns/j2ee"
    version="1.4">
  <display-name>Diary EAR</display-name>
  <module>
    <web>                                        WAR file hosted
      <web-uri>diary.war</web-uri>               at /diary
      <context-root>diary</context-root>
    </web>
  </module>
```

```
<module>
  <ejb>diary-core-persist.jar</ejb>       EJB JAR
</module>

<module>
  <java>diary-core.jar</java>
</module>
<module>
  <java>jdom.jar</java>               Other JAR files in a
</module>                              JBoss-only mechanism
<module>
  <java>rome.jar</java>
</module>
</application>
```

If Ivy had retrieved the files with their version markers, the application.xml file would have had to contain the same inline version properties as the Ivy file, and then we would have had to use a <copy> with a nested <expandproperties/> filter-chain element:

```
<target name="application.xml" depends="ear-libraries">
  <copy file="ear/application.xml"
    todir="${ear.lib.dir}">
    <filterchain>
      <expandproperties/>
    </filterchain>
  </copy>
</target>
```

By dropping the revision counter from the retrieved artifacts, we avoid this step and can use the XML file directly in the <ear> task, that being the final step of creating the EAR file.

Building the EAR

The Ant task to create an EAR file is called <ear>; it's another extension of the <jar> task:

```
<target name="ear" depends="ear-libraries,war">
  <ear destfile="${diary.ear}"
    appxml="ear/application.xml">
    <fileset file="${diary.war}"/>
    <fileset dir="${ear.lib.dir}" includes="*.jar"/>
  </ear>
</target>
```

The <ear> task extends <jar> with the appxml attribute, which takes the application.xml file and saves it to META-INF/application.xml. There's no attempt to validate the XML file itself.

Running the new target creates the EAR file:

```
ear:
   [ear] Building ear: /home/ant/diary/persist-webapp/
         dist/diary.ear
```

There. The EAR file is built, with all the libraries it needs. We're ready for deployment.

14.6   DEPLOYING TO THE APPLICATION SERVER

The EAR file can be deployed using the deploy-by-copy process from chapter 12, selecting the destination directory from property files in the `persist-webapp/` `deploy/` directory. We've edited the build file so the default filename for deployment is now `jboss.properties`:

```
deploy.name=diary
deploy.dir=/home/ant/jboss-4/server/default/deploy
deploy.port=8080
```

To deploy, Ant reads in this properties file and copies over the EAR to `${deploy.dir}`. The main change is that the destination filename has the extension `.ear`, rather than the previous one of `.war`.

In use, the `deploy` target will build and deploy the EAR file:

```
deploy-by-copy:
     [echo]
     [echo]    Deploying /home/ant/diary/persist-webapp/dist/
               diary.ear to
               /home/ant/jboss-4/server/default/deploy/diary.war
     [echo]    URL: http://localhost:8080/diary/
     [echo]
     [copy] Copying 1 file to home/ant/jboss-4/server/default/deploy

deploy:

BUILD SUCCESSFUL
```

If JBoss is running and the destination directory is correct, the server will now load the application. The code is compiling, the EAR is packaged with all libraries, and it has been copied to the server. We're ready to run!

Setting up the Java projects and build files for the persistent classes, the web application, and the EAR file itself is hard work. Once they're in place, the build files should stay stable while classes are added and the project evolves. We can play with the deployed application, and we can finally get down to testing the application.

14.7   SERVER-SIDE TESTING WITH APACHE CACTUS

The application is deployed. The existing web front end is there, generating an RSS feed from events, and behind the scenes the calendar is now being saved to a database. How can we be sure this happening? By testing, of course!

The HttpUnit tests of chapter 12 act as a regression test of the application. After doubling the `<waitfor>` timeout to twenty seconds to allow for a longer startup, these tests pass. On the surface things are working. What about underneath? How can we test the internal classes and APIs of the application?

We need unit tests against the internals of the system, alongside the functional tests of HttpUnit. As Web and Java EE applications run only on an application server, we cannot directly run such unit tests under <junit>. Something devious is needed here, which is where Apache Cactus comes into play.

Cactus tests server-side code by running JUnit unit tests inside the application server. Cactus operates in a client-server design, meaning a client-side JUnit run manages the test run on a remote server. All the tests run remotely, with the results fed back to the client where they are presented as the output of a normal JUnit test run.

There's some profound work going on behind the scenes to achieve this testing. The test classes need to be present at both ends of the system, as the JUnit test runner still has to instantiate them. Requests to run each test method are then relayed to the server over HTTP and delivered to a Cactus servlet. The servlet creates the real test cases, runs the test methods, and feeds the results back. It's as if you're running the <junit> task inside the server.

Figure 14.2 shows the Cactus architecture. If you're doing anything complex server-side, download Cactus from http://jakarta.apache.org/cactus/ and start writing server-side tests.

14.7.1 Writing a Cactus test

Writing a Cactus test case is like writing any other JUnit test. The big differences are that the class must extend ServletTestCase, and enough server-side libraries must be available for <junit> to create the class in its own JVM.

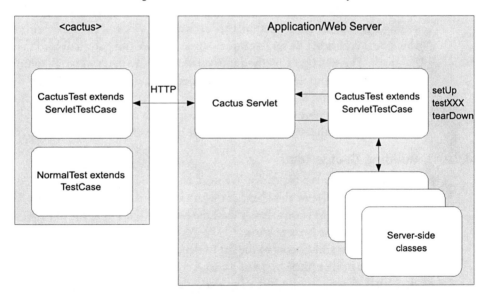

Figure 14.2 How Cactus runs tests on the server. The client program relays test requests to the server over HTTP; results come back the same way.

Listing 14.3 shows a test of the `CalendarSessionBean` class. It looks just like any normal JUnit test class, except it's designed to work inside the application server.

Listing 14.3 A Cactus test case to run on the server

```
public class CalendarSessionTest extends ServletTestCase {
    private CalendarSession calendar;

    public CalendarSessionTest(String string) {
        super(string);
    }

    protected void setUp() throws Exception {
        super.setUp();
        calendar = JBoss4Calendar.getSession();
    }

    public void testAddAndRemove() throws Exception {
        Event e = new Event(UUID.randomUUID(),
                new Date(),"test","test adding");
        calendar.addOrUpdate(e);
        Event found1 = calendar.findEvent(e.getKey());
        assertEquals(e, found1);
        calendar.removeEvent(e.getKey());
        assertNull(calendar.findEvent(e.getId()));
    }
}
```

This test uses the `CalendarSession` interface, creating an event then removing it, testing the state of the collection after each action. We can use server-side classes—in this case `CalendarSessionBean`—provided we can get them into the `<junit>` classpath. The `setUp()` method runs on the server, so that's where all setup operations must go. It's absolutely critical that this method is used for configuring the test, and not the constructor, because that is called in the `<junit>` JVM as well as the server.

With this test and some others coded, it's time to return to the build file, which must compile the classes and run them on the server.

14.7.2 Building Cactus tests

Building the tests is a bit tricky. We need to add the test classes to the EAR and extra server-only libraries to the client for `<junit>` to run. That is because JUnit creates instances of the test classes. Every class the test case links to needs to be present, or else we'll see a runtime linkage error.

We need to add Cactus to the list of dependencies for the test classpath, alongside `junit.jar`, `httpunit.jar`, `jtidy.jar`, and of course the compiled application itself. Cactus is one more Ivy dependency, albeit without its dependencies on Xerces and Cargo:

```
<dependency org="cactus"
    name="cactus"
    rev="${cactus.version}"
    conf="test->default">
  <exclude org="xerces"/>
  <exclude org="cargo"/>
</dependency>
```

The Cactus version has to join the version list in `libraries.properties`:

```
cactus.version=13-1.7.1
```

With Cactus added, the existing `test-compile` target will build the Cactus tests.

Setting up the classpath is also a problem on the server side, because Cactus needs to add its code and the test classes to the application. This is a job for the Cactus Ant tasks.

14.7.3   The Cactus Ant tasks

The compiled test classes need to get into the EAR file along with the Cactus and JUnit JAR files. Rather than rework the `<war>` and `<ear>` targets, we get Cactus to do the merging for us, modifying the existing EAR file.

Cactus ships with five Ant tasks, which are listed in table 14.4. Three tasks configure WAR and EAR files for testing, while the remaining two tasks can run the test suites themselves.

Table 14.4   The Ant tasks of Cactus

Task Name	Function
`<cactifywar>`	Add Cactus and tests to an existing WAR file.
`<cactifyear>`	Patch Cactus and the tests into an EAR file.
`<webxmlmerge>`	Merge in `web.xml` files to add the Cactus servlet to an existing application.
`<cactus>`	Extended version of `<junit>`.
`<runservertests>`	Predecessor to `<cactus>`; do not use.

To use Cactus, we must declare the tasks using the classpath created for compiling the tests, a classpath which contains everything we need. First, the build file declares the name of the WAR file to create and the URL by which it will be known;

```
<target name="cactus-init" depends="deploy-properties">
  <property name="cactus.war" location="${build.dir}/cactus.war"/>
  <property name="cactus.destfile"
      location="${deploy.dir}/cactus.war"/>
  <property name="cactus.url"
      value="http://${url.server}:${deploy.port}/cactus}/"/>
</target>
```

A dependent target declares the tasks, using the `test.compile.classpath`:

```
<target name="cactus-tasks" depends="test-classpaths,cactus-init" >
  <taskdef resource="cactus.tasks"
    classpathref="test.compile.classpath"
    uri="http://jakarta.apache.org/cactus/"  />
</target>
```

All the tasks are now ready for use, the first use being patching up the EAR file.

14.7.4   Adding Cactus to an EAR file

There are two tasks to patch Cactus tests into an application, <cactifywar> and <cactifyear>, for WAR files and EAR files, respectively. We need to patch the EAR file:

```
<target name="cactus-ear" depends="cactus-tasks,packaged"
    xmlns:cactus="http://jakarta.apache.org/cactus/">
  <cactus:cactifyear srcfile="${diary.ear}"       ←❶
      destfile="${cactus.ear}">                    ←❷
    <cactuswar srcfile="${diary.war}"              ←❸
      context="cactus">                            ←❹
      <classes dir="${test.classes.dir}"           ❺
        includes="**/*.class"/>
    </cactuswar>
  </cactus:cactifyear>
</target>
```

This task takes the name of the source EAR file ❶ and that of the output file ❷. It will then add a new WAR file to the archive by way of the nested <cactuswar> element ❸. This takes the name of the source file, the context under which the web pages will be deployed ❹, and the list of test classes to include ❺.

When the task runs, it creates a new WAR file inside the EAR file. This web application includes all the test classes and whatever Cactus class files are needed to run the tests, as well as a patched web.xml file to relay Cactus messages. The task then adds the new web application to the EAR file's application.xml entry:

```
cactus-ear:
[cactuswar] Analyzing war: /home/ant/diary/persist-webapp/dist/
            diary.war
[cactuswar] Building war: /home/ant/diary/persist-webapp/cactus331531
            493cactus.war
[cactus:cactifyear] Building ear:
                /home/ant/diary/persist-webapp/build/cactus.ear

BUILD SUCCESSFUL
```

This creates a new EAR file. With the test code and servlets, it shouldn't be deployed to a public server for security reasons. It's for development systems, for <junit> to test against.

14.7.5 Running Cactus tests

With the EAR built, we can run the tests. There's a special <cactus> task to do this. This task extends the normal <junit> task with integrated deployment to an application server. We don't need this, as we have our own deployment process already set up. We need to copy the new EAR file to the deployment directory, then wait for it to be deployed—after which the tests can run. This is exactly what the existing HttpUnit tests of the web application did, and the build file is almost identical. The big change is that the <junit> task needs the URL to the Cactus application; this is highlighted in listing 14.4. It is the URL to the base of the Cactus-enabled web application, here "http://localhost:8080/cactus".

Listing 14.4 Targets to deploy the EAR file and run the Cactus test suite

```
<target name="cactus-deploy" depends="cactus-ear">
  <copy file="${cactus.ear}"
    tofile="${cactus.destfile}"
    overwrite="true"/>
  <echo>deployed: ${cactus.destfile}</echo>
</target>

<target name="cactus-run"
  depends="test-classpaths,cactus-init,cactus-deploy,wait">
  <get src="${cactus.url}/happyx.jspx"
    dest="${build.dir}/happyx.html"/>
  <junit
    errorProperty="cactus.failed"
    failureProperty="cactus.failed">
    <classpath>
      <path refid="test.classpath"/>
    </classpath>
    <sysproperty key="cactus.contextURL" value="${cactus.url}"/>
    <sysproperty key="server.url" value="${cactus.url}"/>
    <formatter type="brief" usefile="false"/>
    <formatter type="xml"/>
    <batchtest todir="${test.data.dir}">
      <fileset dir="test">
        <include name="**/*Test.java"/>
      </fileset>
    </batchtest>
  </junit>
  <delete file="${cactus.destfile}"/>
  <junitreport todir="${test.data.dir}">
    <fileset dir="${test.data.dir}">
      <include name="TEST-*.xml"/>
    </fileset>
    <report format="frames" todir="${test.reports.dir}"/>
  </junitreport>
  <fail if="cactus.failed">
```

```
      Tests failed. Check ${test.reports.dir}
    </fail>
  </target>
```
■

The command line to run the tests is ant cactus-run, with the tail of the results as follows:

```
cactus-deploy:
    [copy] Copying 1 file to /home/ant/jboss-4/server/default/deploy
    [echo] deployed:
          /home/ant/jboss-4/server/default/deploy/diary.ear
wait:

cactus-run:
    [get] Getting: http://localhost:8080/cactus/happy.jsp
    [get] To: /home/ant/diary/persist-webapp/build/happy.html
  [junit] Testsuite: d1.webapp.test.EventFeedTest
  [junit] Tests run: 1, Failures: 0, Errors: 0, Time elapsed: 1.334 sec
  [junit] Testsuite: d1.webapp.test.HappyPageTest
  [junit] Tests run: 4, Failures: 0, Errors: 0, Time elapsed: 1.889 sec
  [junit] Testsuite: d1.webapp.test.IndexTest
  [junit] Tests run: 1, Failures: 0, Errors: 0, Time elapsed: 1.159 sec
  [junit] Testsuite: d1.webapp.test.cactus.CalendarSessionTest
  [junit] Tests run: 1, Failures: 0, Errors: 0, Time elapsed: 0.843 sec
 [delete] Deleting:
          /home/ant/jboss-4/server/default/deploy/diary.ear
[junitreport] Transform time: 4066ms

BUILD SUCCESSFUL
```

This test run not only runs the new Cactus tests in the server, it runs the existing HttpUnit tests. These run in the local <junit> JVM, not in the server. Cactus tests and classic JUnit tests can live side by side. If tests fail, the reports will even include remote stack traces from the server. Together, the Cactus and HttpUnit tools extend JUnit to test the internal state and external behavior of a server-side application. Cactus is so unique and invaluable that it's the main reason this book has stayed with the JUnit 3.8.x codebase instead of JUnit 4.x or TestNG. Until Cactus or an equivalent works with the newer test frameworks, the test suites for Java EE applications need to stay with JUnit 3.8.x and Cactus.

14.7.6   Diagnosing EJB deployment problems

The tests are working. However, they'll probably fail the moment we deploy to a different application server, where things are always subtly different.

We need to be able to debug what's going on, even remotely. One early problem we had was getting JNDI directory lookups right, meaning it was difficult to track down the fact that a "full" installation of JBoss didn't include EJB3.0. The EAR would load without the session bean.

JBoss has a management console with a Java Management Extensions (JMX) management bean that shows the JNDI directory. In the JNDI global namespace, there should be an entry `diary/CalendarSessionBean/local`. If it's absent, JBoss 4.0.x is without EJB3 support.

We like to automate things, especially diagnostics. Accordingly, we added a new static method to our `FindClass` class, one that can check that a JNDI entry resolves. Here it is in our updated `happy.jsp` page, looking for the data source and the session bean:

```
<table>
  <tr><td>
    <%= FindClass.ldapLookup("java:/DefaultDS")%>
  </td></tr>
  <tr><td>
    <%= FindClass.ldapLookup("diary/CalendarSessionBean/local")%>
  </td></tr>
</table>
```

The `cactus-run` target of listing 14.4, on page 383, does a `<get>` of this page before it even tries to run the `<junit>` tests. This lets us detect deployment problems early. The best bit: anyone can browse to the JSP page and see the diagnostics. The deployment problems encountered in development have been turned into health checks for the operations team.

14.8 SUMMARY

This chapter has entered the realm of Enterprise Java, looking at how to make entity bean and session bean classes by annotating the source. As the annotations are processed by the Java compiler, this is straightforward: `<javac>` with the right classpath will build everything, and `<jar>` will package the output.

Packaging and testing get more complex. The web application is part of a bigger program, and the WAR file must be deployed inside an Enterprise application archive, an EAR file. In theory, this is a portable distribution package, which can be deployed onto any application server. In practice, EAR files often need to be targeted for specific application servers, adding needed JAR files and removing those that cause problems. The various XML files in the packages, `persistence.xml`, and `application.xml` may also need customization for different machines, which can complicate the build further. Ivy comes into its own here, pulling in files at compile time, and again when setting up the libraries that the `<ear>` task can package into an EAR file.

EAR files can be deployed like WAR files by using a `<copy>` task. Once deployed, they can be tested. Alongside the functional tests of HttpUnit comes Apache Cactus, which can run JUnit tests on the server. Cactus is a great way to test server-side Java code.

We've barely scratched the surface of Enterprise Java. What we have shown is how to package, deploy, and test Enterprise Java applications. The key thing that readers should probably remember is this: Apache Cactus runs unit tests in the server.

We'll return to the problem of deployment in chapter 16, when we show you how to take an application into production. Before then, let's see how continuous integration can transform a development process.

Continuous integration

This book has now covered the entire process of building an application with Ant, from a simple library with a few unit tests, to a server-side application that's tested by running functional tests on a client or by running unit tests inside the application server.

There's one more thing that Ant enables that can transform how your project works. Instead of running the builds by hand, why not delegate all the work to a machine? A machine that can rerun the builds and tests nightly, hourly, or whenever you feel the need? Running builds repeatedly is useful, but far too boring to do by hand. That's the kind of dull, repetitive work that machines are for, and where Ant can help.

This chapter is going to cover setting up a machine to run builds for you, not just to save developer time but also to transform your entire development process. It's a bit of a change from the previous chapters, as there are more screen shots than XML listings. This doesn't make it any less important. Indeed, the earlier a project sets up a continuous-integration system, the better.

This chapter will use Luntbuild, which is a web application that can be set up to run Ant builds on demand. But before we can get down to the application itself, we have to understand the concept of continuous integration.

15.1 INTRODUCING CONTINUOUS INTEGRATION

Continuous integration is the practice of setting up a system to do your build for you all the time. This is one of the most profound changes you can make to your development process. If you have a machine always building and testing your project, then you can see at a glance whether all is well or not. But you don't need to check: if things break, the machine can email everyone a warning of the problem. It may even be able to identify what change broke the build and who checked it in.

Nightly builds have long been a feature of software projects: it's a famous aspect of the development of Windows NT and its successors. But a nightly build has to handle everything checked in during the day. You don't find out until the morning that something broke, and then nobody can work with the latest code—it's broken. The whole team ends up wasting half the day finding out what went wrong and fixing it, only having half a day to write new code. And then the whole process repeats itself the next day.

With continuous integration, you find out minutes after any change gets checked in whether it breaks the build or the tests; this lets you fix it before anyone else notices.

Ant builds can be scheduled and automated by using operating system job-scheduling services, such as the Unix `cron` tool, but that's still not enough. Dedicated tools can deliver much more, such as the following:

- Automated builds
- Build logs
- Application deployment to test servers
- In-container test suite runs
- Direct reporting of failures to the appropriate developers
- Build numbering and tagging in the SCM repository
- Web-based reporting

Martin Fowler and Matthew Foemmel introduced the term continuous integration in their 2001 paper *"Continuous Integration."*[1] This paper showed the benefits of the concept and introduced a tool, CruiseControl, that enabled it. Figure 15.1 shows the architecture of this product. The core of the tool is the build loop, a thread that polls the source code repository every few minutes looking for changes. Any change triggers the bootstrap-and-build process, in which the changed files are retrieved and the build initiated. After running a build, the results are published, along with notifications to developers and other interested parties.

In CruiseControl, the build loop was configured by a single configuration file, `config.xml`. The web application was a separate process that does little, other than

---

[1] http://www.martinfowler.com/articles/continuousIntegration.html

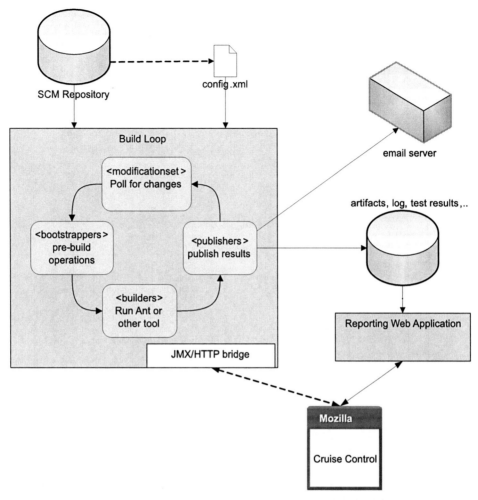

Figure 15.1 CruiseControl was the first continuous-integration server. The build loop polled for changes, ran the builds, and published reports; the web front end displayed the results. Everything was driven by the `config.xml` file.

present results. A servlet could act as a front end to the Java management extensions (JMX) beans in the build loop process so it could trigger builds, but all configuration was through that single XML file.

CruiseControl is the venerable king of continuous-integration tools, and one we've used extensively in the past. However, there are many challengers for the crown, some of which are listed in table 15.1. It's a competitive area, with products competing on features, ease of use, and integration with other processes.

CruiseControl is hard to get up and running; it often needs a bit of nurturing to restart it or fix some problem. This is the main reason why we're not covering it, looking at Luntbuild instead. Luntbuild is very representative of the latest generation

Table 15.1 Some of the continuous-integration tools that work with Ant.

Product	URL	Description
Anthill	http://www.urbancode.com/	A tool with good web-based configuration
Bamboo	http://atlassian.com/	Released in early 2007; integrates with the JIRA bug-tracking system
Beetlejuice	http://www.pols.co.uk/beetlejuice/	Commercial; free to open-source projects
Continuum	http://maven.apache.org/continuum/	A new tool from the Maven team
CruiseControl	http://cruisecontrol.sourceforge.net/	The original tool; widely used
Gump	http://gump.apache.org/	A hosted build of open-source Java
Hudson	https://hudson.dev.java.net/	Sun's open-source continuous integration tool
Luntbuild	http://luntbuild.javaforge.com/	An easy to set up, full-featured tool
TeamCity	http://www.jetbrains.com/teamcity/	From the people that wrote IntelliJ IDEA

of tools, with web-based configuration and cross-project integration. It's one of the continuous-integration servers that a team could try out before committing to a specific product.

15.1.1 What do you need for continuous integration?

If you have a project in an SCM repository with a build file that can run to completion without human intervention, you're ready to begin. What else do you need to bring up a continuous-integration system? You need five things:

- A dedicated server
- A new user
- A build that runs to completion
- A continuous-integration tool
- Free time

That's all. It's well worth the effort.

A dedicated server

You need a dedicated machine for running the builds. Don't try to reuse a developer's own machine, as the developer can break the build by running tests at the same time, or by changing the system configuration in some incompatible way. Find an old but reliable box, add more memory, install a clean OS release, tighten up security, and then install Java and Ant. If you don't have a spare machine, try running a Linux system under VMWare, Xen or something similar.

A new user

Create a special user account with an email address, SCM login, and an IM account. This user will be used for sending out notifications and for accessing and labeling the SCM repository.

A build that runs to completion

You need a build file that runs. This is such a minimal requirement that you can start with a continuous-integration service the moment you start a new project. The one thing to avoid is taking a build that doesn't work and trying to host it on the server. You should avoid doing this because it's so hard to distinguish problems related to the continuous-integration server from those of the build itself. If you have this problem, set up the server to build a target that succeeds, skipping failing parts of the build such as the tests. You can turn on the tests once the continuous-integration build is functional.

A continuous-integration tool

You need a program to run the build and notify people when it fails. Some people try to do this in Ant, using its `<cvs>` and `<mail>` tasks, but this is a wasted effort. There's a lot of work alongside the build, including polling the repository for changes, assigning blame, and generating the status web pages that Ant doesn't do. People have written tools to do all of this, so use them.

Free time

Allocate half a day to bring up a continuous-integration server. The more ambitious you get about running functional tests on the server or using different reporting mechanisms, the longer things will take.

Of all these requirements for continuous integration, time is the most precious, especially on a late project. Start early. A continuous-integration system is harder to bring up the more complex the build, so using a simple build from the start of a project makes setup easier. More subtly, just as writing tests from the outset changes how people code, having a machine continually building the application and running the tests changes how people work. It's better if this new lifestyle is lived from the birth of a project, rather than forced onto the team later on when they already have a defined style of working.

The rarity of free time in a project is also why we prefer Luntbuild over older tools such as Cruise Control. The easier it is to start using a continuous-integration system, the more likely you are to start using it and keep it running.

15.2 LUNTBUILD

Luntbuild is an open source project, whose homepage is http://luntbuild.javaforge .com/. It's very easy to install: all configuration is done through web pages. It also has a strong notion of dependencies across projects. You create a separate entry for each project, and can link them together, rebuilding and testing a project if a dependency changes.

It has a self-contained mode, using a private database and servlet engine, or you can host it on your own web server and switch to another database, such as MySQL. That means that it could be used in a managed production environment, with the application running under a central server, sharing a central database. You could even have extra reporting programs running through the build information in the database.

Luntbuild uses the following terms, which we'll explain in a moment: *users, projects, VCS adaptors, builders,* and *schedules.*

User

A Luntbuild *user* is someone with password-protected access to the site. Each user can have email, instant messaging, and weblog contact information. Different users can have different rights.

Version Control System (VCS) adaptors

Luntbuild uses the term version control system, with the acronym VCS, to refer to a software configuration management (SCM) repository. A *VCS adaptor* is a binding to a specific SCM repository, including login information. The tool supports CVS, Subversion, Perforce, ClearCase, StarTeam, AccuRev, and Visual SourceSafe.

Project

This represents a software *project.* It binds a VCS configuration with builds and schedules. Every project also maps accounts in the SCM/VCS repository to Luntbuild user accounts, so it knows who to contact when things break.

Builders

A *builder* builds projects. It can be Ant or any other command-line program. Builds can be clean or incremental; incremental ones preserve the results of the previous build, and are faster, though they can be contaminated by previous builds.

Schedule

Luntbuild builds things to a *schedule.* Schedules can be triggered by the clock, by changes in the repository, or by manual requests.

Projects can have multiple builds and schedules, so a clean build can run every night, incremental builds every fifteen minutes, and tests run every hour. Builds can depend on other builds, even across projects.

15.2.1 Installing Luntbuild

Luntbuild comes with an installer JAR, which installs the server, asking a few questions on the way. The simplest installation is a self-contained server using a private database. Follow these steps to install Luntbuild:

1 Download the `-installer.jar` version of the application, such as `luntbuild-1.3final-installer.jar`.

2 Install the program on a disk with plenty of space.

3 In the "web application configuration" page,

- Increase the session timeout from 30 minutes to something longer.
- Leave the "path to war deploy dir" field blank. This enables a standalone installation.

4 For the database, select HSQLDB and leave the option fields alone.

5 Skip the LDAP server integration page.

6 Install the documentation as well as everything else.

7 Don't bother with the automated installation script.

Hosting the tool under Tomcat or JBoss would ensure that the program restarts after it reboots, while a binding to MySQL may scale better. Tomcat and JBoss also increase the installation effort, which is why they're left alone.

15.2.2 Running Luntbuild

To start Luntbuild, run the application giving your hostname and a socket port that you aren't using.

```
java -jar luntbuild-standalone.jar k2 8088
```

If you're using Ivy for library management or checking source out from a remote Subversion repository, you may need to add proxy settings to the command line:

```
java -Dhttp.proxyHost=proxy -Dhttp.proxyPort=8080 \
    -jar luntbuild-standalone.jar k2 8088
```

Make sure the output shows that the program is listening on the server's external network address:

```
21:18:59.096 EVENT  Starting Jetty/4.2.23
21:18:59.870 EVENT  Started WebApplicationContext[/luntbuild,Luntbuild]
Luntbuild : --> context initialization started
Luntbuild : --> context initialization finished
21:19:06.112 EVENT  Started SocketListener on 192.168.2.68:8088
21:19:06.112 EVENT  Started org.mortbay.jetty.Server@1a2961b
```

If you aren't careful, Luntbuild may just listen on the local loopback address such as 127.0.0.1:

```
>java -jar luntbuild-standalone.jar localhost 8088

21:19:42.996 EVENT  Starting Jetty/4.2.23
21:19:43.491 EVENT  Started WebApplicationContext[/luntbuild,Luntbuild]
Luntbuild : --> context initialization started
Luntbuild : --> context initialization finished
21:19:49.956 EVENT  Started SocketListener on 127.0.0.1:8088
21:19:49.956 EVENT  Started org.mortbay.jetty.Server@1a2961b
```

This means the web page is only accessible to users on the same machine, not for anyone else on the network. Start Luntbuild with the raw IP address if you cannot prevent the system from mapping from a hostname to a loopback address:

```
java -jar luntbuild-standalone.jar 192.168.2.68 8088
```

Next, browse to the location of the service:

```
http://192.168.2.68:8088/luntbuild/
```

You'll be prompted for username and password; use `luntbuild` for both. This should
then bring you to the home page of the program, from where you can configure it.

15.2.3 Configuring Luntbuild

Luntbuild claims you can be up and running in half an hour. It's relatively straightforward, and best shown through screen shots.

Creating users

The first step is to create users, both for login and for notification. Figure 15.2 shows
the dialog for a single user. The various notification options—Lotus Sametime, MSN,

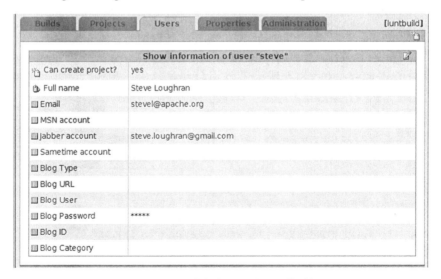

**Figure 15.2   Adding a user to Luntbuild. You can be notified by email, IM, or
blog postings.**

CHAPTER 15   CONTINUOUS INTEGRATION

Jabber, and blog login information—are all for notifications. The email address matters; the rest can be added later.

The password is set on the same page as the other options. This forces you to re-enter the password whenever updating any other setting, which means that whoever manages the users needs to know all the passwords. Don't consider reusing any sensitive passwords in this tool.

Once the users have been entered, you should have a list such as that of figure 15.3. Different users can work on different projects and can have different rights. We tend to run a relaxed house on a private network, but you may want to lock down the system.

Creating a project

After creating the users, you can create a project. Navigate to the "projects" tab. Create a new project by clicking on the new document icon on the top-right corner of the page. Give the project a name. Add all the users you want on the project.

As anonymous users still appear to have read access to all projects and builds, you cannot keep builds private from anyone with access to the web server.

Binding to an SCM repository

The "VCS Adaptors" tab of a project is where you set up the repositories of a project. Every project needs at least one VCS adaptor, with one module underneath. The settings for the Ant book are shown in figures 15.4 and 15.5. As well as declaring a repository, you also must define a *module*. This represents a subsection of the repository and may be a specific branch or label.

Being able to mix branches and labels of different parts of the repository is an interesting feature. It may let a team build and test multiple branches of a project.

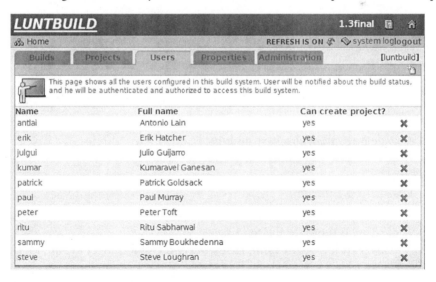

Figure 15.3   A server populated with a full set of users

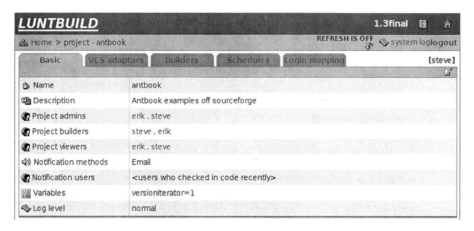

Figure 15.4   A Luntbuild project is bound to a source code repository and can have different builders to build parts of the project on defined schedules.

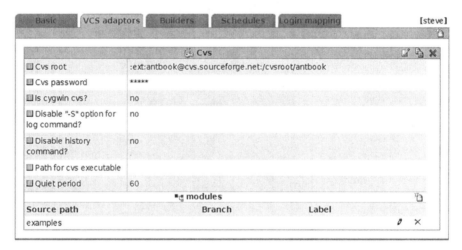

Figure 15.5   The VCS Adaptor to check out the project from SourceForge

A single project can also have multiple SCM/VCS repositories. We haven't tried that; instead, we just create different projects for each repository.

Creating a builder

The builder is where we have to set up Ant builds. The configuration to build the whole diary is shown in figure 15.6.

This is an important form, as it's where the tool bridges to Ant. It has the fields shown in table 15.2.

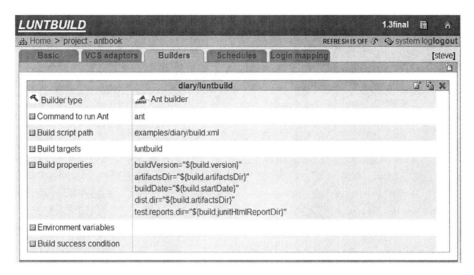

Figure 15.6 Luntbuild configuration of our builder. To create a new builder, click the "new document" icon on the top-right corner.

Table 15.2 The options to configure an Ant builder

Option	Meaning
Command to run Ant	The path to Ant; ant will suffice if it's on the path.
Build script path	The path to the build file from the base of the repository.
Build targets	One or more space-separated targets to run.
Build properties	Properties to pass down to Ant.
Environment variables	Any environment variables to set before Ant runs. To set up Ant's JVM, set up the ANT_OPTS variable here.
Build success condition	How to determine if a build was successful.

The build properties field comes pre-populated with some Luntbuild options to be passed down to Ant, which we extended with three more:

```
dist.dir="${build.artifactsDir}"
test.reports.dir="${build.junitHtmlReportDir}"
no.sign.jar=true
```

These properties will place the distributable files in a place where Luntbuild users can browse and download them, with test reports available under the "reports" tab of the build results. The `no.sign.jar` property tells our build file to skip targets that prompt for the keystore password and to sign the JAR files.

The last field of the form is "Build success condition," which, for an Ant build, defaults to `result==0` and `logContainsLine("BUILD SUCCESSFUL")`, checking both the return code and the last line of output. Delete the contents of this condition to make it default to using the return code, if you ever plan on editing ANT_OPTS to select a different logger, such as Ant's time-stamped logger. The moment your text output changes, the string comparison fails, and Luntbuild thinks the build was unsuccessful. This is why the build machine should be separate from any developer's box. It's too easy for developers to change their system in a way that breaks the scheduled builds; a tweak to ANT_OPTS is enough to confuse Luntbuild.

Creating a schedule

With the builder configured, Luntbuild knows how to build a project. But it doesn't know when. For that we need a schedule, which is a set of rules about what triggers a build. A project may have different schedules, such as a clean nightly build and full test and a more frequent incremental build with partial testing. A schedule has a trigger, which can be manual, simple (every few minutes), or cron, which can be used to set an absolute date or time for a schedule to start. Figure 15.7 shows the schedule for the incremental build of this book's examples. It runs every 17 minutes,

Incremental	
Execution status	success at 2006-03-10 13:27
Description	antbook incremental
Next build version	antbook-incremental (build 3)
Work subdirectory	
Trigger type:	simple
Repeat interval(minutes):	17
Build necessary condition	dependencySuccessful and (vcsModified or dependencyNewer)
Associated builders	diary/luntbuild
Associated post-builders	
Build type	increment
Post-build strategy	do not post-build
Label strategy	label if success
Notify strategy	notify when status changed
Schedules current schedule depends on	
Dependency triggering strategy	do not trigger any dependent schedules
Build cleanup strategy	keep builds by days (3)
Latest build	antbook-incremental (build 2) success at 2006-03-10 13:27

Figure 15.7   The schedule contains the settings to run an incremental build of our project. It declares dependencies on other schedules, the builder to run, and the actions to take on success.

and builds if anything in the repository has changed or something it depends upon has been successfully rebuilt.

The schedule configuration is quite complex, especially once you turn to the dependency system. Any schedule can be marked as depending on any other schedule. The schedules can then be set to trigger builds of everything they depend on, or everything that depends on them. We haven't found that feature to be too useful, because it ends up making builds slower and slower. If every component builds on its own schedule, that should be all you need. The exception is configuring one big "clean build of everything" target to run sporadically, such as every night.

Different schedules have notification policies. That's good for builds triggered by check-ins just to notify the individual team members by email or IM, so they can fix the problem before anyone else is disturbed. Nightly builds can be set up to notify the team mailing list, so the problem becomes more obvious.

One useful feature of a schedule is a post-build strategy. This is a list of builders to invoke after a project builds. For example, a builder could be set up to deploy the application after a successful build or to create a distribution package. Luntbuild would run these dependent builds only if the main build succeeded. We could use this build to have a scaled-up set of tests, with the long-lived performance tests starting only if the functional tests of the system pass.

Login mappings

The final piece of project configuration is the mapping between user names in the SCM repository and Luntbuild users. This is so that Luntbuild knows who to blame when things break. Figure 15.8 shows our mapping.

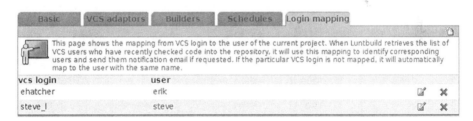

Figure 15.8 Mappings from usernames in the repository to Luntbuild users

The default mapping uses the repository username as the email address of the recipient, and sends notification messages over email as the notification.

Triggering a build

Once a schedule has been defined, it can be run by pressing the green arrow icon on the schedule's page or on the big list of all builds. Doing so will queue the build for execution. If the schedule requires predecessor builds to be built first, all the predecessors will be built. Similarly, if dependent schedules are triggered after a build, then they will be queued to run if the scheduled build completes successfully.

While getting Luntbuild to work, it's handy to have a schedule you can run whenever you feel like it. To do so, set the trigger condition to `always` to ensure that it runs even if the repository files haven't changed.

15.2.4 Luntbuild in action

With everything configured, Luntbuild should run continually, polling the SCM repositories for change and executing builders—which run the Ant builds and targets of the project—on the predefined schedules. Figure 15.9 shows our example server, which is running a set of schedules from three different projects.

The builds have quite a complex interdependency. Every build publishes its artifacts to the local Ivy repository, to be picked up by dependent builds. The (currently failing) test run, `Test`, is decoupled from the run `Incremental` that builds the artifacts. This decoupling enables the builds of all the dependent projects to continue even if a test fails upstream. The failing test run will not be ignored, but fixing it is something that can be dealt with in a relaxed and methodical manner. The `clean` build of the `Clean Release` schedule of the `smartfrog-core` is active, so its status line is animated; a button lets a logged-on user halt this run.

Despite the high number of scheduled builds, the daytime load on this system is light. The tool may poll for changes quite frequently, but builds are triggered only when source or dependencies change.

| Builds | Projects | Users | Properties | Administration | | [luntbuild] |

This page shows build information for all projects. Status of a schedule and build is denoted using icon: GREEN icon means success, the animation gear icon means building, and RED icon means build failed. Schedule status is different from build status, and it means whether or not the schedule has been successfully triggered. Trigger of the schedule may or may not generate a new build, it depends on the current build strategy and repository changes. The system log and build log contain detail information about the execution of a schedule.

Build filter:

Project	Schedule	When to trigger	Latest build		
antbook	Clean	at 0 0 1 * * ?	antbook-clean (build 3) [2006-03-10 13:31]		
antbook	Incremental	every 17 minutes	antbook-incremental (build 2) [2006-03-10 13:27]		
antbook	Manual	manually	no builds yet		
deployment	scheduled	every 17 minutes	deployment (6) [2006-03-08 15:59]		
smartfrog-core	CDDLM implementation	every 47 minutes	cddlm (14) [2006-03-10 13:04]		
smartfrog-core	Clean Release	at 0 0 1 * * ?	clean (6)		
smartfrog-core	Incremental	every 23 minutes	incremental (16) [2006-03-10 12:57]		
smartfrog-core	Manual-always	manually	luntbuild-1.11 [2006-03-03 13:50]		
smartfrog-core	Test	every 60 minutes	test (8) [2006-03-10 13:13]		
smartfrog-core	jetty incremental	every 37 minutes	jetty (1) [2006-03-10 13:00]		
smartfrog-core	www incremental	every 37 minutes	www (11) [2006-03-10 12:59]		

Figure 15.9   The Luntbuild status page. The book is building; some of the other projects are failing. A clean build is under way.

This status page can act as an at-a-glance status page for a big project, showing which bits are working and which bits are not. To determine what's working and what isn't, you need to subdivide a project into modules that can be built and tested independently. It can take time to do so, but the benefit is that it's immediately obvious which parts of a project have problems.

In use, the biggest problem we've found is that nothing kills builds that take too long. Luntbuild will happily let a test run all weekend. This may be what you want, but it if isn't, then other builds get delayed while one build has hung. After we encountered this situation, we made sure that all our <junit> runs gained the attribute timeout="600000", to stop them from running after ten minutes.

We also found it a bit tricky to track down failures, especially when learning to use the tool. There's a link in the top of the page to the "System Log," which shows all the log output from the tool related to problems checking out files from the repository. If a schedule fails to run and there's no build log, turn to the system log page to see what went wrong.

15.2.5 Review of Luntbuild

Luntbuild is an excellent example of a second-generation continuous-integration system. The tool authors have looked at the worst bit of CruiseControl—getting it to work—and addressed that problem through a web-based configuration mechanism.

Where they've really been innovative is when managing dependencies between projects, and when integrating scheduled builds with triggered releases. Scheduled builds let you run a big overnight "soak test" alongside commit-triggered builds, which can stop at the unit tests. The goal of the soak test is not to finish as quickly as possible, but to act much like a real application, even with realistic pauses if that's how end users are expected to interact with the server. Such tests find problems with memory leakage, concurrency, state management, and other aspects of a system that a normal test suite can miss. By their very nature, they are slow, so you run them overnight. Luntbuild will let you do that.

Strengths

- There's no need to edit configuration files.
- If you use MySQL as the repository, other programs can access the data.
- It's got a good installer; the default options are the best way to get up and running.
- The dependency chain logic can demand-rebuild a project if something needs it.
- Displays the HTML-formatted output from <junit> test runs.
- It's easy to add new projects.
- The post-build actions let you run deployment and redistribution build file targets, which can be triggered after the main build or test run completes.
- You can give multiple people the right to create new projects, which lets developers add new builds without unrestricted access to the host.

Limitations

- The more builds and schedules you add, the more the configuration GUI becomes a limit to scalability.
- It doesn't automatically kill builds that run for a long time.
- It takes time to learn your way around.
- We wouldn't trust the user accounts system to keep the build status private.

It's easy to install, so it's worthwhile investing an hour or two in getting it running. If it isn't suitable, there are the many alternatives listed in table 15.1, on page 390, to try out.

Alongside the technical problem of bringing up a continuous-integration server is the social one: having the team adapt to a world in which errors get caught in minutes. That's the final challenge of continuous integration.

15.3 MOVING TO CONTINUOUS INTEGRATION

The hardest part of getting a continuous-integration system up and running is not the software; it's changing how developers work.

With a continuous-integration server, you know within minutes if the program has stopped compiling. Perhaps a newly created file was omitted, or perhaps there was an error in the source. Compilation failures will be caught before the developer has finished the next cup of coffee. Indeed, if the server can page their phone, they get summoned back to their keyboard before the coffee has cooled enough to drink. Test failures can take longer to show up if a project has a thorough enough test suite. Even so, you should expect to see errors from the unit and functional tests within half an hour of a defect being checked in. If nothing went wrong: silence.

If the team cares about the error messages, then the problem gets fixed. The idea is that the best time to fix a problem is immediately after adding the problematic code. If the fix takes, then the application is working again. The result is that a program is rarely broken. It may not be complete, but the source will always compile, the build files will always work, and the tests that the server is set to run will pass.

That's a profound change. There's no more uncertainty about the state of the program: anyone can look at the server status page and check that all is well, reviewing the tests to see what the build tests. Furthermore, the entire history of builds can be preserved, so anyone can go back and look at what changed. This capability helps with blame assignment—finding out who or what broke the system. It's also a good way of keeping management happy without them bothering you for status reports: the server lets everyone know what's going on.

For this reason, continuous integration is more than just setting up a server somewhere to run builds; it's changing how you write code. Is it worth it? Very much so. One of our projects has two servers running constant builds, one on Linux/Java1.5 and the other on Windows Server 2003/Java1.4. The Java 1.4 build acts as a check that everything can still build on that version of Java. The different operating systems verify that the application is portable. They also deploy the system and run all the single-host functional tests, which take about 30 minutes to complete. If the servers are happy, the program is probably in a shippable condition. Sometimes the test fails, with problems that can take some days to fix—particularly if the problem is fundamental, or a new test is added that shows a new fault in the system. In that situation, someone has to sit down and fix the problem; it's a team problem, not that of any particular individual. Everyone has the right to fix any part of the program in order to get the build passing again.

It isn't easy adopting such a process, particularly if the cause is not "your part of the program." However, it's critical for everyone to care about the overall status of the build and for management to care enough about it to let developers spend time fixing the build, as opposed to adding new features.

In the project mentioned previously, the team has debated setting up a separate continuous-integration server for every branch, and having developers work on short-lived branches of only a few days, rather than share the main SVN branch. This setup would give every developer a private continuous-integration build, with the main branch hosting working code that has passed all the tests. With Xen/VMWare-hosted servers, having one background build per developer is possible.

Developers

If warning emails from the server are ignored, there's no point in having an automated build service.

A common reason for ignoring a message is the belief that someone else will fix the problem, because it's in their part of the project or because they broke the build. This is a mistake. As more changes are added, soon the build will be broken in many places, making the effort to fix the build that much harder. Sometimes tests fail for no apparent reason: if everyone assumes it's some else's problem, the build may not get fixed for a very long time.

At the very least, the initial failure report should trigger some discussion about what broke and why. Any developer should be able to get their hands dirty and fix the build. If it's in some part of the project that they don't understand yet, a broken test is an ideal excuse to learn their way around that bit of the system.

Management

Developers will fix a broken build only if they care about it. This should happen once they have adopted the process and recognize the benefits. But how do you convince developers that time spent fixing the build is more important than other things? That's where management has to help. Whoever is in charge of a project needs to encourage the developers to care about the notification emails and the build's status.

In an open source project, the team leaders need to set an example by caring about the build status. When failure notifications come in to the mailing list, team leaders could start discussions about the problem, fix it wherever they can, or ask others to fix it. The leaders also can credit people who put in the effort to fix the build.

Private projects have a management chain that the developers have to listen to, so if the managers say, "the continuous-integration build must work," then developers will keep it working. That is, "I spent yesterday fixing the build" has to be accepted as a legitimate reason for a feature being delayed. If managers think that testing matters, they have to support anyone who gets a broken build working again.

One subtle way of getting management support is to use the status page as a way of tracking changes and watching the status of the project. If the developers know that their manager uses the status page as a way of measuring a project's health, then they'll try to keep that page "green."

The less-subtle way to do this is to force a halt to all other work until the build is fixed. It certainly makes priorities clear, but it's an option that should come out only in emergencies, at least after the first couple of times. Developers themselves need to care about the build; the problem for management is working out how to make developers care.

Despite all of these warnings, a team can adopt a continuous-integration tool and build a development process around it. Even developers who are too lazy to run the tests can start to rely on the server to test for them. It takes time, and the gradual addition of more and more work to the background builds. The key to success is support from the team leads—management, key developers, and architects. If the senior members of a project embrace continuous integration and change how they work, the rest of the team will follow.

15.4 SUMMARY

Continuous integration is the concept of having a dedicated program that continually builds and tests an application. The continuous-integration server polls the source code repository on a regular basis, and, whenever it has changed, triggers a rebuild. If the build fails, the developers get email. If everything works: silence.

Luntbuild is one of the many continuous-integration applications you can install; it's one of the easiest applications to get up and running, yet it has support for complex inter-project dependencies. This lets you build up a background build process, with clean nightly builds and incremental ones running throughout the day.

Continuous integration transforms how projects are developed. It hands off the repetitive work of building and testing to machines that are happy to do it all day long, leaving developers to write the code and the tests. More subtly, by integrating everything all the time, different parts of a big system are able to work together.

Looking back at past projects, the biggest mistakes we've done with continuous integration are

- Not starting off with it at the beginning of the project
- Not paying enough attention to failures

We used to delay using it, primarily because CruiseControl was so painful to set up. Tools like Luntbuild make it so easy to get up and running that there's no such excuse anymore. A single server can build many projects, whether they depend on each other or not. Every project should adopt continuous integration, ideally as soon as the project is started.

CHAPTER 16

Deployment

We've been deploying web applications since chapter 12. It's now time to look at deployment in detail—all the way to production. Before we start, we need to revisit the question: *What is deployment?*

According to application server vendors, deployment is just "deploy-by-copy," such as copying a WAR or EAR file into a directory. Since all application servers now support this, isn't deployment done? Hardly. The real problem is not getting the application to the remote machine, or even getting the application loaded by the application server. It is *getting the whole system working.*

A web site cannot be described as successfully deployed until the database is up and running, the web site can talk to that database, and its pages are externally visible. This is what deploy-by-copy forgets about: copying a file to the application server is a tiny piece of the problem.

Just as we've automated the building and testing of our applications, so can we automate deployment. It's going to be hard, because deployment itself is complex. But it is possible, and it can transform your development if you can manage it.

In this chapter, we're going to explore the final piece of Ant's built-in deployment support—database setup—then look at how Ant can delegate advanced deployment to another tool, SmartFrog. The chapter will show that development processes need to evolve to embrace deployment, instead of fearing it.

16.1 How to Survive Deployment

We clearly think deployment is hard. Why? Mostly, it comes down to complexity.

- *Complex server configurations.* Production systems are far more intricate than a single developer's box. There's a database server, multiple application servers, and a router. Every difference between the development systems and the production systems can break the application.

- *Complex organizations.* Organizations often have a split between *developers* and *operations.* Developers write the code, but operations have to keep everything working.

- *Optimistic schedules.* Since server-side deployment is viewed as easy, everyone neglects the problem until the application is due to go live, at which point it's too late to automate, leaving nothing but chaos and delays.

There's a very simple test to see if the deployment process is working. If you have to go into the air-conditioned server room on a weekend, deployment is broken. If you're scared of the phone ringing, deployment is broken. If you're a week away from going live and you haven't started bringing up the server, then deployment is broken—you just don't know it yet.

It's possible to survive deployment, just as you can stay on top of the rest of the software development process—by having a process to keep it under control. Table 16.1 shows what you have to do:

The idea of integrating deployment into the development process is very leading-edge. It's something that some companies appear to do, though they don't talk about it much. Our proposed process is based on applying test-centric development to the deployment process. Test, automate, and iterate: that's the secret. What do we propose?

Table 16.1   Keep deployment under control by integrating it with the development process

Action	Rationale
Start working on deployment early.	Deployment is too important to leave until the last minute.
Work with operations.	You cannot just throw the application over the wall to the operations team and expect it to work.
Target the production system.	Even during development, target the application server, database, and OS of the production system.
Automate deployment.	With a fully-automated deployment process, you can eliminate errors in the deployment process and deploy to more machines.
Test the deployment.	Deployment problems—usually configuration problems—are testable. So write the tests.
Track deployment defects.	Deployment problems are bugs, just like anything else. So treat them as such.

Start working on deployment early

Your project needs to recognize that deployment will be a problem from the outset, something that needs to be part of the development process. Start now.

Work with operations

Developers have to build a system that meets the needs of the operations team—a system that is secure, manageable, and doesn't generate support calls late at night.

The key is to treat the needs and problems of operations as just another part of the software development process, with use cases, tests, and defect tracking.

The management tasks on the system—creating, backing up, and restoring the database; tracking down why a user cannot log in; blocking the IP address of a malicious client—are all use cases that the system needs to support, one way or another. Work with operations to find out what they want to do, and support it. Then find out what causes them trouble, and avoid it.

Target the production system

Differences between production and development servers cause problems, so reduce them with development systems that match the production one. That's very expensive to do with dedicated hardware, but you don't need dedicated hardware if you make use of *virtualization*.

A virtual machine (VM) is a complete image of a computer hosted under the real operating system (OS). The virtual machine can have its own virtual disk, with its own OS, and its own virtual display and network card. Most programs and operating systems run perfectly on such virtual machines. Products that implement VMs include VMWare, Xen, and Parallels Desktop. The latest x86 CPUs can run a VM at almost the same speed as real hardware.

Virtualization transforms application testing. Every developer can have a whole set of virtual hosts to deploy and test onto. These machine images can be set up to resemble the production systems, with separate hosts for the application server and database server. Virtualization also allows a large database to be pre-populated and saved to a disk image that's rolled back at the end of every test run, giving tests a realistic database with almost no set-up time.

There are some costs with the technology. It cannot be used for performance testing, and all host systems need more memory and hard disk than normal. Most critically, every OS image stored to a virtual disk drive is another OS to maintain. The operations team needs to be in charge of the virtual hosts.

Automate deployment

The entire act of bringing up a new physical or virtual server should be fully automated and, ideally, hands-free. If this can be achieved, then you can reliably create servers that work the first time.

The goal is to automate the entire deployment of the application server, the database, and the applications on top of the server. That includes the OS, with Preboot Execution Environments (PXE), which is something for the operations team to worry about. The stuff above the OS is something to work on together.

Everything above the OS—the application server, the database, or any other application—all need to be automatically installed. Sometimes the products can create their own repeatable installation script, which can be used to replicate an install.

One tactic is to use the package management features of the underlying OS in order to get the OS management tools to push out software. There's an Ant `<rpm>` task around the `rpmbuild` program, and the dotnet Antlib contains a `<wix>` task to generate MSI files for Windows. The weakness of these tools is that only system administrators can install the packages. There should be no need to have super user/administrator rights to install or run Java applications, unless they need access to locked-down parts of the machine.

Alongside the application goes the data. The database needs to be installed, then populated with a realistic dataset. Once the database is populated, it can be backed up and reused in test runs. Either the relevant database directories can be backed up and restored before each run, or the complete virtual machine can be copied. That snapshot of the database server can be brought up whenever a test run needs a server with a database full of test data.

Test the deployment

When the deployment fails, developers can write tests to isolate the problem. These become regression tests on server configurations. For example, imagine if a network filestore's clock is wrong, confusing a housekeeping routine into deleting new files instead of just old ones. It's easy enough to fix the problem on a single system, but why not write a test routine? This routine would verify that the timestamp of created files is within a few seconds of the system clock. Ant does exactly this when you run `ant -diagnostics`, checking that files can be written to `${java.io.tmpdir}`. Why? Because the problem has occurred in Ant often enough.

The book's application has been doing something similar. The `happy.jsp` page and its tests for various classes are the foundation for a testable deployment. As more problems arise, new tests can be added to show the problems and to verify that they aren't present in deployed systems.

Having health checks in a web page makes it easy for humans to check that a system is happy; they just point their browser at it. The real secret is that machines can do the testing too. In Ant, `<get>` or HttpUnit can probe the pages. In the production system, monitoring tools can check the page every few seconds and restart the server if one system is unhappy.

This monitoring only works if the system has a thorough set of health tests, which will come by writing them during development. Just as the benefit of unit tests grows over time, the value of having tests to validate a deployment grows over the life of the system.

Track deployment defects

Every deployment problem is a defect, one that will come back later to haunt you. Treat them as such, with entries in a defect-tracking system. For the defect database to be useful, its symptoms must be noted with a statement such as "JSP pages do not compile," the cause, such as "javac not found," and the fix, i.e., "added JDK/bin to the path." This is all obvious stuff. What's essential is that the defect tracking should begin the moment you start developing the application on your local server. The developers gain more experience in the issues than anyone else. This knowledge needs to be passed on to the rest of the team.

This whole problem of deployment is beyond anything a single tool can address. PXE Preboot tools can install an OS onto a clean server, and OS-level system management tools can configure the OS so that it meets the project's needs. Ant can help with these tasks by preparing artifacts for deployment and by integrating deployment with the build process.

16.2 DEPLOYING WITH ANT

Ant was the first build tool with built-in support for distribution and deployment. It knows how to compile, test, and package Java programs. It also knows how to redistribute the created artifacts by SSH, email, and FTP. Even so, it's still a build tool. It doesn't talk over the network to other copies of Ant. It is unlikely to be able to run for months, and its workflow is very simplistic. It runs a build to completion or it stops in an indeterminate state. Sometimes you can tell tasks to ignore failures, but that isn't real fault handling.

Ant is used all the way through to deployment, cropping up as a startup script or launcher application. This happens because it's the closest thing Java has to a cross-platform scripting language and because there are third-party tasks to simplify the process. And that's the secret to getting Ant to deploy properly: delegate deployment to other tools.

Ant is just part of the tool chain, something that's best at building and testing. It's the program you can start from the IDE, the command line, or the continuous integration tool, so it's a great way to start the deployment. If Ant cannot deploy or undeploy the program, you cannot integrate deployment into the build and test cycle. However, Ant by itself just isn't up to the job of performing complex deployments and undeployments, especially remote ones. It needs help from tools such as Cargo and SmartFrog.

Cargo is a small open-source project, hosted at http://cargo.codehaus.org/. Its specialty is deploying WAR and EAR files to application servers, and starting and stopping those same servers. It can even install middleware by fetching and unzipping an archive, and database deployment is next on its to-do list. Cargo ships as a set of tasks for Ant, and as a plug-in for Apache Maven that can deploy applications. It can also be used inside Apache Cactus, as a way of deploying the WAR or EAR file containing the tests. Lack of space prevents us from covering Cargo, but the http://antbook.org/ web site has some details on it, along with the build file to deploy the application.

The reason we're skipping over Cargo is that we've chosen to look at a more ambitious tool—SmartFrog. But before we do that, there's one last thing we want from Ant: a database. Now, SmartFrog can do the database setup itself, but one reason to do it in Ant is that it's easier to mix SQL operations into Ant targets, with the clean target also deleting tables from the database or having a target to create a user that sets the password from an Ant property.

16.3   DATABASE SETUP IN ANT

Back in chapter 14, Ant used Cactus to deploy the diary application onto an application server and test it. However, we used HSQLDB as the database, which is a pure-Java database that can run in the process creating the JDBC connection. For our production system, we want a real database, such as MySQL. Following our "target the production system" rule, that means we should be testing against MySQL, which will need to be installed and configured with a diary database and user. Following the "automate deployment" rule, we have to automate the installation and setup of MySQL. At the very least we can set up the database before we run the tests, cleaning out the old data and creating the user account.

Before Ant can talk to the database, we need to install MySQL. An automated installation of MySQL is possible, but it's also beyond the scope of this book. Here are the steps to install MySQL by hand:

1 Download MySQL from mysql.com and install the product. For Linux it comes in various formats and in many distributions. For Windows it comes as an installable application.

2 Set an administrator password.

3 Set `mysqld` to start as a Windows service or a Linux daemon.

4 Test that it works from the command line. Type `mysql` to get the MySQL command line, then type `status` to see the database status.

5 Download the JDBC driver from http://www.mysql.com/products/connector/j/

6 Read the license: the driver is GPL, with special terms for open-source projects.

The licensing situation is complex. Understand it before redistributing MySQL or applications that depend upon it or its JDBC driver.

16.3.1 Creating and configuring a database from Ant

Ant's `<sql>` task can issue SQL commands to a database over a JDBC link. To use this with MySQL, we need to set it up with the MySQL JDBC driver on the classpath and the password of the root account.

Ivy can fetch JDBC drivers in a new configuration, "sql."

```
<conf name="sql" description="SQL drivers"/>
```

The `ivy.xml` file must also contain a list of all drivers we may need:

```
<dependency org="mysql" name="mysql-connector-java"
    rev="${mysql.version}"
    conf="sql->default"/>
<dependency org="hsqldb" name="hsqldb"
    rev="${hsqldb.version}"
    conf="sql->default"/>
```

The relevant versions go into the `libraries.properties` file:

```
hsqldb.version=1.8.0.7
mysql.version=3.1.13
```

These changes set Ivy up to retrieve both the MySQL and HSQLDB JDBC drivers, drivers that can be passed to the `<sql>` task through its `classpathref` attribute. We can then use `<presetdef>` to define two new tasks:

```
<target name="mysql-init" depends="ivy-resolve"
  xmlns:ext="http://antbook.org/d1/ext" >
  <ivy:cachepath pathid="sql.classpath"        Set up the JDBC
    conf="sql" />                               driver classpath

  <property name="mysql.root.pass"
      value=""/>                                Define database
  <property name="mysql.diary.pass"            passwords
      value="secret"/>

  <presetdef name="mysql-admin"
      uri="http://antbook.org/d1/ext">
    <sql driver="com.mysql.jdbc.Driver"         Define a new task to
      classpathref="sql.classpath"              issue SQL command
      userid="root"                             to the local MySQL
      password="${mysql.root.pass}"            database
      print="true"
      url="jdbc:mysql://localhost/mysql"
      expandProperties="true"/>
  </presetdef>
  <presetdef name="mysql">
    uri="http://antbook.org/d1/ext">
    <ext:mysql-admin                            Define a task to issue
      userid="diary"                            commands to the diary
      password="${mysql.diary.pass}"           DB as the 'diary' user
      url="jdbc:mysql://localhost/diary"/>
  </presetdef>
</target>
```

The `<sql>` task needs to know the name of the driver to use, via the `driver` attribute, and the JDBC URL to the database. If you don't know about JDBC, this task isn't really the place to learn, although it does let you improve your SQL knowledge through experimentation.

To simplify SQL coding, we've written two preset tasks, one for administrator operations on the root database, and a second one extending the first to run against a diary database under the login of the diary user. These can issue administrator- or user-level commands, respectively. One absolutely critical aspect of these declarations is that `expandProperties="true"` is set in the `<sql>` task. This ensures that Ant expands Ant properties in the SQL text. Otherwise, `${property}` strings get passed down unexpanded from nested-text SQL commands. With the `expand-Properties` attribute set and the drivers downloaded, Ant is ready to talk to the database.

16.3.2 Issuing database administration commands

Our `<mysql-admin>` preset task can issue commands to the database. Here are a pair of targets to drop the database (if present), to create a new database with full rights to the `diary` account, and to set the password of that account. This sequence of operations implicitly creates the `diary` account if it doesn't already exist, using the password in the Ant property `mysql.diary.pass`.

```
<target name="mysql-drop-db" depends="mysql-init"
  description="create the database and account">
  <ext:mysql-admin onerror="continue">
    DROP DATABASE diary;
  </ext:mysql-admin>
</target>

<target name="mysql-create-db"
  depends="mysql-init,mysql-drop-db"
  description="create the database and account">
  <ext:mysql-admin>
    CREATE DATABASE diary;
    GRANT ALL PRIVILEGES ON diary.* TO 'diary'@'localhost';
    SET PASSWORD FOR 'diary'@'localhost' =
      PASSWORD('${mysql.diary.pass}');
  </ext:mysql-admin>
</target>
```

The `mysql-create-db` target depends on the `mysql-drop-db` target to destroy the database before it's rebuilt. To avoid an error if the database is missing, that `<sql>` call has `onerror="continue"` set. When we call the `mysql-create-db` target, it creates the new database.

```
mysql-drop-db:
[ext:mysql-admin] Executing commands
[ext:mysql-admin] 1 rows affected
[ext:mysql-admin] 1 of 1 SQL statements executed successfully
```

```
mysql-create-db:
[ext:mysql-admin] Executing commands
[ext:mysql-admin] 1 rows affected
[ext:mysql-admin] 0 rows affected
[ext:mysql-admin] 0 rows affected
[ext:mysql-admin] 3 of 3 SQL statements executed successfully
```

We can then use our newly defined <mysql> task to issue commands to the newly created diary database, such as setting it up in advance of a run:

```
<target name="mysql-create-events" depends="mysql-init"
    description="create the event table">
  <ext:mysql>
    CREATE TABLE EVENTS (
    EVENT_ID varchar(64) not null,
    EVENT_NAME varchar(255) not null,
    EVENT_DATE timestamp not null,
    EVENT_VERSION integer,
    EVENT_LASTMODIFIED timestamp,
    EVENT_TEXT varchar(8192),
    primary key (EVENT_ID));
  </ext:mysql>
</target>
```

This target will create the EVENTS table, which is ready for the web application:

```
mysql-create-events:
[ext:mysql] Executing commands
[ext:mysql] 0 rows affected
[ext:mysql] 1 of 1 SQL statements executed successfully
```

Although the EJB runtime can create a database schema on demand, in a production system the database administrator (DBA) owns the problem. The DBA should give the developers the SQL statements they need to set up the database and give the operations team the data binding files the application server needs to bind the web application to it. The <sql> task can run those commands. If they're in a separate file, the src attribute can be used to load, parse, and run the file.

There's one thing to be careful of when working with the <sql> task. The task will execute a sequence of SQL statements inline, from a file specified with the src attribute, or in nested <transaction> elements. The task has to parse the text, breaking it into separate statements, before calling the database via the specified JDBC driver. It tries to recognize comments that start with -- or //, but the code that does this is very temperamental. Avoid comments in the file, or any non-standard SQL that the JDBC driver will reject.

To summarize: if you're using a database in an application, then database creation and configuration is one of the tasks you need to automate. The <sql> task can do this. What it cannot do is install and configure the database itself, or bind the application server to the database. For that, we need another tool.

16.4 DEPLOYING WITH SMARTFROG

What if you need to install and configure the application server? What if you need to add the JDBC drivers to its classpath? What if the database needs to be set up on a different machine? What if the LDAP server on a remote system needs to come up before the database or the application server does?

Those are the kinds of problems that real applications encounter. Deployment is a complex problem, with configuration of different parts of the system and choreography across parts of the system a key issue. Ant cannot handle this; it's beyond the scope of a build tool. What can? SmartFrog, an open source application from HP Laboratories, can do all of this from its Ant tasks.

Before we proceed, know that Steve works on SmartFrog as his day job, addressing the challenges of large-scale deployment. Expect some bias in this section.

16.4.1 SmartFrog: a new way of thinking about deployment

SmartFrog is a Java-based framework for deploying and configuring applications across one or more machines. It is to deployment what Ant is to building things: a language, a runtime, and a set of components for configuring and deploying applications. View it as the machine-readable version of the fifty-page file telling the operations team how to install and configure the database and application servers, then deploy the application on top. That's what we want to automate. We want to run an Ant target that deploys our application across our multiple test servers, then later onto the production systems, as shown in figure 16.1.

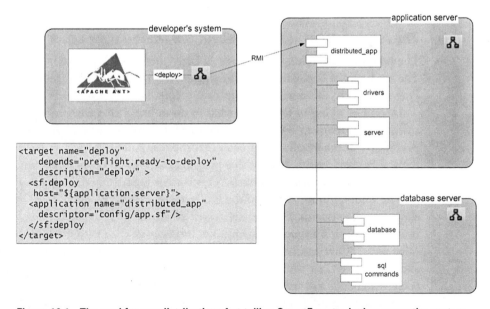

Figure 16.1 The goal for our distribution: Ant telling SmartFrog to deploy our entire system, including setting up the application server and the database

Lots of tools can configure classes, such as Spring, Plexus, and HiveMind. These all work within a single JVM, binding classes together, and perhaps binding classes to a database. The goal of these tools is to make it easier to build an application by connecting together smaller components. SmartFrog is more ambitious than these, because it tries to build a complex distributed application by connecting together code, classes, and programs across machines.

Here are some of the things it can do:

- Deploy the middleware: the database and the application server
- Set up a database with test data
- Deploy the web and enterprise applications
- Configure intimate details of deployed applications, such as the handlers of a SOAP stack, the mime types of a web application, or its Log4J policies
- Run JUnit tests on multiple host machines, aggregating the results
- Start VMWare or Xen images, then deploy other things onto these images
- Test the health of all deployed components
- Shut down everything just deployed

How can it do all this? Primarily because it's nothing but a large distributed system itself, one that can configure, start, and stop components on the machines. Everything else—the things that get started, the sequence of how they are started and stopped—is all implemented in SmartFrog components. It's these components that can handle complex deployments.

The fundamental concept behind SmartFrog

The core concept behind SmartFrog is fairly profound: *deployment is configuration*. The hard part of deployment is configuring everything to work together. The Smart-Frog solution to this mirrors the problem: *configuration is deployment*.

Instead of trying to remember what to do to bring up a complex system, or have a fifty-page document listing the actions to take, operations and developers create a description of the installation process that the computer can itself understand. Something that people write, but which a program can take and turn into a functional system, deployed over the target hosts. This is what SmartFrog does.

The underpinning of SmartFrog is effectively a *domain-specific language* for modeling complex systems. Each model describes what is to be deployed, and how it is to be configured. It's a simple language, not much more than nested templates of name-value pairs. What it adds is two unique things. Firstly, all templates can be inherited and overwritten, so you do not need to repeat definitions. Base templates can be taken, extended, and used to describe specific installations on specific systems. Secondly, it has the ability to cross-reference values. If two parts of a deployment description take the same value, such as the port of a web server, then that value is not duplicated by cut-and-paste. Instead, the value is cross-referenced, so that the port is defined in one place and shared wherever it's needed.

A language that describes complex configurations is useless unless you have a way to turn it into a running deployment. That's the job of the SmartFrog *runtime*. It takes a description and deploys it. It builds up a graph of nested templates, expands all inherited templates, resolves the references and produces an expanded, resolved graph of name-value pairs. The runtime then turns these templates into deployed *components*.

Every SmartFrog component represents something that can be configured and started. Running components can be pinged to see if they are healthy and, eventually, stopped. The actual sequencing of starting and stopping components is handled by the container components in which the child components are declared. These components are just Java classes with an RMI interface for remote access. Simple components implement their functionality inside the class, just as Ant tasks do. More complex components bind to native applications, such as the Apache HTTPD web server.

To summarize: SmartFrog is a language for describing configurations, a runtime to instantiate those configurations, and an extensible set of components that can be deployed and undeployed.

16.4.2 The concepts in more detail

That was a quick overview of the concept, a configuration-centric system for distributed deployment. Now let's look a bit deeper, focusing on how to use SmartFrog for deploying our web application and database. For our deployment, we need to get the MySQL JDBC driver into a directory in the application server where it can be used to set up the data source. Inserting the JAR inside a WAR or EAR file doesn't work, because it isn't visible to the right classloader. A manual deployment document, would say something like "download the MySQL JDBC driver version 5.0.4, verify its checksum, and copy it into the lib/ subdirectory of the chosen JBoss configuration." We need a SmartFrog descriptor that does the same thing, somehow marking the destination directory as something that will be defined later.

The SmartFrog language

SmartFrog comes with a new language—it isn't XML. The language's author, Patrick Goldsack doesn't think XML documents are easily writeable or, more importantly, readable by humans, and sometimes you have to agree with him. Instead, a new language has been written, with the JavaCC tool used to create the parser.[1]

The language itself is very simple, and quite Java-like. It consists of templates, surrounded by curly-braces and name-value pairs inside the templates. Listing 16.1 shows the descriptor to install the MySQL JDBC driver.

---

[1] Puppet, a Ruby-based configuration management tool, has a very similar non-XML syntax. It's clearly the new trend of post-XML programming.

Listing 16.1 A SmartFrog file to fetch and deploy the MySQL JDBC driver

```
#include "org/smartfrog/services/os/java/library.sf"
#include "org/smartfrog/services/filesystem/components.sf"

InstallDrivers extends Compound {          This template extends the
                                           "Compound" template

    destDir TBD;        This attribute is
                        "To Be Defined"

    repo extends Maven2Library {        This component can fetch
    }                                   JARs from ibiblio.org

    jdbcJAR extends JarArtifact {    <—  The JDBC driver to fetch
        project "mysql";
        artifact "mysql-connector-java";
        version "5.0.4";
        sha1 "ce259b62d08cce86a68a8f17f5f9c8218371b235";
        library LAZY PARENT:repo;    <—  The component
    }                                    to fetch it

    copyJdbcDriver extends CopyFile {       Copy the artifact after it
        source LAZY jdbcJAR;                has been downloaded
        destination LAZY PARENT:destDir;
        overwrite false;
    }
}
```

This template solves one tiny part of the bigger deployment and can be reused wherever we need to install the MySQL JDBC drivers.

Putting aside how it all works for a moment, the language has some interesting features. Every template here extends some other template. Where did the templates come from? They came from the files named in the #include statements at the beginning of the document. These are all resources in JAR files on the classpath. Component developers provide the initial templates with the implementations of the components, so that component users can import them and start using them immediately.

The next point to note is that although the names of things appear to be simple, values can be more complex. There are some primitive types—string, integers, and Boolean values among them—but there are a few that are different, like LAZY PARENT:repo. That is a *reference*, a link to the attribute repo of the parent component. It's marked as LAZY, meaning this reference should be dynamically resolved at runtime. Non-lazy references are evaluated earlier on, before the runtime starts bringing up the components.

The reference mechanism is incredibly powerful. A complex path can be built up by chaining template names, such as InstallDrivers:jdbcJAR:version. This refers to the version attribute of the jdbcJAR template in the Install-Drivers template.

Being able to cross-reference things, be they simple values or complex nested templates, eliminates the need to duplicate information. The other trick is that when components deploy, they can add new attributes. A LAZY reference to an attribute can refer to something that isn't defined in any descriptor, but is picked up at deployment time. This can be used for things such as setting the absolute path of a created file or the JDBC URL to a running database.

There's one other interesting attribute value, the TBD declaration:

```
destDir TBD;
```

This means that the destDir attribute is *To Be Defined*. That value must be set in the template before deployment begins, but this particular template doesn't know what the value will be. It means the template can be deployed only as part of something bigger.

The power of composition

The deployment descriptor that sets up the database driver describes one small, albeit critical, part of a big deployment. It's useful only as part of a bigger system. How does that happen? Through composition. Just as a big program is built from small classes, a big deployment is created from small deployment descriptors, each of which solves a specific problem. Listing 16.2 shows the deployment descriptor that deploys the application server, the database, the web application, and a component that checks the resulting site's "happy page."

Listing 16.2   How to compose a system from components

```
#include "deploy/webapp.sf"
#include "deploy/database.sf";          Import the templates we
#include "deploy/jboss.sf"              need to use or extend
#include "deploy/install_drivers.sf";


System extends Compound {
    port 8080;     <—  The web server port

    hostname "localhost";    <—  The web server hostname

    jboss.home TBD;
                        "To Be Defined"
    jdk.home TBD;

    database extends MySQLDaemon {       The MySQL database
        username "diary";                with login information
        password "secret";
    }

    drivers extends InstallDrivers {     Install the JDBC driver into
      destDir LAZY server:libDir;        JBoss's library directory
    }
```

```
server extends JBoss4Server {     ⊲—  The application server

    port PARENT:port;
    jboss.home PARENT:jboss.home;          Bind the configuration of JBoss to
    jdk.home PARENT:jdk.home;              the parent component's settings

    sysProperties [
        ["mysql.url",LAZY database:url],       Pass down the
        ["mysql.user",database:username],      database binding
        ["mysql.passwd",database:password]     as JVM properties
        ];
}
webapp extends DiaryApp {               Deploy the diary
    server LAZY PARENT:server:deployTo;      webapp on the server
}
happy extends Delay {
    time 60000;
    action extends LivenessPage {       Wait 60 seconds,
        page "diary/happy.jsp";         then start polling
    }                                   the happy.jsp page
}
}
```

This descriptor describes the system in about forty lines. It configures the database, copies the JDBC JAR to the application server's library directory, and shows the web application where to go. It also has a monitoring component, which, after a sixty-second delay, starts checking the health of the application.

This is the secret of making big things manageable, by inheriting templates, then expanding or overriding them. This description is nearly ready to be deployed. We just need to fill in those attributes that aren't yet there, those marked as TBD, or the deployment will not even begin.

The SmartFrog runtime

The SmartFrog runtime takes a description and turns it into deployed components. Here is one that fills in all the undefined attributes with data that's valid for a target Windows system.

```
sfConfig extends System {
    jboss.home "C:\\Java\\Apps\\jboss";
    jdk.home "C:\\Java\\jdk";
    webapp:examples "C:\\antbook\\examples";
}
```

This description can be deployed on any Windows system that has JBoss, the JDK, and the diary application in the configured locations. This single-host configuration can be kept under revision control, with descriptors for different hosts and platforms alongside it.

This descriptor can be deployed by handing it to the SmartFrog runtime and asking for it to be deployed. Every host that can be a target for deployment must run a copy of the SmartFrog daemon. This is the core SmartFrog runtime running as a service or Unix daemon. It listens on the network port 3800 for requests to deploy a tree of SmartFrog templates and an *application,* turning them in to deployed components. If part of the graph needs to be hosted on another machine, then it hands off that part of the graph to the remote system. There is no central controller of the machines—just a set of hosts that trust each other. All communication is via Java Remote Method Invocation (RMI) over SSL. This is Java's built-in distributed object framework. It does have its limitations, primarily versioning, long-distance communications, and the problem of distributed garbage collection. SmartFrog works best between hosts on the same site.

After reading in the descriptor, the SmartFrog runtime creates a distributed graph of things to deploy. By default, every component is deployed in the same host and JVM as its parent. To deploy our multi-tier application across a cluster of machines, we would need a new descriptor, one that declares new locations for some components, simply by declaring target hosts inside the descriptor:

```
HomeLinuxCluster extends System {
    sfProcessHost "pelvoux";          <-❶
    database:sfProcessHost "eiger";      <-❷
    happy:sfProcessHost  "eiger";      <-❸

    hostname "deployment.antbook.org";
    home LAZY PROPERTY user.home;          <-❹
    jboss.home home ++ "/java/apps/jboss";
    jboss.home home ++ "/antbook/java/jdk";
    jboss.home home ++ "/antbook/examples";
}
```

This descriptor uses the sfProcessHost attribute to tell the runtime where to host the different parts of the template graph and, later, the components. The application is deployed on the host "pelvoux" ❶, as will all children except for the database ❷ and the happy page ❸, which are hosted on "eiger." The home directory is picked up from the Java property user.home on the remote system ❹. That gives us a two-tier server and, by hosting the happy page remotely, checks that the web site's firewall is open. Figure 16.2 shows what happens. The description is taken and turned into a graph of component descriptions across machines.

The way the sfProcessHost attribute of the database and happy templates were set shows another trick of the SmartFrog language. Deployment descriptors can *inject* data into templates, by giving the full path to the attribute, here database: sfProcessHost. This is useful for putting last-minute information in, although it's a bit like using Ant properties to configure an existing target. It's useful, but does make the deployment more brittle, as you effectively code in more assumptions about the structure of the template.

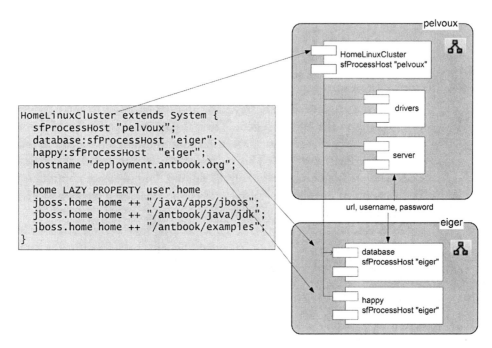

```
HomeLinuxCluster extends System {
  sfProcessHost "pelvoux";
  database:sfProcessHost "eiger";
  happy:sfProcessHost  "eiger";
  hostname "deployment.antbook.org";

  home LAZY PROPERTY user.home
  jboss.home home ++ "/java/apps/jboss";
  jboss.home home ++ "/antbook/java/jdk";
  jboss.home home ++ "/antbook/examples";
}
```

Figure 16.2 The SmartFrog daemons build up a distributed graph of things to deploy. Cross-references are still valid across the network.

Once deployed, the components will run on two different machines. Even though they are now distributed, the graph of components is still intact; components can navigate around and locate their parent or other components. This allows components to share runtime information, by adding new attributes or changing existing ones. They can also talk directly to each other using the Java RMI protocol. Having a single graph of components across multiple servers lets the developers and their build files have control of the complete deployment. Our build file can start or stop the application in one go.

SmartFrog components and their lifecycle

Once the deployment graph has been built up, the next step is to instantiate the components. The runtime instantiates the top node in the graph, here the HomeLinux-Cluster node, and starts to deploy it.

This is quite a complex process, as the SmartFrog runtime tries to move all components through their lifecycle according to the policy implemented by their parent components; deployment is choreographed. Figure 16.3 shows the lifecycle of a single component; child components follow the same lifecycle by default.

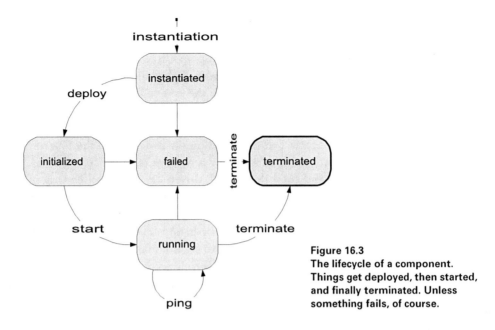

Figure 16.3
The lifecycle of a component.
Things get deployed, then started,
and finally terminated. Unless
something fails, of course.

The lifecycle of an *application*, a hierarchical tree of components, is shown in table 16.2:

Table 16.2   Lifecycle actions that SmartFrog components support, and how they react

The graph is *constructed*	The graph of component descriptions is created, with each template on its chosen host.
The root component is *instantiated*	The Java class implementing the root component is created and bound to the graph.
The root component is *deployed*	The class's sfDeploy() method is called; attributes can be read or written; children can be instantiated and deployed. The node's RMI interfaces are exported.
The root component is *started*	The class's sfStart() method is called to start actual work, such as the database or the application server. Children may also be started.
The root component is *terminated*	The component stops what it's doing, unexports its RMI interface, and cleans up. Programs are stopped, files are deleted, and so on.
A component is *pinged*	The class's sfPing() method is called. It should check its health and throw an exception if it's unhappy. Children also should be checked.
A component is *destroyed*	Once all references to a component are lost, the JVM may garbage-collect the class behind it.
A component *fails*	If the component fails to deploy, start, or respond to a ping request, it is considered to have failed. This is reported to any parent node.

This is quite a complex process. Under the hood, SmartFrog components do resemble Ant tasks: they are both Java classes that you configure through text files; they merely know more about deploying and cleaning up afterwards than Ant tasks. The biggest difference is that by default, parent nodes deploy all their children in parallel—Ant executes tasks in sequence, except inside the `<parallel>` container task.

The component lifecycle in action

When our `HomeLinuxCluster` application is deployed, the SmartFrog runtime instantiates, deploys, and then starts the components. Some components, such as the ones to download and copy the MySQL driver, are contained entirely in the implementation classes. Others, like the JBoss and MySQL support components, are separate processes—Java and native, respectively. They are started by the framework's equivalent of `<java>` and `<exec>`. The happy component is special in that it only deploys its `action` child after a sixty-second pause; it's an instance of the `Delay` component, which manages its child's lifecycle according to its own policy.

The final deployment is that of figure 16.4. The application server is running, and the diary WAR file has been deployed to it by copying into the deploy directory of the

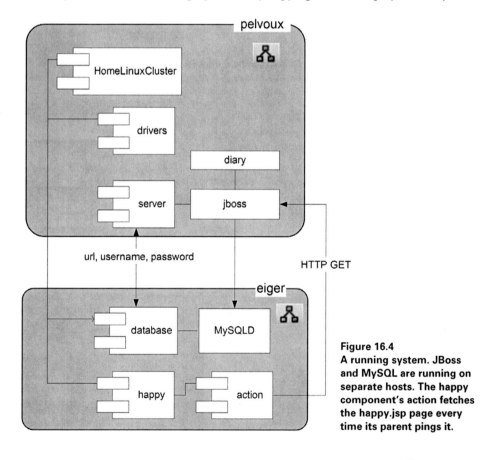

Figure 16.4
A running system. JBoss and MySQL are running on separate hosts. The happy component's action fetches the happy.jsp page every time its parent pings it.

active configuration. When the JBoss JVM process started, it was passed the database connection information—the URL, the username, and the password—information that has been picked up and used to bind to the database.

While the system is running, the root runtime will ping the HomeLinux-Cluster. The server will be healthy if JBoss is still running; the same for the remote database. The happy component considers itself happy if it can retrieve the happy.jsp JSP page from the web site. If it gets an error code or cannot connect, it reports an error to its parent. The result is that it becomes impossible to deploy an unhappy application.

16.4.3 The SmartFrog components

Just as Ant has built-in tasks and third-party tasks and Antlibs, SmartFrog has components, which come in JARs that contain the template .sf files, RMI interface and proxy classes, and the implementation classes. The daemons can download classes and SmartFrog descriptors using Java's remote classloading facility. A list of URLs needs to be supplied the daemons on startup, or they can be set in a deployment descriptor. Table 16.3 lists the main components currently available.

Table 16.3 Packages of SmartFrog components

Component package	Function
Ant	Invocation of Ant components during deployment or termination.
Anubis	A fault-tolerant tuple space for building a high-availability system out of a cluster of machines. This is cutting-edge, distributed-system research—the SLP package is simpler.
Database	Database deployment and table population. Similar to Ant's <sql> task.
Filesystem	Files, directories, temporary files and directories, self-deleting files, copy, touch, mkdir, and the like.
Java	Start Java programs; retrieve artifacts from repositories.
xunit/junit	Components to deploy tests on different hosts and processes; then collect the results.
LoggingServices	Log integration with Log4J and commons logging.
Networking	Networking components, supporting DNS, FTP, email, and SSH.
OS	OS-specific features and program execution.
SLP	A Service Location Protocol server and clients, for LAN-based discovery.
SSH	SSH client code, to connect to remote machines and issue commands.
Workflow	Components to choreograph child components in different ways.
WWW	Jetty, Tomcat, and JBoss deployment.
Alpine	A prototype lightweight "Alpine Style" SOAP stack.
CERN openlab	A third-party package to manipulate .ini, text and XML files, install SSH keys and bring up Grid service platforms.
SmartDomains	CERN components to deploy Xen virtual machines; SourceForge hosted.

The web application sticks to the WWW and database packages, along with foundational content such as workflow, OS, filesystem, and Java. We also have experimented with the testing framework, which can integrate testing with deployment. All of these packages come as separate JARs, which need to be on the classpath of the daemons, either on startup or through dynamic downloads.

Running SmartFrog

For operations, the SmartFrog daemon can be started on the command line, or as a service when the machine boots. For developers' use, there's a broad set of Ant tasks that can deploy and undeploy applications, start and stop the daemons, and even bring up a management window to view the system and its log. There are also Eclipse and NetBeans plugins for in-IDE work. We will use the Ant tasks, of course.

16.5   USING SMARTFROG WITH ANT

That's enough of a description of the tool. Let's use it to integrate deployment of local and clustered applications into the build.

Installing SmartFrog

The project's home page is http://smartfrog.org/. There you can find the latest releases, documentation, and links to the source code repository. When you are starting off with the tool, you will need

- SmartFrog Core: the base runtime
- SmartFrog Components: the equivalent of Ant tasks

The core comes with documentation and a set of Ant tasks for calling SmartFrog from Ant. Follow the instructions to install it and add its bin directory to the path if you want the command-line tools. If it isn't included in the distribution, download the sf-www JAR file containing web application support and add it to SFHOME/lib, where SFHOME is the SmartFrog directory.

Be aware that the tool is released under the Lesser GPL (LGPL) license. This has implications if you were to redistribute modified versions of the JAR files to third parties, but not if you only use the tool internally.

The Ant tasks

Table 16.4 lists the tool's Ant tasks. Two of these tasks, `<faultingwaitfor>` and `<functionaltest>` are general-purpose tasks used for testing SmartFrog itself. The rest are for starting and stopping daemons and for deploying, pinging, and undeploying applications.

To use them we need the SmartFrog JARs, including the `sf-tasks` JAR on the task's classpath. Ivy can do this with a new configuration, "smartfrog":

Table 16.4   The tasks built into the SmartFrog sf-tasks Antlib

Task name	Function
`<deploy>`	Deploy applications to a SmartFrog daemon.
`<gui>`	Start the SmartFrog editor application.
`<management-console>`	Start the management GUI, targeted at a named host.
`<parse>`	Parse a SmartFrog file and pre-validate it before deployment.
`<ping>`	Probe an application to verify it's working.
`<run>`	Run one or more applications in a new process.
`<sign>`	Sign JAR files with a SmartFrog certificate.
`<startdaemon>`	Start a SmartFrog daemon.
`<stopdaemon>`	Stop a SmartFrog daemon.
`<undeploy>`	Undeploy an application.
`<faultingwaitfor>`	A copy of `<waitfor>` that will fail on timeout.
`<functionaltest>`	A task that integrates startup, a `<waitfor>` condition, and a shutdown sequence into a `<junit>` run or other sequence of operations.

```
<dependency org="org.smartfrog" name="sf-www"
  rev="${smartfrog.version}"
  conf="smartfrog->default" />
<dependency org="org.smartfrog" name="sf-tasks"
  rev="${smartfrog.version}"
  conf="smartfrog->default"/>
<dependency org="org.smartfrog"name="sf-database"
  rev="${smartfrog.version}"
  conf="smartfrog->default"/>
```

As usual, Ivy's `<cachepath>` task sets up the classpath:

```
<target name="smartfrog-classpath"
    depends="ivy-resolve,tests-packaged">
  <ivy:cachepath pathid="smartfrog.libraries.classpath"
    conf="smartfrog"/>
  <path id="smartfrog.classpath">
    <path refid="smartfrog.libraries.classpath"/>
    <pathelement location="${test.jar}"/>
  </path>
</target>
```

This target depends on the `tests-packaged` target and adds the test classes as a JAR. This is in case we want to deploy a component that runs JUnit tests, integrating testing with the deployment. With this classpath set up, we can declare the tasks:

```
<target name="smartfrog-tasks" depends="smartfrog-classpath">
  <taskdef uri="antlib:org.smartfrog.tools.ant"
      classpathref="smartfrog.classpath"
      onerror="failall"/>
</target>
```

The `sf-tasks` JAR declares the tasks in an `antlib.xml` file under the URI `antlib:`
`org.smartfrog.tools.ant`. All tasks also support a nested `<classpath>` element for adding extra libraries to the classpath—but it's easier to declare the tasks with everything needed on the classpath.

16.5.1 Deploying with SmartFrog

SmartFrog deployment descriptors are files with the `.sf` extension. Although we've shown some examples of them, the full language and how to write deployment descriptors and components are beyond the scope of this book. We'll just deploy the descriptor to start the web application and JBoss, and deploy it from Ant. First, we need to declare the local configuration, which we do in listing 16.3. Listing 16.3 includes the file in listing 16.2 and makes it deployable by giving values to all the attributes that were marked TBD.

Listing 16.3 The SmartFrog deployment descriptor to deploy everything

```
#include "deploy/ch16-system-listing.sf"    ←❶

WinXPLaptop extends System {
    jboss.home "C:\\Java\\Apps\\jboss";
    jdk.home "C:\\Java\\jdk";                           ❷
    webapp:examples "C:\\antbook\\examples";
}

sfConfig extends WinXPLaptop {    ←❸
}
```

This descriptor takes the abstract system definition ❶ and fills in the system-specific values ❷. Finally, it declares the `sfConfig` template that names what is to be deployed ❸. This name is special; it and everything under it gets deployed.

In the build file, we need to identify this file and the host for the deployment:

```
<target name="smartfrog-ready"
  depends="smartfrog-tasks,deploy-properties"/>

<target name="deploy-properties" depends="init">
  <property name="deploy.host" value="localhost"/>
  <property name="application.name" value="${project.name}"/>
  <property name="deploy.sf"
    value="deploy/targets/ch16-winxp-laptop.sf"/>
  <property name="parse.quiet" value="true"/>
  <property name="deploy.jar"
    location="${build.dir}/ch16-sf-deploy.jar"/>
</target>
```

These properties deploy to the local host, with a descriptor explicitly bound to a specific machine. Other systems will have to point to their own descriptor via a build.properties file. The descriptors are all in the directory config/deploy, with machine-specific targets in the targets/ subdirectory. There are currently versions for Windows, Linux standalone, and a Linux cluster, all of which extend the same base configuration and change a few options. Figure 16.5 shows the structure.

We've split the files into two sets. General purpose .sf files contain configuration details for a specific part of the big system, such as JBoss, the database, and the MySQL drivers. In a separate directory, we've added system-specific configurations that hard-code in the locations of MySQL and JBoss on different platforms. Individual developers can add their own custom .sf files in this target's directory, targeting specific machines.

All of these configuration files need to be packaged into a JAR file, so that the operations can be given a JAR file they can sign and use in a secure SmartFrog environment—one in which the daemons only load classes and .sf files from signed JAR files. For now, we just package the JAR and skip the signing:

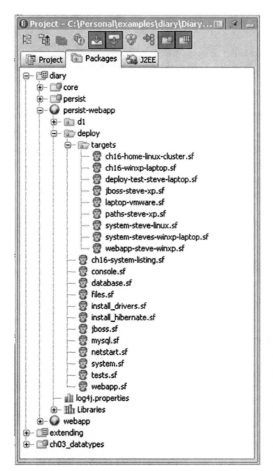

Figure 16.5
Package layout for deployment descriptors. Every descriptor is a resource in a Java package but is built into a separate JAR from the application. That lets us change this JAR and sign it without having to rebuild the application itself. Descriptors in the deploy. targets package are targeted at different machines, while those in the parent deploy package are the reusable templates.

```
<target name="deployment-jar" depends="deploy-properties">
  <jar destfile="${deploy.jar}">
    <fileset dir="config" includes="**/*.sf"/>
  </jar>
</target>
```

This target creates a new JAR file, `build/ch16-sf-deploy.jar`, which contains all of the deployment files for this project. We can deploy them or even check them for validity in advance of a deployment.

Preflight validation

We use the term *preflight checks* for the static validation of the files; it's a term derived from airplane safety checks:

```
<target name="preflight"
  depends="smartfrog-ready,deployment-jar"
  unless="skip.preflight"
  xmlns:sf="antlib:org.smartfrog.tools.ant">
  <sf:parse>
    <classpath>
      <pathelement location="${deploy.jar}"/>
    </classpath>
    <source file="config/${deploy.sf}"/>    ←❶
  </sf:parse>
</target>
```

The `<parse>` task parses the deployment descriptor ❶ and checks that all included files can be found and are syntactically correct. It checks that all attributes marked as TBD have been overwritten with valid data, and that there are no unresolved non-lazy references. Many components have an optional "schema" declaration that lists the type of some attributes and whether they are compulsory or optional. All such schemas are validated during this preflight phase:

```
preflight:

 [sf:parse] Parser - SmartFrog 3.10.00
 [sf:parse] ----------------------------------------------
 [sf:parse] -  Parsing: C:\antbook\diary\
   persist-webapp\config\deploy\targets\ch16-winxp-laptop.sf
 [sf:parse] ----------------------------------------------
 [sf:parse] STATUS REPORT: File: C:\antbook\diary\
   persist-webapp\config\deploy\targets\ch16-winxp-laptop.sf
 [sf:parse]    raw phase: OK   type phase: OK   place phase: OK
   function phase: OK   sfConfig phase: OK   link phase: OK
   predicate phase: OK, parsed in 3665 millisecs.
 [sf:parse] SFParse: SUCCESSFUL

BUILD SUCCESSFUL
Total time: 5 seconds
```

The tool doesn't check whether LAZY references resolve, because they can link to attributes that are created during deployment. This is one disadvantage of runtime binding—you find out what's missing only when you deploy.

Preflight checks are invaluable while working on the deployment descriptors themselves, after which point they mostly become a few seconds of delay. If the property skip.preflight is set, the check is skipped; developers can set this property once the descriptor is stable.

Starting the daemon

To actually deploy the application, we need a running daemon on the target host. One of the tasks, <run>, does a deployment in its own process, blocking Ant until it's finished. This task is easier to integrate with an Ant workflow, but it doesn't give you the option of deploying to a remote host. This makes it less useful than the <deploy> task, which can deploy to the host specified in the host attribute, once a daemon is running on the target system.

A SmartFrog daemon can be started on the command line by running the sfDaemon batch file/shell script:

```
>sfDaemon
SmartFrog 3.10.00
(C) Copyright 1998-2006 Hewlett-Packard Development Company, LP
Graphics mode available
SmartFrog ready... [rootProcess:3800]
```

At this point, the GUI opens up and displays a log window. Closing this window will shut down the daemon. A menu action will bring up the management console, which shows all deployed components and lets developers view their attributes or terminate all or part of a deployed application.

The <startdaemon> task can start the daemon from inside Ant. It doesn't bring up the logging window, so it's useful for unattended operations.

```
<target name="startdaemon" depends="smartfrog-ready"
  xmlns:sf="antlib:org.smartfrog.tools.ant">
  <sf:startdaemon spawn="true">
    <sysproperty
      key="com.sun.management.jmxremote" value="true"/>     ❶
    <propertyfile file="runtime.properties" optional="true"/>     ❷
    <classpath refid="smartfrog.classpath"/>
  </sf:startdaemon>
</target>
```

JVM properties can be set with the <sysproperty> keyword, here used to make the process accessible to the JDK's jconsole program ❶. The <propertyfile> element identifies a file of properties, here marked with optional="true" to indicate that it doesn't have to be present ❷. It's the deployment equivalent of the tradition of the <property file="build.properties"/> declaration in build files, which allow per-developer overrides. These properties let developers provide late binding information outside any descriptor. The PROPERTY and IPROPERTY references resolve string or integer properties from either the process starting the deployment or, if LAZY, the running daemon itself:

```
host PROPERTY target.hostname;     ⟵  Task properties
port IPROPERTY target.port;    ⟵  Task property as integer
temp.dir LAZY PROPERTY java.io.tmpdir;    ⟵  Property in the daemon process
```

This property binding can pass extra information down or pick up state information about the target host, such as the value of the java.io.tmpdir temporary directory property. It's the final bit of customization.

Stopping the daemon

The `<stopdaemon>` task can shut down a local or remote daemon:

```
<target name="stopdaemon" depends="smartfrog-ready"
  description="shutdown smartfrog"
  xmlns:sf="antlib:org.smartfrog.tools.ant">
  <sf:stopdaemon
    failonerror="false"
    host="${deploy.host}"
    timeout="30000"/>
</target>
```

This task will terminate the daemon if it's running:

```
stopdaemon:
[sf:stopdaemon] SmartFrog 3.10.00
[sf:stopdaemon] SmartFrog daemon terminated
[sf:stopdaemon]  - Successfully terminated: 'rootProcess',
  host:localhost

BUILD SUCCESSFUL
```

The failonerror attribute is set to false because it doesn't normally matter if the daemon is already stopped.

Daemons listen for RMI messages on port 3800, so the `<socket>` condition can probe for a running daemon in the `<fail>` or `<waitfor>` tasks. The SmartFrog task suite includes a new task, `<faultingwaitfor>`, that fails the build if the nested condition isn't met:

```
<target name="assert-daemon-running" depends="smartfrog-ready"
  xmlns:sf="antlib:org.smartfrog.tools.ant">
  <sf:faultingwaitfor maxwait="10">
    <socket server="localhost" port="3800"/>
  </sf:faultingwaitfor>
</target>
```

If the task times out without the condition being met, it throws an exception:

```
assert-daemon-running:

BUILD FAILED
    Timeout while waiting for conditions to be met
```

Clearly, we need to go back and run the daemon before deploying.

16.5.2 Deploying with the <deploy> task

After the descriptors are packaged and preflight-successful and after the daemon is started, we can deploy:

```
<target name="deploy"
        depends="preflight,ready-to-deploy"
        description="deploy"
    xmlns:sf="antlib:org.smartfrog.tools.ant">
  <sf:deploy host="${deploy.host}"
    timeout="30000">
    <classpath>
      <pathelement location="${deploy.jar}"/>
    </classpath>
    <application name="${application.name}"
      descriptor="${deploy.sf}"/>
  </sf:deploy>
</target>
```

The task parses the descriptor and expands it completely, resolving all non-LAZY references. It then connects to the target daemon and deploys the descriptor:

```
deploy:
[sf:deploy] SmartFrog 3.10.00
[sf:deploy]  - Successfully deployed:
    'HOST Zermatt:rootProcess:diary',
    [deploy/targets/ch16-winxp-laptop.sf],  host:localhost

BUILD SUCCESSFUL
Total time: 16 seconds
```

Once the expanded and resolved descriptor is submitted to the daemon, the task returns. The deployment is still going on, as the components declared in it get moved through their lifecycle to the instantiated, initialized, and—finally—the running state. We can check this state through the management console.

Checking on the application

We can check what is going on with the deployed application by starting the management console. This lets us see what the actual runtime attributes are and what the application's current state is:

```
<target name="console" depends="smartfrog-ready">
  <sf:management-console spawn="true"/>
</target>
```

This brings up the application of figure 16.6 to view the deployed applications.

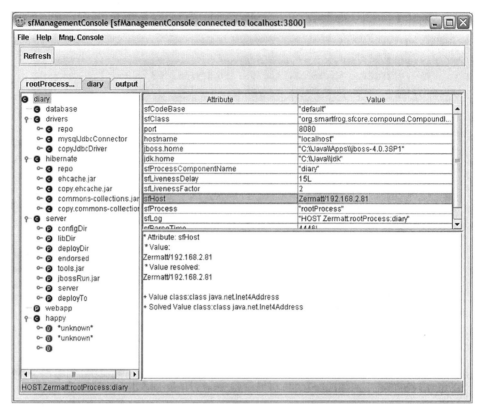

Figure 16.6 The management console, showing the status of the deployed application. The elements under the happy component have not yet been deployed, as it delays for a minute before starting happy page checks.

The console lets you view and manipulate the graph, terminating components or detaching parts of the tree from their parents, so that they can live a separate life.

The basic check of pinging an application to verify that it's alive is so common that it can be run from Ant; there's no need to use the console.

Pinging an application

The <ping> task probes an application to see if it's healthy:

```
<target name="ping" depends="smartfrog-ready"
  description="shutdown smartfrog"
  xmlns:sf="antlib:org.smartfrog.tools.ant">
  <sf:ping application="${application.name}"
    host="${deploy.host}"
    timeout="30000"/>
</target>
```

If the daemon isn't reachable or if the application isn't running, then the task fails:

```
ping:
   [sf:ping] SmartFrog 3.10.00
   [sf:ping] - FAILED when trying PING of 'diary', host:localhost
   [sf:ping]     Result:
   [sf:ping]       * Exception: 'SmartFrogResolutionException::
                    Unresolved Reference: diary
   [sf:ping]         source: HOST Zermatt:rootProcess
   [sf:ping]         path(25)
   [sf:ping]         Cause: Reference not found'
```

This message indicates that there was an unresolvable reference, diary, presumably because there was no active application called "diary." A successful ping verifies that the application is present and healthy:

```
ping:
   [sf:ping] SmartFrog 3.10.00
   [sf:ping] -"diary" was successfully contacted in "localhost".
           Ping time :0.0 seconds
BUILD SUCCESSFUL
Total time: 6 seconds
```

Being able to integrate health checks—such as the happy page checks—into the application's deployment descriptor transforms the notion of what constitutes a valid deployment. All the static and runtime configuration information from the deployment can feed straight into health checks, checks that can be performed by the framework.

Undeployment

Eventually, we need to undeploy the application. The <undeploy> task handles that:

```
<target name="undeploy" depends="smartfrog-ready"
      description="deploy">
  <sf:undeploy classpathref="smartfrog.classpath"
    host="${deploy.host}"
    application="${application.name}"/>
</target>
```

This task triggers a clean termination of the application. All components that have termination routines will do their work. Forked Java and native processes will be stopped, files and directories cleaned up, databases taken offline. The system is returned to its original state.

16.5.3   Summary of SmartFrog

We've just used SmartFrog to deploy our database, application server, and application. With the appropriate configuration files, it can deploy to the local system or to a nearby cluster.

SmartFrog is probably the most advanced distributed deployment framework available and, being open source, is free for anyone to use. However, it does take a bit of time to become familiar with the tool, the language, and the error messages. Once you've learned your way around, you can use it to install, configure, and run applications that span one machine or whole "server farms" of hundreds of machines.

Using the tool, we can trigger deployment from our builds, either to a developer's system or to a cluster of test servers, real or virtual. That not only enables us to automate deployment to the development systems, but to the production systems as well. With automated deployment integrated into the build process, we can then move to a deployment-centric build-and-test cycle.

16.6 EMBRACING DEPLOYMENT

This chapter has looked at how to deploy successfully, by automating deployment and integrating it into the build cycle. But just adding new development tools isn't enough; the process must adapt. Just as adding unit testing to a build file added testing to our edit-and-build cycle, adding deployment can change how we deliver software.

When software is handed off to an operations team, the classic "waterfall" development process starts sneaking in, as figure 16.7 shows.

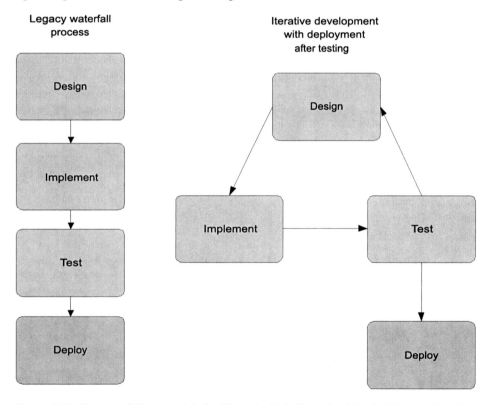

Figure 16.7 The waterfall process is inflexible and widely discredited. But look how an iterative development cycle can revert to a waterfall at the final stage.

By leaving deployment as an afterthought, you don't get feedback from the deployment process or the live system, feedback that could be used to adapt the application to make it easier to deploy and manage. The result can be a hard-to-deploy application that doesn't suit the needs of the operations team.

What can be done? How about integrating deployment with testing and the continuous integration process? The goal is to produce a development lifecycle more like figure 16.8, in which deployment is part of the normal develop-and-test loop.

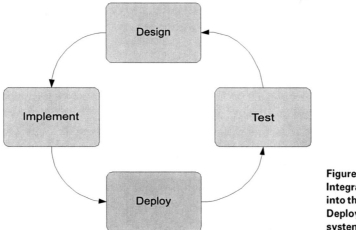

**Figure 16.8
Integrating deployment
into the development cycle.
Deploy to production
systems, then test.**

In this lifecycle, the operations team owns the test hosts. Developers deploy to those machines, running their tests on or against them. This ensures that operations get the experience of deploying and managing the application, while developers can write code that works on the production systems.

There's a small logistical problem here: how to integrate deployment with a test run. We could have Ant block until a condition indicates the application is deployed, and run `<junit>` and `<junitreport>` once the `<get>` indicates the site is live. SmartFrog's own `<functionaltest>` task can do this.

Alternatively, we can take advantage of the fact that SmartFrog deploys anything—including tests! A JUnit test run is just something else to deploy on a host on the network, as is a test listener component to create HTML pages from the results. The `JUnitTestSuite` component takes a list of JUnit 3.8.x tests, tests it can run:

```
HttpUnitTests extends extends JUnitTestSuite  {
  server.url TBD;
  name "HttpUnitTests";
  package "dl.webapp.test";
  properties [["server.url",server.url]];      ← JVM Properties
  classes ["EventFeedTest",          ┌ A list of JUnit test case
    "HappyTagTest",                  │ classes in the named package
    "IndexTest"];
}
```

This component can be deployed under a `TestRunner` component, which can run tests in different processes or on different hosts, relaying the results to a test listener. The HTML test listener creates XHTML pages as the results come in: there's no need to wait for the whole run to finish before the results are created. Admittedly, the pages are not very pretty—there's clearly scope for improving the presentation and analysis of the test results collected from tens or hundreds of systems. But it's a start and, being live, it's convenient on big test runs.

Moving deployment into the core development cycle isn't easy. Developers will have to work with operations earlier than normal; operations have to start supporting many more systems earlier on. This is exactly why you need to do it: the two teams need to work together right from the outset of a project!

Continuous deployment

With deployment automated and testing integrated with the deployment, then one more action becomes possible. The team's continuous integration server can redeploy the application and its functional tests. It could even be set up to redeploy to production on a nightly basis if the functional tests pass, of course!

If you intend to explore this possibility, here's some advice:

- Have the production deployment driven off a tagged branch. This stops code from being released accidentally.

- Restrict the update frequency to a limited rate, such as once per day. If your customers think you can roll out a patch in half an hour, they will demand all bugs fixed within an hour. Having a delay built in to the process reduces stress and encourages better fixes.

- Have a good rollback mechanism and test it.

This whole notion of continuous deployment goes hand in hand with the "everlasting beta" phenomenon of web site development, in which the site is never stable and new features appear daily. It goes even better with web service development, in which you are trying to develop a public API for use by external callers. Just as agile development encourages developers to work with the customers, agile web site and service development requires the team to integrate with operations, and to rapidly evolve the live application based on the experience of real users. Integrating deployment into the continuous integration process makes agile development possible, while exposing a web site or service to outside callers.

16.7 SUMMARY

We've explored the challenges of deploying to production servers and have proposed some ways to survive that phase of a project:

1 Start working on deployment early.
2 Work with operations.

3 Target the production system.

4 Automate deployment.

5 Test deployment.

6 Track deployment defects.

Ant's <sql> task can set up a database setup, while SmartFrog can completely automate the deployment of complex applications. SmartFrog can transform how developers and operations teams deploy things, and it lets you integrate deployment into the build cycle.

We've closed with the idea of continuous deployment—having the continuous integration server handle deployment to the staging and perhaps even the production system. This is one of the many leading-edge techniques you can explore once you have deployment under control.

And that's it! We've reached the end of the part of the book that covers applying Ant. We started the section with a build file for a single library, and we've gone through third-party tasks and Antlibs. We've looked at large projects with multiple-build files, using Ivy for dependency management, and we've applied these techniques to build a web application and then an Enterprise Java application. Then we've shown how to use a continuous integration server to build and test everything, before getting into the world of automated deployment.

The remaining two chapters go low-level into Ant's own source code to look at how to extend Ant with new tasks, datatypes, and resources.

PART **3**

Extending Ant

If you're pushing the limits of Ant's built-in capabilities, chapters 17 and 18 are for you. We first cover writing custom Ant tasks and the essentials of Ant's API. Then, we explore scripting inside Ant build files and, finally, creating your own datatypes. This section enables you to extend Ant to meet the specific needs of your projects and to provide redistributable tasks for your application.

CHAPTER 17

Writing Ant tasks

There comes a moment where it becomes clear that Ant doesn't do everything you need. It may be that something minor is missing, such as not being able to pass all the options you want to <junit> or <java>. It may be that something major is absent, like having no way to run a custom test framework. It may even be that a common Ant task doesn't work quite right. This happens to everyone and there's always a solution.

Ant can be extended through Java classes, and it takes only a small amount of Java coding to write a new Ant task. If the problem lies in the actual Ant source itself, then the fact that an entire Ant source tree is a download away comes into play. If Ant doesn't work right, then it can be fixed. However, this isn't something we advocate—not yet. Ant can be extended without rebuilding it, in many ways:

- Custom tasks, written in Java or a scripting language
- Custom datatypes
- Custom listeners, loggers, filters, selectors, and mappers
- Hosting Ant inside another Java application

This chapter will show you how to write tasks in Java. We'll look at the other extension mechanisms in chapter 18, because knowing how Ant tasks work and understanding the Ant API are the precursors to all extensions of Ant.

17.1 WHAT EXACTLY IS AN ANT TASK?

If a task is written for a project's own use, it is a *custom task*. When used by other projects, it becomes a *third-party task*, and if it becomes part of Ant's own source tree, it becomes a *built-in task*. We've been using the latter two task types throughout the book, but now it's time to write our own, custom tasks.

Here's what we have to do:

1 Write a new class that extends Ant's Task class.

2 Add methods that Ant can use to set attributes and add elements.

3 Write an execute() method that does something useful.

All Ant tasks are implemented by a Java class that extends the org.apache .tools.ant.Task class, overriding the void execute() method to do useful work. Sometimes <macrodef>, <presetdef>, and the scripting languages we will look at in chapter 18 define tasks differently, but behind the scenes a subclass of Task is doing the work. Here's a first task, one that prints out a message:

```
package org.antbook.tasks;

import org.apache.tools.ant.Task;

public class MessageTask extends Task {

    private String message = "";

    public void setMessage(String message) {
        this.message = message;
    }

    @Override
    public void execute() {
        log(message);
    }
}
```

In a build file that compiles the task, we can use the task after it's been compiled by declaring it just as we do for third-party tasks:

```
<target name="messagetask" depends="compile">
  <taskdef name="message"
           classname="org.antbook.tasks.MessageTask"
           classpath="${build.classes.dir}"/>

  <property name="the.message" value="blue scooter"/>
  <message message="${the.message}"/>
</target>
```

Running this target gives the following results:

```
messagetask:
  [message] blue scooter
```

This task is similar to `<echo>` and does nothing but log the value assigned to the `message` attribute. Ant saw that the build file set the `message` attribute and matched that to the `setMessage(String)` method on the task. It then called that method with the expanded string. Before the task saw the attribute, Ant had already expanded the properties. The task printed its output through the `Task.log` method. This is part of Ant's API for tasks: a method in the parent class to log text.

This little task, then, is the foundation of all custom Ant tasks. It has an attribute that Ant supports through introspection and an `execute()` method that does some work through Ant's APIs. Everything else is just "feature creep."

In this chapter we're going explore that feature creep—Ant's task model and API. We'll show the reader how to write and test Ant tasks. Authors of existing Ant tasks should read this chapter, because the testing mechanism and resource API is new—everyone will learn something!

Let's start by looking at how Ant configures and runs a task.

17.1.1 The life of a task

Ant's mapping from XML task declarations to Java classes is a miracle of data binding. We will soon show you how attributes and elements are mapped to Java methods, but before that comes the task lifecycle. There are different stages in the processing of a build file, and the objects that implement tasks are used throughout the stages. Here's how Ant executes a task:

1. When Ant parses the build file, it creates an instance of the task's implementation class for every declaration of the task in the file.

2. Ant then calls methods on the task to tell it about its hosting project and target, as well as which line of the build file contains it.

3. Ant calls the `init()` method of the `Task` class. Most tasks don't override this method.

4. Ant executes the targets in the order it chooses.

5. The tasks inside a target are executed one by one. For each task

   a. Ant configures it with the attribute and element values in the build file, using reflection.

   b. Ant calls the task's `execute()` method.

   c. If any method called throws a `BuildException`, the task has failed. Unless it's somehow caught, that failure halts the build.

   d. Instantiated tasks remain around after they're executed; they may be executed more than once in some circumstances.

Ant requires all tasks to extend its `org.apache.tools.ant.Task` class. It's possible to declare a class that doesn't extend this class as a task; Ant uses a proxy class in this situation. However, such a task will not have access to most of Ant's API, so it is of limited use. Ant's API is the real Ant—the language behind the XML and something tasks make full use of—hence something task developers need to know.

17.2   INTRODUCING ANT'S JAVA API

Behind all Ant tasks comes Ant's API. You don't need to understand all of the classes and structures that make up the Ant codebase, but several key classes are worth knowing about, as they crop up frequently. With Ant's source code being open, it's easy to learn Ant's secrets by looking at the source code and its JavaDocs.

Figure 17.1 shows the main Ant classes. A `Project` hosts `Target` and `Task` instances; targets (and any other `TaskContainer`) can also contain tasks. Task classes are themselves extensions of the abstract `ProjectComponent` class, which is an indirect parent of everything from datatypes to conditions.

There also are a few utility classes that crop up repeatedly, `BuildException` being one of them. Let's take a quick look at some of the main methods in the core classes. Consult the JavaDocs and the source for the full details.

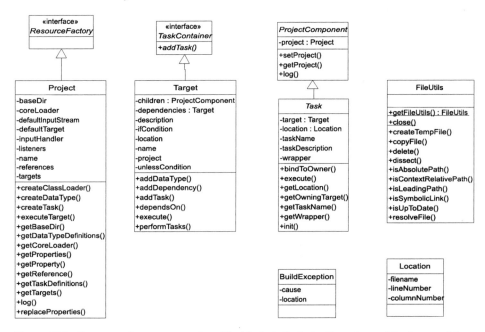

Figure 17.1   Common classes encountered inside Ant. Projects, Targets, and Tasks map 1:1 with the <project>, <target>, and task declarations. The other interfaces and classes are implementation details.

Project

The centerpiece of any build is the project, implemented by the `org.apache`
`.tools.ant.Project` class. With a project reference, you can run targets, read
and write Ant properties, or even add new targets and tasks. A project routes all I/O in
the build, from logged messages to `System.out`, `System.in`, and `System.err`.
It's here that listeners, loggers, and input handlers integrate with Ant.

The project holds the graph of targets and tasks; there are operations to manipulate this graph. Other methods add or retrieve references, create tasks and types, and
log output messages. These references include all those datatypes that are given `id`
values, so that they can later be retrieved using `refid` references—filesets, paths, and
the like.

void addReference(String referenceName, Object value)

This method maps the object to a reference ID in the project, so that when a `refid`
attribute is resolved, the registered reference is returned. All Ant datatypes given an `id`
attribute are registered by the Ant runtime, so they can be resolved in a task. Many
other things internal to Ant are stored as references. It's the best way to add the private
state to a project. For example, the class that helps a project manage properties is
stored as a reference under the name `ant.PropertyHelper`. If you add new private references to a project, pick names that are sufficiently obscure that nobody uses
them for datatype references. Ant's built-in tasks usually prefix all references with
`ant.` and then follow with the task name.

AntClassLoader createClassLoader(Path path)

This method creates an `AntClassLoader` instance classloader from the supplied
path. It's how Ant creates separate classloaders for different tasks and programs run
within Ant.

Task createTask(String name)

This method creates a task with the given name. For example, a Java task instance
could be created in an operation such as

```
Java javatask=(Java)getProject().createTask("java");
```

The trouble with this approach is that it assumes that the type of the task `<java>`
will always be that of the Java task, `org.apache.tools.ant.tasks.Java`.
The moment someone uses `<presetdef>` to redefine the `<java>` task, (perhaps to
give it a new default), its type changes, breaking code inside other tasks. Ant itself had
to undergo a major cleanup once this problem was noticed. Current code just creates
an instance and then configures it.

```
Java javatask=new Java();
javatask.bindToOwner(this);
```

The `bindToOwner()` call copies all binding information from the current task. If
you forget to do this, the created task will probably throw an exception.

Object createDataType(String typeName)
This call creates a datatype of the given name, such as a `<fileset>`:

```
FileSet fileset=getProject().createDatatType("fileset");
```

Again, the warnings of the `createTask()` method apply; this method is rarely used in Ant's own source. Instead, a `new FileSet()` operation is followed by the method called to bind the created class to the project instance.

void executeTarget(String targetName)
This method executes a named target and all its dependencies. This is how Ant runs targets and how tasks like `<ant>`, `<subant>`, and `<antcall>` run different targets.

Hashtable getProperties()
This call returns a copy of the current set of properties. Altering these properties doesn't affect the property values in the project.

String getProperty(String name)
The `getProperty` method returns the value of an Ant property, or `null` if it isn't defined. Ant automatically expands properties in attributes before handing the value to the task, so this method is rarely needed. Tasks that implement `if=` and `unless=` tests for properties use this method.

public Object getReference(String key)
Use this method to look up a reference; return the cached value or null if there is no match.

String replaceProperties(String value)
Here you can expand all properties in a string, returning a new string. This method can be used to patch up any text between the tags of an XML element as, unlike attributes, that text is not automatically expanded.

void log(String message, int msgLevel)
With this method, you can log a message at a certain level. Classes that know which project they belong to, but not which task they are working with, sometimes use this method.

void log(Task task, String message, int msgLevel)
This call logs a message as coming from a particular task. This is what `Task.log()` delegates to.

void setNewProperty(String name, String value)
This method assigns a value to a property. Immutability is enforced here: the property will not be changed if it already exists.

Target

The `Target` class implements the `TaskContainer` interface, telling Ant that it supports tasks nested inside. Targets contain all the information they were given in the XML file—name, depends, `description`, `if`, `unless`—and a list of nested `ProjectComponent` instances. They have a link back to the owning project, their location in the build file, and a list of all the targets that they depend on.

Custom tasks rarely need to make calls on their containing target; they cannot even rely on there being one. Some tasks do look through a project for a specific target and invoke it, using `Project.executeTarget()`.

ProjectComponent

`ProjectComponent` is an abstract base class for anything that can be declared inside a build file. Two direct descendants are the `Task` and `Datatype` classes, as are conditions.

`Project getProject()`

This call returns the project in which the component is executing. This will never be null unless whoever created the task forgot to bind it to the project.

`log(String msg, int msgLevel)` and `log(String msg)`

These log methods forward messages to the `Project` log methods, adding the name of the task. There are five logging levels, listed in descending priority in table 17.1. The basic `log(String)` method logs at the `Project.MSG_INFO` level.

Table 17.1   The mapping from API log levels to build file output levels

Project constant	Description	`<echo>` level
MSG_ERR	Error messages visible at all logging levels	error
MSG_WARN	Warning messages visible at -quiet and below	warn
MSG_INFO	Messages visible by default; at -info	info
MSG_VERBOSE	Messages visible at the -verbose log level	verbose
MSG_DEBUG	Debug messages printed in -debug runs	debug

A `BuildLogger` is capable of filtering the output based on the logging level selected. Normally, tasks print errors and warnings at the relevant levels, diagnostics for build file authors at the verbose level, and internal task debugging information at the lower debug level.

Tasks should normally log liberally, especially at the verbose level, showing the details of what's going on. The `MSG_INFO` level shouldn't be over-used, as it's seen by default. Too many built-in tasks over-log at this level.

The `void setProject(Project project)` method binds a `Project-Component` to a `Project` instance. It's done very early in component initialization.

Whenever a task creates anything that is a subclass of `ProjectComponent`, it should bind it to the task's own project through a call to `setProject()`.

Task

The abstract `Task` class is the base class for Ant tasks and the main unit of work during an Ant build. Most custom tasks extend this class and, at a minimum, implement their own `execute` method. Being an extension of `ProjectComponent`, the `getProject()` and `log()` methods are there to provide access to the owning `Project` and to log messages.

When a task creates a new task to delegate some work, it should call the `bindToOwner(Task owner)` method to propagate shared information—the hosting project, the task name and location, and other things.

It's important to use this method when creating tasks through their constructors, rather than by calling `Project.createTask()`, which, as mentioned earlier, can break if the build uses `<presetdef>` or `<macrodef>` to redefine existing tasks. The robust way to create a task is as follows:

```
Java javaTask=new Java();
javaTask.bindToOwner(this);
javaTask.init();
```

After the `init()` call, you can proceed to configure it and then finally call `execute()`. There's a full example of this delegation in work in section 17.8.

void execute()

Here's where it all happens! The `execute()` method is the heart of a task. At the point this method is called, Ant will have passed down to the task information all attributes and nested content. The `execute` method should validate the task's configuration, then do the requested work.

Location getLocation()

With this call, Ant returns the location of this task—the build file and the task's position within it. If this call is set to `Location.UNKNOWN_LOCATION`, the task doesn't know where it is.

Target getOwningTarget()

This is a method that returns the `Target` that contains this task. If it's `null`, then the task was not declared inside any target: you cannot rely on tasks having an owning target.

void init()

The `init` method is called when Ant encounters a task during the parsing phase of the build file. Tasks that need to do early initialization can override it. Why do that instead of doing the work in the constructor? Because at the time the `init()` method is called, the task has been bound to its owning project. The task can safely do work that involves a `Project` instance.

BuildException

This is probably the most ubiquitous of all Ant classes, and it's used to signal any kind of problem. The class is a `RuntimeException`, which means that it doesn't need to be declared on methods. Any method that Ant calls can throw a `BuildException`. It's the underpinning of Ant's failure-handling, such as in the following attribute setter:

```
public void setTimeout(int seconds) {
    if(seconds<0) {
        throw new BuildException("Positive timeouts only");
    }
    Timeout=seconds;
}
```

Whenever any method throws a `BuildException`, it forces a build failure, with the exception's message being displayed to the user. Any task or datatype that needs to handle problems should be prepared to use a `finally{}` clause to clean up regardless of what happened.

The class has a `Location` attribute that's set to the location in the build file that's at fault. Ant sets this attribute automatically.

17.2.1   Ant's utility classes

Ant contains a set of utility classes that provide common operations for task authors to use. It is much better to use these library classes instead of reimplementing their code, as they are stable, well-tested, and work well across different Java versions. Utility classes include the following:

ClasspathUtils

This can create a classpath and load classes from it. Tasks that dynamically load new classes from user-supplied classpaths need this. There's also a `LoaderUtils` class to provide some extra classloader-related operations.

DateUtils

This class simplifies working with dates, with methods to parse ISO8601 dates and date-time strings down to `java.util.Date` instances.

JavaEnvUtils

This useful class contains operations to work with the JRE and JDK, including determining JRE version and executing programs in the JRE. The static method `getJavaVersionNumber()` returns the version number, "5" for Java1.5, while the `getJdkExecutable(String)` and `getJreExecutable(String)` methods build up platform-specific paths to JDK programs.

FileUtils

The `FileUtils` class is one of the most commonly used utility classes. It contains filesystem support that adapts itself for different platforms, with operations to copy files, resolve filenames, split paths, and convert between filenames and URLs. Call `FileUtils.getFileUtils()` to get a shared instance.

static void close(Writer)

This static method closes the supplied Java I/O class, be it a `Writer`, `Reader`, `InputStream`, or `OutputStream`, catching any `IOException` thrown. If the argument is `null`, nothing happens. This method appears everywhere Ant methods clean up open files, in the finally clause. A `FileUtils.close(stream)` call will safely close the supplied parameter.

copyFile(File source, File dest)

This is a method to copy a file, passing in the source and destination files. Overloaded variations support extra parameters, including overwrite flags, whether to copy timestamps, and a `FilterSetCollection` containing filters to apply during the copy.

boolean isUpToDate(File source, File dest)

This test compares the dates of two files, returning `true` if the destination file is considered up-to-date with the source file. This test compensates for platform-specific timestamp granularities.

File resolveFile(File file, String filename)

This invaluable method resolves and normalizes a file path relative to another `File` if the `filename` isn't already an absolute path. There's a lot of platform-specific logic here.

StringUtils

This class contains some minor `String` and `StringBuffer` operations, most importantly one to split up a `String` into a `Vector` of elements based on a separator. To break up a `String` by lines, use `"\n"` as the separator.

ResourceUtils

This is a utility class providing operations that work on resources, rather than just files. There are operations to compare resources for text or binary equality, `contentEquals()` and `compareContent()`, and others, including `copyResource()` to copy resources.

One of the most interesting methods is the `selectOutOfDateSources()` method, which returns an array listing all resources that are out of date with their destination. Tasks can use this method to select resources for processing, e.g., copying, compiling, or some other action that brings the destination up-to-date.

17.3 A USEFUL TASK: <FILESIZE>

Enough API coverage. It's time to write a useful task. How about a task that sets a property to the size of the file or files passed in? This task—let's call it <filesize>—will have two attributes:

Attribute	Function	Required?
Property	The name of a property in which to store the result	Yes
File	The file to analyze	Yes, and the file must exist

Later, in section 17.6, we'll extend the task to take multiple files as nested elements.

17.3.1 Writing the task

Listing 17.1 shows the task in its entirety. There is no init() for initialization; all the work is done in the execute() method, which first checks that it's configured right and that the file exists, and then sets a property to the size of the file. If any of the preconditions aren't met, Ant throws a BuildException.

Listing 17.1 A task to set a property to the size of a file

```
package org.antbook.tasks.filesize;
import org.apache.tools.ant.Task;
import org.apache.tools.ant.BuildException;
import org.apache.tools.ant.Project;
import java.io.File;

public class FilesizeTask extends Task {
    private String property;
    private File file;

    public void setProperty(String property) {
        this.property = property;
    }

    public void setFile(File file) {
        this.file = file;
    }

    public void execute() throws BuildException {
        if(property==null) {
            throw new BuildException("No property");
        }
        if(file==null) {
            throw new BuildException("No file");
        }
        if(!file.exists()) {
            throw new BuildException("Not found: "+file);
        }
```

```
        long size = file.length();
        log("The size of "+file+" is "+size, Project.MSG_DEBUG);    ◄─❶
        getProject().setNewProperty(property,                  ❷
                        Long.toString(size));
    }
}
```

If the task is set up correctly, the file's size is evaluated, the result logged at the debug level ❶, and then `Project.setNewProperty()` is called to set the property to the value ❷.

This is a fully functional task, with validation and logging in only thirty-five lines. There is just one outstanding question. The task works with its `file` and `property` fields. How are they set? How is this going to work? What's going on?

The answer is "magic," or code complex enough that it may as well be. Ant is automatically translating strings in XML attributes to strongly typed Java classes. It's calling the bean-style setters on the class, then the `execute()` method—all through Java reflection!

Let's run it and see if it works.

Building the <filesize> task

Compiling this new task is easy; listing 17.2 shows the build file to compile and run the task.

Listing 17.2 The build file for the <filesize> task

```
<project name="filesize" default="default">
  <property name="build.dir" location="build"/>

  <target name="init">
    <mkdir dir="${build.dir}"/>
  </target>

  <target name="compile" depends="init">
    <javac srcdir="src" destdir="${build.dir}"/>            ❶
  </target>

  <target name="define" >
    <taskdef name="filesize"
      uri="http://antbook.org/"
      classname="org.antbook.tasks.filesize.FilesizeTask"    ❷
      classpath="${build.dir}"/>
  </target>

  <target name="ready-to-run" depends="compile,define"/>

  <target name="filesize" depends="ready-to-run"
      xmlns:book="http://antbook.org/">
```

```
      <book:filesize/>
  </target>

  <target name="clean">
    <delete dir="${build.dir}"/>
  </target>

  <target name="default" depends="filesize"/>

</project>
```

The `compile` target compiles the task ❶, and the `define` target defines it in its own namespace ❷. That target doesn't depend on the compile stage, because we want to be able to define the task without triggering a rebuild; this will be useful when testing. However, the `filesize` target *does* depend on the compilation stage, so when it's run it should execute the new task.

Running the task

The `filesize` target builds, defines, then calls our new task without any parameters. What's going to happen? There's one way to find out:

```
>ant filesize
Buildfile: build.xml

init:

compile:
  [javac] Compiling 1 source file to /home/ant/filesize/first/build

define:

filesize:

BUILD FAILED
/home/ant/filesize/first/build.xml:24: No property

Total time: 3 seconds
```

It didn't work. Of course not: the task wasn't configured because we haven't gotten Ant to do that yet!

17.3.2 How Ant configures tasks

Tasks are described in a build file as XML data. When Ant encounters a new XML element, it looks up its list of types and creates an instance of the Java class registered for that element. That's the easy part.

The hard part is configuring that instance, passing the XML attributes, nested elements, and body text to the task. Ant handles this using reflection, mapping the XML values to Java types, and then passing them to the instance that it's configuring.

Ant scans the class for specially named methods and invokes them with the data from the build file. It supports both XML attributes and elements. Attributes are simpler, and we'll cover them first.

Ignoring XML namespaces, an XML attribute consists of a name and a string value. Ant takes the value of each attribute and expands all properties with `Project.replaceProperties()` to create the expanded string. It searches for all methods with the name of the attribute prefixed by "set". For our `<filesize>` task, the `property` attribute is mapped to the `setProperty` method:

```
public void setProperty(String property) {
    this.property = property;
}
```

A `String` parameter is the most straightforward attribute type since it can be set directly to the text:

```
<filesize property="new.property"/>
```

A `String` type is only the first of many types that can be used, though. Most of the main Java types can be passed in.

Boolean values

Many times a task simply needs to have a true/false option. By having your setter parameter take a `boolean` or `java.lang.Boolean` value, your task will get `true` (or `Boolean.TRUE`) if the value is yes, on, or true, and `false` (or `Boolean.FALSE`) otherwise.

```
private boolean failonerror = false;

public void setFailonerror(boolean failonerror) {
    this.failonerror = failonerror;
}
```

The task used in the build file is

```
<book:setter failonerror="on"/>
```

Because of implicit attribute expansion, our task doesn't know the difference when the build file writer sets the attribute using a property:

```
<property name="fail.mode" value="true"/>
<book:setter failonerror="${fail.mode}"/>
```

The `setFailonerror` method is invoked with `true` in both cases.

Accepting numbers

Ant supports attributes that accept all the Java primitives numbers and their `Object` equivalents:

```
byte / java.lang.Byte
short / java.lang.Short
```

```
int / java.lang.Integer
long / java.lang.Long
float / java.lang.Float
double / java.lang.Double
```

If Ant cannot convert the attribute value to the desired type, a `NumberFormat-Exception` will be thrown, halting the build.

A single character

If you ever need a single character, implement a setter method that takes a `char` or `java.lang.Character` type. The character passed in will be the first character of the attribute value; Ant will ignore any additional characters.

Files or directories

Many tasks take a file or directory as an attribute. If a task implements a setter with a `java.io.File` parameter, Ant will configure the task with `File` instances. Ant converts the path string in the XML file to the local format, resolves any relative path against the project's base directory, then calls the task's setter method with a `File` object representing the path. For `<filesize>`, the `setFile()` method means that the task has a `file` attribute:

```
public void setFile(File file) {
    this.file = file;
}
```

The task must do its own validation if it wants to restrict the argument to only a directory or only a normal file.

17.3.3 Configuring the <filesize> task

Now let's look at configuring the `<filesize>` task. It's already got the setters it needs—we just need to pass the information down as attributes:

```
<target name="filesize2"
    depends="ready-to-run"
    xmlns:book="http://antbook.org/">
  <book:filesize property="size" file="${ant.file}"/>
  <echo>size = ${size}</echo>
</target>
```

Run this and we see the result we've been waiting for:

```
filesize2:
    [echo] size = 1074

BUILD SUCCESSFUL
```

There we have it—a fully functional task. It has attributes set by Ant, and when it runs, it sets a property in the project. This is a genuine Ant task. A bit of packaging and it will be ready for redistribution. Oh, and the tests of course—we mustn't forget those!

17.4   TESTING TASKS WITH ANTUNIT

All of the Java code in this book comes with tests. Should Ant tasks be any different? Of course not! But how do you test an Ant task?

The original technique was to write JUnit tests that extended the `org.apache` `.tools.ant.BuildFileTest` base class. Each test method would run different targets in the same build file, then check the state of the project and its captured log afterwards. That *was* the original approach, in the past.

Things are different now. Better. There is an Ant task to test Ant tasks: AntUnit.

AntUnit is an Antlib, a library of extra tasks with the filename `ant-antunit` `.jar`. It contains the Java tasks and macros to turn build files into test suites. The `<antunit>` task will load a build file and run every target in it whose name matches the pattern `test?*`, executing the optional `setUp` and `tearDown` targets before and after each test target. The Antlib includes a set of assertion tasks to check the state of the project in the test.

AntUnit is Ant's equivalent of JUnit. It has its own home page, http://ant.apache.org/antlibs/antunit. This web site contains AntUnit documentation and the JAR, `ant-antunit.jar`. The JAR can be added to `ANT_HOME/lib` or `${user-home}/.ant/lib`, or it can be dynamically loaded via a `taskdef` declaration. We keep it in `ANT_HOME/lib`, because we use it so often.

17.4.1   Using AntUnit

To use AntUnit in a build file, you need to declare the Antlib namespace in the project or in targets that use the new tasks:

```
xmlns:au="antlib:org.apache.ant.antunit"
```

This code provides the tasks and types of table 17.2, and the assertion tasks of table 17.3.

Table 17.2   The Ant tasks and types that come with AntUnit, excluding the assertions

Task/type	Description
`<antunit>`	Tests a specified build file.
`<expectfailure>`	Runs a nested sequence of tasks, expecting them to end in failure; a `BuildException` being thrown. The optional `expectedMessage` attribute can list the message that the exception must contain.
`<logcapturer>`	Starts capturing the build log.
`<logcontains>`	Polls a level of Ant's log for a message.
`<plainlistener>`	A listener for AntUnit test results. Prints the output of the test runs to the console.
`<xmllistener>`	Prints the output of test runs as an XML file.

The key tasks are <antunit>, which tests a build file, and <expectfailure>. The <antunit> task takes a nested fileset of build files to test and the name of a listener for test results, two of which are bundled: the <plainlistener> and <xmllistener>. Here's the task calling a test build file:

```
<au:antunit>
  <fileset file="test.xml"/>
  <au:plainlistener/>
</au:antunit>
```

This will test all test targets in the file test.xml, printing the results to the console. These test targets can verify that something worked or, with <expectfailure>, that something failed. The <expectfailure> task wraps a sequence of Ant declarations and executes them in turn. If the sequence completes without throwing a BuildException, the <expectfailure> task throws an exception: the sequence was meant to fail. If an exception is thrown, it is caught and its message verified against the value of the expectedMessage attribute:

```
<au:expectfailure expectedMessage="No property">
  <book:filesize file="${ant.file}"/>
</au:expectfailure>
```

The <logcontains> condition searches the log for a string. This condition works only under an AntUnit-controlled test, when a special logger saves all the output to a buffer. It returns false in other situations. There's no need to use it directly, as it's used inside the <assertLogContains> task.

```
<au:assertLogContains text="The size of " level="debug"/>
```

This assertion is one of the many provided by the toolkit—table 17.3. lists them all. All of them can be used in test targets to check that the Ant task is behaving as expected.

Table 17.3   The assertions that come with AntUnit. All but `<assertTrue>` are actually built from `<macrodef>` statements.

Assertion	Description
`<assertTrue>`	Fails if a nested condition isn't true.
`<assertFalse>`	Fails if a nested condition isn't false.
`<assertEquals>`	Asserts that the expected and actual strings are equal; the casesensitive option defaults to true.
`<assertPropertySet>`	Asserts that the property identified in name is set.
`<assertPropertyEquals>`	Asserts that the property identified in name is set to the string value in value.
`<assertPropertyContains>`	Asserts that the property identified in name contains the string value in value.
`<assertFileExists>`	Asserts that file is present.

continued on next page

Table 17.3 The assertions that come with AntUnit. All but `<assertTrue>` are actually built from `<macrodef>` statements. *(continued)*

Assertion	Description
`<assertFileDoesntExist>`	Asserts that `file` is absent.
`<assertDestIsUptodate>`	Asserts that the dest file is newer than the `src` file.
`<assertDestIsOutofdate>`	Asserts that the dest file is older than the `src` file.
`<assertFilesMatch>`	Asserts that the expected and actual files match.
`<assertFilesDiffer>`	Asserts that the expected and actual files do not match.
`<assertReferenceSet>`	Asserts the reference in `refid` maps to a known reference.
`<assertReferenceIsType>`	Asserts the reference in `refid` maps to a reference of type type, using the `<isreference>` condition.
`<assertLogContains>`	Asserts the log contains the specified `text` at the specified `level`, the default level being `"info"`.

These assertions are used to verify that the tasks being tested have the desired effect. As the underlying task, `<assertTrue>`, takes a nested condition, anything that `<condition>` can test for can also be used in an assertion.

17.4.2 Testing the <filesize> task

We know enough about AntUnit to use it. It's time to add tests to the build by running the `<antunit>` against our own build file:

```
<target name="antunit"
  depends="ready-to-run"
  xmlns:au="antlib:org.apache.ant.antunit">
  <au:antunit>
    <fileset file="${ant.file}"/>
    <au:plainlistener/>
  </au:antunit>
</target>
```

Calling this target will trigger a run against the test targets in the file and the optional `setUp` and `tearDown` targets. The `antunit` target is set to depend upon the `ready-to-run` target, which ensures that the source is compiled before the tests run. The individual test targets *do not depend upon this*. If they did, every test target would also have the complete compile step re-executed, because when AntUnit runs a target, it runs all its dependencies. Instead, the test targets depend on the `define` target, which declares the custom task with `<taskdef>`.

The first test target runs the task with valid arguments and asserts that the property is set:

```
<target name="testWorking"
    depends="define"
    xmlns:au="antlib:org.apache.ant.antunit"
    xmlns:book="http://antbook.org/">
```

```
    <book:filesize property="size" file="${ant.file}"/>
    <au:assertPropertySet name="size"/>
  </target>
```

The next test is more complex. We want the task to fail in the test, so we use
`<expectfailure>` to run the task and look for the exception message it should raise:

```
<target name="testNoProperty"
    depends="define">
  <au:expectfailure expectedMessage="No property">
    <book:filesize file="${ant.file}"/>
  </au:expectfailure>
</target>
```

These test targets still work from the command line. The only tests that must be
run under AntUnit are those that look for logged messages with `<assert-LogContains>`:

```
<target name="testOutput"
    depends="define"
    xmlns:au="antlib:org.apache.ant.antunit"
    xmlns:book="http://antbook.org/">
  <book:filesize property="size" file="${ant.file}"/>
  <au:assertLogContains text="The size of " level="debug"/>
</target>
```

The final test is one that asks for the size of a nonexistent file. Again, it uses the
`<expectfailure>` task:

```
<target name="testNoFile"
    depends="define">
  <au:expectfailure expectedMessage="Not found:">
    <book:filesize property="size" file="bad.file"/>
  </au:expectfailure>
</target>
```

The `expectedMessage` attribute lists only part of the fault string; the full message
contains the path of the absent file, which isn't a constant. The `<expectfailure>`
task does a substring search on the message, so only a portion of the error message
is needed.

17.4.3 Running the tests

With the tests written, let's run the `antunit` target:

```
>ant antunit
Buildfile: build.xml

antunit:
[au:antunit] Build File: /home/ant/filesize/first/build.xml
[au:antunit] Tests run: 3, Failures: 0, Errors: 0,
    Time elapsed: 0.05 sec
[au:antunit] Target: testNoFile took 0 sec
```

```
[au:antunit] Target: testNoProperty took 0 sec
[au:antunit] Target: testWorking took 0.02 sec
[au:antunit] Target: testOutput took 0 sec
```

BUILD SUCCESSFUL

The tests passed, the report is printed, and the build succeeds. What if the opposite had happened, and a test had failed? To see that, we need a test that fails. How about a test that expects <filesize> to fail if it's passed a directory?

```
<target name="testDir"
    depends="define"
    xmlns:au="antlib:org.apache.ant.antunit"
    xmlns:book="http://antbook.org/">
  <au:expectfailure>
    <book:filesize property="size" file="."/>
  </au:expectfailure>
</target>
```

Will this work or not? Without an explicit test for directories, it must depend on what happens when File.length() is invoked on a directory. What happens in the test?

```
antunit:
[au:antunit] Build File: /home/ant/filesize/first/build.xml
[au:antunit] Tests run: 4, Failures: 1, Errors: 0,
   Time elapsed: 0.05 sec
[au:antunit] Target: testNoFile took 0.01 sec
[au:antunit] Target: testNoProperty took 0 sec
[au:antunit] Target: testWorking took 0.02 sec
[au:antunit] Target: testOutput took 0 sec
[au:antunit] Target: testDir took 0 sec
[au:antunit]     FAILED
[au:antunit] Expected build failure

BUILD FAILED
/home/ant/filesize/first/build.xml:44:
Tests failed with 1 failure and 0 errors
```

One of the tests failed, so <antunit> itself failed. This is exactly what we want. Of course, we now have a bug to find.

Debugging a task

How do you debug a task? It's no harder than debugging other Java programs. You need to set the IDE up to run Ant under the debugger, setting up the command line with the build file and target needed to invoke the task.

- The entry point is org.apache.tools.ant.Main.
- The classpath for debugging must include Ant, the tasks being debugged, and any other tasks and optional libraries used in the build file—including AntUnit if it's needed.

- The JVM options should pass down the `ANT_HOME` value with an option such as `-Dant.home=/home/ant/Ant`.
- The command line should include the target to run.
- Any other Ant option can be added, except for `-lib`, `-cp`, `-nouserlib`, and `-nouserclasspath`. These options are all interpreted by Ant's launcher program.

When we run Ant, it will load the build file and create the task, halting at any breakpoints set in the task's source. Debugging the task is then no harder—or easier—than debugging any other Java program.

The limitations of AntUnit

AntUnit is new and still acquiring all the features you expect from a test framework. The biggest limitation is that the test builds are all executed in the same JVM—that of the project calling `<antunit>`. If there's any state stored in static variables, it's accessible to all tasks in all the tests. One build file could contaminate all the other tests, and that would be hard to fix.

17.5 MORE TASK ATTRIBUTES

Having built and tested the task, let's return to the details of how Ant configures tasks. There are two more attribute options we can work with: enumerated attributes and user-defined types.

17.5.1 Enumerations

Many tasks restrict attributes to a limited set of values—an enumeration. All tasks that need to do this and still work on Java 1.4 and below have to extend Ant's `EnumeratedAttribute` class. Doing so provides a basic enumeration that Ant tasks and types can use. It crops up all over Ant's own tasks. With Java 5 things are easier. All you need is a Java enum:

```
public enum Day {
    monday, tuesday, wednesday, thursday, friday, saturday, sunday;
}
```

This enum is passed to the task in an attribute-setter method. The Ant runtime finds the enumeration instance whose name matches the attribute value, passing that instance to the task. Listing 17.3 shows a task that uses this Day enumeration, printing out its name and index value when executed.

Listing 17.3 Java enumerations can be used as task attributes.

```
package org.antbook.tasks;
import org.apache.tools.ant.Task;

public class Weekday extends Task {
    private Day day    = Day.sunday;
```

```
    public void setDay(Day day) {
        this.day = day;
    }

    public void execute() {
        log("the day is " + day.name());
        log("the day index is " + day.ordinal());
    }
}
```

Using Day with the example task, we can pass down an in-range value:

```
<weekday day="tuesday"/>
```

This prints out the value and its index:

```
[weekday] the day is tuesday
[weekday] the day index is 1
```

Ant will throw an exception if the attribute doesn't match a case-sensitive comparison with any of the allowed values. The attribute day="Tuesday" isn't allowed:

```
'Tuesday' is not a permitted value for org.antbook.tasks.Day
```

The AntUnit tests for the two enumeration examples show AntUnit at work. In particular, the test for day="tuesday" being valid uses the <assertLog-Contains> assertion to probe the log for the output messages. Tasks that log information at the verbose and debug levels are easy to test.

```
<target name="testWeekday" depends="define">
  <book:weekday day="tuesday"/>
  <au:assertLogContains text="the day is tuesday"/>
  <au:assertLogContains text="the day index is 1"/>
</target>

<target name="testWeekdayCaseSensitive" depends="define">
  <au:expectfailure
    expectedMessage="not a permitted value">
    <book:weekday day="Tuesday"/>
  </au:expectfailure>
</target>
```

Java enum types are the best way to restrict the value of an attribute to a fixed range. Ant validates and converts the string, so the task developers can work with an enum that can be used in switch statements and the like.

If the enumerated or the built-in attribute mappings don't cut it, there is one last option: a custom, user-defined type.

17.5.2   User-defined types

Any Java class that has a public `String` constructor can be used as an attribute. The `java.math.BigDecimal` class, for example, has no formal Ant support, but its string constructor is enough:

```
package org.antbook.tasks;
import org.apache.tools.ant.Task;
import java.math.BigDecimal;

public class Bignum extends Task {
    private BigDecimal value;

    public void setValue(BigDecimal value) {
        this.value = value;
    }

    public void execute() {
        log(value.toEngineeringString());
    }
}
```

This task takes a very large integer and prints it as an engineering value; any exponent is rounded to the nearest multiple of three. The statement `<bignum value= "1045e17" />` is printed as

```
[bignum] 104.5E+18
```

Any Java class that takes a string constructor is valid, so many classes in the Java libraries can be used as Ant attributes. When in doubt, try it!

17.6   SUPPORTING NESTED ELEMENTS

Attributes are easy to work with, but they're limited. A task can have only one attribute of a given name, and every attribute is just a simple string. Most tasks use nested XML elements for complex or repeated configuration data. For our `<filesize>` task, we want to support lists and sets of files as nested elements:

```
<book:filesize property="java.source.size">
  <fileset dir="${src.dir}" includes="**/*.java"/>
</book:filesize>
```

Like attributes, Ant invokes specially named task methods when it encounters nested elements. There are four distinct scenarios that Ant handles using the specially named methods, listed in table 17.4.

We strongly recommend that you use the `add`, `addXXX` or `add-ConfiguredXXX` methods for nested task elements, because they allow you to support subclasses of the same types. For example, a custom extension to the `FileSet` class could be passed to our `<fileset>` task.

The `addConfigured` method is useful if your task needs a fully populated object immediately, rather than waiting for the `execute` method; however, in practice it's

Table 17.4 Methods that tasks can implement to support nested elements

Scenario	Method
Ant constructs the object using a no-arg constructor; no pre-population.	`public void addElementName(ObjectType obj)`
Ant constructs the object using a no-arg constructor, but pre-population is needed.	`public void addConfiguredElementName(ObjectType obj)`
The task creates the object.	`public ObjectType createElementName()`
The task takes any datatype that implements the interface/extends the base class.	`public void add(ObjectType obj)`

rarely needed. Use the `create-` method in situations when you need to construct the object itself, perhaps because it doesn't have a no-argument constructor or because additional steps are needed beyond what the `add`-prefixed methods provide.

For our `<filesize>` task, if we wanted to support a single collection type, such as a fileset or a filelist, we could add an `addFileset(Fileset set)` or `addFileList(FileList list)` method. Ant uses the type of the method's single parameter to identify the supported datatype, while the method name determines the element's name. A method called `addSource` would take an element called source, independent of its type.

We want to support any Ant resource collection that can provide a list of files, so we'll use the general purpose `add()` method:

```
public void add(ResourceCollection rc) {
    resources.add(rc);
}
```

Tasks that support nested elements need to handle the case where more than one element is supplied. This task adds them to a `Union` instance, which is the class behind the `<union>` resource:

```
private Union resources = new Union();
```

This collection will now aggregate all resource collections passed down to the task. When Ant executes the task, we'll need to get those collections, or at least their inner resources, back. All resource collections have an `iterator()` method that provides access to the nested resources. When our task wants to retrieve the resources, it just asks for this iterator:

```
Iterator element = resources.iterator();
```

It can then iterate through the elements, measuring their size. There's only one slight flaw in this plan. The `<filesize>` task measures the length of files, not strings or any other kind of resource. How can we restrict the task to file resources only?

The solution is to check the type of every resource, only converting it to a `FileResource` if it is one. A `FileResource` is a special resource that represents files, and it has a `getFile()` method to return the file it represents. Our extended execute() method has to iterate across the resources that have been added, halt the build if any is of the wrong type, and otherwise add the file's length to the running total:

```
public void execute() throws BuildException {
    if (property == null) {
        throw new BuildException("No property");
    }
    long size = 0;
    int count = 0;
    Iterator element = resources.iterator();
    while (element.hasNext()) {
        Resource resource = (Resource) element.next();
        if (!(resource instanceof FileResource)) {
            throw new BuildException("Not a file: " + resource);
        }
        log(resource.getName(), Project.MSG_VERBOSE);
        FileResource fileResource = (FileResource) resource;
        File file = fileResource.getFile();
        if (!file.exists()) {
            throw new BuildException("Not found: " + file);
        }
        size += file.length();
        count++;
    }
    if (count == 0) {
        log("No files sized up", Project.MSG_WARN);
    }
    getProject().setNewProperty(property, Long.toString(size));
}
```

This is all we need to support file resources, nested in arbitrary resource collection types. Admittedly, most of those files are going to come in as <filesets>, which are the near-universal representation of files and file groups in Ant, but there are more. By using resources, our task will be flexible and extensible, supporting new collection types from Ant and third parties. There's just one price: we need to know our way around the resource classes.

17.7   WORKING WITH RESOURCES

Ant resources are its emerging conceptual model for files, paths, URLs, and other data sources. Older tasks invariably work with a few datatypes, such as the Path and FileSet types and perhaps the FileList—all of which are now resource collections. Resource-enabled tasks can work with any of these collections as well as new ones. To do so, task authors have to know how they are implemented in Java.

The resource class hierarchy is complex enough that we're going to have to resort to UML diagrams—in plural—to describe them. Consult the Ant JavaDocs and source to explore the resource class hierarchy in more detail. Figure 17.2 outlines the Resource classes that ship with Ant.

The Resource class represents a source or destination of data. Resources have a size, a lastModified timestamp, and a name. Their exists flag is set if the

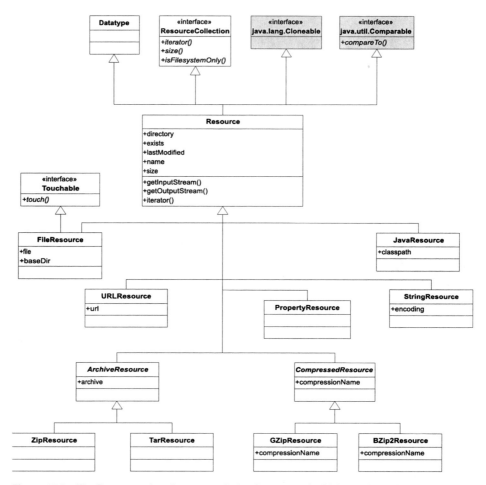

Figure 17.2 The Resource class has many derivatives, any of which can be added to resource collections. The Resource class is in the `org.apache.tools.ant.types` package; all the derivatives go under the `org.apache.tools.ant.types.resources`.

resource actually exists, and the `directory` flag is set if it's a directory. There are public methods to access all of these values, methods that subclasses often override.

The method that all subclasses override is `getInputStream()`, which returns an `InputStream` reading in the contents of the resource. The `Property-Resource` and the `StringResource` resources return the contents of the property or the string as a `ByteArrayInputStream`, while the `URLResource` connects to the URL and returns the source provided by the active `java.net.URL-Connection` instance.

Resources can be aggregated into collections, such as `<fileset>` or `<path>`. These are implemented as classes that implement the `ResourceCollection` interface and its three methods:

Method	Function
isFilesystemOnly()	Returns true if all resources are files in the filesystem
iterator()	Returns an iterator over the contained resources
size()	Returns the number of resources in the collection

The common file datatypes, <fileset>, <filelist>, and <path>, are all resource collections, as are the aggregate containers such as <union>, <intersection>, and <difference>. The Resource class itself implements the Resource-Collection interface, implying that all resources are sources of resources. This is a little trick that makes it easy to treat single resources as single-element collections: the iterator() operator returns an iterator class and then returns the resource itself, once.

Figure 17.3 shows the resource collection hierarchy. It's complex because the ResourceCollection interface was retrofitted to the existing datatypes.

Most tasks don't have to worry about all these details. It shouldn't matter to a task how resources are specified, aggregated, or sorted. All the tasks need to worry about is the contents of the collections.

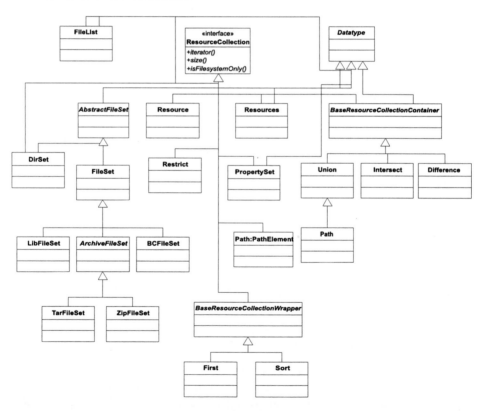

Figure 17.3 A UML outline of the resource classes. The methods and attributes have been stripped off as the diagram is complex enough already.

17.7.1   Using a resource-enabled task

By adding the `add(ResourceCollection)` method to our `<filesize>` task, the task will support all of the resource collections, but only if the underlying resources are all files in the filesystem.

Let's start using this task, first in AntUnit tests. We'll begin with a fileset:

```
<target name="testFileset"
    depends="define">
  <book:filesize property="size">
    <fileset dir="src" includes="**/*.java"/>
  </book:filesize>
  <au:assertPropertySet name="size"/>
```

This task should add up the size of all Java source files. Filesets have a base directory and, when evaluated, return only those files under the base directory that match the nested patterns. This scanning of the directory tree takes place every time the `iterator()` method is called, so it should not be done lightly.

Other collections also can be used. First, a filelist:

```
<target name="testFileList"
    depends="define">
  <book:filesize property="size">
    <filelist>
      <file name="${ant.file}"/>
    </filelist>
  </book:filesize>
  <au:assertPropertySet name="size"/>
</target>
```

A filelist is a resource collection containing an ordered list of files. Unlike a fileset, its `iterator()` returns the files in the list, whether or not they exist. This is why our task has to handle missing files by throwing a `BuildException`.

Paths are also resource collections, so they too can be passed down:

```
<target name="testPath" depends="define">
  <book:filesize property="size">
    <path path="${java.class.path}"/>
  </book:filesize>
  <echo> classpath size=${size}</echo>
</target>
```

Running this task tells us the total size of the JAR files on the classpath:

```
testPath:
    [echo]   classpath size=21018332
```

That code demonstrates why resource-enabled tasks are good. Unless the task has a need for a specific type (like a classpath), the sole reason to not support resources is a need to be backwards-compatible with Ant 1.6. Otherwise: adopt resources!

17.8 DELEGATING TO OTHER TASKS

This chapter has shown how to write and test Ant tasks. It has one big topic left to cover: how to delegate work to other tasks and Java programs, and how to set up the classpaths to do so. Many of Ant's tasks are just simple wrappers around Java or native programs. Most of the SCM tasks simply set up the command line arguments for the native command-line tools. Many of the JDK-related tasks invoke the program bundled in the JDK as a native program (`<genkey>` and `<signjar>`) or by directly invoking the Java entry point (`<javac>` and `<rmic>`). There's a lot of duplicate work going on here, so obviously some shared classes do the heavy lifting. What are these classes? They are the classes behind `<exec>` and `<java>` tasks, tasks we've been using throughout the book.

Many of Ant's tasks delegate work to other tasks. Every Ant task that's implemented in Java can be created in another Ant task simply by calling its constructor. It can then be configured by using its Java API—the setters and other methods designed for Ant to call by introspection.

NOTE   Ant's tasks have a Java API, the `set-`, `create-` and `add-` methods written by the task authors, along with the task lifecycle methods of `init()` and `execute()`. To delegate work to other tasks, create the task, call `init()` to initialize it, configure it, and finally call `execute()`.

We're going to use the `Java` class to run any Java program with arguments built from nested resources. This task, `<runjava>` will have the following attributes and elements:

Configuration option	Role
attribute `classname`	The name of the class to run
attribute `classpath`	The classpath of the program
attribute `classpathref`	A reference to an existing classpath
element `classpath`	A classpath as nested XML
resource collection elements	Arguments to the program

The `<runjava>` task is going to expose only a fraction of the Java task's features. Some options will be set to sensible values, while the rest will be left alone.

Here's the top of the task:

```
public class Runjava extends Task {
    private Union resources = new Union();

    public void add(ResourceCollection rc) {
        resources.add(rc);
    }
    ...
```

This is pretty much the same code as for the `<filesize>` task: support for nested resource collections. The harder bits are the other attributes, especially supporting class and classpath set-up.

If a task has a setter method that takes a `java.lang.Class` parameter, Ant will automatically load the class and pass the `Class` instance down. *Do not use this!* Ant will try to load the class from Ant's current classloader. Tasks are much more flexible if they take the classname string and support configurable classpaths.

Here are the recommended ways to work with classes:

1 Tasks that dynamically load classes should support user-specified classpaths.

2 Classpaths can be specified by a reference to an existing classpath, a path attribute, or as a nested path.

3 Use `AntClassLoader`, which is an Ant-specific classloader.

4 The method `Project.CreateClassLoader()` takes a `Path` instance and returns an `AntClassLoader` containing all the classes listed in the path, both in JAR files and under directories.

5 After classes and classloaders are no longer needed, references to them should be set to null and the `cleanup()` method of the classloader should be called to force it to close any open JAR files. This prevents memory leaks.

Because we are delegating to the `<java>` task, only the first two items are our problem; the rest is the Java task's. Our task needs only a simple string to store the classname:

```
private String classname;
public void setClassname(String classname) {
    this.classname = classname;
}
```

This does, however, leave the problem of setting up the classpath itself, which forces us to look at how Ant handles paths and datatype references.

17.8.1 Setting up classpaths in a task

There are three ways to let build files pass a classpath to a task:

- Write a setter method that takes an `org.apache.tools.ant.types.Path` parameter. This results in an attribute that takes a classpath as a string of colon- or semicolon-separated filenames.

- Write an `add-`, `addConfigured-`, or `create-` method call that takes a `Path` parameter. This results in a nested element that takes a full path datatype.

- Have a setter method that takes an `org.apache.tools.ant.types.Reference` parameter. This creates an attribute that takes the reference ID of a predefined path. By convention, the method should have "refid" or "ref" in its name. The task has to create a path and bind the reference to it.

Tasks that have an add(ResourceCollection) method can also get all nested paths passed down, alongside any other collection type. In such a situation, it's best to treat the <path> elements equally to the other collections. A separate add-Classpath(path) method keeps classpath setup separate.

Our new <runjava> task will support all three methods: the classpath attribute, the classpath element, and a classpathref attribute.

A classpath attribute

First, comes the field to store the path:

```
private Path classpath;
```

Next, the simple attribute setter:

```
public void setClasspath(Path classpath) {
    this.classpath = classpath;
}
```

This attribute will take something like

```
path="${java.class.path}:${build.dir}"
```

A classpath element

The path element is no more complex.

```
public void addClasspath(Path classpath) {
    setClasspath(classpath);
}
```

Robust tasks may check for duplicate attempts to set the classpath and then fail on the second attempt, unlike this example, which will accept the last path given to it by the runtime:

```
<book:runjava>
  <classpath path="${build.dir}"/>
  <classpath refid="run.path"/>
</book:runjava>
```

Incidentally, Ant always adds elements in the order in which they appear in the build file; there's no way to guarantee that the same behavior happens with attributes, as the XML parser can return them in any order. This is consistent with XML's rules, in which the order of attributes is unimportant but the order of elements is highly significant.

A classpath reference

Supporting references to predefined paths is essential for path reuse. To accept a path or other datatype reference as an attribute, use a setter that supports the org .apache.tools.ant.types.Reference type, and then create, configure, and add an instance of the desired datatype:

```
public void setClasspathRef(Reference refid) {
    Path cp = new Path(this.getProject());
    cp.setRefid(refid);
    setClasspath(cp);
}
```

This method creates a new `Path` instance bound to the project, and then calls its `setRefid()` method to set its `refid` attribute. Just as Ant's tasks can be delegated to, all Ant datatypes can be created, configured, and fed into tasks.

The Path class

The `Path` class is so common it deserves a closer look. It's an extension of the `Union` resource collection, with extra knowledge about Java classpath. Some of the most interesting methods are listed in table 17.5.

The `Path` class can be fed into other Ant tasks or used with utility classes such as `ClasspathUtils`, which creates an `AntClassloader` instance from a path instance.

Table 17.5 Useful methods in the `Path` class. It's a resource collection, from which `iterator()` and `add()` are useful methods.

Method	Operation
void add(ResourceCollection)	Adds another resource collection (including a path) to the path
void addExisting(Path)	Adds those elements of another path that point to files/directories that exist
void addJavaRuntime()	Adds the Java runtime JARs to the path
Iterator iterator()	Returns an iterator over the path elements
String[] list()	Returns an array of path elements from the `Path` instance
Resource[] listResources()	Gets all path elements as an array of resources
void setPath(String path)	Parses a string and sets the path to the elements inside
void setRefid	Binds this path to an existing reference
int size()	Returns the number of path elements within the `Path` instance
String toString()	Returns the full path as a completely resolved and platform-specific string
static String[] translatePathProject project, String path)	Provides an array of path elements from a single path containing elements separated by colon (:) or semicolon (;) separators

Delegating to the Java task

After all the path setup, delegating to the Java task is surprisingly simple. The entire `execute()` method fits into about 15 lines of code:

```
public void execute() {
    Java java  = new Java();
    java.bindToOwner(this);
    java.init();
    java.setFork(true);
    java.setFailonerror(true);
    java.setClasspath(classpath);
    java.setClassname(classname);
    Iterator element = resources.iterator();
    while (element.hasNext()) {
        Resource resource = (Resource) element.next();
        java.createArg().setValue(resource.toString());
    }
    java.execute();
}
```

To create a new task, just call the task's constructor. The `Task.bindToOwner()` method then copies some of the delegating task's state to the new class. Some of the information—the project and owning target—is absolutely critical, as tasks always assume that `getProject()` never returns `null`. Other attributes—name, location, description, and type—let the delegate inherit the public name and location of its owner. In the build log, it won't appear to be a separate task.

After copying this data, we call the task's `init()` method to begin its lifecycle. Once initialized, the task can be configured using the appropriate `set-`, `create-` and `add-` methods, mimicking in Java the attribute and element declarations in a build file. In our `<runjava>` task, we set the `fork` and `failonerror` attributes to true, then pass down our `classpath` and `classname`. Setting nested arguments is more complex, as a nested `<arg>` element is created for each one, using `createArg()` to return new instances of the `Commandline.Argument` class. This class crops up wherever Ant tasks set up classpaths, including the `<exec>` and `<apply>` tasks.

Finally, we `execute()` the delegate. This will run the Java program with the specified classpath and arguments, check the return value and report a failure if appropriate, and route all I/O to Ant's own process. Internally, the `<java>` task itself creates and delegates to `<exec>` when `fork="true"`; otherwise, it loads and runs the Java class in its own classloader, under a security manager that intercepts `System.exit()` calls. Delegation is the underpinnings of Ant.

Running the task

As usual, some AntUnit tests verify that everything works. Here's one of the tests:

```
<target name="testClasspathRef" depends="define">
   <path id="run.path" path="${build.dir}"/>       <-①
```

```
        <book:runjava
            classpathref="run.path"        <-❷
            classname="org.antbook.tasks.runjar.ListArgs">
          <resources>
            <file file="${ant.file}"/>
            <string value="a string"/>
          </resources>
        </book:runjava>
      </target>
```

This test creates a path ❶ which we pass by reference to the `<runjava>` task ❷, a task set to run a `ListArgs` program. Two resources are passed as arguments, a filename and a string. What is the program? It's the program we wrote back in chapter 2, the one that lists all of its arguments. We've come full circle and are now running it in Ant via a task we've written ourselves:

```
testClasspathRef:
[book:runjava] /home/ant/ch17_tasks/runjava/build.xml
[book:runjava] a string
```

The program can now be passed anything that fits into a resource collection. It could be a path; it could be a fileset. We've just extended Ant's resource collection support to an external Java program. What's more, we've done it in a reusable manner. If the task is bundled into a JAR, it can be distributed to anyone who needs it. This is why custom tasks are so powerful: they can be reused by anyone.

17.9 OTHER TASK TECHNIQUES

We are nearly through the tour of writing tasks. There are only a few minor aspects of task coding to cover, a mixed bag of techniques that task authors should know of.

Error handling

Ant will catch any exceptions thrown from a task and fail the build. Tasks should throw a `BuildException`, which is a `RuntimeException` subclass, when they wish a build to fail for any reason—including from inside attribute or element setters.

The `failOnError` attribute is a common pattern in Ant tasks; if set to false it implements a simple "ignore any errors" policy. Here's a simple task that can be told to not fail:

```
package org.example.antbook.tasks;
import org.apache.tools.ant.Task;
import org.apache.tools.ant.BuildException;

public class ConditionalFailTask extends Task {
    private boolean failOnError = true;

    public void setFailOnError(boolean failOnError) {
        this.failOnError = failOnError;
    }
```

```
public void execute() throws BuildException {
    if (failOnError) {
        throw new BuildException("oops!");
    }
    log("success");
}
}
```

Tasks that follow this pattern should enable `failOnError` by default, forcing a build file writer to explicitly turn it off, if desired. This is consistent with the design of all new Ant tasks. Swallowed exceptions should still be logged at the verbose level, because it's very useful when tracking down obscure problems.

Handling inline text

Many Ant tasks support plain text inside an XML element. This is very easy to do. Adding an `addText()` method to your task tells Ant to allow nested text. Here's a task that gets this wrong:

```
package org.antbook.tasks;
import org.apache.tools.ant.Task;

public class MessageTask extends Task {

    private String text = "";

    public void addText(String text) {
        this.text = text;
    }

    public void execute() {
        log(text);
    }
}
```

What has gone wrong? Well, for historical reasons (bad planning), Ant doesn't expand the properties in the text before passing it to the `addText()` method. You would not be able to use a property inside the message. A task use such as

```
<book:message>${ant.file}</book:message>
```

would return

```
[book:message] ${ant.file}
```

This would be wrong. We need to explicitly expand the properties in this text, as in

```
public void addText(String text) {
    this.text = getProject().replaceProperties(text);
}
```

This is an easy mistake to make, because attribute setters do expand properties. Some of the Ant tasks themselves (like `<sql>`) have made this mistake in the past. Don't copy them!

Ant's binding from XML to Java makes it easy to write a task or set of tasks. We still need to make those tasks easy to use and easy for developers to pick up and use in their own build file, which means they need to be packaged as an Antlib.

17.10 MAKING AN ANTLIB LIBRARY

Tasks are easier to use if they're bundled up as a library, in a JAR file. To make it even easier, the JAR file can contain property or XML files listing the types and tasks in the library. If this is done, it becomes an *Antlib*.

The first step in building the task library is to compile the source into a JAR. The usual `<javac>` and `<jar>` tasks come into play here. What is absolutely critical is the `<copy>` task that pulls in everything in the source tree with the suffixes `.xml` or `.properties` ❶:

```
<property name="build.dir" location="build/classes"/>
<property name="build.classes.dir"
  location="${build.dir}/classes"/>
<property name="dist.dir" location="dist"/>
<property name="tasks.version" value="1.0"/>
<property name="tasks.jar"
  location="${dist.dir}/filesize-${tasks.version}.jar"/>

<target name="init">
  <mkdir dir="${build.classes.dir}"/>
  <mkdir dir="${dist.dir}"/>
</target>

<target name="compile" depends="init">
  <javac srcdir="src" destdir="${build.classes.dir}"/>
  <copy todir="${build.classes.dir}">
    <fileset dir="src" includes="**/*.xml,**/*.properties"/>    ❶
  </copy>
</target>

<target name="ready-to-jar" depends="compile"/>

<target name="jar" depends="ready-to-jar">
  <jar destfile="${tasks.jar}">
    <fileset dir="${build.classes.dir}" includes="**/*"/>
  </jar>
</target>
```

These targets create the library file `dist/filesize-1.0.jar`. All the library file needs are the configuration files.

Declaring a tasks.properties file

The original way of declaring tasks was a properties file, by convention a file called `tasks.properties` in the same package as the tasks themselves. This file lists the names of the tasks and the classes that implement them:

```
filesize=org.antbook.tasks.filesize.FilesizeTask
resourcesize=org.antbook.tasks.filesize.ResourceSizeTask
```

This file can be used by the `<taskdef>` task:

```
<target name="define-via-properties" depends="jar">
  <taskdef
    resource="org/antbook/tasks/filesize/tasks.properties"
    classpath="${tasks.jar}"/>
</target>
```

At this point, the new tasks are ready for use:

```
<filesize property="size" file="${ant.file}"/>
```

Task declaration through property files is a long-standing feature of Ant. Although this format is easy to write, it's limited, and the tasks aren't automatically loaded when Ant encounters namespaces with `antlib:` URIs. The `antlib.xml` design is better.

Declaring an antlib.xml file

The successor to the properties file is a full-blown XML file, `antlib.xml`, listing the task and types in the library. Most Java developers probably dread another XML configuration file, but there's one nice thing about the `antlib.xml` file: it's an Ant file! To be precise, it is an XML document with a root element `<antlib>`, inside of which can go any Ant task or other element that implements the interface `org.apache.tools.ant.taskdefs.AntlibDefinition`. There are five such tasks built into Ant: `<typedef>`, `<taskdef>`, `<macrodef>`, `<presetdef>`, and `<scriptdef>`; new ones can be added by the adventurous.

When an Antlib is loaded, all tasks inside it are executed inside the current project. The result is that all the tasks defined in the library become available in the project. This technique has a number of compelling features.

1 It lets you define new Ant types and tasks in the same classloader.

2 It makes `presetdef` and `macrodef` declarations act as part of the library.

3 It allows scripting languages to be used to write tasks in the library.

4 It integrates with the Antlib: URI mechanism for automatic library loading.

For our task suite, the Antlib file is just a simple `<taskdef>` sequence:

```
<antlib>
  <taskdef name="filesize"
    classname="org.antbook.tasks.filesize.FilesizeTask" />
  <taskdef name="resourcesize"
    classname="org.antbook.tasks.filesize.ResourceSizeTask" />
</antlib>
```

The `<taskdef>` tasks don't declare any classpath. The Antlib XML file is loaded by the same classloader as the task classes, so it isn't needed. The tasks also omit any XML namespace. This is all handled automatically.

The new Antlib can be loaded just like any of the Antlibs we've been using since chapter 9. The first way is in a `<typedef>` declaration:

```
<typedef
  onerror="failall"
  resource="org/antbook/tasks/filesize/antlib.xml"
  classpath="${tasks.jar}"/>
```

This declaration loads the tasks straight into the main Ant namespace, ready for use. The `onerror` attribute tells the task what to do if the resource file cannot be found: we want the build to halt, instead of display a warning message in the log.

Once the Antlib is loaded, the tasks are ready for use:

```
<resourcesize property="size">
  <fileset file="${ant.file}"/>
</resourcesize>
```

We could instead load the task into another URI:

```
<typedef
  onerror="failall"
  uri="http://antbook.org/"
  resource="org/antbook/tasks/filesize/antlib.xml"
  classpath="${tasks.jar}"/>
```

Most importantly, if the `uri` attribute is set to the `antlib:` URI of the package in which the `antlib.xml` file lives, the file is automatically located:

```
<typedef
  onerror="failall"
  uri="antlib:org.antbook.tasks.filesize"
  classpath="${tasks.jar}"/>
```

This is one step away from full dynamic loading, in which the namespace declaration alone is enough to pull in the tasks:

```
<target name="testAutoload"
    depends="define"
    xmlns:book="antlib:org.antbook.tasks.filesize">
  <book:resourcesize property="size">
    <filelist>
      <file name="${ant.file}"/>
    </filelist>
  </book:resourcesize>
</target>
```

Running this target will force Ant to load the `antlib.xml` file from the classpath when an element in the namespace is encountered; failing with an "unknown task" error if the Antlib cannot be found. You have to set up the build with the task on the classpath, which you can do in the build after the distribution JAR has been created:

```
>ant -f antlib2.xml testAutoload -lib dist
Buildfile: antlib2.xml
```

```
define:
testAutoload:
BUILD SUCCESSFUL
```

At this point, we have a fully functional Antlib. It's now ready to be redistributed.

Adding <presetdef> and <macrodef> declarations

There's one final trick to know: how to make `<presetdef>` and `<macrodef>` declarations in the `antlib.xml` file. Both tasks can be used in the `antlib.xml` file to
define new tasks, tasks that then are available to any users of the Antlib.

However, there's one main problem. What happens when the Antlib library is
loaded into a namespace? How can declarations in the `antlib.xml` file predict
which namespace they will be loaded into, so that they can correctly reference other
things defined in the build file?

```
<macrodef name="echosize"
  backtrace="false"
  xmlns:this="ant.current" >    ◁—❶
  <attribute name="file"/>
  <attribute name="property"/>
  <sequential>
    <this:filesesize property="@{property}"
        file="@{file}"/>                      ❷
    <echo>Size of @{file}=@{property}</echo>
  </sequential>
</macrodef>
```

The problem is solved by having a special namespace URI to refer to the current Antlib, the string `"ant.current"`. It needs to be declared as a namespace ❶, and then
the declared prefix can be used to identify tasks defined in the Antlib ❷. It's a bit of a
hack, but it allows end users to declare the library into any namespace of their choice.
The result is that Antlib authors can write tasks and other Ant types, extend them with
`<presetdef>` and `<macrodef>`, then ship the entire package as a JAR file that build
files can load just by declaring the `Antlib:` URL in an XML namespace declaration.

17.11 SUMMARY

The main way to extend Ant is by writing new tasks. This is normally done in Java,
taking advantage of the full API that Ant provides. With the information in this chapter, you now have an understanding of how to do this and how Ant binds to tasks.
Java introspection and method-naming conventions are the secret.

The trick to writing a good task is to use the core classes such as `Project` and
`Task`, to delegate work to other Ant tasks, and to accept the common datatypes built
into Ant.

Along with the tasks come the tests and packaging. The AntUnit library makes it
easy to write test targets for a new task. As for packaging, Antlib libraries are just

JAR files with an `antlib.xml` configuration file somewhere in the package hierarchy. That isn't yet another XML format to learn, because it's really a tiny subset of Ant itself.

We are now half-way through our exploration of Ant's internals. Now that we've covered writing Java tasks and Ant's own classes, we can go on to write tasks in scripting languages and to match the custom tasks with custom datatypes. These are the tools of the power developer.

C H A P T E R   1 8

Extending Ant further

We've just been extending Ant with custom tasks in Java. Is that all that can be done to adapt it to a project? No, not at all! Some of the other ways that Ant can be extended are by

- Writing tasks using scripting languages with the `<script>` and `<script-def>` tasks

- Writing new conditions for use in `<condition>`, `<fail>`, and other tasks

- Writing custom resources, filters, selectors, and mappers

- Monitoring the build process with custom build listeners and loggers

- Embedding Ant inside your own program

We're going to go through all these extension mechanisms in turn to see what they are and how to write, test, and use them.

In the previous chapter, we looked at writing an Ant task and the Ant API. Although we are extending Ant in different ways in this chapter, everything covered in the previous chapter about Ant's Java API and how to test tasks is still essential. If you haven't already done so, read chapter 17.

18.1 SCRIPTING WITHIN ANT

The first thing we're going to do is extend Ant via scripts—that is, small bits of code implemented in an interpreted language. These code fragments can be placed inline in build files or hosted in text files alongside the build. Almost all of Ant's official extension mechanisms can be implemented in inline scripts, including tasks, conditions, filters, and more. This means you can solve complex build problems without resorting to Java code. Java is good for reusable tasks and datatypes, but it's overkill for a one-off problem.

Ant uses the Apache Bean Scripting Framework (BSF) for its primary scripting support. This is a language-independent way of integrating Java with scripting languages. To use BSF scripting languages inside a build file, Ant needs three things:

1 The Bean Scripting Framework JAR itself, `bsf.jar`. The current version is 2.3.0.
2 The `ant-apache-bsf.jar` JAR file, containing the relevant Ant tasks.
3 The specific JAR files for the individual libraries.

Script authors have a broad choice of languages, the complete list of which is found on the BSF pages at http://jakarta.apache.org/bsf/projects.html. Table 18.1 lists some of the main ones.

Table 18.1 Scripting languages. The language name is used in the `language` attributes of Ant's scripting tasks.

Script language	Description	Home page
beanshell	BeanShell language	http://www.beanshell.org/
groovy	Groovy—a new JVM-specific language	http://groovy.codehaus.org/
jacl	TCL in the JVM	http://tcljava.sourceforge.net/
jruby	Ruby in the JVM	http://jruby.codehaus.org/
jython	Python in the JVM	http://www.jython.org/
netrexx	Java port of the REXX mainframe language	http://www.ibm.com/netrexx/
javascript	JavaScript in Java 6; Rhino	http://www.mozilla.org/rhino/

Of all the languages, those that seem to work best with Ant are Jython, JRuby, and BeanShell. The currently released versions of Rhino and BSF aren't compatible—so you cannot use JavaScript except on Java 6. Otherwise, the choice comes down to which language you know, prefer, or think would be best for your career.

To use any BSF-based script language, you need the language-specific JAR and a compatible version of `bsf.jar` on Ant's classpath. Ant's `fetch.xml` file has a `"script"` target that will pull down BSF with Jython, JRuby, and BeanShell.

Java 1.6 adds a built-in script engine to the JVM, along with a JavaScript implementation. Ant has support for this, which we will look at once we've introduced the `<script>` and `<scriptdef>` tasks.

Running a script

With the BSF and relevant language JARs on the classpath, we can use them in the `<script>` task. Doing so executes a piece of script during the build, as in listing 18.1.

Listing 18.1 An inline BeanShell script

```
<target name="random">
  <script language="beanshell"><![CDATA[
    float r=java.lang.Math.random();
    int num = Math.round(r*10);
    project.setNewProperty("random", Integer.toString(num));
    self.log("Generated random number " + num);
  ]]>
  </script>
</target>
```

The script creates a random number in the range 0-9, sets the property `random` to the value, and prints the value out:

```
random:
   [script] Generated random number 6
```

Any target that depends on this target has access to the result, such as this AntUnit test:

```
<target name="testRandomScript" depends="random">
  <echo>Random number is ${random}</echo>
  <au:assertPropertySet name="random" />
  <au:assertLogContains text="Generated random number" />
</target>
```

The `<script>` task has one mandatory attribute, `language`, which must be set to the language of the script. The script itself can either go inline or in an external file, which is good for complex scripts:

```
<script language="jython" src="update.py" />
```

This works well for Jython, as Python's indentation rules make it tricky to use inline in an XML file.

Implicit objects provided to <script>

The `<script>` task provides two fixed-name implicit objects to the script context: `project` and `self`. The `project` object is a reference to the current Ant `Project` instance, offering all the methods covered in chapter 17. The `self` object is a reference to the `Script` task instance. This reference is useful for logging messages, using the `log` methods that `Task` provides. In listing 18.1 we used both `project` and `self`, calling `project.setNewProperty` to assign a property and `self.log` to generate a message at the debugging level.

Overall, the `<script>` task is fairly low-level. It doesn't integrate well with Ant, and it's showing its age. There are newer ways to use script inside Ant, especially `<scriptdef>`.

18.1.1 Writing new tasks with <scriptdef>

The `<script>` task is very limited. It's a piece of inline code and isn't very reusable. Why not write a whole task in a scripting language, complete with attributes and elements? That is what `<scriptdef>` is for. It lets you define an Ant task inside a build file in a scripting language. Listing 18.2 uses `<scriptdef>` to create a task that sets a named property to a random number.

Listing 18.2   A task written in Jython, using `<scriptdef>`

```
<target name="random-task-jython">
  <scriptdef language="jython"
      name="random"                           ←❶
      uri="http://antbook.org/script">        ←❷
    <attribute name="max"/>                   ❸
    <attribute name="property"/>
    <![CDATA[
from java.util import Random
from java.lang import Integer
max=Integer.valueOf(attributes.get("max"))
property=attributes.get("property")
num=Random().nextInt(Integer.valueOf(max))
result="%d" % num
project.setNewProperty(property, result)
self.log("Generated random number " + result)
    ]]>
  </scriptdef>
</target>
```

This target declares a new task, random ❶ in the namespace `http://antbook.org/script` ❷. We then declare two attributes, max and property ❸, to configure the task. The `<scriptdef>` task can define tasks with attributes and elements but not with nested text, except within elements. Nor can you declare the type of an attribute—they're always strings. That means all the attribute-type conversion magic to set up paths and files is lost, though Ant will expand properties before passing them down to the task.

Our `<random>` task is written in Jython, Python's port to the JVM. Python uses indentation as a way of marking code blocks, the way Java uses the curly braces, so it's sensitive to layout in the XML file. The script uses `java.util.Random` to create a random number; all of Java's and Ant's classes are available to the scripting languages.

Ant creates an attributes hash table containing all attributes that are passed to the task, indexing the attributes by their names. The `attributes.get()` operation returns the value of an attribute. If the attribute is absent, it returns null. Ant expects the script to handle missing elements and attributes itself, either by raising an exception or skipping some work. There's a method, `self.fail(String)`, that throws a BuildException if needed:

```
<target name="random-task-validating">
  <scriptdef language="jython"
      name="random2"
      uri="http://antbook.org/script">
    <attribute name="max"/>
    <attribute name="property"/>
    <![CDATA[
from java.util import Random
from java.lang import Integer
max=attributes.get("max")
property=attributes.get("property")
if max and property :
    num=Random().nextInt(Integer.valueOf(max))
    result="%d" % num
    project.setNewProperty(property, result)
    self.log("Generated random number " + result)
else:
    self.fail("'property' or 'max' is not set")
]]>
  </scriptdef>
</target>
```

The resulting fault trace is pretty messy, as the exception gets passed into Jython and then out again; in the process, Ant somehow ends up with a complete stack trace. Passing exceptions across JVM languages is clearly something that could be improved.

Testing <scriptdef>-defined tasks

We can use AntUnit to test the scripts, just as we did for Java tasks in chapter 17:

```
<target name="testRandomTaskNoProperty"
    depends="random-task-validating"
    xmlns:s="http://antbook.org/script">
  <au:expectfailure expectedMessage="not set">
    <s:random2 max="20"/>
  </au:expectfailure>
</target>
```

AntUnit and <scriptdef> make a very good combination; they let you write both your code and your tests in build files, or at least in interpreted languages. Because the scripting languages have full access to the Ant runtime and the Java libraries, they can do things normal tasks cannot do, yet you have a fast, iterative development cycle.

Nested elements in scripted tasks

Alongside attributes and text come nested elements. These are slightly trickier because the <scriptdef> declaration has to declare the type of the element to create, as well as its name. The task also has to deal with the possibility of multiple elements of the same name being set. Here is a JRuby script that supports a <classpath> element:

```
<target name="nested-task-jruby">
  <scriptdef language="ruby"
      name="nested"
      uri="http://antbook.org/script">
    <element name="classpath" type="path"/>    <-❶

    paths=$elements.get("classpath")    <-❷
    if paths==nil then
      $self.fail("no classpath")
    end
    for path in paths
      $self.log(path.toString())
    end
  </scriptdef>
</target>
```

The <element> declaration has to state the type of the element ❶. This can be a
known Ant type, or it can be the full name of any Java class, a class that must have
a public, no-argument constructor.

When the script is executed, Ant builds up a list for every named element handed
in. All these lists are stored in the elements HashMap, which can then be queried
for a named list ❷. If no element was supplied, the result will be null. Here, in
Ruby, the keyword is nil, but the meaning is clear.

Testing this task is straightforward; a test target invokes it with a couple of paths:

```
<target name="testNested" depends="nested-task-jruby"
  xmlns:s="http://antbook.org/script">
  <s:nested>
    <classpath path=".:${user.home}"/>
    <classpath path="${ant.file}" />
  </s:nested>
  <au:assertLogContains text="."/>
</target>
```

Another test checks that calling the task with no nested elements throws the expected
exception. With element support working, our scripts have access to Ant's full suite of
datatypes: paths, files, resources, and the like.

Once written, our scripted tasks need to be distributed. There are two ways to do
this. The simplest way is to embed the scripts in a build file, perhaps one that's pulled
in via <import>.

The other way is to declare them in an Antlib. Build files can use the tasks just by
declaring the Antlib URI. If you're creating an Antlib for a project, you can declare
<scriptdef> scripts inline in the antlib.xml file itself. When the Antlib is
packaged and distributed as a JAR file, the scripted tasks are available to all users.

There's one limitation here. The file attribute of <scriptdef> takes a file
only in the local file system. That means that developers cannot currently keep all of
the script files in separate .js, .py, or .ruby files in the JAR and then refer to them
in <scriptdef> declarations. That is something that will be fixed in the future.

Before closing our script coverage, let's look at how the script tasks behave under Java 6, where script support is built into the Java runtime.

Ant scripts in Java 6

Java 6 ships with a new scripting API and a copy of the Rhino JavaScript engine in the package `sun.org.mozilla.javascript`. As a result, you can use JavaScript in your Ant builds *without needing any extra libraries*:

```
<script language="javascript"      ◄─❶
  manager="javax">                 ◄─┐
  var r=java.lang.Math.random();    ❷
  var num = Math.round(r*10);
  project.setNewProperty("random", num.toString());
  self.log("Generated random number " + num);
</script>
```

To use this script, we have had to do two things. Selecting `language="javascript"` is the first of these ❶; this tells Ant to use JavaScript. Ant then needs to choose which scripting engine to use. It does this based on the `manager` attribute. The default value, `manager="auto"`, tells Ant to use the BSF manager if it's present and if the requested language is available. By asking for the `javax` manager ❷, we get the Java 6 manager, bypassing BSF. There's also the option of setting `manager="bsf"` to only check the BSF script manager for the specific language.

What that means is that if you don't express a choice of script manager, Ant looks for the script language in both runtimes, BSF and Java 6. You need to set the `manager` attribute only if you really want to select a particular implementation.

The fact that JavaScript is built into the runtime makes it very appealing: if all developers are using Java 6, then the build files can use JavaScript inline without any external dependencies. There's no reason not to use `<script>` or `<scriptdef>`.

18.1.2 Scripting summary

The scripting framework is very powerful. Tasks defined with `<scriptdef>` are true peers of Java tasks, rather than second-class citizens. Why didn't we cover them in the previous chapter? The answer is that Java is the main language for writing tasks today, especially those that integrate with other Java applications or libraries. The other reason is that to introduce scripting at the same time as Ant's internal API would be too much at one time. You need to know Ant's API and how to use AntUnit first.

Once you know how Ant works under the covers and are familiar with at least one of the supported scripting languages, then `<script>` and, more importantly, `<scriptdef>` are very handy tools indeed. There are other places that you can use scripting languages in Ant, which we'll cover as we go through Ant's remaining extension points; we'll start with conditions.

18.2 CONDITIONS

Now, let's go beyond tasks into Ant's other types. A nice place to start is with conditions, which are little classes that evaluate to true or false. Custom conditions can be used in the <condition>, <fail>, and <waitfor> tasks. Some third-party tasks also support conditions, such as AntUnit's <assertTrue> and <assertFalse> tasks. It's easy to write a new condition that all these tasks can use.

To implement a condition, we write a Java class that implements Ant's Condition interface and its boolean eval() method. This method must return true if the condition holds and false if it doesn't. That's it. Attributes and nested elements come via Ant's normal XML binding mechanism. If the condition extends the ProjectComponent class, Ant even binds it to the current project, allowing the condition to log messages or manipulate the project's state. Listing 18.3 shows a simple condition, one that tests for the contents of the value attribute being an even number.

Listing 18.3   A condition to test for a number being even

```
package org.antbook.conditions;
import org.apache.tools.ant.ProjectComponent;
import org.apache.tools.ant.taskdefs.condition.Condition;

public class isEven extends ProjectComponent implements Condition {

    private int value;

    public void setValue(int value) {
        this.value = value;
    }

    public boolean eval() {
        return (value & 1) == 0;
    }
}
```

This is all there is to it. Once compiled and declared, the condition is ready for use in any of the conditional tasks. Compiling is the traditional <javac>; nothing new. Declaring the condition is slightly different from declaring a task, because <typedef> is used.

Alongside tasks, Ant has datatypes. Examples of these are <fileset> and <path> declarations declared outside any task. When Ant encounters a datatype in a build file, it converts it to Java objects. If the type has an id attribute, it stores the converted type instance in the project by using the Project.addReference() method.

Ant's type system also includes any Java classes that implement specific interfaces—in this case Ant's Condition interface. Ant uses introspection to see what a declared datatype can do and to allow the custom types to be used inside tasks or other datatypes. If a task or datatype declares an `add()` method that takes a Java interface, any Ant type with that interface can be added. For Ant conditions, that means any task with the method `add(Condition)` can host the condition.

To tell Ant about our new condition, we use the `<typedef>` task:

```
<typedef name="iseven"
  classname="org.antbook.conditions.isEven"
  uri="antlib:org.antbook.conditions"
  classpath="${target.jar}" />
```

The declaration also can appear in Antlib libraries. Here is the `antlib.xml` for the conditions package:

```
<antlib>
  <typedef name="iseven"
    classname="org.antbook.conditions.isEven" />
</antlib>
```

This declaration can then be loaded via an implicit namespace-driven load or via an explicit `<typedef>` of its own:

```
<target name="define">
  <typedef
      onerror="failall"
      uri="antlib:org.antbook.conditions"
      classpath="${target.jar}"/>
</target>
```

After the condition has been declared as an Ant type, it's ready for use. We can use the condition inside any conditional task, such as `<condition>` itself:

```
<condition property="2.is.even">
  <cond:iseven value="2"/>
</condition>
```

It can also be used in `<fail>`:

```
<fail message="-1 is odd">
  <condition>
    <not>
      <cond:iseven value="-1"/>
    </not>
  </condition>
</fail>
```

We can even use it inside third-party tasks that take conditions, such as AntUnit's `<assertTrue>` assertion:

```
<target name="testZero"
    depends="define">
  <au:assertTrue>
    <cond:iseven value="0"/>
  </au:assertTrue>
</target>
```

Because conditions are so easy to write and because they slot so easily into so many tasks, they are a handy type to add to libraries in which conditional evaluation of some aspect of the system is appropriate.

Scripted conditions

If a project has a one-off test they need to make in a build, the developers can implement the condition in script, using the `<scriptcondition>` condition. Here's the test for a single number "3" being even:

```
<scriptcondition language="ruby">
  <![CDATA[
  $self.value= (3&1)==0
  ]]>
</scriptcondition>
```

The `self.value` attribute is used to store the result of the evaluation. If it's set to true by the script, then the condition is true; if it isn't set or if it's set to false, then condition evaluates to false.

There's no easy way to pass data down to a `<scriptcondition>`, and the script has to be repeated wherever it is used—unless the `file` attribute is used to point to a file containing the script. As such, it's of fairly limited use.

18.2.1 Writing a conditional task

As well as writing custom conditions, you can write tasks that accept conditions and evaluate them. The best way to do this is to extend Ant's `ConditionBase` class. This class supports all the conditions built into Ant and adds an `add(Condition)` method at the end to contain third-party conditions. The class does nothing with the conditions it collects, leaving it up to the subclass, which must implement an `execute()` method. Here's a task that counts the number of nested tasks passing or failing:

```
package org.antbook.conditions;
import org.apache.tools.ant.taskdefs.condition.ConditionBase;
import org.apache.tools.ant.taskdefs.condition.Condition;
import java.util.Enumeration;

public class CountConditions extends ConditionBase {

    public void execute() {
        int passes = 0;
        int failures = 0;
        Enumeration conds = getConditions();        ←— Get the conditions

        while (conds.hasMoreElements()) {            ⎤ Loop through
            Condition c = (Condition)               ⎥ the conditions
                        conds.nextElement();         ⎦

            boolean pass = c.eval();     ←⎤ Evaluate each
            if(pass) {                    ⎦ one in turn
```

```
            passes++;        ←┐  Count passing
        } else {               │  conditions
            failures++;       ←┐  Count failing
        }                      │  conditions
    }
    log("Conditions passing: "+passes+" failing: "+failures);
  }
}
```

This task supports all conditions, both built-in and custom:

```
<cond:count>
  <cond:iseven value="-1"/>
  <cond:iseven value="42"/>
  <istrue value="true"/>
</cond:count>
```

The output of this task is what we would hope—two tests passing and one failing, as shown here:

```
testCount:
Conditions passing: 2 failing: 1
```

It's important to know that simply implementing add(Condition) doesn't give classes access to Ant's built-in conditions, because they aren't actually declared as Ant types. Extending the ConditionBase class is the best way to support the built-in conditions.

To summarize, conditions are found all over build files. It's easy to add a new one, and not that much harder to support conditions in a custom task. Either action makes it easy for Ant extension libraries to integrate with existing tasks and build processes.

18.3 WRITING A CUSTOM RESOURCE

One very interesting extension point to Ant is the resource class hierarchy. In chapter 17, we resource-enabled our <filesize> task, so it could process data from any resource. Equally powerful is that the resource type itself can be extended. To do this, we extend the org.apache.tools.ant.types.Resource class with a custom resource class, overriding the base methods. The key method to override is usually getInputStream(), which returns the contents of the resource as input stream. There are some other methods that can be useful to override, specifically getLast-Modified() and getSize(). These methods return the timestamp of the resource (or 0L if it isn't known) and the resource size, respectively. The base class actually has setSize() and setLastModified() methods that can be used in build files to set the values; this may be adequate for the custom resource.

The example resource we've chosen is one to create a stream of random characters from any cryptographically strong random number generator that is in the Java runtime, using the java.security APIs to access the generator. This resource has no last-modified time, but it will have a size—a size set in the build file. It will have the two attributes `size` and `algorithm` to set the length of the resource and the random number generator to use. Listing 18.4 shows the resource.

Listing 18.4 A custom resource to generate strongly random data

```java
package org.antbook.resources;
import org.apache.tools.ant.types.Resource;
import org.apache.tools.ant.BuildException;
import java.io.InputStream;
import java.io.IOException;
import java.security.SecureRandom;
import java.security.NoSuchAlgorithmException;

public class RandomResource extends Resource
        implements Cloneable {
    private Long seed;
    private String algorithm;

    public void setSeed(Long seed) {
        checkAttributesAllowed();
        this.seed = seed;
    }

    public void setAlgorithm(String algorithm) {
        checkAttributesAllowed();
        this.algorithm = algorithm;
    }


    public InputStream getInputStream() throws IOException {
        if(isReference()) {
            RandomResource that= (RandomResource) getCheckedRef();
            return that.getInputStream();                               ❶
        } else {
            return new RandomInputStream(create(),getSize());
        }
    }
    public boolean isExists() {
        return true;                                                   ❷
    }

    public long getLastModified() {
        return UNKNOWN_DATETIME;                                       ❸
    }

    private SecureRandom create() {       ◁—❹
        SecureRandom generator;
        if(algorithm==null) {
            generator = new SecureRandom();
        } else {
            try {
                generator = SecureRandom.getInstance(algorithm);
```

```
        } catch (NoSuchAlgorithmException e) {
            throw new BuildException("unsupported algorithm "
                +algorithm,e);
        }
    }
    if(seed!=null) {
        generator.setSeed(seed.longValue());
    }
    return generator;
    }
}
```

A Resource is an Ant Datatype; a Datatype is a ProjectComponent. As such, a resource has access to the project and a logger, and Ant binds to it just as it binds to any other XML element—by creating an instance and then configuring it through its XML-to-Java mapping code. There are some subtleties with datatypes. Every setter method needs a call to checkAttributesAllowed(), which throws an exception if the declaration has already been given a refid attribute. There's also the strange stuff in the getInputStream() method ❶, which is the other part of reference handling and is something that we'll cover in section 18.3.2.

Ant requires resources to state whether the data they refer to is present, and when it was last modified. This resource is always found ❷, and it has no last-modified date ❸. The heavy lifting—the random number creation—is implemented in the create() method ❹. This method creates a SecureRandom number source that is then fed into the constructor of a helper class, RandomInputStream. This class implements java.io.InputStream, returning a new random value on every read() until a predefined limit is reached:

```
package org.antbook.resources;
import java.io.InputStream;
import java.io.IOException;
import java.security.SecureRandom;

class RandomInputStream extends InputStream {
    private SecureRandom generator;
    private long size;

    public RandomInputStream(SecureRandom rng, long size) {
        this.generator = rng;
        this.size = size;
    }

    public synchronized int read() throws IOException {
        if(size--<=0) {
            return -1;
        }
        return generator.nextInt(256);
    }
}
```

When the resource is asked for its input stream, a new generator is created and a new `RandomInputStream` is returned. This means that unless a seed is used to set the randomness, the input stream will be different every time `getInputStream()` is called. Every call will result in a new stream of finite length, full of random data[1]— that is, as soon as we can use it in a build file.

18.3.1 Using a custom resource

To use our random data source, we need to tell Ant about it, which brings the `<typedef>` task into play again:

```
<typedef name="random"
  classname="org.antbook.resources.RandomResource" />
```

Once defined, the resource can be used in any task that supports resources, such as the `<loadresource>` task, which fills in a property from a resource:

```
<target name="showload"
  xmlns:res="antlib:org.antbook.resources"
  depends="ready-to-run">
  <loadresource property="result">
    <res:random size="10"/>
  </loadresource>
  <echo> random result=${result}</echo>
</target>
```

This prints out a random set of unreadable characters:

```
>ant showload -q
    [echo]  random result=Ï3A°IáÚG
```

Custom resources can be fed into any resource-enabled task. To save random data to a file, we could use it inside the `<copy>` task:

```
<copy todir="build">
  <res:random name="random.bin" size="8192"/>
</copy>
```

The name attribute had to be set here, so that `<copy>` would know what filename to create at the far end. The result? An 8-KB file full of random numbers.

18.3.2 How Ant datatypes handle references

Datatypes differ from other Ant components in the notion of "references." If we give a datatype, including a resource, an `id` attribute, Ant will file it away for reuse:

```
<res:random size="10" id="testSharedResource" />
```

---

[1] During development the size check was accidentally omitted, so the stream was infinite. Ant did run out of memory eventually.

To use this reference, task declarations declare a generic resource with a `refid` attribute. This could be the simple `<resource>` type:

```
<loadresource property="set1">
  <resource refid="testSharedResource"/>
</loadresource>
```

Alternatively, we could declare a specific resource type, in which case the type of the declared resource must match that of the reference:

```
<loadresource property="set2">
  <res:random refid="testSharedResource"/>
</loadresource>
```

How does this work? Every "relevant" operation on a datatype needs to be redirected to any reference type, if it's present. This explains the code in the `getInput-Stream()` method in listing 18.4. The method had to call `isReference()` to see if it was a reference, and, if so, get the target resource through the call to `get-CheckedRef()`. It is the target resource whose `getInputStream()` method is finally invoked. Every operation that acts on the referenced datatype needs to resolve references this way.

Touchable resources

Any resource that wants to support the `touch(long)` operation should implement the interface `org.apache.tools.ant.types.resources.Touchable`. The `<touch>` task can update the resource with this interface. There's an implicit assumption that touching a resource updates its last-modified time, and that `getLastModified()` will (approximately) reflect the new value.

Resource summary

Resources are a very interesting datatype. New to Ant 1.7, they aren't universally supported across tasks, especially third-party ones. They offer lots of places to improve the build process, as anything that can act as a source of data or locator of files can now plug directly into other tasks. Some projects should be able to do very creative things with them, such as directly feeding remote data into other applications. We may even see custom resource collections, which group resources differently or we may provide sets of resources from new locations. It would certainly be great to have an `<sshfiles>` collection containing files from a remote SSH server, or an `<artifact>` resource giving us direct access to an Ivy artifact on a remote repository. The tools are there—we'll have to wait and see what people do with them.

18.4 SELECTORS

There are three more Ant datatypes we want to look at: selectors, mappers, and filters. Let's start with selectors.

A selector is an Ant type that can filter filesets to decide whether to include a file in a collection. As well as the built-in set, you can add new selectors to a project, writing them in Java or in scripting languages.

A simple example is one that selects read-only files. The ReadOnlySelector that does this is quite short and sweet:

```
package org.antbook.selectors;
import org.apache.tools.ant.types.selectors.BaseExtendSelector;
import java.io.File;

public class ReadOnlySelector extends BaseExtendSelector {

    public boolean isSelected(File basedir, String name, File file) {
        return (!file.canWrite());
    }
}
```

Ant's documentation already provides extensive coverage of writing custom selectors, so we don't cover it in detail here. The main actions are extending `BaseExtend-Selector` and implementing the `isSelected` method. Custom selectors also can take parameters using nested <param> tags. The Ant manual covers this in the "Programming Your Own Selectors" page (http://ant.apache.org/manual/CoreTypes/selectors-program.html).

After the usual steps of compiling the source and creating a JAR file, the selector can be declared with a `<typedef>` command:

```
<antlib>
  <typedef name="readonly"
    classname="org.antbook.selectors.ReadOnlySelector" />
</antlib>
```

A custom selector can support attributes and nested elements and text, through the appropriate `set-` and `add-` methods. Once declared, the selector can then be used inside any fileset, as with this copy operation:

```
<target name="testTypedefSelector" depends="define">
  <copy todir="${temp.dir}"
      xmlns:sel="antlib:org.antbook.selectors">
    <fileset dir="${data.dir}">
      <sel:readonly />
    </fileset>
  </copy>
  <au:assertFalse>
    <available file="${temp.dir}/writeable.dat" />
  </au:assertFalse>
</target>
```

This example is from the AntUnit test that verifies that the writeable file wasn't copied.

Selectors are easy to test in AntUnit; the `setUp` target builds a directory with some files that meet the selection criteria, and some that do not. For our selector, this involves creating stub files with <echo> then using <chmod> and the Windows equivalent (an <exec> of cmd.exe /c attrib +R). The tests themselves copy files from the selection to a temporary directory, which the build file then probes for files that should and should not have been copied. Finally the tearDown target cleans up the temporary directory, ready for the next test.

18.4.1 Scripted selectors

If you don't want the overhead and build stages of a Java selector, a <script-selector> can implement the selector inline. Here's the selector re-implemented as a piece of BeanShell script:

```
<copy todir="${temp.dir}">
  <fileset dir="${data.dir}">
    <scriptselector language="beanshell" >
      self.setSelected(!(new File(filename)).canWrite());
    </scriptselector>
  </fileset>
</copy>
```

Since we've just avoided writing and compiling a Java selector, this is clearly a good way to do a one-off selection.

18.5 DEVELOPING A CUSTOM MAPPER

Many of the same tasks that take selectors also support the <mapper> datatype, which can rename files as they're moved, copied, or imported into archives. Listing 18.5 shows a custom mapper that makes filenames uppercase.

Listing 18.5 A mapper that converts filenames to uppercase

```
package org.antbook.mappers;
import org.apache.tools.ant.util.FileNameMapper;
import java.util.Locale;

public class ToUpperMapper implements FileNameMapper {

    public void setFrom(String from) { }
                                              Ignored
    public void setTo(String to) { }

    public String[] mapFileName(String sourceFileName) {
        return new String[] {
            sourceFileName.toUpperCase(Locale.ENGLISH)
        };
    }
}
```

A custom mapper must implement Ant's `FileNameMapper` interface, which has three methods. We ignore two of the methods, and only implement the `map-FileName()` method. This method takes a string, the path of the file relative to the base of the fileset, and returns an array of strings, the mapped paths. Mappers are free to return multiple mappings for the same source file.

As before, the Ant type needs to be compiled, packaged, and declared using `<typedef>`, possibly in an `antlib.xml` file.

```
<antlib>
  <typedef name="toupper"
    classname="org.antbook.mappers.ToUpperMapper"/>
</antlib>
```

Once declared, the mapper can be used in a `<copy>` operation:

```
<copy todir="build/dest"
  xmlns:map="antlib:org.antbook.mappers">
  <fileset dir="src" />
  <map:toupper />
</copy>
```

The result of this is that files beneath the directory `src` are copied with uppercase file and directory names into `build/dest`. If there was a file `src/package/filename.java`, it would be copied to `build/dest/PACKAGE/FILENAME.java`. The parent directories of the fileset, everything up to and including `src`, aren't mapped. Mappers work only on relative paths, such as turning source directory trees into dotted Java package names.

Mappers crop up a lot in Ant's internals, as they can encode any transformation from input files to output files, such as those of Java RMI stub files. Such mappers aren't declared as Ant datatypes, and they remain hidden from build files. Examine the `<rmic>` and `<java>` tasks in Ant's source to see some at work.

Scripted mappers

You can avoid writing and building a mapper in Java for a one-off file mapping by using the `<scriptmapper>` mapper for coding the mapping inline. Here's the previous `<copy>` task, this time with the mapping in BeanShell:

```
<copy todir="build/dest">
  <fileset dir="src"/>
  <scriptmapper language="beanshell">
    self.addMappedName(source.toUpperCase());
  </scriptmapper>
</copy>
```

Ant calls the script once for every invocation of `FileNameMapper.mapFile-Name()`. The `source` variable holds the source filename, and every call to `self.addMappedName()` adds another mapped name to be returned.

Testing mappers

As with any other Ant extension, we need to test our mappers, which brings us back to AntUnit. Some source files matching the relevant pattern should be set up, then mapped into a target directory and the results validated. The <resourcecount> task, which counts the number of resources in a nested resource collection, comes in handy, as it can count the number of files matching a pattern:

```
<resourcecount property="files.missing">
  <fileset dir="build/dest">
    <filename name="org/**"/>
  </fileset>
</resourcecount>
<au:assertEquals expected="0" actual="${files.missing}"/>
```

This test case asserts that no files matching the (case sensitive) org/** pattern was pulled in by the mapper. A similar check can count the number of files matching ORG/** to assert that uppercase files were created instead.

18.6   IMPLEMENTING A CUSTOM FILTER

Just as mappers can transform the names of files, filters can transform their content. They are Ant types that are chained together during some operations. Once set up in a filter chain, the entire data source is pumped through a character at a time, with each filter fetching the character from its predecessor, possibly transforming it, and then passing it up to the next entry. Filters are the equivalent of piped commands in Unix. We introduced them in chapter 6, and we've been making use of them in <java>, <exec>, and <copy> tasks.

Custom filters can perform custom transformations on the data stream, including adding or removing data from it. The simple filter of listing 18.6 converts lowercase text to uppercase.

Listing 18.6   A custom filter to convert read text to uppercase

```
package org.antbook.filters;
import org.apache.tools.ant.filters.BaseFilterReader;
import org.apache.tools.ant.filters.ChainableReader;
import java.io.Reader;
import java.io.IOException;

public class ToUpperFilter extends BaseFilterReader          This class
    implements ChainableReader {                             is a filter

    public ToUpperFilter() {
    }

    public ToUpperFilter(final Reader in) {                  This constructor takes the
        super(in);                                           source of data to read in
    }
```

```
public Reader chain(Reader rdr) {
    ToUpperFilter filter=new ToUpperFilter(rdr);       Create the filter
    filter.setProject(getProject());                   for this chain
    return filter;
}

public int read() throws IOException {
    int ch=super.read();                               Read in the next character
    return Character.toUpperCase(ch);                  from the chain and convert it
}
}
```

Filters use the standard `java.io.Reader`, which is implicitly available as the `in` member variable from the parent class `BaseFilterReader`. The `chain` method comes from the `ChainableReader` interface and allows our class to be linked to another filter, passing the modified stream through to it. The most important method is `read()`, which Ant calls when another character is needed. Our implementation calls the predecessor in the chain and then returns the result of converting lowercase characters to uppercase in the process.

As with the other Ant types, you need to declare the filter before use:

```
<typedef name="toupper"
    classname="org.antbook.filters.ToUpperFilter"/>
```

We can now test this class inside the `<concat>` task, passing a string through the filter chain:

```
                                              Print to
<concat destfile="build/README"      ←┘      a file
  xmlns:f="antlib:org.antbook.filters">
  <string value="Hello, World!" />   ←—  Our message
  <filterchain>
    <f:toupper/>   ←┐  Convert
  </filterchain>   └ the case
</concat>
                                          Print the
<concat>                                  result
  <file file="build/README" />   ←┘
</concat>
```

What is the output? It's what we hoped for:

```
showConcat:
   [concat] HELLO, WORLD!

BUILD SUCCESSFUL
Total time: 0 seconds
```

Admittedly, case conversion is a pretty simple operation, but it shows what can be done. Arbitrary post-processing can be performed on the input to or output from a Java or native program.

Scripted filter readers

If we don't want to write Java for a quick bit of text filtering, the `<scriptfilter>` type can help. This can host a piece of script that will be invoked once for each token to be filtered. Here's the AntUnit test for a scripted filter:

```
<target name="testScripted">
  <loadresource property="uppercase">
    <string value="Hello, World!"/>
    <filterchain>
      <scriptfilter language="beanshell">
        self.setToken(self.getToken().toUpperCase())
      </scriptfilter>
    </filterchain>
  </loadresource>
  <au:assertEquals expected="HELLO, WORLD!"
    actual="${uppercase}"/>
</target>
```

The test uses the `<loadresource>` task to load a string into a property by way of the filter. Every character gets converted into uppercase during the read, which is what we then test for.

Filter summary

Filters are the last of the main Ant extension points, though a thorough browse of the Ant documentation will undoubtedly uncover a few more. Filters are useful for pre- and post-processing of text, such as input to or output from a native program. They can do pretty complex things. Whenever you `<copy>` a file with property expansion, that's a filter at work. If you need to process streamed data in a build, then write a filter either inline or in Java. Remember: they're just like Unix pipes.

That's the end of our coverage of Ant types. The other way that Ant can be extended is much more low-level. You can write new classes that change how Ant prints out the build or handles input. You can even host Ant inside another application. That is the last thing this book will cover. Let's build up to it by hooking into Ant's I/O and eventing infrastructure.

18.7   HANDLING ANT'S INPUT AND OUTPUT

It's time for the final bit of extending Ant—time to go low-level and look at topics that most people avoid. We're going to look at the internals of Ant, first by customizing its I/O mechanisms.

Ant lets developers monitor its progress during execution. Ant prints to the console, and in IDEs Ant's output appears in windows in the editor. How does Ant do this? Through two tightly related concepts: *listeners* and *loggers*. These receive lifecycle events and the output of a build, and both can be extended by custom versions. Let's first take a look at the UML for the `BuildListener` and `BuildLogger` interfaces, shown in figure 18.1.

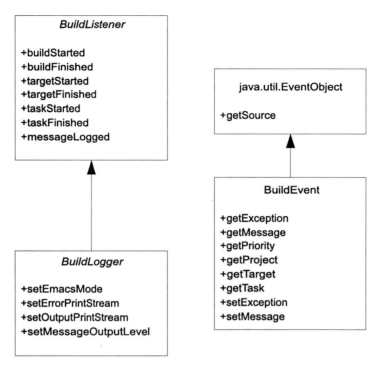

Figure 18.1 The `BuildListener` and `BuildLogger` receive lifecycle events, events which are described by BuildEvent objects.

A `BuildListener` is a Java class that receives notifications of various build, target, and task lifecycle events during a build. The events are build started/finished, target started/finished, task started/finished, and message logged. A project can have any number of build listeners. Ant internally attaches some of its own build listeners to catch events, particularly the build-finished event, which triggers cleanups. Each of the events is handed a `BuildEvent` instance. This `BuildEvent` encapsulates all the details of the event being triggered, as listed in table 18.2.

Table 18.2 The different `BuildListener` callbacks and the `BuildEvent` data they can expect. For all the finished events, a non-null exception inside the `BuildEvent` implies that the task, target, or build failed.

`BuildListener` event	`BuildEvent` contents
buildStarted	Project
buildFinished	Project and possibly an exception
targetStarted	Project and target
targetFinished	Project, target, and possibly exception
taskStarted	Project, target, and task

continued on next page

CHAPTER 18 EXTENDING ANT FURTHER

Table 18.2 The different `BuildListener` callbacks and the `BuildEvent` data they can expect. For all the finished events, a non-null exception inside the `BuildEvent` implies that the task, target, or build failed. *(continued)*

`BuildListener` event	`BuildEvent` contents
`taskFinished`	Project, target, task, and possibly exception.
`messageLogged`	Message and its priority. The Project attribute is always set, and depending on where the message originated, the target and task attributes may also be set.

The `BuildLogger` interface builds on its parent `BuildListener` by adding access to the output and error print streams. Two additional methods that the `BuildLogger` interface extends beyond `BuildListener` allow for setting the emacs mode and the message output level. The `DefaultLogger` reacts to the emacs switch by generating output formatted for IDE integration, as its formatting of error locations in files is something most IDEs can parse. The message output level is used to filter the output based on the logging level.

Every Ant project has one and only one logger, which is hooked up to the output streams and attached to the project as a listener to receive lifecycle events. Users can select a specific logger on the command line via the `-logger` switch; otherwise they get the default one. Using `-emacs` enables the emacs mode. The `-quiet`, `-verbose`, and `-debug` switches can move the logging level up or down from its default of "info." Because only one logger is allowed, IDEs don't let you switch from their custom loggers, which are needed to integrate Ant with the editor.

18.7.1 Writing a custom listener

As we stated, a listener is a Java class that implements `BuildListener`. Listing 18.7 shows a custom listener we've pulled together. It records the frequency of start and finish events and then, when the build finishes, prints them to `System.out`.

Listing 18.7 A listener that collects statistics

```
package org.antbook.listeners;
import org.apache.tools.ant.BuildListener;
import org.apache.tools.ant.BuildEvent;

public class StatsListener implements BuildListener {

    private Tracker builds = new Tracker("Builds");        These log
    private Tracker targets = new Tracker("Targets");      events
    private Tracker tasks = new Tracker("Tasks");

    public void buildStarted(BuildEvent event) {           The build
        builds.enter(event);                               has started
    }

    public void buildFinished(BuildEvent event) {          The build
        builds.exit(event);                                has finished
        System.out.println(builds);
```

```
        System.out.println(targets);          Print the
        System.out.println(tasks);            results
    }

    public void targetStarted(BuildEvent event) {    A target has
        targets.enter(event);                        started
    }

    public void targetFinished(BuildEvent event) {   A target has
        targets.exit(event);                         finished
    }

    public void taskStarted(BuildEvent event) {      A task has
        tasks.enter(event);                          started
    }

    public void taskFinished(BuildEvent event) {     A task has
        tasks.exit(event);                           finished
    }

    public void messageLogged(BuildEvent event) {    Ignore logged
    }                                                messages
}
```

This listener delegates most of the work to a helper class—the `Tracker` class—which tracks notifications. This class tracks the start and finish events for each category, as well as the last exception thrown on a failure:

```
package org.antbook.listeners;
import org.apache.tools.ant.BuildEvent;

public class Tracker {                     What is
    private String category;       ←┘     tracked      The total
    private volatile int count;        ←┘              entry count    The current
    private volatile int depth;              ←┘                       depth
    private Throwable thrown;       ←—  Any exception thrown

    public Tracker(String category) {        Store the category
        this.category = category;            during creation
    }

    public synchronized void enter(BuildEvent event) {
        count++;                                             Entry: increase
        depth++;                                             count and depth
    }

    public synchronized void exit(BuildEvent event) {
        depth--;
        if(event.getException()!=null) {                     Decrease the
            thrown=event.getException();                     depth and cache
        }                                                    any exception
    }
}
```

CHAPTER 18   EXTENDING ANT FURTHER

```
    public String toString() {
        StringBuffer state =new StringBuffer();
        state.append(category);
        state.append("=");
        state.append(count);
        if(depth>0) {
            state.append(" depth=");
            state.append(depth);
        }
        if (thrown !=null) {
            state.append(" (failure)");
        }
        return state.toString();
    }
}
```

Construct and return a string containing everything that has been recorded

This class's `toString()` method prints the statistics for that particular category. When a `StatsListener` instance receives a `buildFinished()` notification, it prints out all the trackers' statistics at that point. Assuming that we receive such a message at the end of the build, this should give the statistics of the build.

There's no test suite for listeners and loggers, no equivalent to AntUnit. Ant's original test-harness JAR can be used to run Ant from JUnit tests, setting up a project and making JUnit assertions about the results. Suspiciously, there are no tests for any of Ant's own listeners or loggers, just a `MockBuildListener` that appears in notification dispatch tests.

We'll break our test-first rule and mimic the Ant team by running our code, instead of rigorously testing it. To run our listener, all we need to do is run Ant from the command line with the `-listener` argument pointing to the new class and the newly created JAR appearing on the classpath:

```
ant -listener org.antbook.listeners.StatsListener \
    -lib dist/antbook-log-1.0.jar dist

Buildfile: build.xml

init:

compile:

jar:

dist:

ready-to-run:

ready-to-install:

install:

installed:
```

```
default:

BUILD SUCCESSFUL
Total time: 0 seconds
Builds=1
Targets=9
Tasks=16
```

This is actually mildly interesting, especially on a big project. A quick check of a work-related build showed 596 targets and 3456 tasks. The project count remains at one, even when multiple <ant> calls have invoked other build files. Listeners are notified only on the big builds starting and finishing, not on subsidiary projects. It is, however, possible to start targets and tasks before the previous one finishes, using <parallel>, <antcall>, and the like.

What happens on a failing build? For that, we need a build file that fails, such as that in listing 18.8.

```
<project default="fail">

  <property name="ant.build.success"
    value="Well done, ${user.name}"/>
  <property name="ant.build.failure"
    value="Better luck next time, ${user.name}"/>

  <target name="fail">
    <fail message="Example build failure"/>
  </target>
</project>
```

Running the test now gives us a failure message:

```
ant -listener org.antbook.listeners.StatsListener \
    -lib dist/antbook-log-1.0.jar -f test/fail.xml
Buildfile: test/fail.xml

fail:

BUILD FAILED
/home/ant/listeners/test/fail.xml:7: Example build failure

Total time: 0 seconds
builds=1 (failure)
targets=1 (failure)
tasks=3 (failure)
```

This build file shows that when a task fails, the containing target and build file also are notified. There's one more experiment to do: use the Ant-contrib <trycatch> task of chapter 9, which can catch and discard exceptions, and see what the statistics are if a task's failure is caught and ignored:

```
Buildfile: test/nofail.xml

nofail:

BUILD SUCCESSFUL
Total time: 0 seconds
builds=1
targets=1
tasks=6 (failure)
```

This shows something mildly useful. If a task fails, it is signalled as such to a listener, even if an outer container catches the failure and discards the exception.

18.7.2 Writing a custom logger

The next coding exercise after a custom listener is a custom logger, which is a class that implements `BuildLogger`. This is simply a `BuildListener` with four additional methods to handle the system output and error streams as well as the setting of some output options. The easiest way to do some logging, if all you want to do is slightly tweak the normal output, is to extend Ant's `DefaultLogger` class, which is Ant's normal logger. Listing 18.9 is an example of this.

Listing 18.9 A new logger, an extension of the normal one, that replaces the normal success/failure message with one from project properties

```
package org.antbook.listeners;

import org.apache.tools.ant.DefaultLogger;
import org.apache.tools.ant.BuildEvent;
import org.apache.tools.ant.Project;

public class PersonalLogger extends DefaultLogger {
    private static final String SUCCESS = "ant.build.success";
    private static final String FAILURE = "ant.build.failure";
    private String result;

    @Override
    public void buildFinished(BuildEvent event) {
        String name;
        name = event.getException() == null ?
                            SUCCESS          │   Select the property
                          : FAILURE;         │
        Project p = event.getProject();    ◁— Read it
        result = p.replaceProperties("${" + name + '}');   ◁— Expand it
        super.buildFinished(event);
    }

    @Override
```

```
protected String getBuildFailedMessage() {       Return the message
    return result;                                 to print on failure
}

@Override
protected String getBuildSuccessfulMessage() {    Return the
    return result;                                 success message
}
}
```

This logger replaces the usual BUILD SUCCESSFUL and BUILD FAILED messages at the end of a build with whatever the evaluations of the `${ant.build.success}` and `${ant.build.failure}` strings are, respectively. The parent class, the `DefaultLogger`, calls `getBuildSuccessfulMessage()` or `getBuild-FailedMessage()`, depending on the build's outcome. All our logger needs to do is evaluate the appropriate property at the end of the build. Instead of reading the property using `Project.getProperty()`, the logger just creates the appropriate `${property}` string and asks the project to expand it. When the property is undefined, the message will become the name of the property to set.

We can use this logger on the command line:

```
>ant -logger org.antbook.listeners.PersonalLogger -q \
   -Dant.build.success=well-done!

well-done!
Total time: 0 seconds
```

Here the `-logger` option set the classname of the new logger, which was already on the classpath. The `-q` option turned off all the output except for errors and warnings, a feature of the `DefaultLogger` class that subclasses get for free.

Being able to change the message in advance is one thing, but setting it inside the build is something else that's potentially useful. In the build file of listing 18.8, the success and failure properties were set in the build; these are the properties that should propagate to the output text:

```
ant -logger org.antbook.listeners.PersonalLogger -f test/fail.xml

Buildfile: test/fail.xml

fail:

***Installation failed, call Julio for support ***
/home/ant/listeners/test/fail.xml:9: Example build failure

Total time: 0 seconds
```

This build file gives us a custom error message for our end users. We do need to make sure the new logger is selected for every build. This can be done with the `ANT_OPTS` environment variable, such as here in a bash configuration file:

```
export ANT_OPTS="-logger org.antbook.listeners.PersonalLogger"
```

This will switch to the new logger on all command-line runs.

Avoiding trouble in custom listeners and loggers

The Ant documentation warns against loggers or listeners printing to `System.out` or `System.err`, because doing so can create an infinite loop. The logger is handed two `PrintStream` instances for output; it should use these. Listeners are not really meant to generate output, but if they must, they should do it to some other device such as a file. In fact, you can get away with printing to `System.out` and `System.err`, as long as you don't do so in `messageLogged()` events.

One trouble spot is the state of a project during lifecycle events. When a listener receives a `buildStarted` event, the project isn't yet fully configured. Its tasks aren't defined, and the default properties aren't set up. The project isn't ready for serious use. Similarly, when a listener has its `buildFinished()` method called, the build is already finished. The listener can examine the project and its properties, but not run any targets or tasks.

A project calls all the listeners in sequence, in the build's current thread. Slow operations will slow the build down. When the `<parallel>` task is used to run tasks in a new thread, the notifications from those tasks are raised in the new thread. Listeners need to be thread-safe.

18.7.3 Using loggers and listeners

Historically, Ant loggers have been used for generating custom reports. The `MailLogger` creates emails, and the `Log4JListener` and `CommonsLogging-Listener` (which is actually a logger) generate more complex reports, including pretty HTML logs that can be emailed around.

Nowadays, it's the job of the continuous integration server to generate the HTML reports and the emails, and the IDE has probably taken over from the command line as the main way of launching Ant. In either situation, *do not attempt to use your own loggers*. The IDE and continuous integration developers will have written their own loggers, loggers that should be left alone.

If you want Ant to send out emails when a build fails, have a continuous integration tool do the work. It will catch and report problems that the loggers won't get, such as a missing `build.xml` file. There's no need to re-implement what existing continuous integration tools can do better.

Listeners are less troublesome, as a project can have any number of active listeners, and listeners can be added or removed during the build. There aren't any tasks to do this, other than the `<record>` task, which records events to a file. However, a custom `<scriptdef>` task could easily create the desired listener, configure it, and then call `Project.addBuildListener()` to add it to the project, or `remove-BuildListener()` to prevent it from receiving events.

18.7.4 Handling user input with an InputHandler

The opposite of Ant's output system is its mechanism for handling user input. Although Ant is designed to run without user intervention, sometimes builds use the `<input>` task to ask for input from the user. Doing so delegates the task to an `InputHandler`, which is a class that handles all input from the user. The default handler reads from `System.in.`, expecting input from a user at the console. Ant ships with two other handlers, the `PropertyFileInputHandler` and the `GreedyInputHandler`. The first of these handlers reads input from a property file, while the `GreedyInputHandler` reads the whole input stream into a single `<input>` request. Selecting this handler with the `-inputhandler` option lets Ant integrate into a Unix-style pipes-and-brackets setup:

```
find / -name build.xml -print | ant exec -inputhandler \
        org.apache.tools.ant.input.GreedyInputHandler
```

New classes can act as input handlers; they have to implement the `org.apache.tools.ant.input.InputHandler` interface and its `handleInput(InputRequest request)` method.

IDE developers do all this work to stop the `<input>` task from hanging under their IDE. We aren't covering the details of how to write a new InputHandler—only mentioning that it is possible. If you're writing an IDE or continuous integration tool, then consult Ant's documentation and source for details on how to integrate Ant's input handling.

18.8 EMBEDDING ANT

The final way to extend Ant is to embed it inside another Java program. This isn't as unusual as it sounds. Java IDEs do this to integrate Ant with their GUI. Many other programs use it internally. It crops up in products such as Apache Tomcat, where `<javac>` compiles down JSP pages into `.class` files. When embedded, Ant becomes a library that can execute built-in or custom tasks. It has become a simple workflow tool with tasks for compiling and running Java programs.

Ant can be used within any Java program. You can either create a `build.xml` file and hand it off, or create a `Project` instance with tasks and targets via Java operations. Interestingly, there's one way that is hard to use Ant: its static entry point, `Main.main()` calls `System.exit()` at the end. If you want to embed this class, you have to subclass its `Main` and override its `exit()` method. You can still use Ant's launcher application, specifying the new entry point via the `-main` argument. However, we'll ignore this route, as fully embedded Ant is more interesting.

Listing 18.10 shows Ant running inside another Java program. It doesn't do much—just runs the `<echo>` task. What's important is that a `Project` instance has been created and set up, with logging all wired up and running at the "info" level.

Listing 18.10 A private run of Ant

```
package org.antbook.embed;

import org.apache.tools.ant.Project;
import org.apache.tools.ant.BuildException;
import org.apache.tools.ant.DemuxOutputStream;
import org.apache.tools.ant.DefaultLogger;
import org.apache.tools.ant.taskdefs.Echo;
import java.io.PrintStream;

public class Embedded {

    private Project project;

    public Embedded() {                                      Create a
        project = new Project();          <──┘               project
        project.init();
        DefaultLogger logger = new DefaultLogger();
        project.addBuildListener(logger);                    Wire a logger
        logger.setOutputPrintStream(System.out);             up to the output
        logger.setErrorPrintStream(System.err);              streams
        logger.setMessageOutputLevel(Project.MSG_INFO);
        System.setOut(
          new PrintStream(
            new DemuxOutputStream(project, false)));          Route output
        System.setErr(                                        through the
          new PrintStream(                                    project and log
            new DemuxOutputStream(project, true)));
        project.fireBuildStarted();       <──┐   Start the
    }                                        │   build

    public void run() {                          Create
        System.out.println("running");          a task
        Echo echo=new Echo();             <──┐
        echo.setTaskName("Echo");            │   Bind to the
        echo.setProject(project);         <──┘   project       Initalize
        echo.init();                                   <──┘     the task
        echo.setMessage("Hello, world");   <──  Configure it
        echo.execute();           <──  Execute it
        project.log("finished");
        project.fireBuildFinished(null);   <──  Stop the build
    }

    public static void main(String args[]) {
        Embedded embed=new Embedded();   <──  Create our class
        try {
            embed.run();   <──  Run it
        } catch (BuildException e) {
            e.printStackTrace();   <──  Log exceptions
        }
    }
}
```

To configure the <echo> task, we just call the relevant set-, add-, or create-methods of the task, passing in the data we want. That's all it takes to configure the task. If we had wanted to expand properties or resolve paths, we would have had to invoke the relevant Project methods before calling the task methods.

To test this program, we can run it under Ant itself, in a forked <java> task:

```
<target name="exec" >
  <java classname="org.antbook.embed.Embedded"
    failonerror="true"
    fork="true">
    <classpath>
      <pathelement path="${target.jar}" />
      <pathelement path="${java.class.path}" />
    </classpath>
    </java>
</target>
```

Here is our test run of Ant inside the output of the <java> task:

```
exec:
    [java] running
    [java]      [Echo] Hello, world
    [java] finished

    [java] BUILD SUCCESSFUL
    [java] Total time: 0 seconds
```

This shows that we've written a new entry point to Ant. It isn't as complex as Ant's own Main class, but it shows the basic techniques of running Ant and Ant tasks. You just create a project, create and configure tasks, then bind them to the project before you run them.

Tips on embedding Ant

- Don't expect a very long-lived build not to leak memory. Supporting builds that last multiple days isn't a priority for the tool's development.

- If you distribute a version of Ant that can be directly invoked by end users, or if you put your version of Ant on the CLASSPATH—which has the same effect—you take on all support responsibilities. The Ant team doesn't support any problems related to random redistributions of Ant.

- Never use an Ant task without creating a Project and binding the task to it with setProject(). Tasks depend on a project instance for logging and many other operations, and they break horribly if getProject()==null.

18.9 SUMMARY

This chapter finishes our coverage of Ant with a look at the final ways to extend Ant. Alongside Ant tasks come Ant types—types that are defined with <typedef>. Many of the extension points explored here—conditions, resources, mappers, filters, and selectors—are all different dynamically configured Ant types.

We've introduced Ant's scripting support in `<script>` and `<scriptdef>`, and we've shown you the script bindings to conditions, filters, and selectors. There's nothing wrong with a bit of script to solve a problem that Ant cannot normally handle.

Custom conditions let you add new tests into a build. Ant can set properties from the condition or block until it passes. You can even write custom tasks that accept nested conditions, both built-in and third-party.

Ant resources are one example of an Ant datatype—an XML element that can be shared between tasks. Resources can provide a source of data to any resource-enabled application. They let any such task access data from any source, without having to know or care where it comes from.

Custom mappers and selectors can control how Ant processes sets of files. Mappers translate one filename to other filenames, and a custom one can provide new mapping rules. Selectors nest within filesets, allowing sophisticated filtering of files within a directory tree. Writing a custom selector can add enormous capabilities to file selection, such as the read-only file selector we developed here. Mappers are useful to identify the output files generated from source files, which is why they're used internally in many tasks.

Filters allow for powerful data transformations, and chaining filters together accomplishes something similar to piping commands from one to another in Unix shell scripting.

Finally, there's the low-level side of extending Ant. These are not ways to enhance a build file; rather, they are new ways to integrate Ant with other applications. Build listeners and loggers let you capture output or generate new messages. You can also embed Ant inside another Java program, simply by creating a new `Project` class and adding configured task classes.

The most important point we can leave you with is this: familiarize yourself with all of Ant's out-of-the-box capabilities before beginning customizations. Very likely, you will find that Ant can already handle your needs. Consult Ant's documentation, this book, and online resources such as Ant's user and developer email lists, where you'll find a helpful and often quick-responding crew of Ant users from around the world—including ourselves.

Installation

If there is one area where Ant could be improved, it's in the area of installation. It still has a fairly manual installation process, and a few things can go wrong. Here's a summary of how to install Ant, and also a troubleshooting guide in case something goes awry.

BEFORE YOU BEGIN

Before installing Ant, check that a Java SE Software Development Kit, otherwise known as JDK, is installed on the target system. Type `javac` at a command prompt; if a usage message doesn't appear, then either a JDK needs to be installed or the PATH environment variable path isn't set up correctly. Sun distributes their versions under http://java.sun.com/javase/—you need to download the appropriate JDK for your system.

On Windows, install the JDK on a path without spaces in it, such as `c:\java\jdk`, instead of a path such as `C:\Program Files\Java`. Spaces in paths can confuse Ant and other programs.

After installing the JDK, Ant requires the environment variable JAVA_HOME to be set to the directory into which it was installed. You should also append `JAVA_HOME\bin` to the PATH environment variable, so that you can run the SDK's programs from the command line. Some Ant tasks depend on this, since they run these programs.

THE STEPS TO INSTALL ANT

The core stages of the Ant installation process are the same regardless of the platform:

1 Download Ant.

2 Unzip or untar it into a directory.

3 Set up some environment variables to point to the JDK and Ant.

4 Add Ant's bin directory to the command line path.

5 Add any optional libraries to Ant that you desire or need. (This can be done later.)

The exact details vary from platform to platform, and as Ant works to varying degrees on everything from laptops to mainframes, it isn't possible to cover all the possible platforms you may want to install Ant onto; instead we'll cover only the Windows and Unix/Linux platforms.

Ant distributions come as source or binary distributions. Binary distributions should work out of the box, whereas source editions need to be built using the Ant bootstrap scripts. It's probably safest to hold off getting the source editions until chapters 17 and 18, when we look at extending Ant's Java code.

When downloading a binary version, get either the latest release build, or a beta release of the version about to be released. Nightly builds are incomplete and built primarily as a test, rather than for public distribution.

SETTING UP ANT ON WINDOWS

Download the binary distribution zip file from http://ant.apache.org/ to your local disk. Then unzip it to where you want the files to live, making sure that the unzip tool preserves directory structure. The `jar` tool built into the JDK can expand the archive:

```
jar xvf apache-ant-1.7.0-bin.zip
```

Let's assume you unzipped it to `c:\java\ant`. This new directory you've created and installed Ant into is called "Ant home."

You should add the bin subdirectory, here `c:\java\ant\bin`, to the end of the `Path` environment variable so Ant can be called from the command line. You also should set the `ANT_HOME` environment variable to point to the Ant home directory. The batch file that starts Ant can usually just assume that `ANT_HOME` is one directory up from where the batch file lives, but sometimes it's nice to know for sure.

You can set environment variables in the "system" section of the control panel, in its "Advanced" tab pane, under "Environment Variables...." This dialog is somewhat cramped and noticeably less usable than a text file, but such is progress. After closing the dialog box, any new console windows or applications started should pick up the altered settings. You can check by typing SET at the command prompt, which should include lines like the following:

```
ANT_HOME=C:\Java\Apache\Ant
JAVA_HOME=C:\Java\jdk
Path=C:\WINDOWS\system32;C:\WINDOWS;C:\Java\jdk\bin;C:\Java\Ant\bin
```

If these variables aren't set, try logging out and in again.

This is also a good time to check that the CLASSPATH environment variable isn't set. If it is, all JAR files listed in it get picked up by Ant, which can cause confusion. If there's a quote inside the CLASSPATH, or if it ends in a backslash, Ant will fail with an obscure error. This variable has made both mistakes:

```
CLASSPATH="C:\Program Files\JARS\xerces.jar";c:\project\classes\
```

The correct setting—if it has to be used at all—would be

```
CLASSPATH=C:\Program Files\JARS\xerces.jar;c:\project\classes
```

As we said, you shouldn't need this at all. It only confuses Ant and other Java programs.

To test that Ant is installed, type ant -version at a newly opened console. The result should be the version of Ant that's installed:

```
Apache Ant version 1.7.0 compiled on December 13 2006
```

The printed version number must match that of the version you've just downloaded; anything else means there's still a problem.

SETTING UP ANT ON UNIX

The first step to running Ant on a Unix/Linux system is to install a JDK. Ant works best with an official Sun JDK. The Kaffe and Classpath projects provide a runtime that's good for running code, but the official JDK is still best for development. Sun provides the JDK at http://java.sun.com/.

Many Linux distributions provide a packaged distribution, such as an RPM or .deb file. Those that are created by the JPackage team at http://www.jpackage.org/ are the best; they integrate the installation with the operating system's library management tools. Their web site shows how you can use yum or apt to subscribe to their releases. Sun provides RPM packages that are not fully compatible with JPackage installations.

With JPackage, the JDK will be installed somewhere like /usr/lib/jvm/jdk_sun_1.5.10; with a Sun RPM, the destination is something like /usr/java/jdk_1.5.10. To stop this value from changing every time you update the JDK, set up a symbolic link, such as /usr/lib/jvm/jdk, to point to the JDK you want to use. Then set up the login scripts of yourself—or all users in the system—to have the JAVA_HOME environment variable set to this location. In the bash script language, it would be something like

```
export JAVA_HOME=/usr/lib/jvm/jdk
```

You should also add the bin subdirectory of the JDK to the PATH environment variable.

To test for the JDK, you should try running java first:

```
> java -version
java version "1.5.0_06"
Java(TM) 2 Runtime Environment, Standard Edition (build 1.5.0_10)
Java HotSpot(TM) Client VM (build 1.5.0_10, mixed mode, sharing)
```

If this picks up another Java runtime from the one you've just installed, then you have an existing runtime installed somewhere. Uninstall it and try again.

Once java works, check that javac is on the command line, as is tnameserv. The latter is available only if the JDK's bin directory is on the path. If it's found, the JDK is installed, and it's time to install Ant.

As with the JDK, the JPackage team provides a version of Ant. You can install it and have it set up Ant to work from the command line. The alternative is to do it by hand.

1 Download the .tar.gz file from http://ant.apache.org/.

2 Expand it using gunzip:

```
gunzip apache-ant-1.7.0-bin.tar.gz
```

3 Untar it using the Gnu tar program. AIX, Solaris, and HPUX users will encounter problems if they use the version that ships with their OS, as it cannot handle long filenames:

```
tar -xf apache-ant-1.7.0-bin.tar
```

4 Set the ANT_HOME environment in the login script

```
export ANT_HOME=/home/ant/apache-ant-1.7.0-bin
```

5 Add $ANT_HOME/bin to the PATH environment variable:

```
export PATH=$PATH:$ANT_HOME/bin:$JAVA_HOME/bin
```

6 Log out and in again.

7 Change to Ant's bin directory:

```
cd apache-ant-1.7.0/bin
```

8 Run Ant:

```
ant -version
```

The result should be the version of Ant that's installed:

```
Apache Ant version 1.7.0 compiled on December 13 2006
```

A different version means that there's a conflicting copy of Ant on the path, perhaps one preinstalled by the system administrators.

There's a place where Ant options (such as ANT_OPTS) can be set in Unix, the .antrc file in the user's home directory, which is read in by the Ant shell script. Other mechanisms for starting Ant under Unix, such as the Perl or Python scripts, don't read this file.

INSTALLATION CONFIGURATION

There are two useful environment variables that the Ant wrapper scripts use when invoking Ant: `ANT_OPTS` and `ANT_ARGS`. These can be used to configure Ant's scripts—but have no effect on IDE-hosted Ant.

ANT_OPTS

The `ANT_OPTS` environment variable provides options to the JVM executing Ant, such as system properties and memory configuration. One use of the environment variable is to set up the proxy settings for Ant tasks and Java programs hosted in Ant's JVM. Declaring two system properties is sufficient here

```
-Dhttp.proxyHost=proxy -Dhttp.proxyPort=8080
```

Remember these are system properties, not Ant properties. They will be visible as Ant properties, but they are interpreted by the JVM, not Ant.

ANT_ARGS

In a similar fashion to `ANT_OPTS`, the `ANT_ARGS` environment variable is passed to Ant's main process as command-line arguments, in addition to the arguments that you specify on the command line. This could be useful, for example, if you always want to use Ant's `NoBannerLogger` to remove the output from empty targets.

```
export ANT_ARGS=-logger org.apache.tools.ant.NoBannerLogger
```

Any Ant command-line parameter can be set in this environment variable.

TROUBLESHOOTING INSTALLATION

Getting started with Ant is difficult: you don't know exactly what to expect, and there are a few complex steps to go through. This is where you discover that a consequence of free, open source software is that nobody staffs the support lines apart from other users of the tool.

Because Ant does work for most developers, any installation that doesn't work is almost always due to some local configuration problem. Something is missing or misconfigured or, perhaps, some other piece of software is interfering with Ant.

The best source of diagnostics is built into Ant—the `-diagnostics` command:

```
ant -diagnostics
```

This will list out Ant's view of its own state. If you get an error instead, something has gone horribly wrong, either with the command line or the classpath. If it works, it will display information about the installation, including Ant's JAR versions, which tasks cannot be instantiated, system properties, the classpath, and other relevant information. This output may help to determine the cause of any installation or configuration problems. It is also important data to include in any bug report filed against installation problems.

If you cannot get Ant to work, consult the Ant user mailing list. Remember that Ant does work on most people's machines, so if there's a problem it is in the local system. These are hard bugs to track down, and nobody else can do it but you. All you are likely to get is advice such as "reset CLASSPATH" or "remove the RPM and try again," because there are no obvious answers to these problems.

Problem: Java not installed/configured

If Java is missing or not on the path, then Ant doesn't work.

Test Run `java` from the command line; if this isn't a known command, then either Java isn't installed or the path is wrong.

Fix Install the JDK; set up `JAVA_HOME` to point to the install location. Add the bin directory to the PATH, and log out and in again.

Problem: JDK not installed/configured

Ant needs to find the JDK so that it can use classes in `tools.jar`, such as the Java compiler. Without the JDK, some Ant tasks will fail with "class not found" exceptions. The environment variable `JAVA_HOME` is used to find the JDK—if it isn't set, Ant will warn you on startup with an error message:

```
Warning: JAVA_HOME environment variable is not set.
```

This may just be a warning, but it's a warning that some tasks will not work properly. More insidiously, if `JAVA_HOME` is wrong, Ant will not notice until some tasks fail, usually `<javac>` and `<javadoc>`.

Test 1 Run `javac` from the command line; if this isn't a known command, then either Java isn't installed or the path is wrong.

Test 2 Use `set` or `setenv` to verify that the environment variable `JAVA_HOME` exists. Verify that the file `tools.jar` can be found in the subdirectory `JAVA_HOME/lib`.

Fix Install the JDK; set up `JAVA_HOME` to point to the install location.

Problem: Ant not on the path

Ant is started by a platform-dependent batch file or shell script, or by a portable script in a language such as Perl or Python. If the path doesn't include Ant's `bin` directory, these scripts aren't found and so Ant cannot start.

Test Run `ant -version` from the command line: a version number and build time should appear. If the command interpreter complains that `ant` is unknown, then the path is wrong. If the error is that the Java command is unknown, then the problem is actually with the Java installation, covered earlier.

Fix Modify the environment path variable to include the Ant scripts, log out, and reboot or otherwise reload the environment to have the change applied.

Problem: Another version of Ant is on the path

Many Java products include a version of Ant, including Apache Tomcat, IBM Web-Sphere, and BEA WebLogic. This may be an older version of Ant, or the installation may be incomplete.

Test   Run `ant -diagnostics` to get a diagnostics output, including `ant.home`.

Fix   Remove or rename other copies of the batch files/shell scripts, or reorder your path to place the version you want first.

Problem: Ant fails with an error about a missing task or library

This can mean that a library containing needed task definitions is missing. The `-diagnostics` command will probe for missing tasks. Usually the problem is missing third-party libraries, though it also can be caused by a custom build of Ant that was compiled without those libraries.

Test   Run `ant -diagnostics` to see if the task is present.

Fix   Consult Ant's documentation to see what extra libraries are needed—download them and install them in the `ANT_HOME/lib` directory.

Problem: The ANT_HOME directory points to the wrong place

If `ANT_HOME` is set, but it's set to the wrong location, much confusion can arise. A warning about `lcp.bat` being missing is one obvious sign when calling `ant.bat`; another is failure to find `ant.jar`, with a Java error about the class `org.apache.tools.ant.Main` not being found.

Test   Look at the value of `ANT_HOME` and verify it's correct.

Fix   Either set the variable to the correct location, or omit it.

Problem: Incompatible Java libraries on the classpath

If you set up the `CLASSPATH` environment variable with a list of commonly needed JAR files, there's a risk that the libraries listed clash with the versions Ant needs.

Test   Look at the value of `CLASSPATH` and verify it's empty.
Run Ant with the `-noclasspath` option to omit the classpath.

Fix   Remove the environment variable.

Problem: Java extension libraries conflicting with Ant

Java supports extension libraries; JAR files placed into `JAVA_HOME\jre\lib\ext` are loaded by the runtime using a different classloader than normal. This can cause problems if any code in the extension libraries (such as `jaxp.jar`) tries to locate classes loaded under a different classloader.

Test   Look in the `JRE/lib/ext` directory for any JAR files that have crept in as extension libraries and that are confusing Ant.

Fix   Move the XML parser libraries to a different directory.

Problem: Sealing violation when running Ant

This exception happens when a library has been marked as sealed but another library implements classes in one of the packages of the sealed library. This exception means there is an XML parser conflict, perhaps from an older version on the classpath or extension library, or perhaps from some other library that contains a sealed copy of the JAXP API. The underlying cause will be one of the two problems above: extension library conflicts or classpath incompatibilities.

Fix   The message should identify which libraries have sealing problems. Use this to identify the conflict, and fix it, usually by removing one of the libraries. You can unseal a JAR file by editing its manifest, but this only fixes a symptom of the conflict, not the underlying problem.

Problem: Calling Ant generates a Java usage message

If the Java invocation string that the Ant launcher scripts is somehow corrupt, then the `java` program will not be able to parse it, so it will print a message beginning with `Usage: java [-options] class [args...]`.

This is usually caused by one of the environment variables, `JAVA_HOME`, `ANT_HOME`, `ANT_OPTS`, or `CLASSPATH` being invalid. Backslashes at the end and quotes in the middle are the common causes.

Test   Examine the environment variables to see if there are any obvious errors.

Fix   Fix any obvious errors. Otherwise, unset each variable in turn until Ant works; this will identify the erroneous variable.

Problem: Illegal Java options in the ANT_OPTS variable

The `ANT_OPTS` environment variable must contain options the local JVM recognizes. Any invalid parameter will generate an error message such as the following (where `ANT_OPTS` was set to –3):

```
Unrecognized option: -3
Could not create the Java virtual machine.
```

If the variable contains a string that is mistaken for the name of the Java class to run as the main class, then a different error appears:

```
Exception in thread "main" java.lang.NoClassDefFoundError: one
```

Test   Examine `ANT_OPTS` and verify that the variable is unset or contains valid JVM options.

Fix   Correct or clear the variable.

Problem: Incomplete source tree on a SYSV Unix installation

The original SYSV Unix `tar` utility cannot handle the long filenames of the Java source tree, and doesn't expand the entire Java source tree—files appear to be missing.

Test   In a source distribution, run `build.bat` or `build.sh`. If it fails, the source tree may be corrupt.

Fix   Untar Ant using the GNU `tar` utility, or download the `.zip` file and use `unzip`.

To summarize, most common installation problems stem from incorrect environment settings, especially the CLASSPATH environment variable, or duplicate and conflicting Ant installations.

If these tests don't identify the problem, call for help on the Ant user mailing list. This is a mailing list where Ant users solve each other's problems, be they related to installing Ant or getting a build to work.

XML Primer

Ant build files are written in XML, so Ant users must understand the language. Here's a brief introduction to basic XML.

Extended Markup Language (XML) provides a way of representing structured data that's somewhat readable by both humans and programs. It isn't the easiest of representations for either party, but it lets people write structured files that machines can parse. The strength of XML is that many tools can work with the XML without knowing what the final use is. Once you've learned XML, you can recognize and navigate almost any XML document.

XML documents should begin with an XML prolog, which indicates the version and, optionally, the encoding of the XML file—usually the string `<?xml version="1.0"?>`. Next comes the XML content. This must consist of a single XML root element, which can contain other XML content nested inside. An XML element has a name, such as `project`, and is started and finished with *tags* of the element in the name inside angle bracket characters (`<` `>`). All Ant documents must have `project` as the root element, so all Ant XML files should have a structure something like this:

```
<?xml version="1.0"?>      ◁⅃ Prolog
<project name="example">   ◁— Root element
                           ◁— Tasks and targets go here
</project>   ◁— Close the root element
```

XML elements can have XML content nested inside them, including other elements. One such element in Ant is `<echo>`, which tells Ant to print a message:

```
<echo></echo>
```

525

This element would only actually print an empty string, because it contains no child elements or other description of a message to print. Empty elements can be written in a special shorthand way:

```
<echo/>
```

To the XML parser, this means exactly the same as the previous declaration—an element declaration with no nested children. Most Ant tasks provide extra information to Ant through child nodes, textual or XML, and attributes of the elements. Attributes are the simplest.

Attributes

XML attributes are name=value assignments in the opening tag of an element. For example, the `<echo>` task supports the message attribute:

```
<echo message="hello, world"></echo>
```

Attributes must be quoted in single or double quotes. The following statement is identical to the one above:

```
<echo message='hello, world'/>
```

This statement uses single quote characters and closes the element within the opening tag. When executed, both Ant task declarations will have the same result:

```
[echo] hello, world
```

Attributes cannot be declared in the closing tag of an element; this is illegal:

```
<echo></echo message='hello, world'>
```

The XML parser will fail with an error before Ant even gets to see the file:

```
BUILD FAILED
build.xml:2: The end-tag for element type "echo"
 must end with a '>' delimiter
```

XML parser errors are fairly low level, and do not always explain the underlying problem. They do usually hint at the problem, and show the file and line at fault. XML-aware text editors are good at showing these problems.

Incidentally, there's no order to an element's attributes; Ant may see them in a different order from that of the XML file. Furthermore, you cannot have duplicate attributes with the same name. For that, nested elements are a better way to represent the information.

Nested text and XML elements

Many Ant elements support nested data. One such type is text, which the `<echo>` task accepts as the message to display:

```
<echo>hello, world</echo>
```

As before, this will print out a message to the screen.

```
[echo] hello, world
```

Sometimes, the child elements are complex XML declarations of their own:

```
<target name="compile">
  <javac srcdir="." destdir="." />
</target>
```

In this example, one XML element `<target>` contains another element, `<javac>`; each element has one or more attributes.

Unlike attributes, there's no limit to the number of duplicate elements you can nest inside another element. Also, the order matters. This allows a `<target>` to contain a sequence of tasks:

```
<target name="compile">
  <echo>about to compile</echo>
  <javac srcdir="." destdir="." />
  <echo>compile finished!</echo>
</target>
```

While elements support nested text, they cannot support binary data. XML files are text files.

Binary data

XML cannot contain binary data; it has to be encoded using techniques like base-64 encoding. This is rarely an issue in Ant build files. A more common problem is that certain characters, specifically ">" and "<", can confuse the parser. Such characters need to be *escaped*, here with the strings `&gt;` and `&lt;` respectively. This should be familiar to anyone who has written a lot of low-level HTML content. Most Unicode characters can also be described in XML by providing its numeric value in a very similar manner: `&#32;` and `&#x0020;` both refer to the ASCII space character. This trick can be useful in dealing with minor internationalization issues. When needed, a line such as

```
<echo message="&apos;&lt;$&gt;&amp;&quot;" />
```

would be translated to an output such as

```
[echo] '<$>&"
```

Escaping characters is most common in XML attributes, such as setting the passwords to remote FTP or HTTP servers. Table B.1 lists the most common symbols that you must escape in an Ant file.

Because escaping characters can become very messy and inconvenient, XML provides a mechanism for allowing unescaped text within a CDATA section. In Ant's build files, CDATA sections typically appear around script blocks or SQL commands. CDATA sections begin with `<![CDATA[` and end with `]]>`. The ending sequence of

Table B.1   How to escape common characters so that the XML parser or Ant can use them

Symbol	Ant XML representation
<	&lt;
>	&gt;
"	&quot;
'	&apos;
newline; \n	&#10;
A Unicode character, such as ß (hex value 00df)	&#x00df;

a CDATA section is the only set of characters that requires escaping internally. A CDATA example is

```
<echo><![CDATA[
    <b>hello</b> world
    ]]>
</echo>
```

Even within CDATA or Unicode escaping, not all characters are allowed. As an example, the ASCII NUL symbol, \u0000, is forbidden, even with an &#00; declaration. The only allowed characters in the range 0-31 are 8, 10 and 13; tab, newline and carriage-return.

Character sets

The default character set of XML files is not that of the local system; it is UTF-8 encoded Unicode. All ASCII characters from 0 to 127 are represented as-is in UTF-8 files, so this subtle file format detail often will not show up. The moment you add any high-bit characters, such as the £ currency symbol, the parser breaks. To avoid having the build failing with an error about illegal characters when you add a string like "München" to the file, you must set the encoding of the XML file in the XML prolog, and save the file in that encoding. For example, to use the European character set, you must declare in the prolog that the file is in the ISO 8859-1 format:

```
<?xml version='1.0' encoding="iso-8859-1" ?>
```

This will tell the parser that the encoding is ISO Latin-1 so that the ISO Latin-1 characters from 128 to 255 are valid.

The other main content that people will find in build files are comments—a good build file is documented.

Comments

XML comments begin with <!-- and end with -->. This is very important in an Ant build file, because documentation of the stages in the build process is so critical. It is also useful for commenting out sections during development. You cannot use double minus symbols "--" in a comment: this is an XML rule that hits some Ant users.

This comment is illegal:

```
<!-- ------------illegal-comment------  -->
```

You have to use something like the following style instead:

```
<!-- ============allowed=============== -->
```

This inconveniences some Ant users, but there's nothing the Ant team can do about it; it's a quirk of history that everyone has to live with.

Together, XML elements, attributes, text, and comments form the core of XML, and all that was needed in chapters 1 to 8 of this book. Chapter 9 introduces XML namespaces, as a way of keeping Ant tasks from different sources separate, so it's important to understand them too.

XML NAMESPACES

XML namespaces let XML files mix elements and attributes from different XML "languages." Ant uses them to make it easy to use Ant tasks in third-party libraries. This section of the XML Primer is therefore only relevant from chapter 9 onwards.

In a namespace aware XML-parser, you can declare elements and attributes in different namespaces and mix them together by prefixing each use with a namespace prefix. Here is our (mis)understanding of the complex rules:

- XML namespaces are uniquely identified by a URL or other valid "URI."

- There is no requirement for any file to be retrievable from any namespace that's given by a URL.

- A namespace is bound to a prefix when the namespace is declared in an `xmlns` declaration, inside an XML element:

  ```
  <target xmlns:pr1="http://antbook.org/1" >
  ```

- Such a prefix can be used in the element in which it is declared and in all nested elements—but not anywhere else.

- To use elements or attributes in a namespace, they must be declared with the prefix in front of the name:

  ```
  <pre1:echo pre1:level="verbose">
    <pre1:number default="5"/>
    <number2/>
  </pre1:echo>
  ```

- Attributes are automatically in the same namespace as their element, so the following are equivalent:

  ```
  <pre1:echo pre1:level="verbose"/>
  <pre1:echo level="verbose"/>
  ```

- Nested elements are not automatically in the same namespace as their parent element; you need to explicitly declare them.

- The name of the prefix is irrelevant; only the URI string of the namespace is relevant. Thus the following prefixes are equivalent:

```
<a:element xmlns:a="antlib:org.antbook.filters" />
<b:element xmlns:b="antlib:org.antbook.filters" />
```

- If you omit a prefix from an XML namespace declaration, it becomes the *default namespace*. This is the namespace into which all nested elements belong unless they have a prefix or the default namespace is redefined.

```
<element xmlns="antlib:org.antbook.filters" />
```

- Do not redefine the default namespace in Ant—the tool does not like it.
- You can redefine any prefix with a new declaration.

That is the extent of the rules for XML namespaces across all XML 1.0-based applications. Ant bends these rules a bit to make nested elements easier to use:

If an element or attribute is in the "" namespace, and yet the name of the element/attribute matches one that a (namespaced) task expects, Ant assumes you meant the element or attribute in the specific namespace.

What does that mean? It means that Ant takes a more relaxed view of namespaces than do most XML tools, because Ant would be unusable without it. This is convenient, but it can teach Ant users bad habits.

Incidentally, you cannot use Ant properties in the namespace URI; this doesn't work:

```
xmlns:prefix="${mytask.uri}"
```

The XML parser does the namespace processing before Ant gets to see it, so the namespace would be `${mytask.uri}`, which isn't legal according to the official syntax of URIs. You can use properties to provide URIs in normal Ant task attributes, just not `xmlns:` attributes.

Namespace best practices

To keep the complexity of XML namespaces manageable in a build file, here are some good practices:

- Use the same prefix for the same namespace across all your build files.
- Never declare a new default namespace in Ant projects; don't use an `xmlns="http://antbook.org"` declaration.
- Declare the namespaces in the root `<project>` element if they are to be used in more than one place, or in the `<target>` that contains the tasks.

Finally, if you want to know more about XML, including a more thorough explanation of XML namespaces, we recommend the *Annotated XML Reference* (Bray 1998) (http://www.xml.com/axml/testaxml.htm), *XML in a Nutshell* (Harold 2004), and *Effective XML* (Harold 2003).

A P P E N D I X   C

IDE Integration

All of the popular Java IDEs support Ant out of the box. This gives the users the best of both worlds—great environments for developing their application, and a build tool that can compile, test, and deploy that application.

Ant doesn't constrain or dictate your choice of IDE. Developers should choose whatever editor supports their needs, without worrying about whether it supports Ant, because the answer is always "of course it does." Even so, there are some differences in features and ease of configuration and use. Here is a quick guide to using Ant in Eclipse, NetBeans, and IntelliJ IDEA, the three main Java IDEs.

HOW IDEs USE ANT

The IDEs parse the build file and make it easier to view, edit, and use. They usually have an Ant-aware editor, which lets you navigate around targets and add Ant tasks to them. Eclipse and NetBeans let you debug Ant, setting breakpoints in a build file. IntelliJ IDEA doesn't offer this feature, but it does determine which properties are unset and highlights them in the text editor—reducing the need for a debugger somewhat.

The IDEs all call Ant directly, rather than going through the normal launcher scripts. This has some consequences:

- JAR libraries in ${user.home}/.ant/lib may not be added to Ant's classpath.
- The property ant.home may not be set.
- The IDE may have its own Java security manager, interfering with Ant's attempts to create one when running <java> without forking a new JVM. If

non-forked Java programs don't work properly, set `fork="true"` to host them in a new JVM. Eclipse lets you run Ant in a new JVM, which can help.

- JVM settings in `ANT_OPTS` will not be picked up.
- Ant options in `ANT_ARGS` will not be used.
- A custom input handler is used to bring up a dialog whenever `<input>` asks for user input.
- Custom listeners and loggers are used to capture the build's output and to aid debugging.
- JAR files added to Ant's classpath may be locked while the IDE is running, especially after an Ant has (somehow) leaked memory, perhaps by saving Java classes to static data structures.

Because a private Ant version is used, the classpath may be different from the command line. JAR files in `ANT_HOME/lib` may not be loaded, breaking the build. To compound the problem, you cannot run `ant -diagnostics` against the IDE's version of Ant, because that is a command-line option. You need to use the `<diagnostics>` task instead:

```
<target name="diagnostics" description="diagnostics">
  <diagnostics/>
</target>
```

IDEs invariably provide some way to add new files to the classpath, either globally or for individual projects. Use this to add essential JAR files to the private Ant runtime's classpath.

The other classpath problem is that of selecting all JARs needed to compile the application. If you're using files in a `lib/` directory, selecting these files is trivial. If you use Ivy, it's useful to have a target to copy all JARs from the `compile` or `run` configurations into a single directory, so that you can point the IDE at them. In either case, if you want the source and JavaDocs for the libraries, you'll need to download them from the relevant projects' sites.

Another issue with IDEs is that there is usually a lag between an Ant version being released and support for it in IDEs. The IDEs usually let you switch the IDE to another version of Ant on the hard disk. This lets you use the same Ant installation for the command line and the IDE. We use this method whenever we can, partly for consistency, but also because as Ant developers, we're always updating our Ant version. The IDEs all support this, although they may not recognize new tasks or types correctly, marking them as unknown or invalid. This is something you just have to accept until a later IDE release ships.

Now, with those details out of the way, let's look at the Ant support in the three main Java IDEs, starting with Eclipse.

ECLIPSE HTTP://WWW.ECLIPSE.ORG/

The IBM-founded Eclipse IDE is a general-purpose development framework targeting Java development, with emerging support for C++, Ruby, and Python. It is clearly the dominant player in the Java IDE market.

Eclipse has quite a strong process model. It assumes that you have all your projects in a single "workspace," and it manages the links between them. Don't fight this system. Eclipse has a way of organizing things, and if you embrace that way, the IDE works. This design can, unfortunately, make it hard to integrate with Ant. Eclipse supports simple Ant-based projects with a single build file for a single module. However, once you have multiple build files importing each other, things can break down.

This is a shame, because apart from this, the IDE supports Ant very nicely. Figure C.1 shows the IDE debugging an Ant build file: you can halt the build at a breakpoint and view Ant's properties. In this run, the IDE has just fielded an <input> request by bringing up a dialog prompting for the data. We can edit the values or continue the build.

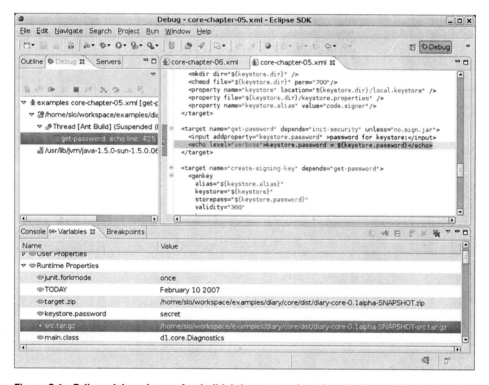

Figure C.1 **Eclipse debugging an Ant build. It has stopped at a breakpoint and is showing the current set of Ant properties.**

Adding an Ant project

Eclipse supports multiple projects in a *workspace*; each project can either live under the IDE's workspace directory, or it can be remotely linked in. For projects that build under Ant, this linking-in process doesn't seem to work that well if you have build files that call other build files through `<import>`. Apart from that, all goes smoothly.

Whenever you open a file called `build.xml`, Eclipse will recognize it as an Ant file and open it in its Ant-specific editor. To open any other XML file in this editor, select the file and bring up the "open with…" dialog with the right mouse button; ask for the Ant Editor. This editor offers

- As-you-type completion of tasks—otherwise known as "Content Assist."
- Templates for some tasks, such as `<property>`, `<delete>`, and `<javac>`. New templates can be added and shared between developers.
- Attribute completion, with a popup listing of values for attributes that take Boolean or enumerated values.
- Control-space completion of known properties after entering `${` to start dereferencing a property.
- Go-to-declaration (the F3 key) to follow the definition of a target in a target's `depends` list.
- The ability to set breakpoints on a line of the build.
- A list of targets, with the ability to navigate to, run, or debug any target.

Eclipse can run build file targets when the user asks to "build" or "clean" an eclipse project. This method offers the tightest integration, as it hands off the important work—the build—to Ant.

To tell Eclipse to build a project with Ant, you need to create a new *builder*, which you can do from the project properties dialog of figure C.2.

Selecting "New…" brings up the window of figure C.3, which offers the choice of an Ant build or another program.

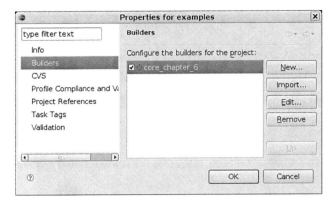

Figure C.2
Eclipse projects "build" through builders. You can add a build file as a builder through the project's properties dialog, where it can live alongside the projects' other builders.

Selecting "Ant Build," brings up the final dialog, which provides detailed control over the build, including the choice of build file, targets, and Ant's classpath, properties, and operational environment. The first action is to select the build file and its base directory, which figure C.4 shows.

Alongside selecting the build file, setting the base directory is the most important action. You must point it at the directory in which the build file lives, after which everything but `<import>`

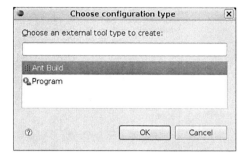

Figure C.3 You can add any program as a new builder, but only Ant has built-in support from the IDE.

should work. Keep the "Set an Input handler" option checked, to ensure the IDE brings up a dialog box when user input is needed.

The "Refresh" tab controls whether the IDE should reload its files after a build. It is safer (albeit slower) to enable a full refresh. More relevant is the tab that lets you bind the targets to run from the IDE actions, the "Targets" tab of figure C.5.

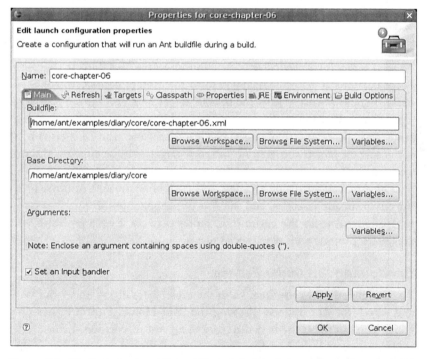

Figure C.4 The first step to setting up the new builder is to set the path to the build file and its base directory. You also can add arguments to the command line, but not -lib or -logger related, as the IDE is in charge of those.

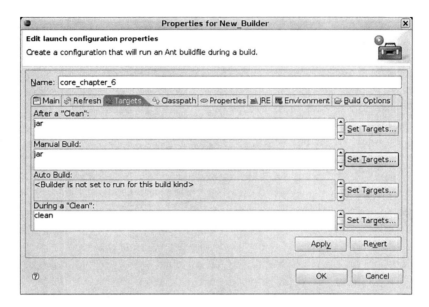

Figure C.5 You can add any number of targets to the IDE actions.
"Auto Build" is the background compile of the application; the "After a Clean"
and "Manual Build" builds are the targets to do a clean and incremental build
of the application.

To set a target for a particular IDE action, press the "Set Targets" button to the right
of each action's target list, which will show the form of figure C.6. For a full or manual
build, Eclipse normally runs the default target of a project, the one declared in the
`<project>` declaration. To change it to another target, you need to unselect the default
target and select the desired target. Navigation through the list is easier in a big project
if you sort the targets and hide all "internal" targets—those targets without any description attribute.

The Ant builder dialog also lets you customize the Ant runtime used—the JRE,
the environment variables, and the Ant implementation to use. It is normally better
to configure Ant for the entire IDE, rather than do it on a project-by-project basis,
except for projects with very special needs.

Configuring Ant under Eclipse

To configure the Ant runtime, go to the Preferences dialog under the Window menu
and search for Ant options. Pressing the "Ant Home" button brings up a dialog in
which you can select the base directory of an Ant installation. Eclipse will then automatically select all the JAR files in the `lib` subdirectory, using this as the base classpath for Ant. *This list does not get updated when new JAR files are added to* ANT_HOME/
`lib`. If you add new JAR files to this directory, you need to update the JAR list in the
IDE by reselecting the Ant Home directory again (figure C.7).

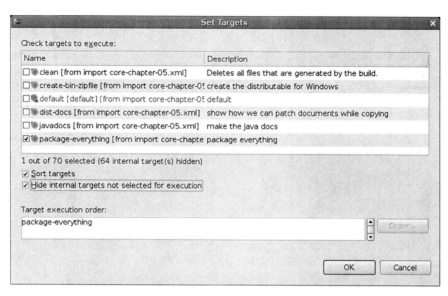

Figure C.6   Selecting targets to run in response to IDE actions. Avoid setting up long lists of targets for each action; it's better to create new targets in the build file with the appropriate dependencies. This lets you use it from the command line and makes it available to other developers.

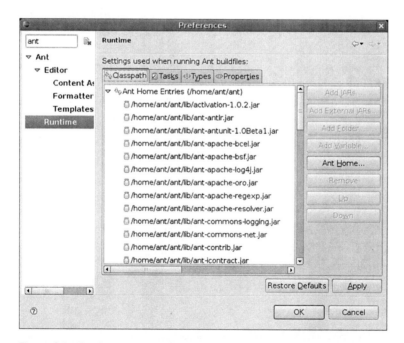

Figure C.7   To choose and configure the Ant runtime in Eclipse, go through the Preferences dialog to the Ant runtime, and select a new Ant Home, the base directory of the Ant installation.

The classpath can also have "Global Entries," files picked up from `${user.home}/.ant/lib` and the JRE itself, and "Contributed Entries." These are JAR files that provide Eclipse-specific tasks and the extra JARs needed to integrate Ant with the IDE. Leave this list alone.

The "Tasks" tab of the settings window lists the extra tasks added to Ant by Eclipse. Build files that run only under Eclipse are free to use any of these tasks, including the JDT compiler adapter, which lets you use the Java Development Tools (JDT) compiler inside Ant. If you want to use any of these tasks on a build outside Eclipse, you need to add the same JARs to Ant's classpath.

The <import> problem

When the IDE creates an Eclipse project from an existing Java Ant project, it seems to copy the build file over to its own workspace. For most tasks this fact is not obvious, because all file references get resolved relative to the base directory of the build, which Eclipse sets to be the original directory of the project. As a result, Ant's normal file resolution process ensures that all file references, including statements such as `<property file="build.properties">` will work.

There is one task, however, that deliberately does not resolve references relative to the `basedir` attribute of a project, and that is `<import>`. This is because it's designed to support chained imports across multiple files, something that wouldn't work if all paths were relative to the base directory of the main build file. As a result, `<import>` doesn't work right under Eclipse.

The easiest way to show this problem is to create a "Java Project from Existing Ant Build File," selecting a build file that uses `<import>` to import another project. The IDE copies over the build file into its workspace directory, setting up a link to the source tree. As a result, all the other files in the project are absent, and so the imported file isn't found:

```
Buildfile: /home/ant/workspace/core-chapter6/core-chapter-06.xml

BUILD FAILED
/home/ant/workspace/core-chapter6/core-chapter-06.xml:20:
  Cannot find core-chapter-05.xml imported from
  /home/ant/workspace/core-chapter6/core-chapter-06.xml
```

This is a serious problem, as the project no longer builds. What can be done about this?

One solution is to include `${basedir}` in the resolution path of an import. The original build file had a statement of the form

```
<import file="core-chapter-05.xml" />
```

This can be changed to

```
<import file="${basedir}/core-chapter-05.xml" />
```

This will make the `<import>` work under Eclipse, yet it will still allow the build to work on the command line. However, it doesn't chain well across multiple imports. If the build file containing this now-modified `<import>` statement was itself imported from a project with a different base directory, the import would fail as `${basedir}/core-chapter-05.xml` would no longer resolve to the target file.

This is pretty bad. A better solution is to create a custom build file purely for the IDE, one that uses a `basedir`-relative import to pull in the main project. Here's an `eclipse.xml` build file that does this:

```
<project name="eclipse" default="default">
 <import file="${basedir}/core-chapter-06.xml" />
</project>
```

This file pulls in the real build file from where it lives, after which all imports will chain properly.

There's one final option: check out the entire source tree as a single project. Once you do that you can set up Ant builders for any part of the source tree. This workaround removes much of the value of Eclipse, however, as you lose most of the Java development tool support.

Of course, projects that avoid using `<import>` don't suffer from this problem. Do we advise this? No, because `<import>` is key to scalable Ant-based projects. Incompatibilities between Eclipse and Ant are something that will have to be resolved, somehow.

Summary

Eclipse is the ubiquitous Java IDE. Apart from the `<import>` problem, it hosts Ant very well, and is an editor that offers task and property completion and build file debugging. At the same time, it likes to take total control of where your files live and how they are built. You need to commit to it—in which case there are workarounds for the `<import>` problem—or avoid it. It's not something you can only use part-time.

SUN NETBEANS HTTP://WWW.NETBEANS.ORG/

NetBeans is Sun's free, open source Java IDE. Currently at revision 5.5, the tool is built around Ant. Whenever you tell the IDE to create a new project, it creates a new Ant build file, one that you can use and extend. Sun also keeps reasonably up-to-date with Ant versions, a benefit of their frequent release cycle. Here are some of the things you can do with Ant under NetBeans:

- Tell the IDE which targets to use to clean, compile, run, and test a project.
- Debug Ant builds, with breakpoints and watched properties.
- Bind menu items and keyboard shortcuts to targets in a build file.
- Define targets and actions for other IDE operations.

Figure C.8 shows the IDE running the builds of chapters 5 and 6: the IDE has popped up a dialog because the `<input>` task has requested user input. There is a breakpoint

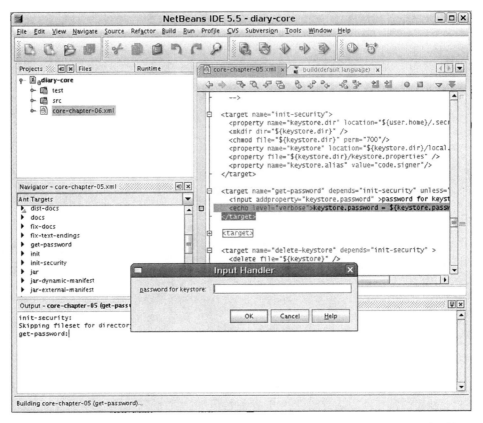

Figure C.8 NetBeans running a build file that prompts for input. It brings up a dialog in this situation. We've set a breakpoint on the following task, so the debugger will halt the build.

on the next task, so when the build continues, the IDE will pause the build with Ant under the debugger, where you can see the current properties.

In some ways it is scary that a build tool needs a debugger, but if you have a build that needs to be debugged, you will be grateful! Consider installing NetBeans for this feature alone.

Another nice touch of the IDE is its JUnit test support. When you run your normal JUnit targets, the reports get pulled into the IDE's JUnit results. Once you have a complex test run—such as those which test remote web sites or Enterprise applications—you will appreciate the value of this.

Adding an Ant project to NetBeans

It's slightly tricky to get an existing Ant project building under NetBeans, because it has strong expectations of what a build file must contain. You need to create a new project, selecting the "with Existing Ant Script" option, as in figure C.9. Before you do this, run the dist and test targets at least once from the command line, to

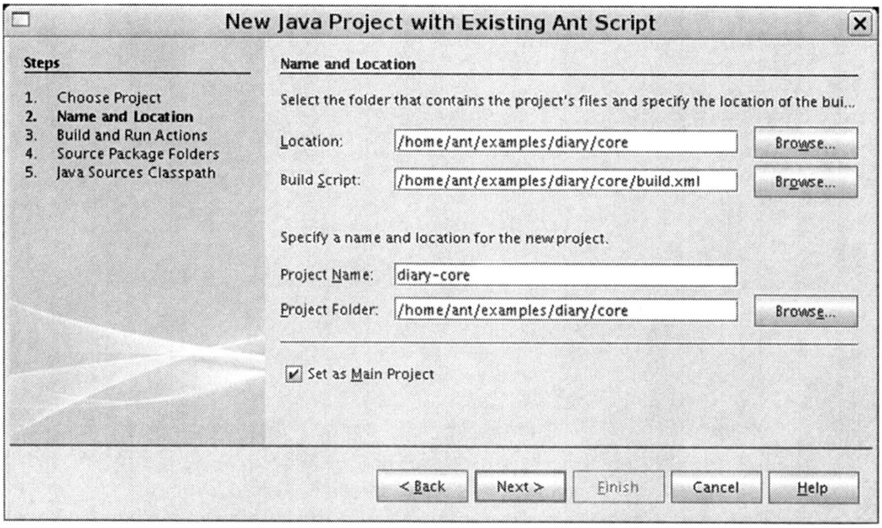

Figure C.9 Adding an existing Ant project to NetBeans. It will create a subdirectory, `nbproject`, to hold extra project information, such as custom build files for the debugging actions.

ensure that all the output directories for source classes, test classes, and JavaDocs have been created. You need to be able to select these directories when setting up the output paths for the build.

The first step to creating the project is to point the IDE at the base directory of the chosen project. It will look for the `build.xml` file and extract the project name from it. If you want to use a differently named build file, this is the dialog to select it.

After binding to a project, you need to map IDE actions to specific Ant targets, as in figure C.10. NetBeans will guess the appropriate target from common names—the only target we hand-entered was the name of the "Run" target.

After the target bindings, two more forms are presented: one to identify the folders for Java source and test files—and the directories into which they are compiled—and the other to add any extra JARs to the compile classpath. This is solely for the IDE to provide type completion and detect errors; it doesn't alter the build file. Once this is done, you're good to go! You can now use the "Build" menu to build the project, or hit the F11 key. For tests, press Alt-F6. This will run your `test` target, presenting the results in the JUnit results pane.

The IDE lets you integrate debugging with the build; it can create a project containing debug targets, targets that set up the `<java>` run with all the debugging options, and run a custom `<nbjpdastart>` target to tell the IDE to start the debugger. The result is a very tight development cycle using Ant for the entire build process—either the built-in Ant or an external copy.

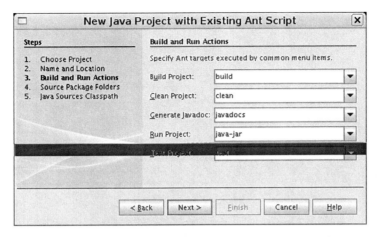

Figure C.10 Binding targets to the stages in the build file. You don't need a target for every action at this point, as you can edit these bindings later

Configuring Ant

NetBeans lets you configure Ant from the "Miscellaneous" section of the Options dialog, where you can change to a new version of Ant other than that built into the IDE, and define new Ant properties. Figure C.11 shows this dialog.

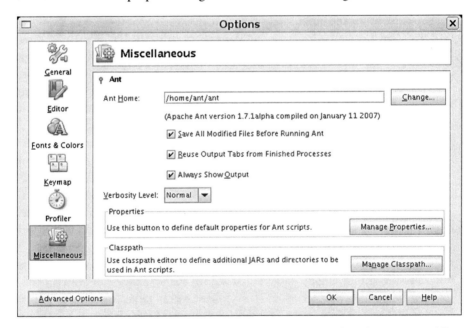

Figure C.11 Configuring Ant in NetBeans. We've entered the location of our command line Ant distribution. The IDE-supplied Classpath option is left alone. Checking the "Save Files" option tells the IDE to save all files before running a build. Always select this option.

One critical option is the "Save Files" check box—set this unless you like to be confused by the IDE building and running out-of-date versions of your code.

The IDE automatically adds all files in `${user.home}/.ant/lib` to Ant's classpath, so there's no need to add any of those files through the "Manage Classpath" dialog. However, if you have any build file that assumes that the `ant.home` property is set, the "Manage Properties" dialog is the place to set it.

Summary

Outside of Sun, NetBeans is a bit neglected. Eclipse has all the momentum. However, from an Ant perspective, NetBeans is a very nice IDE. What's nice about it is that it's much less dictatorial about how your project is laid out than is Eclipse. It doesn't try to tell you how to work, but adapts to you and your Ant build. In particular, there's no need to duplicate any information in the IDE about the build, other than the location of input and output directories, and the library dependencies. Given it also has a good Java application profiler, it's well worth a play.

INTELLIJ IDEA HTTP://INTELLIJ.COM/

This is a commercial IDE, but it's reasonably priced, discounted to individual purchases, and free to open source developers. The tool has led the way in refactoring and testing and is strongly Ant-aware. Here are some of the Ant features that IDEA 6.0 offers:

- Completion of well-known Ant task names, attributes, and elements.
- Property management: renaming; highlighting of undefined properties, jumping to property declarations, and property completion while typing.
- Running of targets, jump-to-source from the target list.
- Background execution, hiding the log on a successful build.
- Ability to mark targets as items to run before/after compilation, and before a run or debug. This is good for code generation, post processing, and deployment.
- Giving targets keyboard shortcuts.
- Binding multiple build files to a single IDE project.

The IDE is very code-centric: it assumes that the core artifacts of your project are JAR files and tests; this is not a process-driven platform. In particular it doesn't try to impose any kind of structure on your code or build files, other than the standard practice of separate source and test package trees.

There's no Ant debugger in this IDE, but it does highlight any properties that it thinks are undefined. It knows which tasks set properties and how, and it detects references to properties that have not been set by any task in any target on the current target's dependency list. This is very useful, although it doesn't extend to third-party tasks or tasks added to Ant after the IDE's release. Figure C.12 shows the IDE warning of unset properties.

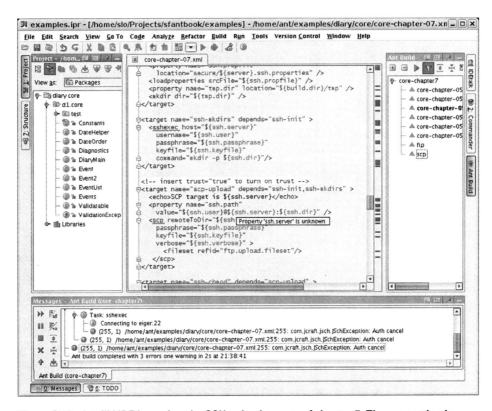

Figure C.12   IntelliJ IDEA running the SSH upload targets of chapter 7. The connection is failing, and an error is appearing in the messages window. Clicking on the error brings up the line of the build file. IDEA highlights all unknown properties—here it is marking as unknown all properties loaded from the server-specific properties file.

Adding an Ant project

To add an Ant project you need to create an IDE project which can do the basic compile under the IDE; then you need to add Ant build files to the project.

1 Create a new project, selecting the JVM and directory of the project. Start with a "single module project" and choose the target project type, such as Java, EJB, Web, or Java EE—Java being the simplest.

2 When asked to create a source directory, point it at the existing source directory.

3 Configure the output directory to match that of Ant, such as `build/classes`.

4 Click "finish" to finish with the wizard.

5 In the project browser window, find the build file and click the right mouse button to bring up the context menu; choose "Add as Ant Build."

6 In the same window, select the module at the root with the right mouse button, and bring up the "module settings" dialog. In the "sources" tab, select the test

source tree as test source, then go to the "output" tab to declare the path for generated tests, such as `build/test/classes`.

The goal for configuring the test and source directories is to have the IDE compile into the same source tree as Ant. That lets Ant do the main build, generating classes the IDE will use when running or debugging the application.

That's it! Your Ant build is ready to go. Under the Window menu, select "Ant Build" to see the build window. This is a list of build files and their targets. Double-click a target to run it, or bring up the context menu with the right mouse button for more options, such as the keyboard shortcuts.

Because the IDE is doing the main build, there is some duplication of effort. Whenever you test or run the project from the IDE, it compiles the code itself, rather than delegating to Ant. What you can do is pull Ant actions into the build by selecting any target in the Ant Build menu, popping up the context menu, and picking "Execute On...." You can then request that the target runs before or after the compilation stage. A target that creates Java source, such as a WSDL-to-Java operation, or the Java from XML activity of chapter 13, should be set to run before the build. Post-processing activities such as an `<rmic>` compile can be set to run afterwards. If you select "Execute Target before Run/Debug," you can run the target before running, debugging, or testing the application. Figure C.13 shows the dialog that's presented, from which you can choose which activities require the target to run.

Once you start mixing IDE actions and build file actions it does get a bit hard to determine what exactly is going on. The NetBean policy of "Everything is in the build files" makes it all more transparent, and there's a lot less duplication of settings. However, IDEA let's developers set up keyboard shortcuts to any target and, in so doing, hand off most of the build to the Ant. Even so, it's useful to keep the IDE able to build and test the application, as that way you can start debugging sessions off test runs.

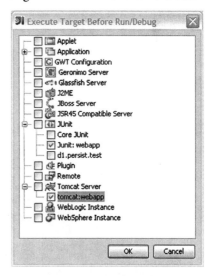

Figure C.13 Selecting the actions for which we want a deployment target to run; here the Tomcat and JUnit activities both trigger the action. You may find that you will need IDE-specific targets for such actions, targets that do not depend on the complete build taking place. This is because the IDE has already taken on much of the build.

Configuring Ant under IDEA

In IDEA, you can configure Ant on a project-by-project basis. After adding or creating a project, select any of its targets in the Ant Build window and request the properties dialog, either by the context menu or the toolbar. Within this dialog you can

- Set Ant properties or other JVM options.
- Switch to any Ant version installed on the local system.
- Add JAR files to the classpath.
- Filter out which targets to see in the IDE.

Figure C.14 shows the dialog where these settings can be changed.

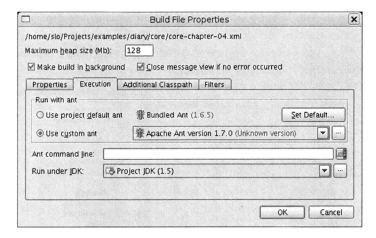

Figure C.14   IntelliJ IDEA lets developers run a version of Ant in the file system, rather than the built-in version, with extra JARS on the classpath and with custom properties.

By telling the IDE to run the build in the background and to not hide the messages window if the build was successful, you can host long-running builds, such as a deploy-and-test sequence, while getting on with writing more code or tests.

The other nice thing the IDE does is that you can tell any run or test activity to run Ant before starting. Any of its "run configurations" can be set to build the application in the IDE first *or to run any Ant target.* That means that you can set up Ant to build the application, including complex activities such as dynamically generating Java source or running the `rmic` compiler against compiled code, before running or debugging an application.

BUILDING WITH ANT AND AN IDE

To use Ant from an IDE, you need to identify and use the best features of each product. IDEs are great at debugging and editing text; Ant is good at building, testing, and deploying. Where IDEs are weak is in team integration: each developer has to configure his IDE projects to work on his own system, and changes in the build do not propagate well. So why try to unify the IDE environments? Ant can be all the commonality of the build process developers need. Here are our recommended tactics to combine IDEs and Ant in a team project:

- Let developers choose their favorite IDEs. The boost to productivity and morale here can outweigh most compatibility issues.
- Have lots of RAM on the machines. Whatever you have, get more.
- Make sure there is a standard IDE installed on everyone's machine, regardless of the developer's ultimate choice of tool. If pair-programming techniques are being used, a common IDE is invaluable.
- Integrate tests into the build process, so they are run every build and deploy cycle. Testing and deployment are key reasons for developers to use Ant over the IDE's own compiler.
- Use a team build file to build the code. Any customizations should be in per-user properties, not private build files.
- Have standard target names across projects (a general Ant best practice).

Some developers may miss the total integration of a pure IDE build; adding unit tests and deployment to the Ant build, surpassing what the IDE build could do, could help bring them on board. Offering them not only the choice of which IDE to use, but also the funding to buy a commercial product, could also help with motivation.

index

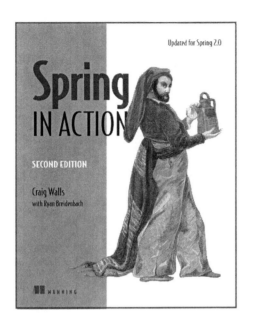

Spring in Action, Second Edition
by Craig Walls and Ryan Breidenbach
ISBN: 1-933988-13-4
600 pages
$49.99
July 2007

GWT in Action
Easy Ajax with the Google Web Toolkit
by Robert Hanson and Adam Tacy
ISBN: 1-933988-23-1
632 pages
$49.99
June 2007

For ordering information go to www.manning.com

9 781932 394801